Banking on Death

Or, Investing in Life:
The history and future of pensions

◆

ROBIN BLACKBURN

V

VERSO

London • New York

For Margrit

First published by Verso 2002
© Robin Blackburn 2002

Paperback edition first published by Verso 2003
© Robin Blackburn 2003

1 3 5 7 9 10 8 6 4 2

Verso
UK: 6 Meard Street, London W1F 0EG
USA: 180 Varick Street, New York NY 10014–4606
www.versobooks.com

Verso is the imprint of New Left Books

ISBN 1–85984–409–X

British Library Cataloguing in Publication Data
Blackburn, Robin, 1940-
    Banking on death, or, Investing in life : the history
    and future of pensions
    1. Pension trusts 2. Pension trusts – Cross-cultural
    studies
    I. Title
    332.6'7254
    ISBN: 185984409X

Library of Congress Cataloging-in-Publication Data
A catalog record for this book is
available from the Library of Congress

Typeset in Bembo by M Rules
Printed and bound in the UK
by Biddles Ltd, Guildford and King's Lynn

Contents

List of Tables

List of Illustrations

Acknowledgements

A large number of people have helped me to understand the pension world and it will not be possible to mention all of them. Family, friends, colleagues, and even casual acquaintances, have tolerantly put up with my none-too-subtle attempts to steer the conversation towards what many find – obviously I disagree – a charmless topic.

Stanley Engerman is the only person to have read and commented on the entire manuscript; I am most grateful to him.

The first research towards this book was begun while I was a Research Fellow at King's College, Cambridge, in 1998–9. Among those who gave me helpful advice at that time were Gareth Stedman Jones and Geoffrey Harcourt. Perry Anderson, Lucy Heller, Andrew Glyn, Richard Minns and Robert Rowthorn furnished helpful comments on my first essay in the field. My colleagues at the University of Essex, particularly Ted Benton, Diane Elson, Miriam Glucksmann, John Scott and Lucinda Platt have offered guidance of various sorts. Likewise colleagues at the Graduate Faculty of the New School University in New York, especially Nancy Fraser, Eli Zaretsky, Mike Hanagan, Oz Frankel and Lance Taylor. I have published three pieces in *New Left Review* relating to the ideas presented here and greatly appreciate the stream of helpful suggestions I received from Sebastian Budgen, Thomas Mertes, Robert Brenner and Susan Watkins. John Grahl kindly read and commented on a portion of the manuscript as did Tony Lynes, Peter Townsend, and Yally Avrahampour. Göran Therborn helped me to get to grips with the Swedish experience, as Manuel Riesco did with the Chilean. The late Joe Simmons, editor of the *Essex Pensioner*, wrote me a long, helpful letter, responding to my *New Left Review* article. I have also benefited from comments from Henri Jacquot.

Fay Lomax Cook, Peter Diamond, Frank Field and Rudolf Meidner kindly agreed to be interviewed by me, helping me to understand not only more about pension policy but also aspects of Swedish, British and US politics which are central to this book.

In different ways Gemma, Christopher and Margrit Blackburn all helped to sharpen my view of the book's subject. Ian Webber kindly helped to proofread the book. I am grateful to Ros Howe for attentive copy-editing. Tariq Ali was very encouraging and helped me find a good title.

I would like to thank the Lippman/Miliband Trust for a grant towards research into pension policy.

Given the character of the book the usual disclaimers apply. Responsibility for the overall approach and for any mistakes is mine alone.

Those who read the book from beginning to end will, I hope, find that the narrative of each chapter carries forward the argument. But those who would like an initial overview should consult the introduction, the summary at the beginning of chapter 7 (pp.431–5) and the first dozen pages of the conclusion.

Robin Blackburn
Wivenhoe, April 2002

Introduction:
It's Pensions, Stupid!

The most unexpected thing to happen to a man is old age.
(Leon Trotsky, 1939)

Once we have understood what the state of the aged really is, we cannot satisfy ourselves with calling for a more generous 'old age policy', higher pensions, decent housing and organized leisure. It is the whole system which is at stake and our claim cannot be otherwise than radical – to change life itself.
(Simone de Beauvoir, *Old Age*, 1977)

there is still a rhetorical presentation of old age, but not one that nobly defends the final age of man against the derision or even contempt of the first. No, it is found mainly on television and consists of a disguised and highly effective attempt to ingratiate potential new consumers. In these advertisements, the elderly rather than the old, to use the more neutral term, appear sprightly, smiling and happy because they can finally enjoy some particularly fortifying tonic or exceptionally attractive holiday. Thus they too have become highly courted beneficiaries of the consumer society, depositories of new demands and welcome participants in the enlargement of the market. In a society where everything can be bought and sold, even old age can become a commodity like any other.
(Norberto Bobbio, 'Old Age', 1996)

Damien Hirst's famous pickled shark is entitled 'The Impossibility of Death in the Mind of the Living'. Perhaps a butterfly case could represent another thought: 'The Impossibility of Old Age in the Mind of the Young (and not so Young)'. We are now living through a remarkable transformation of the human condition as the average life-span lengthens and the birth rate drops. These trends have been most pronounced in the developed world but they are now also well established in many parts of what used to be called the Third World. In the early nineteenth century in Britain and the United States average life expectancy was around forty. By the beginning of the twentieth century it had risen to fifty and at the outset of the twenty-first was approaching eighty. Since many perished in infancy in the past these averages are a little, but only a little, misleading. Those who had already reached sixty years of age in 1900 had a life expectancy of 14–15 more years, whereas today that figure is over twenty more years. Rising longevity and a falling birth rate have begun to transform the age structure but it is only in the present century that the real impact will be observed on a global scale. At the close of the twentieth century there were 419 million people aged sixty-five or over in the world, comprising 6.9 per cent of the total population, rising to 12.6 per cent in North America and 14.7 per cent in Europe. Just over half of those aged sixty-five or over, 216 million, lived in Asia, with 107 million in Europe and 39 million in North America. Life expectancy in China is already seventy years for men and seventy-two years for women. Around the year 2000 those aged fifty or over comprised 17 per cent of the world's population. UN demographers project that, on present trends, the fifty-plus proportion of the total will rise to 27 per cent in 2025, 34 per cent in 2050 and 38 per cent in 2075.[1]

Those who do address the revolution in longevity are often too ready to pigeon-hole it for us as either a bad news story – 'the population bomb', 'the old age crisis' and so forth – or simply a good news story, complete with super-grannies and athletic pensioners – apparently the speeds achieved by the over-sixties Olympic runners in 1998 matched those of the Olympic winners of 1898. In fact, whether all this is a good or a bad story has yet to be decided. At the moment it is a tremendous challenge to our culture and society, demanding forethought, imagination and a willingness to embrace the advantages of a society based on multiple overlapping generations. This book is about how that challenge might be successfully negotiated, bearing in mind that the success to be looked for will always have to come to terms, sooner or later, with individual frailty and mortality.

The aspect of matters that will be centrally addressed is that of economic provision but, as we will see, culture and politics are very much at stake too. Our ageing society is, perhaps, obsessed by youth for similar reasons to the reverence for old age typical of the young societies of the past: partly rarity value and partly the need that every generation has for its successors and predecessors, at both the practical and the symbolic level. Generational interdependence is obvious enough within any primary human group. The human young are dependent for a far more protracted period than any other species and the lengthy learning period this makes possible gives to human culture and society its dynamic quality. The elderly suffer diminishing powers, yet – as the death of a parent brings home to us – without their memory, experience and recognition their children are diminished. The advent of a knowledge-based economy does not abolish these dependencies but rather extends and amplifies them, with a learning process that reaches into old age. But the implications of these developments for a modern economy have yet to be properly worked out. Central to them is the financing of pension regimes and systems of social security.

The provision of pensions seems to be about distributing wealth, not creating it. In economists' parlance it is about 'transfers' and rentier income, which can easily appear to belong to a passive realm of consumption and coupon clipping. Yet the financing of retirement income is related to the central dynamic of the economy. While a good pension regime could help to reinforce a healthy and sustainable pattern of economy, a bad and short-sighted one will compound economic dangers and social distempers. Pension provision has a reputation for being arcane, worthy and boring. Pensions may be thought tedious because they are horribly complicated, or because they sacrifice the present to a remote future, and spontaneity to calculation, or because they embody a vain human attempt to control the future – an attempt never more fruitless, some claim, than in today's ever more uncertain world. These notions are not completely wrong but they get in the way of more important truths.

We live in the present but that present is always in flight towards the future and we are all curious about where we might be going. The act of securing that future for others and ourselves allows us to extend our hopes and energies to a further horizon; it can ensure that all continue to be full members of society. The coexistence of generations three, or even four, deep allows greater perspective. But this is not the only riposte. Those who value the present and proximate future should consider that the world we live in is shaped decisively by the way we organise pensions. Thus even the gut feeling that we should enjoy the present – *carpe diem* – should take account of the fact that today, as never before, our possibilities are dominated by the structures we find already in place to determine the future.

Retirement Funds and Global Capital

The distribution of property is one such future-oriented structure since ownership of property confers rights to go on enjoying it, or to claim the income or rent which it is capable of procuring. This observation becomes doubly true today when so much of the investment which shapes our future is undertaken by pension funds. In fact decisions taken by fund managers, and deeply determined by the legal and incentive structures within which they work, shape the world in which we live. At present the pension funds are integral to a globalised economy which decrees that shopping malls and shiny office blocks will proliferate while parks, swimming pools, libraries and theatres open to all will not, that some regions will boom while others decay, that commercial gain will displace the ethos of public service, that the poorest will have to tighten their belts if economic 'adjustment' is required, that natural resources accumulated over millennia will be consumed in a few short years, and that the abundance of the oceans will be poisoned and destroyed. A central feature of this brave new world is a pervasive commodification in which such items as clean water, fresh air, a good education or security in old age become 'products' to be bought and sold.

In fact the boring world of pension provision now fuels the glamorous world of high finance, property speculation, rogue traders, media and technology mergers, and stock exchange bubbles. Those who market and manage pension products are big players. Underlying the spills and thrills of globalisation is the search by money managers for a better return on the savings of a few hundred million employees, mostly in the First World but some in the Third World too. Though some of the beneficiaries are comfortably off, these people are not the super-rich. In fact they include many modestly paid janitors, factory workers, teachers, lorry drivers, hospital workers, clerks and those in a host of other occupations so long as they are relatively permanent; but conversely they cover fewer of the unemployed, or carers, or those who work in the countryside or in some temporary job.

Employee pension schemes around the world were estimated to have reached a global value of $13 trillion, that is $13 thousand billion or, to spell it right out, $13,000,000,000,000, in 1999.* This compares with world GNP of about $28 trillion and a world-wide value of stock markets of $23 trillion, according to OECD figures for the previous year. Three-fifths of global pension assets, $7.8 trillion, were held for US policy holders, with their stake having grown by 140 per cent since 1994. This growth reflected both booming share prices and the hefty contribution rate of 'baby-boomers' close to their earnings peak. By 1999 the Japanese pension funds held assets worth $1.5 trillion and the British funds assets worth $1.4 trillion.[2] The pension funds own much else besides shares – real estate, government bonds, works of art and simple cash. But the ownership of corporate equities has long dominated the portfolios of the pension funds.

The rise of the pension funds and other institutional investors does not mean the demise of the wealthy individual. Notwithstanding the steady advance of what Peter Drucker once called 'pension fund socialism', and nearly three decades after he first coined the term, the bourgeoisie is still in place and a cosmopolitan capitalist class commands more assets than ever before.[3] At the end of 1999 there were seven million individuals world-wide with liquid assets of over $1 million. There were 2.5 million of these 'high net worth' individuals in North America with a total wealth of $8.1 trillion, ahead of the value of US pension fund assets by what, in this context, we may deem a whiskery $0.3 trillion. In the UK in 1997 there were 147,000 high net worth individuals – in this case those with more than £0.5 million of liquid assets – and their total holdings were worth £659 billion, close to the then value of UK pension fund assets. At the top of the global wealth pyramid at the end of 1999 there were 514 dollar billionaires, including 276 Americans, 115 Europeans and 77 Asians. The 400 wealth-iest US citizens together held property worth just over $1 trillion in 1999.[4]

All these wealthy individuals, whether millionaires or billionaires, hold their assets in a variety of forms, but their shareholdings are big enough to give them huge influence in business affairs. Much of the time rich indi-viduals and large institutions may react in similar ways to market signals and opportunities, though some individuals may be more entrepreneurial. On average, the pension funds have much larger holdings than all except the top echelon of wealthy individuals. There are thousands of pension funds

---

* Throughout, billion is used to mean thousand million.

worth over $1 billion, with dozens in the United States alone worth more than Bill Gates. Even small funds are worth hundreds of millions of dollars. And those who manage the pension funds are becoming more prone to coordinate their strategies. While all investors, individual and institutional, use the facilities offered by banks, brokers and money managers, those with more assets can obtain better terms and their greater resources should allow them to spread risk more advantageously. But the money managers, investment banks and brokers are positioned to secure a high price for their services. We will see that much of the gain reaped by the funds, if not all of it, goes to these intermediaries, rather than to the holders of the pension plans who face a bemusing array of choices and whose legal rights to their 'pot' are very much less clear-cut than the right of wealthy individuals to their investments and assets. So while the institutions may have more leverage than many wealthy individuals, the policy holder has even less leverage over the supposed guardian of his or her interests.

The famous complexity of pension provision has already been mentioned as one of the off-putting aspects of the topic. This complexity afflicts both the pension itself and its implications for the wider society. State pension provision does have its arcane aspects, often to do with the contribution record or other qualifications relating to various levels of provision, especially if 'means tests' are applied. But public pensions are simple compared with the luxuriant variety of private provision. Some of this complexity is, perhaps, inescapable; after all, the pension plan is trying to anticipate different futures and to offer choice. But, inevitably, complexity generates confusion and this offers openings to marketing gimmicks and high-powered salesmanship. In the late 1990s BBC TV's *Money Programme* sent a reporter into the streets of the City of London to find out whether the businesslike citizens striding along its pavements would claim to understand their own pensions; most confessed themselves to be as baffled as the rest of us. When I got my first permanent job, personnel called me in to ask whether I would like my pension 'with profits' or without, much as one might be asked, 'Do you take your coffee with or without sugar?' I discovered that a 'with profits' policy was one which smoothed the ups and downs of the market by withholding some income in good years and paying out from reserves in bad years. But how this was done remained as much a mystery as ever. Only later did I realise that the information necessary to assess a 'with profits' policy is not, in fact, divulged to the mere policy holder. The 'with profits' device, until then the hallmark of responsible risk pooling in the British pensions and annuities industry, was to attract a glare of negative publicity when Equitable Life, a London insurance house founded in 1762, was itself obliged to close its doors to new business in December 2000. The problem – to be discussed in chapter 3 – in fact stemmed not from the 'with profits' device but from a foolish promise to pay a guaranteed rate of interest on some of its annuity products. But the collapse highlighted the 'with profits' policies because it was to be the holders of the latter – about a million of them – who were expected to foot the bill. Even if the policy holders had correctly grasped the small print in their own policy they could still be brought low by the small print in some other policy issued by Equitable.

Writing about the pension scheme options facing a US employee in an occupational scheme in 1983, Laurence Kotlikoff and Daniel Smith observed:

> A typical worker today might face age and service restrictions on plan participation, a graduated vesting schedule, portability with a specified set of co-participating employers, a social security step-rate integrated benefit formula, an optimal peak-years or terminal years earnings base, age- and service-specific early retirement benefit reduction rates, supplemental early retirement benefits, partial actuarial increases in benefits for work beyond the plan's normal retirement age, and limited cost of living allowances.

So long as the policy holder wanted all these wrinkles, getting to grips with them would be plain sailing compared with the laconic rider to this list: 'An informed worker should also understand the investment decisions of the pension fund's portfolio manager.'[5]

The foregoing refers to workers with an occupational pension. Such employees at least find themselves entering into terms negotiated by their union representatives with access to legal and accounting expertise. Those taking out individual pension plans are urged to seek professional advice but to do so is bound to be costly and many are tempted to skip this precaution. The financial industry expends considerable ingenuity and marketing muscle touting its extensive range of pension products. Inescapably, the proliferation of choice from a multitude of providers carries a high, but not immediately visible, price tag. One of the aims of this book is to identify costly structures of provision and to distinguish real difficulties from wilful obfuscation and the mystique of marketing.

However, such questions by no means exhaust the complexity of pension provision. In principle, pension regimes throw up problems whose elucidation requires findings drawn from demography, actuarial calculation, law, micro-economics, macro-economics, welfare economics, social gerontology, generational ethics and, doubtless, several other daunting specialisms besides. Many traditional approaches to economic arrangements have tended to a reductive presentism, giving a cross-section at one moment in time. Even approaches sensitive to issues of social equality and inclusion have asked whether this tax or that benefit would redistribute from rich to poor, or from young to old, without taking proper cognisance of the fact that age cohorts can differ greatly in size. When they do, generational transfers can become very unequal and the same rules applied to successive generations can produce very discrepant results. This does not justify a 'war of the generations' approach to pension provision or anything else. In recent years an alarmist literature has grown up which attempts to compute the supposedly intolerable burden represented by the promises implicit in public pension arrangements, without due account being taken of offsetting factors or of the new opportunities this represents to improve pension financing. Too often the alarmists and partisans of 'generational accounting' themselves adopt a flawed or foreshortened model of the economy and further implicitly assume that pensions can only be furnished either out of today's taxes or out of funds managed by the financial services industry.[6] But the basic point that social justice cannot be achieved without due attention to generational complexity remains valid.[7]

The policies governing the provision of public pensions need not be baffling, and in a number of countries there appears to be considerable understanding of them. The essential workings of the US Social Security system are quite well understood; indeed it has retained its reputation of being the 'third rail' of national life since the late 1930s.[8] US legislators wisely entrusted management of the programme not to a government ministry but to a quasi-autonomous Social Security Administration which is obliged to make annual reports concerning its financial state, complete with demographic projections, assumptions concerning future immigration and so forth. They further required an Advisory Council to investigate the workings of the system at regular intervals. The French public pension system is inherently more complicated but its administration is even more independent and its guiding principle of generational solidarity well understood. In both these countries a steady flow of editorials, articles, books and speeches by different political leaders means that one can truly speak of a national debate on the topic, something that has been less true in other countries, especially Britain. A study of the economics of pension provision in the UK sardonically observes of its tangled confusion and frequently changed nomenclature: 'the only saving grace of a such a complicated system is that no one understands it, thus making it (politically) easy to reform.'[9] Yet, as they show, successive waves of reform by stealth in the UK have created a bewildering patchwork of ill-understood programmes, in which public provision has contracted and private systems of delivery have been encouraged, notwithstanding their inadequate coverage, their history of 'mis-selling' and the failure of the pension funds to foster a healthy pattern of national economy.

Fortunately it is possible, by looking at pension provision as a whole and focusing on key links to the wider political economy, to cut through complexity and concentrate on basic design, leaving detailed refinements for the specialists to sort out. The contemporary debate on pension provision is beset by important but not inherently baffling or intractable questions. What are the respective merits of public or private provision? Does the ageing of the population pose intolerable burdens on pension provision? Should pensions be financed on a pay-as-you-go basis, like most state systems, or is it more prudent to establish a fund, as is usually the case with occupational schemes and personal pension plans? Has the growth of pension funds reached the point where they have an impact on the economic climate as a whole? Should pension provision be thought through in conjunction with a revaluation of the social contribution of older workers and attention to new lifestyles and life choices? While information and expertise are required to answer such questions, so is common sense and a willingness to engage in joined-up thought.

The Prophets of Pension Fund Socialism

In the 1970s *The Unseen Revolution* (1976) by Peter Drucker, the eminent philosopher of management, dramatically widened the scope of the debate by looking at pension funds within the context of the overall course of economic development. He complained:

> The Congress of the United States spent more than two years on ERISA, the Pension Reform Act of 1974, hearing countless witnesses, conducting dozens of studies, and considering a raft of alternative proposals. Yet there is not one mention in those thousands of printed pages of the social and political implications of the pension funds, and very little concern for the economic impacts, on capital market or capital formation, for example. The entire discussion is on actuarial and portfolio management matters only.[10]

Drucker believed that pension funds might be the key to rekindling economic advance. The persistence of low growth, even in the 'recovery' phase of the trade cycle following the oil shock of the 1970s, led to increasing concern with the two issues he had singled out, the functioning of the capital market and the extent of capital formation. Thanks to the 1974

Employee Retirement Income Security Act (ERISA) legislation, private pension provision did grow and channelled a growing stream of savings to the financial services industry. But as economic malaise stubbornly refused to go away opinion divided, with some blaming bloated public programmes for 'crowding out' a healthy recovery and others focusing on what they saw as the malfunctioning of the financial sector itself. Free market economics, marginalised during the postwar boom, was becoming respectable again, with first Friedrich von Hayek, and then Milton Friedman, receiving the Nobel Prize for economics. Proposals began to be aired for swingeing reductions in public expenditure and for the privatisation of public provision and services. The argument was heard that the Social Security system should be privatised to enable more savings to flow into the financial system. In 1976 the International Monetary Fund, an institution founded partly at British initiative according to a British plan, insisted that the London government had to cut back on many of its most popular programmes and impose a regime of stringent austerity. Anthony Crosland, a member of the Labour cabinet, famously declared: 'The party's over'. The London government complied, though its success in reducing wages and social provision eventually cost it the election of 1979.

Peter Drucker's book celebrated the growing importance of funded pension provision, arguing that it embodied an alternative to both free market economics and the big state. His references to 'pension fund socialism', and his claim that if the essence of socialism was that the workers should control the means of production then the United States was 'the first truly "socialist" country in the world', were deliberately provocative and playful but nonetheless serious. He argued that employee pension funds had acquired a potentially controlling stake in most large US corporations. Drucker was exaggerating the situation as it stood in 1974 but over the succeeding decades the pension fund stake was to grow both absolutely and relatively. In his view, pension fund collectivism offered an alternative to both state socialism and free market individualism:

> The pension fund movement is not 'individualism' à la Herbert Hoover. Pension funds are collectives. And the agents are other collectives, the large employing organisations. But they are 'non-government' and, in that sense, 'private'. They offer one example of the efficacy of using private non-governmental institutions of our 'society of organizations' for the formulation and achievement of social goals and the satisfaction of human needs.[11]

In such passages Drucker's claims for pension funds sometimes betray a blindness to, or perhaps underestimation of, the capitalist dynamic which still underlay the 'society of organisations'. On this score, coming decades were to show that pension fund managers single-mindedly focusing on shareholder value were quite unconcerned with 'the formulation and achievement of social goals' or the 'satisfaction of human needs'. Perhaps the reason why Drucker's revolution was 'unseen' was that it had not yet happened. Nevertheless, as we will see, he was on to something.

Drucker also sought to alert his readers to what he saw as a demographic threat to the rate of capital formation. In his view, reorganised pension funds could foster new capital formation in ways that would counteract America's chronic undersaving and a looming social crisis as the population aged. Drucker maintained that as the numbers of retired pension receivers grew in relation to the active labour force, then neither Social Security nor the pension funds would contribute to net savings. The contributions going to Social Security would simply be transferred to pensioners who would spend them; likewise with the pension funds, which by about 1990 would begin taking more out of the stock market than they put in according to Drucker's calculations. Once again, Drucker had anticipated the pension debate of the future even if he placed the dis-savings crisis too early. Drucker believed that it was wrong for banking institutions to manage pension funds since it involved them in conflicts of interest. He did not believe it was either desirable or possible for banks to construct so-called 'Chinese walls' between their business loan departments and their money management departments. In his view, pension funds anyway needed trustees who were independent of banks and employers and who truly represented the interests of the employees whose savings they managed. Only trustees of this sort would have the legitimacy and autonomy needed to act in the long-term interests of pension fund beneficiaries, persuading them, when necessary, to raise contribution rates to ward off inflation and to ensure investment-led growth sufficient to anticipate the rising proportion of the retired and the consequent dis-saving problem.[12]

Drucker had a bolder and more rounded vision but there were others who realised that economic growth and social provision had to be thought through together. This new imperative was recognised by the report of the Wilson Commission, chaired by the country's ex-Prime Minister, on the workings of the British financial system. The report urged a new statute for pension funds, a measure that would help the public authorities to regain leverage over the economy, and withstand the pressure of international finance. However, it appeared at a time when the débâcle of the government of his successor, Callaghan, was sufficient to discredit anything associated with the Labour leadership. Yet, however sorry the performance of the Labour administrations of the 1970s, the fact remains that their encounter with what we now call globalisation was educative for many involved. Tony Benn, a Labour cabinet minister, was advised by Jack Jones, the trade union leader, that finding a way to finance pension promises would have more far-reaching significance than another piecemeal nation-alisation programme. A response to this advice figured in Benn's remarks about the possible role of pension funds in *Arguments for Socialism* (1979) in which he observed:

> the financial institutions . . . do not necessarily use the huge sums put at their disposal in a manner compatible with the common interest. This is one area where there will have to be change. . . . These savings belong to the workers, they are their own deferred earnings. Workers want them not only as income when they retire, but while they are at work, and so to guar-antee that they will retire in a buoyant economy.

Benn went on to envisage trade union representation 'alongside investment managers in the big financial institutions' and to propose that the value of the funds be guaranteed by North Sea oil revenues.[13] But it was to be Margaret Thatcher who benefited from the deals struck with the oil com-panies and Labour was to be out of office for eighteen years. As we will see in chapter 5, Labour's more generous pension arrangements were to be the Conservative premier's first target.

Drucker's visionary thesis attracted little attention on the Left, but there were some exceptions. Randy Barber and Jeremy Rifkind published *The North Will Rise Again* (1978),[14] outlining a bold plan to use employee pen-sion funds for regional regeneration and to prevent the blight of the rustbelt area of the US north-east. Their advocacy did encourage some small-scale experiments in social investment whose fruits will be examined in what follows. Two other books explored the idea that there was an urgent need for a progressive reform of the retirement fund regime: *The Political Economy of Aging* (1982) by Laura Katz Olson, and Eric Shragge's *Pension Policy in Britain: a Socialist Analysis* (1984). Olson combined a per-ceptive critique of the 'medical industrial complex' and prophetic warnings concerning the dangers of privatising care for the elderly with the con-clusion that: 'If employees and communities succeed in wresting control over pension funds, despite some inevitable and fundamental systemic constraints, they can serve potentially as one step toward a fundamental transformation of society.'[15] For his part, the British author Eric Shragge argued that while Drucker's claims were over-pitched, and his proposed programme of reform too limited, he was nonetheless right to draw atten-tion to the collectivist dynamics of the new pension fund regime. In Shragge's view, if groups of workers were allowed to exercise real control of their pension funds this would help to remove the dead hand of state bureaucracy from the socialist model.[16] The British National Union of Miners did try to take up this idea but lost a key legal battle in the mid-1980s as a consequence of which none of the miners' huge pension assets were invested in the regeneration of their own blighted valleys and villages. Margaret Thatcher's victory over the NUM in 1984–85, and over the Labour Party in successive elections, set the scene for a very different experiment in pension reform (to be considered in chapter 5).

Someone who raised similar issues to Drucker quite independently around the same time was Rudolf Meidner, a German refugee who became chief economist at the LO, the Swedish trade union federation. He was one of the architects of the postwar Swedish welfare system and witness to the fierce battle over the funding of secondary pensions in Sweden in 1957–60. This episode underlined the importance of finding ways to guarantee funding for social programmes without overloading the tax system. The Swedish Social Democrats had always encouraged a flourishing private sector but in the mid-1970s Meidner put forward proposals for making sure that this prosperity would be shared more widely and harnessed to industrial policy.

The 'Meidner plan' required that large companies would issue shares to their own workforce, up to a threshold of 20 per cent of their equity, after which further share distributions would be made to public bodies representing wage earners in each region. These corporations, it was argued, could make profits only because of the wider social context and should therefore be obliged to return a portion of these profits – initially 20 per cent – in the shape of shares issued to the wage-earner funds. The funds would commit to maintain these investments in the companies and use the income they would eventually generate in socially useful ways. Unlike taxes, these levies would not go to the state and would not subtract from corporate investment. The 'wage-earner funds' would, it was hoped, ensure that the fruits of economic advance were shared by employees and society at large; although returns to these funds might eventually help to underwrite social or pension provision this was not their stated purpose, which was simply to strengthen the position of wage earners. (Sweden already had a fund for supplementary pensions but it was barred from buying equities.) The Meidner plan was strongly supported by the LO in 1976 – most unusually, the vote at the conference which approved the proposal was greeted by an ovation and the singing of the 'Internationale'. The Social Democrats did not immediately endorse the plan and lost the election held that year. But prior to the elections of 1982, which they did win, the Social Democrats committed themselves to the introduction of a modified version of Meidner's plan, though the party leaders were not fully convinced. Opinion polls showed that the wage-earner funds were popular among Social Democrat voters. The country's business leaders were intensely alarmed and spent five times more money attacking the plan than the cash laid out by all the parties on the 1982 election. The privately owned press ran a sustained and vigorous campaign exploiting every real or supposed weakness in the plan and harping on the equivocations of the Social Democratic leadership. The opposition parties argued that the wage-earner funds would give too much power to trade union leaders, and leave unrepresented those who were self-employed, unemployed or not in a union. Since the initial share distributions went in the first instance to representatives of the private sector companies, public sector workers felt left out. Under assault, support for the scheme ebbed and the Social Democrat leaders believed that it was prudent greatly to dilute the scheme so that the government could concentrate on defending the welfare system.

The Meidner plan was a prototype in need of some refinement and firm articulation. As Rudolf Meidner well knew, time was running out for the 'Swedish home'. Ironically, if fewer compromises had been made and the social purpose of the scheme clarified, support for it could have been maintained. Jonas Pontusson has urged that the 'general interest' served by the wage-earner funds was not sufficiently established.[17] If most of the income from the wage-earner funds had been pledged to boosting pension provision, or to some other specific social purpose, then perhaps this would have countered the impression created by the plan's opponents that its aim was simply to boost trade union power. Implementation of the Meidner plan could have furnished a critical element of protection to the Swedish welfare model by taking some of the strain from taxation and by giving the wage-earner funds a voice and a vote in determining the policies of the large corporations. It would have made it more difficult for the Swedish banks and multinationals to undermine Sweden's welfare system by running down their stake in domestic facilities and siphoning off large resources to overseas investments. Within two or three decades a full-blooded Meidner scheme would have made the 'wage-earner funds' the masters of the economy – which is why bourgeois interests mobilised so energetically against it. The defeat of the scheme left the Swedish financial industry with increased freedom of action. A speculative boom ensued, centred on real estate, first at home and then abroad. In 1990–91 the bubble burst, creating mass unemployment. A haemorrhage of capital had helped to enfeeble the productive base and expose the 'Swedish home' to exercises in social dumping. In the mid-1990s the residual 'wage-earner funds' were wound up and their assets – now worth about £1.8 billion – were used to set up a variety of scholarly research institutes. In consequence, research of all types was to be better funded in Sweden in the 1990s than in other parts of Europe: though Meidner's grand objective was thwarted, even this modest outcome demonstrated the scheme's potential for underwriting social expenditure.

'Old Age Crisis' and Privatisation

Unfortunately, the New Right proved to be better at spotting the far-reaching implications of pension policy than was the Left. For the Left pension provision had to be defended, of course, but few noticed its fundamental significance for the whole rhythm of economic and social advance. As for the representations of the New Right, these had a powerful ally in the shape of the financial industry itself. There were alarmist projections of the future cost of an ageing population and assurances that the best, or perhaps only, solution was to scale back public pensions – or, even better, privatise them outright – and oblige people to save for their retirement relying on the skills of the financial services industry.

In 1994 these themes achieved a new respectability and solidity when the World Bank issued an influential report, *Averting the Old Age Crisis: Policies to Protect the Old and Promote Growth*, whose sub-title already announced an agenda. The report represented a sustained challenge to what it called the 'dominant public pillar' of pension provision. The analysis offered by the World Bank was to inform and legitimate an undermining of public provision and a thrust towards commercialisation which was to influence many governments and was boosted by the real or supposed successes of 'Anglo-Saxon' economics. But in the sphere of pension policy neo-liberal policy proposals have not carried all before them. When attempts have been made to introduce them they have encountered stiff resistance – in the streets, at the ballot box and in an impressive range of research papers and other publications.

The resulting debate throws into relief the wider issues of political economy and social justice posed by pension arrangements, as I seek to demonstrate in what follows. Although I will pay some attention to demographic issues, the fact of an ageing society does not point in a single obvious direction, as some wrongly suppose. A chorus of commentators harps on the theme of the looming demographic disaster. While there are real issues of intergenerational justice I do not believe that the current problem is essentially a war of the generations, pitting 'Generation X' against the 'baby-boomers'. There is a phoney 'youthism' in contemporary Western culture, often peddled by those who are not so young anyway, which seeks to make reckless consumerism seem alluring. Giant corporations who use computers to answer their phones, use teenagers to make their logos sexy. Yesterday's internet entrepreneurs notwithstanding, most executives drawing mega-salaries are well into middle age. And caricatures of 'greedy geezers' or rhetorical flights of 'boomer bashing' typically fail to address the yawning gulf of circumstance and opportunity within each generation. The pension funds have promoted a 'globalised' pattern of increasing inequality, insecurity and pillage which deepens class cleavage and threatens young and old alike.[18]

In itself, the ageing of the population tells us nothing about how best to deliver good pensions to more people. Yet neo-liberal advocates find demographic doom-mongering irresistible. The pay-as-you-go pension systems are vitiated, in this view, by the fact that the ratio of those paying contributions to those receiving pensions has dropped from five or six to one in the 1950s to three or four to one in the 1990s, and perhaps two to one or less as the population ages. The viability of Social Security in the United States was questioned in the 1970s and again attacked in the 1980s after the 1983 Greenspan Commission reforms. By the 1990s the plight of the Italian, French and German systems seemed even worse. It was not difficult to find those predicting that tax payers in these countries would soon have to pay 20 to 30 per cent of their income – or in one case I cite in chapter 4, 70 per cent of their income – simply to finance the state pension system. Governments in these countries produced schemes for postponing or reducing pension rights but these ran into stiff opposition. In the neo-liberal view the answer was to cut back on public pensions and encourage citizens to make provision for their own retirement by contributing to commercial pension funds.

The resulting battles and controversies are examined in chapters 4–6 but for the present it is enough to note that pension-related issues made a contribution to the defeat of right-wing governments in Italy in 1996, France in 1997 and Germany in 1998. Some might add the defeat of the Major government in 1997, since the Conservative record had been tarnished by a gigantic 'mis-selling' scandal and the morale of often Conservative-leaning pensioners had been undermined by the government's financial mismanagement and policy of allowing the state pension to lag far behind the rise of earnings. In the United States President Clinton chose his State of the Union messages in 1998 and 1999 to launch an ambitious plan to refinance the Social Security retirement scheme, arguing that two-thirds of the growing budget surplus should be committed to guarantee the programme. In the 2000 presidential contest this issue furnished one of the few substantial differences between the candidates of the two main parties. While Gore wished to retain and bolster Social Security, Bush urged that employees should be allowed to hold back a proportion of their Social Security contribution in order to set up their own supervised pension plans. Bush, who must be aware of the Reagan administration's defeat when it sought to tamper with the 'third rail' of American politics, of course claims that his goal is to strengthen Social Security. The issues at stake in the US Social Security debate are examined in chapter 6.

Confronted with often overstated and unduly alarmist claims, it is worth asserting that growing life expectancy is a good thing. The concomitant decline in the birth rate in most advanced countries reflects a preference for smaller families and reduces the pressure of population on resources. Rather than being invoked as a source of pessimism or disaster, these developments could lead to more fulfilling as well as longer lives. Certainly it will be important to ensure that older people's livelihoods are maintained but this can be done without sacrificing the interests of succeeding generations, so long as appropriate measures are taken.

The true dimensions of the ageing problem are often misconstrued. Thus the 'shortage of workers' argument ignores several major countervailing circumstances. *Firstly*, the medical advances which lengthen life expectancy also lengthen people's ability to go on working past the standard age of retirement. *Secondly*, if there is a labour shortage in one country it can often be met by immigration from another. *Thirdly*, the decline in the birth rate reduces the number of children, which has the effect of reducing the number of dependants per worker. *Fourthly*, technological advance is continually raising the productivity of labour, meaning that even a reduced workforce could maintain levels of national wealth. *Fifthly*, it is clear that the problems of modern capitalist economies do not principally centre on labour shortage. If they did unemployment rates and early retirement would not be as high as they are in Europe, every country would have Swedish-style free childcare facilities to raise female labour participation rates and the US authorities would take care not to allow large numbers of able-bodied people to fester in prisons.[19]

While all the above considerations mitigate the economic and social consequences of an ageing population they do not, of course, recommend the conclusion that there is no problem. The different factors itemised will only mitigate or ease the strains of an ageing society if new approaches and policies are adopted. Thus the potential of older workers, even of many well below retirement age, cannot be counted on if, as at present, it is frustrated by the ageism of employers. Similarly, public pension arrangements deter older workers from continuing in employment by withdrawing benefit if they do. In effect this means that the earnings of those over the age of sixty or sixty-two are taxed at exorbitant marginal rates. Because of the grotesque inequalities in the world, emigration to the richer countries is likely to increase and will make some contribution to improving their dependency ratios. But the ageing of populations is a world-wide phenomenon. Its consequences will have to be faced in, say, China, no less than in Europe, and no country will be able indefinitely to rely on immigration to solve its ageing problem. Moreover, the governments and peoples of the developing countries will only receive limited help from high levels of emigration. Emigrants do tend to remit money home, or return themselves, but poor areas will not be helped by losing large numbers of expensively educated and trained people. So while migrations will play some positive role, and are both desirable and unstoppable anyway, they will not supply some providential solution.

The real challenge is to find a healthier political economy which could help all parts of an unevenly ageing world to make the necessary adjustments. According to the 1998 revision of UN projections of world population, all regions face the prospect that the proportion of over-sixties in their population will double over the next fifty years. Table I.1 presents the medium range of predictions concerning dependency ratios – the numbers of the old and/or young per 100 working-age adults – made by the UN demographers, together with their best estimates for 1950 and 1998 for comparison. The projections extrapolate from present trends, especially increasing longevity nearly everywhere and declining fertility as development takes place. Such trends change in unexpected ways but it would be irresponsible not to reckon with the possibility that something like these ratios lies in store, whether a little sooner or later than predicted.

Table I.1 shows that while ageing is, and has been, a global phenomenon, its impact on the dependency ratio has so far been offset by the declining number of children, even in the developed world. The notion of 'economic dependence' employed by the categories in the table implies that fifteen is roughly the age at which people enter the workforce and sixty is the age at which they leave it. For the majority of the world's populations, this is probably a reasonable assumption. The actual and predicted ratios

Table I.1 World population age ratios (per 100 adults aged 15–59)

	Overall dependency ratio			Child/adult ratio			Older person/adult ratio		
	1950	*1998*	*2050*	*1950*	*1998*	*2050*	*1950*	*1998*	*2050*
World	74	63	72	60	51	34	14	16	38
Developed countries	64	61	92	45	30	29	19	31	62
Less developed	79	69	69	68	56	34	12	13	35
Least developed	88	90	56	77	81	37	10	9	18
Europe	62	61	97	43	29	28	20	32	68
North America	66	61	82	45	35	31	21	26	51
Oceania	69	64	76	50	42	33	19	22	43
Africa	91	92	56	81	83	38	10	10	19
Asia	76	65	74	65	51	33	12	14	41
Latin America	85	67	74	74	54	35	11	13	39

Notes: *Child*, those aged 0–15; *Adult*, those aged 15-59; *Older person*, those aged 60 and over.

Source: United Nations, *World Population Prospects: the 1998 Revision*, vol. 3, *Analytical Report*, New York 2000, pp. 159-74.

show that the age structure should not have been a burden anywhere in the twentieth century. If dependency was experienced as a burden – or if the young or old were condemned to unemployment – then the cause was economic failure, not demographic pressure. (A possibility to be considered will be that the prevailing regimes of pension provision have been an active part of the problem.) The developed world confronts the definite possibility, according to this medium projection, that the numbers of dependants per 100 adults will rise by a third, from around 61 in 1998 to 92 in 2050. At that time the increased proportion of older people elsewhere in the world will probably be offset by a reduced number of children. But if this is the case, then eventually the same overall reduction in the ratio of working adults to dependants will occur there too as these societies age. When assessing the possibilities and probabilities we should bear in mind that the demographic experts have often underestimated the speed of demographic changes.

Financing the New Life-Course

In later chapters more detailed and near-term estimates are given but the broad correlations indicated by the overall medium-term projections cited above are worth bearing in mind. They imply a need to modify and adapt inherited notions of the life-course. In the classic industrial-age life-cycle individuals would spend at least the first fifteen years of their life as dependants; then they would work for forty or fifty years and contribute taxes to be spent on programmes for the young, old and sick; finally they would spend about half a dozen years, or a little more, in retirement, once more supported by the efforts of the working-age population, just as they had been in their childhood. While these age brackets still had much purchase on the world of 1998, they were already disappearing fast among the global middle class. The life-cycle towards which we are already moving – especially in the developed world but even beyond it – looks very different. The period of education is being extended by five or ten years and the period of retirement by twenty. And the 'contributory' period of work is itself more likely to be punctuated by learning and retraining. Overall – and notwithstanding the important work that may be undertaken by students and retired persons – the period of economic dependency is likely to be extended. Given advances in the social productivity of labour, the 'burden' of providing for this need not be at all unmanageable, so long as it is identified and appropriately anticipated.

As things are now, the size of the real burden of dependency is not easy to assess. The way work is organised does not make the most of our capacities and marginalises the older worker. The different phases of the life-cycle are too clearly demarcated. Thus by the early 1990s unemployment among men aged 55–60 was around a third, and among men aged 60–64 around a half, in most large OECD countries (except Japan, where only 25 per cent of 60–64-year-old men were unemployed).[20] The exclusion of older women from paid work is even greater, so that overall more than half of those aged 55–65 are now typically out of work. Men and women in their fifties who lose a job find it very difficult to get back into employment. Obviously, much more could be done to retrain older workers and find new outlets for their skills and experience. It is not at all uncommon for people to discover new talents in their fifties that went unnoticed because of premature specialisation or simply the stultifying nature of too many jobs. And there can also be rediscoveries of yesterday's achievements – what one might call the 'Buena Vista Social Club effect' – which enhance the prestige of the elderly. In Cuba it is not only mid-century *son* which is newly appreciated but also the traditional cultivating techniques of farmers who did not use chemical sprays or fertiliser.

The benefits to be gained from a more active population of older people are literally incalculable. Instead, many of the elderly have been warehoused in segregated districts and those denied work in their fifties or early sixties are obliged to seek disability pensions. A French study of the retired in the 1970s portrayed it as a time of 'social death',[21] while British researchers analysed the condition of the elderly as being that of 'structured dependence'.[22] More recent social gerontology believes that greater attention should be paid to the everyday strategies whereby the elderly contrive to assert themselves.[23] But a balanced view would have to keep hold of both perspectives, since the official impulse to impose structured dependence has not disappeared.

Thus, while older people have often been treated as passive recipients of public good works, the older worker can also be represented as possessed of the wrong sort of ingenuity and initiative. In recent times British governments, both Conservative and Labour, have claimed that the rise in those receiving disability pensions is a species of welfare fraud. But as Richard Berthoud points out,

> When a stricter medical test was introduced in 1996, about 160,000 claimants were denied benefit. About a quarter of these cases were reinstated on appeal. Crucially only a fifth of those disallowed found any work over the following year. The only effect on the remainder was loss of income. The relationship between impairment and employability is far from straightforward. In the real world, partial incapacity is an important issue. . . . An alternative interpretation of the rise in incapacity claims is based on the effect of long-run labour market changes on the employment prospects of impaired people. As the overall rise in the number of potential workers has exceeded the growth in jobs available, employers have become much more discriminating.[24]

Older workers often compensate for any physical impairment by their experience and interpersonal skills. But employers in an underperforming economy will often prefer to pension off older workers, especially if they can replace them with cheaper, younger workers and if the pension comes from another budget. A more organically productive economy would be able to give suitable employment to older workers, and pay them any pension entitlement as well.

Such observations should not blind us to the probable economic cost of greater longevity. We should not expect, still less demand, that the benefits of a more active 'third age' (as the French call it) should translate into a stream of saleable goods or services. In many cases more resources may need to be expended to make it possible for all this to happen: whatever their other problems, Cuba's veterans of *son* shared a good life expectancy with everybody else because of a well-resourced healthcare system. Rising longevity means many more of the 'old old' whose medical and care needs all have to be met. The healthcare costs of the elderly may well absorb

3–5 per cent of national income. If these are added to the demands of pension provision, it is clear that financing the ageing society will indeed be a demanding proposition.

Fortunately or otherwise, the problems of pension provision will not be ignored. There are large constituencies and powerful lobby groups which will insist they are addressed. People who have reached, or are approaching, pensionable age constitute a larger proportion of the electorate as the ageing phenomenon proceeds. They are often more likely to vote than younger people (though this does not apply to the very old and isolated). In most countries politicians have learnt the importance of cultivating the older voter. Politicians have also discovered that middle-aged voters are influenced by their parents' experience, partly out of filial sympathy, partly because they know they may face the same problems before too long, and partly because they may have to make up for any shortfall themselves.

The contemporary literature on the costs of the ageing society often pits defenders of the viability of existing public welfare and pension arrangements against those who insist that the sharp drop in the dependency ratio – the proportion between active workers and those dependent on transfer incomes – makes imperative an entirely new approach to the problem. In this book I draw on the argument and evidence of works in the former category but the writings of the alarmists and critics of existing welfare arrangements – Peter Peterson's *Gray Dawn* or David Thomson's *Selfish Generations?* – should not be entirely disregarded.[25] Their identification of the problem exaggerates generational tension, fails to address the weaknesses of today's pension fund capitalism and is bereft of real solutions. But the sheer novelty of the generational structure that will very likely characterise the new century could strain prevailing welfare and property arrangements to breaking point. The ageing society is the result not just of increased life expectancy but of dramatically lowered birth rates, leading, in the case of many developed societies by 2020 or a little later, to a contracting population.[26] In itself this development possesses welcome features but it will require innovation to tap them. Labour will become scarcer relative to capital – reversing the trend of the last quarter century. Companies and other employing organisations, which have spent this time eroding labour conditions and rights, will now, instead, have to learn how to woo their actual and potential workforce, including older workers.

Notwithstanding its talk of 'stakeholding' and the 'third way', Britain's New Labour proved a slow learner in this area though, as we will discover in chapter 5, a string of disasters in the year 2000 was to oblige it to pay greater attention. In *The Third Way* (1998) Anthony Giddens endorsed the view that the old redistributive welfare state encouraged welfare dependency and should be replaced by a 'social investment state'. Such a phrase could encompass the approach of a Meidner, or the more radical proponents of 'pension fund socialism', but in fact it does not. Rather than being part of an argument for the pre-funding of social commitments, or a measure aimed at promoting new patterns of social self-management, it is an echo of Tony Blair's claimed prioritisation of 'education, education, education'. Giddens believes that old people should be weaned away from pension dependency and encouraged into greater levels of economic activity:

> The concept of the pension that begins at retirement age, and the label 'pensioner', were inventions of the welfare state. But not only do these not conform to the new realities of ageing, they are as clear a case of welfare dependency as one can find. . . . We should move towards abolishing the fixed age of retirement, and we should regard old people as a resource rather than a problem . . . it makes no sense to lock up pension funds against reaching 'pensionable age'.[27]

There is a good case for ending mandatory retirement ages and for allowing some limited flexibility in access to pension funds. But the first measure will not reverse the burden of social dependency, because, as Giddens himself acknowledges, early retirement – as things are, often of an involuntary character – will offset those who are able to find properly paid employment in their late sixties and seventies. And allowing the early withdrawal of savings, such as happens with many 401(k) funds in the United States, can only mean that larger funds will have to be accumulated in the first place (on which see chapter 2). So the challenge remains that of finding a new pattern of political economy which can absorb the increasing levels of social expenditure – on lifelong learning, certainly, but also on the provision of support and direct care for the elderly that cannot be conceptualised in economic terms as an investment. While being affirmative about the new possibilities of active retirement, and making sure that the resources are there to facilitate it, we should beware of implying that all older persons will be welcome at the banquet – so long as they display youthful style and vigour.

The ageing of the population will double the proportion of those aged over sixty-five in the population in all developed and most developing states. Between 1950 and 1998 the global numbers of those aged eighty or over rose by three and a half times to reach 66 million. These 'old old' are set to increase sixfold, reaching 370 million, by 2050, according to the UN medium projection.[28] While the over-65s – and over-80s – still have a life to live and a contribution to make – and should certainly not be condemned by ageism to some modern limbo of marginalised subsistence – the fact remains that these societies will need to make provision for perhaps a fifth of the population who will consume far more than they can produce. This explains why pension programmes loom so large in public finances and why funded private pension provision, where it is encouraged, soon controls huge resources.[29] Even other large items of expenditure – education, health, the armed forces – do not employ anything like a fifth of the population. Meeting the needs of such a sizeable body of persons is bound to have a large impact on the economy as a whole. Pernicious stereotypes of passive or grasping seniors do not help at all. Only economic security and independence will allow the old to enjoy life themselves and to participate in, and contribute to, society as a whole, whether economically or in a host of vitally significant non-economic ways.

The origins of modern *Homo sapiens* are everywhere marked by burial monuments and grave sites, often accompanied by finely worked tools, or garments, or decorations. The bonds between the generations are integral to personal and social identity. Human societies seem often to have found a value in the experience, or even mere existence, of the elders, perhaps especially older women. Though the numbers surviving past fifty must have been small, those who did survive would often command great respect. The nineteenth-century revivalist distrust of the spiritual capacity of the elderly, discussed in chapter 1, represented an important cultural shift, contributing to the modern cult of youth. A society that lacks a sense of where it is coming from, or negligently abets the tomb robbers, will lose its identity and sense of the future. Thus the prominence of the pension debate reflects questions that go to the heart of social existence.

The resources that will have to be mobilised to meet the economic challenge of pension provision have already whetted the appetite of a shark-like financial services industry, keen to sink its teeth into this abundant shoal of business. The private pensions lobby is already quite strong enough to furnish a flood of advertising to print and broadcast media. This helps to pay for special supplements which discuss the finer points of the different products on offer. Meanwhile, editorialists and financial columnists point out that with the prospect of a cutting back in public pension provision it must make sense to encourage people to take out their own retirement plan. Politicians' promises, they urge, are not to be trusted and it is better to secure the future by accumulating tangible assets. The pension fund, in this view, enables everyone to partake of the benefits of the equity culture. A balanced portfolio will enable the individual to minimise

risk and step on the escalator of national or global prosperity. Encouraging
more to save in this way will, it is claimed, raise the savings rate, making
possible higher rates of investment. If runaway demography is the problem,
then the answer lies in the skills and resources of the financial services
industry. But the state still has a vital covert role.

The classical free market doctrine really did propose a minimal state.
Today's partisans of pension reform, as we will see, invariably propose that
the private pensions industry should be sustained by government-imposed
obligations and favours. Yet the quality of pension provision furnished by
the commercial organisations remains in doubt. Even when stock markets
were booming, and in those countries where private pension fund provision
was extensive and long established – Britain and the United States – the
state pension still remains by far the most important source of income
for the great majority of the elderly. All existing forms of private pension
provision are marked by very uneven coverage. If increasing inequality
and social exclusion have been the fruits of 'Anglo-Saxon' economics
generally, pensions are no exception. So 'neo-liberal' pension reformers
propose to address these problems by herding the whole population into
privately run schemes, with implications that I will be addressing as my
argument unfolds.

I would not have written this book if I did not think that there are real
problems of poverty in old age, that they could get worse and that, especially given the relatively predictable nature of the ageing phenomenon,
they are readily soluble by sensible social and economic planning. Old
age has been reduced in the advanced countries, but not comprehensively
and definitively banished, while in the underdeveloped world it remains a
major problem. Most of the argument and illustration which follows
concerns the OECD countries because they have the resources for universal pension provision. Something will be said about countries like Chile
and China which also have the resources and aspiration to address the economic problems of old age. But there are many poorer countries where
there is no universal state pension, though commercial providers or occupational schemes may still cater to the wealthier classes. Among the evils
which result are, on the one hand, that savings are siphoned off for investment in richer countries, and, on the other, that there is a growing
economic burden of care for the aged on the majority of poorer families.
Although the discussion which follows is based mainly on OECD evidence, it has implications also for poorer countries since good pension
arrangements can promote productive and sustainable economies.

In the advanced countries themselves poverty is by no means confined to pensioners. In both the United States and Europe the number of children in poverty overtook the number of old people in the 1980s. For the young to be stunted and stigmatised by poverty is a terrible fate and one which is certain to exact a price, sooner or later, from the whole society. One of the reasons for the shameful extent of child poverty is that large numbers of parents are unemployed, or lack a decently paid job. Another is the failure of social programmes giving assistance to the excluded, as misplaced economies are imposed. In two recent books on the prospects for social policy in the United States – *The Missing Middle* by Theda Skocpol and *True Security* by Michael Graetz and Jerry Mashaw – the authors conclude that the problem of child poverty is more acute than that of old-age poverty.[30] While this may very well be true it does not mean – nor do these authors necessarily imply – that the two cases of social need should be pitted against one another rather than seen as issues both of which have to be tackled in a generous and enlightened spirit. Public pension provision has raised many out of extreme poverty, but the achievement is both uneven and precarious so there is no cause for complacency.

The further argument of this book is that the scale and nature of the problem of pension provision give it a strategic character. The key to many problems nowadays is 'It's pensions, stupid!' In modern societies economic provision for those in retirement is bound to be costly but there are ways of anticipating and covering this cost that could encourage a more responsible pattern of social relations, one that combats inequality and unemployment by encouraging sustainable development. Pension funds now have enormous power, yet they often do not use this power wisely. Since the pension funds would not exist without the lavish fiscal privileges conferred on them by governments, there is a compelling case, I hope to show, for requiring them to display a proper sense of social responsibility.

Notes

1   United Nations, *Demographic Yearbook 1993, Population Ageing and the Situation of Elderly Persons*, New York 1993, p. 494 (US), p. 518 (UK); United Nations, *Demographic Yearbook, 1998*, New York 2000, p. 109 (US), p. 116 (UK), population over 65, p. 89; United Nations, *Long Range World Population Projections*, New York 2000, p. 23 (life expectancy in China); the projections cited are from the 'medium scenario': United Nations, *World Population Prospects: the 1998 Revision*, vol. 3: *Analytic Report*, New York 2000, p. 60.

2   The pension fund values in this paragraph all come from Financial Indicators, *The Economist*, 20 May 2000, citing a report by InterSec. But see also Richard Minns, *The Cold War in Welfare: Pensions versus Stock Markets*, London 2001.

3   Peter Drucker, *The Unseen Revolution: How Pension Fund Socialism Came to America*, New York and London 1976. This was a perceptive work which is discussed below.

4   Data from Gemini Consulting and Merrill Lynch, *The Wealth Report 2000*, cited in the *Financial Times*, Wealth Survey, 17–18 June 2000.

5   Laurence J. Kotlikoff and Daniel E. Smith, P*ensions in the American Economy*, Chicago 1983, p. 14.

6   This is a problem with two books which raise interesting and important issues but do not succeed in tackling them in a rounded or satisfactory way: David Thomson, *Selfish Generations: How Welfare States Grow Old*, Cambridge 1996; and Peter Peterson, *Gray Dawn*, New York 2000.

7   There is a dearth of 'panel studies' which track the experience of the same generation through a life-cycle. But for a study which examines the evidence available, see Robert E. Goodin, Bruce Headey, Ruud Muffels and Henk-Jan Dirven, *The Real Worlds of Welfare Capitalism*, Cambridge 1999. And for a discussion of the issues involved, see Richard Disney, *Can We Afford to Grow Older: a Perspective on the Economics of Ageing*, Cambridge (MA) 1996, and Norman Daniels, 'Justice and Transfers between Generations', in Paul Johnson, Christopher Conrad and David Thomson, eds, *Workers Versus Pensioners: Intergenerational Justice in an Ageing World*, Manchester 1989, pp. 57–79.

8   Evidence for this is given in chapter 6.

9   James Banks and Carl Emmerson, 'Public and Private Pension Provision: Principles, Practice and the Need for Reform', *Fiscal Studies*, vol. 21, no. 1, 2000, pp. 1–63, p. 55.

10 Drucker, *The Unseen Revolution*, p. 35.

11 Ibid., p. 168.

12 Ibid., pp. 74–101.

13 Tony Benn, *Arguments for Socialism*, London 1980, pp. 150–1.

14 Randy Barber and Jeremy Rifkind, *The North Will Rise Again*, Boston 1978.

15 Laura Katz Olson, *The Political Economy of Aging: the State, Private Power and Social Welfare*, New York 1982, p. 228. See also pp. 100–27. For the critique of the 'medical-industrial' complex see pp. 128–62 and for warnings about privatisation of care services see pp. 187–213.

16 Eric Shragge, *Pensions Policy in Britain: a Socialist Analysis*, London 1984.

17 Jonas Pontusson, *The Limits of Social Democracy: Investment Politics in Sweden*, Ithaca 1992, pp. 186–219, 228–34; Jonas Pontusson, 'Sweden – After the Golden Age', in Perry Anderson and Patrick Camillar, eds, *Mapping the West European Left*, London 1997, pp. 23–54 (for the Meidner plan, see pp. 25–34); and Rudolf Meidner, *Employee Investment Funds: An Approach to Collective Capital Formation,* London 1978.

18 For a critique, see Thomas Frank, *One Market Under God: Extreme Capitalism, Market Populism and the End of Economic Democracy*, London 2001, pp. 136-69,

and Margaret Morgenroth Gullette, '"Xers" vs. "Boomers"', *The American Scholar*, Spring 2000, pp. 105–18. 'Youthism' is splendidly attacked by Tom Nairn in *After Britain*, London 2000, and the commercial exploitation of youth is memorably dissected in Naomi Klein, *No Logo*, London 1999.

19 For a useful corrective, even if it is ultimately too Panglossian, see Phil Mullan, *The Imaginary Time Bomb: Why an Ageing Population Is Not a Social Problem*, London 2000.

20 David Blake, 'Does It Matter What Kind of Pension Scheme You Have?', *Economic Journal*, vol. 110, no. 461, February 2000, pp. F46–81, p. F51; Alan Walker, 'Public Policy and Ageing in the UK: the Social Construction of Economic Inequality', *Hitotsubashi Journal of Social Studies*, vol. 27, no. 1, July 1995, pp. 39–64, p. 52.

21 Anne-Marie Guillemard, *La Retraite: une mort sociale, sociologie des conduits en situation de retraite*, Paris 1972.

22 See, in particular, an essay which brings together an impressive body of research: Peter Townsend, 'The Structured Dependency of the Elderly: the Creation of Social Policy in the Twentieth Century', *Ageing and Society*, vol. 1, no. 1, 1981, pp. 5–28.

23 For a critique of portrayals of passive seniors, see Stephen Katz, *Disciplining Old Age: the Formation of Gerontological Knowledge,* Charlottesville (VA) 1996, pp. 135–41, and Chris Phillipson, *Reconstructing Old Age, New Agendas in Theory and Practice*, London 1998, pp. 55–64, 137–40. These informative accounts offer needed correctives, and identify new dimensions in the social exclusion of the elderly, but they lose sight of economic constraints, down-play overt political action by the elderly and place too much weight on a postmodern evocation of micro-resistance, as if rearranging the chairs in the old people's home constituted an effective dismantling of institutional segre-gation and oppression.

24 Richard Berthoud, 'A Fit and Proper Approach', *Financial Times*, June 2001.

25 Thomson, *Selfish Generations*, Peterson, *Gray Dawn*.

26 These aspects are well covered in Paul Wallace, *Agequake*, London 2000.

27 Anthony Giddens, *The Third Way: the Renewal of Social Democracy*, Oxford 1998, pp. 119–20.

28 United Nations, *World Population Prospects: the 1998 Revision*, vol. 3, *Analytical Report*, p. 172.

29 In nearly all advanced countries the pension programme is the largest single item of public expenditure. In Britain Ewan Davis notes that pension pay-ments were overtaken by spending on the National Health Service in 1994 (*Public Spending*, London 1998, p. 258). But Britain's basic state pension was, and was to remain, at such a low level that those who relied on it qualified for public assistance in the shape of 'income support'. In 1998 the UK spent £32 billion on the basic state pension but a further £12 billion on other pensioner benefits to make a total of £44.4 billion or 5.2 per cent of GDP. A further £20.5 billion, or 2.4 per cent of GDP, was forgone in taxes by the public exchequer in the form of subsidies to private and occupational pension

provision, for a total pension spend of £64.9 billion or 7.6 per cent of GDP.
See Banks and Emmerson, 'Public and Private Pension', *Fiscal Studies*, p. 37.

30 Theda Skocpol, *The Missing Middle: Working Families and the Future of American Social Policy*, New York 2000, pp. 102–39; Michael J. Graetz and Jerry L. Mashaw, *True Security: Rethinking American Social Insurance*, New Haven and London 1999, p. 65, where these authors declare: 'No sensible analysis of which age groups require greater attention to their social insurance protection could possibly conclude that 77 percent of the excess dollars (in US budget revenues) should be devoted to the problems of the elderly.' This statement fails to register that the surpluses that appeared in US budgets in the late 1980s derived from payroll taxes paid by employees specifically linked to old age and survivors' pensions so that the 77 per cent claim of Social Security on these particular revenues was indeed a strong one. For an argument that welfare expenditures in Europe also were too much directed towards the old and familiar risks of old age, and too little towards new risks of family break-down, see Gosta Esping-Anderson, *Social Foundations of Postindustrial Economics*, Oxford 1999, especially pp. 145–69. From the standpoint of the argument I develop in this book the stress of these authors on new risks, with their associated expenses, is fine so long as it does not lead to the non-sequitur that old age expenditures are going to diminish.

1

The Baroque and the Puritan: A Short History of Pensions and Pension Funds

[T]he inequality, dependence and even misery which ceaselessly threatens the most numerous and most active class in our society . . . can be in great part eradicated by guaranteeing in old age a means of livelihood produced partly by their own savings and partly by the savings of others who make the same outlay but who die before they need to reap the reward; or, again, on the same principle of com-pensation, by securing for widows and orphans an income which is the same and costs the same for those families which suffer an early loss and for those which suffer it late.
　　(Antoine-Nicolas de Condorcet, *Sketch for a Historical Picture of the Human Mind*, 1793)

Nous avons servi la patrie
Vous le servez à votre tour.
　　(Adresse des vieillards, Hymne pour la fête de la Liberté, Paris, 1793)

I will consider it a great advantage when we have 700,000 small pensioners drawing their annuities from the State, especially if they belong to those classes who otherwise do not have much to lose by an upheaval and erroneously believe they can actually gain much by it.
　　(Otto von Bismarck, speech in the Reichstag, 1889)

Let mankind enter into a Hobbes–Rousseau social contract in which the young are assured of their retirement subsistence if they will today support the aged, such assurance to be guaranteed by a draft on the yet unborn.
　　(Paul Samuelson, 'An Exact Consumption-Loan Model of Interest with or without the Social Contrivance of Money', *Journal of Political Economy*, December 1958)

French Revolutionary *Festival of Old Age*, Duplessi-Bertault print of a painting by Pierre Alexandre Wille, 1794. Photo Bibliothèque National, Paris

Contemporary pension provision builds on institutions and proposals which can be traced back to the early modern period, especially in those regions of Europe where cash income first and most completely replaced self-provision as the source of livelihood. The pressure of making ends meet in a market society limited what wage labourers could save. As the modern period unfolded, a gradual lengthening of adult life expectancy meant that more now outlived their savings. Some might be able to call on their children for support but a significant proportion would be without surviving children and, for many, family budgets were anyway very tight. In England municipal and parish authorities were expected to make some allowance for the elderly pauper. In the new industrial districts workers formed mutual-benefit friendly societies which stretched to funeral benefit, and perhaps temporary help in sickness, but not to the provision of a permanent income in later life. The ability of offspring to take care of their parents in old age was limited by their own earning power and the family's access to property. In the countryside owning land was the best insurance for old age but in the growing towns and cities of the nineteenth and twentieth centuries only a small minority had family businesses which could offer a similar cushion. In the pre-industrial and early industrial context masters were accustomed to keep on the older worker in less demanding work at lower pay but this paternalist approach became less common as production line methods were adopted. Public authorities feared the cost of accepting responsibility for the aged, and long believed that to do so would encourage improvidence. They grudgingly arranged for local provision of poor relief but were alarmed at the likely cost of a national system of pensions for the rising number of the aged.

As modern bourgeois society established itself in Europe the more comfortable layers of the population could buy public bonds or enter an annuity contract with an insurance house, and in this way provide for their own old age. The development of mathematical techniques for calculating life tables established principles of insurance which could also be used to calculate the cost of supplying a pension to an individual or to a surviving spouse or other relative. While any individual's life-span was unknowable, the insurer could use actuarial principles to predict the cost of annuities for several score or hundred such individuals. The inherent collectivism of this procedure could be adapted to ensure a pension to a larger group of employees or citizens, should the will and resources be present. The first public pension schemes were devised as an inducement to attract or retain favoured or strategic civil servants; a select band of well-established corporations was able to adopt the same practice. Institutions which could furnish pensions, or guarantee them, were able to offer an attractive reward and to obtain a surety of good service. The example of elite schemes prompted emulation from those outside the charmed circle. Consequently the history of pension provision is marked by popular pressure and even class struggle. It is also marked by political and interstate rivalry, as competitors sought to display their ability to furnish coveted social guarantees. While the democratic revolution of the modern epoch raised new demands for income security in old age, even the most conservative authorities were sometimes drawn to pre-empt such a challenge by advancing their own pension proposals.

Culturally the field of pension provision drew on two distinct traditions, the puritan notion of industry, prudence and individual responsibility, on the one hand, and the baroque idea of a well-ordered public space and beneficent, universal public power, on the other. The puritan tradition was nourished by commercial and financial oligarchies from seventeenth-century Amsterdam and London to twentieth-century Boston and New York. It is still invoked by the Anglo-American pension fund industry, with such flagship concerns as the Boston-based Fidelity and the London-based Prudential, while the baroque still finds some echo in the elaborate state-sponsored pension schemes to be found in Germany, France and Italy.[1] The puritan emphasis was always on trust and thrift, probity and self-reliance. It should not, perhaps, surprise us that the world's largest money managers – concerns like Barclays, Putnam and State Street, in addition to the two previously mentioned – parade their Bostonian or evangelical roots to this day. The puritan promise is that individual prudence will eventually reap its reward. The baroque tradition emphasises the pastoral role of the state as an instrument of social harmony. Its roots are in absolutism and the Counter-Reformation, offering the monarch and the Church formulas for re-establishing their authority and leadership by exalting them as instruments of Divine Purpose. Monarchs found in pensions a method to strengthen the central state, to reward those who had given faithful service, to prove their beneficence to all subjects, to banish social exclusion and to exalt hierarchy. Of course baroque claims were always compromised and flawed by the special interests which the royal order protected. Louis XIV awarded pensions to strategic members of the French nobility in a successful attempt to avert another Fronde. But the vision of social harmony which some of the more enlightened servants of absolutism projected was, paradoxically, to resurface in the inclusive social republican tradition, which was to see universal pensions as an engine of communal solidarity. This development, as we will see below, first surfaced in France, homeland of the benchmark absolutism, site of the Great Revolution, its modern history punctuated by great upheavals which have helped to install and extend a pension system built on *répartition*, or sharing. But if republican democracy initially sponsored the idea of universal pension provision, it was first put into practice by Bismarck and the Emperor Wilhelm II in Germany. Thereafter the institution was to be adopted, refined and elaborated by a diversity of states, partly because of the rivalry between them and partly because they were gripped by similar, though not identical, domestic trials. As so often in the evolution of human institutions, there was to be both conscious imitation and unwitting innovation, under the pressure of new economic and political challenges.

Some analysts of the world of pension provision distinguish between the 'Anglo-Saxon model', found in the United States, Britain and other English-speaking countries, and embracing a strong element of private provision, on the one hand, and, on the other, the more collectivist provision, with a 'dominant public pillar', found in continental Europe and some former European colonies. In recent times 'Anglo-Saxon' economics has been twinned with a 'residual' liberal welfare state, with its safety net, while collectivist pension provision has come in both social democratic and corporate paternalist forms.[2] While such classification certainly helps us make sense of contemporary welfare models, the history of pension provision has been marked by imitation and adaptation under the pressure of economic distress and rivalry, social unrest, war and occupation. This has ensured that actually existing welfare and pension regimes embody dynamically evolving hybrids and mixtures. Today, in the epoch of globalisation, there is pressure for all countries to adopt 'Anglo-Saxon' arrangements; and, at the same time, there is resistance to this pressure, even in the 'Anglo-Saxon' states themselves. In Britain this resistance focuses on the failure to tie the state pension to the growth of incomes while in the United States the future of Social Security is at the centre of a major political debate. In the spirit of globalisation all countries are encouraged by the IMF and World Bank to transfer as much pension provision as possible to the financial services industry. Today both the puritan and the baroque images of the good life are menaced by consumerism and by the increasing commercial colonisation of private life and fragmentation of the public sphere.[3]

But the market does not carry all before it. Companies depend on the legal and political contexts furnished by states to defend their property rights and contractual claims. The dependence of private pension providers is even greater since their business would not exist without tax favours. So today the state is being asked to play a far-reaching role as sponsor even by many stern advocates of market discipline. In different ways 'compassionate conservatism', the 'Third Way', 'ethical' funds and a revived social republicanism claim to act as saviours of an imperilled social fabric. The following brief history of pensions and pension funds seeks to trace the origins and variant forms of pension provision.

The First Pensions

In fact, pension promises have been the stock in trade of every rising social institution since the dawn of the modern epoch four or five centuries ago. Notwithstanding their lacklustre reputation, pensions have historically conferred great prestige on the providers and have elicited gratitude from the recipients. Successive ruling institutions – guilds and magnates, absolutist monarchs, commercial oligarchies, the landed gentry network, paternalist corporations, nation-states, political parties, financial institutions – have each in their time identified pension promises as a source of strength. The monarchs and magnates of the late feudal epoch gained prestige from the number of their retainers.

Aspiring absolutist monarchs, like the English Tudors, sought to absorb or control the prebends and pensions which had been in the hands of the guilds or the Church, together with the property which underwrote them. But such arrangements were linked to particular individuals and posts. In 1598 Elizabeth's Parliament voted a pension to soldiers who had fought for queen and country but even this limited measure did not yet become a permanent institution. Colonisation plans in Ireland and the New World drew off large numbers, but there was still a problem of the aged landless poor in the countryside. The possession of land was the best insurance against old age; sons or daughters were rarely able to support their parents but they might help them work land with a view to inheriting it. Those without land, including younger sons, were expected to work until they dropped. Following the dissolution of the monasteries there was greater pressure on the landed gentry to organise public charity. Kett's rebellion of 1548 and similar outbreaks showed the discontent and restiveness that followed in the wake of the spread of capitalist social relations. The Elizabethan Poor Law of 1601 was legislation with national scope, codifying earlier provisions, and a response to the need for social protection in a country where a flexible and disruptive new regime was transforming rural existence. This was a dynamic, decentred agrarian capitalism. Britain had a monarch and a court but very little by way of a central state administration. The Poor Law did not create one; instead it conferred obligations towards the needy, including those too old to work, on each parish. The cost of meeting these obligations was to be met from locally levied poor rates, to be paid by local proprietors and tenant farmers, small and large.

A census of 1570 in Norwich, a rich spinning centre, described three widows of 74, 79 and 82 as 'almost past work'.[4] With the Poor Law, if not before, these women would eventually qualify for an allowance from the parish, providing that they were of good character and had worked until they were no longer able to. The urban poor houses and the rural parish authorities invariably demanded work, and retained discretion as to who they deemed worthy of a measure of support. The Puritan governors of Salisbury in the 1630s made regular church attendance a qualification for poor relief and supplied successful applicants with what they deemed 'essential goods'. According to a law of 1662, parishes were only responsible for those born within their boundaries, or those married to such people, or for those who qualified by dint of long and respectable residence. The individual could appeal against parish decisions to the magistrates but would only encounter the same criteria. Fear of poverty in old age was thus a strong motive for deference to the local gentry and parish authorities.[5]

Provision for the aged pauper was probably more extensive in England in the seventeenth and eighteenth centuries than it was in most parts of continental Europe or than it was to be in eighteenth- or nineteenth-century North America. The decentralised, parish-based Poor Law system helped to conceal this. The conflicts of the seventeenth century resulted in a state geared to the priorities of independent property and trade, but still administratively weak and committed to the view that the burden of poverty could best be identified and shouldered by the proprietors and householders of the parishes. Demographic shifts and the emigration of younger adults meant that in the period 1670 to 1740 those aged over sixty came to comprise a tenth of the English population. Average life expectancy might be only a little more or less than thirty-five years. But this was because of high infant mortality and childhood mortality. Most of those who reached the age of fifteen were likely to live into their fifties or sixties. The responsible exercise of public charity helped the gentry and burghers retain their leadership of a society in which democracy was stirring. Those deemed to be 'past work' received a weekly stipend paid at the rate of a labourer's wage. But many in their sixties or seventies continued to toil. Occasionally, relatives would be given an allowance if they took in an elderly person who could not look after him or herself. Those deemed to be bad characters might find benefit withdrawn.[6] Thus, even though there was quite widespread payment of parish relief to the aged, there was still much that was ad hoc and discretionary about it.[7] Moreover, to be in receipt of poor relief was demeaning. The true pension, on the other hand, has usually been a source of honour or pride to its recipient.

Louis XIV is the grandfather of the modern occupational pension, not because he used pensions to tame potentially troublesome aristocrats or to encourage Huguenots to convert but because his naval ministers established a pension system for naval officers, master mariners and administrators in 1673. France needed to boost its navy, so provision of a pension was a good way to encourage faithful service; the device may also have weakened tension between those born Catholic and the pensioned former Huguenots who were common in the naval professions. Under Colbert and his successors, the French navy was to be more open to merit than the army or other branches of the state.[8] The ability of the monarch to guarantee the future of an entire class of men, and of their widows, was an imposing demonstration of the power of royal administration. The pension fund benefited from the sale of prizes captured by French warships, which gave it a useful source of revenue. It also benefited from the new precision of mathematical calculation. The Ferme Générale, or tax office, also acquired a contributory pension system for its staff in 1681 while the Hôtel des Invalides succoured the army veterans.[9] These monuments to the baroque spirit grew out of rivalry with the Dutch and English.

The Dutch and English local authorities were almost certainly better at looking after the poor, at least those deemed deserving poor, than the institutions of the French monarchy but their approach was piecemeal, discretionary and moralistic. Prior to the Orange restoration in the 1670s the Dutch head of state was actually called the Grand Pensionary, since he was the state's premier salaried official, but the jealous provinces made sure that he had only a modest apparatus at his command. In 1682 England's Charles II established the Royal Pensioners' Hospital, Christopher Wren's imposing Thames-side edifice, for the housing of veterans. Charles also set up pension arrangements for a few key men in the customs and excise department, an example which was to be extended to others in the service in the following century.[10] In 1759 an Act for the Relief and Support of Mariners required seamen to pay sixpence a month, from the proceeds of which they or their widows could claim some benefit. But before long the fund catered only to the ships' masters, not the ordinary tars.[11]

The first state pension schemes were bestowed on military men, offering a reward to those who had risked their life, or senior state functionaries or others who had special leverage and whose fidelity needed to be ensured. Charles III of Spain, an 'enlightened despot', established military pensions in 1762. In the 1780s the rulers of Austria and Sweden introduced pensions for those we would now call civil servants. Sometimes the place holder would have lifetime tenure and the pension was a commitment to ensure that, after his death, his widow and other dependants were not left destitute. Alternatively the pension would allow the office holder to retire and make way for someone younger.

Some of the more enlightened servants of the royal power felt responsible for society as a whole. Turgot, minister of finance to Louis XVI in 1774–6, pointed to the failure of charity or piecemeal measures to meet the afflictions of poverty at a time of economic crisis; he tried to set up charity offices and workshops which would guarantee work to the able-bodied and an income to those unfit for work. The chronic debts of the Crown doomed this scheme. Notwithstanding the universal claims of the late baroque and Enlightenment absolutism, the comforts of a state pension were in practice only extended to functionaries and military men.[12] But the eighteenth century also witnessed the rise of commercial life insurance houses in England and the Netherlands which, armed with Edward Halley's 'life tables' (1698), allowed those with resources to purchase an annuity for a capital sum. By furnishing an income for life to a dependant or a friend, a merchant prince could ape a monarch and a wealthy householder could furnish his widow with a pension. While the royal pensions helped to underpin royal authority the security of commercial annuities derived from the fact that they were invested in government bonds; because the English and Dutch states were based on independent property and commerce, their bonds enjoyed much greater credit-worthiness than the loans made to the absolutist monarchs. Of course annuities, like royal pensions, only covered a tiny minority, leaving the rest of the elderly dependent on family property, paternalistic employers, charity or parish poor relief.

The Revolutionary Idea of Universal Provision

It was not until the epoch of the French Revolution and its Declaration of the Rights of Man and the Citizen that the first proposals were heard for the paying of pensions as of right to all citizens who had reached an advanced age and were in want. Tom Paine canvassed the idea in quite

specific terms in the second part of *Rights of Man* (1792), with calculations
of the likely cost and of the 'progressive taxation' of wealthy estates
whereby it could be defrayed. He envisaged paying to the over-fifties, in
case of need, a pension of £6 a year, with those over sixty to receive £10.
He anticipated that one-third of the elderly – about 140,000 persons –
would be poor enough to require this pension and that the stipend paid to
them could be looked on (as in 'a tontine') simply as the interest of the
sum that they had paid in tax through their life.[13] Paine's ideas had been
influenced by French debates.[14] Whereas his approach required a generous
species of means test, that of his friend Condorcet was to cover all citizens.
Condorcet, a friend of Turgot and pioneering mathematician as well as
outstanding *philosophe* and Revolutionary politician, pointed out that
'tables of general mortality' would allow a universal scheme of social security
to be elaborated on the basis of reliable costings and the calculus of
probabilities. In his insurance scheme the state would help all citizens
to help themselves, by setting up pooled funds. He advocated the erad-
ication of destitution among the elderly by guaranteeing to all who
reached old age a means of livelihood produced firstly by their own savings
and partly by the savings of others who made the same outlay but who
died before they needed the pension. He explained that this species of
collective old age insurance was made possible by 'the application of
calculus to the probabilities of life and the investment of money'. He
pointed out that he was here generalising principles already adopted by the
insurance houses:

> these methods . . . have already been successful, although they have not yet
> been applied in a sufficiently comprehensive and exhaustive fashion to
> render them really useful, not merely to a few individuals, but to society as
> a whole, by making it possible to prevent these periodic disasters which
> strike at so many families and which are such a recurrent source of misery
> and suffering.[15]

He did not envisage only a single national scheme but added that:
'[S]chemes of this nature, which can be organised in the name of the
social authority and become one of its great benefits, can also be the work
of private associations . . .'.[16] What he seems to have had in mind here
was professional, occupational or regional associations rather than commercial provision.

The National Convention decreed that 10 Fructidor was to be the date
of the Fête de la Vieillesse and that there should be old people's homes
established in every department. The figure of the Old Patriot played an
important part in Revolutionary tableaux.[17] The Convention eventually

adopted the principle of a civic pension for the aged in June 1794, just a few months after the abolition of slavery but just a few weeks before the overthrow of the radical Jacobins. By this time Condorcet himself was a victim of factional infighting, and the measure entrusted social insurance to the state alone and not to the associations of civil society as he envisaged.[18] In 1810 the German writer Leopold Krug elaborated a scheme for a pension which combined associationism with state initiative in a proposal for a state-sponsored social insurance fund which would gather in obligatory contributions in order to eliminate poverty in old age.[19]

But whether the state was itself to guarantee social security, or was to use its fiscal powers to allow independent associations to do so, both were equally repugnant to the anti-Jacobin reaction. Britain's rulers did allow self-help organisations, or friendly societies, often sponsored by the Nonconformist Churches, to pool the resources of the deserving poor, but the provision of a regular pension was quite beyond their means and there was no question of the British state helping them out financially, notwithstanding the awesome quantities of public money devoted to the fight against Napoleon. Interestingly enough, the only major pension proposal to find favour in British ruling circles at this time was an Act of 1809 which guaranteed a decent retirement to customs and excise officers, men who held the revenue of the state in their hands.

Social distress in the English parishes during the French wars prompted a rise in the provision of 'outdoor relief', or cash allowances, to paupers. The appearance of English advocates of social republicanism, like Paine and Godwin, and the spectre of further public money being thrown into the bottomless pit of popular misery, so alarmed the Reverend T.R. Malthus and some other early economists that it aroused in them the mother of all welfare panics. Malthus's famous *Essay on the Principle of Population* (1798) carried the sub-title 'as it affects the Future Improvement of Society, with remarks on the Speculations of Mr Godwin, M. Condorcet and other writers'. Malthus was scornful of Condorcet's proposal for social insurance funds for those left in distress by the hazards of life, even funds primed by contributions from potential beneficiaries. Malthus warned that: 'Such establishments and calculations, may appear very promising on paper, but when applied to real life they will be found to be absolutely nugatory.'[20] They would be ruinously expensive, they would blunt the 'goad of necessity' and they would lead to overpopulation since

> were the rising generation free from the 'killing frost' of misery, population must rapidly increase. . . . If the labouring classes were universally to contribute what might at first appear a very ample proportion of their earnings,

for their own support in sickness and old age, when out of work, and when
the family consisted of more than two children; it is quite certain that the
funds would become deficient. Such a mode of distribution implies a mode
of supporting a rapidly increasing and unlimited population on a limited territory, and must therefore, terminate in aggravated poverty.[21]

Malthus was opposed to the universal and collective character of the social
republican proposals. He explained that 'savings banks' which would cater
to the thrifty members of the labouring classes, and would give each individual 'the full and entire benefit of his own industry', would 'greatly
strengthen the lessons of Nature and Providence', though he feared that
the troubled economic climate was not propitious for them.[22]

Even Malthus was prepared to grant that those too old to work and of
good character should receive discretionary cash allowances and not be
obliged to enter the workhouses, as he thought should be the case with
others seeking poor relief. The Anti-Jacobin fear was that popular assemblies, attentive to the 'swinish multitude' (Burke), would introduce
universal welfare arrangements and, in doing so, stimulate runaway population growth and neglect of individual thrift and prudence. However, this
nightmare did not come to pass. The revolutionary democratic movement
in Britain was contained and national energies mobilised for war with
France. Eventually, after growing popular mobilisations and an acute crisis,
the Reform Act of 1832 widened the suffrage a little and made Parliament
more representative of the propertied classes. The new Parliament decided
to reform, not abolish, the Poor Law. The new Poor Law (1834) retained
the principle that the aged poor were deserving of 'outdoor relief' while
other sections of the poor were now required to live in the workhouse as
a condition of help. These workhouses had never offered comfort or dignity but were now to be organised on deliberately punitive lines. Some of
the aged, lacking homes of their own, were forced to live in these gloomy
and forbidding institutions, denounced as 'bastilles' by popular opinion.
Where outdoor relief was provided it could be reduced in amount if the
elderly person was deemed to have sons or daughters who could spend
more on their parents. The aged probably did better than other sections of
the poor but there was still great unevenness. Parishes were combined
together into unions but there was still great scope for the exercise of local
discretion and for harsh criteria to be employed by cheese-paring officials.
Pat Thane points out that

> the percentage of old people receiving regular relief – paid weekly on a six-
> monthly basis – varied from 55 per cent in one [Bedfordshire] parish to 18
> per cent in another. National statistics showed similar extreme variations. 59

per cent of women in their sixties were on relief in Ampthill, 10 per cent in Stourbridge, 8 per cent at Barton-upon-Irwell on the edge of Manchester. Even after age 70 judgements on eligibility for relief, especially of men, related to assessments of their capability for work. In Ampthill up to around age 74 men were always entered on the relief books as 'out of work', 'past work', 'worn out by work'. There were instances of first applications for relief by men aged 80, 85, 79.[23]

The impulse to universalise welfare stimulated by the French Revolution had been denied the circumstances, time and resources needed for it to become effective. The first democratic republics gave birth to an idea but did not author the first universal pension systems. England remained locked into a localistic and discretionary system. In France Napoleon honoured a Revolutionary promise to pay pensions to veterans so that by 1813 payments to 100,000 ex-soldiers comprised 13 per cent of the military budget.[24] The restored Bourbons felt obliged to maintain these pensions, together with those to other servants of the state.

The United States inherited some English Poor Law practices but in a context where actual provision was less widespread and, if anything, even more uneven. The North American republic was to be one of the last of the developed states to adopt a universal system of retirement provision, eventually doing so under the terms of the Social Security Act of 1935. As early as 1775 the Continental Congress had voted a pension to soldiers and sailors who would take up its cause; failure to deliver on this promise led to discontent and revolt after the Treaty of Paris (1783). While more or less ad hoc payments were made to army veterans a navy pension was set up in 1800 which had its own fund, established from the proceeds of prizes captured by US warships. The navy pension fund, with assets of over $1 million at one point, paid pensions to retired naval men until the 1840s when it was wound up and its obligations met from general revenues.[25] While a case could be made for paying pensions to a small number of military men as a way of retaining their services, this was not an example that many wished to generalise.

The politically influential planters of the South were opposed to any schemes which would endow the Federal authorities with fiscal powers and they found some allies in the North. In the farming communities the old would continue to work the land as long as they were able, and, if they owned land, could count on some support from presumptive heirs.[26] The son who stood to inherit would, helped by his wife, support his aged parents while other sons would migrate to areas where land was cheap. In urban centres almshouses and outdoor poor relief were sometimes available but to apply for them was demeaning. In principle, the old were proper objects of public assistance but their claim could easily be jeopardised if they drank or were believed to be of bad character. Many of the leaders of society felt that public charity encouraged improvidence, idleness and viciousness, and some believed that the sufferings of the destitute were providential anyway.[27] Attempts to make municipal provision more generous provoked Emerson's classic outburst against 'alms for sots': 'I tell thee, thou foolish philanthropist, that I grudge the dollar, the dime, the cent I give to such men as do not belong to me and to whom I do not belong.'[28] The Second Great Awakening brought to the fore a Protestant belief in the sacred promise of youth and a disposition to regard the elderly poor both as victims of their own improvidence and as poor prospects for salvation: 'The chills and frosts of old age are about as unfavorable to conversion to God as the frosts and snows of December are to the cultivation of the earth.'[29] The historian Thomas Cole even suggests that contemporary ageism has Puritan antecedents:

> If revival sermons neither prescribe proper conduct toward the aged nor contain comforting advice for old people, they nevertheless radiate a wealth of imagery about ageing and old age – primarily as antipodes to youthful qualities of vigour, immediacy, action, self-control. These sermons often bristle with hostility to old age, that unwelcome reminder both of the oppressive weight of the past and of man's inevitable weakness and dependence.[30]

It would be wrong, however, to think of the United States of the mid-nineteenth century as entirely wedded to individualism, since the sale of 'public land' gave strategic resources to the state and Federal authorities, albeit at the expense of dispossessed Native Americans and Mexicans. Public land was used to encourage westwards migration (the Homestead Law), to establish a free public education system and to subsidise the development of the railroads. Of course the anticipated value of the public land itself reflected the 'market revolution' of 1815–60 and its accompanying celebration of individualism. The public programmes I cite actively promoted expansion via the colonisation of new territory whereas the relief of the aged poor was complicated by it. In such a highly mobile society either the Federal authorities would take the initiative, which was impossible, or nothing effective would be done.

In the aftermath of the Civil War an interventionist Republican philosophy might have gained sway if Radical Reconstruction had not been deflected and defeated.[31] But as it was, the Southern 'redeemers' furnished an ally to those who wished to constrain Federal authority. The sentiments which barred the advance of social security in the United

States centred on the belief that it would discourage thrift, empower the Federal state, sanction tolls on private property, and, last but not least, become an instrument of political patronage and corruption. Federal pensions were established for Union veterans, once again embodying the idea that those who risk their lives in defence of the state deserve to be protected from penury in old age. Between 1882 and 1916 military pensions consumed from 22 to 43 per cent of total Federal expenditure. Since the veterans had the Republicans to thank for their pensions, the scheme was branded a divisive and partisan, rather than universal, measure (though some black veterans managed to qualify). In the Southern states Confederate veterans received much smaller payments from the 1890s.[32]

Bismarck and Lloyd George: State Pensions and Hegemony

The introduction of state pensions was thus left to the Old World. By the 1850s the French state had already extended the categories of civil servant who were entitled to a pension. In nineteenth-century France the pensionable servants of the state came to include university professors, actors in the employ of the Comédie Française, clerks working for the Banque de France and print workers at the Imprimerie Nationale but this was still a long way from the universal citizens' pension of 1794. The unlikely executor of the social legacy of French republicanism was, of course, none other than Otto von Bismarck, chancellor to a Prussian monarchy rooted in absolutist and Enlightenment traditions. The German Empire established the first universal pension system in 1889. The idea of state-sponsored social insurance had been canvassed in a general way by the Social Democrat leader, Ferdinand Lassalle:

> The moral idea of the capitalist is this – that nothing whatsoever is to be guaranteed to any individual but the uninhibited exercise of his faculties. If we were all equally strong, equally wise, equally educated, and equally rich, this idea might be regarded as a sufficient and moral one; but since we are not so and cannot be so, this thought is not sufficient, and therefore, in its consequences leads to serious immorality; for its result is that the stronger, abler, richer man exploits the weaker and becomes his master.

Lassalle urged German workers to develop their own ideal of a 'morally adjusted community', and to show their worthiness to become the new ruling class, by coming forward with proposals to elevate all who were afflicted by wretchedness.[33] In a society where the propertyless were worth no more than the commodity value of their labour power, the state should offer social protection. Lassalle's writings and lectures on these themes had a considerable public impact in the 1860s even though the Social Democrats were not yet a large political force. Bismarck found Lassalle's ideas sufficiently challenging to seek a meeting with him. However, he did not act on social questions until later, after Social Democracy had won a mass following – and he combined Marx's revolutionary new idea that poverty was not part of the human condition with Lassalle's interest in social reform. It was not until the 1880s that Bismarck introduced his own pioneering measures of social insurance, including the old age pension, as a way of taking the wind out of the sails of what he saw as a subversive political force. As he candidly explained to his confidant Moritz Busch:

> Anybody who has before him the prospect of a pension, be it ever so small, in old age or infirmity is much happier and more contented with his lot, much more tractable and easy to manage, than he whose future is absolutely uncertain. . . . In France, even the common man, if he can possibly put by anything, provides for his future by purchasing *rentes* . . . Contentment amongst the impecunious and disinherited classes would not be dearly purchased by an enormous sum. They must be made to understand that the state is of some use – that it does not only take, but gives to boot . . . not as alms giving but as the right that men have to be taken care of when, with the least will imaginable, they become unfit for work. Why should the regular soldier, disabled by war, or the official, have a right to be pensioned in his old age, and not the soldier of labour? This thing will make its own way: it has a future.[34]

Bismarck showed great insight and deserves his starring role in the history of pension provision. His pension policy was one among a number of programmes which asserted the monarchy's ability to lead society as a whole vis-à-vis potential rivals such as the Social Democrats, the Catholic Church (*Rerum Novarum*, the papal encyclical on social issues, was to appear in 1891) or business enterprises (some of which had already established internal pension arrangements some decades previously: the Gutehoffnungshutte as early as 1832, the Bayerische Hypotheken und Wechselbank in 1845, Siemens in 1872 and BASF in 1879[35]). Bismarck was undoubtedly aware of this and his scheme also showed that the monarchy could furnish to all subjects of the Empire an insurance against old age that these corporations could only offer to their favoured employees.

When Wilhelm II dismissed his Chancellor in the year following enactment of the Old Age Pension he was careful to ensure the scheme's continuance. By subsequent standards the pension, which was set at about 20 per cent of average pay, was not generous (though one would have to concede that the British state pension today is set at below this level). The German example was to be followed by two small states nourished by doctrines of social progress, neighbouring Denmark in 1891 and far-away New Zealand in 1899. It was not until 1908 that Lloyd George, the Liberal premier, introduced Britain's Old Age Pensions Act. W.G. Runciman argues that the Act of 1908 and the National Insurance Act of 1911 were 'inspired as much by the example of Germany and need to outflank the Left as by logical recognition of the merits of the philanthropic case'.[36] Gareth Stedman Jones points out why only some of the Liberal and imperial 'reform' proposals which proliferated at this time were to attract sufficient support to make headway. One of the reasons that modest measures of social insurance reached the statute book, and, for example, proposals for 'labour colonies' for the shiftless poor did not, is that the trade unions supported the former and not the latter.[37] Lloyd George, like Bismarck, had an acute understanding of the measures needed to build loyalty to the social and political order.

The extent of urban poverty in Britain had been established by the social researchers Charles Booth and Seebohm Rowntree. Thus Booth's survey *The Life and Labour of the People of London* (1886) found that 39 per cent of the capital's inhabitants aged over sixty-five years were paupers.[38] He showed that many lacked the basics of a decent existence, and this not because of any personal failing but because they could work no longer. Older employees were not automatically dismissed on account of their age and some employers would find lighter tasks for the frail; but not all employers were philanthropic and old workers discovered that if they lost their job during a downturn they would be unlikely to recover it during any subsequent upswing. Booth himself advocated a state pension as a remedy for the poverty of the elderly.

The Trade Union Congress first urged the adoption of a state pension system or, as they sometimes put, it the 'endowment' of old age, in the early 1890s. Trade union leaders knew that their members would prefer statutory provision to reliance on the good will of employers and they believed that a decent retirement system would help to tighten the labour market by removing from it older workers prepared to work for substandard wages. Union leaders demanded a universal, non-means-tested pension, to be paid for by taxing landed property and higher incomes. There should be no means test partly because this was a humiliating Poor Law-style device and partly because some unions ran a superannuation scheme and were anxious that a small income from such savings should not reduce pension entitlement. In their view the endowment of a decent old age should not simply mean raising the aged out of desperate poverty.[39]

The social campaigner Rev. F.W. Stead persuaded several prominent trade unionists to help him form the 'National Committee of Organized Labour for the Promotion of Old Age Pensions'. William Pember Reeves, the New Zealand High Commissioner, George Cadbury, a Quaker chocolate manufacturer, and Charles Booth lent their support to the campaign. In 1899 Parliament established a Select Committee on the Aged Deserving Poor. But not even the pitiful sight of elderly paupers in the capital of the Empire could easily persuade a Parliament crammed with solid bourgeois and landowners to abandon the rigours of the workhouse. It was feared that a state pension would undermine not only thrift but discretionary private provision.

By this time occupational and enterprise pension arrangements were far more common. When Gladstone had introduced income tax in 1853 he exempted contributions to pensions funds. This principle was later to become the basis of the entire pension fund industry but to begin with it was little more than a minor loophole because so few paid income tax. Eventually about a fifth of income tax payers availed themselves of the relief, devoting about 5 per cent of their income to the savings scheme.[40] However, teachers campaigned for a pension and achieved their goal in the 1890s. The more paternalist employers began to offer a pension so long as employees worked as long as they could and gave good service. When his family's chocolate firm introduced a pension scheme in 1906, Seebohm Rowntree explained:

> Many firms may hesitate to adopt a Pension Scheme . . . but it is probable that these very firms carry heavy costs in 'hidden pensions' without realising the fact. If a firm establishes a liberal pension scheme it will doubtless at the same time fix a definite retiring age and will thus never find itself with a number of old workers of low working capacity drawing full pay . . . such employees are very costly, not only does the firm lose on them individually but their presence tends to lower the pace and lessen the output of the whole shop. . . . But they are kept on because they have worked faithfully for a great number of years and the management does not care to dismiss them.[41]

As the new century got into its stride mass production reduced the demand for the type of labour performed by the older worker. Work on the new production lines was to be physically very demanding and craft occupations were to wither. Macnicol detects a remorseless trend to 'jobless' retirement, that is retirement because there were no jobs available, and a decline in the pattern of 'infirmity' retirement.[42] The fact that there were more old people exacerbated, but did not create, the problem. The numbers aged over sixty-five grew from 700,000 in 1841 to 1.5 million in 1901 but, because of population growth, this represented a rise from just over 4 per cent to 5 per cent.[43] Over the next half century, and century, as population growth slowed, the proportion was to rise more swiftly.

It was not until the Liberal landslide of 1906, the rise of Labour and a ferment of social discontent that a very modest British pension measure – set far below the level where it could undermine private arrangements – received parliamentary support. Because the pension was paid from general taxation it was treated as 'socialistic' despite its mean and meagre provisions. It could only be claimed by those over seventy, an age few then reached. At 5 shillings a week it was well below the level of a decent subsistence, and even this was subject to stringent means testing, those with an income of over £31 10 shillings a year receiving nothing. Legislators wanted to confine the pension, which was not based on prior contributions, to those who could prove that they had led a sober and thrifty life but this proved difficult. However, the Act did exclude those who were aliens or had a criminal record.[44]

The means test which limited entitlement to the pension stipulated that an applicant's property would be assessed as if it produced an income of 5 per cent a year. Furniture worth more than £50 was assessed in this way on the grounds that it could be sold if the applicant was really needy. Likewise, if elderly people were in receipt of regular food or lodging from relatives or friends then this would reduce their eligibility. In 1911, 1916 and 1919 the government raised the value of the pension but the means test was retained. The trade unions and friendly societies attacked the means test on the grounds that it penalised thrift and the generosity of relatives or friends. Wartime full employment allowed the trade unions to double in size while the war's appalling carnage prompted a profound questioning of the established order. In 1918 the Labour Party adopted a sweeping programme of public ownership ('clause four') and seemed poised to bid for power. A new suffrage law gave the vote to all men over twenty-one and all women over twenty-nine. Lloyd George, author of the 1908 pension and now Prime Minister, had himself described the earlier measure as merely 'the first step'. Labour supporters widely supported a universal and more generous pension to be paid at sixty-five or even sixty. The evidence given to a government committee set up in 1919 publicised the desperate plight of many old people, whether because of the modesty of the pension or because of their exclusion from it. Pensioners' organisations had by now appeared and they publicised the anomalies and humiliations fostered by the means test. Facing a rising demand for higher pensions and the scrapping of means tests, senior

civil servants from the Treasury and other departments prepared proposals
for a contributory pension scheme, that is a pension financed by special
contributions rather than general tax revenue. Alfred Watson, the
Government Actuary, believed that even the existing means-tested pension
would eventually become unsustainable and that a universal pension paid
from general tax revenue would ruin the national finances. But if all those
in employment were to contribute, then a universal pension could be provided through the administrative apparatus already in place to collect
contributions for health insurance. Furnishing a pension to women who
had no paid employment, or to men or women who had a broken employment record, or to those who were paid very little, remained a problem. But
then a scaled-down version of the 1908 means-tested pension could be
retained for these categories. The Labour Party formed its first government
in 1924 and was widely expected to introduce a Pension Bill. But in its nine
months of existence this minority government failed to act. Winston
Churchill, now a Conservative once again and Chancellor of the Exchequer
in the succeeding Conservative government, seized the opportunity to sow
confusion in Labour ranks and assert leadership at a time of great instability and danger. He introduced a contributory scheme in 1925; in the
following year it fell to Churchill to face down the General Strike. The
workings of the new contributory scheme reflected the thinking of Watson
and other civil servants.[45] This left in place the means-tested pension for
those who could not claim under the new scheme – women comprised 63
per cent of pensioners over seventy. Macnicol writes:

> We should note that at no time was there any serious controversy about the
> need for pensions. The world of the 1920s was very different from that of
> the 1890s, when conservatives could argue that the impoverished elderly
> should take the consequences of their apparent fecklessness and inability to
> save in their past lives. A variety of factors had rendered such a view polit-
> ically untenable – in particular, the pressure of mass democracy, the
> increasing power and confidence of the labour movement, organised lob-
> bying by pensioners and the slow spread of retirement among a growing
> number of old people.[46]

Social Security and the Great Depression

When the United States Congress was eventually persuaded to introduce
a Federal-administered retirement plan, under the terms of the 1935 Act,
at least it was not circumscribed by a means test. The traumatic experience

of slump had shown even the most conservative that thrift offered no guarantees – a lifetime's savings could be wiped out by the collapse of a bank. Home ownership had furnished some with a modicum of property but in 1932 a quarter of a million private dwellings were repossessed by mortgage companies. Many millions of Americans had no resources to fall back on in old age. Company pension schemes had spread in the 1920s until they covered 7.5 per cent of the labour force. But outside public employment the value of such pensions was drastically reduced by long-term service requirements, lack of portability and the discretion accorded to sponsoring companies, many of which anyway went bankrupt.[47] Even the railroad workers, whose pension arrangements dated from the turn of the century or before, faced benefit cuts. But if private provision was in tatters, the idea of the pension as the natural complement to retirement had become well established, and was an aspiration which many could share.

Following the First World War military veterans could claim a pension and around this time university teachers also acquired coverage. Andrew Carnegie had endowed the Carnegie Fund for the Advancement of Teaching (CFAT) in 1901 with the primary purpose of making the career of university teachers in secular institutions look more attractive: he was concerned to limit what he saw as the unfortunate influence of religion on education and research. He hoped that the prospect of a pension would encourage those with the best brains to devote themselves to the further-ance of secular knowledge. The affairs of the CFAT were directed by Henry S. Pritchet, president of MIT, who saw pension provision as being one way to mitigate the excesses of US individualism and extend broadly in society the advantages of an orderly capitalism:

> The question is whether . . . our country will not be compelled to find a means of safeguarding the freedom of the individual up to all reasonable limits and at the same time secure the advantages of the tremendous agen-cies which have been organised in the last fifty years, such . . . as trusts and other industrial organisations. I apprehend that the organisation of the cen-tralised pension system is really only a small part of the larger question.[48]

In this way he hoped that a pension system, with its complex arrangements for the future, would lead the individual to tolerate a measure of collective discipline and provision. The CFAT itself sponsored the setting up of a contributory system in 1919, the Teachers' Insurance Annuity Association (TIAA), destined to become by far the most successful of the early pension schemes, indeed one that has flourished until the present day; now called TIAA–CREF (College Retirement Equity Fund), it is the largest non-commercial pension fund. The TIAA was, of course, helped by the fact that its membership was generally middle-class and removed from the front line of economic fluctuations. While not at all typical, the TIAA and veterans' pensions could still offer an example to employees in the private sector. The spread of new production methods had undermined seniority principles, weakened the demand for craft workers, and tilted many employers' preferences towards the younger worker.[49]

The superannuation arrangements negotiated by railroad employees were the nearest to a modern occupational pension scheme to be found in the United States of the 1920s. These sometimes provided a pension for certain categories of workers, or for those over seventy years of age. The American Express Company, a freight-forwarding enterprise, had introduced pensions for a limited number of skilled employees as early as 1875. By 1900 the Pennsylvania Railroad had a general scheme for all employees who reached seventy years of age. Coverage in the industry then spread as employers were persuaded that pension arrangements helped them to retain valuable workers in their prime and cushioned the blow of compulsory retirement when they were no longer capable. Railroad companies, with their uniformed staff and with the obligatory retired generals on the board, echoed military traditions and mainly employed native-born white male workers. The rail workers' mobility and leverage over critical transport routes gave them significant bargaining power. When the railroad pension schemes ran into the buffers in the early years of the Great Depression it jolted this labour aristocracy into a militant demand that their pensions be guaranteed by the Federal authorities. A body sprang up – the Railroad Employees National Pensions Association (RENPA) – which demanded Federal legislation to compel the employers to introduce a nation-wide scheme enabling all those over seventy to retire on a pension and make way for younger workers. The railroad employees' national network gave it great political strength; the Railroad Pensions Act was to pass the Senate in 1934 by sixty-two votes to zero.[50]

Action to help the railroad workers dramatised the plight of the great majority of their fellow Americans who had no provision for their old age. It also popularised ideas that promised an exit from mass unemployment and constituted an antidote to the disastrous shortfall in consumer demand. RENPA had argued its pension scheme would both open up opportunities to the young and put purchasing power in the hands of the old. These arguments were echoed by the agitators of the Congress of Industrial Organisations who sought to extend the trade union idea to the mass of previously unorganised workers by means of a wave of sit-in strikes. The idea that pensions could help to restore demand was generalised by the so-called Townsend movement which attracted significant middle-class support. The key demand of the movement was that a Federal old age pension should be paid at the handsome rate of $200 a month to retired persons aged sixty-five or over. At this level the pension would be above average manual earnings and would thus ensure that older workers would leave the labour market, making way for younger workers. The monthly stipends were to be paid in a special currency which became worthless if it was not spent within a short period of time – in this way the scheme would give the whole economy the fillip it so desperately needed. The Townsend movement, claiming some three million supporters spread throughout the Union, had an appeal for the elderly, the respectable victims of the slump and all those who believed that the economy needed a massive stimulus. It was manifest that in an industrial economy citizens could no longer live on their own resources when times were bad, as had been possible in the days when farmers, artisans and small producers had typified the social landscape, and when there had been a moving frontier to the west. Only the state, it seemed, could come up with a solution for the problem of old age for society as a whole, though this remained a notion alien to most US employers. The public relations director of the Townsend movement wrote to Roosevelt: 'Big business is too stupid to see that the Townsend Plan will be the means of giving it a new lease on life – that capitalism can only be saved by retiring permanently ten million of our old people, and at the same time giving these old people the means by which to once more restore purchasing power to the United States.'[51]

But such Keynesian ideas were far too advanced and the provisions of the 1935 Social Security Act were very modest compared with the Townsend scheme, offering an average monthly cheque, to begin with, of only $23. Notwithstanding its modest beginnings, the scheme breached the taboo on programmes of government-backed redistribution. Moreover, the restricted principles on which it was initially constructed proved capable of enhancement because it was inherently Federal in scope. Frances Perkins, the Secretary of the Department of Labor, and her assistant, Arthur Altmeyer, urged that the scheme needed its own autonomous administration. They drew on the advice of the economist Barbara Nachtrieb Armstrong to produce a model which blended the social insurance ideas of Isaac Rubinow and John Commons, which had influenced debates and experiments in Ohio and Wisconsin respectively. Several states had some provision for assisting the elderly poor; in time the scheme would reduce the need for such assistance. The important point was to ensure that the states would not feel threatened by passage of the Act. Once fully operational, the Social Security system would tend to redistribute resources from richer states to poorer states. But in the circumstances of 1935 the voters of the more developed regions, with large industrial populations, were clamouring for pension provision and did not see the legislation as a threat. The insurance industry was very unhappy, as were some 'welfare' capitalists who wanted their own workforce to be exempted from the scheme. But the voluntary approach was manifestly inadequate and the experts insisted that the general scheme would need to be comprehensive if it was to work over the long run. The Republican candidate, Alf Landon, denounced Social Security as a 'cruel hoax' and a 'fraud on the working man' which would require the fingerprinting of 26 million Americans if identities were to be properly verified.[52] But since commerce and the market had failed there seemed no alternative to public provision.

Roosevelt insisted that the freedoms Americans cherished required economic security and that the Federal government had the capacity and duty to deliver this. He further acknowledged that in the provision of social security the United States had something to learn from the experience of other countries. According to Altmeyer, the resonant name chosen for the programme – so much at variance with US traditions of individualist self-sufficiency – was taken from Simon Bolivar's famous address to the assembly of Angostura in 1819, in which he sounded the death-knell of Spanish rule and called for the freedom of the slaves, the break-up of the large estates and a 'system of government . . . which produces the greatest amount of happiness possible, the greatest amount of social security and the greatest amount of political stability'.[53] The Social Security programme not only guaranteed benefits to contributors and to partners who survived them but also offered a pension to workers who suffered disability – hence the official rubric OASDI (Old Age, Survivors, and Disability Insurance) used to refer to the programme's provisions.

The fragmentation of the US political system, in league with a pervasive fiscal conservatism, has doomed many attempts to promote social reform: Congress, President, Supreme Court, a minority of the states, each has blocking power. But the Social Security legislation was carefully framed to minimise opposition. The contributory aspect of the scheme meant that no calls would be made on general taxation (though contributions to the scheme functioned as a sort of payroll tax). As agricultural workers were excluded, Social Security laid no burden on the farmer. The exclusion of domestic workers likewise spared those who had hired help.

THE BAROQUE AND THE PURITAN

Both provisions helped to exclude the great majority of black workers, giving the scheme a racial bias which made it more acceptable to the Southern Democrats, a strategic component of the New Deal coalition. Following Roosevelt's convincing second victory in 1936, the Supreme Court, perhaps fearing the charge of 'economic royalism', endorsed the Social Security Act in the subsequent year. The requirement that the programme have its own independent professional administration, the Social Security Administration, helped to alleviate the fear that it would become a tool of political patronage. Moreover, the SSA was charged with the duty of safeguarding the financial integrity of the scheme and coming up with its own proposals for improvements.

The first year or two of the scheme's operation were disappointing. Because of the contributory conditions the number qualifying for a payment was tiny and the amount they received a pittance. Contributions, shared by employees and employers, greatly exceeded payments, so the overall economic impact of the scheme was deflationary, contributing to the new downturn in 1938. The numbers of the elderly requiring assistance from state-supplied relief programmes actually grew. In 1939 Congress was prevailed upon to pass an Amendment which allowed older workers to be credited with contributions they were unable to make because the scheme had not been in existence. This 'blanketing in' of contributions raised entitlements without allowing them to exceed the flow of contributions. While more generous to the older industrial worker, the scheme still excluded most black and women workers. However, the need to mobilise for the war effort was soon to create a labour shortage and encourage a more inclusive approach. The war strengthened the bargaining hand of organised labour, raised popular expectations and justified a raising of tax rates. The Social Security Administration began to move against the scheme's more blatantly discriminatory and inadequate features.[54]

The late 1940s saw the large unions, now at the height of their power, issue vigorous demands for decent pensions, both public and occupational (on the latter more below). With the onset of the Cold War the US government wished to bolster faith in the American system and to make clear that no return to the 1930s would be allowed. Amendments in 1950 and 1954 converted Social Security into a badge of citizenship, a direct link between the individual and the nation. The mostly black workers employed by Southern cotton gins and turpentine works, excluded by the 1939 Amendment, were now brought within the scope of Social Security. The growing numbers of black industrial workers in the North also helped to reduce its racial character. The Republican Party abandoned its hostility and Eisenhower, the party's candidate in 1952, declared: 'Should any political party attempt to abolish social security you would not hear of that party again in our political history.'[55] Social Security had become the famous 'third rail' of American politics and its most celebrated Federal programme.

Contributions plus Universalism: From Roosevelt to Beveridge

The advent of public pension schemes in Germany, Britain and the United States reflected a new social pattern and new demands placed on political authorities. As societies became more urbanised and industrialised, as work became more rationalised, and as the 'demographic revolution' raised the numbers of the elderly, the problem of penury in old age had become more acute – but also more expensive to remedy by means of state pensions. Thus it was only the shock of economic and social crisis, and the pressure of an aroused public opinion, which obliged political and administrative elites to confront the failure of the market. When public opinion demanded government measures, those who saw themselves as responsible leaders opted for contributory schemes. This allowed the language of social insurance progressively to supplant the discourse of poor relief. It was eventually to allow many benefits to be paid without a means test but so long as coverage was incomplete, and benefits fell short of full subsistence, poor relief would still be necessary.

The sums paid out under the early schemes are better seen as supplements than proper pensions, though at a level that had proved beyond the means of popular self-help organisations, trade unions as well as friendly societies. The social insurance approach to pension provision – linking benefits to contributions – had attractions both for trade unionists and independent producers who did not want to undergo a means test or become dependent on 'state alms'. The contributory principle met the objection that pensions would act as a deterrent to thrift. All those with contributions would receive a pension, regardless of their other savings or income. The fact that there would be an incoming stream of contributions to match the outgoings was a vital consideration for those who wished to win over fiscally conservative national assemblies and treasury officials. According to this approach, provision for old age and, perhaps, unemployment, sickness or disability as well, could be afforded so long as every employee was obliged to contribute, with the employer chipping in an equal amount. The scheme would be paid for by the contributions and, in principle, only those who had contributed when they were able to do so, or were the surviving spouse or dependant of a contributor, could claim the benefit. Roosevelt stressed the contributory nature of the retirement pension established by the Social Security Act, well aware that if it risked becoming a charge on the general revenues it would fail in Congress. Indeed, there was alarm in the White House when a funding snag was identified: 'The plan was stopped only by Roosevelt himself, who realized, at the very last minute, that his old age insurance plan would develop a deficit in the 1960s. He ordered Treasury Secretary Hans Morgenthau to make the plan fully funded without the need for general revenues.'[56] Roosevelt believed that a contribution-based scheme would be more likely to pass Congress, withstand legal challenges and weather the political vagaries of the future.

State pensions had been introduced in a number of countries where farmers were politically significant. Such farmers had invariably been highly dependent on the market and yet, when they encountered adverse conditions, they began to find pension proposals attractive. They supplied an element in the class coalitions that backed the first pension legislation in New Zealand, Britain, Canada, Sweden, such US states as Kentucky and Montana in the 1920s or the entire United States in 1935.[57] In 1938 New Zealand went further than any other state with its Social Security Act establishing a citizens' pension to be paid to everyone without a means test and to be financed from general taxation. New Zealanders, whether farmers or townspeople, were used to public bodies playing a large role in social provision and were persuaded that it was most equitable to finance this from general tax revenue. Support for the 'universal', as it was to be called, was underpinned by the idea that civic contributions did not need to take the form of paid employment (farmers and women, the latter enfranchised since 1891, comprised a large majority of the electorate and many of them were not in employment).[58]

When Sir William Beveridge came to draw up his famous report on welfare arrangements for the British government, published in December 1942, he strongly endorsed the contributory principle, to the satisfaction of the UK Treasury.[59] Beveridge's report, broadcast to the world by the BBC, contained resounding affirmations of the principle of universal welfare, and this harmonised with the wartime mood. Pensioners' organisations had publicised the pitiful inadequacy of the 10-shilling pension, delivering petitions signed by millions in 1939 and 1942, calling for a non-contributory pension of 30 shillings (£1.50) to be paid to all, financed by tax revenues. They pointed to New Zealand's Social Security Act as a precedent. But the Treasury insisted that the public purse could not possibly stretch to such an extravagance. In difficult postwar conditions priority would have to be accorded to economic reconstruction, and to education and health. There was lively concern that providing for all those of pensionable age would be hugely expensive and that their numbers were set to grow remorselessly. Pensioners now numbered four million or 9 per cent of the population, compared with the 1.5 million, or 5 per cent of the population, who had been over sixty-five in 1901; moreover, life expectancy was dramatically lengthening due to better social provision. Plans drafted for the late 1940s and 1950s calculated that five million pensioners on £1 a week each would require more than £250 million a year. The pensioners' organisation and left-wing Labour MPs argued that the war itself had shown that revenues could be found where the need existed but the Treasury was anxious about war debts and the cost of reconstruction. Beveridge was anyway inclined to caution on pensions, and after intercession from the Treasury in the form of a series of lunches with John Maynard Keynes, he eventually advised a contributory pension of only 14 shillings (70p) a week in the first instance, set to rise to 26 shillings (£1.30) over a twenty-year period. The latter figure was said to represent a 'subsistence level' income so in the interim needy pensioners would have to apply for means-tested Assistance.

The widespread enthusiasm for a universal approach to social citizenship and Labour's landslide victory in 1945 led to the setting up of the National Health Service and to a new and more generous system of benefits, including pensions. In response to clamour from Labour backbenchers in the Commons, the basic pension was set at 26 shillings (£1.30) in 1948, considerably above the initial level recommended by Beveridge but now, because of inflation, below the measly estimated level of subsistence. The pension was to be financed from National Insurance contributions paid by workers and employers, a victory for the Treasury view and a qualification of universality of provision. But there was to be 'blanketing in' of contributions from those in paid work, though wives acquired entitlement only via their husbands, and widows and spinsters were still to rely on Assistance, as were those with a break in their contributions record. The pension, paid at a flat rate, was to be available only to workers who had retired, with those postponing retirement to receive a small increment.[60]

The National Insurance system was described by Beveridge as a system of 'social security', partly in homage to the US example. But in the UK no equivalent of the Social Security Administration was set up and administration was entrusted to the Whitehall machine. Civil servants deterred their pliable pensions minister from indexing the basic pension, as he had wished. By 1951 969,000 pensioners qualified for National Assistance to eke out a basic pension that now represented a little less than 19 per cent of average manual earnings.[61]

In the UK, as in the United States, the contributory principle seemed at first to ally itself with parsimony. The treasuries liked the fact that contributions and benefits in such a system are likely to be set at a low level so that poorer workers can afford them. This then enables the argument to be made that higher pensions are only possible if there are higher contributions. But in fact this was not an ironclad logic since an element of progressivism could be introduced by levying contributions as a proportion of income (rather than at a flat rate), or by drawing on subventions from general taxation. Once contributory schemes had been in operation for a few years, those who had made contributions began to sense their stake in them, establishing a pro-pension – or in US terms pro-Social Security – sector of public opinion, those who, quite literally, had a 'vested interest'. Once such an interest existed it had some potential to influence politicians to improve pension schemes in the hope of winning votes.[62]

State-sponsored social security, whatever the language used, was a step beyond commercial insurance principles. If the insurance logic had been rigorously carried through, older American and European workers would have received a truly minute pension, if any at all. To begin with, benefits were still rather modest but so long as the system had a large, mandatory contributor base then the pay-as-you-go method of finance together with 'blanketing in' paid pensions to older workers as if they had been contributing. The crediting of notional contributions from older workers was to be a standard feature of post-Second World War pension systems. By paying better pensions to older workers as they retired, this approach reduced the pressure on other poverty assistance programmes. In France, Germany and Italy it could be easily justified in the later 1940s because hyper-inflation had wiped out the value of previous contributory schemes. The position of those – mainly women – who were not in the paid labour force was only reconciled to the insurance principle by the assumption that the male 'bread-winner's' contribution also covered his wife. Notwithstanding such extensions of the contributory principle, it remained a touchstone and helped to ensure that pensions were seen as a right. While the insurance approach limited the generosity of the early state pension schemes, and tended to make women dependent on men, it did at least remove pension provision from the stigmatising effects of public charity and Poor Relief.

The renovated pension schemes were, of course, based on mandatory, not voluntary, contributions. In principle everyone who could contribute had to do so, and, directly or indirectly, everyone would be covered. The British government's White Paper of 1944 evoked the wartime ethos to explain its approach: 'The scheme as a whole will embrace, not certain occupations and income groups, but the entire population. Concrete expression is thus given to the solidarity and unity of the nation, which in war have been its bulwarks against aggression and in peace will be its guarantee of success in the fight against individual want and mischance.'[63] In other states too, the experience of war, whether of victory or defeat or liberation, or some mixture of the foregoing, spurred a collective approach to pension provision and a determination not to repeat the miseries of the interwar years. Esping-Anderson confirms that the Second World War was the 'watershed' and points out that it made acceptable high rates of taxation whose revenues could then be directed at other urgent challenges.[64] The fact that the beneficiaries of 'blanketing in' had often risked their lives for their country helped to justify the practice. The onset of the Cold War was to have a mixed impact. To begin with, it led both East and West to emulate one another's social legislation but sooner or later, as Wilensky has shown, the military expenditure it occasioned was to constrain social budgets.[65]

The aftermath of the war saw far-reaching improvements to pension provision with coverage now often described as being open to anyone. The success of British wartime propaganda was a factor in the adoption of this 'model' by countries, like Sweden and France, which in fact eventually improved on it. The new principle, never quite achieved in the UK, was to devise a pension regime that covered the whole population and rescued all pensioners from poverty. In the immediate postwar years coverage was greatly extended in Western Europe but the pensions paid were meagre and did not offer a basic livelihood. Shortage of resources and the complexity of the new arrangements led to delay. But the advent of full employment helped to boost contributions and entitlements. By the late 1950s France and Germany paid a pension which covered basic livelihood, albeit one with few comforts. Sweden made more generous provision when it linked pension levels to earnings in 1959. In the UK the Labour opposition made waves with a bold proposal for a funded and graduated scheme in 1957 but the Conservative government responded with 'the largest increase since the war in the flat rate pension, just as 500,000 better-off people qualified for the pension for the first time, and one year before a general election (1959), which the Conservatives won'.[66]

In the United States, as we saw above, the Social Security retirement pension only became something like a living pension after the improvements of 1950 and 1954. Between 1940 and 1955 the number of persons covered by Social Security rose from 23 million to 70 million, the number of recipient beneficiaries from 20,000 to 8 million, while cash benefits paid out rose from $35 million to $5 billion. Canada acquired a Federation-wide scheme in 1951 which improved on the minimal provision of 1927 – but not by much. The paying of 'universal' state pensions generally went ahead side by side with the continuation of the occupational schemes to public employees like teachers or postal workers. In France and Italy the basic state pension was linked to special, and usually more generous, arrangements for employees in the public sector, including mines, electricity supply and railways.

The state pensions of the postwar boom moved towards a species of 'universality' still qualified by work record, gender and status. Thus the workings of the contributory principle, even with 'blanketing in' of notional contributions, meant that they did not in fact offer all citizens of a country, let alone all residents, a pension once they reached the age of retirement. 'Blanketing in' itself was usually based on proof that the individual had been in work or available for work. There was a gendered assumption that men were the bread-winners and that women would be covered by wives and widows claiming entitlement via their husbands' work record. In practice women were to be excluded from the full pension if they or their husbands did not have a consistent contribution record, wives therefore being dependent on the punctilio and good will of their spouses. Many unmarried women had no proper entitlement and were obliged to apply for Assistance. And while a widow had a derived entitlement it was often only to a proportion of her husband's pension. Itinerant workers, or ethnic groups suffering social discrimination, or non-registered unemployed, or ex-prisoners, might all find it difficult to attain the minimum contribution record. In the 1960s and 1970s attempts were made to extend coverage because there was political or social pressure for this and because rising national wealth made it more affordable. But exclusions stemming from the contributory principle remained generally in force and some groups in the population, such as recent immigrants or the very old, especially women, had to apply to poor relief programmes. These generalisations applied to all capitalist welfare states (except New Zealand with its tax-based system[67]).

Occupational Schemes: Mobilisation and Compromise

Trade union pressure on employers for second pensions intensified at a time when state provision was still quite meagre, as in Britain during the 1920s and 1930s, or in the United States during the 1940s. The fact that civil servants and teachers had acquired occupational retirement plans at an even earlier date furnished an example to employees in the private sector. From the 1920s US corporations exploited favourable tax treatment of pension funds to take care of senior management. The 1942 Revenue Act, and court-supported IRS rulings based on it, stipulated that pension funds would only qualify for full tax relief if they were open to at least 70 per cent of a company's employees. In order to pay for the war the same Act greatly widened the numbers liable to income tax and also raised corporate tax rates.[68] In this way a situation was created where both employers and employees could find advantage in setting up pension schemes. But militant trade union agitation was required before occupational pensions were introduced across whole industries. The onset of rivalry with the Soviet Union, whose social programmes had been much publicised, and the campaign to destroy Communist influence in the US unions, helped to raise the stakes.[69] In 1946 John L. Lewis led the United Mine Workers in a strike to demand an industry-wide pension plan. With fuel shortages threatening to bring US industry grinding to a halt, President Truman took over the mines and imposed a compromise pension arrangement on both employers and union. After foot-dragging from the employers the first cheques went out in September 1948. Walter Reuther, the leader of the United Auto Workers, sought to extract a pension deal from Ford in 1947 but passage of the strongly anti-union Taft–Hartley Act in the same year (over Truman's veto) boosted employer resistance in this industry too. A similar tangle, with strikes imminent and employers recalcitrant, developed in the steel industry. Truman intervened once again and the Steel Industry Board issued a report in September 1949 which declared that 'a social obligation rests upon industry to provide insurance against the economic hazards of modern industrial life, including retirement allowances, in adequate amount as supplementary to the amount of security furnished by government.'[70] The report was quickly accepted by the steel union and pointed to as a model in the other sectors where organised labour was strong. But the steel employers rejected key elements of the report, arguing that it would be wrong to impose a pension scheme on the whole workforce and that voluntary arrangements would be much better. This reaction provoked the steel union into a strike call. One day before the strike was scheduled to start the United Auto Workers extracted a pension agreement from the Ford motor company, based on the principles which the Steel Board had enunciated. Bethlehem Steel soon decided that the time had come to settle and eventually other steel companies gave up their resistance. In 1950 General Motors came up with a funded pension scheme which envisaged equity investments.

Some of the new pension agreements yoked employers and union leaders together in their management boards, though this was not true of the GM model. Later they were to be heralded as engines of class harmony. But the postwar introduction of mandatory industry-wide, or company-wide, pension schemes had been the product of dramatic class confrontation and struggle. In later years some employers preferred to introduce schemes of their own to pre-empt further bouts of union militancy. The government had helped to impose compromise partly to avoid social strife. But subsequent administrations wished to encourage saving in a bid to dampen inflationary pressures and were consequently often willing to extend major tax incentives to pension schemes, whether collective or individual in character. Another key factor behind the rise of the US industrial pension schemes was the continued willingness of the Revenue Service to treat corporate contributions as a legitimate pre-tax business expense and to allow employees to defer the payment of tax until they actually received the pension.

Prior to the UAW–GM agreement of 1950, pension money had been placed almost exclusively in government securities, a fact which may have helped to recommend these arrangements to the fiscal authorities. But a novel feature of the GM scheme, much stressed by Peter Drucker, is that the pension fund was entrusted to professional management and the managers permitted to invest in equities if they considered this advisable. By the early 1950s the idea of the 'mutual fund' was staging a recovery from the discredit into which it had sunk in the years after 1929. Pension funds copied the spread of investments exemplified by the mutual funds and soon the financial houses offering the latter were being invited to manage the former. The example of the GM scheme was copied in some 8,000 separate agreements made between employers and unions in the subsequent few years. The trustees of these schemes were still legally obliged to obey the 'prudent person' rule but they could argue that investing a chunk of their fund in equities was prudent so long as a balanced portfolio was chosen.[71]

Trade unionists and other employees alike benefited from the fact that contributions to pension funds were tax free. Governments had for some time sought to foster pension-related saving by offering tax concessions. Esping-Anderson cites legislation to this effect in the United States, the UK and Denmark from the 1920s.[72] But in the 1920s tax breaks on pension schemes were of interest only to well-paid managers and specialists. It was not until after the Second World War that the mass of employees paid income tax.

Ann Orloff has argued that the uneven advance of public pension provision reflected the varying ability of states to manage such a programme. Where such a state capacity existed, schemes could be introduced more easily; where it was wanting, there would be delay. Similarly, in the case of employee pension funds, as Richard Minns has pointed out, a crucial facility was the presence of a vigorous stock market.[73] Pension funds made progress in Britain partly because of similar, albeit less dramatic, social pressures to those seen in the United States and also because it possessed a lively equity market and an experienced financial services sector. In the nineteenth century Britain had pioneered the idea of the investment trust with concerns like Foreign and Colonial – still with us in the twenty-first century – offering stakes in funds which held shares in a mixture of companies. In the 1950s 'unit trusts' were established which functioned like US mutual funds. The existence of such financial vehicles furnished a ready-made parallel for the elaboration of pension funds. In 1956 the British government introduced Retirement Annuity Contracts (RACs), a tax-favoured forerunner of today's personal pension plan. When secondary state pensions were introduced in the UK, employees who belonged to occupational schemes were allowed to 'contract out' of them. By 1979 11.8 million British employees were covered by an occupational scheme, 5.6 million in the public sector, with about two-thirds of those covered being men. Contributions rose to around 5 per cent of income from the employee and 7–12 per cent of income from the employer. The schemes' assets rose to £40 billion by 1979.[74] Private pension provision thus shared, or even intensified, the gender and occupational bias of the state pension regime.

Pension funds were also to become important in the Netherlands and Switzerland, countries with historic financial services industries. But in France and Germany social pressure for secondary pensions led to other solutions.[75] While both countries have strong traditions of state *dirigisme*, the postwar context proved more favourable to the emergence of decentralised systems of publicly sponsored saving and pension provision, based on the enterprise or working collective rather than state administration. The experience of the war had undermined the prestige of the state but not the ideal of social provision.

Germany and France Forge a New Social Compact

In the German case the large enterprises were knit into groups by the large banks. They felt able to concede pension arrangements that would be met partly out of company reserves set aside for that purpose and partly from anticipated future growth. The reserves set aside for pension provision often represented a book-keeping device – a claim on the company's future revenues – allowing the contributions to be used in the meantime to boost capacity. Such an outcome was also in keeping with the Weimar tradition of representing employees on one tier of the boards of management (*Mitbestimmung*) and the even older tradition of recognising craft organisation in manufacturing.[76] The German *Wirtschaftswunder* helped the pension arrangement to go with a swing and, reciprocally, the reserves made their own contribution to the miracle, allowing companies to boost investment in productive capacity. In 1980 these book reserves were valued at 115 billion Deutschmarks, or some $45 billion. Georg Heubeck describes the German supplementary pension schemes as 'a necessary addition to the basic protection provided by statutory social security' but also 'a mixture of redistribution and capital accumulation'.[77] There was a risk involved since employees, in effect, found both their savings and their job prospects tied up in the same enterprise. But the German style of industrial organisation, based on bank-led industrial groups, underpinned by cross-holding of shares, minimised the danger of company failure. Since Germany did not possess much by way of a market in equities the US-style pension fund solution was anyway not available. In Italy large companies were also allowed to set aside reserves at a low interest rate as a pension fund for their employees. In France the postwar period witnessed a somewhat different approach to secondary pensions, but one which also by-passed investment in the bourse.

While the German secondary pension system has been based on cooperation between management and workforce, leading to accumulation of 'reserves' within the enterprise, the postwar French system, emerging from the proposals of the Council of the Resistance and the immediate postwar Popular Front-style government, was to see employers and unions cooperate in running a national pension scheme financed on the pay-as-you-go (PAYGO) basis. Current employees make regular contributions which are then paid out to those entitled to a pension. If there is ever a shortfall, governments are expected to cover it. In nearly every country PAYGO is the system used to finance the basic state pension but the French opted to use it for funding secondary pensions too. It is possible to portray this system as an expression of an elementary social contract, along the lines of the famous watchword of French socialism, 'From each according to their ability, to each according to their need'. In fact social republican sentiment helped in the establishment of the French system. But the doctrine of republican social unity did not, in fact, carry all before it in the 1940s. The farmers and the self-employed unwisely refused to join the *régime général*; although its terms were favourable to them they distrusted the left-wing unions controlling the *caisses* which administered the system. Another group to secede comprised the so-called *cadres* or managerial and white-collar employers, who insisted on having their own scheme. Finally, the *régime général* was organised so as not to infringe on the rights and privileges of those already covered by *régimes spéciaux*, schemes which catered to the different branches of the public service.

The coverage of the *régime général* was steadily widened and its provisions became considerably more generous in the years 1968–72, a time when the Gaullist regime faced a reinvigorated challenge from the Left. In Italy a trade union offensive also produced a more generous pension regime in 1968-69 which set the scene for subsequent battles over entitlement. In West Germany the basic standard of pension allocation had been set in 1957 but its provisions were improved in 1972 by the Social Democrat–Free Democrat coalition government, with larger benefits and better provision for women and the self-employed.[78] In 1972 US Social Security benefits were raised by 20 per cent and coverage widened, under legislation prepared by the Democrats but supported by many Republicans including the President, Richard Nixon. In Britain a small graduated element had been introduced by Harold Macmillan's Conservatives in 1961 but generally public pension provision in Britain was rudimentary and mean compared with other West European countries (the Netherlands was also a laggard). The subsequent Labour and Conservative administrations in the UK mooted extensions of secondary provision but it fell to the Labour government of 1974–79 belatedly to place a State Earnings Related Pension Scheme (SERPS) on the statute book. The upgrading of pension provision in several major developed states occurred in the aftermath of social turmoil and their enactment helped to relegitimise the states concerned. But in Canada, in deference to Quebec sentiment and its special standing within the Federation, the necessary legislation was organised and delivered on a provincial basis. In the 1960s and 1970s those in charge of the Quebec Pension Plan used its resources to foster a transformation of the Quebec economy.

The postwar boom raised popular expectations. It also led to rising prices which intensified demands for an overhaul of pensions, to which parties of both the centre Left and centre Right responded. With the advent of a new prosperity it seemed only right to provide more generously for the retired and elderly. In Germany contributions were raised from 14 to 18 per cent of salary, and graduated schemes in other countries also had a tendency to take in more as nominal incomes rose. The continental European pension reforms of the 1960s and 1970s followed the German lead of 1957 in fully incorporating those on middle incomes. In Germany, France and Italy even those earning twice average male wages could look forward to a pension which would itself be well above that average. The male worker on average wages would receive 66 per cent of his former income in Sweden in the early 1970s, and 47 per cent in Germany and France; in Italy the entitlement was growing but delivery lay in the future. In the UK the basic state pension replaced only 20 per cent of average male incomes. In the UK, as in Germany and France, occupational schemes furnished a supplementary pension to those who were covered. Since the UK basic pension offered a flat-rate benefit and embodied better provisions for widows, it gave a better pension to those below half average wages than did the German scheme. In the United States Social Security replaced 48 per cent of the income of a married man of average income on his retirement. The French scheme was more generous than the Anglo-Saxon schemes and more redistributive than the German or Italian. But the most egalitarian and universalist pension provision was that prevailing in Sweden.[79]

I have described the French pension system as financed by the pay-as-you-go method because it was certainly not pre-funded and did pay out the contributions as pensions. Even the contributory schemes incorporated in one way or another into the system in 1947–48 had no funds because of the collapse of the currency, so a reversion to funding was virtually ruled out. The precise form of financing adopted was to be known as *répartition*, in which the rate of contributions was, in principle, fixed in advance, furnishing an income stream which was then shared out among qualifying pensioners, with benefit rates adjusted so as not to exceed the income.[80] In the early decades those who received the pension had some cause to be grateful, even though it was quite modest, because they had contributed little to the system. As the system matured, an expansion in employment, and rising incomes, allowed a better pension to be paid to increasing numbers of retirees. Improvements to the system were assisted by the fact that its administration had a quasi-autonomous character, while both Gaullists and the Left were insistent that it was integral to French citizenship and were usually willing to support top-ups when necessary.

The French *régimes spéciaux* covered a variety of public sector employees but placed strain on the PAYGO financing as the balance between contributors and retirees altered in the branches covered. There have to be complex arrangements to allow expanding areas of employment to subsidise declining ones. Thus in 1970 1.3 million members of the civil servants' pension scheme were paying pensions to 390,000 retirees but only 164,000 miners were paying pensions to 348,000 retired mine workers.[81] In this situation the Ministry of Finance had to come up with a subsidy to boost the miners' pension.

The working of AGIRC, the pension system of the French *cadres*, supplies another example of the working of an unfunded PAYGO arrangement. The scheme originally catered to a restricted number of managerial and white-collar employees. While employers' contributions helped to fund the scheme, the benefit paid out was linked to guaranteeing a pension amounting, overall, to 80 per cent of final salary. To begin with, in 1948, there were 224,000 members but joining AGIRC seemed advantageous. By 1963 the number of members had grown to 600,000 and by 1983 to 2 million. An expanding contributor base meant that the level of benefit could easily keep pace with the advance of national prosperity, indeed could often exceed it. The manifest advantages of the AGIRC scheme attracted new members and made its provisions into a benchmark for the French system as a whole. However, even this scheme encountered financing constraints in 1983, which were met, to the dismay of members, by a reduction in benefit levels. In succeeding years there were to be repeated tensions and clashes over the workings of the French pension regimes. Members of the various schemes, especially the *régimes spéciaux*, fiercely defend their rights in them and public opinion, imbued with social republican principles, has been disposed to come to the defence of pension promises (as we will see in chapter 4) even if this means recourse to public subsidies.[82]

The Logic of Pay-As-You-Go and the Funded Alternatives

Governments arrived at pay-as-you-go (PAYGO) in the case of basic pensions for two reasons. Firstly, it allowed the schemes to come into operation quickly, and secondly it proved a more stable solution than that of accumulating and managing a large fund. Usually care was taken to ensure that the level of benefit furnished by the scheme was adequately covered by the base of employee contributors. Indeed, there was often a surplus on the social security retirement account which governments could spend on other uses. In different ways the postwar boom and the baby boom both helped to ensure the buoyancy of the PAYGO systems. It was not until 1958, however, that economic theory came up with a justification of arrangements which had been dictated largely by necessity. In December of that year Paul Samuelson published a famous essay in the *Journal of Political Economy* which addressed, in what could be taken as reassuring terms, the fear that there was a fundamental incoherence at the heart of retirement provision through Social Security. It is not difficult to present a PAYGO system of financing as a sort of pyramid scheme which is bound to run into difficulties as it matures, with entitlements overtaking contributions. Samuelson showed that it was, indeed, impossible to run a pension system postulating exchanges between living generations because neither the over-65s nor the over-40s would ever be able to reciprocate any economic sacrifice made by the 20–40-year-olds. But if future generations were added into the picture, then the PAYGO system could work. To reinforce the reasonableness of making assumptions about the future, Samuelson observed that money itself, as a store of value, would be worthless without the very same presumption of future productive activity. So far as the economics of a mature pay-as-you-go system were concerned, Samuelson maintained that the real rate of return would be equal to the sum of the rate of growth in the labour force and the rate of growth of productivity.[83] More colloquially, one might say that a rising pension bill can be met so long as output rises because of some mixture of more workers and/or higher productivity. Samuelson was led to formulate what he called the 'Social Security Paradox': the economics of the compact between today's workers and pensioners in a pay-as-you-go system require the ability to lay a claim on those not yet born who, in an infinitely receding horizon, would have a claim on their children or grandchildren (see epigraph to this chapter).[84] An Italian economist, Onorato Castellino, somewhat ominously recast this as follows: 'Perhaps we might say that the burden is imposed on the last generation, the one that comes of age when the pension scheme is abolished or the end of the centuries comes.'[85] Less dramatically, it followed from Samuelson's formula that PAYGO might eventually give diminishing returns if productivity and fertility both dropped significantly, and longevity increased. But in 1958 productivity seemed buoyant, the famous baby boom was well under way, and both these trends were more than sufficient to cover prospective increases in longevity.

Samuelson's real target in this article was free market economics. He pointed out that there were highly advantageous social arrangements which required a degree of 'social collusion', and indeed social 'coercion', to prevent free riders: 'if all but one obey, the one may gain selfish advantage by disobeying – which is where the sheriff comes in: *we* politically invoke force on *ourselves*. . . . Once social coercion or contracting is admitted into the picture the present problem disappears.' More generally he was led to show that individualism needed collectivism:

> That the Protestant ethic should have been instrumental in creating indi-
> vidualistic capitalism one may accept: but that it should stop there is not
> necessarily plausible. What made Jeremy Bentham a Benthamite in 1800,
> one suspects, might in 1900 have made him a Fabian (and do we not see a
> lot in common in the personalities of James Mill and Friedrich Engels?).[86]

These remarks by the leading US economist of his day handsomely acknowledge that the Social Security system did indeed embody a significant element of collectivism. Further, the multigeneration scope of Samuelson's account had greater depth than the life-cycle models of saving and expenditure developed by Milton Friedman.

The PAYGO device was adopted by governments partly because it seemed to work and partly because they were anyway committed to step in if ever there was a shortfall of contributions. The state's fiscal capacities and its ability to legislate for universal coverage put it in a position quite different from that of a commercial undertaking. If the state is planning for everybody, then at least it can be sure that there will be future generations and that it can tax them. If it wishes it can organise secondary or earnings-related pensions on a PAYGO basis too, as happens in France. The British SERPS was set up on this basis in the later 1970s and US Social Security itself has graduated contributions and entitlements. Because of the movement into, and out of, different occupations, the design of such schemes cannot be purely occupational and must be built across the span of occupations. The calibration of contributions and benefits can be arranged to ensure that the scheme diminishes the extent of income inequalities. However, public secondary pensions can also be pre-funded, as is the case in Sweden, with the advantage that the extent of future public obligations is reduced.

But if a pension provider is dealing only with a given group of workers, whether in the public or the private sector, then resort to the PAYGO method for them alone causes problems, because of the risk that the level of employment may fluctuate. This is why occupational pension schemes have usually been pre-funded. Any significant drop in employment would wreck the economics of a PAYGO system applied only within one industry. The rapid decline in the numbers of British steel workers and coal miners in the 1980s would have spelled disaster for an occupationally defined PAYGO system. As it was, the trade unions had pressed for arrangements whereby workers' pensions in these industries were backed by impressive funds. By 1990 Britain's largest pension funds belonged to the miners, the telecom and post office workers, the steel workers and the electricity supply workers (details of this in chapter 2, Table 2.1).

Lacking the constraints and facilities of the French system, British and American employers and trade unions looked to pre-funding if they were to sponsor occupational secondary pensions. Once such a fund was set up, it seemed quite rational to entrust it to a life insurance company, or invest some of it directly in the stock market because equities offered a good rate of return. For their part, governments saw such secondary pension schemes as desirable: in the short run contributions lessened inflationary pressures while in the longer run they allowed more citizens to provide for their own old age. Accordingly, American and British governments maintained favourable tax treatment to money put aside in pension schemes. The contributions made were free of tax, sometimes the pension funds paid little or no capital gains tax, and the eventual pay-out would be taxed at a lower rate than if the levy had fallen on the original contributions. The US ERISA (Employees' Retirement Income Security Act) of 1974 came at a time when the mutual funds and financial services industries were suffering from a troubled equity market and a string of financial scandals, and when there was rising concern at the need to boost savings and investment to meet German and Japanese competition. Following the bankruptcy of the Studebaker motor corporation in the mid-1960s, it transpired that the employees' pension fund was nearly empty. ERISA gave a major boost to the commercial management of pension funds by restoring public confidence and establishing a Pension Benefit Guaranty Corporation (PBGC) which would insure the basic benefits in all schemes in return for a compulsory insurance premium. Tax relief was another attractive feature to all concerned.

Explaining the Pattern of Pension Provision

The foregoing has sketched the main routes to modern pension provision. The end result was that by 1960 state pensions systems had been established everywhere in the advanced world, financed on a pay-as-you-go (PAYGO) basis. In France the PAYGO approach was also drawn upon to provide secondary pensions. In Britain, the Netherlands and the United States, however, the pre-funded approach was adopted for secondary, occupational or personal pensions, with the resulting funds managed either by the financial services industry or by a staff assembled for the purpose by the trustees. In order to administer a PAYGO system a country needed a 'neutral' and quite sophisticated administrative apparatus. And, at least so far as the first wave was concerned, the pre-funded regimes needed access to stock markets. It is worth spelling out the possible combinations and alternatives because then the logic of development in pension provision will become clearer. Pensions can be *delivered* by commercial organisations or the state (or by state-sponsored not-for-profit outfits, as is the case in France). And pensions can be *financed* by direct voluntary contributions or by using the fiscal power of the state, or by some mixture of the two; and, if pre-funded, from investment income as well. In the case of occupational schemes an employer can reduce their voluntary character by making participation a condition of employment. The outcomes so far surveyed do not include any case of a privately delivered PAYGO system, or of a mandatory commercially delivered system, or of a fully funded but state-delivered and mandatory system. These absences strongly suggest a filtering mechanism at work, eliminating approaches which were deemed undesirable or found to be impracticable.

The absence of voluntary, private PAYGO systems relates to the fact that commercial suppliers cannot offer to finance future pensions by, as Samuelson put it, 'drafts on the unborn'. This possibility was filtered out because it seemed so evidently imprudent to allow commercial organisations to collect and spend contributions while accumulating obligations to pay pensions at some future date, counting on new members voluntarily joining the scheme. A firm offering such a deal would usually fall foul of the laws against pyramid schemes. And where such laws did not exist any self-respecting financial community would make sure that they were invented: Charles Ponzi went to jail for fraud in Massachusetts in 1920 despite the fact that his company, because of growing membership, had yet to default on a payment. He was deemed guilty of fraud simply because he had no prospect of maintaining payments other than by continually attracting more members to the scheme;[87] in other words PAYGO, but PAYGO with no possibility of guaranteeing that the membership will go on multiplying.

But if this type of freelance commercial PAYGO is out, what about a state-franchised commercial PAYGO? The government could step in and confer its tax-raising powers on specified commercial organisations. Governments did not adopt this approach anywhere, partly because it might look as if the government was lending its sanction to a dubious commercial practice, and partly because public administrations have always proved equal to the task of running PAYGO systems. Indeed because tax and pension contributions can be collected together, the administrative costs of public pension systems have been very reasonable. However, other ways of privatising pensions have been experimented with in recent years, namely empowering commercial organisations to accept mandatory pension contributions, managing the resulting funds and paying pensions when they fall due. In 1982 the Chilean military government replaced its former PAYGO universal pension system with a mandatory, but pre-funded and commercially organised, scheme. Such an approach had not recommended itself in the prior development of pension policy in the developed countries because governments had not wished to force their citizens into the arms of private companies. Public pensions were introduced in the United States, or expanded in postwar Europe, at times when confidence in commercial arrangements was at a nadir because of bank failures, aggravated in Europe in the 1940s by hyper-inflation. But even once confidence was restored, in the 1950s or 1960s, proposing laws compelling citizens to pay taxes to financial bodies rather than the national government in order to get a pension would have looked inappropriate, and smacked of a return to tax farming. Even with public regulation and guarantees, such an approach, one surmises, would still have been seen as an abdication of government responsibilities and an unjustifiable act of compulsion. In the two small countries which did invite the financial services industry to help organise pension delivery, Switzerland and Chile, these considerations held less weight. In Switzerland the banks and insurance houses had great prestige and the cantons preferred to cede fewer responsibilities to the Confederation. The Chilean case was different. The military government confronted an acute crisis in the early 1980s and had no need to secure assent from any elected body. The coup of 1973 had been aimed against the redistributive and reforming government of the Socialist president, Salvador Allende. The military did not return the state-run copper mines to private ownership because revenues from them helped to defray the military budget. But removing responsibility for future pensions from the state budget seemed like a promising experiment (on which more in chapter 4).

The other approach to pension provision that was generally filtered out or minimised in the developed metropolis was that of a fully or largely pre-funded, publicly delivered, universal pension. The failure to fund is the more curious in that almost everywhere pensions were financed by special, ear-marked taxes or 'contributions', supposedly dedicated to social security or social insurance and nothing else. When pressure built up for public pension provision, as we have seen, treasuries invariably favoured a contributory approach, as it reduced the strain on general revenues and embodied a more responsible fiscal attitude. But a flow of contributions of any sort can easily lead to the accumulation of a fund, even in a PAYGO system. This then poses the problem of what to do with the accumulated reserve. The idea of placing large sums of capital in the hands of public and social bodies invariably made financial institutions and businessmen profoundly uneasy. Indeed such possibilities were sometimes thought to be inimical to a properly functioning capitalist order. A national debt, giving financiers leverage over the state, was one thing. A national investment fund, giving government leverage over business, quite another. When the contributory pension was debated in Britain in the 1920s, the possible appearance of a large national insurance fund attracted criticism from business leaders. While the fund could be sunk in public bonds, in time it could become larger than the national debt and have to be invested in the stock market. W.H. Lever feared the disruption this would cause, seeing it as based on the 'fallacy that there could be investments available for the funds contributed, without entirely destroying and breaking up the very foundation on which the investments in this country rested'.[88] The fear could have been more clearly expressed (was he worried by Fabian Bolshevism or the impact on asset prices?), but was palpable nonetheless. The immediate paying of pensions under PAYGO plus 'blanketing in' reduced the size of the fund and what remained was denominated in special low-interest bonds.

When Roosevelt pushed for old age pensions to be fully funded he also ran into objections from a Treasury committee observing that 'reserves such as become necessary under a full reserves system are unthinkable'.[89] Or perhaps unsayable? Conservative opponents of Social Security were more forthright. The administration's proposal that Social Security funds should be placed in government bonds awoke fears that they would be used for social projects, such as low-cost housing, hospitals and schools or even 'certain types of capital equipment'.[90] There was also the question of what would happen if the Social Security Trust Fund exceeded the national debt. A recent account notes:

> Arthur Altmeyer tells us that he and Senator Vandenberg had an off-the-record discussion about the investment of the trust fund accumulations that were in excess of government debt levels. Altmeyer suggested that a provision could be put in the Social Security Act that would require the Treasury to invest the excess in private securities. He said that the Senator responded by saying, 'That would be socialism'.[91]

This was a jest but one that was close to the bone. Calculations were circulated showing that the trust fund would be worth around $47 billion by 1980 and that 40 per cent of its income would come from investments. The fear that the Social Security fund could be used to underwrite an active policy of public investment made its depletion through PAYGO plus 'blanketing in' more acceptable and led to the residual fund being limited in size and confined to investment in a special type of low-interest Treasury bond that amounted to no more than an official IOU.

The idea of active investment by social pension funds was most calculated to alarm business opinion when organised labour seemed poised to extend its claims. Such reactions also occurred in postwar Sweden. The story of pension provision and welfare financing in Sweden has a special importance since the country was so often the pace-maker for its neighbours. Under successive Social Democratic governments Sweden acquired both a generous welfare state and per capita national income among the highest in the world. In 1947 it had been the first country in the world to index pensions, in 1957–59 it inaugurated a near-universal system of state secondary or occupational pensions. The basic Swedish pension was financed by a PAYGO system but in the 1950s it seemed prudent to pre-finance the secondary pension so that too many liabilities were not stored up for future generations. The result was to be two momentous and very public battles between the Social Democrats and their opponents over the building up of public welfare funds. The first took place in the years 1957–59 and concerned the establishment of a fund to enable the secondary earnings-related pensions to be paid to employees. This plan met stiff resistance from the employers and the 'bourgeois parties', as they are called in Sweden. At the root of the latter's opposition was the fear that the pension fund could be used to dominate or 'improperly influence' the large corporations. After several dramatic clashes – involving a referendum, the dissolution of Parliament, emergency elections, a regular election and commissions of inquiry – the legislation was eventually passed by one vote. Participation in this secondary pension was broad since it included all those paid more than one-third of average male wages. The funding element remained but, as part of the compromise eventually reached, the fund was to invest not in corporate stocks but either in public bonds or bonds issued by banks. The idea of an active public trust fund was excluded, highlighting the determination of the Swedish corporations to retain control of the country's capital market. The pension fund reserves established in this way helped to underpin business credit rather than to underwrite current government spending.[92]

   In successive chapters we will find that the fear of public trust funds lives
on. So far as the financial community is concerned, publicly controlled
pension funds investing in the stock market represent a loss of business.
Perhaps worse was the economic power it might give to public agencies.
Of course the British and US schemes do, from time to time, build up a
surplus of contributions, which are then held as nominal debts against
future disbursements. This cheap finance can be used to balance the public
books but what has not happened in either the United States or the UK is
the setting up of an independent social investment board (or boards)
empowered to invest these surpluses in marketable assets. Ideological opposition to investing pension money in the stock market came from the Left,
of course, as well as the Right. Reformist parties were daunted by the
power such an approach would give to public funds while openly anti-
capitalist parties, if they considered the possibility at all, were likely to deem
it an ineffective, or undesirable, route to the collectivisation of the economy. So long as memories of the stock market crash endured it aroused
popular misgivings.
   But the hobbling of public trust funds was expedient as well as princi-
pled or ideological. In some cases the weakness of the equity market ruled
out such investments while in others governments found that they could
borrow cheaply from public trust funds. Since the government was guaranteeing the value of the fund it seemed not unfair to pay only a low rate
of interest. Governments also found it difficult both to build up the fund
and to pay out current pensions, leading to fund depletion. The first
public pension schemes in Germany and France were meant to build up
funds but these were eventually wiped out by inflation.[93] In subsequent
chapters this issue of pre-funding is probed more deeply and attention
given to recent proposals to set up public pensions funds with the power
to acquire stakes in the private sector. But here we should note that several
successful pension funds were established for state officials themselves, or
for public sector workers at local or national level, without encountering
the same objections – but coverage in these cases was limited and management was not directly in the hands of elected officials.
   Matters were different in some parts of South-East Asia, notably in
Japan, Malaya and Singapore. Here the elites controlling the public bureaucracy identified the potentially strategic role of publicly mobilised savings
for economic development. They also found ways of accomplishing this
without alarming business interests. The Malaysian scheme was established
in 1951 at a time when both Malaya and Singapore were under British
colonial rule. Today's Central Provident Funds (CPFs) in Malaysia and

Singapore directly descend from this institution which has thus stood the test of time. The introduction of the scheme was seen as an enlightened act of colonial policy and as a way of rallying support at a time of Communist insurgency. At the time there were no commercial organisations which could have undertaken pension provision in territories from which the British state was likely to withdraw. The survival of the provident funds reflected both the capacity of the public administration and the buoyancy of the Malayan and Singaporean economies over the subsequent half century. There is good reason to believe that the CPFs helped to stabilise the relatively favourable economic conditions of which they were a part. Whether the CPF should be seen as a powerful lever of social control, or rather as a benign agency of economic construction and nation building, is an issue which is discussed in chapter 4.[94]

In the case of Japan, the role of public pension funds in raising the investment rate is even clearer. Japan had introduced pensions for a few senior officials as early as 1890 and some other special schemes followed in the 1920s and 1930s. It was not until 1941 that a contributory scheme was introduced, aimed at offering a pension to all employees and officially dubbed the Welfare Pension but subsequently known as the Employee Pension Scheme (EPS). In 1948 a committee of the Health and Welfare Ministry urged: 'We must not simply revise the pre-existing systems. We must extricate ourselves from the old customs and privileges for a portion of the population, and establish a revolutionary new system.'[95] But the proposed universal scheme financed by general taxation was deemed too generous by both the US occupation authorities and the Japanese administrative elite, and consequently shelved. In 1951 Japanese companies which offered severance deals to workers they laid off were allowed by the Finance Ministry to make such payments net of tax; this arrangement served as a precedent for company pension schemes. In the mid and late 1950s pension provision was built up on the basis of the wartime EPS and some of the special occupational schemes, such as those for seamen, schoolteachers and state officials. By 1961 Japan, in true baroque style, had six different state pension schemes for different categories of the population.[96]

The EPS was based on contributions with initially modest benefits. In Japanese conditions the scheme began to accumulate a sizeable surplus because of the low level of entitlement, with little recourse to 'blanketing in', and only 5 per cent of the population being over sixty-five. Business leaders and state officials warned that if Social Security benefits were too generous this would undermine the family. The sums collected under the

Social Security programme were lent at a low rate of interest to the Fiscal
Investment and Loan Programme (FILP), a public agency which used
them to undertake far-reaching improvements in the country's basic social
infrastucture, including roads, ports and power supply. The FILP began to
assume responsibility for 40–50 per cent of the state's current account
budget. The FILP also lent money to the Housing Loan Corporation
which was consequently able to offer housing finance on attractive terms.
Writing in the late 1980s, Bernard Eccleston explained, 'in practice the
[Social Security] accounts have shown a huge annual surplus equivalent to
3 per cent of GNP as the accumulated pension surpluses from earlier years
are invested to produce substantial interest earnings.'[97] In the meantime the
dramatic advance of national prosperity had allowed for some improvement
in benefit levels. The proportion of the population over sixty-five rose to
10 per cent in the early 1980s, and was on course to reach 15 per cent in
the early 1990s, 20 per cent by 2010 and perhaps 25 per cent or more by
2030. Such projections did not deter the Japanese bureaucracy from
coming up with a new pension law in 1985 which strove to preserve the
new, higher benefit levels, albeit with some increase in contributions.
Japan had funded private provision and a few argued that now was the time
to let this type of provision take over. Legislation in the early 1960s offered
tax-sheltered savings opportunities to Japanese employees. The Tekikeku
Nenkin (Tax Qualified Pensions) established in 1962 and the Kosei
Nenkin Kikin (Employee Pension Funds) established in 1966 grew over
subsequent decades to embrace 31 million private sector workers. These
pension funds invest in equities, bonds and real estate, with limits set for
each class of asset.[98] But state officials rejected the idea that these supplementary pensions should be extended to replace public provision,
notwithstanding alarming demographic projections. For nearly four
decades the Social Security surplus had made its own notable contribution
to the phenomenal growth rates which had made Japan the world's second
biggest economic power. There was social pressure to ensure the future of
the public system from the Trade Union Federation and the Socialist Party
which complained that the size of the trust fund had been diminished by
the low rate of interest that was paid by the FILP. But the bureaucracy had
its own reasons for defending a system which boosted the state's social prestige and economic leverage – surpluses were set to continue for at least
another decade. Even after some trimming, the benefits available for those
who met a new qualifying condition of forty years of contributions would
replace 67 per cent of pre-retirement income.[99] As we will see, this compares well with pensions elsewhere.

Varieties of Pension Fund and the Answer to a Prayer

Since private and funded pensions exist everywhere, and are particularly important in the 'Anglo-Saxon' model, it remains to explain the different funded approaches. In Britain and the United States occupational pensions schemes were, until recently, organised on a so-called 'defined benefit' (DB) or 'final salary' basis. Those who met the contributory criteria were guaranteed a pension that was a proportion of their final salary. Schemes organised on this basis have advantages for employees, so long as the scheme is insured, inflation-proofed and free of penalties for those who change jobs. The guarantees established by the US ERISA in 1974 sought to address such problems. Partly because of the advantages to employees of a well-designed 'defined benefit' plan, employers came to prefer to sponsor 'defined contribution' (DC) or 'money purchase' pensions in the 1980s and 1990s. Under these the employee is only entitled to whatever sum has accumulated in his or her name by the time of retirement. Whereas the 'defined benefit' schemes place the burden of risk on the employer – who has to ensure that the fund is sufficient to pay the salary-related pension – the 'defined contribution' scheme places the risk of a shortfall on the employee; if there is not enough in the fund, he or she simply has to live with the consequences. And even apart from such downside risks the DB schemes incorporate from the outset an employers' contribution whereas the DC schemes often do not. In the UK individual employees are required to use three-quarters of the 'pot' they accumulate in a DC scheme to purchase an annuity and are thus exposed to any fall in the rate of return on these instruments.

Nevertheless, employees can see advantages in 'defined contribution' schemes because they are often more 'portable', allowing holders to transfer the accumulated balance to another scheme. To meet this problem, some 'defined benefit' schemes now incorporate a so-called 'cash balance' provision whereby the policy holder is allowed to transfer a sum out of the scheme. But whether movers keep an entitlement or claim a balance, they lose the vital inflation proofing and income escalator offered to long-service employees by a DB or 'final salary' scheme. DC schemes may not have an employers' contribution but at a time of stock market buoyancy they seemed a good way of beating inflation. By 1995 the number of 'defined contribution' schemes in the United States overtook that of the 'defined benefit' schemes, though the latter still controlled larger assets. In 1981 37 per cent of US workers were covered by an occupational scheme, a figure which dropped to 23 per cent by 1995. The invention of a new type of employer-sponsored but individually packaged DC plan, the 401(k), in 1981–82 led to a big increase in individual provision. The Individual Retirement Accounts (IRAs) set up by ERISA had only limited success and those with an individual pension of some sort accounted for only 9 per cent of the workforce in 1982. But thanks to the 401(k), the proportion covered by individual pensions rose to 23 per cent by 1995.[100] This is not, of course, to say that the benefits of the 401(k)s were at all evenly distributed; in 1995 nearly half of all holders had $10,000 or less in their accounts.

The 401(k) was named after a section of the US Internal Revenue Code for 1978 which concerned the payment of bonuses rather than pensions. The (k) section had been inserted as a device to allow employers to offer a deferred profits-sharing bonus that would not be taxed until it was paid. As Michael Clowes, editor of the fund managers' journal *Pensions and Investments*, explains:

> The first 401(k) [pension] plan . . . was based on a design by Theodore (Ted) Benna, one of [the Johnson Company's] benefit consultants, and it was literally the answer to a prayer. Benna is a scholarly, religious man. As he tells the story he was working at home on a Saturday afternoon in 1979 trying to devise a new plan for a bank client who wanted to convert a cash-bonus plan to a deferred profit-sharing plan. . . . After a prayer for inspiration, he thought about section 401(k) . . . Benna's solution was for the company to convert its cash bonus plan into a deferred compensation plan under the regulations of Section 401(k).[101]

The regulations established for bonuses under this section could be adapted for pensions, he thought, provided that the scheme was open to any employee, that the tax-sheltered sum did not comprise more than 15 per cent of total pay or over $30,000 in any one year, whichever was the higher, and that membership in the scheme was not overly weighted towards the higher-paid (further details are given in the next chapter). Employers would make the savings plan available, and could contribute something to it as an extra inducement if they wished. But the savings plan itself was to be run by a commercial fund manager. Quaker Oats, one of the first companies to adopt a 401(k) savings plan, offered a deferred bonus and urged employees to add to it up to 5 per cent of their salary. The tax advantages available under 401(k) regulations were considerably more generous than those offered by the IRAs set up by ERISA. It was not until 1982, with Reagan in the White House, that the IRS (Internal Revenue Service) agreed that section 401(k) could be used in this way.

The 401(k) plans could be justified on the traditionally 'puritan' grounds that they encouraged saving and self-reliance – their generous upper limits certainly embodied the principle 'unto him that hath shall be given'. On the other hand, the workings of the 401(k) schemes probably engendered a different psychology, and had a somewhat different impact on the economy as a whole, if compared to traditional savings schemes or collective occupational pensions. Members of the latter tended to think of them in terms of the future pension they would bring. Those who hold a 401(k) scheme are more likely to assess it in terms of how much has accumulated in it – the more so since many 401(k) schemes can, subject to certain conditions, be drawn upon prior to retirement. And unlike traditional savers, the possessors of the 401(k)s had been motivated to contribute to them partly as a way of avoiding tax. Thus during the booms of the 1980s and 1990s the possessors of 401(k)s could experience real satisfaction as the value of their pot climbed. This contributed to the so-called 'wealth effect' which in turn helped to maintain the buoyancy of demand in the United States. At a time of stagnant or even declining US wage rates the role of the 'wealth effect' in maintaining the confidence of the middle-class consumer was considerable.[102] The traditional notion of the 'puritan ethic' had the drawback of entailing a species of asceticism and self-denial. In a consumer society this type of motivational structure was inappropriate. What was needed – the 'answer to a prayer' – was a personalised savings vehicle that stimulated rather than reduced consumer confidence.

Different Welfare Regimes: 'Decommodification', Poverty and Equality

Pension schemes take a long time to come to maturity so it is not surprising that private occupational pensions comprise a large slice of the ownership of shares and other assets while the payments they finance remain comparatively modest. According to Esping-Anderson, payments made by US occupational pension schemes comprised 1.4 per cent of GDP in 1980. In the UK the comparable figure was 1.0 per cent, in Switzerland 1.4 per cent and in Australia 1.4 per cent; by contrast, in France payments from private occupational schemes amounted to 0.3 per cent of GDP and in Germany to 0.5 per cent.[103] These figures do show that occupational schemes were more important in the Anglo-Saxon economies, but public provision was still very important everywhere. State pensions at this time comprised 3.5–5.5 per cent of GNP in the English-speaking countries compared with the range 8–12 per cent for Germany,

Sweden, France and Italy. So far as those over sixty-five were concerned, state pension or social security transfers in or around 1980 represented 78.1 per cent of pensioner income in Sweden, 77.3 per cent in Finland, 71.5 per cent in Norway, and 68.5 per cent in Germany, compared with 54.6 per cent in the UK and 37.3 per cent in the United States – though in the latter two cases those over sixty-five had a relatively high contribution from earnings, comprising about a quarter of their income, because more of them were still in work.[104]

Esping-Anderson develops a 'decommodification' index to measure the degree to which different pension regimes award pensions to all the elderly regardless of contribution or means. Not surprisingly, perhaps, the Scandinavian schemes score highest, ranging from 14 to 17 points, France gets 12 points, Germany and the UK 8.5 and the United States only 7.0 points.[105] Inevitably, such an index embodies some arbitrary values. The scores relate to the arrangements in place in 1980, which would capture the UK public system at its most generous moment, prior to the impact of the Thatcher years (to be examined in chapter 5). Esping-Anderson concedes that Germany is often regarded as having a good pension system but scores it rather low because, while pensions are quite high, the element of redistribution is quite modest. Likewise the US Social Security system was given a low rating because at the time in question (1980) it was funded by a payroll tax and was thus less progressive than if it had been subsidised by general taxation. However, Esping-Anderson did note that US Social Security was a departure from his liberal 'poor relief' model. The index constructed by Esping-Anderson was weighted to score for pension generosity, measuring both income replacement for an averagely paid production worker and the minimum pension in comparison with the latter's wage. In these terms the US and UK basic pension systems delivered less than those of continental Europe.

Esping-Anderson's data confirm that there were three broad types of pension regime corresponding to what he sees as three types of welfare state: liberal, corporatist and social democratic. The pure liberal welfare regime used public funds only to tackle manifest and abject need, established by humiliating means tests, with the rest of the population being encouraged to make private provision (what I have referred to as the puritan ethos being uppermost). The corporatist welfare states developed, he shows, in countries whose political culture had been strongly influenced by absolutism and, though to a lesser extent, Catholicism; in these countries the state guarantees provided quite good, but strongly stratified, retirement incomes, with generous and segregated treatment of senior civil servants, army officers and professional or managerial groups (this category picks up some of the traits of the 'baroque' concept mentioned at the beginning of this chapter). The social democratic regimes offer similarly calculated and fairly generous pensions to all citizens, giving comparatively little weight to contribution record. At the time he was writing, Germany approximated to the corporatist regime, Sweden to the social democratic regime, with France straddling between the two models. While Britain and the United States no longer exemplified the pure liberal regime, the workings of the contributory principle and the modest level of income replacement they offered put them into a residual liberal category.

Using data from a selection of high-income countries (all members of the OECD), Esping-Anderson successfully demonstrates that his three types can indeed be identified in the clustering of key performance indicators, though there is some overlap.[106] Thus both corporatist and social democratic regimes move in the direction of 'decommodification', and social democracy can be seen as a more egalitarian version of absolutist or baroque paternalism. France and Austria score highly for corporatism and etatism, because of their large number of distinct public pension schemes and because of the level of expenditure on pensions for state employees; these help to push them up the 'decommodification' scale but still leave them short of Sweden and Norway.[107] The liberal approach to pension provision – with its 'puritan' ethos – only gradually lost ground in the UK and United States as the market was seen to fail the needs of a growing elderly population. Today's 'Anglo-Saxon' states – Australia and Canada as well as the United States and UK – still retain many features of a liberal regime, with flourishing private provision and many poorer pensioners obliged to seek public assistance to eke out inadequate basic pensions. However, at their more generous, the principles enunciated by those who campaigned for pension provision in Britain and the United States have pointed towards an ideal of social citizenship which is close to the social democratic model.

Esping-Anderson's main indicators related to the year 1980. In the mid-1990s his main contrasts and conclusions were underlined by a study which brought together the results of panel studies relating to the United States, Germany and the Netherlands. This study tracked the impact of social security pensions and taxation (including social security contributions) on the extent and duration of poverty 'spells'. The study shows the 'social democratic' Netherlands to be better than Germany in reducing 'pre-government' poverty, and both these states to be much better than the United States, whose government interventions still left more than a tenth

of the population in poverty. But these effects are somewhat weaker in the
area of old age pensions and the United States actually scores slightly
better than Germany, and only slightly worse than the Netherlands, when
it comes to measuring the extent to which immediate post-retirement
income replaces immediate pre-retirement income. In all cases state pensions were contributing to a high replacement rate.[108] The fact that the US
system is good at 'replacing' (i.e. reproducing) an initially unequal pay
structure qualifies this finding, notwithstanding the fact that it shows US
Social Security to be mildly more redistributive than Germany's 'corporatist' institutions – though bear in mind that German wages are high and
income distribution is more equal to start with.

'Decommodification' correlates inversely with the conceptually distinct category of pensioner poverty. The decommodification index is based
on financing method as well as pension levels, so it seems that there is a
link between the two, with less commodified pensions tending to be
higher. Poverty is usually measured by how many pensioner incomes fall
below 50 per cent of average income, or 40 per cent of median income or
some such relative scale. I would like to cite a further work that gives us a
nuanced picture of the impact of different pension regimes on pensioner
poverty. In a thorough comparative exercise, researchers found that fifteen
studies relating to the period 1984–92 showed Sweden scoring the least
poverty among thirteen countries in twelve of the studies, with one second
place and two thirds. The Netherlands, Norway and France came in
behind Sweden in slots two, three and four, with the Netherlands occupying the first position when Sweden did not. By contrast, the United
States, United Kingdom, Canada and Australia mostly took the seventh to
thirteenth places. These studies sought to log pensioner income from all
sources but the comparisons are complicated by: (1) the income unit
selected, whether individuals or household; (2) whether the income is
logged pre- or post-deductions for housing; and (3) different ways of calculating the average which sets the poverty line. And within the overall
category of pensioners there are often particular categories – notably older
women – who may be doing badly even within some of the otherwise
better welfare regimes. The researchers computed the poverty rates for
those with below 50 per cent of average income, as set out in Table 1.1.

The figures for poverty in the population as a whole also furnish a check
on poverty among the elderly, since the growth of poverty due to unemployment brings down average incomes without making pensioners any
better off. If we think in terms of absolute poverty then Table 1.1 sets a
stiffer challenge for high-income countries like Germany and the United

Table 1.1 Those with incomes below 50 per cent average income equivalent (mid-1980s in percentages)

	Ages 65–74	75+	Total population
Netherlands	2.1	1.4	9.1
Sweden	2.5	7.7	7.2
France	5.0	4.2	12.6
Germany	8.2	15.1	8.5
UK	8.2	8.4	11.9
US	21.2	32.3	21.4
Australia	30.3	30.4	16.7

Source: Peter Whiteford and Steven Kennedy, Social Science Research Unit, University of York, *Income and Living Standards of Older People*, Department of Social Security Research Report no. 34, HMSO, London 1995, p. 53.

States than it does for those lower in the OECD rankings like the UK. Using purchasing power parity and an absolute poverty measure, US seniors received a median income of 119, compared with 103 for Luxembourg, 102 for Canada, 92 for France, 90 for Germany, 76 for Sweden and 72 for Netherlands and the UK. But inequality among older people was much greater in the United States and Canada than in Germany, France or Sweden. The bottom tenth in the United States (and UK) were absolutely worse off than the bottom tenth in France, Germany, Sweden and the Netherlands. But, correspondingly, the richest tenth of American over-65s were much better off, having incomes more than twice as high as the wealthiest tenth in Sweden, the UK and the Netherlands, prompting the researchers to observe: 'If nothing else, this explains why more older Americans are seen as tourists in the countries of our study.'[109] This being a government publication, the authors neglected to add the rider that the distributional pattern would also explain why European visitors to large US (or British) cities would be more far likely to see the homeless and elderly beggars on the street than they would in continental Europe. And, as classic works by Michael Harrington and Peter Townsend had shown in studies conducted long before the troubles of the 1980s, poverty meant real deprivation for the worst-affected in the Anglo-Saxon countries.[110]

Esping-Anderson was as interested in the form of pension provision as in its level or share of government expenditure or GNP. With minor exceptions, all the advanced countries had adopted a universal basic pension system by the 1950s, albeit limited in nearly every case by contribution or work record. These basic or first-tier pension systems were all organised on a PAYGO rather than funded basis, as we have seen, and in most cases there was a presumption that general tax revenues might be drawn on in case of a serious shortfall. It is at the secondary level of pension provision that the differences in regime were most striking, with (1) Sweden and other Scandinavian countries offering a public system; (2) France and Germany exemplifying different versions of publicly sponsored but socially managed and corporatist secondary pensions; and (3) Britain and the United States exemplifying reliance on funded occupational and private secondary pensions. Esping-Anderson noted that Australia was the only advanced country lacking a 'universal' basic pension although there the trade unions had won basic provision in most areas of employment while the government furnished means-tested assistance to those without a pension. Since many 'universal' systems in fact relegate those who do not qualify, or do not fully qualify, to assistance programmes – and at levels that are less generous than those found in Australia – this exception really goes to show that all advanced capitalist countries sustain pension provision of some sort for the whole population, albeit in some cases of a residually liberal, poor relief type. The contrast here, at the time of Esping-Anderson's study, was with the less developed capitalist states of the Third World, and the still Communist states of the Second World.

The more developed Latin American states have long aspired to offer old age pensions to their citizens. In the early twentieth century the Uruguay of José Batlle helped to pioneer social welfare while the writings of Arturo Masferrer on the vital minimum anticipated some of the ideas of William Beveridge. By 1952 twelve Latin American nations had old age pension systems catering to most of the population. However, by the 1980s, if not before, hyper-inflation hollowed out pension promises while the failure of the more comfortably off to pay taxes prevented the proper funding of social programmes. While social expenditure accounted for around 15–25 per cent of GNP in OECD countries in the 1980s, in Latin America Brazil's social expenditure was only 4.6 per cent of GNP, Mexico's 2.0 per cent, Colombia's 2.2 per cent, Venezuela's 1.1 per cent, Uruguay's 7.0 per cent, Argentina's 8.9 per cent, Chile's 9.9 per cent and Cuba's 11.3 per cent. Where pensions were a major part of this expenditure because the system had matured they were imposing strain on the public budget, leading to cuts. In other cases pension provision was anyway limited to a few favoured groups, invariably including the armed forces. Some public employees had the leverage to boost their pension entitlement and some occupational funds held inflation-proof assets. Those in the countryside generally received nothing or, as in Brazil, were paid at half rates. But the already threadbare aspiration to a citizen pension was torn to shreds in the 1980s as 'structural adjustment' and austerity stripped out already depleted social budgets.[111]

In most of the newly independent states of Africa and Asia it was also proving difficult or impossible to sustain basic pension provision for a significant proportion of the population. Some exceptions to these generalisations have already been made, such as the CPF in Singapore or the newly established AFPs in Chile. But Singapore had ceased to be a less developed or low-income country while in Chile nearly half the workforce was in practice excluded from the AFPs and the administration had yet to begin paying pensions to those who were covered. In both cases the fate of pension provision was to be bound up with economic performance. Throughout Asia, Africa and Latin America the extent of basic pension provision reflects levels of economic development. Apart from the obvious constraint on resources in poorer states, pension provision also entails administrative costs which are very difficult to meet. Operating a pension system is complex and expensive, especially since pension clerks tend to be comparatively well paid in poor countries, and comparatively poorly paid in rich countries. Administrative costs thus typically absorb a greater share of the stream of contributions in poor states than in rich ones. And contributions, like taxes, are a problem in countries where the poor have minuscule cash incomes and only survive at all thanks to self-provision, barter and the informal economy. This does not mean that the Third World presents a uniform absence of retirement provision, since state officials and professional groups sometimes participate in functioning pension schemes. But it does mean that the mass of citizens, especially those in the countryside and shanty towns, are outside such provision.

The above considerations might lead us back to the idea that pensions should be seen simply as a function or consequence of the level of wealth or economic development, since both chronologically and geographically this seems to be the pattern. To the extent that this is true it is not because the development of capitalism automatically led to pension provision but because it stimulated social demands and movements which, especially at times of system shock, could lead, with more or less obstruction and delay, to the adoption of broader pension provision. The causal sequence also contained a feedback loop, such that broader pension coverage itself furnished part of the formula for economic and social development, with 'decommodification' correcting imbalances thrown up by capitalist accumulation. The United States adopted Social Security at a time when it had suffered a catastrophic fall in GNP – and the raising of pension levels in 1950 itself contributed to the buoyancy of demand in the 1950s and 1960s. In postwar

West Germany and Japan the channelling of pension contributions into investment, whether at enterprise level (West Germany) or in national infrastructure (Japan), helped to finance their rapid economic advance.

Then there is the experience of the Soviet Union and Eastern Europe to be considered. The Communist autocracies also used universal social services to promote economic mobilisation in countries where the initial level of development was low to middling. Indeed, competition between the states of Western and Eastern Europe helped to prompt an expansion of social provision on both sides of the Iron Curtain.[112] In 1964 Soviet collective farmers were brought into the central All Union pension scheme and by 1970 there were 32.6 million pensioners in the Soviet Union, drawing 37 per cent of average wages, retaining the right to continue working part-time and benefiting from low prices for necessities. In Eastern Europe pensioner incomes were low but subsidies to housing, health and basic consumption goods meant that they covered subsistence; there were extra entitlements for managerial and professional strata. Because of full employment many pensioners could continue part-time work.[113] While pension coverage in China's urban sector was nearly universal, those in the countryside were dependent on family resources or on local and municipal authorities. The collapse of the Soviet and East European Communist regimes after 1989 led to the rapid erosion of effective pension provision, as inflation ripped and empty treasuries stopped payments. The abject poverty of the old helped to skew the composition of demand away from domestic output and towards luxury imports, exacerbating the results of so-called shock therapy.

With slower growth and rising unemployment in continental Western Europe and the onset of problems in Japan, the 1980s and 1990s witnessed a growing attempt to represent the private sector of the 'Anglo-Saxon' pension regime, or at least a reformed and idealised version of it, as a global standard or norm to which all countries could aspire. Associated with this was an insistence that demographic trends, notably increased longevity and reduced fertility, would doom public PAYGO pension systems, in the UK and United States as well as everywhere else. But if there were already difficulties – and there were – with the financing of public pensions in most developed countries in the closing decade or two of the century, the reasons were not mainly demographic. As was seen in the introduction, the overall 'dependency ratio' of the over-60s and under-15s to those aged 15–59 was very similar in the 1980s and 1990s to what it had been in 1950 throughout the developed countries. The numbers of elderly had grown but the drop in the birth rate had kept the overall proportion of those likely to be dependent fairly steady. While an imbalance would eventually appear, and require some recalibration of public programmes, the problems already encountered were to do with the malaise that overtook the capitalist world with the ending of the great postwar boom, the *trente glorieuses* – stagnant wages, high levels of unemployment and weak productivity. Any pay-as-you-go system will immediately reflect overall employee remuneration because the contributions to them function like a payroll tax. So long as wages and salaries are buoyant even quite severe demographic shifts can be dealt with by building up a fund. In fact, some attempts were indeed made to use the period when the baby-boomers were at their earnings' peak to build up a fund. But the prevailing dogma of the post-Thatcher and post-Reagan era was that this would have to take the form of private, commercially managed pension funds. Eventually this view found authoritative expression in the World Bank report, *Averting the Old Age Crisis* (1994). In chapters 4 and 6 the detailed argument of this report will be assessed, and in chapters 5 and 6, respectively, the British and US experience and debates will be recounted. But an essential preliminary, to which the next two chapters are devoted, is to analyse the workings of the 'Anglo-Saxon' pension funds, both their success in delivering pensions, and their contribution to the overall economic and social climate.

Notes

1   The indispensable starting point for grasping the 'puritan' impulse is still Max Weber, *The Protestant Ethic and the Spirit of Capitalism*, London 1930. For the 'baroque' as used here, see José Antonio Maraval, *The Culture of the Baroque*. And for the tension between the 'pastoral' function of the state and puritan identity, see Michel Foucault, 'Governmentality', in C. Gordon, and P. Miller, eds, *The Foucault Effect: Studies in Governmentality*, Hemel Hempstead 1991, pp. 87–104.

2   These categories are taken from Gosta Esping-Anderson, *The Three Worlds of Welfare Capitalism*, Princeton (NJ) 1990. This landmark study pays considerable attention to the variable evolution of pension provision, see especially pp. 48–54, 79–104, 120–38. Esping-Anderson's work demonstrates that the variant types of pension regime stemmed from the particular outcome of a variety of impulses in each national setting, including the scope of macro-social transformation (urbanisation, industrialisation), demographic change, the pressure exerted by organised labour and other social movements, the voting influence of the elderly and the institutional configuration of pension provision. Valuable insights can also be drawn from Peter Baldwin, *The Politics of Social Solidarity: Class Bases of the European Welfare State 1875–1975*, Cambridge 1990; John

Myles, *Old Age in the Welfare State: the Political Economy of Public Pensions*, Lawrence (KA) 1989; and Harold Wilensky, *The Welfare State and Equality: Structural and Ideological Roots of Public Expenditures*, Berkeley 1975.

3   The impact of globalisation on pension provision is trenchantly surveyed in Richard Minns, *The Cold War in Welfare: Pensions versus Stock Markets*, London 2001.

4   Quoted in Pat Thane, *Old Age in English History: Past Experiences and Present Issues*, Oxford 2000, p. 90.

5   Ibid., p. 107.

6   Richard M. Smith, 'Ageing and Well-Being in Early Modern England', in Paul Johnson and Pat Thane, eds, *Old Age from Antiquity to Post Modernity*, London 1998, pp. 64–95.

7   Thane, *Old Age in English History*, pp. 149–50.

8   Hervé Alexandre and Pierre-Yves Chanu, 'Régimes spéciaux', in Pierre Khalfa, *Les Retraites au péril du libéralisme*, Paris 1999, pp. 87–110, p. 90; R.A. Beattie, 'France', in Thomas Wilson, ed., *Pensions, Inflation and Growth*, London 1974, pp. 253–304, p. 256; Geoffrey Symcox, *The Crisis of French Sea Power, 1688–97*, The Hague 1974, pp. 15–30.

9   Jean-Pierre Gutton, *Naissance du vieillard*, Paris 1988.

10   Thane, *Old Age in English History*, p. 237.

11   Leslie Hannah, *Inventing Retirement: the Development of Occupational Retirement in Britain*, Cambridge 1986, p. 11.

12   Alexandre and Chanu, 'Régimes spéciaux', p. 90.

13   Thomas Paine, *Rights of Man*, with an introduction by Eric Foner, London 1984, p. 243. Paine describes his scheme as one which will render 'comfortable' the condition of the aged poor, estimated at one-third of the total elderly population. The word 'pension' is reserved for the government stipend received by his antagonist Edmund Burke. While their past labours and taxes gave the aged poor an entitlement to modest levels of assistance, Burke had, in this view, allowed himself to become a hireling and a burden on the public finances.

14   Gregory Claeys, *Thomas Paine's Social and Political Thought*, London 1989, pp. 75–84, 96–101, 213–16.

15   Antoine Nicolas de Condorcet, *Sketch for a Historical Picture of the Progress of the Human Mind*, London 1955, p. 181. This text was written by Condorcet while he was in hiding in 1793. However, the basic idea here had already appeared in 'A General Survey of Science – concerning the application of calculus to the political and moral sciences (1793)', which will be found in *The Political Theory of Condorcet*, vol. 2, translated by Fiona Sommerlad and Iain McLean, Oxford 1991, pp. 4–23.

16   Ibid.

17   Gutton, *Naissance du vieillard*, pp. 212–15; David Troyansky, *Old Age in the Old Regime, Image and Experience in Eighteenth Century France*, Ithaca (NY) 1989.

18   See Emma Rothschild, 'The Debate on Economic and Social Security in the

Late Eighteenth Century', United Nations Research Institute for Social Development, DP 64, May 1995.

19 Leopold Krug, *Die Armenassekuranz das einzige Mittel zur Verbannung der Armuth aus unserer Kommune*, cited in Winfried Schmahl, 'Avoiding Poverty in Old Age by an Obligatory Contribution-financed Minimum Insurance', in Jurgen G. Backhaus, ed., *Essays on Social Security and Taxation*, Marburg 1997, pp. 14–34.

20 T.R. Malthus, *An Essay on the Principle of Population*, London 1890, p. 299. For an illuminating discussion of Malthus contra Condorcet, see Emma Rothschild, 'Social Security and Laissez Faire in Eighteenth Century Political Economy', *Population and Development Review*, vol. 21, no. 4, December 1995, pp. 711–44, p. 726. Rothschild also traces the connection between Turgot's approach to the social question and that of Condorcet.

21 Malthus, *An Essay on the Principle of Population*, p. 523.

22 Ibid., p. 525

23 Thane, *Old Age in English History*, p. 169.

24 Michael Mann, *The Sources of Social Power*, vol. 2, Cambridge 1993, p. 500–1.

25 Robert L. Clark, Lee A. Craig and Jack W. Wilson, 'The Life and Times of a Public-Sector Pension Plan Before Social Security: the U.S. Navy Pension Plan in the Nineteenth Century', PRC WP 99–10, June 1999, Pension Research Council, Wharton School, University of Pennsylvania. During the Civil War the Union navy was once again able to seize many valuable prizes, leading it, for a time, to be funded once again.

26 Carole Haber and Brian Gratton, *Old Age and the Search for Security: an American Social History*, Bloomington (IN) 1994, pp. 66–71.

27 This discourse on poverty is examined in Michael Meranze, *Laboratories of Virtue: Punishment, Revolution and Authority in Philadelphia, 1760–1835*, Chapel Hill (NC) 1996, pp. 150–7, 265–72. But see also Michael Katz, *In the Shadow of the Poorhouse*, New York 1986, who points out that aged paupers were visible, rather than numerous, because they comprised between a quarter and a half of the inmates of the poor houses (p. 57).

28 Quoted in Max Lerner, *America as a Civilization*, New York 1957, p. 130.

29 The Reverend Albert Barnes quoted in Thomas R. Cole, '"Putting Off the Elderly": Middle Class Morality, Antebellum Protestantism, and the Origins of Ageism', in Davis van Tassel and Peter N. Stearns, eds, *Old Age in a Bureaucratic Society*, Westport (CT) 1986, pp. 49–65, p. 60.

30 Ibid., p. 55.

31 Eric Foner, *Reconstruction: America's Unfinished Revolution, 1863–1877*, New York 1988, pp. 460–565.

32 Theda Skocpol, *Protecting Soldiers and Mothers: the Political Origins of Social Policy in the United States*, Cambridge (MA) 1992. For the difficulties encountered by early proposals for old age pensions in the United States see also the informative study by Ann Shola Orloff, *The Politics of Pensions: a Comparative Analysis of Britain, Canada, and the United States, 1880–1940*, Madison (WI) 1993, especially pp. 215–39. And for the historical peculiarities of the

American state which made it resistant to state intervention in social life, see also Daniel Lazare, *The Frozen Republic*, New York 1997, and Eric Foner, *The Story of American Freedom*, New York 1998.

33 Ferdinand Lassalle, 'The Working Man's Program' (1862), in Theodore S. Hamerow, ed., *The Age of Bismarck, Documents and Interpretations*, New York 1973, pp. 207–9.

34 Hamerow, *The Age of Bismarck*, pp. 257–9. See also John Myles, *Old Age in the Welfare State*, Boston 1984, pp. 32–9, and Gaston Rimlinger, *Welfare Policy and Industrialisation in Europe, America and Russia*, Toronto 1971, pp. 118-21.

35 François Charpentier, *Retraites et fonds de pension: l'état de la question en France et à l'étranger*, Paris 1997, p. 127.

36 W.G. Runciman, *Social Theory*, vol. 3, Cambridge 1997, p. 53. Runciman goes on to observe that 'as always in social evolution it is not the origin of practices which counts, but its subsequent function'. In this case the function of encouraging patriotic mobilisation and alleviating some extreme poverty went hand in hand. Wolfgang Abendroth argues that welfare measures did help European governments to secure the loyalties of their workers to the state as the continent headed for the slaughter of the First World War; see his *Short History of the European Working Class*, London 1972. It is true, as Runciman asserts, that the hopes of the more radical reformers and socialists who had campaigned for social insurance were to be disappointed since 'the egalitarian implications were modest and the sanctity of private property remained untouched' (p. 54). But, seen in a longer perspective, the more generous hopes which inspired social insurance could return to challenge its workings.

37 Gareth Stedman Jones, *Outcast London, a Study of the Relationship between Classes in Victorian Society*, revised edn, Harmondsworth 1984, pp. 335–6.

38 Cited in Thane, *Old Age in English History*, p. 174.

39 John Macnicol, *The Politics of Retirement in Britain, 1878-1948*, Cambridge 1998, pp. 137–47.

40 Hannah, *Inventing Retirement*, p. 5.

41 Quoted in Thane, *Old Age in English History*, p. 243.

42 Macnicol, *The Politics of Retirement*, p. 12.

43 Ibid: see also Hannah, *Inventing Retirement*, pp. 122-36.

44 Macnicol, *The Politics of Retirement*, pp. 137-63. The 5 shillings a week would afford only the most rudimentary existence: see the classic study by Maud Pember Reeves, *Round About a Pound a Week*, London 1914.

45 Macnicol, *The Politics of Retirement*, pp. 167–99.

46 Ibid., pp. 215–16.

47 Caroline Weaver, *The Crisis in Social Security*, Durham (NC) 1982, pp. 47–8.

48 Quoted in William Graebner, *A History of Retirement: the Meaning and Function of an American Institution, 1885-1978*, New Haven (CT) 1980, p. 118.

49 David Hackett Fischer, *Growing Old in America*, New York 1977.

50 Steven Sass, *The Promise of Private Pensions; the First Hundred Years*, Cambridge (MA) 1997, pp. 18–37.

51 Graebner, *A History of Retirement*, p. 197.
52 Robert C. Lieberman, *Shifting the Color Line: Race and the American Welfare State*, Cambridge (MA) 1998, p. 77. See also Alice Kessler Harris, *In Pursuit of Equity: Women, Men and the Quest for Citizenship in 20th Century America*, Oxford 2001, pp. 117–69
53 Orloff, *The Politics of Pensions*, pp. 269-98; Sylvester J. Scheiber and John B. Shoven, *The Real Deal: the History and Future of Social Security*, New Haven (CT) 1999, pp. 17–76; for the Bolivar quote, see p. 39. As a German American of anti-fascist views, Altmeyer was doubtless reluctant to acknowledge the German example; following improvements to the Bismarckian model, pension coverage was now higher in Germany than in any other European country (Esping-Anderson, *The Three Worlds of Welfare Capitalism*).
54 Lieberman, *Shifting the Color Line*, pp. 67-117; Foner, *The Story of American Freedom*, pp. 195-218.
55 Lieberman, *Shifting the Color Line*, p. 115.
56 Edward Berkowitz and Kim McQuaid, 'Social Security and the American Welfare State', *Research on Economic History*, Supplement 6, 1991, p. 578.
57 The role of farmer–labour class coalitions in the introduction of social insurance is highlighted by Esping-Anderson, *The Three Worlds of Welfare Capitalism*, pp. 30–4. See also Peter Baldwin, *The Politics of Social Solidarity: Class Bases of the European Welfare State 1875–1975*, Cambridge 1990, pp. 65–76, 83–94.
58 Francis Castles, 'Needs-based Strategies of Social Protection in Australia and New Zealand', in Gosta Esping-Anderson, ed., *Welfare States in Transition: National Adaptations in Global Economies*, London 1996, pp. 88–115, p. 88.
59 Macnicol, *The Politics of Retirement in Britain*, pp. 200–24, 347–85.
60 Ibid., pp. 385–99.
61 Thane, *Old Age in English History*, p. 371.
62 Henry Pratt, *Gray Agendas*, Ann Arbor (MI) 1993, p. 76.
63 Quoted in Tony Lynes, *Paying for Pensions: the French Experience*, London 1985, p. 18.
64 Esping-Anderson, *The Three Worlds of Welfare Capitalism*, p. 100.
65 Wilensky, *The Welfare State and Equality*, pp. 70–85.
66 Thane, *Old Age in English History*, p. 377.
67 Francis Castles, 'Needs-Based Strategies of Social Protection in Australia and New Zealand', in Esping-Anderson, ed., *Welfare States in Transition: National Adaptations in Global Economies*, pp. 88–115, pp. 88–9.
68 Christopher Howard, *The Hidden Welfare State: Tax Expenditures and Social Policy in the United States*, Princeton (NJ) 1997, pp. 120–1.
69 For this conjuncture, see Mike Davis, *Prisoners of the American Dream*, new edn, New York 1999, pp. 82-93.
70 Quoted in Steven Sass, 'The Heyday of US Collectively Bargained Pension Arrangements', in Paul Johnson, Christoph Conrad and David Thomson, eds, *Workers Versus Pensioners: Intergenerational Justice in an Ageing World*, Manchester and New York 0000 pp. 92-113, p. 101.

71 Peter Drucker, *The Unseen Revolution: How Pension Fund Socialism Came to America*, New York and London 1976, pp. 5–7. A weakness of Drucker's account is that he does not evoke the class tensions which furnished the background to the emergence of the GM formula. However these great trade union battles constituted something of a last hurrah for the wave of labour mobilisations which began in the mid-1930s. The late 1940s also witnessed red scares, McCarthyism and the purge of Communists from many unions. It could be that GM would not have proposed their pension scheme in a country like Italy or France where anti-capitalism still had a mass basis in the labour movement. On the recovered prestige of mutual funds in the late 1940s and early 1950s see Diana B. Henriques, *Fidelity's World: the Secret Life and Public Power of the Mutual Fund Giant*, New York 1995, pp. 103–19.

72 Esping-Anderson, *The Three Worlds of Welfare Capitalism*, p. 95.

73 Orloff, *The Politics of Pensions*; Minns, *The Cold War in Welfare*.

74 Hannah, *Inventing Retirement*, pp. 72, 139, 145.

75 Richard Minns has drawn attention to the link between pension regimes and financial systems. See Minns, *The Cold War in Welfare*, pp. 46–50.

76 For the significance of which see Maurice Glasman, *Unnecessary Suffering*, London 1996, pp. 56–85, and 'The Siege of the German Economy', *New Left Review*, no. 225, September–October 1997.

77 Georg Heubeck, 'Occupational Pension Schemes in the Context of the Evolution of the National Economy', in *Occupational Pension Schemes*, International Social Security Association, Copenhagen 1983, pp. 81–98, p. 97. See also Wendy Carlin, *West German Growth and Institutions, 1945–1990*, Discussion Paper no. 896, Centre for Economic Policy, Birkbeck College, University of London 1993, pp. 37–9.

78 Anne M. Menzies, 'The Federal Republic of Germany', in Wilson, *Pensions, Inflation and Growth*, pp. 45–109.

79 The information in this paragraph and its predecessor is mainly taken from Thomas Wilson, 'Comparative Analysis', in Wilson, *Pensions, Inflation and Growth*, pp. 337–97. But see also Goran Therborn, *European Modernity and Beyond*, London 1995, pp. 91–4, which also gives information on Soviet and East European pension schemes, whose scope and benefits were also improved in the 1960s and 1970s.

80 Lynes, *Paying for Pensions: the French Experience*, distinguishes *répartition*, or sharing of a given income stream, from pure PAYGO in which, he claims, it is benefits which are fixed and contributions which vary in order to cover them (p. 41).

81 R.A. Beattie, 'France', in Wilson, *Pensions, Inflation and Growth*, pp. 253–304, p. 254.

82 Alexandre and Chanu, 'Régimes spéciaux', p. 94.

83 Paul Samuelson, 'An Exact Consumption-Loan Model of Interest with or without the Social Contrivance of Money', *Journal of Political Economy*, December 1958, pp. 219–234.

84 Ibid., p. 479. The notion of reciprocal obligations here is similar to one that was being enunciated at the same time by John Rawls in his essay 'Justice as Fairness', *Philosophical Review*, vol. 67, 1958.

85 *Public Finance*, 1971, p. 465n, quoted in Thomas Wilson, 'Issues and Responses in Europe and the USA', in Wilson, ed., *Pensions, Inflation and Growth*, London 1974, pp. 3–42, p. 40. The French case does not contradict the argument that commercial organisations cannot claim a 'draft on the yet unborn' and thus cannot operate PAYGO pension arrangements (short of becoming outright pyramid schemes). The French scheme was not run by the government but it was backed by legislation and state guarantees; management was entrusted to joint committees and there was no commercial element.

86 Samuelson, 'An Exact Consumption-Loan Model', pp. 480, 481. That Samuelson was aiming his critique at the free market economics of the Austrian school is clearly indicated by the following, where he deploys the notion so much decried by Hayek of macro-economic process government by a single mind: 'The economics of social collusion is a rich field for social analysis, involving fascinating predictive and normative properties. Thus, when society acts as if it were maximising certain functions, we can predict the effect upon equilibrium of specified exogenous disturbances. And certain patterns of thought appropriate to a single mind become appropriate even though we reject the notion of a group mind' (p. 481). Hayek had advanced his argument concerning the single mind fallacy in an article in the *American Economic Review* in 1945. Samuelson's multi generational approach also contrasted with life-cycle models which plotted savings and consumption for an individual or household. See, e.g., Milton Friedman, *A Theory of the Consumption Function*, Princeton (NJ) 1957.

87 Ponzi's ostensible source of profit came from selling cheaply acquired postal return coupons but it could be shown that all coupons in existence could not justify the investments he had collected. Robert Shiller, *Irrational Exuberance*, Princeton (NJ) 2000, pp. 64–6.

88 Quoted in Pat Thane, 'Non-contributory versus Insurance Pensions', in Pat Thane, ed., *The Origins of British Social Policy*, pp. 84–106, p. 103.

89 Berkowitz and McQuaid, 'Social Security and the American Welfare State', p. 177.

90 Scheiber and Shoven, *The Real Deal*, p. 76.

91 Ibid., p. 70.

92 Dorothy J. Wilson, 'Sweden', in Wilson, *Pensions, Inflation and Growth*, pp. 155–200, pp. 162–4; Therborn, *European Modernity and Beyond*, p. 94. Although the fund established for the pension system did not invest in equities its management was kept separate from the national budget so that it did not encourage government spending. See Alicia H. Munnell and C. Nicole Ernsberger, 'Foreign Experience with Public Pension Surpluses and National Savings', in Carolyn Weaver, ed., *Social Security's Looming Surpluses; Prospects and Implications*, Washington DC 1990, pp. 85–118, especially pp. 90–9. The

Meidner plan referred to in the Introduction can be seen as an extension of the logic of the Allmanna Pensionfoden (AP), or National Pension Insurance Fund, but tilted this time towards the wage earners.

93 Mulligan and Sala-I-Martin find a historical tendency for funded schemes to relapse into PAYGO in their study of several scores of countries. See Casey B. Mulligan and Xavier Sala-I-Martin, 'Gerontocracy, Retirement, and Social Security', NBER Working Paper no. 7117, May 1999, p. 39.

94 For contrasting answers see Christopher Tremewan, *The Political Economy of Social Control in Singapore*, Oxford 1994, and Michael Hill and Lian Kwen Fee, *The Politics of Nation Building and Citizenship in Singapore*, London 1995.

95 John Creighton Campbell, *How Policies Change: the Japanese Government and the Aging Society*, Princeton (NJ) 1992, p. 55.

96 Noriyuki Takayama, *The Greying of Japan: an Economic Perspective on Public Pensions*, Oxford 1992, p. 1.

97 Bernard Eccleston, *State and Society in Postwar Japan*, Oxford 1989, p. 97. For the establishment of the Japanese social security system see also Mutsuko Takahashi, *The Emergence of Welfare Society in Japan*, Aldershot 1997, pp. 35–72.

98 Naoto Yamauchi, 'The Effects of Aging on National Saving and Asset Accumulation in Japan', in Michael D. Hurd and Naohiro Yashiro, *The Economic Effects of Aging in the US and Japan*, Chicago 1997, pp. 131–51.

99 Campbell, *How Policies Change*, pp. 328–48.

100 James Ridgeway, 'Hijacking the Future: Wall Street Taking Over Workers' Pensions', *Dollars and Sense*, September–October 1999.

101 Michael J. Clowes, *The Money Flood: how Pension Funds Revolutionized Investing*, New York 2000, p. 188.

102 Robert Pollin, 'Anatomy of Clintonomics', *New Left Review*, no. 3, May–June 2000, pp. 17-46; Robert Brenner, 'The Boom and the Bubble', *New Left Review*, no. 6, November–December 2000.

103 Esping-Anderson, *The Three Worlds of Welfare Capitalism*, p. 83.

104 Ibid., p. 86.

105 Ibid., p. 50.

106 Ibid., pp. 105–38.

107 Ibid., pp. 50, 70.

108 Robert E. Goodin, Bruce Headey, Ruud Muffels and Heck-Jan Dirven, *The Real Worlds of Welfare Capitalism*, Cambridge 1999, pp. 152–72, 209–10. These authors selected the Netherlands as their 'social democratic' state because panel information was available there, as it was not for Sweden. The Dutch Labour Party introduced a universal pension system in 1947 whose provisions were greatly extended in the 1960s; by 1980 the Netherlands held top place for social spending among OECD states (Goodin *et al.*, *The Real Worlds of Welfare Capitalism*, pp. 63–7).

109 Peter Whiteford and Steven Kennedy, *Incomes and Living Standards of Older People*, Department of Social Security Research Report no. 34, HMSO London 1995, p. 56.

110 Michael Harrington, *The Other America*, second edn, New York 1972, and Peter Townsend, *Poverty in the United Kingdom*, London 1979.

111 Evelyne Huber, 'Options for Policy in Latin America', in Gosta Esping-Anderson, ed., *Welfare States in Transition: National Adaptations in Global Economies*, London 1996, pp. 141–91; Carmelo Mesa-Largo, *Ascent to Bankruptcy: Financing Social Security in Latin America*, Pittsburgh (PA) 1989.

112 Eric Hobsbawm, *The Age of Extremes*, London 1994.

113 Guy Standing, 'Social Protection in Central and Eastern Europe: a Tale of Slipping Anchors and Torn Safety Nets', in Esping-Anderson, *Welfare States in Transition*, pp. 225–55; Basile Kerblay, *Modern Soviet Society*, New York 1983, pp. 28–9; for East European pension provision in 1970 see Therborn, *European Modernity and Beyond*, pp. 94–5.

2

Pension Funds and the Returns to Grey Capital

One of his jobs was to arrange for the mortgaging of several hundred peasants to the Trustee Council . . . the most brilliant idea that ever came into a man's head suddenly dawned on our hero . . . Why, were I to buy up all the peasants who died before a new census is taken, were I to acquire them for, say, a thousand roubles, and the Trustee Council gave me two hundred a soul: why there's already a fortune of two hundred thousand roubles! And now is just the right time! There's been an epidemic . . . It is true that it is impossible to buy or mortgage serfs without land, but then I shall be buying them for re-settlement. Land in the Taurida and Kherson provinces is distributed today free, provided you settle peasants on it. That's where I shall settle them! To the Kherson province with them! Let them live there!

(Nikolai Gogol, *Dead Souls*, 1842)

The rapid decline of the Enron Corporation has devastated its employees' retirement plan, which was heavy with company stock, and infuriated workers who were prohibited from changing their investments as the stock plunged.. . . . At the end of last year, the 401(k) plan had $2.1 billion in assets. More than half was invested in Enron. . . . Since then, the stock has lost 94 per cent of its value. At Portland General Electric, the Oregon utility acquired by Enron four years ago, some workers have lost hundreds of thousands of dollars. The utility has lined up grief counselors to help them work through their problems. . . .

(Richard A. Oppel Jr., 'Employee's Retirement Plan Is a Victim as Enron Tumbles', *New York Times*, 22 November 2001)

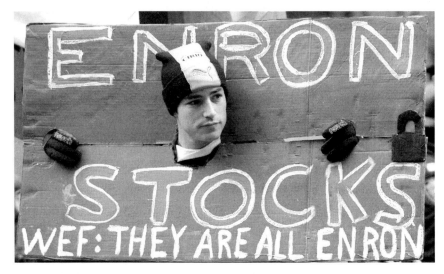

Enron Stocks Demonstration, (Demonstration, New York, January 2002, Reuters)

Pension provision today in Britain and America combines a basic state pension – at best a bare subsistence – with secondary occupational pensions and individual plans unevenly covering about half the working population. A pincer operation by politicians and financial concerns is creating a situation where everyone needs supplementary provision to avoid a penurious old age. Generally, where state provision is mean, private pensions flourish. Pension funds have thrived in the United States, Britain, the Netherlands, Switzerland, South Africa, Japan and Australia. In these countries state expenditure on pensions was less than 10 per cent of GNP – and for most in the range 4–6 per cent – in 1995. But note that private supplementary pension coverage only reached about half of the labour force in these states, Switzerland and Australia excepted. The value of pension assets was equal to, or greater than, that of GNP by 2000 in the UK, the United States, Switzerland and the Netherlands. In France, Italy, Spain, Austria and Germany, by contrast, annual state expenditure on pensions was more than 10 per cent of GNP in 1995, and by 2000 the value of pension fund holdings in these countries was equal only to between 5 and 15 per cent of GNP, but growing. In Chile, Argentina and Brazil, pension funds also now represent about 5–15 per cent of GNP and state provision is declining.[1]

In this chapter I chart the variety of pension holdings and examine their impact on the structures of economic power. The pension funds receive favourable tax treatment because they constitute savings for retirement – whether or not this goal is achieved is also addressed. I concentrate here on the performance of retirement funds in the United States and UK because they are widely held to furnish a benchmark and model, and because their modus operandi is well documented. Currently there is a concerted campaign both to introduce US and British-style pension funds to all European Union countries and to reduce the scope of state pensions in the UK and United States so as to leave more room for private provision. Chapters 4 to 6 survey this drive to extend private pension delivery. Here the aim is to assess a record which already stretches back about half a century.

In the early days pension money was invested in safe and boring ways, with government gilt-edged securities dominating the portfolio. But those days are long gone. New perceptions of risk and some regulatory relaxation have led US and UK pension funds to devote most of their resources to holding stock in publicly quoted companies, so long as the holdings are sufficiently diversified within this asset class. Large British and US pension funds still buy some public bonds, and also hold cash and invest in real estate, but shares and corporate bonds typically comprise by far the largest asset category, ranging from 60 to 99 per cent of the total. And, notwithstanding a fiduciary duty to invest prudently, the philosophy of diversification and the proliferation of new financial instruments have also led some funds to dabble in junk bonds and derivatives.

The funded sector of pension provision mushroomed over half a century to become a defining feature of the stock exchange-based economic systems. This is partly a simple matter of quantitative expansion. US pension funds had assets of $7,000 billion in 2000, mostly held in the form of corporate stocks and shares, while the UK pension funds had holdings of £850 billion. In 1955 American pension funds owned only 2.3 per cent of total equity holdings, and insurance companies 3.2 per cent. By 1997 pension funds held 24 per cent and insurance companies 5.7 per cent of total US holdings. Households held 93 per cent of all US equity in 1945; this proportion had dropped to 42.7 per cent by 1997. In 1963 British pension funds held 6.4 per cent of all shares, and insurance funds 10 per cent; by 1996 pension funds held 27.8 per cent of all shares and the insurance funds 21.9 per cent, for a combined total of just under 50 per cent.[2] I include the figures for insurance funds here since, especially in the UK, pension plans are often based on the purchase of an annuity from an insurance house at retirement, so a large slice of insurance assets are tied to pension provision. Even on the most narrow reading, pension funds comprised a quarter of the stock market while the tax-exempt institutional sector to which they are affiliated – a sector which includes educational foundations and charitable endowments – owns more than half of quoted equity holdings in these two countries. These institutional funds are, like pension funds, held for policy-holders, stake holders or community interests, as well as enjoying considerable tax privileges. It is this tax-exempt sector of 'institutional funds' which is of chief interest in what follows but the term can be used more broadly to refer to all those funds managed by the large financial institutions, such as mutual funds and unit trusts. The personal pension can be quite like a mutual fund or unit trust, and many pension-related vehicles contain such assets. All these assets are held indirectly and are managed by the institutions, but personal pensions are usually less flexible. While the broader context of institutional finance needs to be taken into account, so do the specific procedures and problems of funds which are tax exempt and held under special pension-related fiduciary rules.

Pension funds themselves are diverse in character, and we also need to distinguish occupational from personal funds. The traditional occupational fund was set up by the employer, administered by the employer and managed by trustees largely nominated by the employer. Trade unions sometimes had a role in this and in a few cases the pension fund has actually been subject to de facto union control. But generally unions were content for employers to absorb the cost of administering pensions. Such occupational schemes can readily be distinguished from 'personal pensions' such as those introduced by British governments in 1988 or the Individual Retirement Accounts (IRAs) established under the terms of the US ERISA legislation, in 1974. These personal pensions reflected a contract between the individual and a commercial provider without the employer playing any role. We should, however, note an important hybrid, exemplified by the 401(k) in the United States or the new stakeholder pension in the UK. In these cases the employer does play a role in selecting a range of schemes, making them available to employees and forwarding contributions to a commercial provider.

Most traditional occupational schemes are 'defined benefit'; that is, as explained in the last chapter, the eventual pension is based on the salary earned by the employee. If the fund is unable to afford this then the sponsoring employer is contractually obliged to make up the difference. However some occupational schemes and all 401(k)s are organised on the so-called 'defined contribution' (DC) basis, which means that the pension paid out is based on the sum accumulated in the fund by the contributing individual. Since there is no target pension there is never a (legal) shortfall (expectations are another matter). Thus, although the employer plays a role, those in a DC scheme are in a similar situation to the holder of a personal pension or IRA and must hope that they have a big 'pot' when the scheme comes to maturity.

The occupational schemes represent a tally of the compromises reached between employers, employees and the state in the twentieth century. Some of the largest blocks of capital in today's stock markets are held for such class warriors of yesteryear as Arthur Scargill's miners or Walter Reuther's auto workers. Table 2.1 gives the top UK pension funds in 1990 and 2000. The list is headed by employees of formerly public utilities and industries, reading like a muster roll of organised labour's praetorian guard. The pension funds of local government employees are also important but did not make the lists because they are not aggregated on a national basis (in 2000 the Strathclyde Pension Fund reached £6.7 billion and the Greater Manchester fund £6.1 billion). The employees of banks and a few blue chip companies also figure in the lists, with membership of the pension scheme being an inducement to long service.

Table 2.1 Largest UK pension funds

1990 (in billion 1990 £)		2000 (in billion 2000 £)	
British Coal	12.0	British Telecom	29.7
British Telecom	12.0	British Coal	26.1
Electricity Supply	8.5	Electricity Supply	22.0
Post Office	7.5	University Superannuation	22.0
British Rail	7.0	Post Office	18.0
University Superannuation	5.8	British Gas	13.2
British Gas	5.7	Lloyds/TSB	12.9
Barclays	5.2	BP Amoco	12.5
ICI	5.1	Barclays	11.4
NatWest Bank	4.0	Shell	11.4
Steel Workers	4.0	British Airways	10.5
		NatWest Bank	10.0
		Corus (steelworkers)	9.1

Sources: 1990 – David Blake, *Pension Schemes and Pension Funds in the United Kingdom*, Oxford 1995, p. 286; 2000 – Paul Myners, *Institutional Investment in the UK: a Review*, HM Treasury, London 2001, p. 30.

Even funds that have little direct relation to past industrial battles can still give rise to conflict with the employer in the present. Consider the following:

> An old-style industrial mass meeting of 1,500 British Airways pensioners has voted overwhelmingly to oppose a BA plan to raid a £6 billion pension fund to raise capital at a time when its profits have fallen by £355 million in 12 months. Only seven people voted against a postal ballot to test the views of members. BA has stirred up vehement protest among some of its pensioners because it wishes to merge their fund with another, valued at £3 billion, introduced just before BA was privatised. The merger would result in an immediate surplus of £276 million, which would lead to a reduction of BA's contributions of £90 million over the next four years.[3]

The policy holders only had a say in this case because a change to the basic contract was at stake. Over many vital questions of fund management, as we will see, members' views could be safely ignored.

Thus the sponsors of defined benefit (DB) schemes can unilaterally decide to close them to new members. In April 2001 British Telecom, after saddling itself with a mountain of debt to acquire third-generation mobile phone licences, did just that and, in place of the DB arrangement, offered their employees a defined contribution scheme:

> BT says the defined contribution scheme is 'not a money-saving exercise'. Instead, the measure gives it peace of mind through predictability and cost-containment. But contributions are likely to fall. Over the last three years, BT's average contribution to employees in the defined benefit scheme was 9.5 per cent of salary. Under the new scheme, the average is expected to be 6 per cent.[4]

While BT's decision was hailed as a sign of the times, eighty-three of the companies in the FTSE 100 still offered a defined benefit scheme at that time.

Table 2.2 Largest US pension funds in 2000

Defined benefit funds ($ billion)		Defined contribution funds ($ billion)	
Calpers	156	Federal Retirement Thrift	85
New York State	111	General Electric	26
California Teachers	98	General Motors	22
Florida State	93	Lucent Technologies	21
New York Teachers	82	Boeing	21
Texas Teachers	79	IBM	19
New Jersey	74	SBC Communications	19
General Motors	70	Proctor and Gamble	18
New York City	63	Ford	18
Wisconsin	58	Bell Atlantic	17

Sources: *Pensions & Investments* web-site pionline, August 2000 and January 2001.

The top US pension funds in 2000 listed by *Pensions & Investment* (see Table 2.2) are dominated by teachers and other public employees, with the funds for employees of major corporations also featuring. Here, too, unionisation rates are high among those covered, as they are not among the workforce as a whole. The largest DB fund was Calpers (California Public Employees Retirement System) with $156 billion. (The magazine lists TIAA-CREF, which furnishes pensions for university and college teachers, separately as a money manager with $291 billion under management.) In the list of the top ten DB funds nine are operated on behalf of public employees, with the General Motors fund being the only corporate entrant. But note that General Motors also sponsors one of the top ten DC funds; the combined assets of the GM funds came to $91 billion. If other leading corporate pension funds of different types are aggregated, then the General Electric Funds were worth $71 billion, the Lucent Technologies Funds $62 billion, and the IBM funds $62 billion.

The roll call of large occupational funds shows only the tip of the iceberg of tax-favoured retirement provision, with hundreds of thousands of enterprises offering 401(k)s and millions of individuals investing in IRAs. The pensions schemes, large and small, now supplied a substantial amount of business to companies in the retail finance field, with DC funds worth nearly $2 trillion by the close of the 1990s compared with nearly $5 trillion in the DB occupational funds. The older public sector funds have a definite institutional personality and, albeit to a lesser extent, the same can be true for large private sector DB and DC schemes run specifically for the employees of a given corporation. By contrast, the 401(k)s and IRAs are closer to the world of the mutual fund supermarkets, with the difference that the policy holder is tied into a stream of payments. These schemes reflect the decline of lifetime occupations – though the coverage they offer is slim since many in the newly casualised labour markets cannot afford the contributions needed for an adequate fund.

The growing share of DC funds in the United States in the 1980s and 1990s was helped by the rise of 401(k) plans, which fall under the DC heading. These plans qualified under the terms of the Revenue Act of 1978, as noted in chapter 1. Their regulations sought to deter employers from simply feathering their own nests or those of senior staff but were not concerned with underlying cost structures. The regulations allow employees to set aside a proportion of their income completely tax free – up to a ceiling of $6,000 in 2000 – to be invested in a selection of funds marketed by the financial industry. Sometimes employers will match a proportion of the contribution, or will contribute company stock. The employee has the opportunity to choose between a limited number of stylised asset allocation mixes offered by the nominated broker or money manager. These typically embrace 'short-term' funds which invest in the money market, 'income funds' which invest in intermediate bonds and mortgages, or 'growth funds' which invest in equities, or 'balanced funds' which invest in both types of asset.

Employers also often encourage their employees to hold stock in the company. In the early 1990s, 23 per cent of the assets in 401(k)s took the form of stock in the employing firm, 32 per cent in GICs (Guaranteed Investment Contracts, linked to a stock market index but offering lower risk and return), 14 per cent in balanced portfolios, 19 per cent in equities and 7 per cent in bonds. However, those with access to 'participatory advisory services' held 51 per cent in equities, 9 per cent in bonds, 5 per cent in balanced portfolios, 15 per cent in GICs, and 18 per cent in the employing company. As the 1990s boom continued, so did a shift to equities. By the end of 2000 42 million US workers held more than $1,800 billion in their 401(k) accounts. The distribution of assets for all funds now approximated the 'advisory' pattern with, on average, 51 per cent of plan balances invested in stock funds, another 19 per cent in company stock, 10 per cent in GICs and 8 per cent in balanced funds. The average amount held of the employer's stock – at nearly one-fifth – was still rather high. In a swathe of major corporations the proportion was a half or more: Nortel, Lucent, Coca-Cola, Proctor and Gamble, Pfizer, General Electric, Texas Instruments, McDonalds, AOL Time-Warner, and many others – including Enron and Global Crossing.[5] Awarding stock or options to employees did not make demands on cash flow, stimulated loyalty to the company and allowed all to express their corporate patriotism. If employees suffer hardship because of illness or losing their job, they may be permitted to make a distribution from the funds in their account but they will have to pay a 20 per cent tax on the withdrawal. Convenient as this may appear, it erodes the funds held for retirement and will weaken the contribution which 401(k)s will be able to make to future pensions.

Once the employees have made their choice of plan they tend to stick with it, so providers engage in a big marketing spend to attract this premium custom. From zero in 1981 the number of 401(k) plans rose to 10.3 million worth $105 billion by 1985, and reached 18 million participants with funds worth $475 billion by 1993. Both employers and employees tended to opt for well-known brand names so that by 1996 77 per cent of total 401(k) assets were being managed by just twenty companies, while the top ten firms accounted for 56 per cent of total assets: these were Fidelity, Vanguard, State Street, Merrill Lynch, Bankers Trust, Barclays, Prudential, UAM, Principal Financial and T. Rowe Price.[6] The 401(k)s allowed these firms to sell either their well-established products or new ones devised to appeal to those planning a pension.

The state is heavily implicated in all these schemes, because of the special laws and privileges it lays down for them. The fiscal exemptions offered to occupational and personal funds have now ballooned into major items of 'tax expenditure'. The latter were worth £17.5 billion in 1998 in the UK and $109 billion in the United States in 2000–1.[7] These subsidies were justified as measures favourable to employees struggling to make proper provision for their retirement and as a way to encourage a healthier macro-economic balance between savings and expenditure. But do these arrangements deliver results in terms of benefits and coverage which meet these objectives and justify the forgoing of public revenue?

Pension funds as we know them today are a creature of legislation, since they would not exist without tax breaks. Yet the growth of the funds has placed huge reservoirs of financial power at the disposal of fund managers run by the world's leading banks and brokers. While some of the subsidy may accrue to the benefit of the fund members, much of it swells the profits of the financial services industry. Are the fund managers properly answerable for their stewardship of the pension funds either to the policy holders or to any representatives of the general public interest? Of course they are asked to respect the law, but do they conduct themselves in ways that justify the great cushion of tax subsidy on which the pensions industry rests? It is to these questions that we turn in this chapter and its successor.

The Lever of Finance

We rightly worry about the unaccountable power of multinational corporations. But these often command fewer assets than, and in crucial respects are dependent upon, the pension and insurance funds and their managers. In 2000 the largest US money managers, ranked by asset value, were Fidelity Investments with $1,074 billion under management, Barclays Global Investors ($784 billion), State Street Global Advisers ($681 billion), Deutsche Asset Management ($589 billion), Vanguard ($564 billion), Merrill Lynch ($557 billion), Morgan Stanley ($425 billion), Putnam ($391 billion). It can easily be seen why institutional investors often control half the equity in large corporations, giving their funds leverage over even the largest multinationals.[8] Around the time of the foregoing valuations General Electric, the world's most valuable company, had a market worth of $460 billion and Microsoft a market capitalisation of $353 billion. These are the super giants. 'Large cap' companies start at a valuation of $5 billion, with only a handful topping $100 billion. The top ten individual US pension funds had assets in the range $75–156 billion in August 2000, with some trustees responsible for more than one fund. The overall value of 'tax-exempt institutional funds' in the United States was $7,769 billion with the top 100 firms managing assets worth $6,055 billion. The fourth largest concern – TIAA-CREF – was the self-managed pension fund for university teachers which manages total assets worth $285 billion. Most of the other top 100 were subsidiaries of the financial services industry. These firms each offer hundreds of financial investment products so that tax-exempt pension funds and retirement schemes are run alongside mutual funds and other investment vehicles.

The large money managers do not flaunt their power and, for reasons to be explored, often adopt practices which limit and conceal their potential influence. Barclays looms large in the institutional league table because of its success in running 'passive' index trackers. Nevertheless pension funds have a special salience for the money managers and for the corporations both because of their size and because they are more predictable than the mass of independent investors. The holders of mutual funds can simply cash in their shares when they feel like it. The trustees of pension funds are much less volatile, staying with a manager at least for a few years at a time and often longer (in the UK the average has been seven years). Several of the larger funds are run in-house by management teams assembled by the trustees and sponsors. Others make use of up to a dozen fund managers.

It is not unusual for an employees' pension fund to be more valuable than the company the employees work for. The pension fund at General Motors had assets that were worth almost twice the company's value in September 2000. Lockheed Martin had a stock market valuation of $13 billion while its defined benefit pension fund had assets valued at $24 billion. Boeing's market value was $39 billion and its pension fund was worth $37 billion. The UAL Corporation, owner of United Airlines, was worth $3.5 billion but had pension assets of $8.3 billion. These figures reflect the fact that older companies often have more retirees than workers.[9] In the UK recent valuations showed the ICI pension fund to be worth £8.2 billion when the company was worth £2.9 billion, the British Airways pension fund was worth £8.9 billion while the company itself was worth £3.8 billion and the Rolls Royce pension fund was valued at £3.9 billion when the company was worth £3.3 billion.[10] Because companies which sponsor DB schemes are committed to maintaining their viability the performance of the pension fund often has a large impact on profitability.

DB funds are still very large because they have been running for decades and because they tend to have lower costs, and a higher net return, than personal schemes. Private sector DB funds in the United States were worth $1,782 billion in 1998 and public sector pension funds, mainly DB in character, were worth $2,344 billion, giving a combined total of $4,126 billion. The US DC-type funds, many based on the 401(k) or IRAs, were worth $2,199 billion in 1998. In addition, trade union-sponsored funds controlled $350 billion of assets. Trade unions also have some formal representation on DC funds worth $343 billion and DB funds worth $757 billion, in both cases because the funds were set up as a result of collective negotiations.[11] While, for reasons to be explained below, this trade union representation has limited significance, at least such funds cannot be wound up or closed simply at the whim of the employer, as is the case with the funds which were not set up in this way. Employers' recourse to 'termination' , whether 'healthy' or otherwise, is also explored later in the chapter. For the time being, the importance of the figures in this paragraph is simply that they indicate the value of the holdings of the different types of US pension fund.

That the pension fund-managing institutions are now hugely important to 'Anglo-Saxon' capitalism is beyond dispute. But do they behave in distinctive ways? Does quantitative growth translate into qualitative impact? Pension funds may be as large as, or larger than, major industrial or communications companies, but surely it is the giant multinational corporations which bestride the world economy, with the institutions as their pliant handmaidens? The pension funds or tax-exempt funds, taken together, may own between a quarter and a half of the shares of the major companies but, following the rule of diversifying risk, they have to spread their holdings widely so that a particular fund often holds no more than a tiny percentage of the shares of any given company.

Another circumstance apparently limiting the power of the financial institutions is that corporations can finance by far the larger part of their investment – usually well over 80 per cent – from their own revenues. The issuing of shares makes a negligible contribution, 1 or 2 per cent or less, to the financing of the investment programmes of large US or British corporations. Bank loans and corporate bonds are more important, though far behind self-financing. Finally, it can be urged, the financial institutions of today are not so novel. They have simply taken over the role of mobilising popular savings once monopolised by other concerns, such as the large retail banks. Indeed, the fund managers are usually concerns set up for the purpose by investment companies (Merrill Lynch, Fidelity), insurance companies (Prudential, Equitable Life) or banks (Barclays, State Street). While managing the pension funds furnishes such financial concerns with lucrative new opportunities, it does not radically change the nature of their business or their relations with non-financial corporations.

In seeking to gauge the respective strength of large corporations, pension funds and financial institutions it is important to register that they each operate at distinct and different levels. The corporation encounters competitive rivals on its own level and needs financial allies. As in any jungle, there is a food chain and intimate host–parasite relations. The corporations are large-scale employers, and the world in which we live is directly shaped by their investments, their rivalries, their supply policies and their marketing strategies. The financial services industry is also an employer, albeit on a smaller scale. Its significance is that it shapes the environment in which both corporations and individuals take decisions. The investment banks, supplying services to corporations, need to be well connected to the brokers, retail banks and insurance houses which hoover up savings. The rise of the pension funds added a crucial new fount of capital formation. Retail banks and insurance houses used to be the principal way in which the savings and positive balances of a host of individuals and small companies were drawn into the financial system. Now the pension funds also play this role and pension fund management is an important source of profit in its own right. By using a bank, small depositors gained greater security and useful access to facilities for handling receipts and payments. While depositors paid bank charges, the banks could use their deposits as the basis for the credit they offered. Today's pension funds give the policy holder a tax break on deferred compensation, a nominal lien on the fund's assets and the prospect of income in retirement. The charges vary according to the type of pension arrangement but can be stiff. The more flexible pension arrangements often entail higher charges. Those with low charges usually make it costly or impossible to recover contributions prior to the maturation of the policy. Most people in a pension plan are locked in, the only significant exception being 401(k)s where life emergencies are held to justify withdrawals. Compensating for this is the fact that, once they have chosen a provider, the holders of 401(k) plans rarely switch schemes.

The stream of contributions funnelled by pension fund executives and trustees to the financial industry gives them some leverage over the corporations but they only rarely exercise it. Unless funds manage their own assets, the trustees do not have much of a staff. They rely on consultants for monitoring the performance of money managers and reviewing their mandate. The large corporations have to be attentive to the fund managers since the latter own so many of their shares and are closely connected with the institutions they rely on for financial services. The corporations may be able to undertake investment from revenue but this certainly does not mean that they can afford to be indifferent to the financial institutions. Their credit rating and the price of their shares are critical factors in their day-to-day operations. The financial markets will form a view of the investment projects of a large corporation. A lowered credit rating will raise the cost of borrowing and encourage suppliers to ask for tougher terms of payment. A share price which falls seriously below that of the sector and market as a whole will further constrain the strategic management of the company, first by making acquisitions difficult, and then by exposing it to a boardroom coup or takeover. The limited supply of appropriate replacements exercises some restraint on the financial institutions, as do a certain fellow feeling and mutual respect between financial and corporate management.

On the whole, the share price will benefit when a company makes profits, and profits will be easier to make when revenue is strong. Basic data concerning sales, costs, inventory, assets and profit can be manipulated a bit but financial managers know the devices well and are aware that auditors can be lenient to their clients. Where management does have scope is in the story it tells about where the company is going. Strictly speaking, the share price is determined by investors' view of future profitability and the company's ability to make good use of its assets. Thus management has to be careful not to indulge in what the market regards as overinvestment, even if the company is making good profits, since if it does it could be punished by a declining share price, and become a tempting target for a predator. This is one of the reasons for the widespread practice of the buyback, in which boards disburse large sums buying back their own shares; another reason for the practice is that capital gains carry a lower tax than dividends.[12] As holders of share options, senior executives also stand to gain if the result is a boost to the share price.

If a sector is thought to have peaked, then ploughing more resources back into it will attract negative attention. In this way stock exchange systems do exercise real discipline over apparently mighty corporations. And companies themselves learn to internalise such disciplines. John Grahl points out that in a globalised context external finance is likely to define opportunity cost for both lenders and borrowers: 'Once industrial borrowers begin to take the external cost of capital as the key hurdle for investment projects, and their customary creditors start to regard yields on organised asset markets as a base-line rate of return, then market terms and costs will inevitably start to be internalised – even if insider finance continues to prevail in a quantitative sense.'[13] If financial intermediation has a more pervasive scope in the era of globalisation, then the rise of the pension funds has contributed to it. With their captive contributors, they have indeed functioned like the banks of old, but on a larger scale and more reliably. The fund managers, themselves tributary to the financial complex, need a steady supply of liquid or semi-liquid assets and encourage others to find ways of securitising or commodifying assets.[14]

The financial institutions have the resources to monitor corporations on a daily basis but they are discreet about this since the latter are potential clients. Since the fiercest struggles take place between those occupying the same economic niche, rival corporations will pay generous fees to obtain the best financial backers. Investment banks such as Goldman Sachs or Morgan Stanley Dean Witter have the contacts that will be vital in negotiating mergers and acquisitions. In a highly competitive climate it can be advisable for the corporate leaders themselves to canvass the pension fund managers. Consider the following example. In 2000 Chris Gent, CEO of Vodafone, launched a takeover bid for Mannesmann worth $185 billion. Prior to formalising his offer, the financial press explains, he 'spoke with all of Mannesmann's key institutional investors, both as a goodwill gesture and to gather support for his bid. Esser [CEO of Mannesmann] did not meet with investors before the bid and concealed details of what many stockholders would later call a knock-out internet strategy that could have changed their minds.' The same report also noted:

> Mannesmann also missed an opportunity to sway Vodafone's big holders, such as Schroder's Asset Management, Mercury and Gartmore, when Institutional Shareholders Services, a highly influential Maryland-based group that represents the interests of 500 money managers, was to issue a report advising US shareholders on whether they should approve Gent's takeover proposal. The Vodafone shareholders' meeting was scheduled for January 24th, but ISS analyst Jenny Chin Paik had to make her report by January 12th to give her clients the time to vote by proxy. Vodafone contacted Paik and arranged a video conference. . . . No one from Mannesmann called Paik until after the report was out, even though Paik says she tried unsuccessfully to get Mannesmann's arguments.[15]

The triumph of Vodafone was highly significant as a victory of the Anglo-Saxon 'shareholder value' approach over the more conservative German bank-finance system. Yet it also saw Gent manipulating shareholders for his own ends, for example in his use of shareholder research: 'One of Gent's trump cards, courtesy of D.F. King, was the knowledge that 40 per cent of Mannesmann's shareholders were also Vodafone shareholders. By promoting the takeover of Mannesmann as a make-or-break deal for Vodafone, he [Gent] effectively put these investors in his back pocket from the beginning.' If the bid failed, then the shares of both concerns would drop and these investors would take a double hit. In such accounts the role of the investment banks advising the contenders is usually not foregrounded. That does not mean that it was not important, simply that the adviser, Goldman Sachs being Gent's in this case, would not wish to appear too aggressive or to be thought the author of all Gent's gambits (one of them being an ill-judged jest at the expense of Esser's German accent and highbrow tastes). Just as fight promoters do not get into the ring themselves but need doughty pugilists to take and give punishment, so the

financial institutions need business stars, men or women who can build a
business or mastermind a string of acquisitions. Hence the popularity of
business leaders such as Bill Gates, Jack Welch and Jeff Bezos with the institutional investors and money managers. The restless search for better
returns also makes the financial industry susceptible to the wiles of ener-
getic operators of every type. In their day, such men as Michael Milken,
Ivan Boesky, James Goldsmith, Robert Maxwell and Jim Slater had the
elite institutions eating out of their hands – as Rupert Murdoch still does,
sometimes with help from Milken.

In the aftermath of the Mannesmann takeover Gent prevailed on his
colleagues to offer him a £10 million bonus package on top of his salary,
a move that angered the institutional investors whose attention he had
himself solicited. They objected to him collecting a bonus long before it
was at all clear whether the takeover had been a success; and perhaps some
of them resented the way they had been manoeuvred. In response to these
well-publicised complaints, the Vodafone board offered a coded apology
and promised it would not happen again while Gent declared that the cash
he had received would be used to buy Vodafone shares. An individual
described as 'the head of voting services' at the National Association of
Pension Funds welcomed these tokens but another UK body, the Pensions
Investment Research Consultancy (PIRC), dismissed Gent's gesture as 'a
pretty small sop'.[16]

From accounts of takeover battles it emerges that the fund managers,
and the financial complexes within which they are embedded, can play a
key role and that they behave quite unlike a completely atomised shareholder body. In such a situation the investment banks retained by the
rivals will canvass support and themselves lend a certain organisation to the
proceedings. The role of the larger representative bodies, like the UK's
National Association of Pension Funds, is different. They see themselves as
defending the general interests of those commercial concerns which
manage pension money. The smaller PIRC, supported by local government pension funds worth £25 billion, tries to foreground trustee or
policy-holder interests. In the United States the Council of Institutional
Investors, founded in 1985, has sought to link the activities of 500 pension
funds, with a total asset value of over $1 trillion. It has encouraged greater
shareholder 'activism' over issues connected with corporate governance
and has played a role in ousting underperforming CEOs. But it otherwise
remains faithful to the long tradition of running pension funds in exactly
the same way as any other fund.

It might be thought that pension funds, with their distinctive long-term purposes, would have distinctive long-term investment styles and objectives. Yet the pension funds are notorious for 'short-termism' and, for the most part, behave like other institutional funds. The great majority of trustees on both sides of the Atlantic have long been content to hand their fund assets over to be managed by the leading financial concerns: Fidelity, State Street, Barclays, Merrill Lynch, Schroders, or one or more of the few hundred other money managers. There is a small number of self-managed pension funds – that is, pension funds whose trustees establish their own management structure – which have pioneered shareholder activism and concern for corporate governance issues. Such funds include several giants run of behalf of teachers and other public sector employees – like TIAA-CREF or Calpers (California Public Employees Retirement System), or the funds attached to the Florida State Board of Administration or the State of Wisconsin Investment Board. In the UK the University Superannuation Scheme and other public sector retirement funds have begun cautiously to follow the example of their US counterparts. These internally managed funds have gradually and tentatively developed a more distinctive approach after decades during which they deferred to the corporate establishment. But even the more 'activist' pension funds are still prone to apply rigidly orthodox financial criteria, and to confuse entrepreneurialism with ruthless asset stripping.

Grey Capital and the 'Double Accountability Deficit'

The division of responsibility between trustees, money managers and consultants, the power of the sponsor and the limited rights of the policy holders or members, all conspire to ensure that retirement funds will be 'grey capital'. I use this term because the property rights represented by the funds represent a grey area in terms of law and political economy – that they are also funds held to finance old age is a source of vulnerability to those whose sacrifices have established them. And as it happens in contemporary financial parlance the shadow market in shares about to be released is called the 'grey market', no doubt because deals concerning that market take an anticipatory and conditional form. Pension funds are anchored to specific property claims in the present but the income flows they are to sustain lie in a variable future.[17]

The legal deficit at the heart of the pension fund statutes has a double aspect. It renders the interests of scheme members more vulnerable and it deprives major sectors of the economic system of consistency and direction.

Sponsoring employers and fund managers wield many of the powers that stem from the accumulation of employee savings but they must ultimately give primacy to the interests of their own shareholders. The focus of the present chapter is on the impact on the policy holder of 'sponsor risk' and 'eroded returns'; in the next chapter the discussion turns to the implications of grey capital for the economy as a whole. But a few preliminary observations, refining and illustrating the analysis of financial and corporate power so far offered, will indicate why it is that the usurpation of weak policy–holder claims by sponsors and fund managers lies at the root of both problems.

In classical capitalism the entrepreneur or capitalist had command of, and responsibility for, property in means of production, whether these were factories, machines, ships, telegraph wires, shops or offices. The capitalist, or the manager he or she appointed, was responsible for deciding what investments to make and how to allocate the stream of income generated by the enterprise. In the mid-twentieth century it was claimed that owners had been eclipsed by managers who represented a powerful independent stratum whose command of the imposing apparatus of the large corporations made them largely independent of the scattered mass of atomised shareholders. This thesis of a 'managerial revolution', as it was called, greatly exaggerated the independent power of the managers. The latter were, of course, happy to carve out a niche for themselves. But they were tied by powerful strands of interest and common outlook to the large property owners, whose ranks they often joined. In the postwar period managers could often count on the support of major blocks of shareholders in pursuing long-term strategies of investment. The managers' strategies had to bear fruit or they would render themselves vulnerable, firstly to the disapproval of their bankers, and then to a boardroom coup or a takeover. But the market in corporate management skills was restrained – the major shareholders knew that if they lightly or frequently dumped managers they would find it difficult to find competent replacements. Capitalist corporations in this way found a discipline which bound together owners and managers. The industrialist, financier, corporate manager or small entrepreneur all put their reputations and economic prospects on the line when they made a major investment decision. Without endorsing every claim of the so-called 'Austrian school' of economists – notably Friedrich von Hayek and Ludwig von Mises – they were not wrong to stress that the capitalist had a key role to play in capitalism. This role is weakened in the 'managerial capitalist' type of organisation. The owner's keen interest in, and commitment to, his or her enterprise encouraged a rational attitude to risk, one which would pursue advantages but avoid speculating with key assets. The entrepreneur wished not just to make a one-off windfall gain but to construct a valuable on-going business. Moreover, the structure of the market would tend to weed out the frivolous from the ranks of capitalists/entrepreneurs; of course, there was luck, too, but even good luck requires the ability to exploit it. The capitalist's stake in his business, and a context of eco-nomic rivalry, acted as a check and constraint, discouraging both gambling and a refusal to innovate.[18]

With the rise of the large-scale corporation it was necessary to ensure that senior corporate functionaries served the demands of capital rather than simply pursuing a comfortable career. Devices were elaborated for monitoring the work of top managers and for giving them incentives to serve the best interests of the owners. Audit and accounting procedures were tightened and the major exchanges laid down new reporting condi-tions so that, for example, directors had to report any dealings they had in the company's shares. Pay could be linked to profit targets, and stock options offered an extra incentive to improve market valuation. Losses or poor profits would soon lead to trouble. Credit rating agencies would sound the alarm if they saw rocks looming and the shareholders would rush for the life boats. A declining share price generally weakens a com-pany's position, making credit more expensive. If nothing else, the threat of takeover persuades CEOs to keep shareholder confidence by pursuing 'shareholder value'. So long as managers deliver this very tangible goal, they have great scope to conduct the affairs of the corporation as they wish. They may even be able to corrupt or confuse their auditors and bankers. But if revenue drops and the shares slide then they are likely to face a harsh day of reckoning.

Shareholders' formal consent is generally required at AGMs for the re-election of the board and for approval of special resolutions. Shareholders also have to give their approval for rights issues, or for any placing of shares outside normal guidelines. A company which issues high-yield bonds is potentially setting up a rival claim on its future streams of revenue, so there can be tensions between shareholders and bond holders. But the money managers invest in both types of instruments and will be wary of such developments. In general they subscribe to bond issues which promise to boost the overall success and value of a company – by financing an acquisition, for example. Because the exercise of shareholder votes is cum-bersome – requiring countersigned paperwork from the trustees establishing a mandate – money managers have long been accustomed to minimising formal proxy voting and relying on informal contacts or the simple power of exit.

Many of the routine tasks associated with shareholding and trading are not actually performed by the money managers but are contracted out to 'custodians', usually a large bank. In the United States the lion's share of the custodian business is in the hands of the Bank of New York, State Street, J.P. Morgan Chase Manhattan and Citigroup, while in Europe HSBC, BNP Paribas and Deutsche Bank handle much of the work. The custodian discharges the 'back office' or 'mid-office' functions, tasks generally regarded as humdrum. Custodians can arrange for proxy votes to be cast and can give legal guidance. As money management becomes ever more competitive and explores new territory custodians may become more important since it is up to them whether important scale economies in administration can be delivered. But, for the time being at least, they do not have anything to do with stock picking or deciding how shareholders' votes are cast.[19]

From the mid-1980s institutional investors were more inclined to use shareholder power to ensure that underperforming managements were removed. In the United States money managers and pension trustees were concerned that such managements could use 'poison pills' to prevent takeovers and in this way insulate themselves from shareholder pressure for better results. But 'poison pill' defences – for example, those giving the existing board a controlling raft of share options in the event of a challenge – usually required the consent of existing shareholders. Seeing that such arrangements would reduce their influence on management, and hence their ability to demand good returns, the institutions used their existing voting power to block poison pill devices. And boards which nevertheless managed to adopt them found that their share price suffered. In 1987 the chairman of GM was prepared to pay over the odds to buy out Ross Perot's shares in the company and to remove this troublesome colleague from the boardroom. The Council of Institutional Investors was worried by the implications of this action and one of its members tabled a motion of censure, though this was eventually withdrawn following negotiations. In 1992 the institutional investors secured the replacement of the new chairman, Robert Sempel.[20]

It is now common for corporations to have an investor relations manager with direct access to senior management; his or her task is to keep the institution happy, or to assist the chairman or CEO in this endeavour. Robert Reich, the former US Labor Secretary, notes: 'In recent years, institutional investors have been active in ousting chief executives at IBM,

AT&T, Sears, General Motors, Xerox, Coca-Cola, Aetna, Compaq Computer and other blue chip American corporations that didn't boost share prices enough.'[21] Reich indicated that the financial demands of retirement funds lay behind this pruning process. His post at the Department of Labor had left him keenly aware of the way in which ruthless pursuit of the bottom line by certain large pension funds had helped to promote corporate downsizing.

In a wide-ranging comparative study John Scott has identified the crucial role of institutional funds, and the 'constellations' of interest they represent, in setting the parameters of control over corporations throughout the English-speaking world.[22] When companies get into real difficulties Britain's National Association of Pension Funds has been accustomed to set up an in-house IPC (Investor Protection Committee) representing the major investors and charged with securing a new management plan or a board recomposition. The existence of the IPC is not divulged publicly. Its representations will be kept confidential so long as the management is cooperative; if it is not, then hostile stories will appear in the financial press. It is believed that resort to formal IPCs was less common in the 1990s than in the 1980s but that informal alliances of the leading institutions came to play a similar role. A study by Mathur Gaved of forty-seven UK companies where the chief executive was removed after shares underperformed in 1995 found that there was strong or circumstantial evidence of institutional shareholder initiative in eighteen cases. The usual pattern was that the largest three or four shareholders, with 20 per cent or more of the total shares, would encourage one of their number to play the lead role in reconstructing the failing management.[23]

The emergence of proxy shareholders in the shape of institutions means that managers have to contend with close and informed invigilation. No longer is it plausible to portray the shareholders as scattered, bemused and powerless in the face of corporate boards because large shareholdings are now concentrated in the hands of powerful agents. Gaved, who interviewed a large number of fund managers, quotes one as making the following observation about a manager: 'We knew his markets were in trouble in the US because I had seen his biggest US competitor, which was having problems, and between them they have around half the market. There was no hint of any problems when I had a meeting with the company; they only finally admitted there was a problem when the preliminary results came out a couple of months later.' [24] But the new leverage of the money managers benefits them much more than their clients. The institutions themselves have to worry about their own shareholder value. They need to retain the loyalty of sponsoring companies and the pension fund trustees they nominate. And this very fact influences their use of proxy shareholder power. The large financial institutions see all corporations as potential clients and do not wish to alienate them. Gaved notes: 'Clearly a corporate client, although strictly speaking only the indirect source of pension fund manager business (because in law the fund and its trustees are independent and separate legal entities from the company), will not appreciate coming into conflict with the manager of its own pension fund.'[25] In extremis fund managers may act to remove underperforming CEOs, but they prefer a cosier relationship with corporate boards. And given the diversity of services performed for companies by the financial institutions (underwriting new issues or assisting with mergers and acquisitions), they can use their leverage to advance their own business interests more than those of the policy holders.

Alaistair Ross Goobey, a leading UK fund manager, reviewing a book by Allen Sykes, whom he describes as a 'distinguished executive manager', writes that

> problems arise from the well-documented fact that ownership rights and executive powers are held by two separate professional agents – fund managers and company managers. What shortcomings are there in 'double agency' or the 'double accountability deficit', as Mr Sykes terms it? In his view, agents of the beneficial owners, the institutions, do not take action to control or correct real problems in companies because, inter alia, they are on short-term investment contracts, have conflicts of interest and are not paid to intervene. As a result, a strong management, with a self-perpetuating oligarchy of board membership, can write its own terms and conditions and manage the company less optimally for many years at no risk for themselves. The institutional shareholders shrug their shoulders, sell the shares of the underperformers and move on to more promising territory.[26]

After offering this account of Sykes's argument in *Capitalism for Tomorrow* (2000), Goobey observes: 'I can agree with the overwhelming bulk of Mr Sykes's analysis of the problems, but his proposed solutions seem much less compelling. He believes that the market cannot solve the identified problems and that government action is needed.' In Goobey's opinion, he and his colleagues were beginning to clip the wings of errant managers but the situation was worse on the other side of the Atlantic: 'The real danger is infection from the US, where most shareholders have been supine in the face of astounding corporate self-aggrandisement.'[27] While we should not forget the CEOs sent packing by shareholder pressure nor should we overlook their extravagant 'compensation' (on which more below). The insider indictments of a 'double accountability deficit' point as much to the exclusion of beneficiary owners as to the relative autonomy of one of the sets of managers.

The policy holders, whose contributions and pension rights underpin the whole edifice, do not have to be much considered because their rights and powers are weak and unclear. They cannot remove trustees or impose policies on them. For their part, the trustees themselves take comfort from the use of money managers since this is accepted legally as meeting their fiduciary responsibility. They normally employ a consultancy like Watson Wyatt, Frank Russell or William Mercer to help them pick or review a manager; this further reduces the fiduciary onus weighing on them. Whatever happens, they can say they acted on advice. Trustees of a DB scheme will also need to take the advice of actuaries, or may obtain this from their consultant, to make sure that the size and structure of the fund are well calibrated to the likely needs of members. In recent years some trustees have cautiously opted for a modicum of shareholder activism but here they encounter the often arcane complexity of shareholder 'democracy'. Certain vital decisions, such as that of approving the issuing of new shares – sometimes a crucial aspect of a merger or acquisition – will exceed the normal power of attorney and will require new instructions from shareholders or their designated manager. Antiquated and prone to mishap as the mechanisms of shareholder consultation may be, they do yield decisions as to whose will is to prevail.[28]

With exceptions to be considered later, it can be said that pension assets represent a large cloud of indefinite, irresponsible and ill-defined property rights. The fund managers are not owners, and do not behave like owners. They are functionaries of the financial services industry. The mechanisms making them responsive to their own shareholders are stronger than those linking them to fund trustees, and far stronger than those linking them to policy holders. There is thus a chain of principal/agent problems and, in some cases, even doubt about the identity of the principal. The fund manager has an inducement to be attentive to those who dispose of the mandate but these are the sponsor-nominated trustees and certainly not the scattered mass of policy holders. The fund managers have huge resources at their command but are themselves, unlike any true owner, removed from the constraints and opportunities of any specific context. Supposedly dedicated to the single-minded pursuit of the highest rate of return, the funds they manage typically underperform the market. But this should not be seen as unrelieved failure since the financial concerns for which they work often outperform the market, and grateful shareholders in these

Figure 1 Shareholder control – the contemporary reality
Largely passive shareholders and unaccountable managements – executive
directors implicitly 'trustees for the public good'

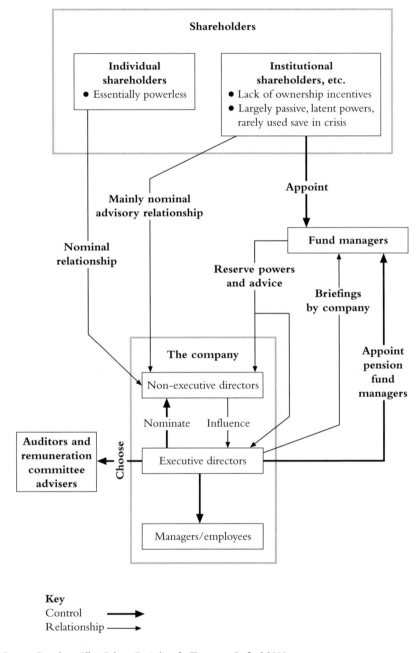

Source: Based on Allen Sykes, *Capitalism for Tomorrow*, Oxford 2000.

concerns are content to see the money managers collect handsome salaries and bonuses.

Policy Holders as Dead Souls

The policy holders in a pension fund, whatever the type, have no direct purchase or control over the assets which are held to finance their pension. They do not even have the option exercised by investors in a mutual fund or unit trust who can at least sell their holdings if they wish. Legal prohibitions and financial penalties make the cashing-in of pension plans either impossible or, at best, difficult and costly. If pension scheme members seek as individuals to gain control of their 'pot' they find that it will shrink or even vanish. With 'defined contribution' pension funds, other than 401(k)s, the so-called 'pot' is an accounting device and there are no assets ear-marked for particular individuals. If they withdraw from the scheme the transfer value may be less than the nominal pot and if they seek a distribution there will be tax to pay and possible penalty fees as well. In this respect holders of 401(k)s are in the same position. In defined benefit schemes the employee whose rights are 'vested', because they have been contributing for, say, five years, will retain their rights to a pension at 65 or 60.

Interestingly enough, the less individualised the policy holders' claim to fund assets the better the prospects of a good return. This is because costs of administration rise steeply as attempts are made to tie particular assets to particular individuals. Thus defined benefit schemes generally deliver a much better return to those who stay in them than do individual pension

---

Figure 1 Shareholder control: This is the view of Allen Sykes, a well-informed participant and observer. Note that fund managers are appointed both by the 'executive directors' and by the 'institutional shareholders'; this is because, in the private sector, the executive directors generally nominate the key trustees. The claim that the influence of shareholders, whether private or institutional, is only 'nominal' is polemically overstated since they have been able to secure a focus on 'shareholder value' and to dismiss CEOs who fail to deliver it. The public sector pension funds, not included in the diagram, have often played the part of the 'activist' shareholders. Note also that it is diagrammatically difficult to represent the fact that there are many thousands of companies and only a few dozen large fund managers. The 'consultants', who advise trustees, and the 'custodians', who handle the administrative functions of share ownership, are not represented in the diagram, presumably because they play no direct part in corporate governance.

plans. But DB schemes have their own serious drawbacks, even where portability and 'vesting' problems have been reduced. An employee who leaves a company at the age of forty-five after, say, ten or twenty years and who has contributed over that time to a DB scheme will very often find that the pension he or she eventually receives is extremely modest. The reason for this is that the pension will be based on the salary at the time of leaving. It will not reflect inflation or a potential 'final salary'. But if the employee stays with the company the pension will be pegged to earnings, which should supply an element of inflation proofing and is also likely to reflect promotion or seniority. Employers themselves were always aware that their pension arrangements acted as bronze or silver handcuffs in this way; they were partly adopted with the hope of retaining experienced staff. The drawbacks and inflexibility of DB schemes have reconciled employees to individualised 401(k)-style schemes despite their higher charges, enhanced risk and the frequent absence of an employer contribution.

The problem of loss on changing jobs in DB schemes is somewhat mitigated in the case of some public sector and professional DB schemes, such as most teachers' schemes, since they do allow for a degree of portability within the sector or profession with no loss of entitlement and an earnings link. The public sector DB funds have generally also been far better than the schemes in the private sector when it comes to protecting the value of pensions from inflation. Even long-service members of schemes run by blue chip companies like GE can find that there are lengthy intervals between the uprating of their pensions, leading them to suffer real hardship. What Leslie Hannah has to say about the UK is relevant to the United States as well:

> Why was there not greater progress towards paying pension benefits in the real terms which are, after all, the terms in which pensioning needs are naturally and rationally expressed? The basic problems were costs and employers' objectives. The generous inflation-proofing offered in the public sector could be worth one-third of the whole pension entitlement, and increases in cost of that magnitude cannot be borne by most private schemes. It is, of course, true that pension funds would have been obliged to pay pensions in real terms in the absence of inflation: but it may, of course, have turned out that they would have not been able to do so.[29]

The absence of inflation proofing and the buoyancy of markets in the 1980s and 1990s allowed many corporate sponsors to enjoy lengthy contribution holidays. Members of the GE scheme whose benefits had stagnated pointed out that the sponsoring company had made no contribution for fourteen years yet was paying an average benefit of only $700 a month in 2000.[30] The company sponsoring a DB scheme can make pre-tax contributions to the fund, build up a surplus and then use that surplus to take a contribution holiday while paying out inflation-eroded pensions to retirees. As awareness of such practices spreads, the attractions of fund membership to employees diminish. In the UK an official desire to promote good practice in the wake of the Maxwell affair, and other problems highlighted by the Goode report (1993), led to a tightening up of the rules relating to DB funds in the Pensions Act of 1995. DB funds were now required to provide for price indexation of plan benefits up to 5 per cent annually as well as to conform to a 'minimum funding requirement'. However, from around this time few new DB plans were to be introduced and many old ones were to be converted to a DC basis.

The policy holder needs a good and responsible agent to husband his or her investments and to achieve economies of scale by performing the same service for large numbers in a like situation. But Anglo-American law has not been developed to respond to the new needs of the policy holders. Instead, they have been handed over to a legal and business system built for other purposes, one which, as it turns out, is dedicated to minimising the leverage or input of the policy holder. Thus pension funds are put in the hands of trustees bound by the 'prudent person' or 'prudent expert' rule. The institution of trusteeship developed in early modern England and in the early American colonies as a means of managing the assets of those deemed incompetent to handle their own affairs – children, lunatics and women. Widows sometimes managed to wrest control of their estates, notwithstanding prejudice against their sex. But the task facing today's policy holders is scarcely less daunting. A large number of pension plans allow for no direct representative of employees or beneficiaries on the board of trustees. And it is virtually ruled out in 401(k)-type holdings in ready-made financial products. When a defined benefit fund runs a surplus the law usually allows employers to reduce their contributions, and, on termination of the scheme, they may be able claim it back (on which more below). Law courts in the United States and UK have a queue of cases concerning the disposition of pension funds and their 'surpluses'. While the precise terms of the original pension contract may help to adjudicate property rights in these funds, the fact remains that nobody really owns them: they are instead simply held for certain purposes. That purpose is to pay the policy holder, and perhaps the policy holder's spouse, a pension. Once that function has been discharged (on the death of the beneficiary), then the assets concerned are not inherited by the policy holder's heirs but remain in the common pool where they will continue to generate income for other policy holders.

Most DB plans lay on the sponsor the duty of topping up the fund, if necessary, to ensure that 'final salary' provisions are met. But this require- ment should strengthen the claim of the plan members not only to the fund and to any surplus in it but also to future profit in the sponsoring company. In 1983 Jeremy Bulow and Myron Scholes published a paper arguing that such pension plans were inherently collective in character and had a claim on the sponsor. They wrote that 'employees, with the salaried pension plan, should be looked at not as individuals but as a group'. These authors noted a variety of anomalies that pension fund obligations set up − such as that between accrued and future benefits noted above − and showed that they stemmed from the nature of the pension contract. In their view in the case of any problem: 'The group [of employees] negotiates with the stockholders of the firm (the board of directors of the firm or its management representatives) over the division of the profits earned by the firm.'[31] In seeking to plumb the economic logic of the arrangement, the two eminent economists found the terms of the legal contract failed to yield a clear-cut decision.

A recent attempt to analyse the legal character of policy-holder claims develops the notion of 'non-private property', as distinguished from pri- vate, common or communitarian property. The author, John Harris, argues that: 'We may suppose, as to some resource, that it ought to be sub- ject to protected storage but we should avoid borrowing ownership notions in relation to its use or disposal.'[32] Policy holders may not be reas- sured to learn that other entities that qualify as 'protected non-property holdings' are embryos, human organs and corpses. While Harris's account captures an important aspect of the legal reality, the fact remains that pen- sion fund assets are possessed of qualities which exceed those needed for the purpose of administering the pension. In principle equities − even non-voting shares − confer a degree of leverage over management, espe- cially when large concentrations of them are owned by institutions which have the possibility of pooling information. The hollow rights generally accorded to policy holders do not allow them to wield this power. They are like the 'dead souls' in Gogol's novel, or serfs fixed to the estate (the fund) whose futures are being gambled by absentee landlords in market places remote from their own daily settings. The institutions find them- selves in a false situation where they have more power than they can properly use.

Notwithstanding the law, it is the spontaneous belief of many pension scheme members that they are, collectively, the effective owners of the pension fund and entitled to a share of any surplus that develops. This sentiment is reinforced by the fact that inflation can erode the value of a 'defined benefit' pension so that the surplus appears as compensation for this. The stakes are considerable; in 1997 the value of the surpluses in British company pension funds was £60 billion and the phenomenon is just as common in the United States.[33] When takeovers occur there is resentment if the surplus is simply scooped up as a prize by the predator. The former employees of the Trustee Savings Bank protested at the appropriation of the surplus in their pension fund when Lloyds–TSB was formed because the terms of their 'final salary' scheme left them drawing pitifully small amounts.[34] In another case, the surplus in the pension fund of the former National Bus Company was simply appropriated by the government when the company's services were privatised. Thanks to the determined efforts of Frank Wheeler, a maverick trade unionist opposed even by his own union, the Pensions Ombudsman eventually decided that the £200 million surplus should, on a strict reading of the original deed of trusteeship, have been paid into the Bus Superannuation Trust (BEST).[35] Some recent legal decisions in the UK relating to pension fund surpluses slightly extended policy holders' rights. They ruled that although policy holders do not own their pension fund, nor do their employers, and policy holders do own the benefits they have been promised and hence 'provisions which increase the security of those benefits' (such as surpluses which might enable pension promises to be kept if there is a downturn).[36] In July 1999 this approach was qualified in *Edge* vs *The Pensions Ombudsman* where the judge ruled that the trust deed would be decisive. In most cases the trustees are deemed the arbiters of the trust deed. This gives the initiative to employers. Some of the latter believe it to be unwise to assert their rights over the surplus too greedily, but others, BA being a recent case in point, do not scruple to seize the surplus.[37] In 2001 and 2002 companies contending with a fall in profits also found themselves obliged to report deficits in their pension funds because of new accounting standards. This led more firms to close down their DB pension schemes as a way of preventing a deterioration of their bottom line.

The decision of companies to close their DB schemes also short-changed their employees. In the case of BT, mentioned earlier, the company used an earlier fund surplus to claim a contribution holiday but then decided to withdraw when the fund went into deficit. The not normally squeamish FT Lex column was moved to comment:

[A]fter pocketing the benefits of strong equity markets in the 1990s, it could be rational [for BT] to shift future investment risk from shareholders to employees. The problem is that employees, investing over a single lifetime of employment, have limited ability to diversify their risk. They value defined benefit schemes. Companies which end such schemes should expect to pay higher salaries and receive less loyalty. It may still be in shareholders' interests to end defined benefit schemes but it is anything but a cost-free decision.[38]

Among companies closing their schemes in 2001 and 2002 were ICI, Sainsbury, Whitbread, Lloyds TSB, Iceland, and Ernst and Young.

In the United States the employers' role as fund sponsor also enables them to nominate most of the trustees. There are multi-employer schemes in which trade unions have prominent representation but this is the exception and in some cases, even when the scheme was really promoted by the union, it is still the employers who act as sponsors. ERISA did try to ensure that pension schemes would not be used by managers simply to feather their own nests. In order to qualify for tax-favoured treatment a pension plan had to meet certain conditions and not discriminate against less well-paid employees. All employees were to be informed about any pension scheme and free to join it if they wished. A series of tests ensure that the scheme either covers 70 per cent of all 'non-highly compensated employees' or meets a 'ratio test' or an 'average benefit test' that shows the 'non-highly compensated' proportionately benefiting from the scheme. The 'highly compensated employee' was set in 2000 as someone who earns more than $80,000 and is among the highest-paid 20 per cent of employees. The legislation also set ceilings on the size of tax-free contributions and of benefits paid under the scheme. Thus in a DB scheme in 2000 no annual benefit could be more than the average of the employee's best three years of earnings or $135,000, whichever was the lower. In the same year the ceiling on contributions to a defined contri-bution scheme was the lesser of $30,000 or 25 per cent of salary.[39] These arrangements allowed the better-paid substantial participation while still setting a limit on it.

So far as surpluses in DB funds were concerned, the rights of the spon-soring organisation had priority, leading employers in the 1980s to terminate schemes, pay off existing participants and seize the remaining surplus (on which more below). Legislation now makes this more difficult but nevertheless in the overall running of a pension plan the initiative and the power rest with the sponsor, and only employers can be sponsors. When the employer is a public body, or where many employers are brought together by a trade union as collective sponsor, then the leverage of the employees is likely to be greater; and this does correlate with a different investment performance and style.

While it might seem reasonable to deny full control of pension assets to a policy holder who only has a claim to an income stream for a given period of time, it seems strange to deny any rights to the collective entity of policy holders. Yet this is what Anglo-American law generally does in the case of pension schemes covering a particular industry or company. Indeed, both managers and the law have usually been particularly hostile to attempts by employees to establish any collective say over the disposition of assets in a pension fund. Thus in the mid-1980s Britain's National Union of Miners sought to influence the investments of the Coal Industry Pension Fund, urging it to make some investments in the economy of the mining regions and not to increase its stake in overseas assets. When this was resisted by the Coal Board the judge, Sir Robert Megarry, found against the union, citing as a precedent the US case of *Blakenship* vs. *Boyle* in which it was declared that it would be a 'breach of duty' for a trade union-sponsored pension fund to invest money in such a way as to enhance the position of the union rather than single-mindedly follow commercial criteria – for example, by declining to invest in profitable non-union companies. Megarry also ruled that the fund should not be prevented from investing in any asset class, such as oil stocks or overseas shares, since the prudent pursuit of good returns would involve seeking out a broad and diversified range of investments. Megarry insisted that the fund trustees should confine themselves to a narrow interpretation of their duty to concern themselves only with the best interests of the beneficiaries and that 'the best interests of the beneficiaries are normally their best financial interests'.[40]

It goes almost without saying that 'best financial interests' can easily be subjected to further narrowing and refining. The prudence of the 'prudent expert' or 'prudent person' in an Anglo-American financial context is institutionally defined. As Teresa Ghilarducci explains in her study of US pension funds, since 'expertise and prudence are whatever passes for standard practice by members of the pension fund industry', then US law 'requires the industry to abide by the standards the industry itself defines. The prudent person rule sanctions management practices that would be used "in the conduct of an enterprise of like character and aim".'[41] With this cautionary observation in mind, it is now appropriate to look at the investment policies and commercial practices of the pension fund industry in the United States and Britain. In doing so, we will have to explain why an industry that supposedly pursues the best financial rate of return for its customers so often fails to deliver it.

Adventures in Speculation

In the course of the 1980s the dominant investment style in the Anglo-Saxon world was set by deregulation and the increasing scope for playing the market, both globally and domestically. Legislation eased the restraints on the types of assets that pension fund managers could invest in and the buoyancy of equity markets rewarded those funds which increased their equity holdings. Money managers did not wait for an AGM to punish managements they did not like; they simply sold stock in the company and bought into another concern. In Albert Hirschman's terms, they used 'exit' rather than 'voice'.[42] Getting involved in the affairs of any one concern was likely to be time-wasting and costly, as well as implying a concentration of assets which might break the rule of reducing risk by diversifying investment. The resulting investment style has come to be famous for 'short-termism' and the 'herd instinct'.

As managers chased higher rates of return they were drawn in the 1980s towards increasingly speculative purchases of junk bonds, which offered those rates. This could be reconciled with the prudent expert rule by the argument that the more diversified the assets in a portfolio, the safer it was. Buying junk bonds broadened the spread of asset types. Managers had vast sums to invest and their main rule was to spread risk by diversification. The architects of corporate restructuring and downsizing often found it easier to deal with a few pension fund managers than to raise the finance they needed in other ways. In the short run the results were often good because takeover battles boosted share prices. Soon pension funds lost their sedate image and found themselves embroiled in some famous scandals. Even experienced managers working for long-established concerns like Fidelity found it difficult to resist the attractive returns delivered by Michael Milken, the junk bond king. By 1983 more than a third of the assets managed by Fidelity came from institutional trustees.

As its name implies, Fidelity had always marketed itself as a supremely reliable concern. Like the other Boston-based financial giants, State Street and Putnam, its early directors numbered several members of that city's WASP or 'Brahmin' elite and, just in case these hints were missed, its flag-ship product was the Puritan Fund. But the hectic atmosphere of the late 1970s led to some jazzing up of the image with the launch of the

Aggressive Income Fund in 1977, which was to specialise in the acquisition of junk bonds. (This homage to Mammon reflected involvement in a
market symbolised by Merrill Lynch's bull and the ram of T. Rowe Price.)
Fidelity, like most money managers, did not itself directly sponsor corporate buy-outs but it could buy stock from those who did, like Milken's
operation at Drexel Burnham. In this way Patsy Ostrander, a leading
Fidelity manager, was found to be implicated in Milken's corrupt schemes
for the peddling of junk bonds; like Milken, she was to spend time in jail.
Stung by her colleagues' failure to stand by her, Ostrander alleged that her
actions were simply the product of a corporate culture in which company
officials would use the placement of clients' funds, or knowledge relating
to those placements, to advance other interests.[43]

Deregulation and greed also lay behind two further scandals that
afflicted the savings industry in the late 1980s and early 1990s, the Savings
and Loan débâcle in the United States and the pensions mis-selling affair
in the UK. Speculation and corruption went hand in hand in the S&L
fiasco which eventually cost the US tax payer $175 billion because deposits
were covered by a Federal guarantee. The S&Ls had been established in the
1930s to finance the construction of new homes during the Depression.
They offered mortgages to home buyers at reasonable rates and depositors
had the added reassurance that their money was insured with the Federal
Housing Loan Insurance Corporation (FHLIC) and that the operations of
the S&Ls were supervised by the Federal Home Loans Bank Board
(FHLBB). The advent of high inflation in the 1970s put a strain on these
previously sound, if unexciting, 'thrifts'. They were prevented from offering more than 5.5 per cent return on new deposits at a time when inflation
was running at 13 per cent. The 1980 Depository Institutions
Deregulation and Monetary Control Act and the 1982 Depository
Institutions Act allowed S&Ls to charge higher rates of interest and to
invest in a wider range of assets including commercial real estate. In a parallel move, the FHLBB sought to encourage the growth of S&Ls by
dropping the requirements that these thrifts have at least 400 stock holders and that no stock holder could own more than 25 per cent of any one
S&L. While the rules were loosened in this way deposits in the thrifts were
still covered by Federal insurance with the limit on the insured amount per
depositor raised to $100,000. Reagan quipped, 'I think we've hit a home
run', and later told S&L executives that the legislation was the
'Emancipation Proclamation for America's savings institutions'.[44] In fact,
the S&Ls had been rendered vulnerable to gamblers and crooks. They had
always been subject to state as well as Federal legislation but the deregulated

regime led to new arrangements at state level as well. The staff employed by the California Department of Savings and Loan fell from 172 full-time examiners in 1979 to fifty-five in 1983 while the number of S&Ls shot up and the scope of their operations widened. California and Texas, the two states worst hit by the crisis, were also the states which deregulated most thoroughly. The S&Ls whose operations led to criminal convictions were newly established or had recently experienced a change in control. So-called 'thrifts' could be purchased and turned into money machines for corrupt depositors or fraudulent borrowers. However, the size of the eventual losses incurred was greatly in excess of the outright corruption involved. The indictment of high-profile S&L executives for fraud and a rising toll of failures forced a general liquidation of S&L holdings in commercial real estate and bonds at a time when the market was depressed. The fire sale allowed astute private investors to make acquisitions at bargain rates. Some accounts were to suggest that it was the Federal guarantee of deposits, or 'incomplete' deregulation, which promoted 'moral hazard', fraud and speculation. Yet over the previous fifty years, when S&Ls were much closer to being community-controlled, not-for-profit concerns, neither fraud nor speculation had ever been a significant problem. Even without the guarantee, the thoroughgoing commercialisation and commodification of S&L control and membership would have fostered speculation and malpractice. After all, neither Charles Ponzi's pyramid scheme nor Michael Milken's junk bond scams needed a Federal guarantee.[45]

Following new legislation in the UK in 1987, money managers were allowed to persuade those already covered by an occupational scheme or the State Earnings-Related Pension Scheme to abandon these arrangements in favour of a personal pension plan. High-powered salesmen, themselves under pressure from marketing managers, often made false promises of superior performance for pension schemes burdened with much higher charges than was characteristic of the schemes they were urging clients to cash in. These higher charges reflected the fact that individually supplied commercial pension plans are bound to have higher marketing and administrative costs than mandatory occupational schemes. A government in the grip of the dogma of privatisation neglected this basic factor and sponsored a promotional campaign that gave credence to the salesmen's pitch. Subsequent legal action has identified about 1.5 million people who were gulled into taking out a personal plan when they already had a better arrangement. Those guilty of fielding the salesmen responsible constituted a roll call of the British financial establishment. Following legal action by the GMB trade union, the Prudential, the flagship of that establishment, was ordered to pay an average of £25,000 to 44,000 policy holders.[46] The overall cost of compensation to those lucky enough to live to claim is likely to be in the region of £13.5 billion.[47]

Britain's mis-selling scandal spotlighted the high charges and disadvantageous costs attached to personal pension plans. But at least these British pension fund holders had been advised by accredited agents to leave occupational schemes which could be used as a reference point in legal actions. The mass of those taking out a new plan, whether in the UK or the United States, have not usually been in this advantageous situation and it is this − not the superior qualities of the plans they have subscribed to − which deprives them of grounds for legal action. The DB plans that have been legally withdrawn by the sponsor, leave the employee with no alternative but to find a (generally inferior) alternative.

E.P. Davis points out that there are structural reasons why personal pension plans will often prove to be a bad deal:

> Given the information asymmetry between seller and buyer, the one-off nature of the transaction, and the lack of purchasing power of the purchaser, personal defined contribution plans are particularly vulnerable to agency problems vis-a-vis financial intermediaries, as well as the ability of the seller to impose high commissions on the purchaser. But there are also economic reasons for high costs, such as the need to construct individual contracts, as well as the need for expenditures on advertising, marketing, and public relations.[48]

The problems itemised by Davis have always afflicted personalised financial instruments accessible to those without large asset holdings. It makes sense for someone with a high net worth to engage specialists who will help to get a good return on their liquid assets. The swanky investment banks in New York or London will generally require a minimum of at least £1 million ($1.5 million) in liquid assets before they offer personal banking services. But those with a smaller sum − say $0.5 million − might still find it reasonably cost-effective to invest it with the help and advice of a bank or broker, though much is then likely to be placed in mutual funds with their own charges. A financial agent who handles a lump sum of this sort is bound to charge much less than the same agent if required to handle the same sum spread out over thirty years of monthly contributions. Such agents usually find it more costly to collect contributions than do employers who can simply dock them from the monthly pay cheque.

The managers of pension funds themselves show significant 'returns to scale', that is the cost of managing a fund declines as a proportion of asset value as the size of the fund grows – up to a value of $3.5 billion, according to a recent study of mutual fund management.[49] The financial services industry gives pension funds some access to these savings, though naturally they charge a fee for this. US mutual funds and UK unit trusts even give the small investor access to expertise and scale returns but at an even stiffer price. In the 1950s and 1960s that price was certainly enormous and some charge-gauging practices were to survive much longer, especially in the UK. An 8.5 per cent sales commission or 'load', paid to the broker, was standard for mutual fund deposits and was followed by management fees and administration expenses charged to the fund, and redemption charges when the holding was cashed. Purchasers who were tempted by salesmen to flit from fund to fund paid heavily. The Securities and Exchange Commissioner, alarmed at high redemption rates, observed: 'The high redemption rate is a reflection of the quality and adequacy of existing selling techniques . . . I suspect that the majority comes from mis-directed salesmanship and deliberate "switching".'[50] But the warning was not heeded.

In the 1960s respectable fund managers like Dreyfus and Fidelity found themselves attracted to Bernie Cornfeld, a Geneva-based super-salesman whose Investors Overseas Services exploited the eagerness of those with piles of dollars to store them away in tax-free offshore mutual funds. Cornfeld sold US mutual funds on commission and was especially fond of contractual front-end load plans, which were to be purchased by a programme of payments, with the salesman collecting his 8.5 per cent commission on the whole deal up front. At one point Cornfeld's operation controlled $2 billion of assets, an extraordinary sum for the mid-1960s, before collapsing in scandal in 1968, having enriched many of its salesmen and executives but ruined many of its investors. Cornfeld was a deep embarrassment to the institutions that had dealings with him, but the tax-free contractual plans which had been his staple bore a family resemblance to personal pension plans.[51] And if mutual funds were to avoid becoming tainted by dubious fund touts, then they had to be prepared to invest in their own costly sales teams.

The personal pension plans adopted many of the practices of the mutual funds and unit trusts but with the plan purchaser having even less leverage than the small investor. The contributor was locked into a programme of payments and could only exit at great cost. The tax advantages of the pension plan seemed to compensate for the rigidity of the contract. Legislation to protect the purchaser and competition between suppliers did eventually discourage some of the more blatantly unfair arrangements. But, as Davis notes, many of the charges levied by the personal pension plan industry corresponded to real costs. Competition and legislation could not reduce these and sometimes actually increased them. When new corporate schemes were established in the period 1950 to 1980, the 'defined benefit' type of fund was invariably chosen, covering all or most employees, leaving the personal plans to those unfortunate enough not to have access to a DB scheme. Administration costs were quite low and marketing costs non-existent. Contributions would be deducted from the pay packet at negligible extra expense. But, as we have seen, notwithstanding lower costs these schemes also had their downside.

The corporate sponsors see the DB funds as an element in their general financial planning. In good times the fund can serve as a tax-protected shelter or offer a contribution holiday, in bad times winding up the fund and claiming its surplus, or anticipating its recovery, can serve as a crutch. While the *Wall Street Journal* notes that: 'accounting rules allow excess pension income to flow to the bottom line, where it can boost operating income and boost earnings,' the *New York Times* reported that the median company in the Standard and Poor 500-stock index assumed pension earnings of 9.2 per cent in 2000 when actual earnings were 5 per cent.[52] These ulterior calculations did not prevent DB funds growing when the stock market was buoyant but the sponsors were not single-mindedly concerned with good pensions or even fund performance. As we will see in the next section, they practised trade-offs inimical to the interests of scheme members. With an occupational DC fund, matters are different since the sponsor does not have to maintain any predetermined level of viability for the scheme. It would certainly look bad if the scheme bombed, but so long as the results are not too far below the average for pension funds then there is no problem. If a reputable commercial provider is involved and a consultant consulted, then the fund executives and trustees are in the clear. But this approach can also deliver poor returns to hard-earned contributions.

Miscreant Managers – and Employers Who Help Themselves

In the large corporate defined benefit pension scheme both trustees and managers are remote from policy holders while close to the sponsoring corporation. Two researchers into the functioning of US pension funds report the following characteristic exchange with the executive at 'Industrial Co' responsible for managing its pension fund: "'*Do you have any contact with the beneficiaries of the fund?*" "None whatsoever." "*It never happened?*" "None whatsoever." . . . "*What kind of reporting is done to the beneficiaries every year?*" "The legal requirement under ERISA." "*What does it look like on paper?*" "I'm trying to remember".[53] This study, undertaken by two anthropologists, describes an organisational culture in which pension fund executives were keen to limit responsibility, and hence blame; they therefore followed procedures and kept away from corporate governance issues. While communication with fund holders was minimal, much attention was devoted to nurturing good personal relations between trustees and fund managers. The pension fund advisers Keith Ambachtsheer and Don Ezra find the picture quite convincing and estimate that the fund management industry generally suffers from an underperformance of 66 basis points or 0.66 per cent per year which they consider 'highly material' since annual returns are in single digits.[54] Evidence to be cited later shows that pension funds often underperform the market by considerably more than this but, as experienced advisers, these authors are aware of the cost factors which tend to this result and are seeking to pinpoint the element of poor design and judgement.

There is usually a close relationship, as I noted above, between sponsors and managers. The sponsoring company and fund trustees will be coached in their duties by the fund manager and the latter will usually be part of, or linked to, a bank, insurance house or investment company. In these financial conglomerates there are, supposedly, 'Chinese walls' between fund managers and those underwriting shares for companies or lending them money. The laws against insider trading prohibit the use of privileged information for personal enrichment and the legal statutes relating to pension funds limit the scope for 'self-dealing'. But where there are complexes of interlocking companies self-dealing is harder to prove. And anyway commercial fund managers evolved a general style which was (and often remains) indiscriminately supportive of corporate management, because it would benefit the financial institution to be known as a helpful and cooperative concern. The institution can earn good fees by handling corporate public offerings, or negotiating corporate loans, or playing a part in mergers and acquisitions. In this situation money managers often opt to be passive shareholders or use their voting power at AGMs to endorse board proposals. If managers lack confidence in a company then they sell its shares, but the financial institution will normally be discreet about this. The sell-side analysts engaged by the financial institutions are notorious for their boosterism. Studies have shown that only about 1 per cent of their recommendations are to 'sell'; if they are unhappy about a stock they prefer to mark it down from 'strong buy' to 'buy', or from 'buy' to 'hold'. The main reason for this is that institutions realise that they need corporate business and good will. It is these very same corporations that will come to them to help carry out a rights issue or plan an acquisition. The financial institutions make fatter fees from these activities than from fund management. Since sell–side analysts themselves are dependent on the corporations they monitor for access to advance information they have a further reason for discretion. Finally, the major financial concerns wish to maintain or improve general market levels.[55] Large pension funds and pension fund managers use buy–side analysts to sift the propaganda emanating from investment banks and large corporations, but only the largest have the scale and resources to monitor the whole market in which they invest, leaving them somewhat reliant on the story they are receiving from the sell–side analysts.

The aftermath of the stock market bubble in 1998–2000 cruelly exposed the hucksterism of the Wall Street 'analysts'. A report in the first days of 2001 noted:

In the past few months as former stock market favorites crashed to earth, many top analysts remained maddeningly upbeat all the way down. Consider Mary Meeker, the analyst at Morgan Stanley Dean Witter & Co, who became known as the Queen of the Internet for her prognostications on electronic-commerce companies like Amazon.com and Priceline.com. In 1999, as internet stocks soared and new companies were taken public in droves, she made $15 million, according to news reports. Now that internet stocks are in pieces on the ground, she has become decidedly less vocal – but no less optimistic. In her reports, she rates all 11 internet stocks she follows as 'outperform' even though as a group they are down an average 83 per cent. Of the 11 companies she remains positive on, eight had securities underwritten by Morgan Stanley.[56]

The independent self-managed, mainly public sector, pension funds which have pioneered shareholder activism, occasionally dragging commercial managers along with them when things are really bad, do not experience the same pressures. But the willingness publicly to challenge management is a recent development and one mainly practised by a few high-profile self-managed funds which have developed the confidence and resources occasionally to buck the trend set by the financial establishment. And these flurries of shareholder activism do not change the structural character of commercial money management. The independent self-managed funds may be critical of the failings of particular CEOs but remain typically focused on short-range definitions of shareholder value. And their greater sensitivity to public opinion should not obscure their general commitment to the norms and procedures of the financial industry.

One of the most notorious cases of fund trustees doing the bidding of the sponsoring corporation came in the early 1990s when trustees allowed Robert Maxwell to use £400 million of pension assets in a desperate attempt to shore up the share price of his companies. No trustee was ever convicted over this affair, so it is a 'crime without a criminal'. An official report published nearly ten years after the event criticised, among others, Goldman Sachs and the accountants Cooper & Lybrand for having helped to make possible the plundering of the pension funds but no new sanctions were proposed. However, this extreme and blatant example of 'sponsor risk' prompted the Goode report (1993) to come up with proposals for a tightening of regulations, some of which found their way into the 1995 Pensions Act. Sue Ward, a member of the Goode Committee, observes that regulating the large number of occupational pension plans is an extraordinarily demanding task. The Occupational Pensions Regulatory Authority (OPRA) set up following the Act is, she writes, 'a much more limited body than that proposed by Goode' with vital aspects of regulation entrusted to other bodies or left without proper enforcement. Thus: 'Certain sections of the Act, covering indexation of pensions, and equal treatment, are specifically excluded from OPRA's ambit.' Furthermore: 'Though it can remove trustees if it decides they are unfit for the job, and replace them with others, it does not have a general supervisory role over the behaviour of trustees outside their statutory duties. Breach of trust is left to "private law" enforcement, that is by individuals taking the trustees to court, or going to the Ombudsman.' Ward concedes that there are inherent difficulties in regulation when there are many tens of thousands of plans, modest resources, and much reliance on good will:

> There is a fundamental problem with regulation, when something is vol-untary for employers to provide, and where they are not going to incur a profit – in fact they are going to incur a cost – when they do. Why should they bother? In that situation if you impose rules the employer considers burdensome – even if in fact they are plain common sense or good man-agement – some at least of them will find other ways of doing the same thing, or give up doing it altogether.[57]

In the United States the ERISA of 1974 set up the Pension Benefit

Guaranty Corporation (PBGC) to monitor the management of occupational funds; the PBGC is supported by a levy on the funds and its highly qualified staff have reason to make sure that funding levels are maintained. Britain does not have any equivalent to the PBGC. As previously mentioned, the Pensions Act also laid down a 'minimum funding requirement' (MFR). Although not scheduled to come fully into effect for several years, the MFR has been blamed by the financial services industry for dragging down performance by obliging funds to invest in a small proportion of long-term bonds. As noted earlier, the introduction in 2000 of a new accounting standard, FRS17, obliged companies to declare pension fund deficits or surpluses in their annual accounts, a requirement that was unwelcome to many and which prompted more companies to freeze, or close down, their DB pension schemes.

Because it was given greater powers and responsibilities than OPRA, the PBGC has been a more effective instrument for bringing the 'sponsor-related' problems of US pension funds to light. The latter have been analysed by Teresa Ghilarducci under the headings of 'healthy terminations', chronic underfunding of schemes, and surreptitious 'self-dealing'.[58] These practices mainly refer to the 'defined benefit' schemes. The 1974 Act, which supposedly guaranteed the security of pensions, nevertheless gave sponsoring corporations the power to nominate most trustees and to alter the rules of the pension scheme, or even wind them up when they deemed this necessary. The years 1975–89 were to witness the termination of 12,000 schemes, double the number of terminations in the years 1950–74.[59] While some were dictated by adverse conditions, others appear to have been 'healthy terminations' where the sponsoring corporation had the motive of dodging liabilities or appropriating a tempting surplus in the fund. As we have seen, during good times companies could store pre-tax gains in the pension fund. Corporations and trustees had, and still have, considerable discretion in deciding how big a fund should be if it is to meet its eventual liabilities. The fund's current liability, if wound up immediately, will always be much less than its projected future liability. The pensions paid to employees will be specified as a proportion of the last or best year, or years, of salary paid to them and it will take several years of contributions before their rights in the pension are fully 'vested'; prior to that they are only entitled to claim back a portion of their contributions. Since vesting entitlements and salary levels rise as employees remain in a company's employ, the liabilities chargeable to the pension fund will also increase substantially. When corporate finance officers come to estimate liabilities and how they will be met they have great scope for adjusting the respective figures. What rate of interest do they assume and what salary levels do they think reasonable? Present circumstances can easily be brought to bear on these calculations. If a fund is deemed to be in surplus, then the sponsoring corporation can take a contribution holiday.

The phenomenon of the 'healthy termination' could be prompted by a takeover or simply by a board realising that it was sitting on a gold mine. The termination of a pension fund would release assets both to employees (usually in modest amounts) and to the corporation (the surplus). An Internal Revenue Service (IRS) ruling of 1983 – No. 83–52, 1983–1 C.B. 87 – confirmed the sponsoring corporation's rights just at the moment when several were to find this convenient. Plan terminations were to release $20 billion into corporate coffers in the course of the decade, though from 1987 a 15 per cent tax was to be levied on these redemptions. Corporations terminating plans included Ford, Eastern Airlines, GATX and Santa Fe.[60]

Ghilarducci also identifies underfunding as a real problem. According to the terms of the 1974 Act, the liabilities of pension funds had to be insured with the PBGC and this body had to be satisfied that fund viability was being maintained by an appropriate level of employer contributions. Companies which encountered serious difficulties could sometimes persuade the PBGC to suspend contributions in the interests of survival. Alternatively such companies, with or without the approval of the PBGC, could adjust their calculations to reduce the size of the contribution needed to maintain scheme viability. Ghilarducci cites a case where a group of tyre companies that were in difficulties anticipated average future returns to the pension fund of 11.3 per cent at a time when IBM was anticipating a 5.5 per cent rate of return on its fund. Likewise, GM boosted its first-quarter profits in 1989 by increasing the investment return assumption in its pension portfolio and correspondingly reducing the contribution that had to be made to the fund.[61] The willingness of the PBGC to condone large-scale underfunding was justified on the grounds that the employees had a lively interest in the survival of their employer. A staff economist at the PBGC explained that there would be advantages in employees beginning to see themselves as, in effect, shareholders with a long-term interest in the company.[62]

The willingness of the PBGC to pursue its own 'industrial policy', as Ghilarducci puts it, marks a singular departure from the conventional Anglo-American understanding of fiduciary or trustee obligations. Its role as a guarantor and monitor allowed it to act in ways that would not have been permitted to fiduciaries. The willingness to consider a wider construction of policy holder interest could be seen as a positive precedent. But in many cases existing pensioners were short-changed in an attempt to bail out management. The PBGC was not set up to pursue an industrial strategy and had no resources of its own. When large steel companies were threatened with bankruptcy, the size of future pension obligations was a huge factor in the balance sheet compared with the write-down costs of plant and machinery; consequently, lenient treatment could offer an extra lease on life for the corporation – or a convenient way of offloading an obligation. If the company survived, those who were still its employees might benefit; but in the meantime it might have shed labour and shed obligations. Gordon Clark allows that lenient treatment could sometimes have been justified: 'LTV's strategy of pension liability shifting was probably one of the more benign management-designed pension-oriented restructuring strategies.'[63] The essence of this strategy was to rely on the PBGC to take care of the pension obligation and to use all available resources for company survival: 'LTV acted legally in pursuing its mergers strategy, but it did so knowing that the pension costs of this strategy might be ultimately borne by the PBGC.'[64] In this case the company's retirees were three times the number of its current workforce and pension liabilities totalled $2.3 billion out of total debts of $4 billion. At Continental Can management strategy singled out employees whose pension rights were close to being vested: 'Employees eligible for early retirement were identified and permanently laid off.'[65] International Harvester, the company founded in the 1830s by Cyrus McCormick, was found to have sold a subsidiary, Wisconsin Steel, to a concern that manifestly lacked the resources to assume its outstanding pension liability. The purchaser was a small environmental consulting agency with only twelve employees and negligible working capital. It was found that the calculation was that everything would be all right because 'the downside risk' was 'to be assumed by PBGC and the WSC's employees'.[66]

The workings of the PBGC guarantee, and similar IRS waivers, can be seen as classic instances of 'moral hazard' since they encouraged behaviour they were designed to insure against. Yet it should be recalled that the United States was going through a wrenching process of industrial restructuring. In France the numbers of steel workers also plummeted in the 1980s and there was distress in the regions involved. Because of French *dirigisme* and *répartition* the pension rights of French steel workers were better protected and the restructuring a little less painful. In the United States the 'industrial policy' pursued by the PBGC was better than no policy at all but still left many without a job and with prematurely terminated pension rights. Most of the employees of TWA or United Airlines kept their jobs, and eventually recovered their pension rights, as a result of lenient treatment from the PBGC and IRS; indeed United employees now own most of the company. But, even apart from the absence of wider social planning, there was something wrong with a system that concentrated rather than pooled risk. To lose your job because your employer goes bust is bad but to lose much of your pension at the same time is a double blow. To have permitted the pension funds to invest in the opening of other employment possibilities in their region might have been more justifiable in many cases. More generally, there are manifest disadvantages in workers placing their savings in the company which employs them, especially if this company is threatened with going under.[67]

The consequences of the practices itemised by Ghilarducci were prejudicial for policy holders. Those whose plan was terminated before their rights were vested were left with nothing, notwithstanding the contributions they had made. Even for those lucky enough to have vested rights, plan termination meant that their future pension, pegged to their salary or wages at termination, would be much eroded by inflation by the time they came to draw it. Any early termination deprives the policy holder of the inflation proofing and earnings-linking which is intrinsic to any DB, 'final salary' scheme. Attempts have been made by the Financial Accounting Standards Board (FASB) and by subsequent legislation to remedy some of the worst abuses itemised by Ghilarducci. Workers who have continuously paid into a scheme for five years were deemed to have vested rights under the terms of the 1987 Pension Protection Act. Directives and Statements from the FASB now require company accounts to calculate both the ABO (Accrued Benefit Obligation) and the PBO (Projected Benefit Obligation) of a company. But as the rules governing DB plans tightened the number drawn up fell, with employers massively opting for 401(k) schemes instead. In the next section we will see that – even short of an Enron-style collapse – individual DC schemes are plagued by high costs and low yields.

Investment Performance and Rates of Return

The performance of pension funds and mutual funds shows considerable variation but over the long run it is much more strongly related to costs than it is to investment returns. The money managers are paid fund management fees based partly on the size of the fund and partly on 'relative performance evaluation' (RPE), that is how well they have performed compared to their peers or a market benchmark – with peer benchmarks being common. Managers also have to operate in an environment where most of their assets must be liquid, where their performance will be assessed at quite frequent intervals and where the mandate will be up for review every one to three years. Retaining the mandate is more important than small rewards for outperformance.

A wide-ranging quantitative study of British DB funds by David Blake and Michael Orszag reveals their generally mediocre results:

> we found that the majority of (DB) fund managers delivered a very similar performance over time, suggesting evidence of possible herding behaviour of fund managers. Also, the typical UK fund manager underperformed the market average by 0.45 per cent p.a.: and this is before the fund manager's fee is taken into account. Furthermore only 42.8 per cent of funds outper- formed the market index. Nevertheless 80 per cent of all funds are within one percentage point of the average market return. This suggests that despite their claims to be active fund managers, the vast majority of UK pension fund managers are closet index matchers, yet charge fees for active management.[68]

This harmonised with another conclusion reached by these researchers when they separately identified the factors which explained the rate of return actually achieved. Pension fund trustees are legally required to stip- ulate minimum holdings in the various major asset classes, such as domestic shares, overseas shares, domestic bonds, overseas bonds, cash and so forth. Trustees make such recommendations on advice from actuaries and con- sultants, who take account of the maturity structure of the scheme and the holdings needed to meet the statutory minimum funding criteria laid down by legislation. Research into US fund management has long stressed that asset allocation is more important that stock picking. Blake and Orszag found that 98.47 per cent of the total return generated by UK fund man- agers can be explained by the strategic asset allocation: 'This is the passive component of pension fund performance . . . the overall contribution of active fund management was just over 1 per cent of the total return, which is less than the annual fee that many active fund managers charge.'[69]

The UK fund managers operated within a system which rewarded aver- age returns (or those just below average), but was risk averse. Less than 1 per cent of their assets were invested in venture capital concerns, and smaller companies or equity stakes were avoided. Fund managers knew that the consultants would not tolerate serious underperformance but nor would they reward outstanding success. Hence the rationality of herding behav- iour: if you are together with the rest you cannot be singled out. A *Financial*

Times survey reported that the interaction between managers and consultants had 'produced a rigidly conservative style of investment in the UK which, many outsiders believe, limits returns and is bad for pensioners'.[70]

However, consultants should not take all the blame. British unit trusts share many of the failings of British pension funds. David Blake and Allan Timmerman have compared the returns achieved by 2,375 unit trust funds over the period 1972–95 with those of the relevant benchmark index. They write: 'We find that the average UK equity fund appears to underperform by around 1.8 per cent per annum on a risk-adjusted basis.'[71] The British funds underperformed in the United States where they were unable to match the local firms' access to attractive new issues, timely research, cheap trading facilities and so forth. In their home market the managers complained of the fact that the range of shares they could pick was too limited and that in consequence most portfolios comprised only around sixty stocks. In these circumstances the British fund managers devoted resources to devising an extraordinary variety of overseas growth stocks.

British pension funds, influenced by the example of the unit trusts, place about 30 per cent of their equity investments overseas. A study of 247 pension funds' international equity holdings by the previously cited authors revealed that over the period 1991–97 they underperformed local benchmarks by 70 basis points, substantially more than was the case with their domestic investments. The source of this 'home country bias' was partly that the fund managers face 'information asymmetries' overseas. But even more important were their poor market timing and 'poor performance in allocations of funds between major international markets'.[72] The discovery that overseas allocations were a source of underperformance is interesting in the light of an earlier study by David Blake where he found that such funds made a disproportionate contribution to fund managers' fees: 'Fund managers typically charge an extra 0.5 per cent for trading in overseas securities. This additional charge provides an incentive for managers to engage in churning, that is, excessive trading in overseas securities. According to *Financial Statistics*, the overseas equity portfolios of UK pension are turned over more than twice as quickly as their UK portfolio.'[73]

In another study David Blake, Bruce Lehmann and Alan Timmerman find that basing the manager's fee on a charge of about 1 per cent of the size of the fund, plus various transaction charges, offers only a weak incentive to managers to improve performance – one which is outweighed by the risks.[74] Thus raising the size of the fund by, say, 8 per cent instead of 4 per cent would double the return to the fund but only increase the fee by 4 per cent. Other charges could have a larger effect and anyway the manager's main consideration, as noted above, will be mandate retention and what is believed to be safety-first investment. The tireless David Blake has also joined forces with John Board to come up with an overall estimate of the reduction in yield (RiY) resulting from charges on UK personal pension plans. The RiY amounted to 1.2 per cent each year for a 25-year plan and 2.5 per cent each year for a ten-year plan in 1999. Unfortunately, many who purchase these products find it difficult to maintain the payment schedules – after four years, for example, membership drops to between 57 and 67 per cent. Adjusting for policy lapses raises the five-year RiY to 18.2 per cent and gives an overall rate of return on contributions of minus 9.2 per cent.[75] These authors also suggest measuring shortfalls in terms of the difference between gross contributions before charges and effective contributions after charges on the grounds that this is more likely to be understood by the lay person. Where there is front-loading of charges, and because of compound interest, the reduction in contributions (RiC) will rise over time despite a falling RiY. Thus a plan with a 1.7 per cent reduction in yield over twenty-five years would produce a drop in effective contributions of 22.9 per cent.[76]

One conclusion reached by Blake and Board is that it makes far more sense to judge a pension plan supplier by its charges than by its investment performance record. For any given type of plan, charges vary by supplier in fairly predictable ways while performance tends to cluster and is unknowable (it does not correlate with past performance). Consequently, commercial providers should be compelled to publish comprehensive information concerning all charges and deductions, including trading costs. The investigations and conclusions I have cited have had a cumulative impact on British policy debates, and have led the framers of the stakeholder pension to attempt to limit charges (to be considered in chapter 5).

In the late 1990s the chief British fund managers began to fall to foreign takeovers from US or European concerns with larger resources but the problem of underperformance remained. In 1998 the median UK-invested pension fund rate of return was 3.2 per cent behind the All Share Index.[77] The normally placid world of British institutional investing began to be riven by discord:

> Merrill Lynch Mercury, the UK's largest pension fund manager, has denied claims that it was negligent in managing some clients' funds, but admitted it made some poor investment decisions. It emerged last month that Unilever's pension fund was investigating the possibility of seeking compensation from MLM following an underperformance of 10 percentage points against a benchmark set by Unilever in 1997.[78]

(For its part Unilever was to face irate policy holders who complained that it had misappropriated fund surpluses.[79])

In March 2001 the British Treasury published a report by Paul Myners which confirmed and amplified the by now familiar litany of criticisms of British institutional investment. After a perfunctory tribute to the industry, it found fault with the consultants because of their conservatism, the trustees because they lacked necessary skills or training, and the fund managers because of their herd behaviour, short-termism, weak results, timidity in tackling failing management, neglect of venture capital, and high/disguised charges. The report turned a spotlight on the 'soft commissions' paid to brokers and investment houses for their dealing and research services, pointing out that since these did not figure in the management fee, the institutional client rarely had any way of checking the costs thereby incurred. Myners, on secondment from Gartmore, was referred to in some sections of the financial press as a 'poacher turned gamekeeper' and many of his conclusions – a ban on soft commissions, training and pay for trustees, replacement of the Minimum Funding Requirement, greater clarity in fund management objectives, full reporting of charges, more willingness to invest in start-ups and so forth – were to prove highly controversial. However, Myners's approach was scarcely draconian. His recommendations envisaged a trial period of voluntary implementation, with legislation to follow if this failed to change matters. Clearly the intention of the report, to which we return in chapter 5, was to encourage the financial services industry to put its house in order. In the process, however, it had succeeded in showing that cleansing these Augean stables would indeed be a Herculean task.[80]

Several counts of the indictment of UK pension fund managers and trustees have also long been levelled at their US counterparts. Thus Diane Del Guercio has argued that the 'prudent man' requirement has persuaded trustees and managers to favour conservative investment strategies that concentrate on large, well-known companies since nobody is going to be found wanting in their fiduciary duty if they invest in Coca-Cola, General Motors or IBM. Stocks are chosen because of reputation and liquidity (they are easy to sell) rather than because of future potential. Del Guercio observes: 'what the courts accept as a prudent investment has been based primarily on the characteristics of assets in isolation, and ignores the role the asset plays in the overall portfolio.'[81] She points out that huge streams of institutional money have been used to create portfolios comprised overwhelmingly of blue chip stocks, with the inevitable result that these become overpriced: 'if a sizeable portion of investors choose stocks because they are "glamour" or "good" stocks, and not on the basis of objective risk characteristics, this may raise the required return on small unknown firms and lower the return for the well-known glamour stocks.'[82] In the mid-1990s there is little doubt that blue chips were trading at inflated prices for these reasons. During the dotcom bubble in 1998–2000 some small companies suddenly became 'glamorous' but this did them few favours when the bubble burst. Robert Snigoroff anticipated one of Myners's themes when he charged that US pension fund trustees have too little professional training, resources and staff and are thus not capable of properly steering their investment portfolios: 'there is a surprising lack of resources devoted to the pension fund's own internal management.'[83]

As it happens, the performance of the US pension funds during much of the 1980s and early 1990s was rather worse than that of their counterparts in the UK, as measured by returns. In the years 1981–92 British pension fund managers underperformed the market by an average of 0.3 per cent, only beating the benchmark indices in two of the years. But this was better than the record of US pension fund managers who underperformed the benchmark by an average of 3.0 per cent over this period, not managing to beat the index in a single year.[84] Of course the poor performance of the pension funds did not mean that the managing companies themselves were making poor profits. A factor contributing to fund underperformance in the United States as in the UK was excessive turnover or activity, generating fees for the manager. Fund managers may be unable or unwilling to invest in venture capital concerns or small companies but they often believe that they can spot market anomalies affecting the larger concerns, buying or selling ('scalping') their stock in anticipation of market corrections. But in chasing what often turns out to be the will-o'-the-wisp of a quick gain, they incur transaction charges which wipe out the fund's profit. It is this type of consideration which explains why 'inactive' US funds (with a rate of turnover of under 15 per cent p.a.) obtained a 30-basis points premium in returns over funds with a turnover of over 70 per cent.[85] The problem of such hyper-active 'churning' was to prompt an essay on the topic by the chief economist of the PBGC.[86]

It might be thought that the injection of massive, regular new funds into the mutual market via 401(k)s would have allowed a dramatic reduction in costs. In fact, management fees and other charges mostly rose. On the whole the rise of the 401(k) plans has coincided with a decline in the practice of 'front-loading', that is of levying an initial sales charge. Apart from its bad reputation, this practice was inappropriate anyway for those making a commitment to regular payments. But other charges have proliferated, relating to fund management fees, brokerage charges, administration and advertising. Average fees in mutual funds increased steadily from just over 0.8 per cent of assets in 1986 to just under 1 per cent in 1996, management fees rising by 11.8 per cent and other expenses by 22 per cent. Companies with heavy charges usually achieve a lower rate of return. As a wider choice of funds was introduced, many ancillary fees had to be met for auditing, legal work, brokerage, customer services and so forth. Competition for market share and name recognition led to heavy advertising. The SEC introduced Rule 12b-1 which allowed funds to charge advertising costs to current investors, using the argument that the latter would eventually benefit if more people joined their fund. The maximum permissible charge under this heading was 1.25 per cent of asset value but it was subsequently dropped to 0.75 per cent, with an extra 0.25 per cent to compensate registered representatives – unusual in the case of 401(k) plans.[87] The device of passing along the costs of acquiring new business to existing customers is also characteristic of the companies which contribute to the mutual funds 'supermarkets' run by Charles Schwab, Fidelity and others; barred from charging the new customers the distribution fee exacted by those organising the supermarket, they add it in as a service charge paid by all their customers.[88]

A study of the actual performance of US mutual funds in the period 1970–99 found that, prior to costs and charges, they outperformed the market by 1.3 per cent per year but that after costs and charges there was a net underperformance of 1 per cent. Transaction costs and expenses averaged 1.6 per cent of assets a year which, together with underperformance of 0.7 per cent associated with non-stock holdings (cash or bonds or real estate), explains the 2.3 per cent gap between gross and net performance.[89] Another study found that the managers of funds which underperform during the first half of the assessment period (usually a calendar year) have an incentive to take on extra risk in the hope of catching up, while those which outperform in the first half tend to shed risk and seek to 'lock in' their gain.[90] Herding effects are found in the United States as in the UK but the much larger scale of the fund market allows for a wider spread. While balanced mainstream funds hew to a benchmark there are niche growth products with higher charges and greater volatility. Those investing in mutual funds as part of a 401(k) might have to meet extra expenses for any change in administration or contributions consequent upon changing jobs and for the subsequent conversion of their pot into an annuity, though from the individual's point of view these costs could be absorbed by the tax subsidy received.

The large fund managers spend liberally on expertise, equipment and promotion. Globalisation has favoured those managers with the best sales staff and most expensive computers. When the UK's Mercury Asset Management, one of the top five UK money managers, sold a controlling stake to Merrill Lynch it was argued that Mercury would gain access to the 'thundering herd', as the US company's 10,000-strong sales force is known. Shortly thereafter, in December 1997, Merrill Lynch announced that it was hiring 2,500 sales staff in Japan previously employed by the failed Japanese house Yamaichi Securities. By the close of 1999 Merrill Lynch peaked at over 70,000 employees of all types world-wide. But already the company, under pressure from brokers like Charles Schwab, had realised that the web and e-mail were making its sales force too cumbersome and costly, and was investing huge sums in boosting its capacity to do business on-line. The paper economy had been burying Merrill Lynch's London offices under a pile of 5,000 research reports on companies world-wide every Monday morning – these were now put into hypertext and made machine readable. Its institutional offerings were assembled on one site – mlx.com – and another site – Multex.com – gathered together research.[91] When it comes to the new information systems, the resources of the large investment banks give them an edge – Fidelity spends $500 million a year on IT. The new technology enables them to process global market movements, to spot profitable new openings, to dangle customised bargains in front of clients, and to grade the latter according to their purchasing habits. State-of-the-art IT makes it possible to execute programme trades such as 'index arbitrage', or basket trading, which exploits the difference between prices on the current and futures market by buying and selling all quoted stock. Of course accidents can still happen – in late May 2001 a young trader at a London equities desk hit the wrong key when executing a programme trade just before the close of the market and brought the whole FTSE 100 down by over 3 per cent.

The money managers have spent more as more individualised pension schemes have appeared. They need to offer incentives to salesmen or brokers or 'independent financial advisers', and they strive to ensure name recognition by advertising. Standard textbook theory argues that providers of goods whose quality only becomes manifest over the long term need to advertise more heavily. The suppliers of personal pension plans are in just this position. Supposedly, this signals to the customer the confidence the provider has in the product.[92] Yet in fact the providers do not themselves know whether their stock picks will prove correct or not. All they do know is that the more customers they can sign up and commit to regular contributions the greater their fees will be. Thus the rational check on marketing spend is not confidence in the product but simply diminishing returns to advertising: at a certain point in a well-supplied market the new business generated by advertising dips below the cost. The threshold concerned is not very constraining because the pension providers will be looking not at the customer's outlay for the first month, quarter or year but for many years ahead. As noted above, once people have made their choice, they do not switch 401(k)s or personal pension plans very readily. So the large commercial providers of pensions become locked in a marketing-spend arms race, which raises costs and detracts from yield.

Competition in the financial sector presents monopolistic or oligopolistic features because large providers are better able to meet the costs involved. Some purchasers may feel that if they purchase a Fidelity product then they have acquired a stake in or guarantee from Fidelity. This is, of course, not at all the case. They have simply purchased a share in a self-standing fund which has a management contract with the famous Boston finance house. So the money spent on advertising reflects the strength of its sponsor rather than a fund's intrinsic resources. In 2000 the Net Net fund marketed by Framlington, itself a subsidiary of HSBC, lost 75 per cent of its value. The directors of Framlington were not out of pocket – in fact they shared a bonus of £75 million.[93] The large financial providers like to offer a gamut of funds ranging from the staid to the adventurous since in this way they also raise the cost of entry to their business.

While advertising, sales staff and computing power push up costs, so do extravagantly rewarded 'star' managers who scour the globe in search of speculative gain. Promotional campaigns dwell on investment performance, not costs, so managers who produce good numbers are at a premium. The rise of 401(k) plans in the United States and individual tax-favoured retirement savings vehicles in the UK has helped companies like Fidelity and Merrill Lynch to maintain or improve their ranking vis-à-vis the leading investment banks which do not deal with individual savers. But the retail providers can only cover their huge marketing and administration costs by charging higher fees.

Surely an extra 0.5 per cent or 1 per cent charge is no big deal? But this is to underestimate the impact of decompounding, the obverse of the 'miracle of compound interest' on which the salesmen like to dwell. Spread over forty years, an asset-based 1 per cent charge will reduce the size of an individual's 'pot' by 20 per cent (this is similar to 'the reduction in contribution' effect, cited above, elaborated by Blake and Board). While many mutual funds deduct charges equivalent to 1–2 per cent of assets

annually, large DB schemes and collective DC schemes have charges ranging from 0.15 to 0.30 per cent a year of assets. The annual expenses for
401(k) schemes have been found to vary between 0.84 per cent and 1.27
per cent, excluding loads, while the charges levied by TIAA-CREF range
between 0.29 per cent and 0.42 per cent, with no load.[94]

The term 'load' needs explanation, as do practices common in the
mutual fund and retail pension sector which disguise charges. Estelle James
and her co-authors, focusing on mutual fund performance in the year
1997, have explained the difference between what they term the 'total
fund expense profile' and the 'reported expense ratio', with the former
adding two extra categories to the latter, 'average brokerage costs' and
'annualised front-loaded commissions'. In 1997 the total fund expense
profile across all the funds came in at 1.85 per cent of assets compared with
a reported expense ratio of 1.28 per cent. However, if the expenses are
weighted by assets then these ratios fall to 1.43 per cent and 0.91 per cent
respectively, because the large funds with the most assets have lower costs.
Because most fund sponsors (i.e. companies like Fidelity and Charles
Schwab) are private they are not required to file returns which would make
it possible to identify when the reported expenses are incurred. James
notes ten problems with establishing cost levels:

1. Until 1996 there was no disclosure of brokerage costs.
2. Brokerage fees can cover research or other expenses of the fund or its
   manager (the 'soft commission' problem identified in the UK by the
   Myners report).
3. Some investment returns are reported net of cost.
4. Income from lending operations and securitisation can be offset against
   custodial and other expenses (managers don't just keep assets quietly in
   the portfolio but loan them out for a fee to other institutions for
   short periods).
5. The consolidation of shareholders in omnibus accounts makes it difficult to track costs per member.
6. 'Investment advisers temporarily waive some fees, especially fees of
   new funds, as a business strategy to attract new customers, but may
   later reinstate them; these temporary fees may not reflect real costs.'
7. 'The data set includes only funds that were still operating in 1997 and
   it therefore suffers from survivorship bias.'
8. Many shareholders pay a front-loaded one-time sales charge directly to
   brokers or other sales agents.
9. There is an 'invisible diseconomy of scale' caused by the fact that

when very large funds buy or sell a stock their action may be big enough to alter the price adversely.

10. 'Most mutual funds are members of a mutual fund complex (e.g. Fidelity or Vanguard). Certain activities, such as advertising and new product development, are jointly supplied to all members of the complex by the common investment adviser. The allocation of these expenses among the funds may be influenced by estimates of where the expenses can be absorbed with least loss of clients'.[95]

There is every reason to believe that individualised pension funds, many of which incorporate mutual fund share ownership, replicate these problems while also often adding to them an extra layer of charges relating to the stream of contributions and any changes in their amount or timing.

Employees in a good DB or large, collective DC scheme, with reasonable 'portability' conditions, enjoy better returns because they do not have to cover marketing expenses or many of the items listed above. Those in such schemes are thus generally better off than those relying on 401(k) plans for their retirement supplement. Employers like 401(k) schemes because they absolve them from onerous future obligations. And employees who lack a better alternative can still be happy because their scheme garners tax favours which absorb the extra charges involved. Of course from a public policy perspective the tax subsidies are really being swallowed by the financial services industry, which often enjoyed levels of profitability far above those of industry and services in the 1980s and 1990s.

Michael J. Clowes, editorial director of *Pensions & Investments*, summarises the impact of the rise of the 401(k) on the individual employee in the following candid terms:

> The switch to 401(k) plans has been a mixed blessing for employees. Those whose defined benefit plans were replaced with 401(k) plans generally lost in the change. Whereas before they had a set pension benefit paid for entirely by the employer and guaranteed not only by the assets of the fund and the financial health of the employer but also by the Pension Benefits Guaranty Corp., now they have an uncertain pension benefit for which they pay most of the cost. In addition, the size of their retirement income depends on how much they contribute each year and on their investment success with their 401(k) assets. Furthermore there is no Pension Benefit Guaranty Corp. to help out if poor investment results leave them with an inadequate pension. Finally, employees often spend all or part of their assets in their 401(k) account when they change jobs, thus devouring part of their future retirement income. On the other hand, many employees who had no pension benefits when there were only defined benefit plans, now have

some benefit coverage through a 401(k) plan. Many employers who would not start a defined benefit plan because of its cost and complexity started 401(k) plans which are simpler and less expensive. In addition, the employees can take their 401(k) assets with them when they change jobs, whereas in a defined benefit plan they usually had to leave them behind, sometimes to be collected years later when they ultimately retired.[96]

Employers are responsible for choosing which 401(k) schemes will be made available to their employees and, notwithstanding high charges and poor performance, Clowes notes that the 401(k) plan was 'still by far the least expensive pension plan for the employer to offer'.[97] As the markets went into a steep decline in 2000–1 those who had taken out 401(k)s found their retirement savings contracting by 20–40 per cent in less than two years. 'Aggressive' funds were hardest hit but all were affected.

The poor performance of many money managers in the 1990s led many to conclude that the answer was to invest in index tracker funds. Fund management fees would be much lower and fund growth much the same, leading to better returns. Some fund trustees and consultants were taken with this logic. But the trackers proved to contain hidden risks. It turned out that the leading indices had a lopsided character that was risky in the turbulent conditions that periodically swept the markets after 1997. Tracking led to disastrous stock selection. An article in the *New York Times* Mutual Funds Report by Gretchen Morgenson warned: 'Many investors may think they are protected from stormy markets by investing in a large-stock index fund. They couldn't be more wrong. . . . After years of soaring performance, investing on auto-pilot has gone into stall.' Morgenson explained that index funds had been obliged to pay 'outlandish' prices for new entry stocks, meanwhile reducing their exposure to stocks that had done badly; in other words, 'they are buying high and selling low'. The article also presented a table of the best and worst performing funds supposedly tracking the same index, the Standard and Poor 500. Over the period of a year there was a 5.1 per cent gap between the best and the worst, with many lagging the leader by 1–3 per cent, in a reflection of differing transaction costs, expenses and interpretations of the index tracking function. The trackers with the best results often invest in only a sample of the target index, declining to take expensive positions in illiquid shares. Such funds can approximate index performance while more faithful trackers lag the index. In the first quarter of 2000, for the first time in five years the majority of actively managed funds – 66 per cent of them – beat the S&P 500. In 1999 just under half – 47 per cent – had done so; in 1998 only 18 per cent, in 1997 only 11 per cent, in 1996 27 per cent, and in 1995 16 per cent.[98]

The performance of the main indices in the United States and UK in 2000 bore out the warnings offered by critics such as Morgenson and showed that passive investors would pay a stiff price in a bear market. Thus both the Standard and Poor's 500 index and the FTSE 100 index lost more than 10 per cent over the year while the NASDAQ dropped by a half from its peak in March. The passive funds did worst but the active funds, many 'closet trackers', were not far ahead of them. The *Financial Times* reported:

> Britain's fund managers had one of their worst performances for 25 years in 2000, according to figures released by CAPS, the performance measurement company. Only six fund managers – out of 65 that run flagship pooled with property funds – recorded a positive return. . . . Some of the best-known names, including Gartmore, Merrill Lynch Investment Managers and Friends, Ivory and Sime, failed to match the industry average. . . . Alan Wilcock, CAPS research and development director, said: 'The performance was very disappointing for pension funds. It was not just the managers at the margins (that underperformed)'.[99]

The same newspaper had warned in an editorial a few days earlier that the pension funds were courting danger since the main British indices were heavily weighted towards a few large companies: just three – Vodafone, BP Amoco and Glaxo-SmithKline – comprised 22 per cent of the FT All Share Index at the close of 2000. 'In the period to March last year [i.e. 2000], those pension fund trustees that entrusted their money to indexed managers were no doubt delighted with the outcome. But many of them were squeezed as index managers scrambled for Vodafone stock at its peak, which had become artificially scarce after its acquisition of Mannesmann.' Vodafone shares halved in price over the next twelve months.

> The damage done from these distortions would be limited if pension fund managers focused on the long term. Yet a third of all medium to large pension funds consider changing their fund managers every year. Many of those that fired an active fund manager in 2000 will have done so on the basis of bubble-distorted figures. As well as incurring costs on the change, they will have suffered post-bubble underperformance from the new passive managers.

Addressing what could be done about this, the *FT* observed: 'Too little attention has been devoted to the role of pension fund trustees and their investment consultants. . . . Trusteeship badly needs improving.'[100] Those firms offering indexed funds nevertheless managed to sell a lot of policies so that, overall, the size of tracker funds in the UK grew by 9 per cent – but for their negative investment return they would have grown by 15 per cent[101] – a momentum that will be assisted by the Labour government's Stakeholder Pensions, most of which are trackers, if they recover from their weak launch in 2001.

The collapse of many 'growth' stocks led to the rehabilitation of 'value' investors like Warren Buffett in the United States and Phillips and Drew (P&D) in the UK. While actively managed funds did significantly better than the index trackers, the value investors did best of all. The UK's P&D, bottom of the tables in 1999, moved to top in 2000, as a *Sunday Times* report explained:

> The world looks a very different place from a year ago. Last winter's unques-
> tioning faith in technology has gone. . . . This turn in the market has proved
> an immediate boon for value investors . . . P&D's chief executive estimates
> that the firm's returns on British equities last year were 7 per cent to 8 per
> cent better than the FTSE All Share index, and 4.5 per cent to 5.5 per cent
> better off than the average return achieved by industry rivals. In the cautious
> world of pension fund-management, this is a terrific result.

The report mentioned that several large clients had withdrawn after P&D did badly in 1999: 'Rough estimates suggest that the clients – such as Kent County Council – which abandoned P&D last year, may have cost them-selves £600 million.' But doing better does not remove the stigma of being different. The head of investment consulting at William Mercer, Andrew Kirton, was quoted as observing:

> 'A lot of us admire P&D's commitment to the way it invests money. But
> clients have had to ask themselves whether they can accommodate the kind
> of volatility that a value manager is going to bring.' Kirton says even one
> year of serious underperformance can impose real pain on a pension fund
> because of the need to meet the minimum-funding requirement test. Failure
> to meet this requirement could require higher pension contributions from
> the sponsoring employer.[102]

The ability of a potential purchaser of a 401(k), mutual fund, unit trust or similar vehicle to assess performance in turbulent times is reduced as the promotional departments get to work massaging the figures. Because each of the large providers has scores or even hundreds of funds, they will always be able to find some which have done a bit better. While attention is lavished on these, weaker funds will be amalgamated, rebranded or folded. In some cases successful flagship funds are closed to new members but reference to their outperformance still plays its role in company pro-paganda. Others are quietly wound up and their policyholders transferred to a new fund. In March 2001 the Lipper consultancy announced that over 200 funds had changed their name over the previous six months, with the word 'growth' or its cognates being widely jettisoned for the word 'value'. An article in the *International Herald Tribune* noted 'survivorship bias' in the public records of mutual funds. Thus in 1970 there were 350 equity funds but by 2001 there were only 186 equity funds with thirty-year track records. Thus industry-wide measures of performance relating only to these survivors will ignore the less happy fate of those funds which failed. Indeed, of the fifteen best-performing funds in the 1960s only four still existed.[103] There is solid research backing for 'survivorship bias' on both sides of the Atlantic. The previously cited study of UK unit trusts by David Blake and Allan Timmerman covered 973 dead funds as well as 1,402 live ones. They estimate that the average survivor bias – 'the difference between the mean return on the surviving funds and the mean return on the full set of funds' – was 0.8 per cent a year. This large bias, similar to that found in the US mutual fund business, underlined for them the importance of 'having access to the full set of funds' before assessing a rate of return.[104]

I have cited criticism of the pension fund managers for their conservatism but many of them allowed their funds to be drawn into the extraordinary stock market bubble of 1996–March 2000. To some extent, the herding logic could explain this. But as markets continued to soar in 1999 and early 2000 there were voices of caution and very little sign that any but a few of the money managers heeded them.[105] Private investors may have been even more prone to herd than the institutions, but then they generally lacked the information and expertise of the elite institutions. The latter, as we have seen, had a quite lucrative stake in high-tech IPOs but it could be that the structure of the fund management business, and the incentive structure of managers, made its own contribution. Smaller fund managers certainly saw the craze for new technology stocks as a battering ram allowing them to break into the big time with high-profile funds. And then the big companies themselves found that a punt on the technology stocks might work for them too. Basically the leaders of an oligopolistic financial industry discover, firstly, that they must respond to new entrants taking risks and then that they can bear these risks better than the newcomers.[106] A model like this might explain the really prodigious excesses of the bubble: not the dotcoms launched for a hundred million or two, but the tens or even hundreds of billions sunk in the global telecoms industry.

Whatever the performance of a fund, the time comes when it must be used to finance a retirement income. One way of doing this is to purchase an annuity with the accumulated fund. But here another source of risk and loss is encountered. The 1990s trend from defined benefit schemes to defined contribution schemes, and from plans covering an occupational collective to more individualised arrangements, exposes more and more policy holders to annuity rate risk. In the UK once a pension plan matures the policy holder is obliged to buy an annuity with 75 per cent of the pot. In the course of the 1990s annuities became increasingly expensive. Whereas £100,000 would purchase a 65-year-old man an annuity of £8,000 p.a. in the mid-1980s, by 1999 the annuity purchased by this sum was only a little over £5,000. Lower yields on long-term government bonds and increasing longevity both contributed to this decline.[107] Similar trends are at work in the United States. If US contributors to a DC plan wish to ensure themselves an income for life the most straightforward procedure is to buy an annuity. Yet, as Olivia Mitchell points out, 'the retail market for individually-purchased annuities is skewed by adverse selection because people who buy individual annuities are likely to live longer than the population average.' She continues: 'For this reason, a firm-based or occupational pension plan can afford workers a valuable precommitment device, namely access to a group survival risk pool early in life.'[108] Thus, if a group of employees enter a collective scheme in their twenties, then a proportion of them will die or disappear over the forty years before they reach retirement age and the contributions of these individuals will boost the eventual pension that can be paid to survivors. Less obvious, perhaps, is that in individual plans a portion of the gain from the contributions of those who drop out of the scheme accrues to its commercial organisers. Some collective DC schemes capture the 'wastage rate' gain for the employees but 401(k) schemes do not. As in the case of expenses of administration, the more collective the pension arrangement the better the deal received by the pensioner.

The Financial Cost Disease

The argument of this chapter is that pension sponsors, and commercial pension fund managers, often delivered a rather poor return to policy holders in the 1980s and 1990s. In some cases the sponsors exploited lax regulations for their own benefit, in others it was the pension providers who took advantage of deregulation. Poor returns could reflect the fund managers' attentiveness to the sponsoring companies rather than to the mass of policy holders. And as pension provision became more commercialised and individualised in response both to legislation and to the 'new economy', so marketing and administration costs took an increasing toll. Remedial legislation finds it hard to keep up with a financial services industry which is inventive and restless. The regulatory flaws which allowed for the Maxwell affair prompted many features of the UK Pensions Act of 1995, by which time 'mis-selling' and excess charges were more clearly identified as a problem, leading eventually to the stakeholder legislation of 2000, by which time the crisis at Equitable and the stock market slide were highlighting other risks. In the United States the Studebaker collapse led eventually to ERISA, which permitted 'healthy terminations' in the 1980s, prompting the 1987 Pension Protection Act; by which time junk bond scams and the S&L disaster were attracting attention, in turn arousing concern at the 'moral hazard' created by Federal insurance guarantees at a time when the next big threat to the integrity of the US financial system was to be deregulation and the hubris of the hedge fund managers and energy traders. Meanwhile legislation to improve DB schemes led more employers to offer 401(k)s instead, just in time for an orgy of bubble economics and the Enron collapse. The macro-economic implications will be explored in the next chapter but none of this has been good for policy holders, employees or citizens more generally.

So far as the pension funds are concerned, the problem is that they are still at the mercy of sponsoring companies and/or fund managers who have their own shareholders to consider and who are caught up in an increasingly deregulated and 'financialised' environment where traditional accounting and reporting standards no longer yield reliable information. When the whole market was rising the trustees and their fund managers could appear to be doing well. But pension funds have to withstand the test of the bad years as well as the good. Unfortunately the policy holders were powerless to ask awkward questions. As unions became weaker in the private sector it became clear that there was no constant and vigilant counter-pressure coming from the policy holders. The historic public sector pension plans could be, and can still be, rigid and constraining. But they do deliver better value in terms of pension provision. Their costs were kept down by the fact that they did not have to compete for members since participation in the occupational scheme was mandatory for most grades. Those which engaged commercial fund managers naturally had to pay a price, and sometimes found themselves locked into a financial network with a logic that led to below-par returns. But often they were obliged to give at least some representation to the unions and to the local authority.

Being a member of an Anglo-American pension fund in the 1980s or 1990s might be compared to taking an economy-class long-distance flight. If all goes well it gets you to the destination with some discomfort but without the luxurious trimmings, and limousine on arrival, of business and first class. If you can buy a discounted ticket the flight may be cheap but the route and schedule very rigid; otherwise your 'full economy' fare may prove to be very expensive. Many policy holders in a defined benefit, final salary, scheme arrived at retirement with a pension that had risen in line with their earnings, even though it lagged far behind those with stock options or a significant personal stake in finance sector shares. But those who had changed jobs found the value of their benefits plummeting. Even some of those who stayed with the same company found themselves with depreciating pensions if the scheme was underfunded and the sponsoring employer in difficulties – in the recessionary climate of 2001–2 this was to become a major problem. A DC scheme would be more portable, but just as vulnerable to a downturn and higher charges would make it much more expensive. Whatever the pension fund type, there was very little transparency. In terms of the airline analogy, the policy holder could be left in a crowded departure lounge not knowing what was happening but hoping that the regulatory small print would offer some insurance.

The pension funds could be sub-optimal in a variety of other ways, both to policy holders and in terms of the wider public interest, yet also furnish rates of return which encouraged funded pension provision and left policy holders in a better position than that of the great majority of those outside such schemes. The stock exchange booms of the 1980s and 1990s meant that the funds were almost bound to do well, notwithstanding a rough patch after 1987 and the fin-de-siècle roller coaster. Pension fund managers could achieve double-digit investment returns yet underperform the stock market. Pension funds need to deliver results over thirty or forty years, not ten or fifteen. If they underperform poor markets as well as good ones, as tends to be the case, then they find it difficult to meet this test. And spon-sors also find it harder to maintain their contributions during a downturn creating, for some, a problem of underfunding.

Poor returns are still much better than no returns at all. Many of those who retired in the 1980s or 1990s welcomed the extra help supplied by an occupational or personal pension. However, there were few for whom the private pension, by itself, would be their principal source of income. According to US figures for Social Security in 1998, the state retirement pension was in aggregate the single most important source of income for all except the richest 20 per cent of pensioners; for the less wealthy three-fifths it supplied, overall, more than 50 per cent of their income. Private pensions furnish a useful boost, raising some out of poverty but still leav-ing many on very modest incomes. Many of these pensions, as we have seen, were not protected against inflation. Of course, most in the lower quintiles receive nothing at all from private pensions. A study of pension coverage in 1988 found that 51 per cent of white men were covered in their current job compared with 43 per cent of white women, 42 per cent of black men and 42 per cent of black women. Interestingly, a higher proportion – 48 per cent of the black men and 49 per cent of the black women – had been covered in a previous job. Coverage of employees in large concerns was much better than for those in smaller companies, with 68 per cent of men and 60 per cent of women being covered in companies employing over 100 workers.[109] A study which focused on the incomes of the over-65s found that 57.2 per cent of married white males had a pension, compared with 44.3 per cent of married black men and only 35.4 per cent of married Hispanic men. For married women, the figures were 53.8 per cent for whites, 50.8 per cent for blacks and 53.5 per cent for Hispanics. While the median income for elderly white couples was $19,000, it was only $11,000 for black couples.[110]

The rising value of Anglo-American pension funds did not mean an increase in the quality of coverage. The numbers with supplementary pension coverage in the United States rose steadily from 9.8 million in 1950, representing 18.6 per cent of the workforce, to reach 35.8 million in 1980, representing 48.1 per cent of the workforce.[111] The absolute number of those covered by a DB pension scheme stood at about 40 million in the late 1990s but they constituted a smaller proportion of a larger labour force. While public sector workers continued to enjoy good coverage, the same was not true of the private sector where DB schemes had a stagnant membership. Short-term contracts and part-time employment spread in ways that did not favour pension coverage. Even those who paid into a scheme could afford only a little and might dip into the fund between jobs. DB plans accounted for 80 per cent of all schemes in 1979 but this fell to 50 per cent by 1996. The growing number in the 401(k) schemes are likely to reap inadequate pensions, because employers contribute much less, employees struggle to maintain payments, costs devour returns, and 'stock market risk' replaces employers' guarantees. Despite the spread of 401(k)s after 1983 a study of pension wealth found that for two-thirds of all US households it did not grow at all between that year and 1998, and that it grew only by 19 per cent for those at the 80th percentile.[112]

In the UK a similar pattern emerges. DB schemes have been in decline and the personal pensions which often replaced them were demonstrably inferior. Private pensions of whatever description can make an important difference to those who have them but the state pension remains the main source of income in retirement, notwithstanding the fact that its value relative to earnings has declined sharply since 1980. For the three least well-off quintiles (that is, the poorest 60 per cent) of married men, the state pension supplied the bulk of their income. Those in the fourth quintile were reliant on the state pension for nearly a half of their income. So it was only those in the top quintile (the top 20 per cent) who were able to live on private pensions and other property income. However, private pensions still played a role in lifting some above the poverty line – though not far above it – at a time when the state pension was falling behind national prosperity. In 1979 pensioners as a group had constituted 47 per cent of those in the poorest fifth of the population; by 1995–96 the proportion of pensioners in the poorest quintile had dropped to 25 per cent. But the numbers of pensioners in the next poorest quintile rose from 24 per cent in 1979 to 33 per cent by 1995–96, so 58 per cent of pensioners fell into the category of being in the poorest 40 per cent of the population. Thus married male pensioners in the next-to-bottom quintile received an average of just £22 a week from private sources but it was enough to push them into this category; their total weekly income was only £106, about 28 per cent of average earnings.[113] It should also be borne in mind that the numbers of the unemployed tripled between 1979 and 1995–96, so that the relative improvement in the position of some pensioners was as much a consequence of a general rise in poverty as it was of any improvement in the situation of pensioners.

Those with a stake in occupational or private pensions have been not just the better-paid, though the latter do of course take up their allowance. Members of trade unions and workers in the public sector – overlapping but not identical categories – are among those with the highest rates of coverage in both the United States and the UK. Also well covered are better-paid white-collar and professional employees. Most pension arrangements set a ceiling on tax-favoured contributions. So while the better-off do well out of pension schemes, some limit is set on this. The truly wealthy have other ways of avoiding tax, like going offshore. Those most likely to be excluded from pension plan coverage are poorly paid part-time and temporary workers, and those employed by smaller companies; some of these may later move to jobs which allow them some coverage, though not if casualisation proceeds apace. The impact of pension plans on tax arrangements is not progressive; most of the poor do not benefit, but much of the working class and middle class find that a supplementary pension makes a real difference.

While registering the limitations on coverage, the theme of this chapter is that even in the 1990s boom the pension funds delivered more weakly than they should have done, and failed to replace the state pension for most of those who were covered. The poor returns, we have seen, stemmed partly from risks of being short-changed by sponsors or providers, but also from the multiple costs of commercial provision and individual customisation in the saving and pension delivery process.

Some analysts of public sector finance argue that public services are afflicted by what they call a 'cost disease'. The generally labour-intensive character of, say, education or healthcare – sectors where the need for individual care and attention is paramount – limits the scope for raising productivity. With growing national prosperity, the salary cost of providing these services has to grow, hence the unjustly named 'cost disease'. With increasing numbers of persons over the retiring age, the expense of pensions is also bound to rise. But the administrative cost of delivering public pensions is not great. Matters are different with the private pension delivery systems, which are afflicted with what can quite properly be called a 'cost disease' of enormous proportions. They find it expensive to market their products, to manage funds, to cover transaction expenses and to keep track of contributions. Those whose pot is diminished by competitive excess have little choice; they are opting for this type of product because a good state scheme or occupational scheme is not available to them. It is still too early to know how 401(k)s will perform in the long run. The workings of UK personal pensions have been dire. Michael Orszag has pointed out that prior to delivery the typical UK personal pension has to be divided by three charge ratios relating to losses involved in: (1) fund management and administration (the *accumulation ratio*); (2) switching between funds (the *transfer ratio*); and (3) purchasing an annuity (the *annuity ratio*). He writes:

> Reasonable figures for the UK are an *accumulation ratio* of roughly 75 per cent (consistent with a 9 per cent equity yield, a 50 basis points fund management charge, and a 5 per cent annual fee), an *annuity ratio* of 85 per cent and a *transfer ratio* of 90 per cent. The total charge ratio is therefore 1–0.75 multiplied by 0.85 multiplied by 0.90 = 0.57, so that 43 per cent of the pension is lost in charges. In other words the value of a private account in the UK is roughly cut in half by administrative and other costs.[114]

Clearly these are calculations of average cost which only apply to commercially provided personal pension plans. Occupational defined benefit funds would provide better ratios and those that are organised in the public or professional sphere would be better still. The focus here is on overall delivery costs. From the point of view of the individual recipient, these can be outweighed by tax advantages, a good rate of return (if achieved) and the absence of alternatives. Most public pension systems are not pre-funded, and do not invest in the equities market. Although their delivery costs are very good their investment rate of return may not be. But from a social point of view the 'cost disease' which afflicts private pensions is highly significant since, even at far more favourable ratios than those cited by Michael Orszag, they would entirely absorb the tax subsidy.

Pensions have been described as a species of retirement income insurance. With threats to the level of public provision and the rise of individualised private schemes, there has been a notable contraction of the quality and range of insurance provided, notwithstanding the immense sums which have been given by trustees to the commercial suppliers. The insurance provided by today's DC-oriented schemes focuses on pooling risk among a cross-section of the population at a given point in time. The workings of capital markets constrain corporations from carrying risks related to future event shocks. Both the traditional DB schemes and classic PAYGO sought to insure against long-range risk, striving to build up reserves and carry out smoothing to this end. Large corporations increasingly decline to offer such insurance, leaving the individual employees with flattened and foreshortened protection at a time when 'event risk' and global turbulence are growing.[115] The classic retirement protection mechanisms were put in place after the system shocks of depression and world war. But they could be tackled because government, enterprises and trade unions had the authority and nerve to take responsibility for the future, to 'plan'.

A New Dimension in Alienation

The world of 'grey capital' is plagued by an absence of authority or commitment. Because the policy holders are deprived of a real say in the use of their savings they cannot use them as an economic lever to advance the interests of their families and of the communities where they live. Peter Drucker was right to prophesy that pension funds would be of growing importance but wrong to suppose that this would necessarily empower the working class. Indeed, what has happened is rather a reduplication of that alienation of the worker under capitalism of which Karl Marx wrote. The essence of this alienation, in Marx's view, was that the producers lost control of the means of production and found themselves increasingly oppressed by the products of their own labour. The modern twist on this is that employees lose control of their own savings and then find this money siphoned off to remote settings while their own neighbourhoods decay. Many of those covered by the original occupational schemes were employed by traditional smokestack industries which began to decline in the 1970s or 1980s. Yet trustee and fiduciary law prevented their pension funds from helping to furnish alternative sources of local employment. To prevent pension funds from being used to shore up failing concerns would have been reasonable. But to prevent pension funds from investing in local infrastructure or alternative employment was perverse. Instead, pension funds were allowed to become the reserve army of the corporate raiders. Certainly Michael Milken, James Goldsmith and other raiders of the 1980s and early 1990s found the pension fund managers a ready source of support and finance. Even some of the shareholder 'activism' promoted by pension funds was aimed at breaching the defences of existing managements, in support of raiders who promised, and sometimes delivered, more 'shareholder value'. Thus Calpers entered the lists to defeat and suppress the 'poison pills' which protected established boards from takeover – by, for example, triggering a flood of cheap options available to the defenders. As Teresa Ghilarducci explains, 'the stewards of capital – labor's capital – used pension funds in speculative investment activity, which closed plants and strangled communities.'[116] The Enron collapse of 2001, to be considered in the next chapter, was to show that labour's capital was still insulated from employee control and exposed to sponsor risk.

The pension funds have been awarded a fiscally privileged status by government to encourage their members to help themselves. Yet these members and their local or regional elected authorities are prohibited from exercising the power of a proprietor. Proprietorial capitalists necessarily take risks, committing their credit to producing a good or service for a particular market in a particular way. Because the world is constantly changing, they have to be prepared to innovate or adapt. David Harvey, following Marx, has argued that the financing of such entrepreneurial activity often requires 'fictional capital' which only becomes 'real' as the enterprise justifies the hopes and efforts placed in it.[117] Grey capital, hobbled by trustee law and nobbled by the financial industry, cannot play this role. If the pension funds were rooted in and responsible to working collectives, or the residents of a region, or the members of an affinity group, they might be capable of social entrepreneurship – of committing themselves to a project that met the needs of their community. If they had power perhaps they would make mistakes but, as it is, others make mistakes for them and no one is really responsible. Of course such a model of social entrepreneurship cannot exist simply at the level of one enterprise but would need to fit into an alternative overall framework to that of the frenzied and deracinated compulsions of grey capitalism. The volatility of grey capital, as we will see in the next chapter, now increasingly defines not just the 'Anglo-Saxon' model but the whole process of globalisation.

Notes

1   For state pension expenditure see Organisation for Economic Cooperation and Development, *Ageing in OECD Countries: a Critical Policy Challenge*, Paris 1996, pp. 38–40; for pension fund coverage see Richard Minns, *The Cold War in Welfare*, p. 9; for the value of pension funds in 2000 see *European Pension Fund Managers Guide*, vol. 1: *The Market Place, 2000*, William M. Mercer, London 2000. For Latin America see Juan Yermo, 'Institutional Investors in Latin America', in OECD, *Private Pensions Systems and Policy Issues*, Paris 2000, p. 213.

2   US Board of Governors of the Federal Reserve Bank, *Flow of Funds Accounts of the United States, Annual Flows and Outstandings*, Washington, DC, various years; *Promoting Prosperity: a Business Agenda for Britain*, Report of the Commission on Public Policy and British Business, London 1997, p. 97. In the 1990s the proportion of UK shares held by UK institutions appeared to reach a plateau and then dip, but this was because of the rising proportion held by foreign investors, a large proportion of which were also institutions: Paul Myners, *Institutional Investment in the UK: an Enquiry*, HM Treasury 2001, p. 27.

3   Keith Harper, 'BA under Fire for Pension Fund Raid', *Guardian*, 24 August 1999.

4   Simon Targett and Michael Peel, 'Pensions' Proud Tradition Loses its Pull', *Financial Times*, 19 April 2001.

5   *The Economist*, 15 December 2001; Michael Littlewood, *How to Create a Competitive Market in Pensions*, Institute of Economic Affairs, London 1998, p. 229; Elizabeth Wine, 'Even the 401(k) is No Longer Sacred', *Financial Times*, 21 November 2001.

6   Investment Company Institute Research Department, '401(k) Plans: How Plan Sponsors See the Market Place', in Robert C. Pozen, ed., *The Mutual Fund Business*, Cambridge (MA) 1998, pp. 402–10, and Cerulli-Lipper Annual Report, 'The State of the Defined Contribution–401(k) Market 1996', in Pozen, *Mutual Fund Business*, pp. 411–20.

7   The Government of the United States, Budget Office, The Budget for 2001; HM Government, *A New Contract for Welfare: Partnership in Pensions*, Cm 417, London December 1998, p. 21. See also Christopher Howard, *The Hidden Welfare State: Tax Expenditures and Social Policy in the United States*, Princeton (NJ) 1997, pp. 20, 26.

8   Rankings, *Pensions & Investments*, pionline.com web-site, 31 January 2001.

9   Vineeta Anand, 'Some Pension Plans Surpass Firm's Value', *Pensions & Investment*, pionline.com web-site, January 2001.

10 Targett and Peel, 'Pensions' Proud Tradition Loses its Pull'.

11 Catherine Sauviat and Jean-Marie Pernot, 'Fonds de pension et épargne salariale aux États-Unis: les limites du pouvoir syndical', *Fonds de pension et 'nouveau capitalisme'*, Association Recherche et Régulation, *L'Année de la régulation,* vol. 4, Paris 2000, pp. 89–116, p. 94.

12 Tom Nobel and Vefa Tarhan, 'Share Repurchases and Firm Performance', *Journal of Financial Performance*, no. 48, 1998, pp. 187–222.

13 John Grahl, 'Globalized Finance', *New Left Review*, no. 8, March–April 2001, pp. 23–48, p. 37. Note that the buying and selling of shares has more of an impact on corporate finance than 'flow of funds' information suggests, since the latter is a net figure subtracting buy-backs from rights issues and initial public offerings (IPOs).

14 E.Philip Davis, 'Pension Funds, Financial Intermediation and the New Financial Landscape', Discussion Paper PI-2010, The Pensions Institute, Birkbeck College, July 2000.

15 David Lanchester, 'Why Shareholders Chose Vodafone', *Institutional Investor*, vol. 25, no. 4, April 2000, pp. 33–40.

16 Charles Pretzlik, 'Gent Tries to Placate Investors', *Financial Times*, 25 July 2000.

17 David Blake has pointed out that the financial structure of the DB pension can be replicated using an implicit long put option and an implicit short call option on the underlying assets of the fund, both with the same exercise price which equals the present value of the DB pension at the member's retirement age: 'The put option is held by the scheme member and written by the scheme sponsor, while the call option is written by the member and held by the sponsor. If, on the retirement date of the member, which coincides with the expiry date of the options, one of the options is in-the-money, it will be exercised. If the value of the fund assets is less than the exercise price, so that the scheme is showing an actuarial deficit, the member will exercise his or her put option against the sponsor who will then be required to make a deficiency payment.' David Blake, 'Does it Matter What Kind of Pension Scheme You Have?', *Economic Journal*, vol. 110, no. 461, February 2000, pp. F46–F81, F64. While apparently more simple, the DC scheme will lead to the payment of a variable lump sum which may or may not be used to buy an annuity, producing a similar complex 'futures' structure.

18 Mary O'Sullivan, 'The Innovative Enterprise and Corporate Governance', *Cambridge Journal of Economics*, vol. 24, no. 4, July 2000, pp. 393–415; and for the 'Austrian School', see Andrew Gamble, *Hayek: the Iron Cage of Liberty*, Cambridge 1996.

19 Simon Targett, 'Global Custody 2001', *Financial Times*, 5 July 2001.

20 Michael J. Clowes, *The Money Flood: How Pension Funds Revolutionised Investing*, New York 2000, pp. 218–19, 248–9.

21   Robert B. Reich, 'Look Who Demands Profits Above All', *Los Angeles Times*, 1 September 2000.

22   John Scott, *Corporate Business and Capitalist Classes*, Oxford 1997, especially pp. 49–50. For the United States Michael Useem gives the following judgement: 'The challenge to the managerial revolution came with a novel twist. Ownership power was resurgent, but not from the original founder-entrepreneurs . . . The new exercise of ownership muscle came instead from major institutional investors, takeover specialists and financial professionals.' Michael Useem, *Executive Defense: Shareholder Power and Corporate Reorganization*, Cambridge (MA) 1993, p. 243. Further discussion of 'ownership-disciplined alignment' of management will be found on pp. 28–57, 234–8. For another assessment see Mark S. Mizruchi and Linda Brewster-Stearns, 'Money, Banking and Financial Markets', in Neil S. Smelser and Richard Swedberg, eds, *The Handbook of Economic Sociology*, Princeton (NJ) 1994, pp. 313–41, especially pp. 325–8.

23   Mathur Gaved, 'Ownership and Influence: the Debate about Shareholder Influence on Listed Companies', Ph.D., London School of Economics, 1997, chapter 9.

24   Ibid., p. 61.

25   Ibid., p. 107.

26   Alaistair Ross Goobey, 'A Rallying Call to Supine Shareholders', *Financial Times*, 5 September 2000.

27   Ibid.

28   John Plender, 'Butterfly Balloting Comes to the City', *Financial Times*, 13 January, 2001.

29   Leslie Hannah, *Inventing Retirement: the Development of Occupational Pensions in Britain*, Cambridge 1986, p. 113.

30   For this and other information about GE and its pension scheme see the website gecontract2000.com/pensionfact.htm

31   Jeremy Bulow and Myron S. Scholes, 'Who Owns Assets in a Defined Benefit Pension Plan', in Zvi Bodie and John S. Shoven, eds, *Financial Aspects of the United States Pension System*, Chicago 1983, pp. 17–36.

32   J.W. Harris, 'What is Non-Private Property?', in J.W. Harris, ed., *Property Problems from Genes to Pensions*, London 1997, pp. 175–89, p. 185.

33   *The Times*, 14 June 1997.

34   'Pension Move by Lloyds-TSB Rouses Fury', *Guardian*, 29 September 1997.

35   See the excellent account of this saga in Paul Foot, 'Taken for a Ride', *Guardian Review*, 15 November 1997, pp. 22–9.

36   Richard Nobles, 'Pensions as Property and Pensions as Contract', in Harris, *Property Problems from Genes to Pensions*, pp. 89–102, p. 97.

37   Linda Tsang, 'Scrapping over the Fate of the Fund', *Financial Times*, 26 March 2001.

38   The Lex Column, *Financial Times*, 23 April 2001. See also Targett and Peel, 'Pensions' Proud Tradition Loses its Pull' and Nicholas Timmins, 'Pension Decisions that Ministers May Pay For', *Financial Times*, 11 February 2002.

39 Dearborn Financial Planning, *Pensions and Profit Sharing*, New York 1999, pp. 4–5, 35–50.
40 George Helowicz, 'Pension Fund Investment', in Bernard Benjamin *et al.*, *Pensions: the Problem of Today and Tomorrow*, London 1987, pp. 83–115, p. 105. See also E. Philip Davis, 'Regulation of Private Pensions – a Case Study of the UK', Discussion Paper no. PI-2009, The Pensions Institute, Birkbeck College, London, and Richard Nobles, *Pensions, Employment and Law*, Oxford 1993, pp. 38-63.
41 Teresa Ghilarducci, *Labor's Capital: the Economics and Politics of Pension Funds*, Cambridge (MA) 1992, p. 90.
42 Albert Hirschman, *Exit, Voice, and Loyalty: Responses to Decline in Firms, Organizations and States*, Cambridge (MA) 1970.
43 Diana Henriques, *Fidelity's World: the Secret Life and Public Power of the Mutual Fund Giant*, New York 1995, pp. 224–6, 337–46. The self-exculpatory context should certainly lead to some caution here but reasons will be given below for accepting the general point that money managers are not solely guided by the interests of policy holders but also manage pension funds in ways found agreeable by sponsoring companies.
44 Kitty Calavita, Henry N. Pontell and Robert H. Tillman, *Big Money Crime: Fraud and Politics in the Savings and Loan Crisis*, Berkeley and Los Angeles 1997, p. 12.
45 Calavita *et al.* stress that systemic weakness, deregulation and fraud should be seen as complementary, not rival, explanations (e.g. ibid., pp. 17–45, 169–90).
46 'Union Forces Pru Pensions Climb Down', *Guardian*, 21 January 1997.
47 Jane Croft, 'Urgent Cases Still Waiting for Pensions Redress', *Financial Times*, 8 December 2000.
48 E. Philip Davis, *Pension Funds: Retirement Income Security, and Capital Markets, an International Perspective*, Oxford 1995, p. 236.
49 David Latzko, 'Economies of Scale in Mutual Fund Administration', *Journal of Financial Research*, vol. XXII, no. 3, pp. 331–9.
50 Harry McDonald quoted in Henriques, *Fidelity's World*, p. 113.
51 Henriques, *Fidelity's World*, pp. 141–51, 164–6, 175–8.
52 Floyd Norris, 'Guaranteed Profits: the Fiction of Pension Accounting', *New York Times*, 7 December 2001; Ellen R. Schultz, 'Companies Find Host of Ways to Pare Retirement Earnings', *Wall Street Journal*, 27 July 2000. Quoted in Daniel Ben-Ami, *Cowardly Capitalism: the Myth of the Global Financial Casino*, Chichester and New York 2001, p. 120, where examples from the US and UK are cited.
53 William M. O'Barr and John M. Conley, *Fortune and Folly: the Wealth and Power of Institutional Investing*, Homewood (IL) 1992, p. 107.
54 Keith P. Ambachtsheer and D. Don Ezra, *Pension Fund Excellence: Creating Stakeholder Value*, New York 1998, p. 14–15.
55 See Charles Batchelor, 'Analysts' Reports: to be Taken with a Large Pinch of Salt', *Financial Times*, 26 July 2000, and 'Selling Bull', *The Economist*, 14 November 1998.

56 Gretchen Morgenson, 'Analysts: Salesmanship Takes Precedence over Research', *International Herald Tribune*, 2 January 2001. This report was taken from the *New York Times*.

57 Sue Ward, 'Regulation of Pensions in the UK', in Gerard Hughes and Jim Stewart, eds, *The Role of the State in Pension Provision: Employer, Regulator, Provider*, Boston 1999, pp. 63–74, pp. 66, 68.

58 Ghilarducci, *Labor's Capital*, pp. 85–110.

59 Ibid., p. 87.

60 Ibid., pp. 90-1.

61 Ibid., pp. 95, 102-3.

62 Richard Ippolito, 'The Labor Contract and True Economic Pension Liabilities', *American Economic Review*, vol. 75, no. 5, December 1985, pp. 1031–43.

63 Gordon L. Clark, *Pensions and Corporate Restructuring in American Industry*, Baltimore (MD) 1993, p. 36.

64 Ibid., p. 133.

65 Ibid., p. 38.

66 Ibid., p. 110.

67 Ghilarducci, *Labor's Capital*, pp. 95-7.

68 David Blake and J. Michael Orszag, *Towards a Universal Funded Second Pension*, Birkbeck College, University of London, October 1997, p. 9.

69 Ibid., pp. 9–10. For the US see David Swenson, *Pioneering Portfolio Management*, Glencoe (IL) 2000, p. 53.

70 William Lewis, 'The Closed World of Pensions', *Financial Times*, 7–8 June 1997, Money Section.

71 David Blake and Allan Timmerman, 'Mutual Fund Performance: Evidence from the UK', *European Finance Review*, 2, 1998, pp. 57–77, p. 58.

72 Allan Timmerman and David Blake, 'Determinants of International Portfolio Performance', Discussion Paper PI-2011, The Pensions Institute, Birkbeck College, September 2000, p. 2.

73 Blake, *Pension Schemes and Pension Funds in the UK*, p. 440.

74 David Blake, Bruce Lehmann and Alan Timmerman, 'Performance Clustering and Incentives in the UK Pension Fund Industry', Discussion Paper PI-9901, The Pensions Institute, Birkbeck College, London.

75 David Blake and John Board, 'Measuring Value Added in the Pensions Industry', *The Geneva Papers on Risk and Insurance*, vol. 24, no. 4, October 2000, pp. 539–67, p. 544.

76 Ibid., p. 543.

77 'Pension Returns Hit 15 Year Low', *Guardian*, 5 April 1999.

78 'MLM Denies Negligent Fund Management', *Financial Times*, 19 April 1999.

79 'Unilever Soft Soaps its Pensioners', *Daily Telegraph*, 2 April 2000.

80 Myners, *Institutional Investment in the UK: an Enquiry*.

81 Diane Del Guercio, 'The Distorting Effect of the Prudent Man Laws on Institutional Equity Investment', *Journal of Financial Economics*, vol. 40, 1996, pp. 31–62, p. 32.

82 Ibid., p. 33.
83 Robert Snigoroff, 'The Economics of Active Management', *Journal of Portfolio Management*, vol. 26, no. 2, Winter 2000, pp. 16–24, p. 22.
84 Davis, *Pension Funds*, p. 155. This was part of a broader picture of institutional underperformance, see Josef Lakonishok, Andrei Scheifer and Robert W. Vishny, 'The Structure and Performance of the Money Management Industry', *Brookings Papers on Economic Activity, Microeconomics*, 1992, pp. 339–79.
85 Ibid., p. 156.
86 R.A. Ippolito and J.A. Turner, 'Turnover Fees and Pension Plan Performance', *Financial Analysts Journal*, November–December 1987, pp. 16–26.
87 Alfred Fredman and Russ Wiles, 'Sorting Out Costs', in Pozen, *Mutual Fund Business*, pp. 516–25; Jason Zweig, 'Your Funds May be Making You Rich . . . But You're Also Being Robbed', in Pozen, *Mutual Fund Business*, pp. 531–7. This reader also contains an attempt to contextualise these developments in ways that justify them: Lipper Analytical Services, 'The Third White Paper: Are Mutual Fees Reasonable?', in Pozen, *Mutual Fund Business*, pp. 538–47.
88 Ellen E. Schultz and Vanessa O'Connell, 'No Free Lunch: "Supermarket" Fees Lift Costs', *Wall Street Journal*, 18 September 1996.
89 Russ Wermers, 'Mutual Fund Performance: an Empirical Decomposition into Stock-picking Talent, Style, Transaction Costs, and Expenses', *Journal of Finance*, vol. 55, no. 4, August 2000, pp. 1655–703.
90 K.C. Brown, W.V. Harlow and L.T. Starks, 'Of Tournaments and Temptations: an Analysis of Managerial Incentives in the Mutual Fund Industry', *Journal of Finance*, vol. 51, 1996, pp. 85–110.
91 'Merrill Lynch's Internet Conversion', *The Economist*, 9–15 June 2001.
92 For example David Begg, Stanley Fischer and Rudiger Dornbush, *Economics*, 4th edn, London and New York 1994, p. 170, but note too p. 169 on the role of advertising in building up a range of brands and thus deterring new entrants. These authors later observe: 'Since a large fraction of the stock market is held by pension funds and insurance companies which will eventually make payments to workers, monopoly profits may indirectly pay income to some relatively poor people' (p. 296). Clearly this ignores monopoly power in financial intermediation. The sort of costs I have explored above are likely to wipe out these supposed gains from monopoly.
93 Kirstie Hamilton, 'Top Framlington Executives Share out £75 Million Bonus', *Sunday Times*, 15 April 2001.
94 Olivia Mitchell, 'Administration Costs in Public and Private Systems', in Martin Feldstein, ed., *Privatizing Social Security*, Chicago 1998, pp. 403–52, pp. 433, 440, 449.
95 Estelle James, Gary Frier, James Smalhout and Dimitri Vittas, 'Mutual Funds and Institutional Investments: What is the Best Way to Set Up Individual

Accounts in a Social Security System?', National Bureau of Economic Research, Cambridge (MA), March 1999, pp. 9–10.

96 Michael J. Clowes, *The Money Flood: How Pension Funds Revolutionized Investing*, New York 2000, p. 272.

97 Ibid., p. 268. For the weak performance of the most popular 401(k) plans see pp. 259–60.

98 Gretchen Morgenson, 'Why an Index Isn't a Mirror of the Market', *New York Times*, Mutual Funds Report, 9 April 2000.

99 Simon Targett, 'Top Fund Managers Suffer Poor Results', *Financial Times*, 23 January 2001.

100 'Benchmarks and Bubbles', *Financial Times*, 9 January 2001.

101 Barry Riley, 'Portfolio Managers Face Cyclical Dilemma', *Financial Times*, 24 January 2001.

102 Paul Durman, 'After Much Suffering During the Technology Boom Value Investors are Suddenly Back in Fashion – and Profit', *Sunday Times*, 7 January 2001.

103 Conrad de Aenile, 'Survivorship Bias: Dead Mutual Funds Don't Count in Industry Measures', *International Herald Tribune*, 31 March 2001.

104 Blake and Timmerman, 'Mutual Fund Performance: Evidence from the UK', pp. 58, 75. For the US see S.J. Brown, W. Goetzman, R.G. Ibbotson and S.A. Ross, 'Survivorship Bias in Performance Studies', *Review of Financial Studies*, vol 4, 1992, pp. 111–42.

105 Alaistair Ross Goobey, 'Followers of the Internet Fashion Beware', *Financial Times*, 2 March 2000. In this piece the chief executive of one of London's large pensions managers chided his colleagues for their 'lemming-like' investment decisions. The most thorough study of the psychology of the end of the century bubble is Robert Shiller's *Irrational Exuberance*, Princeton (NJ) 2000, a work the more impressive for having been sent to press while the mania was at its height. It would have been interesting, however, to have had more in this work on the role of the institutional investors.

106 Frederick Palomino, 'Relative Performance Equilibrium in Finance Markets', CEPR Discussion Paper no. 1993, London 1998.

107 Philip Coggan, 'Age of Discontent', *Financial Times*, 11 August 2000.

108 Olivia Mitchell, 'Developments in Pensions', PRC WP 98-4, Pension Research Council, Wharton School, University of Pennsylvania, 1998, p. 8.

109 Sophie M. Korczyk, 'Gender Issues in Employer Pensions Policy', in Richard V. Burkauser and Dallas L. Salisbury, *Pensions in a Changing Economy*, Washington, DC, 1993, pp. 56–66, pp. 60, 64.

110 Donald Snyder, 'The Economic Well-Being of Retired Workers by Racial Hispanic Origin', in Burkauser and Salisbury, *Pensions in a Changing Economy*, pp. 67–78, pp. 71, 77.

111 Alicia Munnell, *The Economics of Personal Pensions*, Washington 1982, p. 109.

112 Richard Ippolito, *Pension Funds and Employee Performance: Evidence, Analysis and Policy*, Chicago 1997, p. 79; Jeff Madrick, 'For Most in US No Pension Windfalls', *New York Times*, 22 February 2002.

113 Report by the Pension Provision Group, *We All Need Pensions – the Prospects for Pension Provision*, Stationery Office, London 1998, pp. 18, 21.
114 J. Michael Orszag, 'Individual Accounts: Lessons from the UK Experience', paper presented at a White House Conference in December 1998, available on the web-site Network Democracy Social Security Briefing Book. The depletion of fund values wrought by these ratios is further explained in Mamta Marthi, J. Michael Orszag and Peter R. Orszag, 'Administative Costs under a Decentralised Approach to Individual Accounts', in Robert Holzmann and Joseph Stiglitz, eds, *New Ideas About Old Age Security*, Washington (DC) 2001, pp. 308–35, p. 316.
115 On pensions as insurance see Zvi Bodie, 'Pensions as Retirement Income Insurance', *Journal of Economic Literature*, vol. 28, 1990, pp. 28–49; and on the impact of the economic environment on corporations see F. Allen and D. Gale, 'Financial Markets, Intermediaries and Inter-temporal Smoothing', *European Economic Review*, vol. 39, 1995, pp. 179–209. See also Davis, 'Pension Funds, Financial Intermediation and the New Financial Landscape', pp. 17–18.
116 Ghilarducci, *Labor's Capital*, p. 130.
117 David Harvey, *The Limits to Capital*, London 1999, pp. 95–6, 265–71, 276–80, 300–9.

3

Pension Funds and 'Anglo-Saxon Economics'

Within Enron, according to documents made public Monday, traders used strategies with the code names Fat Boy, Ricochet, Get Shorty, Load Shift and Death Star to increase Enron's profit from trading power in California – techniques that increased the cost of electricity as well as congestion on power transmission lines.
(Richard Oppel Jr. and Jeff Gerth, 'Enron Forced Up California Energy Prices, Memos Show', *New York Times*, 8 May 2002.)

Spitzer's 10-month investigation into Wall Street's generally mediocre performance focussed on Merrill Lynch's vaunted team of Internet analysts. What he learned from 30,000 internal e-mails is that at the height of the dot-com mania only the clients were deluded, not the analysts. In these e-mails, Merrill analysts routinely dismissed stocks recommended by the firm as a 'powder keg', a 'piece of junk' or worse.
'Mischief on Wall Street', New York Times, *International Herald Tribune*, 12 April 2002.)

It is a serious mistake for public figures to acquiesce in the stock market valuations we have seen recently; to remain silent about the implications of such high valuations, and to leave all commentary to market analysts who specialize in the nearly impossible task of forecasting the market over the short term and who share interests with the investment banks and brokerage firms. The valuation of the stock market is an important national – even international – issue. All our plans for the future, as individuals and as a society, hinge on our perceived wealth, and plans can be thrown into disarray if much of that wealth evaporates tomorrow. The tendency of speculative bubbles to grow and then contract can make for very uneven distribution of wealth. It may even cause many of us, at times, to question the very viability of our capitalist and free market institutions.
(Robert J. Shiller, *Irrational Exuberance*, Princeton, 2000)

Maxwell Companies' Pensioners, 1992 (Reuters)

The pension funds have played an indispensable, albeit discreet, role in the evolution of the Anglo-American or 'Anglo-Saxon' economic model. The corporate pension schemes helped to underpin the surge of growth in the 1950s and 1960s; in this 'golden age' the 'welfare enterprise' developed as a complement to the welfare state. With the onset of a more troubled period of 'stagflation' from the early 1970s, the pension funds maintained their holdings in a wide range of established 'blue chip' companies because this was consistent with the dictates of prudence. For safety, the fund managers would also invest in government bonds — these actually gave a better rate of return than equities in the early 1970s. And to diversify their portfolio and pep up performance the managers would back real estate developers or buy junk bonds or foreign assets. The willingness to invest in junk bonds and to back the corporate raiders of the 1980s made the fund managers into the accomplices of those who downsized industry. However, throughout the 1980s and 1990s the core holdings of the funds continued to be stock in the Standard and Poor 500 or, in the British case, shares in the FTSE 100. By the 1990s this dull fare was spiced up by the acquisition of overseas privatisation issues or some dabbling in 'emerging markets'. As the century and millennium were ending, the money managers discovered — and stampeded into — new technology stocks, only to stampede out of them as the bubble burst.

Over three or four decades the money managers were much better at moving resources away from declining sectors and regions than at fostering the growth of new productive complexes. From the mid-1970s the large Anglo-American corporations were not themselves the source of innovation and began to cut back on both investment and employment. They sought to withstand East Asian and European competition by exploiting their strong market position and their already developed production facilities. The money managers went along with this not wholly unsuccessful rearguard action, no doubt believing that they had no alternative. In an emblematic development the largest industrial corporations in the United States and the UK — Jack Welch's GE and Arnold Weinstock's GEC — elected to turn their corporations away from engineering and towards finance. The money managers also helped to promote such an involution when they backed the corporate raiders and underwrote a wave of mergers and acquisitions. The corporate raiders' strategy was to take over traditional concerns and restore profitability by cutting outlays to the bone while siphoning off remaining cash flow to other purposes. This process could be financially quite successful without giving birth to new businesses. Much of the diversification in the 1980s went into reflector-glass office blocks or showy shopping malls or overseas investment. By the 1990s the pursuit of shareholder value and the pressure for share buy-backs also discouraged many big corporations from large-scale investments. Only at the very end of the decade was there a willingness to invest in the ill-fated 'new economy'. For two decades Wall Street played a negligible role in fostering new technology. The financial industry's obsession with global brand-name companies and privatisation stocks, asset-stripping and secur-itisation showed good returns but an earlier and more consistent investment in new technology could have done better. As it was, the roller-coaster ride of companies which relied on NASDAQ listings did little good to those involved. Meanwhile the fund managers channelled pension money towards hedge funds, energy traders and credit derivatives only to discover belatedly the new, concentrated risk involved.[1]

Secrets of the Anglo-Saxon Model

Notwithstanding well-known stereotypes – 'free market' Anglo-Saxon economics versus Japanese or French *dirigisme*, or German corporatism – public expenditure in the United States did far more to encourage tech-nological advance than did its financial institutions. And in some crucial areas – higher education and the military – the absolute and per capita levels of public spending were far ahead of those found in the other lead-ing states. These public expenditures were hugely important in seeding the component parts of the 'new economy', from computers to biotechnology, the web to miniaturisation. Publicly financed bodies – and not-for-profit incubators of new technology attached to university development parks – had the stamina and commitment to pursue new technical possibilities, qualities which many Anglo-American companies notably lacked.[2] The web itself was the product of university-based research groups, and Tim Berners Lee, the man who did most to perfect it, understood that seeking to put commercial limitations on it would destroy its potential.[3] And while commercial software giants sought to colonise cyber-space, the 'open source' movement has developed Linux, a highly successful operating system, owned by no one and given away free, yet preferred by many to Microsoft equivalents.[4] In Britain the success of pharmaceuticals, in contrast to the disappointing performance of other main industrial sectors, was helped by the purchasing policies of the country's National Health Service as well as by the historic research strengths of its universities.

The mainstream financial institutions based in New York and Boston – and the pension funds which they managed – did not even do much to promote the commercialisation of advances in information technology, usually leaving this to new start-ups in outlying locations. The Kansas-based money manager Janus, founded in the 1980s and owned by a railway company (Kansas City Southern), was quite exceptional in spotting the first stirrings of the new economy in the early 1990s, hugely outperforming its rivals in consequence. The West Coast did produce some successful development banks, like Hambrecht and Quist in San Francisco, and commercial internet incubators such as Campsix (San Francisco) and Ignition (Seattle), but the older financial centres were left far behind. The retail financial concerns, like the brokers Charles A. Schwab, maintained offices in California to tap into the state's burgeoning personal wealth, but in the 1990s they discovered a lucrative new vocation there as venture capitalists, enabling them to reposition themselves in the Wall Street hierarchy.

However, Fidelity and Merrill Lynch, which showed no particular prescience about 'new technology', and which concentrated on the short-term pursuit of 'shareholder value' throughout the 1980s and 1990s, managed to lever themselves into the 'bulge bracket' of top Wall Street companies during this time. The secret of their success was their ability to attract both pension funds and small savers, notably those opting for tax-favoured vehicles like the 401(k) and IRAs (Individual Retirement Accounts). Their predominant investment strategies contrived to be both conservative – in the sense of concentrating on well-known brands and blue chip companies – and speculative – in the sense that they would slavishly follow market fads, helping to drive stock exchange prices far above historic price/earnings ratios and, indeed, far above the level thought appropriate by Alan Greenspan, the chairman of the Federal Reserve Bank who famously attacked the market's 'irrational exuberance' in early 1997.[5] The major institutions were easily discouraged and unimaginative when it came to the long-term and arduous endeavour of investing in productive innovation or in social regeneration. But they were indefatigable and highly ingenious when it came to devising new financial instruments and new ways of commodifying assets or securitising income streams. They invariably prefer buying publicly quoted shares, which can contribute to price bubbles, rather than taking an equity stake, which contributes resources for real investment.

Notwithstanding the thirty- or forty-year period over which pension policies mature, most trustees believed that they would be vulnerable to challenge if they sought to formulate strategies for transforming the pattern of an industry or region, with complementary and sequential investments. And such an approach would not even occur to the commercial money managers since they needed to produce good quarterly and yearly figures. The benchmark performance used by consultants and trustees would be that of the major stock market indices, so the best policy was to invest in the corporations comprising them, perhaps altering the composition marginally or finding a small side bet with a tiny sliver of funds. Of course once businesses like Microsoft and Amazon.com were thriving, then the institutions piled in – and piled out when unsettling news came along. Some large corporations did develop their own internal telematic networks to cope with problems of data processing, procurement and marketing; but these 'intranets' did not add together and even blocked the emergence of the internet. The 'new technology' revolution drew on the inspiration of a myriad micro-entrepreneurs who tapped into decades of university research, drew on locally improvised finance and linked up with collaborators around the world. The size of the US market was, nevertheless, certainly a further, decisive factor for the first commercial applications of NT; most of those applications are about transactional gains in how the market works, whether it is business to consumer or business to business. This means that some of the major application breakthroughs are only likely to be made in a market that is large and buoyant – the latter condition being absent during much of the period 1975–94 – or one where there is the sort of concerted effort to achieve social and economic advance seen in the early postwar period.

The new technology did not emerge from the already existing large corporations but was linked to the emergence of new enterprises, usually located far from the traditional financial centres. Most of the pension funds were run by Wall Street or the City of London and were therefore implicated in the siphoning away of resources from industrial giants and the failure to sponsor new economic complexes. The performance of the US pension funds, however, was not monolithic, since some of them were not run by Wall Street money managers. Supposedly, US pension funds as a whole devoted 5 per cent of their assets in the 1990s to venture capital projects, compared with 0.5 per cent in the case of the British pension funds (more on the implications of the dismal British figure below).[6] But such figures relate to venture capital projects of all types, and they reflect the disproportionate contribution of the self-managed public employee funds. The public sector funds and multi-employer trade union funds on the West

Coast – they included such large funds as Calpers, the California State Teachers Retirement System, the Regents of the University of California, the Washington State board, Oregon State Employees Retirement System and the West Coast Teamsters Fund – both made their own specific investments in the local economy and boosted the resources available to local financial institutions, like Brentwood Venture Capital or Redpoint.

Another section of the pension funds played a specific role in the time of troubles, namely the defined benefit schemes in large corporations hit hardest by restructuring. In the 1980s, as we saw in the last chapter, the occupational pension funds in a number of sectors – especially steel, automobiles and aircraft – bore some of the strain of restructuring. To the extent that they did indeed help their enterprise to survive, fund participants benefited, both because they kept their jobs and because stocks given to the fund in lieu of financial contributions acquired some value. So for those who retained their jobs the sacrifice was probably worth it (at least until 2001–2 when a new downturn hit many of the same companies and DB funds). Overall, the decline of employment in these sectors contributed to the decline in defined benefit corporate schemes, those who still belonged becoming a relatively privileged layer.

So the balance sheet for the pension funds in the period 1975–95 was a mixed one. A few public sector unions managed to play a part in fostering the advance of their region. Some occupational funds were used by the IRS and PBGC to underwrite the restructuring of some traditional sectors of the economy. But the great mass of employees' savings were committed to conservative blue chip companies or to financial speculations of a new type, notably those characteristic of what people were learning to call 'globalisation'. The total sums involved were very large. The multi-employer funds, on which trade unions have direct representation, had assets worth $350 billion in 1998; public sector funds as a whole were much larger, at $2,344 billion. Defined benefit and defined contribution schemes managed by the financial services industry were worth $3,881 billion; of the latter, assets worth about $1 trillion were held by schemes which were the product of some negotiation with unions.[7] The enormous financial power conferred by these accumulated funds was thrown into the conventional pursuit of shareholder value, whatever the cost to communities or indeed the policy holders themselves.

The experience of the majority of Americans and Britons in the period 1975–95 was an unhappy one. In the United States hourly wage rates actually fell while unemployment remained high. In 1969–76 hourly US wage rates for non-supervisory staff were $13.17 while in 1993–98 the same hourly rate was $12.37 (both figures given in 1998 prices). And while the unemployment rate averaged only 4.8 per cent in 1961–68 it rose to an average of 7.1 per cent in 1981-92.[8] As more women joined the labour force there was an increase in households with two earners; and as a result household income held up better than wage rates. But the growth of poverty, distress and insecurity was palpable. Many blamed worsening conditions on free trade and the decision of large corporations to invest in cheap labour zones overseas. Public discontent produced the campaigns of Ross Perot, and Bill Clinton's slogan, 'It's the economy, stupid'. The question that has to be asked is what institutions were responsible for over two decades of economic misery. And were, perhaps, the workings of the pension fund industry part of the economic stupidity involved?

Notwithstanding the talk of a Thatcher miracle, the 1980s were a time of economic suffering for many in Britain too, a fact acknowledged in its own way by the Conservative Party in 1990 with its unceremonious ejection of Margaret Thatcher as it searched for a more compassionate image. Unemployment in Britain soared from less than half a million in the early 1970s to over three million in the 1980s; those in employment did see wage rises but their pay still lagged far behind that of German or French workers. Employment in manufacturing dropped by 40 per cent between 1979 and 1994; though productivity rose, output remained flat. In 1997 compensation per hour in British manufacturing was just 54 per cent of German rates, 85 per cent of US rates and 86 per cent of those in France.[9] (The high pound actually flattered these figures.) Around the same time per capita national income was $34,630 in Japan, $25,860 in the United States, $25,580 in Germany, $23,470 in France, $23,360 in Singapore, and $18,850 in the UK.[10] The international financial markets gave their own verdict on the strength of the British economy when they forced the pound out of the European Exchange Rate Mechanism in 1992, a humiliation that led to a collapse in public confidence in the Major government from which it never recovered. In the last chapter mention was made of the pension mis-selling scandal which burdened 1.5 million policy holders in the years 1987–94 with costly plans. Another, and in its own way worse, scandal had its roots in one of the Thatcher government's first big decisions: to remove the guarantee that the modest, flat-rate state pension would be increased in line with average earnings. Lacking this link, the state pension sank from being 20 per cent of average earnings in 1979 to 15 per cent in 1997. Once again, responsibility for these woes must certainly be placed at the doors of political leaders (on which there will be more in chapter 5). But the financial industry bears its share of responsibility, partly because it lobbied for commercialisation of pension provision and partly because it did not use its great strength to restore the fortunes of the wider British economy.

As noted above, only about 0.5 per cent of British pension fund assets were invested in venture capital undertakings in the late 1990s. Curiously, the Coal Industry Pension Fund, which had blocked union attempts to obtain influence in the 1980s, was one of very few British funds to take an interest, setting up CINVIN as a vehicle for its venture capital investments. In June 2000 the British Venture Capital Association was able to release a report prepared by the WM Company showing that its members' combined performance of 27.2 per cent over five years compared with a FTSE 100 index rate of return of 21.8 per cent and a pension fund return of 16.3 per cent over the same period. Over ten years the venture capital funds achieved a 20 per cent return, the FTSE a 15.6 per cent return and the pension funds a 12.5 per cent rate of return.[11] The British economy in the late 1990s was still showing the effects of several decades of low investment. If the strong pound was undoubtedly one factor making for uncertainty and stagnation in the manufacturing sector, another was the adverse capital stock/labour ratio compared with other advanced economies. Indeed, over a period of twenty years British capital stock had grown by only 1 per cent a year.[12] This deficit was largely to blame for labour productivity lagging the United States, Germany and France by between 15 and 35 per cent. Over this period modest improvements in labour productivity stemmed only from overall shrinkage of the industrial sector and some foreign direct investment.

The financial institutions specialise in arbitrage and are uncomfortable with entrepreneurship. Exploiting price anomalies requires technical skill, which they have in abundance. Identifying the ways in which existing resources could be put to good new uses is more demanding and requires the sort of specific knowledge not often found on Wall Street or in the City of London. The rise of the pension funds simply confirmed this basic pattern and predisposition.

Gordon Clark argues that the conservatism of the pension funds stems from the trustees' desire, reinforced by consultants and communicated to managers, to purchase assets with three principal characteristics: (1) '*the option for liquidity*, being able to enter and exit the position at will'; (2) '*risk pooling*, diversifying risk across a range of positions or circumstances'; and (3) '*risk sharing*, having a small stake or share in the investment relative to the total investment required'.[13] A fund combining different types of government bond and a wide range of equities in large, listed public companies meets the criteria. But an investment in a new technology start-up does not. Trustees need to check on the value of their fund at regular intervals; sinking significant resources into new unquoted or fledgling enterprises introduces an unsatisfactory element in the asset list, as they will be unlikely to 'perform' for a considerable time.

However, the Anglo-American financial services industry is nothing if not ingenious when it comes to ways of repackaging assets and risk. Some pension funds would be willing to make an investment in constructing a shopping mall or office complex but many would not because it would be contrary to each one of the previously cited criteria (though in the case of property at least, there are always tangible assets whose value could appear in balance sheets). However, it was perfectly possible for the money managers to find shares in real estate investment trusts (or REITS) which would span a number of projects – some mature and yielding rents, others not – and thus meet the criteria. Other assets that could be securitised and repackaged might include mortgages, student debt or just about anything that could produce income, even if discounted income (since in that case the price would be low). The multiplication of derivatives, the loaning of assets overnight, swap options and hedge fund products showed that the financial markets could devise solutions to problems no one had previously thought of. But the 1980s and early 1990s saw few attempts to package problems of urban and industrial regeneration in such a way as to make them attractive to the fund managers or trustees. At the limit, some US trade unions represented on the boards of multi-employer funds persuaded their trustees to back what were called Housing Investment Trusts and Building Investment Trusts (HIT/BITs). These projects built social housing using trade union labour in areas where there was a shortage; leases furnished a reasonable income stream even when below-market prices were charged.[14] However, such schemes held no appeal for Wall Street and, like the piecemeal and reactive approach of the PBGC, they were too limited to lead on to large-scale attempts to, say, furnish alternative employment in declining regions.

Large Company Bias

A characteristic problem of Anglo–Saxon stock exchange capitalism has been that it privileges the large, visible companies at the expense of the mass of medium and small businesses, which find raising resources for develop- ment far more difficult. The global operations and elitism of the City of London make this a notorious and long-standing feature of the British system.[15] In the United States the decentralisation of retail banking historically furnished some counterweight to the big financial centres. But the rise of the institutions and their pension funds channelled resources to the financial centres, weakened many local and regional manufacturing networks, and brought about a transformation in the way financial markets assessed corporations. In the period 1926–79 it was generally reckoned that there was a 'small stock premium' of about 4 per cent per year. In the period 1980–96 the large institutional investors bought heavily into the leading corporations, nearly doubling their share of all publicly quoted stocks. While the 100 largest financial concerns held 19 per cent of common stock in 1980, they held 37 per cent in 1996. This inrush of funds was overwhelmingly concentrated on the stock of the larger companies worth billions and helped to drive up their value further. The fund managers liked large companies because their shareholdings could be readily 'marked to market'. Not only was there no problem valuing their holdings but the market for these shares was highly liquid and so there was never any difficulty disposing of them. Small companies, by contrast, worth only a few hundred million, were difficult to research and the market for their shares tended to be sluggish and illiquid. Under legislation enacted in 1935 and 1978 all companies worth more than £100 million must report their shareholding structure to the SEC. Two scholars who have researched the pattern of ownership revealed by these reports conclude:

> We find that the level of institutional ownership in a stock can help to forecast its future return, and provide evidence that the predictive power is due to shocks resulting from the compositional shift in ownership towards institutions. Overall, the compositional shift tends to increase demand for the stock of large corporations and decrease demand for the stock of small corporations. With unit-elastic demand for both types of stock, the compositional shift by itself can account for a nearly 50 per cent increase in the price of large-company stock relative to small-company stock. This price appreciation translates into an extra return of 2.3 per cent over the sample period and can explain part of the disappearance of the historical small-company premium.[16]

It may well be imagined how the disdain for 'small' companies hindered their access to credit. By 2000 even indices that supposedly catered to 'medium cap' or 'small cap' stocks were actually stuffed with large firms. Thus 16 per cent by value of the S&P Mid Cap 400 index consists of companies with a capitalisation of $8 billion or more. In the S&P Small Cap 600 some 15 per cent of the companies were actually above the threshold – $1.2 billion – for a mid-sized company.[17] The internet craze did allow even micro-companies to get a listing and see their valuation rise like a rocket. But this correction was very short-lived.

In Germany local savings banks, or *Sparkassen*, have played a key role in financing business within each *Land* or state. Companies could also use some of their pension reserves. The result was the historic strength of the German *Mittelstand*. In Britain and the United States the huge significance of the top financial institutions, coupled with concentration on a small number of money centres, skews investment towards large companies which the institutions find easy to monitor. If pension funds had to be managed by concerns headquartered in the region where their contributors live, the centralising logic might have been somewhat curbed. For employees to invest in their own company concentrates risk but for them to invest in their own region helps to preserve its vitality. In both the United States and the UK the 1980s and 1990s witnessed a strong prejudice against companies that made things, especially if this involved metal bashing. This outlook is pungently summarised by the financier Jim Slater in his cult book, *The Zulu Principle*: 'Look for self-financing companies which generate cash. Avoid companies that are capital intensive and are always requiring money for new machinery or even worse, for the replacement of old machinery at a vastly higher cost.'[18]

The short-termist pressure of the share market encourages many corporations to skimp on R&D but at the same time it supposedly provides another route to the acquisition of superior technologies and products, namely takeovers. Financial operations of this sort can exact a heavy toll in 'collateral damage' and can easily become an end in themselves, especially since they seem to promise swifter profits than the hard graft of research and development itself. While it is obvious enough that many employees of the target company will suffer, it is significant that research shows that, after the initial buzz has worn off, no benefit accrues to the shareholders of the acquiring company. The merger and acquisition movement of the 1980s lowered rather than raised spending on R&D while a study of 100 large deals in the years 1994–97 showed that two-thirds of them underperformed the market after a year.[19]

The constant pressure for returns, and the turbulence which is its byproduct, are also a distraction. Allan Kennedy gives the following as the average length of time various shares were held by managers in 1998–99: Amazon.com 7 days; Yahoo 8 days; Dell 3.7 months; Delta Airlines 6.3 months; IBM 13.8 months; Exxon 29.6 months; GE 33.1 months.[20] While all institutional investors feel pressure to make short-term gains, the evidence of portfolio renewal rates suggests that the pressure is stronger on mutual fund managers than on managers of occupational schemes, and stronger on managers of occupational schemes than on the managers of the public sector employee funds. This is indicated in Table 3.1.[21]

Table 3.1 Portfolio renewal rates in % p.a.

	1993	1995	1997
Enterprise pension funds	33.2	24.8	36.3
Public sector pension funds	13.3	20.7	19.3
Mutual funds	48.2	42.3	42.5

Source: see note 21 (p. xx)

The time horizon of trustees and money managers is suggested by the following exchange in which a pension fund executive explains procedure with respect to monitoring fund performance as a whole:

What is the horizon in evaluating performance? No one is really sure. What we do is that it's calculated monthly. At the same time we provide year to date information, calendar year to date, and then one, two, three, four, five years, and inception numbers. . . . You look at the long term, but if you see a guy that's coming up with a bunch of poor months you're going to have poor quarters, and you're going to have poor years, and poor years turn into poor three years performance, and so on and so forth.[22]

If a three-year sag is unacceptable, then consultants or trustees would have to act after eighteen months of bad results. There is a specific reason why the defined benefit schemes sponsored by large companies are structurally prone to short-term horizons. John Plender explains this pressure with respect to Britain but the same logic applies in the United States:

If overall income goes down, the trustees may have to ask the company to pay increased contributions, on the basis of the actuaries' advice, into the pension fund pot. Note, however, that a majority of the trustees of company pension funds are directors of the company that runs the pension scheme. They themselves are anxious to secure the best possible return to protect the company's profits from increased pension contribution costs.[23]

GE and Marconi: Finance Rules

The story of GE, the world's mightiest corporation, and of the British companies GEC (subsequently renamed Marconi) and GKN, repository of hopes for the regeneration of British electronics and engineering, reveals much about the logic of Anglo-Saxon economics. Arnold Weinstock, who led GEC from the 1960s to the mid-1990s, owed his long tenure partly to the consistent support he received from the financial institutions, notably the Prudential, and partly to his legendary skill at 'financial engineering'. The latter comprised a ruthless approach to costs and a sharp attention to the details of the monthly financial ratios which each of his divisional managers was required to submit. Weinstock kept his company in a commanding position within UK electronics by fostering good relations with the Ministry of Defence and with public utilities like BT. GEC successfully merged the giants of British electrical engineering. It developed strategic stakes in telephony, office machines, power generation and consumer electrical goods. While these businesses were skilfully reorganised, pruned and sold, or leased out, none developed into solid world-class undertakings. Partnerships with Siemens and the US GE, covering computers and consumer goods respectively, left others to undertake technical development, while GEC was left flexing its famous financial rigour. Indeed, John Plender, who is by no means entirely negative about the Weinstock record, concedes:

> reflecting the wider picture in the British economy, GEC spent less on research and development and filed many fewer patents than most of its big international competitors. The individual businesses within the group tended to know very little about each other, because their lines of communication were almost exclusively to the centre at Stanhope Gate. The scope for cooperative exploitation of GEC's scientific and technological knowledge base was thus limited.[24]

When Weinstock was in his seventies his stewardship of GEC was still being zealously defended by the Prudential. When he stepped down in 1995 the company's manufacturing divisions were weakened and it had missed out on mobile phones, but at least it had cash and investments worth £1.5 billion and one or two promising acquisitions. The immediate returns obtained from its holdings kept shareholders reasonably happy even as the core business wilted. Weinstock's successors believed that the company's future could only be secured by a clearer focus on a core business combined with a corporate makeover. The company was renamed Marconi and the board sought to concentrate on telecommunications equipment while disposing of subsidiaries like the Picker medical systems business. For a while, during the technology stocks bubble of 1998–99, this new orientation saw the company's shares rise from £3.09 to £12.50. But the company was still hobbled by its weak R&D; its Picker subsidiary was sold for much less than expected; and it did not have the technological edge to dominate any particular niche in the communications sector. When the tech bubble burst it was left without a lifeline. The company's shares dropped vertiginously to £1.12 by 6 July 2001, a twenty-year low and less than 10 per cent of its worth ten months before.[25] Relegation from the FTSE 100 loomed.

One of the very few British manufacturing companies to retain its global edge in the 1980s and early 1990s was GKN, a world leader in the making of constant velocity joints for front-wheel-drive vehicles. But the company's management issued a warning in evidence to the House of Commons Select Committee on Trade and Industry that it was finding increasing difficulty in resisting pressure from institutional investors, with their unrelenting demand for cash returns:

> The consequence is that UK companies distribute a relatively high propor-
> tion of earnings as dividends, putting pressure on the company to earn
> high rates of return and reducing the internal funds available for reinvest-
> ment (in times of recession, surplus funds can be eliminated completely).
> Consequently, British companies are relatively risk averse and tend to seek
> growth through acquisition. There is also pressure, particularly during a
> recession, to reduce discretionary costs such as R&D in order to protect div-
> idends: a reduced dividend can have serious consequences in terms of lower
> share price and possible predatory takeover.[26]

Another way of fending off such pressures, much resorted to in the 1990s and with many of the same consequences, was to spend money buying back shares.

The story of Jack Welch's GE shows some of the same pressure towards 'financialisation' and growth through acquisition, albeit on a very much larger canvas. A diversification strategy embarked on in the early 1980s led to the setting up of overseas divisions, the cutting of the company's US labour force by 125,000, and the development of new interests in the area of leasing and finance in the United States itself. By 1998 the company had just over 40,000 workers but very healthy profits, 40.8 per cent of which came from financial activities. It is the boast of GE that it has a very com-municative corporate culture yet much of its growth has come from GE Capital, its financial wing. In 1997–99 GE Capital spent $51 billion acquir-ing more than 100 different companies. In order to finance the purchase and development of these and other concerns, GE Capital had borrowed a total of $200 billion, of which $129 billion was short-term debt. These highly levered financial operations now make GE a financial group more than an engineering corporation, with all the opportunities and risks that this entails. While GE is now heavily involved in such exciting fields as collecting unpaid bills on behalf of shoe shops, it almost missed the growth of business-to-business internet commerce notwithstanding its possession of GE Information Services (GEIS) which at one point was the only internet B2B of any size. As a report explained: 'The reason was a bad case of conglomeritis. GE . . . offers vast opportunities to use technology inventively. But its obsession with earnings growth means that it suffers from an inherent conservatism. . .'[27]

GE's orientation to finance is, of course, not bereft of a logic of its own. It can help to corral business for the remaining manufacturing side. Welch sought to crown his stewardship of the corporation by negotiating a merger with Honeywell in 2000 that, among other things, would have allowed GECAS, the company's powerful aircraft-leasing arm, to make finance for its global network of customers – many of the world's leading airlines – conditional on the purchase of avionics from the new merged entity. This initiative was blocked on competition grounds by the European Commission in the summer of 2001, leaving GE listing towards an increasingly troubled financial sector.[28]

While GE is a far stronger, as well as far larger, company than GEC/Marconi, its contribution to its own domestic environment as an employer and producer has declined sharply. As part of its cost-cutting strategy, it has reduced pension contribution burdens dramatically. The company was able to take a contribution holiday for more than a decade after 1987, because of a reduced benefit obligation for its smaller labour force, and because of good returns from the pension fund's investments. The company made modest cost-of-living adjustments to its pension obligation in 1991 and 1996 but this still left the pension plans overfunded. Trade union pressure for an improvement in the benefit formula, which averages only $700 a month per retiree, has been resisted.[29]

Enron and 'Financial Engineering'

Welch and Weinstock were hugely admired as business leaders even if they were sometimes accused of turning manufacturing corporations into banks. The rise of 'financialisation' in the 1980s and 1990s encouraged large companies to behave like hedge funds. Many export-oriented firms would find themselves taking positions on the futures markets for currencies, or scarce inputs, simply to reduce uncertainty. Others found this activity itself a source of profit. And still others came to themselves organise spot and futures trades, as a promising extension of their ordinary business. One of the most admired practitioners, dominating the spot and futures energy market and offering over 3,000 other contracts, was Enron. The year before its collapse *Fortune* ranked Enron as the seventh largest US corporation by turnover. The new technology boom helped the company but its stock continued to rise well into 2001, because of its apparently strong revenues and profitability. It was, after all, not a dot.com start-up but a company that owned tangible assets (pipelines, power stations, reservoirs and the like) and that had large revenues from its trading business. Yet by December of 2001 it had filed for bankruptcy. Neither auditors nor regulators had reported any problem. By dint of offering generous consultancy fees to its auditors, Arthur Andersen (and employment to nine former Andersen employees), it escaped rigorous assessment. In 2000 and 2001 Andersen earned more from Enron in consultancy fees than from its auditing work. The company also put on its board Wendy Gramm, a former public regulator whose rulings had let the energy traders rip and whose husband, Senator Gramm, helped to slash regulatory requirements in the United States. It also gave a board seat to Lord Wakeham, the former UK energy minister, who had supervised the privatisation of Britain's electric power industry.

Though Enron acted like a financial corporation, it was not subject to the reporting standards of a brokerage, or the deposit conditions of a bank. One might suppose that Enron's own bankers would have been keenly aware of the lax regime enjoyed by its client and would have had sources of information other than audited accounts. But nevertheless, these banks, among them the conglomerates J.P. Morgan–Chase and Citibank, issued large loans to the company. The banks were able to lay off much of the risk involved in this by constructing and selling to others two complex financial instruments, collateralised debt obligations (CDOs) and the pooling of loans in asset-backed securities (ABSs). Those who purchased these loans stood to gain if they were redeemed in a timely way, but were exposed to heavy losses in the case of default. A report in the financial press explained that these credit derivatives became very popular with insurance houses and fund managers in the 1990s:

> The Bond Market Association estimates the asset-backed securities market in the US alone grew from $315 billion in 1995 to $1,048 billion in 2001. Collateralised debt obligations grew from $1 billion globally in 1995 to $300–400 billion last year [2001] . . . It is now becoming clear that existing accounting and regulatory regimes were unprepared for the explosion in financial engineering. . . . Enron was a classic case . . . The FSA's concern that insurance companies may not have known fully what they were doing in buying such instruments is plausible. Even sophisticated financial companies

have admitted that they had trouble understanding the complex instruments marketed by Wall Street . . . Because some of the risk–transfer products such as CDOs are weak credits dressed as strong ones, some pension funds and mutual funds may have invested in products that have exposed them to unwanted risk and volatility.[30]

The large pension funds are suing Enron and Andersen as shareholders but those who purchased Enron-related credit derivatives also took a heavy hit. The Florida state employees pension fund lost $325 million on its share account, with the fund's manager continuing to buy as Enron stock plunged. Altogether the public pension funds lost $5–$10 billion with the private funds probably losing even more. Among those affected were the state employees pension funds in Ohio, New York City and Georgia, and the pension and endowment fund of the University of California, which lost $145 million.[31] Generally these funds will have taken care that their holding in any one company would not be large enough to much affect their overall performance. But some will also have had exposure to Enron-related CDOs or to stock declines in concerns that suffered from the 'Enron effect' – including the company's banks, other energy traders, or other companies with suspect accounting practices – with a consequent deterioration of their risk profile.

Some pension funds also invested in Enron's infamous off–balance sheet partnerships ('special purpose entities' or SPEs) like the so-called 'Raptor I, II and III', or 'Jedi I and II'. The SPEs hid liabilities and allowed Enron to practise self-dealing; at the October 2001 meeting of the LJM partnership it was reported that all but 11 per cent of its transactions had been with Enron or its affiliates. Fund managers seemed sometimes to have been flattered to have the opportunity to invest in such a leading edge concern. Others will have been reassured by the involvement of highly respectable financial advisers: 'Merrill Lynch handled the sales pitch for one such concern, LJM2 Co-Investment. According to claims and counter-claims filed in a Delaware court this month, many of the most prominent names in world finance – including Citigroup, JP Morgan Chase, CIBC, Deutsche Bank and Dresdner Bank – were still involved in the partnership, directly or indirectly, when Enron filed for bankruptcy.'[32]

Among those who invested in these partnerships were Calpers and the Arkansas Teachers Retirement System. Calpers earned a 23 per cent return on the $250 million it contributed to the formation of Jedi I in 1993 but had problems when it sought to reclaim its capital stake three years later. The California employees fund was eventually persuaded to convert its claim into a $500 million stake in a new Raptor-style vehicle.[33] Perhaps

Calpers believed that Enron was upgrading the state's power supply; if so, it was to discover how wrong it had been (on which more below).

Enron notoriously encouraged its own employees to become investors on a large scale. As the company imploded many employees discovered they had lost their savings as well as their jobs. At the close of 2000 more than a half of the $2.1 billion of assets in their 401(k) retirement plans were invested in Enron. About 57 per cent of Enron's 21,000 workers were members of the plan. While board members sold stock worth $117 million in the period between January and August 2001 many employees found that their holdings were frozen, either because of a two-week technical overhaul of the 401(k) programme or because they had not yet satisfied vesting conditions. True to its reputation as a communal benefactor and considerate employer, one Enron concern, Portland General Electric, hired grief counsellors to console its stricken workforce. And as one report noted: 'Stock plunges similar to Enron's have also wiped out the savings of many employees of the Nortel Networks Corporation, Lucent Technologies Inc. and Global Crossing Inc.'[34]

Enron and Andersen helped to make the political weather. The company's chairman, Kenneth Lay, known as 'Kenny Boy' to George W. Bush, distributed largesse to politicians of all parties so that Enron would enjoy light regulation and political favours. The President himself had received half a million dollars in campaign contributions and several senior members of his administration had been on the Enron payroll, including his economic adviser and Army Secretary. Arthur Andersen had also lobbied energetically and successfully in both Washington and London. Legislation that would have forbidden auditors to earn consultancy fees from their clients was squashed, with help from, among many others, Senator Joseph Lieberman. In the UK, Enron sponsored events for the Labour Party while Andersen composed for the Treasury a highly positive report on New Labour's cherished Private Finance Initiative. Subsequently Andersen received a juicy contract to assist a government-sponsored PFI that would break up the London underground system (a project strongly opposed by the capital's elected mayor). When the US Congress came to investigate the Enron collapse it transpired that, of the 248 members of Congress who sat on one or another of the 11 committees of the Senate or House involved in the investigation, no fewer than 212 had been in receipt of money from either Enron or its auditors.[35] These two companies were held in the highest official esteem, not despite, but because of, their skilful practice of crony capitalism. The débâcle of Enron was significant not just because of its size – other concerns that failed at this time, like K-Mart or LTV, actually had more employees and pensioners – but because it was the very embodiment of 'Anglo-Saxon economics', and of the promise of a new world of deregulated financialisation.[36] Enron's momentum came not from productive investment or innovation, or even skill in arbitrage, but from financial manipulation. By 2001 the profits it was making even on its trading activities were being squeezed by rivals. Its relentless pressure for deregulation reflected a wish to escape competition by opening up new pastures.

Given its extraordinary network of contacts, it has to be asked why no attempt was made to organise a bail-out for Enron, as in the case of Long Term Capital Management in 1998. The Enron crisis crept up slowly, and, at first, just looked like the sort of stock slide that was affecting many companies in 2001. By the time that bankruptcy loomed many had already lost a lot of money. In the case of LTCM the Federal Reserve Bank acted, it was said, because if it had not done so the collapse of the hedge fund would have had a devastating impact on the financial system. Many banks, even some central banks, were using LTCM to hedge their positions. If it had been allowed to go under it would have taken a lot of other concerns down with it. Because of this it was possible for the Fed to persuade 14 banks to put up $3.6 billion as part of the bail-out.[37] The situation of Enron was quite different. Its crash certainly brought losses on a huge scale – perhaps as much as $60 billion. But these losses were spread around thinly between a large number of institutions. As we have seen, the banks were careful to play pass-the-parcel with the insurance houses and fund managers. Enron's collapse caused serious pain for many but did not by itself bring down any major financial concern (though others thought to be afflicted with 'Enronitis' came under close scrutiny). Some in the financial community say the lesson had been learnt and the right precautions taken. While financial institutions had protection, the same could not be said of Enron's employees or, indeed, for tens of millions of others whose 401(k)s or pension schemes were invested in Enron shares, or, via the Osprey fund, in Enron bonds, or in credit derivatives or SPEs like Jedi II and LCM II. It may well be that a popular President, his ratings riding high in the aftermath of victory in Afghanistan, thought that he could scarcely be blamed for the débâcle anyway. In the event Bush did fear paying a political price and, as will be seen in chapter 6, began rather unconvincingly to talk of the need for rigorous standards and accountability.

The hit taken by credit derivatives in the Enron collapse draws attention to the way a sophisticated financial system is nourished by apparently low-grade debt. Credit derivatives are based on consumer as well as corporate

debt. As pointed out above, GE Capital is now heavily involved in consumer credit. Citibank, which adroitly off-loaded much of its Enron
exposure, purchased Associates First Capital in September 2000 for the
impressive sum of $31 billion. Eyebrows were raised that a financial giant
like Citibank – America's largest bank – should be interested in a concern
notorious for its 'predatory lending' to the poor, an outfit which had
waxed fat by deploying, as *The Economist* put it, 'the tactics of the loan
shark and the con man'.[38] Citibank's acquisition allowed it to loan out at
20 per cent the money given to it by its depositors. During the years of the
bubble many consumers, encouraged by the rising value of their 401(k)s,
got themselves heavily into debt. While most will have kept out of the
clutches of Associates First Capital, many ran up credit-card debts that
could also cost close to 20 per cent annually to service. With consumer
debt rising to 116 per cent of income by 2000 the financial sector was in
good shape even if the US economy was not.

The Price of Short-termism

British industrialists have often attacked the City finance houses for
neglecting the needs of domestic investment. In an ironic twist of fate, the
investment banks and brokers of the City of London, whose lack of commitment and short-termism had led to the decimation of British
manufacturing, themselves became the target of a wave of takeovers in the
1990s. One by one, over a few short years, the great names of British
banking either came under US, Dutch, Swiss, French or German ownership, or found themselves obliged to sell off their investment banking
operations. The famous brokerage houses went the same way. According
to an insider's vivid account – Philip Augar's *The Death of Gentlemanly
Capitalism* – responsibility for the astonishing liquidation of a three-
centuries-old financial complex lay with nerveless management and timid
pension funds and fund managers. Thus when Barclays sold BZW, its
investment banking arm, one of those involved explained to Augar:

> 'It's the difference between ownership and management', he said. 'There is
> no one in Barclays able to take a long term view. The chief executive prob-
> ably thinks he's only got a year or two to sort it out. The institutional
> shareholders are working on an even shorter time horizon. Building an
> investment bank is a thirty year process and Barclays are about a third of the
> way through it but no one is around for that long.'[39]

Another victim was NatWest Markets:

> Derek Wanless, who as NatWest's chief executive was on the receiving end
> of much of their criticism, does not blame the fund managers: 'I've got
> more sympathy with the fund managers than you might think. Their sole
> brief is to perform so that's what they try to do. Pension fund trustees are
> where the problem starts: they set the rules for the fund managers. It's
> wrong to blame the fund managers for the problems of capitalism.' The fund
> managers at the institutions work in an industry that is every bit as com-
> petitive as corporate finance and equities. Performance league tables are
> issued quarterly for each fund and are pored over by consultants who report
> to boards of trustees. Fund management houses that regularly underperform
> are sacked. It is no wonder therefore that shareholders pressurise the com-
> panies for short-term results.[40]

This leads the author to conclusions that others had reached when they
had been let down by the City: 'when strategic issues are at stake,
institutional ownership is inappropriate and that is why it is important for
the government to protect the public good. That, after all, is why we
have governments.'[41]

The Bubble and the 'New Economy'

At the end of the 1990s many believed that a more hopeful note could be
struck. The traditional industrial behemoths might have disappeared, or
transmogrified into holding companies, but new corporations like
Microsoft and Amazon, Nokia and Vodafone were taking their place.
Massive investment in information technology promised breakthroughs in
industrial organisation and productivity. The United States bounced back
in the late 1990s in ways which seemed to redeem two decades of troubled performance. Output, profits and even productivity rose, while
unemployment fell. But with the bursting of the bubble in 2000–1 the
limited nature of the gains became apparent. The 1990s boom did not
replicate the sustained growth of the 1950s or 1960s. Growth rates were
lower and the new national wealth was shared far more unevenly. The
stock exchange rose sharply but increasingly unsteadily for eight years
from 1993 to 2000, as investors lurched into, and then out of, 'new economy' stocks. The long-run potential of the information and technology
industries became the excuse for an extraordinary speculative bubble. In
Britain, the other prime stock-exchange-dominated economy, the recovery was less marked and the bubble even less justified by solid evidence of

economic transformation; the 'old economy' had certainly been run down in the UK but a few patches of 'new economy' growth like Vodafone or Smith-Kline-Beecham were unable to fill the yawning gaps left by industrial shrinkage. (And note that though Vodafone has its head-quarters in Britain this is not where its phones are manufactured.) In Europe as a whole 'Anglo-Saxon economics' made dramatic headway during the 1990s boom (on which more in the next chapter). But the first attempt to use stock exchange finance to sponsor a major industrial re-orientation was not auspicious. Institutional investors used their new clout to back hugely expensive rival attempts by telecommunications consortia to capture the market in third generation mobile phones. In 1998-9 about £300 billion was devoted to this but, as the potential scale of wasteful and costly duplication became apparent, investors' enthusiasm was to collapse, raising the question as to whether this was the best way to launch a new communications system

In the United States some elements of a new technology-based econ-omy were in place but sceptics argued that the late 1990s growth in productivity stemmed from cyclical rather than structural factors. Robert Gordon, the most pertinacious of the sceptics, granted that there were pro-ductivity advances in the computer industries themselves but otherwise the gains were just what should be expected in an upswing.[42] The reversal of productivity gains in the first half of 2001 suggested that Gordon's argu-ment had much substance at the level of the economy as a whole.[43] But at the level of individual enterprises there is evidence that increased investment in IT in the early 1990s correlated with improved productiv-ity by the late 1990s.[44] Indeed, the question arises of whether the Anglo-American pattern of economic organisation is really capable of making the most of the promise of the new technologies or whether micro-economic advances are not being choked off by the macro-economic context. While there was undeniable growth of income and GNP in the 1990s boom, the quality of that growth was uneven and questionable. Incomes and output grew at the expense of social cohesion and ecological sustainability. Inequalities yawned. The rising tide lifted all lucky enough to have a boat – but flooded those in low-lying areas. And when the waters receded unwary boatsmen found themselves stranded. Partly because of the boom the United States failed to make any progress towards the targets it set itself at the summits on the global environment in Rio de Janeiro and Kyoto. Because of the existence of North Sea gas, the UK did make progress on this front but maintained a most unenviable reputation for marine pollution and disease-ridden livestock. In both countries, the reduction in unemployment was accompanied by a rising prison population – doubling to reach nearly two million in the United States in the course of the decade.

Private Affluence, Public Squalor

By the end of the 1990s it was also clear that deregulation and privatisation had led to a perilous rundown of strategic public utilities. In 1997–98 the New Zealand city of Auckland was deprived of electricity for six weeks because the privatised power company had failed to invest in sufficient capacity. In December 2000 California's major electric power suppliers, Edison and PG&E, announced that they wished to raise prices by 20 per cent as one-third of the state's generators were closed for repairs. As a feature in the *FT* explained: 'That California's energy deregulation has gone awry is beyond doubt . . . Economists see the crisis as a further sign that, after years of low investment, the state's infrastructure is in no condition to sustain growth'.[45] Subsequently the state attorney entered a law suit accusing the PG&E holding company of having siphoned off over $4 billion from its generating business since 1996.[46] The knock-on effect of the failure of California's leading suppliers led to the tripling of free market electricity prices in the north-west and persuaded Alcoa to cut aluminium output at its smelters by one million tonnes, equivalent to 5.5 per cent of world production. Several of Alcoa's smelters were protected against electricity price hikes by contracts with the Federally operated Bonneville Power Administration but Alcoa closed them down anyway because they could make more money selling the electricity than by making aluminium.[47]

President Bush set up a task force under the chairmanship of his Vice President to come up with a new energy policy. Kenneth Lay and other Enron officials met with the task force on six different occasions, and played a key role in shaping its conclusions (for example: 'Direct the Energy Secretary to work with the FERC [Federal Energy Regulation Committee] to relieve transmission constraints by the use of incentive rate-making proposals') . Lay supplied a list of nominees to serve on the FERC and two of these were duly appointed. The chairman of the commission also reported receiving a phone call from Lay to the effect that 'he and Enron would like to support me as chairman, but we would have to agree on principles.'[48] Enron's collapse just a few months later made it clear that the company was far more interested in maximising trading opportunities than in the unexciting business of producing electricity. The pressure on Enron to embellish its results came in part from the exorbitant profits expectations that grew up in the course of the 1980s and 1990s. To aim for anything less than double-digit *annual* returns looked extremely wimpish. In the public utilities sector this approach led to the use of inappropriately high hurdle rates for investment projects. An investment in a new power station or an upgrade to the electricity grid might take over a decade to pay off and then only at half the rate that the financial engineers regarded as interesting. The speculative bubble did allow for some real investment in new technology equipment but everywhere else the share-buying frenzy killed more projects than it kindled.

Lack of investment also caused Britain's rail network to seize up for months following an accident in October 2000. The accident killed four people and injured thirty-four, four seriously, against a background of previous accidents which killed thirty-eight people. Privatisation in 1994–95 had been followed by a rise in passenger traffic and the introduction of more high-speed trains. This heavier traffic had not been supported by track investment, with a consequent proliferation of broken rails and other safety problems. Britain was experiencing 0.36 deaths per billion kilometres, compared with Italy's 0.10 and France's 0.27, while in Japan not a single passenger had been killed on an express train since 1964.[49] As the dimensions of the problem became clear, rail services were slashed and 20 mph speed limits imposed, pending a five-month repair programme. The chairman of the company responsible, Railtrack, complained that privatisation had passed 'like a tornado' through the British rail system. Nevertheless his company had made excellent profits. Thus the 'Anglo-Saxon economics' of the 1980s and 1990s supplied an extra twist to that mixture of 'private affluence and public squalor' of which J.K. Galbraith warned in his classic study, *The Affluent Society* (1959). The Labour government elected in the UK in 1997 failed to reverse this bias. A report in November 2000 noted: 'Public investment fell sharply in Labour's first three years of office and shows little sign of picking up this year'.[50] Because of the weakness of the opposition, New Labour won the general election of 2001 but observers plausibly attributed a 12 per cent drop in turn-out to public dissatisfaction with the parlous state of the health, education and transport services. In the United States the mid-term elections of 1998 gave evidence of a concern to improve, rather than scrap, public services. The election of 2000 saw a strong showing for Bush but he took care to stress the need for public spending on education and Medicare.

Limos for Life (and other Trophies of Executive Privilege)

Even on a narrowly economic reading, the 1990s were disappointing for many in the Anglo-Saxon economies, where growth was accompanied by escalating inequality, a proliferation of low-wage casual employment and the corrosive penetration of commercial values into every area of public service and social life. The pension funds had helped to create a new world of work, yet characteristically many of the new employees were themselves unable to take out pension coverage, either because they were part time or because the level of their wages left no margin for saving. In the late 1990s US average wage rates were still close to the levels already reached in the mid-1970s. Wage rates had dropped by 5.7 per cent between 1978 and 1988 and by 3.3 per cent between 1989 and 1996, so there was much lost ground to be made up. In 1997 wage rates grew by 1.3 per cent, in 1998 by 2.4 per cent, and in 1999 and the first half of 2000 they rose at a rate less than 1 per cent ahead of the rise in consumer prices.[51] In Britain decades of slow growth pushed wages towards the bottom of the league table for the advanced countries. In both the United States and Britain two decades of restructuring, casualisation and 'financialisation' left many employees haunted by insecurity and unsure of the future. Many older workers who lost their jobs in these exciting times found themselves excluded from the chance to work and had to content themselves with early retirement or a disability pension. Younger workers found it easier to get a job but this often meant long hours, few rights or protections and no confidence in the future.

Top managers and those employed by the financial services industry enjoyed handsome salary rises, with stock options for top executives and bonuses for bankers and money managers. There are various ways to measure inequality but in the case of the United States and UK all of them told the same story over the period 1980–2000. One approach is to measure movements in the gap between the income of those close to – but not at – the top, and the income of those close to – but not at – the bottom. Thus in 1979 the income of those at the 95th centile of US income distribution received three times the median income and thirteen times the income of those at the 5th centile; by 1996 these multiples had widened so that those at the 95th centile received four times the median income and twenty-three times the income of those at the 5th centile.[52] Another method, that of the Gini coefficient, according to which zero is absolute equality and extreme inequality (one person earning all income) would measure 100, showed that between 1977 and 1998 the Gini coefficient moved from 40 to 45 in the United States and from 23 to 33 in the UK.[53] These figures will become more tangible if some examples are considered.

The annual *Business Week* survey of executive pay in April 2000 pointed out that 'during the early years of the bull market, there was a disconnect. A lot of mediocre executives effortlessly reaped millions from their stock options.'[54] While noting that stock options had failed to yield similar windfalls for some in the turbulent conditions of 1999, it observed:

> For now, however, the suffering is relative. Overall pay continues to explode. In 1999, the average total pay garnered by CEOs at 362 of the largest U.S. companies again shattered the record, rising 17% from 1998's $10.6 million to an average of $12.4 million. . . . That $12.4 million is more than six times the average CEO pay check in 1990. The raise was smaller than the 36% boost in 1998 – perhaps because CEOs in some underperforming sectors chose not to exercise their options, the biggest component of a top pay-check these days.[55]

The report went on to note that the top twenty unexercised share option 'treasure chests' had values ranging from $296 million to $2.2 billion. Jack Welch at GE held $436 million in such options while Louis Gerstner at IBM held $481 million of options. The top actual payout for 1999 was $655 million given to Charles B. Wang, the CEO of Computer Associates International, with all but $4.6 million coming in the form of restricted shares. At the bottom of the top twenty Kenneth Lay of Enron received a salary of $5.4 million and shares worth $49 million. The range among the top ten executives who were not CEOs went from $47 million to $359 million. The rationale given for these extraordinary payments was that they were necessary to retain key personnel or that they reflected an agreed rise of share values. As *Business Week*'s writer puts it: 'A perceived scarcity of talent has desperate boards ponying up sums that would make a potentate blush.' The reporter further noted that 'some of the most lavish pay packages aren't the upstarts but rather the big, established companies'. The idea that these payments helped retain key executives was not convincing: the report noted that 'accelerated options vesting has redefined "successful executive retention" to mean as little as one and a half years'. Two large payments at Computer Associates had been motivated by the retention argument, but the market was not convinced: the share price suffered when news of the compensation deal was announced. In this case shareholders sought to contest the pay package legally on the grounds that certain formalities had not been observed. This and other reports in *Business Week* generally reflect shareholder exasperation when CEO compensation is at odds with, or harms, share prices. It also highlighted the practice of repricing executive share options to raise the compensation rate in cases where trigger prices had not been reached. The 1998 *Business Week* report on executive pay had drawn attention to the grotesque contrast between executive greed and the modest stipends of the great mass of employees. It also commended the State of Wisconsin Board of Investment for seeking to ensure that all executive pay packages should receive the prior approval of shareholders.[56] According to some calculations the options awarded to top executives in 1994–98 amounted to 5 per cent of the value of all shares in their corporations; in less buoyant conditions this might have depressed share prices.

In the UK executive pay also rose dramatically, though never quite reaching US levels. In 1999 more than 110 top executives received £1 million or more each, and average executive compensation rose by 16.5 per cent or four times as fast as average employee earnings. The range of remuneration among the top ten CEOs ran from £1.8 million at Glaxo to £15.2 million at Colt Telecom. Two Vodafone executives received £21.2 million and £16.2 million. Share options realised are included in these figures, as were bonuses, but not those granted. In the case of Vodafone, the board's remuneration amounted to 27 per cent of the cost of the company's entire workforce.[57] By British standards these were gigantic salaries. In the early 1990s there had been a public outcry against fat cats when the top executive of a privatised water company had received annual pay of less than £400,000.

In the United States the average CEO package at the 362 largest companies was 475 times larger than the pay of the average American manufacturing employee. In Britain chief executives of the hundred largest companies received twenty-four times the average manufacturing salary, making the widest gap in Europe. In Germany and Sweden the multiple was 13, in France 15 and in Japan 11.[58] Evidently 'Anglo-Saxon' economics had something to do with the growth of yawning inequalities, presided over by the politicians of the 'Third Way'. This also emerges from a survey of all publicly listed companies published by the British journal *Management Today* in August 2001. Its findings are summarised in Table 3.2, which does not reveal the full extent of the gap between workers in 'Anglo-Saxon' and other states since non-wage entitlements and rights were also generally meaner in the former. Redundancy pay for manufacturing workers was three or four times larger in Japan, Sweden, Germany and France than in the UK or United States and holiday entitlement more generous.

Table 3.2 Average salary of CEOs and manufacturing workers (in £)

	CEO	*Manufacturing worker*
US	993,000	31,603
UK	509,000	20,475
Australia	457,000	21,034
Japan	386,000	36,779
France	398,000	24,574
Sweden	311,000	23,034
Germany	296,000	25,124

Source: *Management Today*, August 2001, p. 47; CEO figures rounded to nearest £000.

By the turn of the century the level of executive compensation was a target of shareholder activism on both sides of the Atlantic. But this was a belated and still fairly weak response. Pressure from trustees and public opinion repeatedly induced UK institutional investors to raise issues of excessive boardroom pay rises in 2000 and 2001, both with relatively successful companies like RBS and Vodafone and with deeply troubled concerns like Railtrack, BT, Marconi and Marks and Spencer. The repricing of executive share options, following falls in the share price, aroused particular fury. Often issues concerned with executive compensation are used to signal wider shareholder concerns. A report in July 2001 noted: 'The biggest factor in the awakening of shareholder activism is the economic downturn, which has affected the share-price of many companies.'[59]

Anglo-Saxon economic institutions are meant to have devices for aligning the interests of executives with those of the shareholders. Stock options are meant to be one of those devices and yet the exercise of these options contributed in a big way to the extravagant rewards executives were garnering. The options give the executive an interest in rising share valuations, allowing them pure gain on the upside with no penalty on the downside. If executives can find some way of boosting the share price they can then take their gain by selling their shares. It might seem that at least the shareholders are benefiting from this arrangement. But the shareholders only benefit if they sell their shares at the same time as the executive sells shares (or options). In the nature of things many institutional investors will not sell at this time. If what happens next is a sharp decline in the share price then investors who have remained faithful to these shares will begin to feel gulled. This will especially be the case if they can identify executive actions which did not really conduce to the company's long-term health but simply gave a short-term boost to the share price. In some now notorious cases conscious and premeditated fraud may have been involved. Perhaps this will be proved in the case of Enron. But even honest executives are expected to talk up the prospects of their companies and to act in ways that will sustain the share price. The practice of the share buy-back whose recent prevalence was noted in the last chapter is, other things being equal, good for the share price. In theory this helps the stock market to allocate capital more efficiently. But in practice companies can and did borrow from the bank in order to finance a share buy-back pro-gramme. Substituting debt for equity in this way was unlikely either to strengthen the company or to reallocate capital in a more efficient way but it was personally beneficial to executives. The board members and senior executives who arranged the bank loan to finance the buy-back operation could cash in their own options before the market realised what was happening. Robert Brenner writes:

> . . . it is increasingly clear that as the 1990s progressed, mounting buy-backs were increasingly driven by the desire of corporate executives, taking an increasing part of their salaries in the form of stock options, to drive up company stock values simply to line their own pockets. They have had no hesitation in resorting to ever more debt to accomplish this. By 1999 the corporate debt-to-equity ratio of S&P 500 companies had shot up to 116 per cent compared to 84 per cent at the end of the 1980s, when the cor-porate debt crisis had paralysed both banks and corporations. In the years 1994–99 inclusive, borrowing by non-financial corporations amounted to $1.22 trillion. Of that total, corporations used just 15.3 per cent to fund capital expenditures, funding the rest of such purchases out of retained earnings plus depreciation, while they devoted no less than 57 per cent or $697.4 billion, to buying back stock – an amount equal to 75 per cent of their retained earnings and 18 per cent of their cash-flow.[60]

During the stock market bubble the mass of shareholders were content to see the value of their shares rocket. Once the bubble burst executives who could be seen blatantly to have manipulated the share price might became unpopular, and a few may have suffered in consequence. But not many, because the end of the bubble seemed like a force of nature, beyond the control of any board or executive. Competent executives, concerned for their reputations and able to spot profitable new possibilities for their companies, might shun the path to financially engineered gains. But whether competent and honest or not, few could resist enrichment through options, increasingly seeing it as their due. Perhaps there was a real difficulty in finding genuinely profitable new openings. At all events Anglo-Saxon executive culture simply became used to the extraordinary rewards available. But at least some institutional shareholders were uneasy, or even angry, as the great share slide set in.

The independent self-managed pension sector in the United States was better placed to respond to the orgy of executive self-indulgence. In March 2000 TIAA-CREF issued a warning, though one which still fell far short of denouncing the unseemliness of the greed on display. 'We see executive pay as a window through which the effectiveness of the board may be viewed', the fund's head of corporate governance was quoted as saying. 'Large compensation awards to executives despite poor company performance . . . gives shareholders strong reason to believe that directors are not looking out for their best interests.'[61] And, as noted earlier, the award of a bonus of £10 million to Chris Gent, the CEO of Vodafone, aroused the ire of shareholders and extracted a token response from him.[62] (He was, of course, well aware of the even bigger handouts to two of his colleagues in the previous year, mentioned above.)

The advent of the bear market exacerbated the problem of the gap between executive performance and reward, highlighted the contrast between top management and workforce and showed that shareholder complaints had yet to make any real impact. Thus in August 2001 both Lucent and Honeywell announced packages for departing top executives: 'In Lucent's case, it took a 15-page attachment to cover the terms for its former senior executive, Richard McGinn, and former chief financial officer, Deborah Hopkins. In contrast, less than a page of Lucent's quarterly report covered its decision to lay off 10,500 employees. Mr McGinn, who presided over the troubled company for barely three years, received the most money: almost $13 million. Ms Hopkins did slightly better, based on time in office. She was CFO for less than a year and received almost $5 million.'[63] The Economist rightly drew attention to some bizarre features of these loss-of-office packages. As part of the agreement, McGinn was able to receive a previously restricted 'incentive' grant of shares as an absolute grant. Further, it pointed out,

> Mr McGinn borrowed money on the 'assumption of continued active employment', which, it is safe to assume, is true for most people who take out a loan. Unlike most people, though, when employment was discontinued, his former employer bailed him out, granting him a new $4.3 m loan, presumably on better terms. He retains an annual pension of $870,000, as well as health and life-insurance benefits equal to those that other retired senior executives receive. Like Mr McGinn, Ms Hopkins was given her restricted stock, and she also received $30,000 for 'financial counselling' (not something you would expect a CFO to need). Both she and Mr McGinn

retain their share options. . . . This, presumably, ensures that both root for their successor.[64]

The same report noted some similarly remarkable clauses in the $9 million settlement received by Michael Bonsignore, the ousted CEO of Honeywell, in the same month: 'M Bonsignore's termination agreement says he will be treated like a chief executive, with "executive transportation" and "financial and tax planning services", among other things, for the rest of his life. All this without the bother that comes from actually running a company.' In contrast the 1.5 million workers laid off in the United States in 2001 usually received a pittance – in the case of Enron employees who lost their jobs when it declared bankruptcy, just $4,500 in severance pay was distributed to each.[65]

Most money managers' objections to lavish pay-outs to executives were so muted and belated for one very simple reason – namely, that they were overcompensated themselves. CEOs of financial institutions were on a par with their counterparts in the large non-financial corporations while those who ran particular funds could claim annual salaries in seven figures and bonuses reaching to eight figures. A survey of the remuneration of some 10,000 fund managers in the UK, United States, Canada, Singapore and Hong Kong found that the British managers, with an average salary of £142,000 ($200,000) a year, came in ahead of the US managers, whose average annual salary was $190,000, even though the UK funds were not nearly as large as their US counterparts. Top fund managers, with ten years' experience, received $1.1 million a year in the UK and $900,000 in the United States.[66] These figures do not take full account of bonuses. The remuneration would be excessive, however good the managers' performance. In the light of the mediocrity of fund returns (documented in the last chapter), and of the failure of the funds to reallocate social resources in entrepreneurial and progressive ways (the theme of this chapter), the levels of pay were simply grotesque.

The overall trend towards pronounced, indeed extreme, inequalities in the United States and Britain reflected the openness of these two market societies to the impact of globalisation; similar trends in Germany and Japan were largely, though not completely, contained. When considering the apparent social acceptability of extravagant increases in top executive pay, it should be borne in mind that they were accompanied by more modest but often still very substantial increases for most of those earning above the median income as pay differentials widened throughout the spectrum. Media commentators who themselves earn seven-figure annual salaries are not well placed to voice indignation at the remuneration of business leaders. A look at the entire spectrum of pay differentials, especially the persistence of low pay at the bottom, suggests that the process of exporting lower-paid jobs to developing areas in Asia and Latin America weakened the bargaining power of less skilled workers in the United States and UK. But by itself the rise of the Asian tigers and other Third World producers would not have led to this result, had new jobs been created in the UK and the United States. A.B. Atkinson suggests that where business elites feel constrained by the need to protect social cohesion, whether because of the strength of the labour movement or out of respect for national ideals of communal solidarity, they moderate their own demands and seek to cushion the impact of the trade cycle on employees.[67] But the leaders of US and British business failed to generate a level of advance in the 1980s and early 1990s that could compensate for the ravages of deindustrialisation. The weakness of the Anglo-American economies over the whole period 1975–95 boosted unemployment in ways which undercut the bargaining position of trade unions as well as of unorganised employees. In Japan and Germany there was sufficient growth in the 1980s to forestall this logic, allowing trade union pressure in Germany, and a more generalised ideology of social cohesion in Japan, to prevent the growth of Anglo-American levels of inequality. Even in the 1990s, when both the Japanese and the German economies slowed markedly, prevailing social mores and institutions largely constrained pressures towards explosive inequality. By the late 1990s there were at least small signs that the balance of social forces and opinion was moving against the executive fat cats in the United States and UK and that trade unions were again acquiring a modicum of leverage. But the protests of the fund managers were belated as well as often muted. After all, if the institutional investors had made a concerted effort in the 1970s or 1980s – even as late as 1985 when the Council of Institutional Investors was formed – to chart a more dynamic future for US industry, bringing it into a cooperative relationship with the universities, then more good new jobs would have been created and the vicious spiral of inequality might have been avoided.

Wall Street's attention was fixed, as we have seen, on furthering the needs of large corporations and helping the newly wealthy to invest advantageously. But towards the end of 1992 some people must have been impressed by a politician who promised redress: 'Do you know that in the 1980s, while middle class income went down, charitable giving by working people went up? And while rich people's incomes went up, charitable giving by the wealthy went down?' He pointed out that CEOs had 'raised their pay in the last decade by four times the percentage their workers' pay went up'. And he attacked the outgoing president for truckling to Wall Street: 'When Salomon Brothers abused the Treasury markets, the president was silent. When the rip-off artists looted our S&Ls, the president was silent. In a Clinton administration, when people sell their companies and their workers and their country down the river, they'll get called on the carpet.' Just a little while later this man, William Jefferson Clinton himself, as the reader will have divined, declared that he offered a 'New Covenant for economic change that empowers people' and argued that corporations should not be allowed to deduct more than $1 million from their taxable income for CEO compensation: 'never again should Washington reward those who speculate in paper, instead of those who put people first'.[68] These declarations, it need hardly be said, have a peculiarly hollow ring in the light of the Clinton administration's abysmal failure to chart a different course despite favourable circumstances. The long boom of the 1990s showed that something was coming right for the US ruling stratum even if precious little trickled down to the average wage earner.

Notwithstanding its social divisiveness, in the 1990s the proponents of Anglo-Saxon economics were increasingly confident that it held the secret of globalisation. US and UK money managers ended the decade celebrating new technology just as they had begun it, by gorging themselves on the world-wide privatisation of public assets, by plunging into 'emerging markets', by exploiting the scope for the 'securitisation' of assets, and by patronising the rise of hedge funds. The mainstream financial institutions centred in London, New York, Boston and Chicago could and did scour the globe for profitable opportunities. Many did well out of the privatisation of public assets because governments put very low prices on them to guarantee success – the proceeds were anyway seen as a windfall gain by public treasuries inexperienced in the art of maximising gains from the auctioning of assets. Emerging markets furnished a more mixed experience but the IMF and/or the US Treasury could be relied on to organise the necessary bail-outs (Mexico 1994, South Korea 1997).[69] The global scope of financial markets allowed positions in one market to be hedged by those in another, but, once again, when the experts of arbitrage were skewered by their own miscalculations the financial authorities would step in to limit the damage, as they did when they organised the rescue of the hedge fund Long Term Capital Management in 1998.

Another problem is that of the lack of commitment typically shown by the Anglo-Saxon financial system. In the last chapter I cited the case of Mary Meeker, the Morgan Stanley analyst who was still forecasting a bright future for tech stocks underwritten by her own firm despite the collapse in their share price over the previous months. A colleague defended her on the ground that her choices had been 'made for the long term'.[70] While this would be a more impressive defence if Meeker and her employer had no stake in the outcome, it is not impossible that the stock corporations selected were promising but in the market meltdown they stood no chance. The lucky enterprises in the sector were those which came to market just at the peak and used their windfall wisely, making the whole investment process more like a game of musical chairs than rational economics.

There is a common line of criticism of Anglo-Saxon economics which stresses its speculative character. Susan Strange's books *Casino Capitalism* (1987) and *Mad Money* (1998) drew attention to this aspect of matters. If one considers the demise of Long Term Capital Management or the high-tech bubble of 1996–2000, then it is clear that many investors, large and small, were indeed taking a punt on the market – or had even convinced themselves that the stock market had become a money-machine. Robert Shiller published *Irrational Exuberance*, a well researched and withering critique of the mentalities involved, just before the slide began.[71] He shows that some of the bets being made rested on such extreme assumptions that a type of collective delusion must have been in operation. Yet he also stresses that, most of the time, it does indeed make sense to emulate one's fellows – there is an economy of effort involved as well as an awareness of one's own limitations. The money managers may not have led the way but they had no scruple about joining in. In an article entitled 'Churning Bubbles', Franklin Allen and Gary Gorton in 1993 pointed to the fact that the upside-only performance-related element in the fees earned by money managers allows them to benefit from rises in the market while not paying a financial penalty if it subsequently drops. They conclude: 'The call option form of portfolio managers' compensation schemes creates the possibility of bubbles.'[72]

The money managers who happily churned the bubble knew that their reputation was protected by the safety of numbers. Daniel Ben-Ami argues that the money managers are the very reverse of bold entrepreneurs or reckless speculators. In fact, he believes, a paralysing risk aversion is the central creed of today's financial services industry, inducing what he calls 'cowardly capitalism'.[73] This author, previously editor of *Investment Adviser*, an *FT* publication, points out that derivatives are, in the great majority of cases, used to reduce uncertainties: for example, an exporting company will buy forward its own currency in order to be able to know what income to expect. Investors and money managers can use convertibles – fixed income bonds that can be turned into shares above a strike price – as a way of insuring themselves against downside risk while still standing to gain if the shares rise steeply. Likewise, most of the procedures observed by money managers, consultants and trustees – especially those which give rise to 'short-termism' – are rooted in risk aversion. By contrast, if pension funds invest in the needs of their own community they will often be flouting the prudent expert rule or sinking resources in entities which are less than fully liquid. Yet, paradoxically, it is the insistence on marking all assets to market that can lead to huge gambles when that market overshoots, as markets regularly do. The committed social investor, by contrast, has a degree of insurance if the investment meets a local or regional need.

It is interesting to note that family ownership and control of large corporations survives in sectors like automobiles where there is an exceptional need for the commitment of owners. This is an industry which requires not only long-range planning but also a willingness to bear the strain of sometimes lengthy downturns. Whether in the United States, Europe or Japan, family ownership has often displayed the resilience required. The financial services industry itself is also a sector where restricted ownership has furnished an element of protection.

The growth of the US and UK economies in the 1990s was accompanied by a wave of mergers and acquisitions that was just as rapacious and speculative as its 1980s predecessor. The ballooning of share prices swelled the war chest of a new breed of takeover tycoon. The forced marriage of high tech and blue chip or the restructuring of old economy giants often led to job shedding or prepared the way for it when the bubble burst. While Japanese corporations doggedly retained their workforce, the large Anglo-Saxon firms were willing to declare many thousands redundant at the first hint of a slowdown. In the last days of 2000 John Plender highlighted the role of investment banks:

> it is possible that the largest wave of takeovers and mergers in business history may finally have peaked after a last burst of activity in the telecommunications, media and technology sectors. . . . The US players, led by the mighty trio of Goldman, Morgan Stanley and Merrill Lynch, are the shock troops of globalisation. While McDonald's and Coca-Cola rank higher in the post-Seattle demonology, the US investment banks are having a more profound impact in the ministries, boardrooms and workplaces of Europe and Asia. Their model of market capitalism, which emphasises

shareholder value, is the yardstick on which global markets are converging. It has huge potential for creative destruction and economic efficiency. . . . In the Anglo-American world they have helped impose an increasingly transactional culture on business. Yet the evidence that takeovers are economically beneficial is, at best, mixed. As the UK economist John Kay points out, investment bankers are prone to argue that companies add value when they merge and add value again when they demerge. This, he adds, is the financial equivalent of the perpetual motion machine – wonderful for investment bankers but not necessarily for investors in the companies concerned. That said, it is not difficult to put a case that takeovers in the more mature sectors of continental Europe and Japan can enhance the productivity of capital. Yet the hostile takeover mechanism is also profoundly subversive of those elements of European and Japanese business culture that foster long-termist, non-opportunistic behaviour. It is also potentially damaging in the UK and US in businesses where human and social capital are important. Since leaders of the pharmaceutical industry switched from organic growth to acquisitions, many of the scientists in their employ are more reluctant to share knowledge or make investments in human capital that have no value outside their own company. In other words takeovers reinforce those pressures that encourage managements to regard employees as a cost rather than an asset. And it is a measure of how far investment banker values have influenced the political agenda that a left-of-centre government in Britain objects violently to a proposed European Union directive that might slow the takeover process.[74]

Plender cited the case of Vodafone, touched on in the last chapter, as an example of the unclear logic of growth by takeover, adding '[a]nalysts meanwhile are reluctant to criticise the company in case their investment bank is excluded from participation in Vodafone's endless string of lucrative deals.'

Plender also notes:

A paradox in all this is that many investment banks are themselves immune from the disciplines of the takeover cult of which they are the high priests. At Goldman, for example, there is a dual voting structure. The board of directors, since Goldman recently ceased to be a partnership, can issue preferred stock with multiple voting rights to dilute a potential bidder. Removal of its directors or amendments to its constitution require no less than a whopping 80 per cent of the outstanding votes. Such obstacles, which are not unique to Goldman, usually elicit hostile comments from US analysts and bankers when encountered in Europe. If this were not Wall Street, the stock would be dubbed junk equity. Yet the investment bankers could claim that these devices protect human and social capital. The interests of the employees, who own a large bite of equity, are said to be aligned with those of outside shareholders.

Plender doubted whether lavish bonuses to staff – termed 'unusual compensation pressure' by Morgan Stanley that Christmas – bore this out. But his most sobering conclusion was that it was 'the world's tax payers who perhaps have the most to fear' since, like LTCM, the investment banks are too large to be allowed to fail. His conclusion also left little doubt that it was pension and insurance money which had fuelled the investment wave: 'The top three have more than $1,500 billion of other people's money under investment management.'

The Anglo-Saxon Model Vindicated?

I have argued that the performance of the Anglo-Saxon economies in the 1980s and 1990s was accompanied by dire social side-effects and that by the year 2000 there were more than a few portents of trouble in store. Nevertheless, in the 1990s the Anglo-Saxon model increasingly prevailed over its rivals. Indeed, by the end of the decade the contrast was sufficiently stark to embolden a whole genre of triumphalist commentary such as *The Lexus and the Olive Tree* by Thomas Friedman and *The Commanding Heights* by Daniel Yergin and Joseph Stanislaw. The message of this literature was that the collapse of the Soviet Union, the taming of the Asian tigers, and the chronic underperformance of Euroland showed that the new globalised order would ruthlessly punish economies which did not wholeheartedly embrace deregulation, flexible labour markets and all the paraphernalia of Anglo-Saxon stock exchange capitalism (including pre-funded pension provision). It is, of course, true, as I have acknowledged above, that there was a reality to the US recovery of the 1990s – the UK numbers for growth rates, productivity and profits were, of course, far weaker while other vaunted Anglo-Saxon economies like Canada, Australia and New Zealand were stagnant and in difficulties. The 1992–2000 boom in the United States was stronger as well as longer than the Reagan boom of the 1980s, with some recovery in profitability, and eventually culminating in some productivity gains. The bubble economy of the late 1990s gave a fillip to new technology expenditure but its collapse furnished a harsh test for enterprises still in the throes of experimentation. There is still reason to believe that the web will be able to improve the ways for companies to do business with one another and the consumer. Biotechnology also has enormous potential – in the double sense of being both large and, if purely commercially driven, pregnant with enormities. To give the devil his due, one might say that Anglo-Saxon capitalism had siphoned off financial resources from traditional sectors and regions, allowing them to be reallocated – albeit tardily, clumsily and without commitment – to growth points like Silicon Valley and the university industrial parks. Some new technology giants appeared from nowhere and are likely to endure. The analysts of Anglo-Saxon finance capitalism have stressed that a system giving leverage to 'outsiders' rather than 'insiders' would ensure that successful companies would not overinvest.[75] In some simple models of competition under capitalism the purpose is to switch resources from unprofitable to profitable undertakings. But in this tougher version, the idea is to switch resources from still very profitable sectors to very promising, even if loss-making, sectors. Of course bank-integrated systems and centrally planned economies also try to allocate towards the new growth points but those in control may be reluctant to contemplate radical shifts away from their own apparatus.

In the 1970s the invention of the micro-chip and an exponential growth of computing power was seized on by Soviet planners and Japanese and German manufacturers, as well as by a new generation of US technology firms. In the Soviet Union the growth of computing power proved of little help since the bureaucratic economy failed to generate rational prices or accurate information on stocks and sales. The computers given to the large enterprises were often used for nothing except the calculation of the monthly wage bill. Those installed in Gosplan lacked the essential information they needed on costs and the capacity of enterprises to satisfy real demand. The Soviet Union became the world's largest producer of electricity, cement, steel and oil but much of this output was wasted. Gigantic industrial fiefdoms straddled the economy, with steel works running farms and operating construction businesses to make sure their own workers were fed and housed.[76] However, post-Soviet shock therapy took no account of the need to build up new, more effective structures before destroying the old, and in consequence managed to produce a terrible, decade-long slump rather than the growth seen in China, where the Township and Village Enterprises, mainly under public ownership, played a strongly positive role.[77]

The Japanese and South Koreans proved very adept at manufacturing PCs but not at exploiting their potential for constructing new decentralised and fluid economic networks. While their economies remain formidable in many ways, there was a check to the growth in popular living standards. The French minitel programme sought to develop an information system that could link citizens to services and retail outlets but was a centralised system that eventually proved inflexible compared to the internet. For much of the 1960s and 1970s Japan, France and Germany outperformed the United States and they may do so again in the future. But their under-performance in the 1990s was a sign that the dominant banking and industrial complexes were, indeed, too inflexible and insider dominated. During this time the Anglo-Saxon system allowed for large-scale disinvest-ment and deindustrialisation without hitting on a new winning formula.

In the United States the real potential of the computer revolution was missed for nearly two decades and even after this it was only very partially realised. The vast majority of PCs were destined to be used as a new gen-eration of electronic typewriter or as a speedy calculating machine. During the 1980s and much of the 1990s there was no evidence that the purchase of tens of millions of increasingly powerful computers was making any impact on productivity. But eventually the military and the universities did develop the internet and its possible commercial applications were enthu-siastically, if belatedly and stumblingly, explored. It took the United States a long time to begin to fathom the potential of the micro-chip and its rivals proved even more inept. But the attempts made in France, parts of South-East Asia and Scandinavia to open up universal access to communications technology may well prove to have a critical role in the further tapping of the information technology revolution. California may have led the world in ICT in the 1980s and 1990s but the failure of government to ensure broadband access and the yawning disparities between its constituent com-munities and regions presented an obstacle to obtaining the best social return from the new possibilities. Only a tenth of US households and small businesses had access to broadband high-speed, high-capacity cables in December 2001, limiting the pool of those who could make use of advanced applications. In fact, the highest indices of 'connectivity' are to be found in the Scandinavian countries, with their relatively more egali-tarian social structures. Finland has more internet servers per 10,000 citizens than California while Swedish employees are twice as likely as their US counterparts to be connected to the net. Nokia and Ericsson, the Scandinavian mobile phone companies, benefited from government-prescribed common technical standards, some pooled facilities, and deep markets, first in Scandinavia and then in the European Union; however, Europe's lead in this area was subsequently to be compromised by a spec-ulative and competitive – 'Anglo-Saxon' – approach to the introduction of the third-generation mobile phones.[78]

The economic strength and the global leverage displayed by the United States during the 1990s do not reflect a situation where it trumped rivals by playing the new technology card. American business and political leaders prevailed because they had strong cards in their hand, in fact something of a grand slam:

1. The size of the US market gives its own producers great advantages and allows US negotiators to drive a hard bargain with all those who wish to gain, or preserve, access to it.
2. The leading US corporations still had the scale, strength and reserves to meet Asian and European competitors once they had secured their own sources of supply in cheap labour zones.
3. Lower population densities in North America, compared with Japan or most of Europe, allowed US firms access to cheaper building land and the productivity gains of 'greenfield development', albeit at great environmental cost.[79]
4. Japanese banks and pension funds, and European corporations, saw in the purchase of US assets a useful hedge, mitigating the problem of adverse trade balances and low domestic savings rates.
5. The IMF and the World Bank were obliged to defer to Washington and were anyway generally dedicated to Anglo-Saxon economics.
6. The strength of the United States in the culture industries and the dynamism of US popular culture furnishes a helpful background.
7. The United States was able to assert itself as the political and military leader of the advanced world from the Gulf War to the Kosovo War.[80]

It is only after reckoning with the strength of each and all of these assets that the as-yet-little-realised potential of new technology could be added to the list.

And it should be noted that even the combination of these factors does not make the case for some intrinsic superiority in the supposedly market-led Anglo-Saxon model. I have already made the point that it was the universities, not the stock exchange, that developed the new technology. Most of the other factors enumerated above stem from the advantages accruing to the United States because of its size, resources and special history as a land of immigration, and as a continent lucky enough to have escaped a war on its soil since the 1860s. Wall Street has been able to benefit hugely from US advantages without repaying the debt by contributing to the healthy and balanced development of its host society. In fact, the pressures exerted by the financial industry have instead helped to exacerbate social frustrations and divisions, and deepen inequalities and insecurities. By contrast, the social and economic advances registered in the United States in the 1940s and 1950s received much of their impetus from the expanded role of the state, the programmes of the New Deal and the pressures of the labour movement. Wall Street itself played little part in setting the scene for the Golden Age and was eventually to become the instrument of the forces which destabilised it. Military expenditure did have productive spin-offs but because of its inherently wasteful character made far less of a contribution to the impressive US performance of the 1950s and 1960s than the construction of the interstate highway system or the huge boost to 'human capital' deriving from public educational expenditures.[81] The booms of the 1980s and 1990s were weaker because linked to military expenditures in the 1980s and growing inequality in both decades.

The Big Wireless Gambles

Even if undeservedly, a connection was naturally perceived in the 1990s between US strength and the strengths of the US economic model. This perception certainly lent extra prestige to Anglo-Saxon economics, which already showed a considerable, one might say almost insidious, power, even in the 1980s at a time when US economic leadership appeared to be compromised and challenged. The cultures and structures of consumerism and individualism are very bad at identifying social cost or valuing social cohesion, hence the divisiveness and destructiveness of 'turbo-capitalism'. But they are very good at inserting themselves into the motivations of people contending with the pressures of a capitalist society. The idea of maximising exchange value along every possible dimension is one which will recommend itself to many economic actors in a competitive market society. Thus, for example, even if one doubted the wisdom of privatisation, the purchase of stock in newly privatised assets could be a good buy. The logic of 'financialisation' encourages individuals and business to lease out any assets they possess which are lying fallow, or to take on debt in order to acquire a supposedly more advantageous mix of assets. Support is gathering for new 'fair value' accounting methods which would enter all a company's assets and work-in-progress into its books not at 'historic cost' but at the price they would command if sold at the end of the period. Yet any innovative enterprise will have projects which cannot be instantly marked to market and the value of even more tangible assets and liabilities would fluctuate with interest rate oscillations.

While continental Europe is still wedded to greater collective provision of health and social insurance, the 1980s and 1990s witnessed large-scale privatisations and a growth in market capitalisation. In 1990 stock market capitalisation in France and Germany lay between a quarter and a third of

GNP; by the end of the decade it had grown to over 70 per cent.[82] The European contribution to the late 1990s bubble took the form of 'the big wireless gamble' as giant privatised telephone utilities and new mobile phone companies sunk hundreds of billions into developing third-generation mobile telephony. The rise of the mobile phone had demonstrated the ability of European capital to steal a march on its US competitors. But with the rise of the equity culture all the phone companies, old and new, were sucked into betting the bank on their ability to dominate hand-held access to the net, seen as a hugely lucrative market. Each concern spent tens of billions, and borrowed tens of billions, purchasing licences, building infrastructure and developing the handsets.[83] It seems unlikely that all can win this hugely expensive race and it is not impossible that the prize itself will be much less than glittering. The giant telecom companies are probably too big to be allowed to fail and changes to the licences may subsequently permit the saving of some of the vast waste incurred by needless duplication. But if the costly and cut-throat scramble for 3-G is compared with the cooperative and thrifty development of the World Wide Web in the first place, then it can be seen that the states of the European Union have already allowed themselves to be more than half colonised by 'Anglo-Saxon' economics.

The United States will share in what the *Wall Street Journal* calls the 'Epic Telecom Debt Debacle', though in the US case the emphasis is on surplus landline capacity:

> It is shaping to be one of the biggest financial fiascos ever, with losses to investors expected to approach the $170 billion US government clean-up of the savings-and-loan industry a decade ago. What is unprecedented, besides the staggering debt totals – is how little assets of the troubled telecoms companies are likely to be worth as the restructuring plays out. Past bankruptcy waves, such as those that swept the rail, retail, steel and movie theatre businesses, left bondholders with about 40 cents on the dollar. However bond investors may not be able to salvage much more than 10 cents on the dollar from the telecom restructurings, with banks also taking a hit, according to analysts. One reason: The industry's high-tech gear becomes outdated at such a rapid speed.

In the view of the *WSJ* staff writers, deregulation set the scene: 'The bust had its origins five years ago, when US Congress lifted restrictions on who could sell voice, video and data services in the local phone markets.' The result was an orgy of competitive landline laying across America. But by 2001 97 per cent of fibre optic capacity was unused and many of the concerns involved were teetering towards bankruptcy:

Companies that spent the past few years digging up streets, highways and
ocean floors, such as Level-3 Inc., are burning through hundreds of millions
each quarter . . . the troubles will likely weigh on the overall growth of the
economy for the next several years because the telecom sector has become
so big. In the past six months more than 10 telecom providers have filed for
bankruptcy.[84]

By the close of 2001 only 3 per cent of broadband capacity was being used
and only 10 per cent of homes and smaller businesses were connected to
it. And in January 2002 the giant Global Crossing was added to the list of
those filing for bankruptcy.

The over-investment and surplus capacity which precipitated recession in
2001 was nowhere more evident than in telecoms. It might be thought that
the telecom roller coaster, whether in the United States or Europe, is a classic case of investors playing the game of casino capitalism. And there can be
no doubt that the institutions were deeply implicated. But many money
managers became part of the great gamble by sticking to what they believed
were safety-first principles. Their main stakes were in the blue chip majors,
not in the start-ups. The former had healthy balance sheets and their stock
was ultra-liquid. The start-ups were generally supported by venture capital,
with modest institutional participation since even the venture capital companies do not have the sort of assets which meet fiduciary requirements. But
the appearance of the start-ups, backed by some mavericks, induced panic
in the well-established market leaders who proceeded, as they saw it, to
make sure that their companies survived a perceived 'telecoms revolution'.
The market leaders continued to have a healthy cash flow and this inspired
a degree of confidence when they sought to raise money by selling bonds
or making rights issues. The nature and size of the gamble being taken by
the money managers was not clear to them. The firms in which they were
investing dominated the big indices and the supposedly super-prudent
tracker funds were heavy on them anyway. The executive directors of the
telecom concerns must have been well aware of the risks being taken but
felt caught in a situation where the only way to finish ahead was to double
the stakes. The non-executive directors seem to have been either totally
bemused or remarkably complaisant. As the institutions slowly awoke to the
situation, they made their presence felt – in the UK they removed the CEO
of BT in April 2001 – but by then it was really too late. Governments also
played their part by encouraging wasteful duplication of transmitting equipment rather than using their potential monopoly control of this to gain
good terms from the operators.

Indeed, while political leaders – notably Vice-President Gore and Prime Minister Blair – liked to orate on the huge potential of the 'information superhighway', they signally failed to propose that the government should step in and construct a capacious new system, including broadband cable and a unified relay system. In the 1950s the administration of President Eisenhower, a Republican, gave a decisive impetus to the construction of the interstate highways. In doing so, it certainly contributed to the wider productivity gains of the golden age, even if the US corporations were to be allowed to compromise the new transport system by their neglect of safety and fuel economy, and by their successful attempts to cripple rival mass transit systems. The new scope offered to the automobile, the bus and the lorry required public support, and could have been far less destructive if introduced with more planning, as Europe's more balanced transport systems attest.

While ambitious social plans set the tone during the 'golden age', today the whip hand is held by hedge funds whose rapacity makes Milken and Boesky look like Boy Scouts. Despite the débâcle of LTCM the period of market turbulence did not kill off the hedge fund. Indeed, in a falling market investors, both private and institutional, were attracted to the supposedly 'market-neutral' strategies of the hedge fund managers. The latter sought to spot overvalued stock no less zealously than undervalued assets. They then aggressively short shares in companies they deem to be overvalued, reaping large returns if they prove to be right. In 2000 and 2001 the sums at the disposal of the hedge fund managers grew rapidly as investors sought to make money out of a falling market. In July 2001 there was estimated to be more than $400 billion in about 6,000 hedge funds 'completely unregulated and highly leveraged'.[85] The charges levied by the hedge fund managers are very stiff, often over 5 per cent of capital appreciation. If the speculation fails, then it is, of course, the client's funds which shrink. So the 'bubble churning' aspect of the incentive structure is very marked, with the difference that bubble bursting is the indicated strategy for a bear market. The success of the hedge funds reflects the failures of the passive or inept institutional investors, or the naivety of small punters. Corporate management now often faces the tricky problem of deciding whether to cooperate with hedge fund managers who thoroughly research their operation and insist on answers to the most sensitive questions. The hedge funds often take a keener interest than the real shareholders, yet their scenario will be to drive down the value of the company in a large-scale shorting operation if it is in a fragile condition. While the hedge funds are unpopular they should be seen as a symptom of the deficit of accountability and commitment that characterises institutional finance and corporate management.

Anglo-Saxons Lose the Propensity to Save

A curious feature of the rise of Anglo-Saxon economics, with its emphasis on individualism and its echoes of the Puritan ethic, has been its
association with low, and in the United States even negative, savings rates.
One sign of this was an import boom fuelled by domestic consumption
but involving a mounting trade deficit. Investment rates in the United
States were sustained not principally by domestic saving but by an influx
from Japan and later Europe. Japanese companies typically invoice their
overseas customers in dollars; the Japanese authorities then extend credit
in yen to these concerns so that they can keep these earnings in dollars,
which are then invested or recycled through the banking system to allow
other Japanese concerns to invest. The net effect is that Japan's trade surplus helps to offset the trade deficit of the United States.[86] The US
economy in the 1990s became the 'consumer of last resort', helping to
maintain the faltering dynamic of advance in Europe and South-East
Asia. Analysts believe that this formula cannot be sustained for ever. For
the purposes of the present discussion, however, the important point is
that the phenomenal growth of the pension fund and mutual fund business did not lead to a growth of net savings across the economy.
Conventionally, this was attributed to the 'wealth effect' generated by the
stock market boom. The move from DB pension scheme, where there is
no sense of an individual pot, to DC schemes, especially 401(k)s, where
people can track the changing value of funds in their account, will have
boosted this wealth effect. As Americans watched the value of their
assets – including mutual and pension fund holdings – grow, they felt
richer and were more inclined to spend than save. In April 1999 Larry
Summers, then Deputy Secretary of the US Treasury, somewhat
defensively argued that if one regarded unspent capital gains as saving
then according to this 'different concept', saving was at an all-time
high! But he did nervously concede that there was easy credit for
consumers and 'a tremendous focus on consumer goods in our society'
and that this explained disappointingly low savings rates in conventional terms.[87] There are signs that the same low level of saving and
dedication to consumption were visible in other Anglo-Saxon economies
even though in their case the offsetting factor of booming stock markets
was far less significant. As a *Financial Times* columnist put it in April
2000: 'a similar decline in savings has occurred in Canada, Australia,
New Zealand and the UK. The stock markets in those countries have
lagged well behind Wall Street.'[88] As we will see in chapter 6, Martin

Feldstein and other advocates of privatising Social Security have long maintained that the existence of public pension systems discourages citizens from saving. But in an international perspective, the relatively more generous pension systems of Germany and France have been linked to higher savings rates.

The financial industry has grown mightily in the United States, Britain and some other countries in the last half century as a result of voluntary, tax-favoured pre-funding of retirement. But to the more ambitious financial concerns and the more ideological proponents of neo-liberalism or Anglo-Saxon economics around 1990, the glass seemed half empty rather than half full. The pension funds and money managers became committed to globalisation, so naturally the idea arose of exploring the potential of other markets. The 1990s were to be a decade of intensive proselytisation of Anglo-Saxon economics, with international organisations, lobbyists and consultants arguing that it was imperative for the rest of the world to attend to the issue of pension reform. This meant adopting policies more favourable to private pension funds. Simply legalising these financial instruments was not enough, they should also be given tax favours and the public system of pension provision wound down. The first priority was to tie up the more affluent sections of the global middle class but, as a few were beginning to realise, the logical terminus of reform would be to make private pensions compulsory. Only then would the financial services industry have the captive market it wanted, and only then could the neo-liberal ideologues tackle the low savings problem in a politically correct, if thoroughly illiberal, fashion.

As we will see, a key argument deployed by those campaigning for private pensions was to be the real or supposed crisis of public provision. This argument was invariably pitched in terms of the imminent prospect of a looming demographic crisis as the massed ranks of the postwar baby-boomers retired from the workforce. Without doubt, the rising numbers of the aged will place greater demands on pension finance. Yet an aspect of the problem too little considered was that the two wasted decades of low growth of employment incomes (roughly 1975–95) in most advanced countries was bound to lead to declining revenues for public pension systems financed by pay-as-you-go methods, as the yield of payroll taxes and National Insurance contributions is directly linked to these incomes. Likewise the onset of recession in 2001 will depress social security revenues. So in this way sub-standard economic performance itself weakened the financial situation of the public schemes – and gave ammunition to the privatisers.

Notes

1   The best study of the weaknesses of the US recovery of the 1990s is Robert Brenner, *The Boom and the Bubble: The US in the World Economy*, London and New York, 2002.

2   The role of the US higher education complex is stressed by Michel Aglietta, *Le Capitalisme de demain*, Fondation Saint Simon, Paris 1998, pp. 14–16. On the poor performance of large Anglo-American corporations as innovators, see Mary O'Sullivan, 'The Innovative Enterprise and Corporate Governance', *Cambridge Journal of Economics*, vol. 24, no. 4, July 2000, pp. 395–415, and William Lazonick and Mary O'Sullivan, *Corporate Governance and Sustainable Prosperity*, New York 1998. For the development of the internet, see Manuel Castells, *The Network Society*, London 1997, pp. 29–64.

3   Tim Berners Lee, *Weaving the Web*, London 2000, p. 115. For a warning that growing commercialisation and tighter enforcement of intellectual property rights are stifling innovation see Lawrence Lessig, 'The Internet's Undoing', *Financial Times*, 29 November 2001.

4   Glynn Moody, *Linux and the Open Source Revolution*, London 2001.

5   Robert Shiller, *Irrational Exuberance*, Princeton (NJ) 2000.

6   Simon Targett and Patrick Jenkins, 'Venture Capital: Not Simply a Fairy Story', *Financial Times*, 22/23 July 2000. Clowes argues that pension funds made a vital contribution to US recovery in the period after 1985. I find this overpitched but note that his argument relates to DB and public sector funds not to Fidelity, Merrill Lynch and the retailers of 401(k) schemes, which he sees as doing little or nothing for venture capital. See Michael Clowes, *The Money Flood*, New York 2000, pp. 1–17, 265–76.

7   Catherine Sauviat and Jean-Marie Pernot, 'Fonds de pension et épargne salar-iale aux États-Unis: les limites du pouvoir syndical', in 'Fonds de pension et "nouveau capitalisme"', *L'anneé de la régulation*, vol. 4, 2000, pp. 89–115, p. 96.

8   Robert Pollin, 'Anatomy of Clintonomics', *New Left Review*, second series no. 3, May–June 2000, pp. 17–46, pp. 29, 36.

9   Martin Wolf, 'Sick Man of Britain', *Financial Times*, 2 August 1999.

10 Fitzroy Dearborn, *Book of World Rankings*, Chicago 1998, p. 80.

11 Simon Targett, 'Venture Capital Performance Figures: Funds Beat Companies in the FTSE 100 Index', *Financial Times*, 14 June 2000.

12 Andrew Glyn, 'Manufacturing: Time to Take (Capital) Stock', *Financial Times*, 8 July 1998.

13 Gordon L. Clark, *Pension Fund Capitalism*, Oxford 2000, p. 150; the emphasis is mine.

14 Teresa Ghilarducci, *Labor's Capital: the Economics and Politics of Pension Funds*, Cambridge (MA) 1992, pp. 124–5; Clark, *Pension Fund Capitalism*, p. 202.

15 See, for example, Geoffrey Ingham, *Capitalism Divided? The City and Industry in British Social Development*, London 1984, and 'Commercial

Capital in England', *New Left Review*, no. 172, November–December 1988, pp. 45–66.

16 Paul A. Gompers and Andrew Metrick, 'Institutional Investors and Equity Prices', *The Quarterly Journal of Economics*, vol. 116, no. 1, February 2001, pp. 229–59, p. 257.

17 Gretchen Morgenson, 'Why An Index Isn't a Mirror of the Market', *New York Times*, 9 April 2000.

18 Jim Slater, *The Zulu Principle: Making Extraordinary Profits from Ordinary Shares*, 2nd edn, London 1997, p. 20. This much reprinted work comes garlanded with praise from City giants like Lord Hanson; it is assigned reading on courses for fund managers as well as popular with private investors. It bears out the well-established critique of the anti-industrial bias of the British financial institutions: Geoffrey Ingham, *Capitalism Divided?*, Will Hutton, *The State We're In*, London 1994, and Perry Anderson, *English Questions*, London 1992.

19 Mark Sirower, 'Manager's Journal: What Acquiring Minds Need to Know', *Wall Street Journal*, 22 February 1999: quoted in Dean Baker and Archon Fung, 'Collateral Damage', *Second Heartland Labor-Capital Conference, Final Report*, vol. 1, Duquesne (PA) 1999, p. 20.

20 Allan Kennedy, *The End of Shareholder Value*, London 2000, p. 167.

21 Mary O'Sullivan, 'Le socialisme des fonds de pension, ou "plus ça change..."', in 'Fonds de pension et "nouveau capitalisme"', *L'Année de la régulation*, vol. 4, 2000, pp. 47–88, p. 74.

22 William M. O'Barr and John M. Conley, *Fortune and Folly: the Wealth and Power of Institutional Investing*, Homewood (IL) 1992, pp. 164–5.

23 John Plender, *A Stake in the Future*, London 1997, p. 63.

24 Ibid., p. 85. This book assesses GEC at length, mainly on pp. 81–90 and 137–9.

25 Thorold Barker, 'The Hangover after the Spending Spree', *Financial Times*, 5 July 2001; Simon Targett and Thorold Barker, 'Investors Lose Faith in Marconi', *Financial Times*, 6 July 2001.

26 Trade and Industry Select Committee, *Second Report 1993–4, Competitiveness of UK Industry*, Memorandum of Evidence, HMSO London 1994, quoted in Plender, *A Stake in the Future*, p. 61.

27 'While Welch Waited', *The Economist*, 19 May 2001.

28 'Welch Squelched', *The Economist*, 23 June 2001.

29 Allan Kennedy, *The End of Shareholder Value*, London 2000, pp. 166–70; John Plender, 'GE's Hidden Flaw', *Financial Times*, 31 July 2000; and for the GE pension fund the web-site gecontract2000.com/pensionfact.htm.

30 Charles Pretzlick and Gary Silverman, 'What Goes Around', *Financial Times*, 31 January 2002.

31 Elizabeth Wine, 'Florida Looks to Join Legal Battle', *Financial Times*, 31 January 2002.

32 Andrew Hill and Stephen Fidler, 'Enron Ties Itself Up In Knots, Then Falls Over', *Financial Times*, 20 January 2002.

33 Ibid. See also Rebecca Smith and John R. Emshwiller, 'Fancy Finances Were the Key to Enron's Success and Now to Its Distress', *Wall Street Journal*, 8 November 2001.

34 Richard A. Oppel Jr., 'Employee's Retirement Plan is a Victim as Enron Tumbles', *New York Times*, 23 November 2001. The executive share sales total is from the web-site of the *Houston Chronicle*, 15 January 2002.

35 Don Van Natta, '212 Out of 248 on Congressional Panels Received Enron Donations', *International Herald Tribune*, 26–27 January 2002.

36 Paul Krugman, 'The Enron Scandal is a Turning Point for America', *New York Times*, 30 January 2002.

37 Nicholas Dunbar, *Inventing Money: The Story of Long Term Capital Management*, New York 2000, p. 223.

38 'Predatory Lending in America', *The Economist*, 10 March 2001.

39 Philip Augar, *The Death of Gentlemanly Capitalism*, London 2001, p. 314.

40 Ibid., p. 315.

41 Ibid.

42 Robert Gordon, 'Not Much of a New Economy', *Financial Times*, 24 July 2000.

43 Gerard Baker, 'Miracle or Mirage', *Financial Times*, 8 June 2001; Philip Coggan, 'Confidence and Concern', *Financial Times*, 11 July 2001.

44 Cited in 'Special Report: The New Economy', *The Economist*, 12 May 2001, pp. 99–102.

45 Christopher Parkes, 'Power Failure', *Financial Times*, 27 December 2000.

46 Tim Reiterman, 'State Sues Parent of Troubled PG&E', *Los Angeles Times*, 11 January 2002.

47 Gillian O'Connor, 'Alcoa to Cut Production in Northwest US', *Financial Times*, 8 January 2001.

48 Duncan Campbell, 'New Enron Scandal Link to Bush', *Guardian*, 2 February 2002.

49 'Another Crash, Another Crisis', *The Economist*, 21 October 2000.

50 'Public Investment: They Can't Spend It', *The Economist*, 25 November 2000.

51 Robert Pollin, 'Anatomy of Clintonomics', pp. 17–46, p. 36. The *Economist's* 'Economic Indicators' showed real US wage growth below 1 per cent in its issue of 19–25 February 2000; and in its issue of 12–18 August 2000 this section noted: 'American workers received pay rises of 3.7% in the 12 months to July but failed to see any gains in real terms'.

52 G. Burtless, 'Growing American Inequality', *Brookings Review*, winter 1999, vol. 17, no. 1, pp. 31–5.

53 A.B. Atkinson, 'The Tall Story of Widening Inequality', *Financial Times*, 16 August 2000. For evidence suggesting growing inequality in the UK in the late 1990s see Tom Clark and Jane Taylor, 'Income Inequality: a Tale of Two Cycles', *Fiscal Studies*, vol. 20, no. 4, December 1999, pp. 387–408.

54 Jennifer Reingold, 'Special Report: Executive Pay', *Business Week*, 17 April 2000, pp. 100–14.

55 Ibid.

56 *Business Week*, 20 April 1999.
57 'Rewarding the Boardroom: A Survey', *Guardian*, 22 August 2000.
58 Charlotte Denny, 'Gazing in Awe at Executive Salaries, US-style', *Guardian*, 23 August 2000.
59 Simon Targett, 'The Institutional Investor Starts to Stir', *Financial Times*, 23 July 2001.
60 Robert Brenner, 'The Boom and the Bubble', *New Left Review*, second series no. 6, November–December 2000, pp. 5–44, p. 24. See also Peter Martin, 'Buy-outs without the Buy-in', *Financial Times*, 17 April 2002.
61 Daniel Bogler, 'Executive Pay Increases Come under Attack', *Financial Times*, 14 March 2000.
62 Charles Pretzlick, 'Gent Tries to Placate Investors', *Financial Times*, 25 July 2000.
63 'Money for Nothing?', *The Economist*, 18 August 2001.
64 Ibid.
65 Ibid.
66 Astrid Wentland, 'UK Fund Managers Beat US on Pay', *Financial Times*, 25 June 2001.
67 A.B. Atkinson urges that market forces alone do not explain these trends but also a decline in egalitarian 'pay norms', and the social solidarity to enforce them. See 'The Tall Story of Widening Inequality'.
68 These quotes all come from Daniel Gross, *Bull Run: Wall Street, the Democrats, and the New Politics of Personal Finance*, New York 2000, pp. 85–7.
69 Robert Wade and Frank Veneroso, 'The East Asian Crash and the Wall St-IMF Complex', *New Left Review*, no. 228, March-April 1998, pp. 3–24, and 'The Battle over Capital Controls', *New Left Review*, no. 231, September–October 1998, pp. 3–27.
70 Gretchen Morgenson, 'Analysts: Salesmanship Takes Precedence over Research', *International Herald Tribune*, 2 January 2001.
71 Shiller, *Irrational Exuberance*.
72 Franklin Allen and Gary Gorton, 'Churning Bubbles', *Review of Economic Studies*, vol. 60, 1993, pp. 813–36, p. 832.
73 Daniel Ben-Ami, *Cowardly Capitalism: the Myth of the Global Financial Casino*, London 2001.
74 John Plender, 'Globalisation's Troops: Investment Banks have Brought their Model of Market Capitalism to Companies around the World', *Financial Times*, 21 December 2000.
75 Steven Kaplan, 'Corporate Governance and Corporate Performance: a Comparison of Japan, Germany and the United States', *Journal of Applied Corporate Finance*, vol. 9, no. 4, Winter 1997. See also Franklin Allen and Douglas Gale, *Comparing Financial Systems*, New York 2000.
76 I analysed the reasons for the failure of the Soviet model in 'Fin de Siècle: Socialism After the Crash', *New Left Review*, no. 185, January–February 1991.
77 Axel Leijonhufvud, 'The Nature of the Depression in the Former Soviet Union', *New Left Review*, no. 199, May–June 1993; Peter Nolan, *China's Rise,*

Russia's Fall, London 1995; Stephen Cohen, *Failed Crusade: America and the Tragedy of Post-Communist Russia*, New York 2001; Joseph Stiglitz, *Whither Socialism?*, Cambridge (MA) 1994, pp. 175–6.

78 John Lloyd, 'Sweden 2.0: The Information Nation', *The Industry Standard Europe*, 1 March 2001; Daniel Stedman Jones with Ben Crowe, *Transformation not Automation: the e-government Challenge*, Demos 2001, pp. 22–3; Christopher Brown-Humes, 'High-tech Haven Braced for the Slowdown', and Rafael Behr, 'Technology', in 'Finland' survey, *Financial Times*, 5 July 2001.

79 The point is well made by Adair Turner, *Just Capital: the Liberal Economy*, London 2001, pp. 155–6, 244–5. For the failure of the state in the US to support broadband technology see Karen Kornbluh, 'The Broadband Economy', *New York Times*, 10 December 2001.

80 Leo Panitch, 'The New Imperial State', *New Left Review*, second series no. 2, March–April 2000, pp. 5–20.

81 Stanley Engerman, 'Human Capital, Education and Economic Growth', in Robert W. Fogel and Stanley S. Engerman, eds, *The Reinterpretation of American Economic History*, New York 1971, pp. 241–56. See also Claudia Goldin and Lawrence Katz, 'The Legacy of US Educational Leadership', *American Economic Review*, vol. 91, no. 2, 2001, pp. 18–23.

82 Turner, *Just Capital*, p. 177.

83 'The Wireless Gamble', *The Economist*, 14 October 2000.

84 Gregory Zuckerman and Deborah Solomon, 'Epic Telecom Debt Debacle', *Wall Street Journal*, 14 May 2001.

85 For the activities of the hedge funds see Barton Biggs, 'The Hedge Fund Bubble', *Financial Times*, 9 July 2001, and John Plender, 'The Hedge Funds', *Financial Times*, 18 August 2001.

86 Taggart Murphy, 'Japan's Economic Crisis', *New Left Review*, second series no. 1, January–February 2000, pp. 5–24.

87 Press Briefing by Director of the National Economic Council Gene Sperling and Deputy Secretary of the Treasury Larry Summers, The Briefing Room, The White House, 14 April 1999, available on the web-site of the Network Democracy Social Security Briefing Book .

88 Philip Coggan, 'Surplus up, Savings down', *Financial Times*, 4 September 2000. He was commenting on a paper, 'Opposites Attract', by Ian Morris of HSBC, New York.

4

The Global Drive to Commodify Pensions

The systematic search for the highest value possible for the share-holder is nothing other than the disguised expression of rentier interests, with a strong preference for the future over the present, a translation of the power of Anglo-Saxon pensioners (who are the only ones to save so strongly) over the whole of world society, in short of old, or ageing, Americans and Britons to the detriment of young people of all other countries. Have we already succumbed to this new form of serfdom? Let us forget for a moment frontiers and national-ities: within each of us, to put it another way, old age is in charge of what we do. The high rates of interest we have known for nearly twenty years, are they not the expression of this new domination, of governance without debate? . . . Indeed we find that today's work-ers have no say over how their savings are invested and the activities of the most powerful financial interests are legitimated.

(Jean Peyrelevade, president of Crédit Lyonnais,
Commentaire, autumn 1998)

To bolster the pillars of the European economy, the ECB [European Central Bank] is intent on using its authority to promote a reform of European labor markets, wage cartels and welfare state. . . . Amid the grand rhetoric of the midnight changeover, one of Mr. Duisenberg's most revealing comments came when he said Europe needed to adopt American-style free market policies.

(John Schmid, 'New Era for ECB', *International Herald Tribune*,
2 January 2002)

Italians Warn that Pensions are like High Tension Cables; Do Not Touch! (Mimmo Chianura, AGF, 1994)

In the first chapter I pointed out that privately managed pension delivery first arose in countries where stock markets were already flourishing. Also noted was the Chilean government's move in 1981 to wind down its public pension system and replace it with a 'mandatory' privately managed system. Because it was replacing a universal state scheme, the new arrangement also claimed to be universal; hence the obligatory contributions which were to be invested in property, shares and other marketable assets. Thus pension funds were being introduced to a country with a weak stock market, indeed, at that moment, a very weak economy altogether. However, the country did have some long-established financial institutions which, following introduction of the mandatory contributions, were able to set up pension funds (AFPs) which could henceforth rely on a steady stream of business. The scheme was introduced by a finance minister trained at the University of Chicago and one of its merits in his eyes was that it reduced the weight of the state in the economy. Other measures that accompanied the introduction of the AFPs were the privatisation of state assets, completion of the agrarian reform and a 'shock therapy' programme. As noted in chapter 1, the huge state-owned copper mine, CODELCO, much of whose revenues were hypothecated to the military, was left well alone. The pension entitlements conferred by the public system had been reduced to a pittance by raging inflation. The new AFPs were not due to pay out their first pensions for over a decade. In the meantime they were the recipients of a steady stream of contributions from all those in regular employment, as required by law, a dose of compulsion necessitated by this particular 'free market' measure. The AFPs pumped resources and liquidity into Chile's fledgling market economy, strengthening its financial system and playing a much-needed part in the recovery from the desperate conditions of the early 1980s. The military government was persuaded by burgeoning domestic opposition and international pressure to hold a referendum, which it lost, in 1988. The rigour of shock therapy was somewhat abated as the elected government found a Harvard-trained economist to replace the 'Chicago boys'. This also helped the recovery. By the mid-1990s the AFPs had built up assets of $25 billion which seemed promising. The 'Chilean example' was sufficiently established by the early 1990s to play a part, together with Margaret Thatcher's 'market revolution' and privatisation programmes, in a general assault on

welfare entitlements and public provision. Much less attention was paid to
a Swiss law of 1982 which also established mandatory private secondary
pensions but accompanied with a guaranteed 4 per cent rate of return
annually on deposits.[1]

Efforts would be made to promote the idea of mandatory private pensions in many parts of the world, not excluding the United States itself
which still, after all, had a Social Security retirement system in which
Wall Street played no role. International advice to other Latin American
countries and to the former Communist states often proposed some variant of the Chilean 'model'. Japan already possessed a mixed regime of
public and private pensions, and the early 1990s – the aftermath of the collapse of the 'bubble economy' of the late 1980s – scarcely seemed the right
moment to compel citizens to put their life savings in the stock exchange.
However, the European Union seemed readier to embrace the new
'market-friendly' message which the World Bank preached in its 1991
annual report. The European Left and labour movements were groggy
from a series of defeats. The sinking of the Common Programme of the
French Union of the Left government in 1982, after massive capital flight,
had been followed by a demoralising accommodation to market economics. The major parties of the European Left suffered a string of electoral
setbacks in the 1980s and early 1990s. The failure of Gorbachev's peres-
troika and the collapse of the Soviet bloc in 1989–91 for a time weakened
the Left everywhere. Yet most countries belonging to the European Union
still had generously conceived and publicly run pension arrangements –
and practically no commercial pension provision at all. The schemes in
France, Germany and Italy had close to universal coverage and delivered a
pension of 60–70 per cent of pre-retirement earnings. These deeply
entrenched public pension systems, and the collectivist welfare arrangements of which they were a part, represented a stand against the now
triumphant formulas of free market economics. At the same time, they
acted as a barrage against the ambitions of the global financial services
industry – unless it was breached, the impetus to 'financialisation' would be
kept at bay in the world's second-largest economic zone.

Since the Christian Democrats and the Gaullists had helped to build
Europe's collectivist welfare capitalism, weaning them away from these
arrangements would not be easy. The only reason for hope of this happening was that the European economy had been underperforming for
some time, with lower profits and rising unemployment. Above all, the
German miracle was fading and German business was finding it harder to
meet US and East Asian competition. The custodians of financial

orthodoxy argued that if the Europe of the 1990s was to remain competitive and restore profit levels, then it needed to keep down social costs. Some sections of the European financial services industry, notably the French insurance houses and some of the German and Swiss banks, became strongly committed to pension reform since it would open up impressive new business opportunities. Jacques Delors, the president of the European Commission, wanted to see the Commission entrusted with a large public works programme to lift the European economy out of recession. But the central bankers, above all the Bundesbank, vetoed the idea on the grounds that it would stoke up inflation and ruin the chance to restore the competitive edge of European products in export markets. Most of the central bankers were just as convinced that welfare, especially pensions, had to be drastically scaled down. But while the politicians would not defy the Bundesbank by embarking on Delors's grand scheme of Keynesian expansion, they hesitated to question popular and well-entrenched welfare programmes. Clever arguments and moral support would be needed to stiffen the confidence of politicians before they were brave enough to take the cause of pension reform to the people – and risk being mowed down by their opponents in the process. The World Bank obliged in 1994 by publishing a report on pension provision and the global phenomenon of ageing populations.

The World Bank and *Averting the Old Age Crisis*

The World Bank's report, to be entitled *Averting the Old Age Crisis*, was commissioned in the early 1990s at a time when its Chief Economist, Lawrence Summers, was increasingly convinced of the necessity to push back the type of public provision once advocated by his uncle, Paul Samuelson, and to embrace the free market doctrines of Milton Friedman, an early advocate of pension privatisation. As he later explained: 'Milton Friedman . . . was the devil figure in my youth. Only with time have I come to have large amounts of grudging respect. And with time increasingly ungrudging respect.'[2] The first embodiment of the Bank's more market-friendly approach was its 1991 *World Development Report,* but *Averting the Old Age Crisis* was a logical sequel because pensions absorb so much public money and because pension financing is bound to have large implications for the overall economic pattern. In the Preface to *Averting the Old Age Crisis*, written by Summers's successor as Chief Economist, it is claimed that the report was the 'first comprehensive global examination of this complex and pressing set of issues'; indeed it 'synthesises what is known, analyses policy alternatives, and provides a framework for identifying the policy mix most appropriate to a given country's needs'.[3] The authors of the report, a team led by the US pensions economist Estelle James, had indeed assembled much information and spoken with many leading authorities. While adopting the mantle of balance and judiciousness, it was, in fact, quite boldly prescriptive, with implications for the core developed OECD states, with their ageing populations, as well as for 'young countries', emerging markets and those 'in transition'.

The starting point of the report was that public pay-as-you-go (PAYGO) systems were 'financially unsustainable', not just in less developed countries, with their weaker economies, but everywhere. The report was able to quote some unguarded comments by Paul Samuelson, the man who, more than anyone else, had furnished PAYGO pensions with credibility among economists. In a 1967 *Newsweek* article Samuelson wrote:

> The beauty of social insurance is that it is actuarially unsound. Everyone who reaches retirement age is given benefit privileges that far exceed anything he has paid in. . . . How is this possible? It stems from the fact that the national product is growing at compound interest and can be expected to do so for as far ahead as the eye cannot see. Always there are more youths than old folks in a growing population. More important, with real incomes growing at some three percent a year, the taxable base upon which benefits rest in any period are much greater than the taxes paid historically by the generation now retired. . . . A growing nation is the greatest Ponzi Game ever invented.[4]

By 1994, with ageing populations and after two decades of low growth and stagnant or even declining earnings, the game was up for PAYGO. The report was able to cite a contrite Samuelson himself warning about the 'primrose path' of unfunded, or inadequately funded, pension programmes, when population and income growth had stalled.

As the analysis of the report unfolded, public pension provision, and the payroll taxes used to finance it, were indicted as major culprits for stagnation, firstly because of the economic distortions they generated and secondly because they stood in the way of private pensions which would expand the capital market: 'behind the government's fiscal crisis lies the deeper crisis of labor and capital markets that are malfunctioning, preventing the growth that is ultimately the only way out of these difficulties.'[5] Payroll taxes (i.e. the levies, like National Insurance contributions in the

THE GLOBAL DRIVE TO COMMODIFY PENSIONS   231

UK, which go towards social insurance) deterred employers from taking on workers, leading to unemployment and a growth of the 'informal sector'. Combined with generous public pensions, the taxes promoted early retirement and, especially in Europe, a consequent decline in labour participation rates for those over fifty. Moreover, the early retirement of skilled workers was a dead loss to the economy; younger, unskilled workers did not take their place. And the impact on capital markets of overweening public systems was as nefarious as the impact on labour markets, squandering savings, deterring private entrepreneurs and blocking the inventiveness of the financial services industry.

The report advocated, in a seemingly even-handed fashion, a 'multi-pillar' approach to pension provision comprising: (1) a mandatory state pension, run on a pay-as-you-go basis, paid from taxes and acting as a safety net; (2) a mandatory privately managed pillar, in the shape of a personal or occupational pension, fully funded and managed by the financial services industry; and (3) personal savings of a voluntary character.

The prescriptive bias of the report was directed against the 'dominant public pillar',[6] which was the problem, and towards mandatory personal savings plans, which were the solution. State pensions, where they were fully operational, needed to be curtailed. They were cursed by increasing dependency ratios, overgenerous and ill-thought-out benefits, overmaturity and negative side-effects. In most OECD countries, existing schemes were 'financially unsustainable' in their present form because they could only be paid for by doubling or trebling payroll taxes that were already too high. The United States and the UK would need to increase the tax take of GDP by 4.4 per cent and 4.8 per cent respectively to finance pension promises, but for Germany an extra 6.2 per cent of GDP would have to be claimed in taxes; in France 5.5 per cent, in Japan 6.8 per cent and in Italy no less than an extra 11.9 per cent of GDP.[7] The 'tough choices' imposed by the unsustainability of the PAYGO systems included cutting back benefit levels, raising the retirement age, raising taxes – or moving to a new regime where state pensions no longer bore the brunt of retirement provision but instead acted as a safety net.

The introduction of mandatory privately managed and fully pre-funded pension schemes would help to take the strain from public systems. For this second pillar, 'defined contribution' occupational plans were preferable to 'defined benefit' versions, because they were more likely to be portable and non-discriminatory. It is conceded that occupational schemes can be implemented through payroll deductions, but personal plans supplied by the financial services industry had the further advantages of enabling the purchaser to benefit from scale economies and avoiding other inconveniences of the occupational schemes, such as impeding labour mobility and economic restructuring. The following conclusion is reached after a judicious weighing of 'seeming' advantages and real disadvantages: 'Overall, personal savings schemes would seem to have the edge for the privately managed mandatory pillar.'[8]

The critique of the payroll taxes used to finance state pensions stressed employee interests. Unlike income tax, payroll taxes were not 'progressive', that is they do not take more from the rich than the poor; indeed, even when contributions are graduated, they are often regressive, taxing lower- or middle-income employees at a higher rate. Over successive generations this effect can even be intensified, since early generations do much better out of the system than the later generations. The report also noted that workers actually bore the cost of so-called 'employers' contributions' in all cases where the supply of labour would be maintained despite a decline in real wage rates:

> In industrial countries, the supply of labor is relatively inelastic with respect to wages: most workers, especially prime age males, continue working when a tax lowers their disposable income. In that case, workers pay not only their share but also their employers' share as well, in lower wages, since wages fall enough to keep everyone employed. Although wages fall, output does not fall and the tax is not inefficient. In the few situations in which wages cannot fall any further because a legal or social minimum has been reached, employers pay the tax and may cut back on employment and output as a result. This is inefficient. This line of thought suggests that the rise in payroll tax rates in OECD countries over the past two decades may be one possible explanation for the rise in unemployment and the more general slowdown in the growth of real wages. This process redistributes income away from workers but in an opaque way (less employment, slower growth) that may lead workers to pressure for a larger public pension plan than they would want if they realized the full cost.[9]

What had been a 'line of thought', a suggestion of a possibility, hardens a little even in these few lines. A few pages later we read a complementary assertion: 'public pay-as-you-go schemes may have dampened long term saving and capital accumulation relative to what would have occurred under fully funded schemes.'[10] Notwithstanding their apparently tentative initial formulation, these points are repeatedly invoked and are central to the argumentative thrust of the report. The demographic arguments, in themselves, yield no conclusions about the best way of delivering pensions. If the proportion of, say, over-65s is set to rise from 11 per cent of the population to 22 per cent over two or three decades, then either pension provision doubles or pensioners suffer. If the 11 per cent who are pensioners receive, say, 6 per cent of GDP today, then in future they will need to receive roughly 12 per cent of GDP unless their already below-average income is to decline. Private delivery systems are subject to the same mathematical laws as public delivery systems. The report was ready to attribute a multitude of negative side-effects to public provision but it did not go so far as to attack it for keeping more people alive or to recommend private systems on the grounds that they would thin out the ranks of the elderly. The critical argument was therefore that raising payroll taxes would be counter-productive and inefficient. But even if this argument were to be accepted, then some other taxes could be found – on sales, incomes, property or consumption. The report did not offer a comprehensive critique of taxes but instead counted on the assertion that, whatever their form, they could not be raised. And then there was the problem that contributions to the proposed mandatory system would themselves function very like a payroll tax.

While the authors of the report rule out tax increases as politically unfeasible, they instead assume that citizens will accept compulsory deductions from their earnings so long as they are put into approved, tax-favoured personal or occupational funds. At this point their argument could amount to demanding that social insurance contributions really should go into a fund and not be treated as another tax and that the public social fund should be visibly more accountable to those it was set up to benefit. But the report is, in fact, hostile to any such approach. Instead, it insists that pension funds must be commercially managed and subject to lighter public regulation. It claims that those forced to pay contributions will see them as the price they are paying for a purchase and that this perception will banish all the negative aspects of payroll taxes.

While singing the praises of privately furnished pension schemes, the report seemingly balances this by airing criticisms of some of their limitations. It concedes that the coverage of private pension funds is often too narrow: that is why a mandatory approach is needed. The report urges that pension funds should be freed from political interference and should be 'liberated' – an 'idea whose time has come' – from such irksome restraints as minimum holdings of public bonds or controls on the export of capital. It helpfully explains: 'Easy capital outflow helps to stimulate capital inflows, because a prime concern of international investors is to be able to get out of a market quickly when the need arises.'[11]

Employees would accept the obligation to pay a proportion of their earnings to the financial services industry because the returns would be good and fund members would have the satisfaction of seeing their fund grow. The capital markets would receive a much-needed boost and the employment-harming effects of high taxes, especially high payroll taxes, would be avoided. Tax breaks were to continue. The pension fund industry, having been created in its present form by lavish tax concessions, was thus now to be further boosted by compulsory and government-subsidised contributions from the entire workforce. And the report's recommendations applied also to poorer countries, where state pensions are burdensome because of a shortage of the requisite administrative resources. In the case of private pension plans this need be no obstacle: 'The shortage of local expertise in many developing countries may be overcome by using foreign fund managers in joint ventures with local firms. Developing countries reluctant to use joint ventures may have a hard time assembling the expertise needed to run pension funds well, especially in the early years.'[12]

The report, as we have seen, mildly favoured personal savings plans over occupational funds, but strongly favoured private funds of any description over state-sponsored provident funds – despite what was admitted to be the higher administrative and marketing charges involved in the former. Administrative charges in the Chilean system had been very high to begin with and had then come down to 2.3 per cent of assets in 1990. Although employees had to join a scheme they could choose from more than a score of AFPs and, if they became unhappy, could switch. This led to intense competition between rival sales teams and consequent expense. By contrast, the Central Provident Fund of Singapore, a public scheme, had annual administrative costs of only 0.16 per cent of assets a year in 1990 and the Malaysian Provident Fund, also a government scheme, had expenses of 0.18 per cent. However, the investment returns of the AFPs had been 7.5 to 10.5 per cent in 1990 while the Malaysian return was 4.82 per cent and that in Singapore 2.86 per cent.[13] The AFPs had yet to pay out any pensions, which should have reduced costs. And the Singapore CPF, as the report noted, had a remit to help participants buy their dwellings or meet some other permitted expenditures (e.g. training fees), lowering the current rate of return but with some returns to come in the future. *Averting the Old Age Crisis* offered a strategically located table on investment rates of return which signalled the superiority of private over public fund management – though in fact no information was given on administrative charges and the public funds in question were obliged to invest almost exclusively in specially denominated public bonds. Covering periods of between five and ten years in the 1980s, the table showed that the rate of return on public funds in Peru, Zambia, Venezuela, Egypt and

Kenya had been negative, sometimes strongly so; but no information was supplied on conditions in these countries, including rates of return on equity capital. The public bonds given to the funds in exchange for contribution income had steadily lost value, usually because of inflation. This funding device was, in effect, a means whereby the governments concerned treated pension contributions as tax income. The table, not surprisingly, showed better rates of return for the advanced countries, though once again public funds have usually been required to invest in special government bonds. The surplus in the US Social Security account was allotted interest of 4.8 per cent annually. Again, this was a reflection of a government-sanctioned Treasury diktat. The investment income reaped by privately managed funds was higher, according to the table. During the 1980s Dutch occupational schemes returned 6.7 per cent annually, compared with 8.0 per cent for US occupational funds and 8.6 per cent for those in the UK. The Singapore CPF return averaged 3.0 per cent in the 1980s and the Malaysian CPF 4.6 per cent, while the Chilean AFPs came top of the class with 9.2 per cent. The conclusion: 'Privately managed funds beat publicly managed funds hands down'.[14]

In fact, this conclusion was produced by fixing the contest in advance, with no account taken of charges, no information on the returns of personal pensions in the UK or United States and the exclusion or misattribution of evidence concerning public or social funds that were not commercially managed. If information had been given concerning individual pension plan holders in the UK and United States, some would have shown negative or very low returns where participants had been penalised for not maintaining payments. And the figures given in the table lumped the rather successful public sector pension funds in Britain, the United States and the Netherlands into the 'privately managed' category. The exclusion of costs also tilted the comparison against the public funds. The Chilean AFPs were lauded but no attention was paid to the fact that in certain respects they did not exemplify the 'liberated' model of a pension fund since they were prevented from investing outside the country – exactly the sort of regulation deplored by the report. On the other hand, the specifically commercial aspects of the AFP, such as their costly marketing campaigns or special inducements for new members (which led to disruptive fund hopping), promised to be a serious drag on their eventual ability to deliver.

The report did not completely ignore the possibility of overcharging and competitive waste in privately run schemes. It also noted criticism of fund managers' 'short-termism', herd-like behaviour and elitism vis-à-vis the local or small scale. It conceded that small companies and start-ups might have suffered. But whereas the failures of private pension schemes posed 'regulatory issues' which had to be addressed, those of funded public schemes mean that they should simply be abandoned. In fact the 'public funds' to which the report paid most attention scarcely deserved the name but were simply accounting devices used by public treasuries. If the record of public sector funds had been scrutinised, no doubt some problems would have been encountered but financial performance would not generally have been among them But the report was not interested in exploring ways of improving non-commercial pension funds. Indeed, the very possibility that pension funds could be pre-funded and run by the state, or by autonomous non-commercial social institutions, was scouted. This would, it warned, pose a threat to free enterprise capitalism. The authors of the report worried that if 'centralized provident funds' were to 'invest in corporate equities, public officials could gain control of corporate affairs, a back door to nationalization'.[15]

The message of the report was global in scope. Notwithstanding the references to the 'multi-pillar' approach, few readers could miss the emphasis on, and the novelty of, the proposal for mandatory personal savings plans. Indeed the strong standpoint emanating from the report and the wide range of evidence it marshalled helped, together with the Bank's authority, to make this a benchmark study.[16] As such, it has attracted its share of critiques, the most searching of which, co-authored by its former Chief Economist, Joseph Stiglitz, will be considered in chapter 6.[17] In July 2001 the director of the Bank's Social Protection Unit claimed that '[t]he World Bank has been and remains one of the main drivers behind the pension revolution' and noted that mandatory private schemes now operated in eleven Latin American countries and three former Communist states.[18] However, there may well have been disappointment at the slow rate of progress in Europe since the major pension systems incarnated the approach which the report found wanting, that of the 'dominant public pillar'. A brief review of attempts to reform pensions in the 1990s in the core countries of continental Europe will give some idea of the social and economic forces at work once attempts were made to move towards privatisation of pension delivery.

The European Battlefield

The 1990s were to represent a decade of repeated challenges to the corporate arrangements of welfare capitalism in Europe. Politicians and state officials knew that pension provision was going to be increasingly expensive and that this would mean higher taxes. The paying of pensions was already the largest single social programme almost everywhere and as the population aged it would go up steeply, just as the World Bank warned. In several countries many in their fifties took early retirement or were able to claim a disability pension. The European economies continued to suffer from what was called 'hysteresis', a combination of slow growth and high unemployment. The argument that the welfare-related payroll taxes made employment too expensive, and hampered competitiveness, was echoed by many neo-liberal economists. The rise in unemployment rates was indeed troubling, and reduced contributions to social funds. But the European continental economies still had great strengths. In fact, they had raised output and incomes over the previous generation more successfully than the Anglo-Saxon economies. The malaise of the early and mid-1990s manifestly related as much to adverse macro-economic conditions and the severely deflationary implications of the Treaty of Maastricht (1992) as it did to European welfare arrangements.

Indeed, some saw in 'Rhineland capitalism' a superior model to the stock exchange-based systems. Will Hutton argued in his bestseller, *The State We're In* (1994), that the Anglo-Saxon economies themselves had a lot to learn from Germany. The close ties between German banks and industrial corporations allowed them to pursue long-term strategies and to achieve a less painful restructuring. The interests of other 'stakeholders' played a role in corporate policy because workers were represented on the management board (*Mitbestimmung*). And German politics, with its strong *Länder* governments and proportional electoral system, was more decentralised, open and supportive. Some dissident economists also showed that a German-style pension system with reserves could effect a more equitable smoothing of retirement income between generations than was possible through the Anglo-Saxon market finance approach.[19] There was much truth in these observations but implicitly they overestimated the willingness of the German political and business elite to resist the conventional dictates of financial orthodoxy and the process of globalisation that lay behind it. The German government had seized the great prize of unification but knew that it would have to pick up a heavy bill. The Bundesbank reluctantly acceded to Chancellor Kohl's politically driven decision that Ostmarks should be exchanged at parity with Westmarks but was thereafter bound to opt for the greatest caution. In these circumstances Germany insisted on tough conditions for European monetary union, conditions that would include a tight rein on social expenditures. Within the milieu of the central bankers monetarism anyway held sway, in deference to domestic rentiers and foreign investors. At Maastricht the other European states endorsed the doctrines of 'central bankism', and thereby made inevitable a series of attempts to 'reform' (cut) pension benefits.[20] They undertook to bring public sector deficits to within 3 per cent of GDP and to reduce public debt. And Jacques Delors's Europe-wide infrastructure programme was put back on the shelf.

It was not only central bankers who were persuaded that a radical new dispensation was needed. The financial industry in both Europe and America was looking for new grazing pastures. The UK pension funds already invested over 30 per cent of their assets abroad in 1990. The US funds made a smaller allocation to overseas assets but in absolute terms the sums they had available for placement were even larger. So long as the right conditions existed, then overseas investment would contribute to asset diversification. The 'right conditions' meant, in this context, legal security of the investment and an ability to monitor the financial data of the concern in which investment was being made. From this standpoint, the countries of the European Union were bound to be more attractive prospects to US investors than most other alternatives. Hence the impatience to see Europe swept by a market revolution.

By the mid-1990s the Anglo-Saxon model of stock exchange capitalism was beginning to make strategic inroads in the principal European economies, encouraged by a spate of privatisations of publicly owned industries and utilities. The Maastricht 'convergence criteria' dictated the sell-offs, rather than any inherent rationality in disposing of public assets. Indeed, while the sale of profitable public assets makes a once-and-for-all windfall gain, in the medium and long term it reduced the European governments' sources of income. The French insurance houses acquired shares in the concerns privatised by the French government but there was still plenty of action for the 'Anglo-Saxon' pension and mutual funds, which thus acquired control of significant chunks of French industry. (It is to the French that we owe the term 'Anglo-Saxon economics'.) The leverage of the bourse over all sectors increased. Many of the European financial concerns envied the free-wheeling behaviour of their Anglo-Saxon counterparts. But to play at the same table as the large American banks meant gaining access to more high-denomination chips. There was a steady rise in the hubbub about pension reform in the financial sections of the newspapers. The bad news was unaffordable state pensions but the good news was the great promise of a private pension system. If employees paid lower payroll taxes to the government, then they could begin to pay contributions – tax free! – to the financial institutions. This was not just a routine sales pitch but an invitation to a more exciting, mobile and flexible lifestyle. Unfortunately, before the seeds of this attractive and high-yielding new variety could be sown, it was necessary to clear an overhanging forest of inherited social institutions. Without public pension austerity there could be no private pension bonanza.

The ways in which pensions in Europe might be cut were easy to identify, but fairly large measures that would take effect quickly were needed. There was some hope of extending the age at which benefits could be claimed and breaking the index link to earnings. The British government had successfully broken the index link between pensions and average earnings in 1980 and the savings on the pension bill were already quite noticeable. The US government had achieved some economies in Social Security expenditure by making early retirement less attractive and by raising the age of retirement for women. The problem for the governments in Paris, Bonn and Rome was that similar measures would provoke a storm of opposition and were anyway inadequate, or would take too long to achieve the required economies. When the Spanish government had sought in 1988 to cut pension entitlements it sparked off a general strike which obliged it to back down; but at least the Spanish economy was growing reasonably fast at the time.[21]

Already in 1980 the French Commissariat du Plan had forecast that the prevailing pension regime would face a crisis within twenty to thirty years. Dominique Strauss-Kahn, a Socialist economist, published a book arguing for pre-funding of pension commitments in 1982. However, the Common Programme came to grief in the same year and for the rest of the decade the parties of the Right and Left alternated without summoning up the energy for a reform of the pension system. The first politician in France to propose a reassessment of pension benefits was Michel Rocard, the Socialist Prime Minister, in a White Paper in 1991. He proposed raising the qualifying number of years to be worked for entitlement to a full pension and some other economies. The White Paper did not propose privatisation but it did suggest that it would be wise to build up a reserve fund so that *répartition* and taxation did not have to cover the full burden as the pension bill rose. Rocard was shortly thereafter replaced as prime minister and before long his party suffered a crushing political defeat, reflecting weariness with a Socialist administration that allowed unemployment to grow, failed to tackle social exclusion and was tainted with corruption. The Socialist defeat was not specifically related to the pension question on which no action had been taken. In the wake of Soviet collapse the Communist Party offered no rallying point, so that the early 1990s marked an epochal low point for the Left in France, as in several other countries. The subsequent government of Édouard Balladur profited from the collapse of the Left to steer pension economies through the Assembly with little debate – these indexed several private sector schemes (including AGIRC, the scheme for managers and administrators) to prices rather than earnings and extended the qualifying contribution period for a full pension from 37.5 years to 40 years, thus selectively adopting ideas floated in Rocard's earlier White Paper. But Balladur did not tamper with the *régimes speciaux*, covering workers in the public sector and state enterprises (then including railways, electricity, mining and telecommunications). Furthermore, he sought to offset the impact of pension economies by a tax-financed 'solidarity fund' to ensure pensions to those who had a poor contribution record.[22] But a widespread impression remained that he was no friend to the country's self-managed welfare arrangements and would push for greater private provision. In the 1995 presidential contest Balladur was defeated by Chirac, a Gaullist whose campaign stressed social protection and the need for a war on unemployment.

Alain Juppé, Balladur's successor as prime minister of the centre-Right government, came under heavy pressure to bring down projected public borrowing to enable France to satisfy the Maastricht criteria. With state pension expenditure comprising over 12 per cent of GNP it was obviously a prime candidate for pruning. Juppé took up the cause of pension austerity in 1995, targeting the *régimes speciaux*, and proposing that in future their administration would be transferred from the *caisses*, with their trade union-nominated staff, to the government apparatus. The government also announced a reduction in the size of the rail network. By this time trade union density, always on the low side in France, had halved, reaching the dismal level of 9 per cent of the workforce, and Juppé believed that overcoming union resistance would be easy. The welfare reform plan was launched with little preparation and immediately provoked the protracted public sector strike of November–December 1995. The strike was centred on the transport system, which was consequently paralysed. Electric supply and telecommunications workers appeared in the large demonstrations of solidarity which took place in the principal cities. The course of public debate and the evidence of the polls showed that the strikers' cause was identified with defence of the Republic and its social tradition. Indeed, the strike received more public support than the famous events of May 1968.[23] The government felt obliged to back down to restore normal working and to prevent a spread of the strike. This humiliation crippled Juppé's government and set the scene for the victory of the new leader of the

Socialists, Lionel Jospin, in elections held eighteen months later. The Juppé government had tried to introduce legislation giving better tax treatment to private pension funds but Jospin delivered on a promise to prevent its ratification.[24]

Social resistance to pension reform was not limited to France. In Italy the *tangentopoli* scandal ripped like a tornado through the Italian political system in the early and mid-1990s, destroying the previous parties of government. But when the media magnate Berlusconi sought to reassemble a right-wing coalition in 1994–95 the issue on which his government foundered, after only nine months, was pension reform. Italian trade unionists rallied to the defence of the earnings link, with hundreds of thousands taking to the streets in the largest demonstrations seen for twenty years. It became clear that most Italians thought it wrong to tear up contracts entered into many years ago. The interim administration of Lamberto Dini was able to make some amendments to pension entitlements, with tacit support from much of the parliamentary Left.[25] However, as a proportion of GDP the projected cost of Italian pension obligations remained much higher than its equivalent in any other European country. But in a rather unsatisfactory way the 1995 legislation weakens commitments to contributors.

In Germany Helmut Kohl trimmed some benefits but failed to make serious headway with pension reform since it aroused such widespread opposition.[26] Nevertheless, the voters blamed him for his attempts to qualify pension benefits. The Social Democrats gave a prominent pledge in its manifesto to pensions: 'A government led by the SPD will ensure that the so-called "generation contract" between the older and the younger generations remains in force. The cuts in retirement pension . . . have reduced many pensioners, both men and women, to the status of people on welfare.'[27] The SPD promised to reverse those cuts and to overhaul the basic pension so that no pensioner needed to claim supplementary assistance. The robust defence of social provision figured as a major item in the Social Democrat and Green victory in the election of 1998.

The previous administrations having been ousted because of their attempt to reduce pension provision, the new governments of Lionel Jospin in France, Romano Prodi in Italy and Gerhard Schroeder in Germany now proceeded to wrestle with the issue of 'pension reform', subject to many of the same pressures as their (more) conservative predecessors. Many of those who opposed neo-liberal solutions had no difficulty in seeing that they were up against a new model of capitalism as well as a specific measure of social austerity. Thus French commentators were worried that Merrill Lynch, Fidelity and their ilk were bent on sucking France into the global casino economy. Michel Aglietta, an adviser to Jospin and doyen of the 'regulation school' of French political economists, saw the rise of the pension funds in the United States as a menacing development which he analysed in the following terms:

> The system of market finance . . . has decisively changed the constraints on the accumulation of capital by changing the way in which proprietary control is exercised. The old form of managerial control accepted pay deals based on stable distribution of the added value of the firms. Long-term stability of accumulation was the management objective. Institutional investors with holdings in a company, by contrast, insist on performance criteria elaborated by the financial markets. They compel firms to maximise their equity value in the short term, under the constraint of hostile mergers or leveraged buy-outs. This form of company management breeds an obsession with cutting wages without thought for future development.[28]

The Anglo-American funds were able to make a large splash in the small pond of the Parisian bourse and some 40 per cent of the shares quoted were in foreign hands by 1998. The overall value of shares quoted on the exchange is equivalent to only one-half of GNP in France compared with around 100 per cent in the United States and a little more in the UK. Nevertheless, the encroachments of foreign capital and the threat to social provision already caused great concern. The outburst from Jean Peyrelevade, president of Crédit Lyonnais, printed as an epigraph to this chapter, portrays the Anglo-Saxon pension fund model as one which menaces French *joie de vivre*, yokes young people everywhere to the retirement plans of ageing Anglo-Saxons and enthrones the conservative rule of the rentiers.[29]

The German privatisations, notably the sale of Deutsche Telekom in 1996, also attracted inward investment. But the extensive formal and informal arrangements of the German banking groups remained a formidable obstacle. Large concerns were protected from takeover and bankruptcy by cross shareholding. Instead the interlocking groups, centred on various leading banks, supported failing concerns by injecting funds and, if it was thought necessary, installing new management. The practice of holding book reserves ear-marked to finance pensions added another source of support; tax does not have to be paid on these funds and in the meantime they can be used to finance investments.

There was relentless propaganda throughout the 1990s alleging that Germany had to reduce its pension benefits and set up independent pension funds. In a 1996 report widely cited in the German press, the McKinsey consultancy argued that while there had been three workers for every German pensioner in the 1960s, there were two workers per pensioner in 1996, and that by 2030 there will be only one worker for each German pensioner. After taking account of the fact that the burden could be somewhat alleviated by increasing the proportion of those aged between 20 and 65 actually in work, and by delaying the age of retirement, the report still forecast the need for taxes at 25–30 per cent of income simply to finance the state pension.[30] The report concluded that the only prudent course was to begin funding now for the looming granny and grandpa boom. In the same year a similar exercise, undertaken by the European Federation for Retirement Provision, a commercial association, salivated at the thought of the $12.71 trillion that, it claimed, ought to be accumulated by 2020 so long as the necessary legislation, together with the appropriate 'investor mentality and risk perception', could be generated.[31]

Representative of the panic which the press sought to sow on the subject of the population bomb is a *Washington Post* report carried on the front page of the *International Herald Tribune*. It began:

> Elizabetta Valle, 50, is on the leading edge of an oncoming European financial crisis that threatens to bankrupt nearly every major government on the Continent. Her daily schedule does not show it, Ms Valle spends her time ferrying her 11- and 14-year old children to school, running errands, shopping for groceries, making snacks, taking the children to swimming practice, then bringing them home to the family's apartment along the Tiber River and cranking up the homework. But once a month her routine varies a tad: She cashes her pension cheque. Like 5 million other Italians under the age of 65, Ms Valle is a youthful retired pensioner. . . . Retirement was a rational choice for Ms Valle nearly three years ago, when the school where she worked eliminated the architectural-drawing classes she taught.[32]

Aware, perhaps, that this little vignette lacked truly flesh-creeping qualities, the reporter went on to summon up the vision of 113 million pensioners, 'aging baby boomers', in Europe by 2025 who would be

> an unprecedented drain on their governments and children. . . . The pension plans 'are so generous it's almost like giving money back to the government if you work longer,' said Jan Mantel, a consultant to the brokerage firm Merrill Lynch & Co, which published a report on European pension reform last year. . . . According to Merrill Lynch, only 7 per cent of EU workers are covered by corporate pensions and only 0.9 per cent by private savings plans. Thus nearly all workers will be entirely dependent on government paid benefits when they retire . . . Europe's time bomb has been ticking for some time now . . . as it comes closer to exploding . . . it is harder to imagine the euro union holding together . . . experts say the

pension situation reflects the defects of the Old Europe, the Europe of the
welfare state . . . The 'special regimes' as they are called, chew up 27 per
cent of all retirement spending in France and are heavily subsidised by general revenue. . . . As for Ms Valle and her husband, they fear the future
financial burden on their children. Do the children worry? 'We haven't told
them yet,' she said.[33]

Corny, or what?

Throughout the advanced world there was a tendency in the 1980s and
1990s for the numbers of over-fifties and over-sixties in employment to
decline, because of early retirement, disability or simply loss of employment.
Even the above story related to a woman who had lost her job rather than
voluntarily retiring. While inflexible payroll taxes and overgenerous benefit schemes have been blamed for the drop in employment among older
workers, the real responsibility lies with macro-economic recession, the disappearance of many traditional industrial jobs, and employee exhaustion
after decades in frontline or exceptionally demanding jobs (train driving,
coal mining, production line work, some types of teaching, policing and so
forth). Those who have lost jobs in their fifties, and who own a house in a
declining region, find it virtually impossible to move or retrain. Even those
in more dynamic regions will be passed over by youth-oriented employers.
That some may be able to claim a disability benefit or early retirement pension is not only humane but could also allow them to take up some less
demanding occupation – so long as they do not thereby forfeit their pension entitlement. In Italy it is well known that many who have taken early
retirement can easily be tempted back to work by the right job offer. A
reform of pension and benefit provision which encouraged such developments would be welcome – but this is usually the very reverse of what
pension reform means. As it is, globalisation itself provokes widespread
awareness that pension entitlements are a vital cushion against the mass sack-
ings that are meted out to staff in the wake of economic rationalisation.

The events in France, Italy and Germany, embracing both impressive
demonstrations and strikes, followed by major electoral setbacks for the
Right, showed that strong campaigns could be mounted to defend the specific pension rights of particular groups of employees, even where these
were set at levels above general pension provision and where early retirement was at stake. Many can be persuaded that pension promises, however
expensive, should be kept – as a matter of principle, out of respect for solidarity between the generations and as a measure of insurance at a time of
growing insecurity. When groups of employees – railway workers in
France or teachers in Italy – took strike action in defence of occupational

provision they attracted strong support. Underlying this activism was both a generalised sense of civic entitlement and a specific sense that past contributions had established a binding commitment to future benefits. A recent study explains:

> The French trade unions view the social-security system as not being part of the state apparatus, but as some sort of collective insurance plan covering all salaried employees. . . . The management of social security was not given to civil servants, but to joint committees composed of representatives of employers and employees. It should be noted that this perception of social security as something which belongs to the world of employment rather than to the state is not a peculiarity of France. A similar view is also found among German trade unionists.[34]

The author adds: 'Generally, earnings-related schemes of Bismarckian inspiration (France, Germany) provide generous benefits which constitute the main source of income for retired persons.'[35] He points out that while 70 per cent of the French population is solely reliant on the state pension, the corresponding figure for Britain is less than 50 per cent and that the coverage of the supplementary State Earnings Related Pension Scheme (SERPS) was much less – rendering it more vulnerable to 'reform' in the Thatcher and Blair years, as we will see in the next chapter.

The reasons for the depth of popular commitment to prevailing pension arrangements in France, Germany and Italy are illuminated by Table 4.1 which measures pensioners' retirement income as a percentage of average male wages in each country for each of three income thresholds: (1) those who were on half average male wages; (2) those who earned the average male wage; and (3) those who earned twice the average male wage.

In the Netherlands, Canada and New Zealand public pensions are paid at a flat rate so the same figure appears in each column. The US replacement rate had improved on the UK rate, as the British state pension shrank as a proportion of earnings, and as US earnings dipped, allowing indexed Social Security payments to gain slightly. All the foregoing can be referred to as 'Anglo-Saxon', because the public pension is considerably below average male wages for every level of earner, thus impelling those who can to join a private or occupational scheme. The French system guarantees a high degree of income maintenance to each income category while redistributing from the top; the German and Italian systems deliver a similar relative pension as US Social Security to low earners, better pensions to average earners and much better pensions to those on twice average earnings. The special French mixture of egalitarianism and corporatism had been defended not just by Gallic logic or republican notions of

Table 4.1 Public pensions as a percentage of average male wages arranged by income category (*c.* 1995)

	Half average male wage	*Average male wage*	*Twice average male wage*
Canada	50	51	51
France	48	95	165
Germany	34	72	150
Italy	32	82	192
Netherlands	41	41	41
New Zealand	38	38	38
UK	25	34	48
US	32	55	64

Note: In the case of Germany and the US employee's entitlements reflect their overall average earnings whereas in other cases it is the years approaching retirement that count.

Source: P. Johnson, *Older Getting Wiser*, Sydney 1999; quoted in James Banks and Carl Emmerson, 'Public and Private Pension Spending: Principles, Practice and the Need for reform', *Fiscal Studies*, vol. 21, no. 1, pp. 1–63, p. 37.

citizenship but by the 'acts of resistance' of November–December 1995.[36] The Dutch arrangements are really closer to the continental than the Anglo-Saxon model. The flat rate state pension had a somewhat higher replacement rate than that of the Anglo-Saxon states and it was accompanied by extensive secondary coverage. In the Netherlands many sections of employment, embracing 80 per cent of the workforce, were covered by mandatory secondary pensions organised by not-for-profit institutions.[37]

While the solidaristic aspects of these pension systems had made it extraordinarily difficult for politicians of the Right to tamper with them, the pressure to mitigate the cost, and to allow tax favours to private pension providers, remains incessant. And it was yet to be seen whether politicians of the Left might not succeed where those of the Right had come to grief.

As Europe headed for the launch of the euro it continued to be afflicted by high unemployment, sluggish growth and a sense of crisis over the future of pension provision. There were now left-wing governments in eleven out of the fifteen EU states, most of them publicly pledged to raise employment levels and defend social provision. The spread of financial crisis from East Asia to Russia and the West in the summer of 1998 posed a clear challenge. At a meeting in Portschach, Austria, on 26–27 October 1998 the leaders of the fifteen EU states pledged themselves to the pursuit of an expansion and harmonisation plan designed to combat unemployment and 'social dumping' and to ensure a resumption of growth. Oskar Lafontaine, the German Finance Minister, and Dominique Strauss-Kahn, his French opposite number, sought to lend substance to this attempt to give a new lead to the Union and to break the veto of the central bankers. Together, these two finance ministers helped to sink the Multi-Lateral Investment Agreement, a pet project of the free market economists and target of popular campaigns, in November 1998. This seemed a good basis from which to reassert the primacy of public programmes and of growth in Europe. Under trade union pressure the French, German and Italian governments were all committed to the introduction of a 35-hour week. Lafontaine and Strauss-Kahn also emphasised the need to impose a Tobin tax on cross-border currency movements. Lafontaine publicly advised the new European Central Bank to lower the interest rate. He was attacked for meddling in the affairs of the bank and for advocating an old-fashioned Keynesian plan to stimulate the European economy.[38]

This approach might have had its problems but it was not adopted. The just-launched euro declined on the exchanges and by March, Oskar Lafontaine, feared by the bankers and blamed for the 10 per cent slide, resigned his post; Strauss-Kahn followed soon after, accused of obtaining money for his party by corrupt means. With the departure of these two men, most particularly of Lafontaine, the option for a neo-Keynesian solution disappeared. The euro continued to subside. So the European economy received a fillip from the undervaluation of the euro rather than from an internal stimulus. Currency devaluations can promote growth and the German and French economies responded well for a time – helped in some cases by the new flexibility that had attended the introduction of the 35-hour week. A significant factor in the decline of the euro was a migration of European capital to North America, as German and French firms bought important stakes in US industry. The message was that by 1999 leading businesses deemed that long-term prospects were better in North America than they were in Europe. In the short term this was wrong. The low euro helped exports and there was better growth in Europe in 1999 and 2000. But there was no clear new model and business confidence was lacking.

Clearly the advent of the euro required positive, continent-wide economic governance aimed at boosting employment and renovating social infrastructure without rekindling inflation. The common currency had yet to win wholehearted public support in any major European country. If there had been real harmonisation of social arrangements, buttressed by a well-financed social and development fund, the citizens of the new Europe might have begun to see tangible advantages. The 35-hour week made real headway in France, Italy and Germany and helped to encourage a more progressive social model. But it needed to be concerted with other measures aimed at sustainable and investment-led growth. As it happens, a seminar sponsored by the European Federation of Trade Unions had met in Barcelona in June 1997 and advocated a new pensions regime for Europe which would have gone some way to plugging the gap. While strongly supporting existing pension provisions, the seminar also recommended steps to establish a new tier of continent-wide pension funds which would be responsive to employee interests and social objectives. The minutes of the meeting record: 'Everybody strongly underlined the need to direct part of the funds towards ethical investments, social investments creating jobs etc.' They also noted: 'All speakers insisted on the necessity of trade union participation in the management of the pension funds.'[39] In a report to the seminar Gunval Grip, a financial analyst for a trade union-owned Swedish insurance house, stressed that pension rights should be seen as 'deferred pay', explaining:

> conceiving of pensions as deferred pay also entails knowing who owns accumulated pension capital. It is the individual or individuals who have deferred their pay who own the accumulated pension capital. This in turn has significant implications for power over the financial market since a large slice of the capital on that market consists precisely of pension capital.[40]

The pension fund he proposed would be fully transferable ('portable') within the EU and would enjoy the same tax concessions in all member states:

> The main rule concerning investment policy for this pension fund is that the capital should be invested in the EU. This promotes capital growth in the EU, which in turn promotes job-creation and, thereby, economic growth. This is also the overriding reason why the pension fund should be subject to the same treatment for tax purposes within the EU and be granted tax concessions in all the EU's member states.

Unfortunately, European Left parties and movements are still inclined to advance their social objectives at a purely national level – the campaign for a 35-hour week was exceptional in this regard. If the case for a European pension fund had been well established, then it is possible that it might have complemented the 'Keynesian' approach of Delors or Lafontaine. But the Barcelona gathering had little direct political weight. The proposals aired at it may attract support in the future but they emerged too late to influence the introduction of the new currency.

The European Left is still somewhat suspicious of funded social security.

The generous public commitment to future pensions in France, Italy and Germany has been, as we have seen, unfunded. And – exaggerations aside – the warnings about the strain on public finances posed by these commitments have some substance. The gradual pre-funding of pension commitments could both render more manageable the future burden of pension provision and prise current economic policy loose from the grip of the rentiers and central bankers. The effect of pre-funding of pension commitments is similar to a reduction in public debt. Such pre-funding would have to be part of a package aimed at stimulating a healthier and more sustainable pattern of growth within the European Union. The World Bank had been wrong to claim that only the financial services industry can hope to organise the task of pre-funding. In fact, governments could make provision for this pre-funding far more efficiently and cheaply. One way of funding the pension obligation would be to endow pension boards throughout the Union with ownership of selected national assets not actually run by the state – such as car companies, banks and airlines. Those enterprises marked down for future privatisation could thus be 'socialised' instead, thus forestalling further ravages of the equity culture. Furthermore, the proceeds of a continent-wide annual levy on all profits, and on salaries above the national average, could feed into a pension fund linked to investment centres in every region of the Union. The precise size of the levy could vary according to the economic conjuncture. The new capitalised pension funds could foster a better quality of growth than would be created simply by large and showy outlays on motorways, air-ports and high-speed trains (the EU's stand-by public works programmes). The real priorities remain rehabilitating the old rustbelt areas, cleaning up the Baltic, North Sea and Mediterranean, raising the technical level of industry and establishing more far-sighted relations of exchange and devel-opment with Eastern Europe, including Russia, and the South, especially Africa and the Middle East.

At present the European Union has no common programmes binding together its constituent states, other than the Common Agricultural Policy and the Convergence fund which are both small in size (relative to Union GDP) and specialist and restrictive in scope. As James Galbraith, Pedro Conceiçao and Pedro Ferreira have pointed out, Europe possesses no pro-gramme like US Social Security which binds together all citizens of the Union, and this means that the amount of regional redistribution brought about by the Union is very much less than that achieved by the US Federal budget. They advocate both a 'truly European welfare state, with a continental retirement programme' and 'the creation of major new universities of the first water . . . in the beautiful, lower income regions of the European periphery and the full funding of students to attend them'.[41] Such an approach would aim to help break the grip of 'hysteresis' on the continent-wide economy, in which from 20 to 50 per cent of 18–25-year-olds and 55–64-year-olds are out of work. Pension funds taking a low-interest equity stake could supply the liquidity which innovatory small and medium enterprises in Europe now find it so difficult to obtain. In 'An Alternative Stability Pact for Europe', an article in the *Cambridge Journal of Economics*, three authors write that the continent is in the grip of the 'new monetarism' because there is no effective counterweight to the European Central Bank. They urge that the European Investment Bank, a body founded in 1959, could play this role if it had greater resources and a more extended charter. The EIB would be the natural depository for Union-wide pension funds, though it would need to work with development boards in every region.[42]

Following the withdrawal of Lafontaine, the destiny of Europe was now in the hands of the central bankers, flanked by centre-Left governments proclaiming the Third Way or *Neue Mitte*. Given an unparalleled opportunity to turn Europe in a new direction, they chose, instead, to push for greater privatisation, on pensions as in other areas. Chancellor Schroeder and Prime Minister Blair believed that governments did not have the answers and that the financial services industry must be given the opportunity to take the problem off their hands. Only in France were there serious reservations about this course. Earlier opposition to the use of demographic alarmism to promote pension cuts and privatisation welled up again in the wake of the Charpin report at the beginning of 1999. Responding to this concern, Lionel Jospin rejected the report's conclusions and announced that his government would seek to establish a new reserve fund to guarantee the future of the pension system. The latter mechanism reflected ideas put forward in the 1991 White Paper, and adapted by Aglietta and other prime ministerial advisers:

> The fund will be financed through the surplus on Social Security, a part of the profits derived from privatization, as well as through taxation and social duties in companies and capital incomes. On the whole, it has been estimated that this fund will represent an amount totalling Fr 1,000 billion (roughly £90 billion or $130 billion) in 2020. The objective here is to help the pay-as-you-go system to overcome the financial difficulties of the 2005–2010 period, when the baby-boom generation retire.[43]

The proceeds of the sale of third-generation mobile phone licences were ear-marked to be paid into this fund. However, this sale raised less than expected, so it remains unclear where adequate resources will be found to allow the fund to meet the funding gap.

In 1999–2000 there were dramatic and probably decisive changes in the modus operandi of the continental European, and especially German, economies. The takeover of Mannesmann by Vodafone in the spring of 2000 signalled that change was under way, as did the prior collapse of Philipp Holzman, the country's second largest construction group. But the decisive event was a major new tax law in July 2000 which permitted large German companies to offload their cross-holdings in other companies without paying capital gains tax; at the same time corporation tax was lowered from 40 per cent to 25 per cent. The future that beckoned was 'Rhineland, USA'. But there was a still a problem since there were no large German pension funds to play their part in the new scenario. As John Plender had explained the previous December: 'The generosity of German state pensions and the absence of a significant private-funded pension sector leaves an ownership gap that has been filled by foreigners. Mannesmann, where more than 60 per cent of the equity is in the hands of non-domestic investors, demonstrates the point.'[44]

The government of Gerhard Schroeder, like its Christian Democrat predecessor, found pension reform a far more difficult issue to tackle because voters readily grasped its import, as they did not when the capital gains tax had been reduced. As noted above, the SPD had won the election of 1998 because it and the trade unions had opposed attempts to cut the pension benefit system. In the summer of 2000 Schroeder's famous negotiation of the new system of corporate taxation was balanced by an initial rebuff on a projected reform of the pension system. This reform, presented by Walter Reister, the labour minister, did anticipate trimming benefit in a few decades' time as part of an attempt to encourage younger workers to make more provision for themselves. It offered full tax relief on up to 4 per cent of gross income that was devoted to contributions to private or occupational pension schemes. The projected cost of the tax subsidies was to be £6.4 billion by 2008 and the approval of the CDU was needed for this if it was to pass the upper house. But the Christian Democrats announced they would not be supporting the reforms. The *Financial Times* report concluded:

> Stefan Bergheim, senior German economist at Merrill Lynch in Frankfurt, said there was a 'chance' of agreement on reform, 'but the question is how useful the reform will be'. Mr Reister has watered down his plans significantly. According to revised projects, state pensions would not fall below 64 per cent of average net wages until at least 2030, compared with 80 per cent

at present, raising the question mark over what incentive there would be for employees to make private provision.[45]

The pension reform plan was so important to the government's whole strategy that the Chancellor took time out from his summer holiday in 2000 for a two-week tour of the East German *Länder*. Schroeder was reported to be willing to back extension of the Federal aid programme for the east but in return expected eastern representatives in the Bundesrat, the upper house, to back his proposed pension reform, including the proposed tax-favoured treatment of contributions to supplementary plans.[46]

According to another report published around this time, Romano Prodi, president of the European Union, 'did his best in a speech to Europe's leftist leaders in Florence to frighten them at the sheer scale of the looming pensions crisis they face'.[47] To this end, Prodi was able to draw on the following OECD projections of the proportion of GDP that would have to be devoted to pay for public pension commitments in coming decades if policies remained unchanged (see Tables 4.2 and 4.3).

In the original OECD report the quoted figures were accompanied with lower expenditures to illustrate the extent to which 'cost containment' and 'later retirement' (actually retirement at seventy) could meet the problem.[48] The message of statistical exercises of this sort was to recommend the commitment-shedding and privatisation approach exemplified by the UK. According to the report, Prodi believed that 'the root of the problem' was that 'fewer people are working to pay for more retirees. By 2030, 25 per cent of the population in the five largest EU countries . . . will be over 65. . . . In 1950 that figure was just 9 per cent.' Once again, the Commissioner failed to note that there was a massive labour surplus – 10 per cent unemployment – and a long queue of Albanians, Moroccans and so forth, willing to help out. Realisation of the prediction that a quarter of Europe's population will be over sixty-five would be good news. Obviously it is the job of the Commission president to identify future funding problems, but not to assume that the only way to solve them is to cut pensioners' entitlements. The newspaper report went on to say that the European Commission 'is looking at how to encourage a single market in pensions and how private schemes could be regulated at European level. It is also examining issues such as the investment policy imposed on pension funds at national level.'[49]

As in so many reports and discussions, the impression is created that only more commercial provision and deregulation will solve the 'problem'. But according to the OECD forecasts in Tables 4.2 and 4.3, in the year

Table 4.2 Public pensions as a percentage of GDP

	1995	2000	2010	2020	2030	2040
Belgium	10.4	9.7	8.7	10.7	13.9	15.0
Denmark	6.8	6.4	7.6	9.3	10.9	11.6
Germany	11.1	11.5	11.8	12.3	16.5	18.4
Spain	10.0	9.8	10.0	11.3	14.1	16.8
France	10. 6	9.8	9.7	11.6	13.5	14.3
Ireland	3.6	2.9	2.6	2.7	2.8	2.9
Italy	13.3	12.6	13.2	15.3	20.3	21.4
Netherlands	6.0	5.7	6.1	8.4	11.2	12.1
Austria	8.8	8.6	10.2	12.1	14.4	15.0
Portugal	7.7	6.9	8.1	9.6	13.0	15.2
Finland	10.1	9.5	10.7	15.2	17.8	18.0
Sweden	11.8	11.1	12.4	13.9	15.0	14.9
UK	4.5	4.5	5.2	5.1	5.5	5.0
US	4.1			5.2		7.1
Japan	6.6			12.4		14.4

Sources: OECD, *Ageing in OECD Countries*, Paris 1996; *Financial Times*, 23 November 1999, 10 November 2000.

Table 4.3 Population over sixty in selected OECD countries: actual and projected

	1990	2000	2010	2020	2030	2040
France	18.9	20.2	23.1	26.8	30.1	31.2
Germany	20.3	23.7	26.5	30.3	35.3	32.5
Italy	20.6	24.2	27.4	30.6	35.9	36.5
Japan	17.3	22.7	29.0	31.4	33.0	34.4
UK	20.8	20.7	23.0	25.5	29.6	29.5
US	16.6	16.5	19.2	24.5	28.2	28.9

Sources: OECD, *Ageing in OECD Countries*, Paris 1996; *Financial Times*, 23 November 1999, 10 November 2000.

2030 the money going to pensioners will be a considerably smaller proportion of GNP than the proportion of over-60s or over-65s in the population. According to the OECD projection, Italy's over-60s population will be 36.5 per cent in 2040; if this actually comes to pass – and no one can predict with much accuracy birth, death and immigration rates that far ahead – then pension expenditure of 21.4 per cent of GNP might be advisable. These projections suggest that pensioners in the main continental European countries are likely to be on below-average incomes. The economic problem is not so much the amount that should be spent on pensioners – which might well be more than the amount indicated – but the best way of ensuring that decent pensions can be paid. The public pension systems carry out the basic function of delivering the pension at much lower cost than commercial providers. Whether or not there should be a degree of pre-funding is another matter, to which I will return, but it is anyway wrong to conflate commercial provision with pre-funding.

One way to grasp the real economic problem is to consider the rate of growth of the retired population and to compare this with the expected rate of growth of the labour force and of labour productivity. In any PAYGO system the latter will determine its 'rate of return' and capacity to produce a higher yield. While these relationships are clear enough, there remains great difficulty in making the projections. Those incorporated in Table 4.4 are based on an exercise by David Blake.

Table 4.4 Projected growth of population, productivity and the retired 1990–2050 in per cent per annum

	Working population	*Productivity*	*Retired population*
UK	0.0	2.1	0.7
Germany	−0.7	2.5	0.8
Netherlands	−0.3	2.1	1.2
Sweden	0.1	2.8	0.6
Denmark	−0.3	1.9	0.5
Switzerland	−0.2	1.5	1.1
US	0.4	1.6	1.4
Canada	0.4	2.6	1.7
Japan	−0.6	4.1	1.4
Australia	0.5	1.8	1.9

Source: David Blake, 'Does It Matter What Kind of Pension Scheme You have?', *The Economic Journal*, vol. 110, no. 461, February 2000, p. 51.

The dimensions of the pension provision problem are indicated by the right-hand column, showing the rate of increase of the population over retirement age. The left-hand column gives an estimate of likely changes in the size of the working population, given present trends. The middle column gives an extrapolation of past productivity trends. At a distance of decades these projections are all very speculative, with that relating to productivity being particularly difficult to forecast. Nevertheless, the orders of magnitude do show that the probable rise in those reaching retirement will not be offset by an expansion of the working population and in several cases the latter will decline. It is the figures for rises in productivity which give some cause for concern. While at historic levels they often match the problem, there is sometimes little to spare. Such an exercise suggests two important challenges: firstly, achieving these or better rates of increase in productivity; and, secondly, finding a pension financing method that will deliver decent pensions and retain social support. The most obvious solution is to use the funds raised from additional pension funding directly to address the productivity problem. Blake himself observes:

> High labour productivity requires high capital per worker, but net investment (additions to the capital stock after taking depreciation into account) in the United Kingdom and many other parts of Europe has been inadequate; it has typically been considerably less than gross investment and, indeed, net investment by public sector corporations has frequently been negative. The long term consequence of inadequate investment is illustrated by the decline of the coal, steel and ship-building industries across Europe. On top of this, and despite the headline stories of inward direct investment from abroad . . . during the 1980s outward direct investment from Europe was occurring at more than twice the rate of inward direct investment (as a proportion of GNP).[50]

Unfortunately the British government, which should have been backing a Europe-wide renaissance of investment in infrastructure and sustainable technology, instead lectured its partners on the excellence of its own neo-liberal structures, its flexible labour force, its bustling railways, its audacious telecom companies, its thriving service sector, its newly responsible animal husbandry, its dynamic financial structures, and its savvy cultural products, many of which were given a dazzling showcase in the Millennium Dome. While we may imagine the incredulity and even amusement of many of Britain's partners as they listened to such homilies, the fact remained that Anglo-Saxon economics exercised a growing fascination for European elites.

In 1999 the European Commission had published a report arguing that the pension problem could only be grasped by means of a holistic approach addressing the reciprocal interaction of retirement and economic growth. But it entirely failed to deliver on this perfectly valid intuition. The tone and balance of the report was very different from *Averting the Old Age Crisis* but it supplied no true alternative thrust, contenting itself with banal observations to the effect that there was 'no design panacea, and adequate reforms take time and may themselves be painful'. It recommended that workers should be dissuaded from early retirement and recognised that this required 'higher employment rates in general'. While holding out the hope that basic pensions levels could be sustained, it was by no means hostile to an expansion of private provision. Indeed, in a muffled echo of the World Bank, it envisaged a 'sustainable mix of mutually-supporting pension pillars based on legislation, collective agreement and private contract'.[51]

However, the Commission does not have responsibility for member countries' policies on taxation, social insurance and benefits, including pensions. All these matters are still reserved to national governments. Its initiatives on more technical issues are therefore of greater moment. Thus in 1997 the Commission had published a Green Paper on 'competition aspects' of pension fund management which also discussed the project of pension reform, employing World Bank-style references to the famous three 'pillars'.[52] The Green Paper argued that the Commission only had competence to adjudicate on aspects of these policies that affected the free movement of labour and capital, or prevented financial concerns in different member countries from competing on an equal basis. In effect the Commission cannot propose changes in basic pension provision, but will try to secure the support of the Council of Ministers for an EU-wide basic framework for private pension funds. This framework could be minimal or maximal. It could, for example, insist that pension funds operating within the Union should be allowed to invest in any assets they like, so long as they conform to basic reporting and accounting standards. The privatisation lobby might persuade the Commission to recommend the introduction of a commercially delivered, universal and mandatory pension to replace existing national regimes – but obviously this would need to be endorsed by national governments. In the first place it is more likely that the privatisers will plump for an optional but tax-favoured commercial platform which could be used to undermine existing national pension schemes – but this approach will still require legislation to dilute existing public provision. If organised labour and other social movements get behind the EFTU proposal for an EU-wide pension linked to a decentralised social fund, then this too could gain support within EU institutions – in the first place, perhaps, from the European Parliament. The framework of EU law could be used to give policy holders a role in the running of pension funds, and these could be obliged to invest given proportions in various asset classes. Funds could even be required to submit their investment programmes to a social audit.

An important issue to be decided at EU level will be the criteria for deciding whether a given pension-providing body is a commercial undertaking within the meaning of Articles 85 and 86 or is a public undertaking as specified in Article 90 of the Treaty of Rome. Commercial undertakings have to show that they are not abusing a monopoly or dominant position in any market. Article 90 allows for specific exemptions from the competition laws for bodies offering a public service. As may be imagined, the judges have considerable latitude in deciding such questions. In 1993 the

European Court of Justice decided in the Poucet & Pistre case that two French pension schemes were not commercial organisations because they were based on the principle of solidarity in the benefits offered to members; that is, members received benefits related to some estimate of their need rather than in proportion to their contribution. However, in another case involving two Dutch pension schemes the European Commission argued in a submission to the court that they were commercial organisations, notwithstanding the fact that they did not select members and paid out benefits adjusted to need. Moreover, under the terms of Dutch legislation, namely the Company Pension Fund (Obligatory Participation) Act, certain categories of employees had no choice about belonging. These schemes did use a fund and offered members some choice in determining the level of contributions and benefits. However, it is not yet clear what might be at stake in these adjudications. So far, all pension schemes are based on national legislation and the possibility for competition has been confined to genuinely commercial bodies. A directive of the Council of Ministers in June 1998 went no further than insisting that any employee who exercised the right of freedom of movement should not suffer loss of established pension rights in consequence.[53]

Significantly, pension reform has probably gone further in Sweden, with its strong Social Democratic Party, than in most other EU countries. Between 1994 and 2000 a series of reforms have remade the pension regime. In Sweden new legislation in 1994 provided for the pre-funding of the secondary, earnings-related pension. In revisions designed to lessen the impact of demographic change, the state pension is now somewhat less generous, and requires a longer history of contributions before the better terms apply. The state secondary system, the ATP, was always funded but the fund was invested mainly in low-yielding Swedish government bonds. In an effort to raise the rate of return, the fund will now be invested in domestic and overseas equities and bonds. Swedes pay 18.5 per cent of their salary into the pension system but, from 2001, 2.5 per cent is set aside in an individual account. The contributions can be put into up to five different mutual funds, each of which has to conform to standards set by the Premium Pension Authority (PPA). The five funds are chosen from over five hundred funds which meet the prescribed standards. If employees indicate no preference, then their contributions will be pooled in a general fund run by the state-owned Seventh Swedish National Pension Fund, which was expected to make up 30 per cent of the total and consists of 20 per cent domestic equities, 65 per cent international equities, 14 per cent index-linked bonds and 1 per cent cash. With news of tumbling international exchanges coming from all parts in 2000–1, it might be wondered why the fund is weighted so strongly to overseas stocks and bonds – and why so many foreign mutual funds have been invited to tender for the individual accounts. The establishment of this scheme was the product of protracted and delicate negotiations. Against the background of past controversies – that over the ATP fund in 1958 and over Meidner's 'wage-earner funds' in the early 19880s – the moderate Social Democratic leadership seems to have been leaning over backwards to prove that it harboured no intention of establishing a strategic stake in the Swedish private sector. There was also a political calculation connected to the Social Democrats' wish to ensure support from their main bourgeois opponents. Nevertheless, whatever the reason, the Swedish move was a crumb of comfort to the European pension fund lobby, mitigated only by the PPA's determination to prove that it would not be pushed around by the financial giants; Fidelity declined to offer its funds because it believes that the obligatory fee structure is too tight. But despite this fee cap, a combination of charges, market turbulence and inexperience may eat into the value of these accounts.[54] In the early months of the scheme about 30 per cent of employees opted for the default, general pooled fund. But towards the close of 2001 the proportion of new entrants to the scheme who declined to choose funds for themselves climbed to reach over 80 per cent, indicating the possibility that the 'privatised' portion of Swedish pensions will be largely state-run after all.

The defeats suffered by pension reform in Europe in the 1990s, together with the stubbornness of electorates and the scope for future legal pitfalls, combined to have a lowering effect on the perennially hopeful financial services industry. In February 2000 an article in *Institutional Investor* magazine entitled 'The Stalled Promise of European Pension Reform' explained: 'Money managers have stormed the continent. But so far they are fighting over scraps.' Italy had introduced a new law in late 1998 allowing personal pension plans, but 'without the tax incentives that make them exciting' and with a high hurdle for foreign money managers. Warning that 'future calamities loom', the article claimed that 'Italian workers by 2050 could be taxed a crushing 70 per cent of their salaries to feed the state pension fund, according to estimates by Morgan Stanley Dean Witter.' After this implausible conjecture it continued: 'extended to Europe as a whole, the situation could be just as grim. The fledgling equity revolution in Europe is at risk, along with the future of economic and monetary union.' European governments had responded timidly to all the interest that had been shown: 'Take a seat on an airplane going to one of the capitals of Europe and the chances that a fellow passenger is a salesman of investment management is high.' Among those who had set up 'base camps' were Goldman Sachs, Morgan Stanley, J.P. Morgan, Invesco, Vanguard and Merrill Lynch. They encountered stiff competition for the modest business available from BNP-Paribas, Caisse de Dépôts et Consignations, Westdeutsche Landesbank and Dresdner RCM Global Investors. The regulations imposed by European governments were generally too tough on the managers and too timid with the employees. The Swedish public pension fund offered only a 'paltry' 0.2 per cent management fee for funds of $3.5 billion or more. 'The bad news for investment managers is that Sweden could become the template of Europe.' This treatment could not be in harsher contrast to Eastern Europe: 'In Poland, at least, the fund managers have been helped in recouping their costs by management fees as high as 10 per cent.' There was also the problem that the European governments had left too much discretion to employees. An Italian occupational scheme was found wanting on these grounds: '"The sign-up for the funds was less than people had hoped for," says Alan Rubenstein, managing director of the pensions group at Morgan Stanley Dean Witter. "The new system needs to be made obligatory".'[55] Here is a business so confident of its products that it believes their purchase should be compulsory!

The various European governments had tidied up some anomalies and absurdities in the public system and removed legal obstacles to private provision but were not yet creating the hoped-for explosion in demand for personal pensions. But the author of the study was not wholly pessimistic. There were some chinks of light. Some large providers thought that bidding for the Swedish fund management would be a paying proposition – the limited fees were, after all, only for fund management and not for other administrative services which would be carried out by the Swedish pension authorities themselves. Another trend noted was that retail banks handling payroll work thought they would be well placed to offer to run personal plans for employers just as soon as governments were willing to make them fiscally attractive. And, in the medium run, it was clear that the governments in Berlin and Paris were set on establishing such schemes.

In an article for *Foreign Affairs*, Fidelity's Robert Prozen argued in May 2001 that tackling pension reform country by country would not be good enough:

> European pension funds could yield even greater returns if pooled across the continent, thus achieving lower costs and greater economies of scale. For example, contributions to Germany's public pay-as-you-go retirement

system are projected to produce annual investment returns of less than one per cent for people born after 1970. Market-based private and employment linked pension plans operating on a pan-European basis could deliver much higher returns, especially if fund managers were free to invest by prudent-person standards. But the cross border barriers to pension funds are even greater than those for mutual funds. Currently European fund managers do not even have a 'passport' for doing business in other EU countries. Some countries insist that their pension funds be managed by individuals physically stationed in a local office or by specialized institutions established in a local jurisdiction. So far the EU has been unable to come to grips with the politically sensitive demand that employment-linked pensions receive equal tax treatment among its member states.[56]

The stubborn rearguard resistance of European institutions, social movements and electorates is likely to be worn down in the long run if there is no alternative which is capable of solving the funding problem and harmonising existing provision on a generous, redistributive and portable basis. An interesting picture emerges from replies to a questionnaire on welfare given by over 5,000 citizens of Germany, France, Italy and Spain. Summarising their study, the authors declare that 'the responses do not offer an encouraging picture for those arguing in favour of a retrenchment of the European welfare state'.[57] They find that there is no majority for retrenchment in any of these large core states of the Union. But they nevertheless believe that the cause of reform is not lost: 'there is scope to package and bundle reforms strategically in order to build a large and mixed coalition of supporters.'[58] They are encouraged to find that proposals for an opt-out from retirement contributions do elicit support so long as they are carefully framed. Thus they find that there is a widespread belief that public pension provision faces a crisis and that the level of pensions will be significantly lower in ten or fifteen years' time. This view gained assent from 82 per cent of French respondents, 81 per cent of German respondents, 72 per cent of Italian respondents but only 42 per cent of Spanish respondents.[59] When asked whether they would support the reduction by a half of both their retirement contribution and the size of the pension they will be able to claim, respondents give a mixed, though fairly favourable, answer. The idea attracts 24.4 per cent of the French respondents, 47.2 per cent of the Germans, 46.9 per cent of the Italians and 18.9 per cent of the Spanish. Part of the resistance to the idea seems to come from a fear that if their compulsory saving for retirement was reduced they would be sorely tempted to spend the extra money in their pocket or purse. If the question is rephrased to ask whether they would like to see half of their existing social security contribution paid into 'an investment fund of your choice', then support for the idea grows, to reach 49.7 per cent in France, 71 per cent in Germany, 67 per cent in Italy and 63 per cent in Spain.[60] It might seem, then, that the highroad to privatisation is open. But the researchers do not see it this way because the support they find for privatisation melts away as soon as 'transition costs' enter the picture. Any opt-out scheme would have to make provision for paying pensions to current pensioners, so it would not be able to promise that the entirety of the forgone contribution would be applied to personal investment accounts. When deductions to take care of the 'transition burden' are brought into the picture, the numbers 'not at all' prepared to envisage an opt-out rise to 62.6 per cent in France, 75.1 per cent in Germany, 73.7 per cent in Italy and 47.9 per cent in Spain.[61] The researchers also found that respondents tended to underestimate the contributions they were making and to be unclear about their nature: 'In Germany, less than half of the respondents realized that all of their contributions are used to finance current pensioners, with nothing going towards their own retirement.'[62] In such a situation there may well be support for some pre-funding, as reality dawns. At the moment, of course, there is a powerful lobby urging that the process should be entrusted to expensive private fund managers and only very few urging that public and social bodies would do a much better and more responsible job. So the likelihood that a privatising coalition will be built in one country after another remains strong.

And this indeed seems to be happening, albeit in a cautious way. In May 2001 Schroeder eventually secured passage of his pension reform legislation, thus notching up a significant gain for the privatisation cause. Under its terms, the German ratio of wages to net benefits is to fall from 67 per cent in 2015 to 64 per cent by 2020. Employees will be encouraged by tax breaks to make up the difference by investing 0.5 per cent of their pay in equities as from January 2002, rising to 4 per cent of pay by 2008. The funds offered to employees will have to meet quite restrictive standards set by a new public agency.[63] The *Wall Street Journal* report conveyed some idea of the significance of this step:

> fund managers are salivating over estimates that more than E260 billion will flow into the new pension funds annually once they are fully implemented. 'You really only find good equity cultures where you have pension plans based on equities,' said Klaus Martini, chief investment officer for global retail equities with DWS Investment, the mutual-fund arm of Deutsche Bank AG . . . Also significant the reform would point the way for other

large European countries facing the same demographic trends and budget constraints. . . . The German reform is 'a political signal to other big countries', said Thomas Mayer, economist in the Frankfurt office of Goldman Sachs and Co. 'It will make it hard for them to ignore this example of reducing generosity'. Fund managers said there were still several shortcomings in the new system. Chief among them is the requirement that the return on private investment is guaranteed, a measure that limits the return potential and the choice of investments – and runs counter to developing an understanding of what shares are about. The condition should shave about two or three percentage points from returns, fund managers estimated. Also the pay out of the benefits is fixed, leaving pensioners no flexibility in managing their holdings once retired.[64]

Irksome though these restrictions no doubt are, they seem to open the way to further doses of 'reform', first of all in Italy under the new Berlusconi government elected in the same month (notwithstanding his promise to raise minimum pensions, commentators widely predicted that he would use a looming budget crisis to cut pension entitlements[65]). But just to remind Europe's rulers of the explosive character of pension policy, the Greek trade unions staged a general strike and May Day demonstration in 2001 which successfully persuaded the Socialist government to abandon a projected pension reform measure.[66]

Chile and Singapore Revisited

Meanwhile, those who followed the repercussions of the Asian financial crisis of 1997–98 were given food for thought concerning the potentially stabilising role of those provident funds about which the World Bank had been so sceptical. Singapore was hugely vulnerable to the South-East Asian crisis because of its small size and its high exposure to foreign trade. Nevertheless, it succeeded in riding out the storm with much less damage than its neighbours. For its part, Chile also survived better than most South American countries. In its case, too, the *dirigiste* features of its national savings regime played a part – though not at all in ways that the World Bank or neo-liberal philosophy usually approves. More generally, both these savings schemes have considerable defects as pension providers even if they have other positive features.

In Singapore the state-owned and managed Central Provident Fund furnishes a mechanism whereby each citizen is obliged to make provision for sickness and old age; this individual fund can also be drawn upon to finance acquisition of a house or the taking of an educational qualification. Such a system encourages individual involvement and responsibility, while allowing for flexibility. Whether it would promote egalitarianism depends on overall government policy, which can always furnish correctives and controls. Employees and employers are both compelled to make contributions to the publicly run scheme, though the principle of compulsion at work here is not so different from that involved in systems of taxation which are not intended to be voluntary. The CPF invests 90 per cent of its money in public bonds, though the government has used these bonds to make its own equity investments. The CPF emerged in the 1950s as a compromise between the colonial state and its nationalist and social democratic opposition. In the 1960s Singapore seceded from Malaysia and the CPF was retained as a potent nation-building programme. Although the CPF has its own management it is firmly subordinate to the Singaporean government's overall control. In 1968 policy holders were permitted to draw on their CPF accounts if they wished to buy a house from the Housing and Development Board, a body whose construction activities were themselves financed by the CPF. This policy has greatly encouraged home ownership and soon 90 per cent of policy holders made use of the mortgage option. The ruling party in Singapore, affiliated to the Socialist International, has run the island state since independence and has not been tolerant of oppositional activity from other parties or from the trade unions. Its leadership is drawn from the majority Chinese ethnic community. While those of Chinese extraction play key roles in the community, those with a Malay or Indian background are well catered for by the CPF. The Singapore government promotes social inclusion hand in hand with social control, making sure that there is little poverty but also little social spontaneity. While the CPF is certainly a part of this picture, it is not difficult to imagine a somewhat similar institution contributing to a more democratic and pluralist society.[67]

In the macro-economic picture, the CPF has functioned as a powerful gyroscope, keeping the ship of state on an even keel, especially when storms well up as in 1997–98. The nominal rate of return to contributions in the Singaporean CPF averaged a not very impressive 3–4 per cent in the 1990s, but this figure, credited to individual accounts, does not register the real social return. Employees contribute 20 per cent of salary to the scheme and can earn a higher rate of return on contributions above this mandatory amount. The scheme also supplies free medical care in retirement. In the chairman's report for 1999 Ngian Tong Dow declared that after a lifetime of contributions members own their own house, have free medical cover and an annuity worth between 20 and 40 per cent of their salary.[68] However, while the great majority do acquire a house or flat – often on good terms – the retirement aspects of the scheme are weak for those who have had a break in their career, or who have dipped into their fund to cover a life emergency. In 1998 the government reduced the employers' contribution from 20 per cent to 10 per cent, to help them weather the crisis, raising it to 12 per cent in early 2000 when growth had returned to around 7 per cent. The Prime Minister explained in an interview in December 1999 that the CPF acted as 'a sort of buffer' for the government in difficult times.[69] In fact, the government uses the CPF as a lever in its economic strategy all the time. It issues bonds to the CPF in return for the contributions; these bonds carry interest of between 3 and 4 per cent, hence the rate of return to contributions. But the money raised in this way is invested in infrastructure or entrusted to the Government of Singapore Investment Corporation, a body which invests in a range of domestic and overseas assets, including equities. The rate of return obtained by the GSIC is likely to be considerably above the 3–4 per cent remitted to the CPF. While the CPF maintains an informative web-site the GSIC is very secretive.

A survey article in the *Far Eastern Economic Review* describes the CPF as 'more like a mortgage finance scheme than a retirement plan'. The houses it sells are cheap partly because of its market power and partly because it finances new construction. But while this aspect of matters may be satisfactory to members, the risk of depletion of assets is not: about a quarter of the members arrive at retirement with an average of $9,250 in their account (though they will probably own their house and have some medical benefits). The article also notes: 'the fact that it [the Singapore government] can use CPF to fund infrastructure projects frees other funds for more profitable investment elsewhere.'[70] The CPF now has financial assets of $31 billion to cover its 1.5 million members, with further sums tied up in property. It is under pressure to offer a higher rate of return and since about 1995 has proclaimed its intention to 'liberalise' itself. By making additional contributions, participants can invest directly in the stock market or in unit trusts, and at the end of 2000 about $5.3 billion were held in this way. In a talk to fund managers in February 2000 the CPF chairman complained that the high charges of Singaporean unit trusts have meant that they have only attracted $423 million while some $5 billion have been 'punted' on shares.[71] Apart from poor returns to the government bonds, the other problem the CPF faces is that changes in occupational structure weaken its contribution mechanism. As the chairman complained in the previously cited report, the spread of self-employment and short-term contract employment has made it more difficult for the CPF to collect employers' contributions. On the other hand, the scheme does still have the advantage of a high degree of 'portability'. After forty-five years during which the CPF helped the island nation to achieve per capita income levels that are among the highest in the world, its people and government will have to decide whether they strengthen and improve this remarkable institution, attending to the needs of its members, or whether they further liberalise and weaken it, by opening it to the island's burgeoning financial services industry.

In the late 1980s and early 1990s the Chilean AFPs registered a rate of return of 7.5–10.5 per cent but their subsequent performance has been more troubled. In 1995 the funds saw a negative rate of return of -4.7 per cent, and losses were also registered in the subsequent year. In 1994 the average AFP rate of return was positive but eleven of twenty-one AFPs incurred losses that, in some cases, reached 50 per cent of equity. A strongly positive return has been registered from the holdings in the privatised electricity companies Enersis and Endesa. Sebastian Edwards notes that AFP support 'has allowed private firms to rely on long term financing for their investment projects. This has been particularly important for the privatized utilities.'[72]

The Chilean AFPs only have 62 per cent coverage of the workforce compared with nearly 100 per cent for Singapore. In many cases Chilean low-paid workers, especially in the countryside, prefer to opt for a type of self-employed status which excuses both themselves and their employers from making proper contributions. These workers are only nominally covered by the AFP system. Likewise, those who are often unemployed have not been able to maintain payments. And with continuing uneven performance figures for the different AFPs, it is clear the pensions that will be paid out will certainly vary considerably from plan to plan.

The Chilean funded pension experiment does not deliver consistent returns to policy holders but it does add an element of stability to the national economy, not unlike the Singapore gyroscope referred to above. Despite its serious flaws, the Chilean case does suggest that pension funds can be an instrument for targeting investment; to begin with, the AFPs were forbidden to invest outside the country and later only 10 per cent of assets could be held abroad. When the backwash from the Asian financial crisis of 1997–98 hit South America Chile's economy survived in better shape than most because it had special deposit rules for foreign investors and because the AFPs were obliged to respect government guidelines on the placing of their investment. This aspect of the role of the AFPs is carefully played down in the privatisation literature. The AFPs now dispose of capital assets of $25 billion. The Chilean trade unions would like to see new rules which would restrain their excessive costs and permit the formation of more employee-run funds; some professional groups have formed their own employee-owned AFPs, though so far their holdings comprise only 2 per cent of the total. Administration costs run at around 2 per cent of assets a year because of the intense competition between AFPs for business; and it should be noted that these current running costs do not include the front-loaded commissions levied when the AFPs were established which further reduce the long-term rate of return.[73]

In 1999–2000 Chileans had their first opportunity to elect a Socialist president since 1973, thanks to the agreement between Christian Democrats and Socialists that has governed the country since the onset of democratisation in 1988. But the arrival of a Socialist in the Moneda Palace will mean business as usual for the AFPs so long as they navigate a darkening economic prospect. Only if unhinged by 'market risk' are they likely to undergo the sort of sweeping reforms advocated by the country's trade unionists.

The Asian-Pacific Awkward Squad

We hear much about the near-absolute constraints of globalisation these days. We are told that governments are no longer able to pursue their own social and economic policies if these displease the international financial community. The thesis is often advanced in a one-sided and exaggerated way but it nonetheless contains a strong element of truth wherever the pattern of an economy leaves it vulnerable to capital flight and speculation. The fleecing of several of the East Asian 'tigers' in 1997–98 furnished striking examples of the problem. But to the extent that they can mobilise domestic savings, as Singapore did, and avoid or reduce exposure to dollar loans, as Taiwan did, some South-East Asian states were able to survive the speculative storm in remarkably good shape. Even in China, believed to be more exposed than in the past, the impact of the 1997–98 crisis in the region was reduced by three factors: (1) the loans taken out by state enterprises were denominated in yuan, not dollars; (2) the dynamic rural industries are mostly collectively owned and geared to local sources of finance; and (3) foreigners were only allowed to hold non-voting B shares in privately quoted securities. In August 1998 the government of Hong Kong found that it also had to expand the public stake in the economy in order to protect its stock market and currency. In August 1998 some £8 billion of public reserves were invested in leading companies, with an enterprise board established to manage these public holdings over the long term.[74]

China's government will soon be obliged to address the pensions issue; its people are living longer and the dependency ratio of pensioners to workers will be very high because of the one-child family policy. Even if immigration is liberalised, given China's size, it could not make that much difference. There are expected to be 400 million people over sixty in China by 2050. In June 2000 the *Financial Times* reported rumours that China was about to embark on a funded pension system:

> Foreign joint-venture mutual funds are expected to be permitted as early as next year [2001], and domestic institutions will be allowed to run open-ended funds for the first time, officials say. Insurance companies are to be allowed to invest progressively more of their assets in the stock market through brokerages. The extra liquidity this generates will, it is hoped, create conditions for a new wave of privatisations to swell depleted government revenues. Some of the proceeds of asset sales may be used to help finance the state pension burden, says one official.[75]

The same report quoted a Beijing-based foreign banker as cautioning: 'As is often the case in China, changes will be phased in gradually. There is no likelihood of a big bang.' Nevertheless, the options indicated in the report have a clear and even pressing logic. The Chinese government still has huge productive assets. Privatisation would offer rich pickings to foreign investors, though they would be choosy and there would be many closures. The money made by selling state assets would soon be absorbed by central government needs and little would remain for funding pensions. Alternatively, a national pension board could be endowed with major state assets and encouraged to manage them in such a way as to ensure itself a future income. Such an institution could help to cement national unity in a country where regional inequalities are threatening it. China has shown that, under the right circumstances, public authorities can be good economic managers: the Township and Village Enterprises (TVEs) have flourished under municipal ownership and the Institute for the Disabled has made generally good use of the large resources entrusted to it. But corruption and waste have also bedevilled a regime that shuns popular inspection and control. The formulation of solutions to China's demographic and economic challenges will be one of the decisive events of the twenty-first century just as its industrialisation was one of the decisive events of the latter part of the twentieth.[76]

Another Asian country with an ageing population is, of course, Japan. After four decades of extraordinary growth, Japan in the 1990s suffered a protracted hangover from the bubble economics of the late 1980s, which proved resistant to traditional remedies. Successive governments sought to spend their way out of misery by the type of FILP-financed or credit-financed public works programmes which had modernised the country's infrastructure in the past (see pp. 77–8 above). But there is a limit to the number of bridges, roads, airports and harbours needed in any economy. Japan's problems in the 1990s stemmed from the anxieties of its own people, the remorseless pressure of globalisation and the crude application of import quotas and other sanctions by the United States and EU. Japanese consumers maintained a high rate of savings, thus depressing demand, in part because they did fear for the future. While the country's industries and exports remained fairly strong, the Japanese economy was unable once again to export its way out of the recession. Its main economic partners used their increased economic leverage ever more insistently to limit access to their own markets while prising open Japan's markets and financial system.[77] Jeffrey Sachs put it like this: 'Japan was told [by Europe and the US] to grow through domestic demand, not through exports to world markets. This was deeply flawed advice, because Japan is a structural net savings surplus economy, in which its ageing population wants to save more than its companies can profitably invest within Japan.'[78]

Japan's formidable economic ministries made several concessions to 'Anglo-Saxon economics' without ever decisively forfeiting their grip. The market for pension provision in Japan certainly aroused interest from international, especially American, providers. But this is a mature as well as a rich market, with a well-established public pillar. As noted in chapter 1, Japan's public pension system was reformed in 1985 to take greater account of the increasing numbers of those approaching retirement. This reform was accompanied by an unusual degree of public consultation for a country with a notoriously highhanded and secretive governing bureaucracy. One civil servant explained the traditional approach with brutal candour: 'when you want to carry through a reform that's tough on the public, you have to make it seem so the problems are difficult to see, make it as confused and vague as possible, then cut a deal with the opposition parties behind the scenes and slip it through fast.'[79] This vividly portrays the pension reform process in most countries but for once things were somewhat different in Japan. The sponsor of reform within the Ministry of Welfare did what he could to stimulate public attention and debate, including the dispatch of an outline of the reform with a questionnaire to several thousand experts and opinion leaders. The reform did entail some trimming of benefits but essentially it aimed to save rather than abandon the public pension system. The bureaucracy finds that the flow of pension contributions gives it significant added leverage while a shared ethos exalts collective support of the aged: Japan has a day in September to mark Respect for the Elderly. The reform plan preserved fairly generous provision – an average replacement rate pension set at 67 per cent of earnings.

Preservation of the public regime somewhat constrains the scope for private provision but Japan has well-established private or occupational schemes, and increasing numbers of would-be foreign providers have entered the market. But all pension funds, whether Japanese or foreign, faced great difficulty in delivering results in the post-bubble economy. If they invested overseas they faced the risk that further appreciation of the yen would undermine the value they were able to deliver to policy holders. But if they invested in Japanese assets – equities, real estate or bonds – then they often reaped a very poor rate of return. These problems, combined with other difficulties of doing business in Japan, limited the inroads made by US or European fund managers. Nevertheless, private pension provision is among the forces reshaping the Japanese model. Japanese funds found in the 1990s that they owned an increasing proportion of major Japanese businesses and their policy holders became increasingly unhappy at dismal fund performance. The fund trustees were drawn to explore the possibilities of shareholder activism. In 1997 the Ministry of Welfare introduced guidelines seeking to make pension fund trusteeship and management more transparent. While fund managers were now more inclined to pursue 'shareholder value' they were doing so in a regime where interlocking financial and industrial groups still held sway. Since 1990 Japanese pension funds have been able to engage the services of financial advisers and it has become more common for funds to try to secure better results from the companies in which they have invested. But this is done by 'voice' rather than impersonal market mechanisms. According to Megumi Suto: 'In the Japanese system, it is not only more realistic but also less expensive to monitor the companies indirectly through trustee bodies than through direct corporate governance by pension fund managers.' The scope for exercising pressure through AGMs is impeded by share blocks – and by the fact that the AGMs of the larger companies are all held on the same few days. The trustees are generally even closer to the pension sponsor than is the case in the United States but that fact itself helps to make possible what Suto calls 'communications-based' governance.[80] While

Japan is certainly exposed to the distinctive procedures, many would say
ravages, of 'Anglo-Saxon economics', well-placed observers predict that
the pace of change will be slow and the results will be mixed.[81]

This survey of distinctive pension arrangements in the Asia-Pacific
region would be incomplete without reference to the Australian approach
to pension provision. While scarcely animated by 'Confucian' values,
Australian pension arrangements are not simply an Antipodean example of
the residual liberal welfare model. Australia's basic state pension does, it is
true, have classic 'liberal' features and was even enacted in 1908, the year
Britain's Liberal government introduced its own old age pension. The
fact that Australia was demographically a 'young country' combined with
widespread home ownership to reduce pressure for generous pension provision. In mid-century, instead of introducing a universal pension, as New
Zealand had done, Australian governments progressively loosened the
means test until it only excluded the relatively well-off. It was not until the
Labour government of 1972–75 that a universal pension for those over
seventy was introduced.[82] In the meantime a strong trade union movement
succeeded in extracting significant social concessions directly from
the employers.

In the mid-1980s, following a stand-off between employers and unions,
the ACTU obtained the Labour government's backing for a type of
deferred wage increase: the employers were to pay 3 per cent of salary into
Superannuation Funds for their employees. Following a wider 'Accord'
between unions and government, and a Labour election victory, this
arrangement, known as the Super, was extended in 1992 to require all
employers to make a contribution of 6 per cent of salary on behalf of all
their employees, with the phasing in of an employee contribution of 3 per
cent. The introduction of the Super led to the setting up of 1,500
schemes administered by trustee boards on which employers and employees were both represented. There are union-initiated industry-wide
schemes, single-employer funds, and master trust funds for the self-
employed and small employers. Interestingly enough, the benefits which it
is hoped the Super will deliver are expressed in terms of the boost it will
provide to the state pension, supposedly to be raised by 68 per cent after
forty years of contributions, to provide an overall replacement rate of perhaps 60 per cent. By the mid-1990s the Super funds controlled assets of
A$200 billion, causing consternation in some circles. As Christopher
Pierson explains: 'There have been critics from the right, who resent the
state's earmarking of such a large element of an individual's personal
income, and from some sections of industry, which resent both the

additional non-wage labour costs and the control of investment decisions by trade unionists which the co-management of Super funds implies.'[83]

By the end of 1999 Super funds were worth A$439 billion and coverage among full-time permanent workers was 98 per cent, with 59 per cent coverage among temporary or part-time workers. Australian assets, especially equities and bonds, comprise just over 80 per cent of holdings in the Super funds. Australia has been said to possess a 'wage earners' welfare state' and the Super is squarely in this tradition. It is possible to make contributions for non-working spouses but only a few thousand avail themselves of this option. Individuals and the self-employed can buy into the schemes but will not, of course, benefit from an employers' contribution. The arrangements made for management of the Super funds represent a spectrum not unlike those surveyed in chapter 2. There are big public sector funds which manage their own funds effectively, and incur only modest administration charges, and there are large, private retail suppliers, who manage a mass of small or individual schemes and whose charges are high. Trade unions are somewhat more prominently represented on trustee boards than is the case in the UK and the United States but the most striking difference is the very high coverage rate among the employed population. However, the still constrained and remote workings of the trustee arrangements combine with pressure to use a commercial provider to reproduce problems of pensioner alienation indicated in earlier chapters. The conservative Coalition government formed after the defeat of Labour in 1996 declined to raise the employers' contribution as had previously been envisaged, exacerbating an already existing danger that the eventual pensions paid out will be too low. Or perhaps it would be better to say that the inadequacy of Australian pension provision stems from the fact that the basic state pension is low and is means-tested. Means testing discourages savings greater than the mandatory amount, or can lead some to spend until their savings come in below the threshold.[84] More generally, trade unionists and other employees found that after a decade of Labour government their position vis-à-vis the employers was weakened rather than strengthened, both in the workplace and in the wider society. The funds in each employee's Super might eventually help them to live a little better in retirement but because they had been largely handed over to the financial services industry they had not been used as an instrument to protect and advance the interests of employees.[85]

All in all, it is not clear why the World Bank report of 1994 did not devote more attention to the Australian Super, which was already on the statute book and came close to exemplifying some of the principles enunciated in *Averting the Old Age Crisis*.[86] Perhaps the role of trade unions in setting up the scheme and helping to run many of the funds explains the omission. Australian workers seem to feel a sense of 'ownership' towards the Super and on some occasions their holdings have been mobilised for trade union and corporate governance campaigns (e.g. at the 2000 AGM of the Rio Tinto company, as I explain in the Conclusion). In pension terms the programme is still very young and there is still scope for its provisions and modus operandi to be developed.[87] Among trade unionists there is debate on the future of the Super and on how it might be improved. The strong performance of the Australian economy through the regional and global turmoil of 1997–2001 may or may not be linked to a stabilising contribution from the Super regime but it was associated with a modest recovery of confidence in the labour movement. This is all in a very different vein to the World Bank's idealisation of commercial provision.

Notes

1   Doris Elter, 'El nuevo sistema previsional chileno: un modelo para la seguridad social?', in Juan Torres López, *Pensiones públicas: y mañana qué?*, Barcelona 1996, pp. 157–74. For the Swiss reform see Stefan Hepp, 'Mandatory Occupational Pension Schemes in Switzerland: the First Ten Years', *Annals of Public and Cooperative Economics*, vol. 69, no. 4, 2001 pp. 533–46.

2   Daniel Yergin and Joseph Stanislaw, *The Commanding Heights: the Battle between Government and the Market Place that is Remaking the Modern World*, New York 1999, p. 151.

3   World Bank, *Averting the Old Age Crisis: Policies to Protect the Old and Promote Growth*, Oxford 1994.

4   Quoted in ibid., p. 105. For Samuelson's famous 1958 article in the *American Economic Review*, see chapter 1.

5   World Bank, *Advertising the Old Age Crisis* p. 138.

6   Ibid., p. 107.

7   Ibid., p. 159.

8   Ibid., p. 246.

9   Ibid., p. 121.

10 Ibid., p. 158.

11 Ibid., p. 192.

12 Ibid., p. 219.

13 Ibid., p. 224.

14 Ibid., p. 95.

15 Ibid., pp. 93–6.

16 For a well-observed comparison of the reports on pensions and ageing by the

World Bank, European Commission and International Labour Organisation, see Steven Ney, 'Are You Sitting Comfortably. . . . Then We'll Begin: Three Gripping Stories About Pension Reform', *Innovation*, vol. 13, no. 4, December 2000, pp. 341–71.

17 This is now published by the Bank in a volume, together with other responses. See Robert Holzmann and Joseph Stiglitz, *New Ideas About Old Age Security*, Washington (DC) 2001. For an early and powerful critique of *Averting the Old Age Crisis* see Ajit Singh, 'Pension Reform, the Stock Market, Capital Formation and Economic Growth: a Critical Commentar on the World Bank's Proposals', CEPA Working Paper no. 2, New School for Social Research, New York 1996.

18 Robert Holzmann, 'World Bank Supports Pension Reforms', letter in *Financial Times*, 11 July 2001. Holzmann also mentions Switzerland, Hong Kong and Australia as having private mandatory schemes but since the Australian and Swiss schemes pre-date *Averting the Old Age Crisis*, only the Hong Kong scheme can be regarded as an example of its advocacy. Holzmann's somewhat defensive claims were prompted by a review of the book he co-edited with Stiglitz. By the time of the book's publication Stiglitz had been forced out of any position at the Bank in circumstances described in Robert Wade, 'Culling the Bank', *New Left Review*, second series no. 7, January–February 2001.

19 Franklin Allen and Douglas Gale, 'A Welfare Comparison of Intermediaries and Financial Markets in Germany and the United States', *European Economic Review*, vol. 39, 1995, pp. 179–209.

20 Alan Milward, 'Rentier Europe', and Edward Luttwak, 'Central Bankism', in Perry Anderson and Peter Gowan, eds, *The Question of Europe*, London 1996, pp. 220–33.

21 Ana Maria Lagares Pérez, 'The Process of Pension Reform in Spain', in Emmanuel Reynaud, ed., *Social Dialogue and Pension Reform*, ILO, Geneva 2000, pp. 97-107. The strength of the Spanish economy in the 1980s is stressed by Miren Etxezarreta, 'Acerca de la Seguridad Social', in Torres López, ed., *Pensiones públicas: y mañana qué?*, p. 15–21.

22 François Charpentier, *Retraites et fonds de pension*, Paris 1999, pp. 18–22. Géraldine Bozec and Claire Mays, 'The Pension Reform Process in France', *Innovation*, vol. 13, no. 4, December 2000, pp. 373-87, especially pp. 379–81.

23 Daniel Bensaid, 'Neo-liberal Reform and Popular Rebellion', *New Left Review*, no. 215, January–February 1996, pp. 109-16.

24 Bozec and Mays, 'The Pension Reform Process in France', *Innovation*, pp. 381–3.

25 Toby Abse, 'Italy', in Perry Anderson and Patrick Camiller, eds, *Mapping the West European Left*, London 1996.

26 For a quite sympathetic account of the reform Kohl was trying to launch see A. Borsch-Supan, 'A Model Under Siege: A Case Study of the German Retirement System', *The Economic Journal*, vol. 110, no. 461, February 2001, F1–23.

27 Cited in Oskar Lafontaine, *The Heart Beats on the Left*, Oxford 2000, p. 63.

28 Michel Aglietta, 'Postface', *Régulation et crises de capitalisme*, 2nd edn Paris 1997, p. 446 (an English version of this 2nd edn has been announced for 2002).

29 Jean Peyrelevade, 'Fonds de pension et gouvernement des sociétés commerciaux', *Commentaire*, vol. 21, no. 83, autumn 1998, pp. 689–90. This author's remarks chime well with Alan Milward's analysis of the forces driving the Maastricht agreement in his contribution to Anderson and Gowan, eds, *The Question of Europe*.

30 *Financial Times*, 9 April 1996.

31 'Pension Funds Seek Bigger Slice of EU Retirement Funding', *Wall Street Journal*, 13 June 1996.

32 Anne Swardson, Washington Post service, 'An Aging Europe Heads for a Pensions Crisis', *International Herald Tribune*, 27 April 2000.

33 Ibid.

34 Giuliano Bonoli, 'Pension Politics in France: Patterns of Cooperation and Conflict in Two Recent Reforms', *West European Politics*, vol. 20, no. 4, October 1997, p. 118.

35 Ibid. Strictly speaking, these contributory systems are not 'of Bismarckian inspiration' but were hybrid products of twentieth-century social insurance thinking and labour movement pressure. For the German system see Borsch-Supan, 'A Model Under Siege'.

36 The power of the social movement is eloquently registered in Pierre Bourdieu, *Acts of Resistance: against the New Myths of our Time*, Oxford 1998.

37 Erik Lutjens, 'Dutch Government Proposals on Earnings-Related Pensions and Mandatory Participation', in Gerard Hughes and Jim Stewart, eds, *The Role of the State in Pension Provision: Employer, Regulator, Provider*, Dordrecht and London 1999, pp. 85–92, pp. 89–90. Other generous social provisions, such as disability pensions, were defended in 1991 by a million-person march in The Hague. Subsequently more stringent tests of disability were instituted but other benefits made easier to obtain. See Robert E. Goodin, Bruce Headey, Ruud Muffels and Henk-Jan Dirven, *The Real Worlds of Welfare Capitalism*, Cambridge 1999, p. 70.

38 Lafontaine gives a sketch of his economic plans, his conversations with Strauss-Kahn and his clashes with Schroeder and the bankers in *The Heart Beats on the Left*, especially pp. 132–60.

39 *The Euresa/ETUC Workshop on Pension Funds*, Barcelona, Spain, 24 and 25 June 1997, pp. 3, 4.

40 Gunval Grip, 'The Pension Debate with Proposals for a European Trade Union Pension Fund' pp. 7, 46. Since Gunval Grip here again uses the notion of pensions as 'deferred pay', it is worth clarifying the point that this is not a denial that the cost of future pensions has to be covered by future production, something this author explicitly acknowledges.

41 James K. Galbraith, Pedro Conceiçao and Pedro Ferreira, 'Inequality and

Unemployment in Europe: the American Cure', *New Left Review*, no. 237, September–October 1999, pp. 28–51, especially p. 51.

42 Philip Arestis, Kevin McCauley and Malcolm Sawyer, 'An Alternative Stability Pact for the European Union', *Cambridge Journal of Economics*, vol. 25, no. 1, 2001, pp. 113–30, especially pp. 127–8.

43 Bozec and Mays, 'The Pension Reform Process in France', p. 186.

44 John Plender, 'Rhineland, USA', *Financial Times*, 7 December 1999.

45 Ralph Atkins, 'German move for pensions reform stalls after boycott', *Financial Times*, 12 July 2000.

46 'Schroeder's Journey', *The Economist*, 26 August 2000. For the shape of the reform see Ralf Nocker, 'The Recent Proposals for individual funded pensions in Germany – Repeating the UK Experience?', The Pension Institute, Birkbeck College, London, September 2000.

47 Deborah Hargreaves, 'Pensions Will Squeeze European Budgets', *Financial Times,* 23 November 1999.

48 Organisation for Economic Cooperation and Development, *Ageing in OECD Countries*, Paris 1996, pp. 38–40.

49 Hargreaves, 'Pensions Will Squeeze European Budgets'.

50 David Blake, 'Does It Matter What Type of Pension Scheme You Have?', *The Economic Journal*, vol. 110, no. 461, February 2000, pp. F46–81, F48.

51 European Commission, *Towards a Europe for All Ages – Promoting Prosperity and Intergenerational Solidarity*, Office of Official Publications of the European Communities, Luxembourg, pp. 13, 15.

52 'Supplementary Pensions in a Single Market', in Leo Stevens, Humbert Drabbe, Gerry Dietworst and Peter Kavelaars, *Pension Systems in the European Union: Competition and Tax Aspects*, London and The Hague 1999, pp. 87–138.

53 For the court cases see Humbert Drabbe, 'Pension Funds and Competition', in ibid., pp. 5–14. The directive is given on pp. 139–44.

54 Nicholas George, 'Complete Overhaul is Underway', *Financial Times*, Survey of European Pension Provision, 10 November 2000; Peter Diamond, 'Social Security Reform, with a Focus on Sweden', MIT website; Giuliano Bonoli, Vic George and Peter Taylor Gooby, *European Welfare Futures: towards a Theory of Retrenchment*, London 1999, pp. 32–3; Mikko Kautto et al., *Nordic Social Policy: Changing Welfare States*, London 1999, pp. 30–2, 50, 90–2, 255–61; Charpentier, *Retraites et fonds de pension*, pp. 173–4.

55 'The Stalled Promise of European Pension Reform', *Institutional Investor*, February 2000.

56 Robert Prozen, 'Continental Shift', *Foreign Affairs*, vol. 80, no. 3, May/June 2001, pp. 9–14, p. 13.

57 Tito Boeri, Axel Borsch-Supan and Guido Tabellini, 'Would You Like to Shrink the Welfare State?', *Economic Policy*, April 2001, pp. 9–50, p. 38.

58 Ibid., p. 10.

59 Ibid., p. 25.

60 Ibid., pp. 28–9.

61 Ibid., p. 31.

62 Ibid., p. 42.

63 Tony Barber, ' Social Democrats Break with Tradition', *Financial Times*, 10 November 2000; Tobias Buck, 'Schroeder Wins Vital Pensions Reform Vote', *Financial Times* 12/13 May 2001.

64 Christopher Rhoads, 'Germany's Pension Reform Approaches its Final Hurdle', *Wall Street Journal*, 10 May 2001; 'Schroeder's Triumph', *Wall Street Journal*, 14 May 2001.

65 James Blitz, 'Hail Berlusconi', *Financial Times*, 15 May 2001.

66 'General Strike Brings Greece to Standstill', *International Herald Tribune*, 27 April 2001.

67 Christoper Tremewan, *The Political Economy of Social Control in Singapore*, Oxford 1994, and Michael Hill and Lian Kwen Fei, *The Politics of Nation Building and Citizenship in Singapore*, London 1995.

68 Chairman's report for 1999, CPF web-site, August 2000.

69 Interview with Goh Chok Tong, *Far Eastern Economic Review*, 24 December 2000.

70 Ben Dolven, 'Where's My Nest Egg?', *Far Eastern Economic Review*, 25 May 2000.

71 CPF chairman's address to fund managers, *Far Eastern Economic Review*, 16 February 2000.

72 Sebastian Edwards, 'The Chilean Pension Reform: a Pioneering Program', in Martin Feldstein, ed., *Privatizing Social Security*, Chicago 1998, pp. 33–62, p. 44.

73 Stephen Fidler, 'Lure of the Latin Model', *Financial Times*, 9 April 1997, p. 31; Manuel Riesco and Hugo Fazio, 'Employee Ownership in Chile', *The Journal of Employee Ownership Law and Finance*, Fall 1995; Manuel Riesco and Hugo Fazio, 'Pension Schemes in Chile', *New Left Review*, no. 223, May/June 1997; World Bank, *Averting the Old Age Crisis*, pp. 224–5. For the Chilean trade unions' reform proposals, see the interview with Apolonia Ramirez, 'La "prevision" social de los chilenos', *Punto Final*, January 1998. The most recent performance statistics for the AFPs together with an assessment of their macroe-conomic contribution can be found on the web-site of CENDA.

74 Robert Wade and Frank Veneroso,'The Battle Over Capital Controls', *New Left Review*, no. 231, September/October 1998, pp. 13–42, p. 24. See also Robert Pollin, 'Finance and Inequality', *New Left Review*, no. 214, November/December, 1995.

75 James Kynge, 'China's Burden of Age', *Financial Times*, 1 June 2000.

76 Naturally the World Bank and global financial services industry make sure to beam their siren song to the Chinese authorities and public. For a volume that explores the topic of 'reform', with the help of contributions from Martin Feldstein and Estelle James, see Jason Z. Yin, Shuanglin Lin, David F. Gates, eds, *Social Security Reform: Options for China*, Singapore 2000. This collection does, however, include a timely warning against privatisation from Henry Aaron of the Brookings Institute ('Chinese Social Insurance Reform: Personal Security and Economic Growth?', pp. 15-38) as well as a somewhat murky

pronouncement from one of China's official social scientists (Lie Tieying, 'Establish Social Security with Chinese Characteristics', pp. 39–60). For the scope of the problem with existing arrangements, see Zhang Jinchang, Chen Jiagui and Hans Jürgen Rösner, 'Current and Future Problems of Capital Accumulation in the Chinese Pension System', *International Social Security Review*, vol. 53, no. 4, 2001. The Chinese government has pledged that privatisation receipts will be applied to social security but this may just mean plugging gaps in the current account rather than building a permanent reserve.

77 Taggart Murphy, 'Japan's Economic Crisis', *New Left Review*, no. 1, January–February 2000.

78 Jeffrey Sachs, 'The Benefits of a Weaker Yen', *Financial Times*, 18 April 2001. Sachs added: 'Amazingly the yen strengthened sharply between 1990 and 1996 while the Japanese economy was grinding to a halt. The US government began to lecture Japan about the virtues of large budget deficits on the erroneous grounds that fiscal stimulus would produce a domestic-demand-led recovery. Instead nervous households simply increased their own savings alongside the widening government deficit.' Sachs's solution was for a resumption of exports and some way to be found for the export of capital in a 'smooth manner' from Japan to its neighbours. 'Intuitively, Japan needs more exports to keep its economy fully employed while the rest of Asia needs Japanese capital goods and technology to keep its own growth on track. But increased Japanese exports to Asia can work only if Japan can reliably provide the financing.' The latter, he thought, would require not only direct Japanese investment but 'a banking system and other financial intermediaries that can once again lend for the long term, without frequent upheavals in the direction and magnitude of lending'. This could be read as an invitation to the pension fund management industry, although many would challenge the latter's ability to deliver smoothly and without the cited upheavals.

79 John C. Campbell, *How Policies Change: the Japanese Government and the Aging Society*, Princeton (NJ) 1992, p. 331.

80 Megumi Suto, *New Development in the Japanese Corporate Governance: Role of Corporate Pension Funds*, Nissan Institute of Japanese Studies, Oxford, 30 July 1999, pp. 2, 22.

81 Ronald Dore, 'Worldwide Anglo-Saxon Capitalism?', *New Left Review*, no. 6, November–December 2000, pp. 101–19.

82 Francis G. Castles, 'Needs-Based Strategies of Social Protection in Australia and New Zealand', in Gosta Esping-Anderson, ed., *Welfare States in Transition: National Adaptations in Global Economics,* London 1996, pp. 88–115.

83 Christopher Pierson, 'Globalisation and the Changing Governance of Welfare States: Superannuation Reform in Australia', *Global Society*, vol. 12, no. 1, 1998, pp. 31–47, pp. 42–3. This informative article places the Australian experience within the wider context of the nature of contemporary social democracy.

84 Ross Clare and Douglas Connor, *The Superannuation Industry in Australia*, ASFA Research Centre, April 2000; Dan Scheiwe, 'Why Australia's Pension System Is Not a Good International Model', The Pension Institute, Birkbeck College, London.

85 John Phillimore, 'The Limits of Supply-Side Social Democracy', *Politics and Society*, vol. 28, no. 4, December 2000, pp. 557–87.

86 There is a brief and cautious reference – see World Bank, *Averting the Old Age Crisis*, p. 246.

87 For an upbeat assessment of the 'Super' which notes both its similarities to, and departures from, the World Bank Model see Diana Olsberg's informative study, *Ageing and Money: Australia's Retirement Revolution*, Sydney 1997.

5

Carrot and Stick Reform: Implicit Privatisation in the UK

It had been Margaret − backed by a majority of the [cabinet] committee − who had argued that there would be no political support for scrapping SERPS unless an adequate replacement private scheme were made compulsory. I disagreed, pointing out that we were the party of individual freedom; that people had different views about how much pension provision they required; and that to make taking out of a particular level of private provision compulsory was wholly contrary to our political philosophy. Margaret replied that compulsory private provision had long been the practice in Switzerland. 'But Prime Minister', I countered, 'it is well known that in Switzerland everything that is not forbidden is compulsory' − a pardonable exaggeration in the circumstances. At least I never had Switzerland thrown at me again.

(Nigel Lawson, *The View from No 11*, London 1992, p. 590)

Mr Blair's Conference speech was a clarion call for a 'new moral purpose, greater equality . . . solidarity . . . and social justice'. How then can he continue pursuing a policy which, in effect, perpetuates a 'social injustice' roundly condemned by him when in opposition and which is resulting in the continuing decline of the basic state pension? 1999, the International Year of the Older Person, coincided with Gordon Brown heralding the best economic prospects for Britain in a generation. How will today's pensioners fare in this bonanza? Current prospects appear pretty bleak. If inflation remains at its current level, today's single pensioners can expect an increase of 75p per week. . . . Today's pensioners have never been so badly off compared with everyone else . . . I would urge the Prime Minister to remember that it was the sacrifices of today's pensioners in the war against fascism, and their contribution to rebuilding a war scarred Britain, that made it possible for him and the Labour party to be where it is today.

(Mike Le Cornu, 'A Gross Act of Social Injustice', *Essex Pensioner*, winter 1999–2000)

Pensioners' Demonstration, UK, 1999 (National Pensioners Convention)

Britain has been a laboratory for grey capitalism because of the weakness of its public pension provision and the historic strength of the financial services industry. It was among the first countries to embark on 'pension reform' and the New Labour government elected in 1997 has maintained the momentum. Margaret Thatcher has been hailed as a hero of pension privatisation almost on a par with the ministers of General Pinochet. But in truth the public system she set about dismantling was of very recent construction, so that few really understood what they were losing.

Notwithstanding the reputation of Britain's postwar welfare state, it did not establish a 'dominant' public sector in pension provision. The Basic State Pension (BSP) set up by the National Insurance Act of 1946 was universal and financed by National Insurance contributions paid by every employee and employer, with both contributions and benefits paid at a flat rate. But, as noted in chapter 1, the BSP did not furnish a basic subsistence to the retired and therefore did not eliminate the need for means testing. In 1948, the first year of the scheme's operation, 495,000 old age and widowed pensioners, and 143,000 of others above pensionable age, applied for and received National Assistance supplements to the BSP.[1] William Beveridge had proclaimed the goal of a subsistence pension but had hoped to phase it in over twenty years; Labour backbenchers had secured an amendment to accelerate this but inflation undermined their efforts. The inadequate level of the BSP, combined with its contribution conditions, meant that it did not eliminate pensioner poverty. Moreover, even if it rose closer to a minimum subsistence level, as it was projected to do by about 1958, individuals would still have every incentive to stay in or join an occupational or private pension scheme. Beveridge believed that a declining reliance upon means tests and a flat-rate benefit would furnish an encouragement to private saving. The fiscal encouragement to private provision was maintained by Labour and enhanced by the Conservative governments elected after 1951. By the mid-1950s the cost in forgone taxes ran at £100 million annually, more than double the £45 million annual cost of the Exchequer's contribution to the BSP.[2] The proportion of male employees covered by occupational pensions grew from 34 per cent in 1953 to 66 per cent in 1967 – over the same period coverage of female employees rose from 18 to 28 per cent. Occupational schemes still had a quasi-collective aura to them so in 1956 the Conservatives introduced Retirement Annuity Contracts (RACs) which allowed individuals to make tax-favoured contributions without doing so via an employer.

Titmuss, Crossman and Castle: Labour's Second Pension

The contrast between the new power of commercial pension funds, enjoying huge tax privileges, and a still miserably inadequate state pension, lagging far behind national prosperity, alarmed Richard Titmuss, a leading social security expert based at the LSE who advised the Labour opposition. Titmuss showed that the combination of a flat-rate BSP and tax breaks for private pension schemes was fostering glaring inequality: 'The flat-rate contribution means benefits pegged to the lowest wage rate.'[3] But if contributions were to be income-related, then there could be both redistribution and greatly improved benefits, even if there was some degree of benefit gradation according to the level of contribution. Titmuss was also alarmed that the insurance houses which operated private pensions placed their funds in commercial real estate at a time when the country's social infrastructure desperately needed renewal. So he proposed that state superannuation should have its own autonomous fund which should be 'boldly invested', both in public bonds, which could finance new hospitals and schools, and in stocks and shares, which would ensure that pensioners shared in rising prosperity. These principles were embodied in a National Superannuation plan which was adopted by the Labour Party conference of 1957 after a speech of passionate advocacy by Richard Crossman, a young MP and journalist who had been converted to the Titmuss approach.[4] The National Superannuation Scheme would allow those who contributed more to receive a somewhat higher pension, but on a sliding scale that gave a better rate of return to the low-paid. Titmuss had attacked the publicly subsidised private pension schemes for chaining their members to a particular employer; having himself spent two decades working for an insurance house, he knew that the losses incurred by those who left schemes were an important source of commercial gain. Under the proposed new arrangements all employees would be covered but private occupational schemes would continue so long as they offered good terms to those who changed jobs. To finance the new scheme, and to take account of the rising birth rate, the National Superannuation fund would build up an investment reserve for the future. Labour declared: 'We must plan for a surplus on pension account and see that this surplus is invested in industry to create a larger national income.'[5] This fund was projected to be worth £4 billion by 1970 and £6 billion by 1980 at 1957 prices (so roughly £400 billion in 1980 terms).[6] The document explained:

> as a provision for contingencies, such a reserve is clearly excessive. It may also be excessive as a psychological guarantee of pension rights. On the other hand, viewed as a national fund for investment, it is not too large. . . . The importance of the investment policy cannot be over-stressed. For there is only one guarantee that any pension commitment, public or private, can be met now or in the future. This is the soundness of the economy. There can be no other. Paper claims to the future national income cannot be honoured unless the working population is producing the goods and services which these claims represent, and is willing to release them to those who stake these claims.[7]

Vigorously written, carefully argued and meticulously researched, the 120-page pamphlet outlining Labour's superannuation policy stands quite apart from the usual run of indifferently thought-out, and slackly or slickly presented, Labour Party policy proposals. It went through five editions in two years and stimulated a considerable public discussion. The Conservatives attacked the scheme, especially the proposed investment fund which was described as a recipe for 'nationalisation by the back door'.[8] Seeing the impact made by the Labour proposals, however, the governing party brought forward its own, promising graduated pensions but dispensing with pre-funding.

The Conservatives obtained credit for the fact that, as foreseen by the original BSP legislation, many qualified for the full pension for the first time in 1958. Capitalising on this, the Macmillan government itself raised pensions in 1959, prior to the election in that year. After re-election it introduced its own version of Graduated Retirement Benefits (GRB) in 1961. Under this legislation higher-paid employees could, if they wished, receive a little more than the flat rate, for which they would pay slightly higher contributions.[9] But they could also 'contract out' of the higher payments if they were members of an occupational or private scheme and claim the larger subsidies and benefits available from these schemes. As a result, the state second pension was clearly second best, and, since many better-paid employees left the scheme, it had little scope to be redistributive.

The Labour governments of 1964–70 had the opportunity to change the pension regime but failed to deliver – despite the fact that Labour received unusually strong support from older voters in 1966.[10] After

wasting three years, Harold Wilson, the Prime Minister, at last made
Richard Crossman, with his pension expertise, Secretary of State for Social
Services. Crossman was still committed to the approach he had worked out
with Titmuss, believing that the basic pension should be 'dynamised'
(indexed to earnings), that a supplementary pension should be introduced
and that it should be pre-funded, in contrast to what he saw as the 'Tory
swindle' of Graduated Retirement Benefits. After a meeting with Tage
Erlander, the Swedish Prime Minister, Crossman noted the advice that a
good pension scheme would be 'an enormous electoral help'.[11] There followed sticky negotiations with the Treasury, which pruned the level of
funding, opposed the investment plan and diluted the proposal for indexation. The fund was only to be invested in public bonds. Crossman faced
combined pressure from the trade unions and insurance houses to allow
those who were already members of occupational schemes to opt out of
the new arrangements. He felt obliged to accept a device then known as
'abatement' by which those in qualifying schemes could remove a portion
of contributions, with a corresponding reduction in benefit.[12] Crossman
nevertheless crafted a major improvement to British pension provision. He
successfully steered his pensions bill through two Commons readings and
a committee stage. Just as the end was in sight Wilson called an early general election in June 1970, which Labour lost. The Labour leader's
willingness to jettison the pensions bill for a mistaken calculation of short-
term political advantage was characteristic.

It was not until Labour's victories in the elections of 1974 that it was able
to resuscitate its plans for a thoroughly indexed BSP and a secondary state
pension. Barbara Castle, the minister responsible, secured approval within
eleven days for the linking of the pension to the price or wages index,
whichever was the higher. She engaged Brian Abel-Smith, a colleague of
Titmuss at the LSE, and other members of Crossman's team of pension
experts. Within just over a year she steered the Social Security Pensions Act
(1975) onto the statute book. This measure adapted earlier plans to establish what was now called the State Earnings Related Pension Scheme
(SERPS).[13] Castle was assisted in advancing matters so decisively by trade
union support for the measure. The unions had just helped to bring down
the Conservatives and their 'social contract' with the government included
an improved deal for pensioners. Following a bruising clash of her own with
the unions in 1969, Castle herself was anxious to mend fences. Jack Jones,
the leader of the giant Transport and General Workers' Union (TGWU),
was particularly committed to the pension legislation. Retired workers
generally remained members of their union, with a continuing voice and

vote on union social policy. At this time the TGWU and other unions still had an extensive membership in the private sector, many of whom were not covered by occupational schemes. Wage indexation of the basic pension helped those who did have occupational membership. The BSP was raised to its highest-ever level at 20 per cent of average male wages, while the SERPS aimed to deliver an extra 25 per cent of previous average earnings. For the first time women's benefits were to equal men's. Women were also helped by a SERPS provision that twenty, rather than thirty-nine, years of contribution were required to qualify.[14] The overall level of British state pensions remained considerably below that of publicly mandated provision in France and Sweden, and those who took out private or occupational pensions could still 'contract out' of the public second pension and continue to receive tax-free contributions to their own schemes. Both the unions and the fund managers were content with these arrangements, which protected and encouraged the occupational schemes that now covered more than a half of all employees. And, of course, the original 1957 proposal for pre-funding and a national investment strategy had been sacrificed. Despite these compromises and limitations, the new arrangements – because of their complexity, not operational until 1978 – were certainly a significant step towards a more generous public pillar.

The social legislation of the Labour government was to be overshadowed by economic crisis and political turmoil. As the price of an IMF loan in 1976, the government embarked on a sustained wage freeze which cut into popular living standards. The unions loyally endorsed this aspect of the so-called 'social contract' for nearly three years, grateful for the repeal of the Conservative labour laws and encouraged by the hope of further social legislation. Some unions were able to negotiate better pension arrangements in lieu of wage rises. But in 1978–9 a rash of strikes swept the public sector in the so-called 'winter of discontent', leading to the ejection of Labour and return of hyper-inflation. As noted in the Introduction, both Harold Wilson and Tony Benn belatedly conceded that the government's difficulties had been exacerbated by the financial institutions of what Titmuss had called 'the irresponsible society'.

Margaret Thatcher and 'Implicit Privatisation'

The government of Margaret Thatcher, elected in 1979, introduced what seemed to many a modest change in the indexation of the state pension in the following year. Henceforth, increases were to be pegged to rises in prices alone and not to earnings. In fact, the medium- and long-range impact of this change was to be very great. Over the subsequent seventeen years it was to mean that the state pension declined from being 20 per cent of average male earnings to being no more than 14 per cent. In the OECD's scary 1996 projection of the future burden of pension provision Britain came near the very bottom of the table with a likely expenditure of only 5 per cent in 2040, and less thereafter, compared with 7.1 per cent for the United States and double-digit figures for the continental European states.[15] In 2030 the Basic State Pension would be worth only 10 per cent of average earnings. Such projections can be made in different ways; another way of putting the change produced by the dropping of the earnings link is to say that the BSP would fall to a half of its former level vis-à-vis average earnings over whatever period it would take to double per capita national income. Thatcher had accomplished at a stroke that radical 'pension reform' that was to elude Reagan in the 1980s and the continental European governments of the 1990s.[16] She was to follow it up by an attack on the value of SERPS in 1986.

Thatcher's success exploited a variety of circumstances. British governments with a workable parliamentary majority are well placed to ram through any measure they are minded to. Technically, the House of Lords can hold up passage of a bill for a year but it is a power that they use sparingly. Notwithstanding the high proportion of peers who qualify for the pension, they did not use their power to defend the earnings-linked BSP. There were some predictable objections from the parliamentary opposition and pensioners' organisations but these aroused little response; Labour's front bench lacked anyone as well informed and capable as Castle or O'Malley (her Minister of State in 1974–5). At this stage few grasped the import of what had happened and there was little by way of a high-profile lobby to defend public pension provision. In France and the United States pension provision is the province of an autonomous social apparatus while in the UK it is simply another branch of a Treasury-invigilated civil service.

It must have seemed to many that price indexation would protect the pension from the scourge of inflation and that this was the main danger – the country had experienced double-digit price hikes in the early and mid-1970s and did so once again in 1980, the year the new arrangement was introduced. At the time few thought that the Conservatives would be in power for eighteen years. If the pension lagged behind national prosperity, then it could easily be uprated in the first budget introduced by a Labour chancellor. When the Thatcher government introduced new pensions legislation in 1986 there was more by way of public opposition; an announced intention to abolish SERPS and replace it with compulsory private provision was eventually dropped in favour of a draconian, benefit-cutting 'reform' of the programme. The preservation of appearances – few understood the detail of SERPS benefits anyway – and the fact that the government had abandoned its original proposal seemed to indicate that it was willing to compromise. But the failure simply to abolish SERPS and replace it with mandatory private provision chiefly reflected the opposition of the Chancellor Nigel Lawson, since the new arrangements promised tax relief for the obligatory contributions to private schemes to make them more acceptable. It could easily be shown that while SERPS payments yielded a good income to the Treasury, the privatised second pension would mean a substantial loss of revenue. Most private pension providers had not been enthusiastic about catering to the low-paid and other bad prospects, since the costs of dealing with a host of petty accounts would be likely to outweigh the gain.[17]

The approach to secondary pensions still very much encouraged what Paul Pierson has called 'implicit privatisation', namely the process of so minimising the attraction of public provision that citizens are impelled to look to the private sector to insure their future.[18] Indeed the Financial Services Act, introduced in conjunction with the SERPS economies, boosted the incentives to opt out of the public scheme by lowering the rate of National Insurance levied on employees who did so. The new arrangements even encouraged many in occupational schemes to switch to a personal pension instead. This legislation sowed the seeds of the notorious 'pension mis-selling' scandal of the mid-1990s. Of the seven million or so who took advantage of the opt-outs over the next five years it was to be legally established that 1.5 million had been persuaded by high-pressure salesmanship to trade in good pension entitlements for inferior personal schemes. Government advertisements appeared on TV showing a man swathed in ropes and chains, symbolising the burden of collective pension schemes, who then achieves liberation thanks to the providential assistance of money managers. By the mid-1990s this clip, repeated in reports of the 'mis-selling' imbroglio, came to haunt the Conservatives.

The diluted SERPS arrangements would replace 20 rather than 25 per cent of average earnings and widows were to receive a half, rather than full, pension. The earnings-related scheme had been in effect for less than a decade and, with its complex promise still largely in the future, few grasped what was happening. The flagship programme of Britain's welfare state had always been the National Health Service. The NHS, a completely new institution, had been introduced by Nye Bevan, the most flamboyant and radical member of the 1945 Labour government, in the teeth of opposition from the British Medical Association and other vested interests. Its workings soon impinged on the lives of every citizen, and it was embraced as the symbol and substance of a new and more humane social order, of which Britons could be proud. The new state pension of 1948 improved on the previous contributory scheme but the change was less dramatic. Margaret Thatcher accurately sensed the different standing enjoyed by these two programmes. Both she and John Major, her successor, were vociferous in their assurances that the NHS was safe in their hands, and took care to raise the health budget in pre-election periods. Of course, Margaret Thatcher was perfectly capable of miscalculating public opinion, as the 'poll tax' fiasco showed, but her policy of downgrading the state pension reflected a sure grasp of what could be done.[19]

On the evidence of the memoirs of Nigel Lawson, the Chancellor, and Norman Fowler, the Secretary of State for Social Services, the influence of the private pensions lobby could be formidable. When Lawson proposed to phase out the tax-free lump sum which can be claimed by private scheme members on retirement, he ran into what he describes as 'the most astonishing lobbying campaign of my entire political career'.[20] He writes of the 'awesome power of the pension fund lobby' which mobilised the Confederation of British Industry and the Trades Union Congress, and 100 backbenchers. And he adds: 'at the boardroom lunches I attended at this time all talk of the state of the economy, or of their own business, was suspended, as directors turned the conversation to the all-important issue of their pensions.'[21] The plan to drop the tax-free lump sum was abandoned. The proposal to abolish SERPS and replace it with compulsory private provision did not appeal to most of the private providers at this time. They were happy with what Lawson himself describes as the 'excessively favourable National Insurance rates for those who contracted out of SERPS',[22] since this promised a flood of grateful customers while the compulsory scheme would turn them into a new species of tax collector. Lawson himself minuted to the cabinet that the compulsory approach 'would be more than a banana skin, it would be a political death wish'.[23] The compulsory scheme strongly appealed to Norman Fowler. But, as he explains in his (in this instance) inappropriately titled book *Ministers Decide*, he felt obliged to abandon it when confronted with opposition from both the Chancellor and the private pensions lobby: 'I was becoming dangerously isolated. I had against me virtually the whole of the pensions industry. . . . They regarded compulsory occupational pensions as several bridges too far and it was clear that they would campaign against my proposals.'[24] Fowler had himself always urged a cut-back on SERPS benefits as an alternative to abolition and was, in retrospect, content to claim some credit for the large numbers who had taken out personal pensions. Thus the policies eventually pursued by the government were not precisely those initially favoured by its strong-willed leader but, when taken in conjunction with the removal of the BSP's earnings link, they amounted to a powerful dose of implicit privatisation and something central to the Thatcher record.

Margaret Thatcher is a politician who prides herself on plain speaking yet the account she gives of her great pension reform in her first memoir, *The Downing Street Years* (1993), contrives to make it appear a valiant defence of pledges given to defend pensioners' interests. She explains that the need for drastic economies was identified as soon as she reached Downing Street but she was bound by prior commitments not to cut spending on health and defence: 'We were also pledged to raise retirement pensions and other long-term social security benefits in line with prices – and to honour Labour's pension increases that year [1979].'[25] In a similar vein we next read: 'The social security budget accounted for a quarter of total public spending, of which the cost of retirement pensions was by far the largest element. But I had pledged publicly that the latter would be raised in line with inflation during the Parliament.'[26] Moving forward a little to 1983, matters become a little clearer when the author notes: 'There continued to be misunderstanding and resentment of the new system by which the pension was uprated in line with prices.'[27] These sparse lines constitute all that Britain's former Prime Minister had to say about the sabotaging of a programme vital to the livelihood of about 15 per cent of the population and that had huge implications for the future of public finances. By contrast she expends seventy-two pages on her government's success in recovering the Falkland Islands.

When Lady Thatcher came to write *Preparing for Power*, published in 1995, what she had to say was more forthright and revealing. She claimed her success in reining in pensions as a major achievement: 'Because we controlled public expenditure effectively in the 1980s – particularly by limiting the basic retirement pension and other long term benefits to prices rather than incomes and scaling back SERPS – Britain already enjoys an advantage over other European countries which failed to take such action.'[28] And Thatcher's account of her political career prior to becoming prime minister brought out the importance of her early three-year stint as junior minister in the Ministry of Pensions, as it was then called. During

that period she had studied every aspect of the question, theoretical and
practical. She was pleased to discover 'Thatcherite' sentiments in Beveridge
('The insured person should not feel that income for idleness, however
caused, can come from a bottomless purse') and dutifully spoke with pensioners and administrators up and down the land. She was impressed, she
tells us, by 'the self-respect of those people I used to refer to as "the proud
ones", who were not going to take hand-outs from anyone'.[29] The political studies literature dedicated to the German Greens in the 1980s claimed
to discover the 'post-materialist' voter. Margaret Thatcher apparently made
her own discovery, a little earlier, of the 'pre-materialist' voter. This was an
individual who resonated powerfully in her own experience:

> In Grantham and in similar towns up and down the country, we understood
> that there were some families where the bread winner had fallen on hard
> times but who would never accept charity – even what they saw as charity
> from the state – being determined at all costs to keep up their respectabil-
> ity. 'I keep myself to myself and I've never taken a penny from anyone'
> would be the way that many a dignified pensioner would put it.[30]

Pierson argues that Margaret Thatcher got her way on pensions because
British public provision had features which weakened its ability to command support. It was 'immature', with many unaware of benefits to come,
it was fragmented, with many opting out, and it lacked its own independently administered trust fund.[31] These aspects of the British pension
regime certainly go a long way to explain its vulnerability. But they also
link up with the peculiarities of the UK political system, the low profile of
pension issues and the politics of social fear in the post-1979 period, factors which also helped a political leader with minority support among
voters – Thatcher's highest all-UK score was 44 per cent in 1979 – to
inflict lasting damage on public pension provision. Both opposition parties
opposed her pension policies and it is likely that not a few Conservative
supporters did so too. But Thatcher had the steam-roller of a parliamentary majority at her command and was able to demonstrate that
'Anglo-Saxon politics' makes its own contribution to the socially regressive features of 'Anglo-Saxon economics'.[32] As we turn to the evolving
base of support for the parties we also discover that voters often have most
to fear from their own kind. Older voters, including older women, were
unstinting in their support for a political leader who knew them well.

For complex reasons older voters in Britain in the 1970s and 1980s were
conservative with a large as well as a small c, notwithstanding Labour's support for improvements to a programme that was so important to them.

The Conservatives received 49.7 per cent of the votes of those aged 65–74 in 1979, and no less than 63.6 per cent of the votes of those over 74. After the 1980 revision, Labour promised to restore the value of the state pension and, on balance, this may have helped it improve its vote a little in 1987 and 1992. But Labour still failed to win anything like majority support among pensioners in these years. By 1987 support for the Conservatives had slipped a bit but was still impressive – 46.0 per cent among voters aged 65–74 and 55.9 per cent among those over 74. The Conservatives won more support from older voters than from any other age group. The last time Labour won majority support among voters aged 65–74 was in 1966. In the period 1974–92 Labour never attracted more than 38.0 per cent of the votes of those aged 65–74 in any general election, or more than 32.9 per cent of the votes of those aged over 74. If we compare this score with the vote among the population as a whole, then Labour did slightly better among those aged 65-74 in 1979, 1983 and 1992, but trailed by 3.2 points in 1987.[33] The Liberals did badly among older voters – except in 1987 when its alliance with the Social Democrats attracted a swing from this quarter, possibly due to the leading role played by Shirley Williams, a former Labour cabinet minister who embodied the liberal reform tradition.

Focusing just on those over seventy-four it is striking that support for Labour lagged between 5 and 11 points behind its support among the population as a whole in 1979, 1983 and 1987, only closing the gap to 2 points behind in 1992. Many older voters were no doubt, like others, susceptible to Conservative patriotic appeals and Cold War scares, and alienated by Labour's splits, disarray and incoherent radicalism in the 1980s. Some older voters may have associated the party of Churchill and Macmillan with generosity to the pensioner, since both had helped to extend state provision. Thatcher notes of the 1979 campaign: 'Since Central Office was telling me that our support amongst pensioners was shaky I wrote out a press release reminding the voters of the record of Conservative governments on this point.'[34]

Since many of the 65–74-year-olds of one decade become the over-75-year-olds of the next, it might appear that the gap between these two groups cannot be put down to different generational experience. Despite Labour's pledge to raise the pension, the Conservatives retained a strong lead among both groups. The achievement of the 1970s Labour government on pensions seems to have been overshadowed for many older voters by other issues, including the distempers of 1978–9 and the memory of double-digit inflation. The exit polls on which the above-cited age breakdowns are based did not include a question specifically on pensions but in 1979, when asked about 'welfare benefits', 50.8 per cent of over-74-year-olds declared that these had 'gone too far', a proportion which dropped steeply to 19.8 per cent in 1983, by which time 59 per cent believed them to be 'about right'.[35] The term 'welfare benefits' would almost certainly not have been understood to apply to the pension.

In interpreting these figures we should bear in mind that two Conservative-leaning groups had greater longevity – women and members of the middle and upper classes. In postwar Britain women were more likely to vote Conservative than men, and they also lived longer. And likewise the strongly Conservative middle and upper classes (AB) voted by 72 per cent for the Conservatives even in Labour's best year (1966) and enjoyed a greater life expectancy than the skilled and unskilled working classes (C2, DE). Labour's bedrock supporters, male workers, were much less likely to reach the age of seventy-five; and women, with their greater longevity, outnumbered men by two to one among the over-75s.[36] These class and gender gaps unfavourable to Labour filtered generational experience – the over-74s of the 1970s and 1980s had been born before the First World War. Prior to 1987 support for the Conservatives among women was usually 5–8 points ahead of their support among men.[37] Of course, the older women were not all gilded daughters of the Belle Epoque. Many had worked hard as teachers or nurses, part-time workers, temporary workers, domestics or housewives but they often had neither the social expectations and outlook, nor the pension rights, of those who had been in full-time employment for all or most of their adult life. SERPS would help women with interrupted employment, and give widows their husband's full pension – but these arrangements barely applied to the pensioners of the 1980s, and not at all to the over-74s. Another characteristic of elderly female pensioners, one which has endured, is that they fail to apply for welfare benefits to which they are entitled, especially those requiring a means test. The 'proud ones' will accept a pension to which they or their husband have contributed, but not National Assistance or income support. Indeed, the pension is believed to be validated not only by prior pecuniary contributions but by the contribution that civilians as well as the enlisted, women as well as men, made to national survival in the troubled twentieth century.

Non-materialist motivations were important, but a significant section of the Conservative electorate had material interests to defend. While state pensions were indexed, this was often not the case for private pensions, with the losses from this lack of protection increasing over time. More than half of the retired population drew income from an occupational or private scheme. In 1987 the richest fifth of pensioners received private income that was twice as large as the sum they received as a state pension while for the second richest fifth private sources comprised just over a third of their total income.[38] The richer pensioners were more likely to vote than the frail and sometimes socially isolated 'old old' who were dependent solely on the state pension and social assistance. Older voters with significant fixed or rentier incomes are likely to have been especially distrustful of Labour's economic competence. But fear of a return to the turmoil of the 1970s was clearly not confined to better-off pensioners who did well during the Thatcher years.

This is not to say that the 'class war' side of Thatcherism always endeared itself to the elderly. Conservative ratings in the polls tended to sag among all voters when its social revanchism was uppermost – for example in 1984–5 during the miners' strike, or in 1990 at the time of the introduction of the poll tax. But in the two years prior to the election of 1992 John Major took care to present a more moderate, caring image, and traditional Conservative philosophy, with a strong accent on economic competence. Labour went into the election of that year with a pledge to fully restore the value of the state pension and at last saw a modest recovery in its support from older voters. Labour attracted 36.8 per cent of the vote of those aged 65–74 in 1992, compared with only 28 per cent in 1987; among those over 74 its support rose from 25.8 per cent in 1987 to 32.9 per cent in 1992. Overall support for Labour rose from 31.2 per cent in 1987 to 34.3 per cent in 1992.[39] Such a modest accretion of support, with those aged 65–74 inclining towards Labour a little more than other voters, was no consolation for the bitterness of Labour's fourth defeat in a row. According to the post-mortem offered by the 'modernising', proto-New Labour wing, voters had been alarmed by the implications of Labour's spending pledges, the most expensive of which was the pledge to restore the 'earnings link' to the BSP.

The spectacular devaluation of the pound in the European exchange rate crisis of October 1992 was followed by a sudden and lasting collapse of support for the Conservatives.[40] The key attribute which voters wanted from politicians at this time was the ability to keep the economic and financial system on an even keel. The troubled economy of the early 1990s had harmed the Conservatives less than might have been expected, because many, including many over-sixties, still thought them the better economic managers. When that confidence was shown to be misplaced – in the ERM fiasco – it proved very hard to restore. Bitter feuds among leading Tories over Europe kept the issue very much alive. The discovery in the mid-1990s that more than 1.5 million people had been 'mis-sold' costly and underperforming personal pensions because of the legislation of 1986–87 intensified disenchantment with the Conservatives among some of those approaching retirement. In 1995 the Major government brought in a massive Pensions Act – it ran to half a million words – whose major purpose was to prevent a repetition of Robert Maxwell's pension fund-looting spree.

As part of a general makeover, the Labour Party – now 'New Labour' – abandoned its pledge to increase the state pension in line with the growth in average earnings. It did so on the grounds that the pledge was expensive and irresponsible. An attempt was made to drop the commitment with as little fuss as possible while focusing attention on changes to the party's constitution but, as we will see below, the case for restoring the earnings link was to return to haunt the new leaders at successive party conferences. New Labour famously committed itself, should it win the election, to remaining faithful to Conservative spending plans for its first two years in office. Later, the size of the Labour victory and widespread joy at the departure of the Tories were to make this seem overly cautious. But in the long run-up to the 1997 election New Labour strategists, terrified of a repetition of past defeats, were obsessed with fiscal prudence. Nevertheless, aware of a shift in public mood, the 'modernisers' also realised that they needed a more enticing vision of the future beyond the first two years. Party spokesmen spoke of the imperative of 'social inclusion' and the need to empower 'the many, not the few'. More cautiously, some began to talk of the virtues of a 'stakeholder' society. This discourse was, in principle, pitched at voters of all ages. The introduction of 'stakeholder pensions' was promised in a Labour policy document in 1996 and repeated in its election manifesto, presumably aimed at younger and middle-aged voters.

The 'Stakeholder' Philosophy and the 1997 Election

In spite of a fairly steady increase in average earnings for British employees in the 1980s and 1990s, the dramatic rise in unemployment and inequality made this a very uneven and unsettling process. Awareness that the already miserable level of the state pension was destined to decline further as a proportion of average earnings certainly helped to compound a sense of insecurity. Against this background New Labour's promise of 'stakeholding' pensions aimed to address this concern while more or less elegantly burying the costly commitment to restore the 'earnings link' and the SERPS. Those who were already pensioners were promised a special winter fuel supplement and given warm words about improvements as resources allowed. The absence of an independent pensions administration and high-profile pensions lobby, such as exists in France or the United States, assisted this repositioning. Though it had been yoked to Labour's new pension proposals, those who advocated a 'stakeholder' society had a broad social ethos in mind. Few of them were specifically concerned with pensions policy, still less with the tactical problems of Labour politicians.

Something called a 'stakeholder' approach or 'stakeholder capitalism' had long been recommended by those advocating improvements in corporate governance. It was given wider currency in the mid-1990s by Will Hutton, author of the much-discussed book, *The State We're In*, and economics editor of the *Guardian*. Two leading financial commentators, John Kay, a business economist who is a regular contributor to the *Financial Times*, and John Plender, a staff member at the *FT*, also canvassed the merits of stakeholding. The proponents of the original 'stakeholder' approach use the term in a metaphorical sense. They argue that chief executives and company boards should be encouraged to regard a company's employees, its consumers, and the communities it affects, as stakeholders in the enterprise. It should, accordingly, take steps to consult them and to bear their interests in mind. A reform of company law and of auditing and accounting standards could help to promote this. These changes would extend the right to consultation to a wider circle but they would not literally endow every citizen with a property stake – something once advocated by classic stakeholder democrats like William Cobbet or Thomas Jefferson, and now championed by Bruce Ackerman and others.

John Plender used the stakeholder idea to criticise the record of British fund managers. He argued that a 'stakeholder' reform to the financial institutions would require them to take a larger view of both their role and the interests of the policy holder and community. He pointed out that British funds adopt the passive policy of invariably endorsing existing management. If fund managers are discontented they jump ship rather than offer positive guidance. He urged that fund representatives should be obliged to attend and vote at AGMs, explaining the reasons for their actions.[41] Frank Field, a Labour MP with a reputation for innovatory proposals on social exclusion and pensions issues, also adopted the language of 'stakeholding'. He proposed that every citizen should acquire a claim to a secondary pension based on a national fund invested in stocks and shares, thus giving all a stake in national prosperity.[42] He advocated this prior to the vogue for the 'stakeholder' concept, but his proposals and Labour's pension promise seemed to link the two discussions.

Tony Blair appeared to endorse the stakeholder concept in a speech delivered in Singapore in the last days of 1995. The South-East Asian city state, with its startling economic success and famous Central Provident Fund, was deemed to supply the appropriate setting for stakeholder advocacy. But the speech received a mixed reception from business circles and the press. Just because the 'stakeholding' approach had first emerged as a management concept did not mean all members of the business community were enamoured of it. Some branded it as a new code word for government meddling. The Labour leader quickly made it clear that he was talking about a general philosophy, not proposing specific legislation.[43] Tony Blair insisted that a New Labour administration would be pro-business and had no plans to challenge corporate governance. The only tangible proposal to be linked to the stakeholding notion was that of pension provision, when New Labour advocated 'stakeholder pensions' in its 1996 document *Security in Retirement*, which also marked a break with the previous commitments to public PAYGO pensions.

The Conservative party believed that New Labour was encroaching on its own ground – after all, it had long advocated a 'property-owning democracy'. It was aware of public concern at the decline of the BSP and fears that it would be almost worthless by the time that many voters could claim it. Shortly before the 1997 election Peter Lilley, Minister for Social Security, published 'Basic Pension Plus', a plan to replace the state pension with a mandatory plan based on contributions of £9 a month that would, he claimed, allow every citizen to accumulate a pension fund worth £130,000 after forty-four years, enough to buy an annuity worth £175 a week in 1997 values. Those unemployed or sick would receive credits, and low earners, whose National Insurance contributions came to less than £9, would receive a top-up. The contributions would be invested via approved private schemes and there would be a guarantee that, in the case of bad performance of the selected fund, all would receive no less than they would have done under the basic state pension. Of course the downside risk here was still considerable as the BSP was due to decline against average earnings and the guarantee would not cover any sums that might have come due under SERPS.

In order to help with the cost of introducing the scheme, notably the 'transition cost' of honouring past entitlements to the BSP, the £9 weekly contributions were not to be tax free – though the money paid out in a pension was to be. (It will be recalled that Nigel Lawson had opposed the

1985 plans for mandatory private coverage partly because it would have deprived the Treasury of tax revenues on contributions.) A *Daily Telegraph* report noted:

> The new scheme is being introduced against a background of continuing concern over the mis-selling of personal pensions in the 1980s, when some people were badly advised to leave their occupational schemes. Ministers insisted yesterday that the same problem would not arise, because the new funds would not be an optional alternative either to the PAYG state pension or occupational schemes. The new scheme will be compulsory.

Perhaps some did not find it reassuring to be forced into the clutches of the very same providers responsible for the mis-selling. However, the compulsory aspect of the scheme also helped to surmount cost objections:

> The Government argued that the cost of participating in the scheme would be low – nowhere near the 15–20 per cent that has been swallowed by some personal schemes. A major part of the cost of providing personal pensions is the cost of persuading people to save. Since the new funds will be compulsory that cost will not arise. The Government intends to consult with the pensions industry to ensure that costs are kept low. If necessary it will regulate to set the level of charges. Rules will also be introduced to prevent 'churning' – artificial and costly inducements to switch funds between schemes.[44]

An already badly-rattled government sought to offer Basic Pension Plus as an innovative solution that would allow everyone to share in the buoyancy of the stock market.

But voters were not impressed and many traditional Conservative supporters failed to turn out for their party in June 1997. Support for the Conservatives from the over-65s fell three points. Support for Labour among the over-65s also fell – by two points – with Liberal Democrats gaining support.[45] The pension proposals of the two main parties may have cost them some support among older voters – the Liberals simply concentrated on the need for a better pension. Labour did arouse enthusiasm among younger voters but doubtless few of these focused very closely on the stakeholder idea. The election was decided not by a minute comparison of policies on pensions or anything else but by a feeling that there was much that was wrong with the country after eighteen years of Conservative rule. If the economy was as strong as the government claimed, why were public services in such a miserable state and why were there still so many unemployed? There was anger at what was seen as a regime of 'sleaze' and official tolerance of 'fat cats' in the newly privatised

industries. Labour promised to levy a tax on these industries' 'windfall
gains' and ensure jobs for young people. Labour won 44 per cent of the
vote, the Conservatives were reduced to 31 per cent. If it is borne in
mind that the Liberals, with 17 per cent, were politically far closer to
Labour than the Conservatives – indeed to the Left of both main parties on
many issues – then it can be seen that the rejection of the Conservatives
was emphatic. And while Tony Blair's direct share of the vote was close to
Margaret Thatcher's in 1979, the closeness of Labour and the Liberals
gave him much wider backing.

'Thinking the Unthinkable': The Rise and Fall of Frank Field

In June 1997 Tony Blair appointed Frank Field to be Minister of State in
the Department of Social Security with special responsibility for rethinking every aspect of welfare policy. It was said that he had been charged
by Blair with 'thinking the unthinkable', which was widely assumed to
mean a drastic downsizing and privatising of welfare provision.

Field had not been an official party spokesman prior to June 1997. As
a maverick backbencher he had latitude to advocate controversial proposals. He looked favourably on workfare schemes, warned of the danger of
undermining incentives to save, and was seen as a champion of the traditional family. While in opposition he made pension provision an area of
special expertise. Field argued that to contribute to a funded pension
scheme was less of a gamble than relying on the conscience of future
politicians and tax payers to maintain the value of pensions – a point he
might have illustrated, but did not, by reference to his own party's
somersaults on the question. Field's ideas had their own consistency and
deserve careful assessment. He dwelt on the need to anticipate growing
dependency and to offer pensions which rewarded the thrifty. But in addition to rehearsing the familiar case for funded pension schemes, Field
sometimes allowed a different and somewhat more radical logic to peep
out of his plans.

Field wanted to pre-fund pensions but he envisaged responsibility for
running them being entrusted to public and social bodies and he believed
that the new arrangements should cover the whole population. He urged
the setting up of a universal plan, managed by a public Pension Board, to
which all employees and employers would be obliged to contribute.
Benefits should not be conditional on a means test since this would discourage personal saving. In a pamphlet co-authored with his then

researcher Matthew Owen, Field urged that universal provision was essential. His approach required a mandatory scheme, similar in some ways to that advocated by the World Bank in *Averting the Old Age Crisis*.[46] But there were new points. He proposed that the government should make contributions on behalf of those who were not in employment. Full-time carers of invalids and of infants under four would be credited with contributions at the rate of 6 per cent of average earnings; this percentage would reflect the 6 per cent of earnings paid into the scheme by employers on behalf of their employees. Non-working parents of children aged between four and twelve were to receive a contribution equal to 3 per cent of average earnings. Field and Owen added: 'For the unemployed, pension provision must ensure that their retirement earnings are not decimated because the government has used them as a weapon to fight inflation. This means contributions being made to their pensions at the same level that they enjoyed when in work.'[47] The idea of crediting contributions to the basic pension on behalf of mothers of young children and those caring for invalids had featured in Labour's 1975 legislation under the rubric 'Home Responsibilities Protection' (HRP). According to the original legislation, HRP was due to be phased into SERPS in 1999, when the whole scheme matured.[48] Field adapted the idea to his pre-funded approach and the Conservatives were to follow suit in their last-minute Pension Plus plan.

Field believed that universal funded pensions would foster social inclusion, enabling all to avoid being left behind by weakly indexed state provision. He finessed the funding problem by pointing to the buoyancy of the equity markets in which the proposed stakeholder funds would be invested. He argued that even with stock market crashes like that of 1987 taken into account money invested in funded pension schemes would keep pace with earnings. And since Field's scheme would require higher contributions for higher-earning workers, it could be more progressive than existing National Insurance contributions. Field noted that those with occupational pensions had done rather well since 1979; during his tenure as minister the DSS published research showing that the top fifth of pensioners saw an increase of 71 per cent in their incomes, and the next fifth an increase of 61 per cent, in the period 1979–95, largely because of the contribution of pension fund income. By contrast, the income of the bottom fifth, and the fifth immediately above it, lagged behind, increasing by only 29 per cent and 41 per cent respectively.[49] The phasing in of SERPS made a contribution to rises among all categories, but especially those in the middle; the richest fifth had rising asset incomes, including private pensions, while the poorest fifth rarely qualified for SERPS. So the existing pension regime was exacerbating inequality and failing those on average or below average earnings. By 1997 as a result of pensions being linked to prices rather than earnings, the UK basic pension had become one of lowest in the European Union, worth less than 15 per cent of average earnings.[50] Field hoped that his scheme could reach those excluded from the rising value of the funds.

Field's system of funded pensions was to be embedded in collective structures of provision and management. He urged that 'friendly societies', trade unions and other social bodies would be the best trustees of stakeholder funds and that the mutual ownership principle should also extend to management of the funds. He also hinted that it would not be right to allow his proposed Pensions or Social Insurance Board simply to be grafted onto the existing institutions of the financial services industry. In 1994 Field wrote that the 'huge sums' accruing to his proposed National Pensions Savings Scheme would have to be invested bearing national interests in mind. 'Decisions over investment will need to be independent of day-to-day political interference. Presumably trustees will take into account the long-term needs of the British and European economies and in this sense will clearly act both economically and politically.'[51] Field's preference was clear even if it could have been more emphatically expressed. His willingness to countenance non-commercial delivery, and his hints that trustees might take account of long-term interests, marked off his proposals from the World Bank approach, notwithstanding points of resemblance, and echoed Labour's National Superannuation plan of the 1950s. Field also spoke vaguely of a role for the financial institutions but, whether out of lack of enthusiasm or in the hope of winning support in the labour movement, this aspect of matters was very much downplayed.

Field's critics argued that his proposed funds for the poorer citizen would not be sufficient and that a general increase in the universal state pension would be a more direct way of tackling low retirement incomes. In fact nearly three million British pensioners were so poor as to be eligible for supplementary benefit. Of the £42 billion received annually by pensioners in the mid-1990s, one-quarter was received as means-tested 'income support' and not as a pension entitlement. Many women pensioners, not qualifying for the basic pension and not possessing a private pension, were entitled to income support, though many did not claim it (Margaret Thatcher's 'proud ones'). Other pensioners received a disability benefit which was not subject to a means test (Labour was to try to introduce one but there was an outcry and it retreated).

Field argued that Labour's promise in 1992 to restore the relationship of pensions to earnings would have meant little or nothing to pensioners in receipt of income support since their pension gain would be matched by benefit loss. On the other hand, the better-off pensioners who were not entitled to 'income support' would gain. There were over 10 million pensioners in Britain in 1997, a figure likely to rise to 14 million by 2020. The loss in value of the state pension between 1979 and 1996 when compared with average earnings was about £1,000 per pensioner. If the basic pension was restored to this level – at a cost of some £7 billion – the pensioners on 'income support' would receive nothing and much of the money would go to better-off pensioners – even if some of it would come back in taxation. Any attempt actually to raise the entitlement of the poorer pensioners to levels beyond that furnished by income support would require expenditure of, say, £8–10 billion. Field believed that this money could be better used by making a more modest improvement for current pensioners and subsidising a universal stakeholder pension.

Those who opposed Field's ideas and their reflection in *Security in Retirement* included many who had played a key role in Labour's pension legislation in 1975, notably Jack Jones, the former trade union leader who now led the National Pensioners' Convention, Barbara Castle and two welfare analysts, Peter Townsend and Tony Lynes, whose work had helped her frame her Social Security Act. This formidable quartet wished to repair the damage that had been done to the state pension. They campaigned for Labour to restore the earnings link to the BSP and to rehabilitate the SERPS scheme.[52] They argued that opponents of restoring the basic pension had ignored the fact that about 800,000 pensioners, including many women on low pensions, who were entitled to 'income support', failed to claim it, either out of ignorance or because they objected to the means test. In a joint pamphlet Castle, Townsend and others argued that the pensioners who would benefit by indexation to earnings deserved the money because of their past contributions and that many were not in fact very comfortably off.[53] They did not deny that a restored BSP and SERPS would benefit many middle-class recipients – but in doing so, it would also build social support for public pension provision. There was an echo here of Richard Titmuss, who used to say that so long as benefits are only for the poor they will be poor benefits.

A motion recommitting Labour to the earnings link at the 1996 Labour Party conference gathered considerable support, so the National Executive offered a review of the question. The earnings link was resisted on grounds of cost and its failure to improve the lot of those claiming 'income

support'. As for the problem of those not claiming benefit, there were said
to be other ways of reaching them, short of handing more public money
to better-off pensioners. When the moment came for the question to be
voted on, the TGWU block vote, influenced by Jack Jones, moved decisively behind the review of the question promised by the National
Executive. Evidently Jones believed that he would be able to extract some
sort of deal from the Labour leadership. At this time and later some of
those who supported a restoration of the earnings link might have accepted
something less than a full upgrading to 1979 levels, so long as there was a
real boost to the BSP and it was wage-indexed for the future. Moreover,
supporters of the earnings link made no proposals to alter the tax concessions and opt-outs given to those in occupational or personal pensions,
viewing these as discretionary adjuncts to the state system. A majority of
trade unionists were themselves likely to be members of an occupational
scheme and thus, when retired, ineligible for means-tested assistance.

Many of Field's opponents rallied to the defence of SERPS, which,
even in its reduced form, had been helping to boost public pension provision. Though the SERPS itself was only indexed to prices, its level did
reflect earnings at the time of retirement and so supplied a boost for
those who qualified. Furthermore, since it was based on the twenty best
earnings years it favoured those who, because of maternity, unemployment or illness, had a break in their employment record. Unfortunately,
since SERPS was indeed 'earnings-related', it did less for the low-paid. It
remained a good scheme for middle-income earners when compared
with much commercial provision, even after its dilution by the
Thatcher government.

Tony Lynes shared the view that the cost of restoring the basic pension's
loss in value compared with earnings would be worthwhile because it
would boost public support for the pension. But because of the expense
involved he did canvass new funding approaches.[54] Lynes formulated a way
to restore and improve the SERPS system but he did so by proposing that
contributions beyond a certain level would feed into a public pension
fund which could be invested in shares and bonds: 'The task of managing
and investing the fund should be entrusted to National Additional
Pension Fund Trustees, who would employ a number of financial institutions as investment managers.' He concluded by evoking parliamentary
oversight without political control: 'The trustees would make an annual
report of the state of the fund and its investments, which would be laid
before parliament.'[55]

New Labour turned its face against any attempt to restore or improve the legislation of the 1970s and instead invited Field to draw up a blueprint. Extraordinary as it may seem, Tony Blair does not appear to have grasped the implications of Field's long-advertised opposition to means testing. By the early months of 1998 there were leaks to the effect that Field's proposals actually involved the channelling of more resources to welfare, not less. A Green Paper drafted by Field on welfare reform was first delayed and then published in censored form, lacking specific financial commitments or institutional solutions. In November 1997 the DSS published a consultative document on 'stakeholder pensions', drafted by John Denman, a junior minister, but reflecting some of Field's ideas. This document outlined the case for a publicly sponsored, funded pension that would give better value than most personal pensions, especially for those not enjoying a high income. It pointed out: 'The level of charges and the way those charges are levied mean that, even for somebody who works throughout their life, personal pension charges can eat up a quarter of their final investment fund.'[56] It declared that members should be effectively involved in decisions on the management of the schemes and that they could be run by trade unions, mutual societies or affinity groups. It otherwise mainly consisted of a long list of questions as to the best method of devising coverage for those able to make some contribution but who were not catered for by occupational and personal pensions.[57] The Green Paper also argued for a revision of the rules governing pension trustees to encourage them to take greater account of 'ethical and socially responsible investment'.[58]

But as Labour finished its first year in office no progress could be reported on new legislation for pensions, only vivid accounts of clashes between Field and Harriet Harman, Secretary of State for Social Security. New Labour's notorious spin doctors put it about that Field was not a practical politician and would be best employed simply on a campaign against 'welfare cheats'.[59] In July 1998, following a ministerial reshuffle which included the sacking of Harriet Harman, Field resigned from the government, declaring that he had not been given the authority needed for a proper reform of the welfare system.

The departure of Field was not a victory for those who had opposed his ideas. The new overall minister at the Department was Alistair Darling, previously at the Treasury, a man determined to produce a speedy and prudent (i.e. cheap) version of the promised legislation on pension provision.[60] Field's schemes had foundered because of their cost, because of his insistence on a universal approach, and because they had not offered enough scope to the commercial providers. Pension policy had not been the only source of conflict between Field and his colleagues but the omens were not good. One story had him explaining to a bemused Prime Minister that his pension plans would cost £8 billion annually, to the incredulous rejoinder, 'Only eight billions Frank?'[61]

'Partnership in Pensions' and the Launch of the Stakeholder

In December 1998 the government's pension proposals were at last published in *Partnership in Pensions*, described by Tony Blair in a Foreword as being 'a new contract for pensions between the State, the private sector, and the individual', a formula which promoted the 'private sector' to new prominence and omitted reference to trade unions, friendly societies and other bodies about which much had previously been heard. The proposals claimed to furnish both immediate improvements for the poorest pensioners and the elements of a 'new contract for welfare'. The Basic State Pension (BSP) was only £69.50 a week, or 14 per cent of average earnings, and would continue to be uprated only in line with price rises. The lot of the poorest pensioners was only to be improved if their lack of other income meant that they qualified for a means-tested 'minimum income guarantee'.

The minimum income guarantee or MIG was to replace 'income support' and was to raise the single pensioner's weekly income by about £5.50 to reach £75 a week, or £116.60 a week for couples. It was promised that the MIG would in future be raised 'as resources allow': 'Over the long run our aim is that it should rise in line with earnings so that pensioners can share in the prosperity of the nation.' The MIG was thus central to the architecture of the reform. Together with other measures for the poorer pensioner – special payments for winter fuel and the like – this was to cost about £750 million annually, or about a tenth of the cost of restoring the basic pension to its pre-1980 relationship to earnings. In keeping with New Labour's custom at this time, *Partnership in Pensions* offered a headline promise: 'Starting from April 1999 we will implement a £2.5 billion package of measures as part of a new approach to tackling the problem of pensioner poverty.'[62] Most readers, especially journalists under deadline pressure, would take this as an extra £2.5 billion annually, though in fact it referred to an increase of £2.5 billion over three years.[63]

While pensioners who claimed income support were to gain some extra cash from the MIG, their incomes were still very low: £3,900 a year for a single pensioner and less per head for couples at a time when average earnings were above £20,000. But the proposal had two flaws. Firstly, whatever the terminology used, between half a million and a million of the poorest pensioners still had a rooted objection to applying for means-tested benefits. The basic pension itself is a big success in terms of take-up by poor pensioners because they believe they have a right to it and it does not involve complex and demeaning inventories of their assets. Contrary to the advice of eminent welfare experts like Peter Townsend, the government was confident that the problem could be overcome by a special publicity campaign. The other flaw was that, for those who did take it up, the MIG was likely to offer a better deal for many low-paid workers than they would be likely to obtain from the new contributory schemes announced in the document, notably the much bruited stake-holder pension.

Partnership in Pensions proposed gradually to phase out SERPS and to introduce a flat-rate State Second Pension (S2P) for the very low-paid: those earning under £9,000 a year would receive twice as much as under SERPS.[64] Of course, the SERPS, an earnings-related scheme, had never been designed for those receiving less than half average earnings. The S2P is best seen as a measure to compensate for the low level of the basic pension rather than as a replacement for SERPS. While the S2P does raise the entitlement of the persistently low-paid, it will not be so good for those who, after a spell of low pay, do a little better, since contributions to it cannot be switched to the stakeholder scheme. While there are some people who may indeed be locked in very low-paid work all their life, there will be many who dip in and out of such work and may qualify for the stakeholder, or even the residual SERPS, at other times. Yet contributions from one scheme cannot be simply transferred to the other because the stakeholder is essentially a commercial arrangement.

The S2P retained a scaled-down version of carer contributions. These are to be made on behalf of a restricted list of 'registered' carers and mothers with pre-school-age children; since this is to be a PAYGO scheme, the initial cost to the state will be very modest. Notwithstanding the carer's contributions, the S2P may have some of the same coverage problems as the BSP since the qualifying contribution record excludes time spent in education, retraining or unregistered unemployment. Those on low wages who find a portion of their hard-won pay going to the S2P may also rue-fully reflect that the pension it will bring is no better than the MIG – so S2P becomes more a tax on the low-paid than a benefit. Such features of the S2P combined with the preservation of the status quo vis-à-vis the BSP, weaken the poverty alleviation features of the proposals.[65] David

Blake described the overall approach as being that of applying both 'stick and carrot': 'the government is effectively abandoning the first pillar of support in old age and obliging everyone to rely on the second and third pillars. The Green Paper talked of building on the BSP, but this implies building on a sinking ship.'[66] The 'stick and carrot' approach echoes the 'implicit privatisation' of Margaret Thatcher who, as we have seen, made personal pensions appealing by degrading the state pension. But what then of the private and occupational 'pillars' proposed by New Labour, and notably the *pièce de résistance*, the new stakeholder pension introduced in April 2001?

The 'stakeholder pensions' are voluntary, subsidised by tax and NIC relief, and managed by commercial providers. In order to qualify as a provider of 'stakeholder pensions', fund management costs have to be no more than 1 per cent of assets a year. By law employers are obliged to offer them to their employees and are expected to bear some of the consequent administrative costs. Since all employers are obliged to offer a stakeholder, the problem of portability is addressed. The new ceiling on charges is at the low end of commercial pension provision though still above the charges on good occupational schemes. Costs are reduced by offering passive index tracker funds which, as seen in chapter 2, may deliver poor returns. And the 1 per cent limit on charges does not apply to dealing commissions. As part of the new package SERPS will be phased out, notwithstanding its potential for delivering good pensions and universal coverage to those on middle incomes. Insistently described as a 'new insurance contract for pensions', the proposals supply some ad hoc improvements but are likely to weaken overall coverage and create new anomalies.

The voluntary stakeholder pension, if it succeeds, will improve the contractual terms on which many acquire pensions. But taken in conjunction with the phasing out of SERPS, it is likely to create a new gap in public coverage among those on around average earnings. Those earning over £18,000 a year, a little under average earnings, would do better out of SERPS than out of the State Second Pension, according to *Partnership in Pensions*. But SERPS will be phased out. So the prime target group for the stakeholder is those with middling to low income, say in 1998 terms £10–20,000 a year, who do not already have occupational coverage. This comes to about five million employees. Under SERPS people had the option of contracting out, in which case they could take their supplementary, SERPS-linked 4.6 per cent National Insurance contribution and put it towards a private pension. Or they remained in SERPS and were obliged to pay the extra 4.6 per cent into this scheme – doing so significantly raised their future pension entitlement. As the new legislation comes in, this element of compulsion will be very much weakened. Employees with no other coverage will be obliged to contribute to the S2P but, as we have seen, this is calibrated for those earning very low incomes. Indeed as the DSS explains:

> Once stakeholder pensions become established, the State Second Pension will move to stage two. At this point it will become flat-rate (based on £9,500 earnings). As it is it will be in the interests of people earning more than £9,500 to contract out into a private pension. . . . They can then continue to benefit from an earnings related pension.[67]

The stakeholder pensions offer a better deal than the personal plans previously supplied by the finance houses because of the cap on charges. Indeed the stakeholder could well be a hit with better-paid employees and their spouses. Some attempt is made to screen out those who are already provided for but it is unlikely to be effective. Those who both earn over £30,000 and belong to an occupational scheme are ineligible. But such individuals can still purchase a stakeholder for their spouse. And if they have self-employed income as well, then the ban against purchasing the stakeholder does not apply. Those who earn over £30,000 and do not belong to an occupational scheme are, of course, free to take out a stakeholder and many are likely to do so. The new scheme could be a considerable success and still miss most of its target group, leaving many millions uncovered.

Some of the provisions for the stakeholder still furnish a muffled echo of ideas ventilated by Field. It was hoped that stakeholder pensions would have a 'collective structure, like occupational schemes, to get the best value for money for scheme members'. As noted above, employers are obliged to offer membership and to cover some administrative costs. They will select the trustees and potential policy holders will have a choice of commercial products but no say in how their savings are invested. In practice, and in the interests of keeping down charges, the contributions will be channelled to the providers with as little fuss as possible and index-tracking funds will be common.[68]

It is revealing that the new pattern of provision is expected to produce large economies in public pension provision. In fact *Partnership in Pensions* projects that whereas in 1998 the state supplied 60 per cent of all pensioner incomes and private pensions 40 per cent, within a few decades, thanks to a continuing decline in overall public provision and an anticipated growth in the stakeholder pensions, these ratios will be reversed and the state will only supply 40 per cent. To begin with, the new State Second Pension will only cost about £0.5 billion annually though in the long run this will rise to £5 billion, with savings on the income-related public benefits which it replaces.[69] The success of the strategy outlined in *Partnership for Pensions* rests on two interrelated assumptions: (1) a large take-up of the stakeholder among those on average and below-average earnings and (2) a buoyant stock market raising the value of the stakeholder funds. The grudging budget allotted to the pensioners, whether in the short or longer term, reflected the priorities that the minister now in charge, Alistair Darling, had brought with him from the Treasury.

Neither *Partnership in Pensions* nor the two pieces of legislation that stemmed from it – the Welfare and Pension Reform Act of 1999 and the Child Support, Pensions and Social Security Act of July 2000 – attracted much public attention. The publication of *Partnership in Pensions* in the week before Christmas was calculated to minimise scrutiny. In the House of Commons Labour's majority was sufficient to carry all before it and the press paid little attention. On the other hand, the financial services lobby certainly had an input even if several providers were unhappy at the capping of their charges.[70]

The stakeholder pension, as outlined in *Partnership for Pensions* and as enacted in 1999, was subsequently found to contain a glaring design flaw. As implementation details were revealed, Frank Field pointed out that the wage-indexed 'minimum income guarantee' (MIG) offers, for nothing, a better income than stakeholder contributors on £14,000 a year will receive after they have contributed £76 a month for forty years. Using projections of the value of the stakeholder pension released by the Financial Services Authority, Field declared that it was possible to 'measure whether the government's stakeholder scheme is a better buy than the one I proposed before resigning as minister for welfare reform'. His verdict was negative: 'The government's scheme is modelled on the last Conservative government's personal pension scheme. Contributors will buy a stakeholder pension from a private company and the value of the pension will depend on how much is saved and what annuitised income this will buy at retirement.' Since the MIG can be claimed by anyone and is pegged to national prosperity, 'for zero contributions, MIG offers a more generous pension than most savers in the target £9,500 to £18,000 salary group would be able to gain under the stakeholder scheme'.[71] The person on an average of £14,000 could put by the considerable sum of £36,000 over forty years and see no return for it over and above the MIG to which they were anyway entitled. To meet such objections – which extraordinarily enough had not been anticipated – government spokesmen began to promise that a 'pension credit' would be introduced in the budget for 2002 allowing for some of the income from savings to be disregarded when assessments are made for the MIG. But given the legislative agenda, this could not be in operation until 2003 or later and will pose some tricky problems. How much income and what types of savings will be covered by the 'pension credit'? Field had always argued against the means-testing aspects of state pension delivery on the grounds that such measures penalise savings (Barbara Castle often made the same point). It is possible that the appearance of the flaw stemmed from a sudden change of plans. If the stakeholder had been mandatory and there had been no MIG, as Field may have originally proposed, then at least the legislation would have been coherent in its own terms. That the legislation could contain a technical flaw as serious as this was nevertheless astonishing. Darling, the new Secretary of State, evidently felt under great pressure to produce results quickly and had been little disposed to heed the warnings of the ousted minister, especially as remedying them would be costly.

I have written about a 'debate' on pension policy but this was conducted between very small numbers of people. Even clashes at the Labour Party conference, or the publication of the Green Paper, or the passage of the resulting legislation, attracted only brief items in the national news media. The provisions incorporated in *Partnership for Pensions* and the resulting legislation did not correspond in major respects to the proposals that had been previously debated. The appearance of the design flaw in the relationship between the MIG and the stakeholder pension was one result of a Whitehall-driven process. In a historical assessment of this and previous legislation, two authors from the Institute of Fiscal Studies write:

> One striking feature of the evolution of the UK system over the last 20 years (i.e. since the introduction of SERPS) is the number of reforms that have been introduced with little or no prior debate. All genuine economic analysis has been conducted after the reforms have been implemented. This is in stark contrast to the US approach of having a long and detailed debate with, as yet, no reform at all.[72]

Of course, the volume of discussion in the United States and the reluctance to undermine the Social Security programme reflected its historic centrality to post-New Deal America.

Partnership in Pensions promised 'decent' pensions without addressing the more precisely defined objectives which pensions experts have identified.

For example, pension levels can be set to achieve such different outcomes as: (1) to alleviate pensioner poverty; (2) to prevent pensioner poverty; (3) to give the retired the resources to play an active part in the community; (4) to enable the retired to retain their pre-retirement standard of living.[73] *Partnership in Pensions* failed to explain what its ambitions were for pensioners. Implicitly it hoped to prevent pensioner poverty, though for the time being it will simply alleviate it. Since objectives (3) and (4) were nowhere referred to, they were evidently not seen as the responsibility of public policy. Wider issues of civic belonging attracted no attention, which is curious since New Labour is not usually coy about appeals to patriotic and community sentiment. Given the option for private delivery, one can see the problem of then seeking to reintroduce the idea that we are all part of 'one nation'. Under the regime of implicit privatisation the notion of the pensioner as an embodiment of a respected national past is destined for euthanasia. Then again there is the question of the link to the overall economic structure and to the governance of pension funds. The new legislation offers more encouragement, more regulation and more business – 'partnership' – to the private pensions industry (with implications to be considered in a later section).

The Third Way and the Question of Compulsion

Notwithstanding the nomenclature of the 'stakeholder' pension, the philosophy of stakeholding had long been eclipsed in the mainstream of New Labour thinking by this time. In 1998 and 1999 the publication of Anthony Giddens's book, *The Third Way*, offered a new framework for making sense of New Labour's philosophy. In the book Giddens urged the need for individuals to become less dependent on collectivist mechanisms and to become 'responsible risk takers'. The text offers an affirmative rhetoric laced with warnings to those who would 'free ride' on social provision.

> Old age is a new-style risk masquerading as an old-style one. Ageing used to be more passive than it is now; the ageing body was simply something that had to be accepted. In the more active, reflexive society, ageing has become much more of an open process, on a physical as a well as a psychic level. Becoming old presents at least as many opportunities as problems, both for individuals and for the wider community.[74]

Such observations have some truth on a descriptive level and could lead to a revision of rigid and paternalistic notions of retirement. But, in the absence of clear policy indications, there remains the likely conclusion that provision for the aged can be scaled back. However 'active ageing' policies need resources and work best when the retired have income security. Moreover, if people are to be encouraged to delay retirement then they should be able to reap extra benefit when they do retire. The passages on pension provision seem to be recommending self-reliance: '[O]ld age shouldn't be seen as a time of rights without responsibilities.'[75] Here any implicit threat would fit in with the 'stick and carrot' approach. As it happens, 'responsible risk takers' have always seen the advantage of pooling risk, especially when anticipating retirement. The result must be some kind of collective approach – should this be commercial or non-commercial? Though there is no review of the costs and benefits of such alternatives in *The Third Way*, the leitmotif is the need for a downsized state.

Whereas the proponents of stakeholding did not disguise their admiration for German-style semi-collectivist economics and welfare, the project of a Third Way had a more transatlantic flavour. In power New Labour had been urging its European partners to emulate the 'flexibility' of British and American labour market practices. However, in the area of retirement provision there were mixed signals from Washington. The Clinton White House was just at this time (1998–99) preparing to mount a campaign to defend collective provision, in the shape of the Social Security programme. No inkling of this, so much at variance with New Labour's approach to British public pension provision, appeared in *The Third Way*. In so far as the book supplies mood music rather than policy prescriptions, it seems to be harmonising with the siren song of privatisation. But in truth there is precious little here that might guide policy making, bar the statement that '[t]here is good reason . . . to support schemes of compulsory saving'. This had been studiously avoided by the architects of the stakeholder.[76]

In dumping Field and opting for a partnership with the private pensions industry, Blair had also shrunk from the World Bank's favourite notion of mandatory personal savings. Notwithstanding the promised pension credit, there are good reasons to doubt whether the stakeholder pensions will plug the yawning gap in provision among those they were aimed at, those on low to medium incomes.[77] The better-paid will take advantage of the tax savings on offer to purchase pensions for their 'nearest and dearest', but few earning £12,000 or £18,000 are likely to feel able to make payments into a pension, especially if they have a mortgage or the expense of a young family. Evidently the government was daunted by the potential costs and political difficulties of introducing a compulsory 'second pillar' comprising privately run personal pensions. It would have been costly because the government would have had to come up with better contributions for those excluded from paid employment. And it would have been politically risky since it would have hit hardest those on below-average incomes. Indeed, any attempt to force the confections of the financial services industry down the gullets of British employees would have had the makings of a New Labour poll tax.

Frank Field continued to advocate universal coverage from the back benches but this approach to secondary pensions would have obliged New Labour both to defy the pensions industry by entrusting delivery to non-commercial bodies, as he wished, and to come up with generous 'contribution credits' for carers, the unemployed and those on average and below-average wages. In the absence of such measures, to threaten those on poor or middling wages with legal penalties (fines? imprisonment?) if they did not contribute hard-earned cash to financial intermediaries notorious for excessive pay and telephone-number bonuses would have been highly provocative.[78]

The Savings Deficit

Partnership for Pensions argued that its measures would boost the national savings rate, simply assuming that a boost for the takings of the financial services industry must raise savings. But this is far from being the case, as the historically low UK and US savings rates testify. Indeed, the inflation of financial assets can lead to a 'wealth effect' whereby spending rises at the expense of saving. Evan Davis, of the Social Market Foundation and BBC, has pointed out that the consumer-led dynamic of Anglo-Saxon capitalism can inhibit savings:

> My decision over saving and spending should in principle be a reflection of my personal desire to trade off consumption now and consumption later when I retire. But in practice my spending now is heavily influenced by everyone else's. If my friends want to eat at expensive restaurants, I find myself doing the same; and it is possible that societies do get caught up in a culture of consumption even though a large number of rational individuals might prefer to draw their spending back.[79]

It is also necessary to track the impact of growing inequality, such a feature of 'Anglo-Saxon economics', on the propensity to save. While affluent young professionals may overspend on expensive restaurants, a large layer of the not-so-affluent, or even the downright badly paid, may have different reasons for not saving after making payments on their house and on their children. Of course, some of those who are poorly paid nevertheless do save but the sums involved are small and very often the motive is precautionary – the saver is anticipating contingencies other than, and prior to, retirement.

The steady decline in the value of the state pension in Britain, and the multiplication of new tax-favoured savings devices like PEPs and TESSAs, should have raised the propensity of households to save but in fact household saving remained stuck in the 1990s at around 6–7 per cent of GDP – somewhat below France and Germany and only a half of the figure for Belgium and Japan (though as Anglo-Saxon economics spreads, social norms favourable to saving may well erode in these countries too). Cash that is spent by British households on mortgage interest, hire purchase interest or even on the lottery seems like saving and displaces it both psychologically and economically. By contrast, National Insurance contributions (payroll taxes) seem like taxes rather than saving, though governments can use them to raise national savings rates, as long happened in Japan. A study published by Demos focusing on Britain's low level of household savings cited evidence not only of social pressures to consume but also failures to review consumption patterns and over-optimism about future earnings. Those on modest salaries see that there is money around and tell themselves that they will be able to clamber aboard the gravy train one day. This study criticised compulsory measures for raising savings rates on the grounds that they are generally too rigid and fail to allow people to vary their savings rate as their overall situation changes (e.g. needs of dependants, employment status of partner and so forth). But it nevertheless believed that people should be provided with some protection from their most improvident inclinations: 'Some compulsion seems sensible for pension provision, whether it is funded through general taxation, National Insurance or payments into a personal or occupational fund. The level of compulsory contributions probably needs raising a little in Britain.'[80] The replacement of SERPS by the optional stakeholder pension will lower, not raise, the element of mandatory savings.

As Labour moved to finalise its legislation on pensions, research was carried out on inequality which had implications for the problem of raising the savings rate. This research revealed that the gaping income inequality bequeathed by the Conservative years was getting worse rather than better. Writing in *Fiscal Studies* in December 1999 two authors reported: 'Evidence from the latest available data suggests that income inequality might be starting to rise again.'[81] A year later this foreboding was to be confirmed in *The Economist*:

New figures show that inequality of income after benefits and taxation rose again in Labour's third year in office, 1999–2000. The commonly used Gini coefficient that measures inequality has risen again to its 1990 peak. Another indicator, the ratio of income at the 90th and 10th percentiles of income distribution tells a similar story. This has risen from 4.4 in 1996–7, the Conservatives' last year in office, to 4.6 in 1999–2000, not far off its previous peak in 1990. Though modest in comparison with the sharp jump in the second half of the 1980s, the rise in inequality has essentially reversed the decline under John Major's Conservative government.[82]

As we have seen, growing numbers of poorly paid workers complicated the task of pension provision since it was deemed risky to attempt to force these people to save. Yet without an element of compulsion, coverage of secondary pensions would be highly uneven. As the stakeholders became available in April 2001 the government propaganda machine sought to woo less well-paid employees with the following tale:

> Parveen is a self-employed fitness trainer in her late twenties, earning around £14,000 a year. She has recently bought a flat with a friend, and now that the initial expenses are out of the way she thinks she can afford to start a pension. She has considered the information on stakeholder pensions, including the 'decision trees' and this helped her to decide that a stakeholder pension would be suitable for her.

The *Guardian*'s Polly Toynbee was intrigued:

> Parveen is the star of the government's guide to stakeholder pensions. Parveen went to work pretty fast, since the Stakeholder pensions were only launched last Friday. So who is this model citizen, this perfect Asian gymnast who has a mortgage and a pension before the age of 30 on a very modest salary? She seems surprisingly certain about her future life. Is she perhaps a lesbian in a settled relationship with a friend who co-owns the flat? That might explain why she is quite sure she will not have children and will not need rainy-day money, her savings untouchable until she is 65. Parveen is a paragon of prudence. With a mortgage on £14,000 pay (she plainly lives far from the South East), *Guardian* personal finance writers, using average mortgage figures, reckon that after tax, national insurance, council tax, mortgage and energy bills, she has about £6,480 a year, or £135 a week to live on. So what made her decide that a pension was right for her? Shouldn't she have put any savings into an ISA where she could get the money back if she ever gets sick, loses her job or just needs it? Did she have a financial adviser? If so she was mis-sold this pension. I called the Department of Social Security in whose stakeholder guide Parveen features. Would it be possible to interview her? The press officer retired to enquire

and returned a bit embarrassed. 'Um, well, actually she's an example.' Oh? 'She's not real.' Just as well since a real-life Parveen might be going hungry to pay for her old age. No, Parveen is just a decoy duck, displayed to entice real life Parveens. There are, the government says, five million sitting ducks at whom stakeholders are primarily targeted. They earn between £10,400 and £20,000, and currently have no pensions. However research suggests that most people on below average earnings can't afford pensions. (A third of those who take out personal pensions default within a few years, losing most of their money.)[83]

The persistence of inequality and low wages sets up its own constraints which make public policy 'path dependent'. It is only by boldly working against the grain of Anglo-Saxon economics that a more egalitarian pattern, that would see all endowed with provision for old age, can be brought into being. In PAYGO systems the device that made possible a step change in provision was 'blanketing in'. In pre-funded schemes the answer is *contribution credits* made by the public exchequer on behalf of the low-paid, with a full credit made for anyone earning less than 60 per cent of median income, tapering off to a zero credit as the median itself is reached. But this was not the approach adopted by the architects of the stakeholder. So despite its name, the stakeholder will not give every citizen a tangible stake in society. Another and better way of earning the nomenclature would have been to retain, improve and pre-fund SERPS, as Tony Lynes had suggested. As it is, the voluntary character of the stakeholder averts immediate clashes and controversies but stores up problems for the future. Some believe that this will soon become clear and that a second-term Blair administration will make the stakeholder compulsory.

Thus the chance for a radical rethinking of the pensions system has been postponed, the meanness of the BSP retained and a confused package of guarantees and secondary pensions assembled. Blair was at pains to observe: 'These reforms mean that the total income of pensioners will rise in years to come, mainly fuelled by raising private contributions. Public spending on pensions will rise too in real terms, but less sharply, and will fall as a proportion of national income.'[84] Why this should be a cause for congratulation was not explained. New Labour, unwilling to challenge the forked-tongue curse of 'grey capitalism', was effectively offering poor relief to the poor and tax relief to the rich. It entered the new century and the new millennium believing that it had delivered on its promise of pension reform and that the predictable complaints of the pensioners could be ignored.

Blair Is Forced to Change Tack

In April 2000 the state pension was raised by the derisory sum of 75 pence a week, in line with inflation. On 16 April the press reported that the chair of the backbench Labour MPs, Clive Soley, had explained in a speech given in the United States that unfortunately Britain's pensioners were 'predominantly Conservative' and 'often racist'. In a leaked or purloined document that appeared in the Conservative press around the same time the New Labour strategist Peter Mandelson was said to have observed that there was 'no mileage' for Labour in chasing the pensioner vote.[85]

Labour evidently believed that it could exploit the language of 'social inclusion' and offer a 'stakeholding society' but pay little or no price for failing to deliver to the pensioners. It had also promised to look after the interests of 'middle England' but had failed to register that people in middle England had parents and grandparents too. To the extent that any poverty-alleviating measures had been possible while respecting Conservative spending limits these had been directed at working families with children, who benefited from more generous tax credits. The continuing expansion of the economy reduced unemployment by about a million and allowed for a moderate advance of earnings at a time of lower inflation. All this allowed New Labour to enjoy good poll ratings. But there were nevertheless some warning signs. There was public disquiet at the government's failure to deliver improvements in health or education. In the 1999 European elections Labour supporters failed to go to the polls and the Conservatives won more votes and seats.

Because of Labour's promise not to raise income tax, its scope for redistribution had been narrowed. But in fact the Labour Chancellor had discovered ways of raising extra resources and the Treasury anyway enjoyed rising returns because of the economic upswing. In his first budget Brown had removed a major concession applying to pension fund investments – namely relief on taxes paid on corporate dividends (ACT or Advance Corporation Tax). This yielded the Treasury the impressive sum of an extra £5 billion a year. Raising money in this way had the political advantage that the tax increase involved was not one directly imposed on individual tax payers and its workings were not widely understood. The likely response of fund managers was to pass the extra costs on to policy holders. Nevertheless, the removal of an undeserved and unearned tax privilege would have been perfectly justifiable if its proceeds had gone to pensioners and if it had been followed up by measures to make the funds accountable to social and economic priorities.

But pensioners did not receive anything like an extra £4–5 billion a year – in fact only £0.8 billion – and no steps were taken to make the funds pay for their remaining privileges. Instead, the unimpressive rise in the BSP in 1999 had been followed by the increase of only 75 pence a week in the March 2000 budget – the price of a packet of peanuts, as pensioners pointed out. The miserliness of this rise at a time of an overflowing budget surplus could not be disguised by other special handouts (a winter fuel allowance for those over sixty and free TV licence for those over seventy-five). In the local elections of May 2000 Labour trailed the Conservatives in a low turnout. In London the official Labour candidate came third behind the Conservative and was soundly beaten by Ken Livingstone, the maverick former Labour left-winger who advocated an increase of £10 a week in the state pension. The raw deal for the pensioners was predictably attacked by their political opponents, though Conservative jibes lacked credibility. More worrying to the government should have been the complaints of well-respected charitable bodies, especially Age Concern and Help the Aged, which were beginning to articulate and publicise the manifest failure to deliver 'decent pensions'. This was not quite a pensioners' lobby, but in some ways the more effective in consequence. The *Daily Express* newspaper undertook its own campaign for more generous treatment of pensioners and even the right-wing *Daily Mail* carried sympathetic editorials.

The pensioner press ventilated criticism emanating from the Labour back benches. It quoted the Welsh MP Llew Smith telling the House of Commons in October 1999:

> Pensioners are not the only ones outraged by the inflation linked pension increase of 75p. If we as a Government allow that to happen, we shall be in the obscene position of having Cabinet Ministers who earn in excess of £94,000 a year lecturing senior citizens on why a 75p rise is adequate, why £67.50 is an adequate sum on which to live. I do not know whether that is the third way but I know that it is wrong.

Moving on to the proposed reforms he pointed out that

> the combined value of the basic state pension and the proposed second pension will reach only about 21 to 26 per cent of the average male wage . . . When the Labour Government included a compulsory second tier, the state earnings related pension scheme, and guaranteed that earnings would rise in line with earnings or prices, whichever was the higher, the two pensions combined were to be equal to almost half the average earnings. That is far better than the proposals in the current pensions

Green Paper, which shows that the government are determined to privatise much of our pension provision despite the scandal of private pensions mis-selling in the 1980s. If anyone doubts that they should take note of what my right honourable friend the Secretary of State said [15 December 1998]: 'If people stay in the state system they will lose money.' That might be an honest statement of intent, but it signals disaster in terms of providing for future pension needs.[86]

Smith drew on figures from the Government Actuary to argue that the break in the earnings link had saved the exchequer £10 billion a year and that the cumbersome machinery of means-testing social benefits was costing £4 billion annually. He pointed out that the National Insurance fund had a surplus of £5.9 billion and that the budget was projected to have a surplus of £12 billion. 'We are an extremely rich country awash with money that could meet the pensioners' demands. Pensioners demand not the third way but justice.'[87]

In June 2000 Tony Blair's advisers were delighted to have obtained an invitation for him to address the Women's Institute's huge annual gathering in Wembley. This would be the perfect backdrop for an address to 'middle England'. Yet as he launched into a chirpy yet chastened account of the achievements of his government he was visibly disconcerted to receive boos, jeers and a slow handclap from this staid and respectable body. It was, *The Economist* unkindly suggested, his 'Ceausescu moment'. Those responsible later explained that the derisory pension rise and the failure to stop the closure of village post offices had fuelled their anger. Labour's own backbenchers were soon demanding that the budget in 2001 should give a really handsome increase to the pensioners, including a special effort to alleviate the plight of the 'old old'. It was by this time clear that the attempt to reach those who did not claim the guaranteed minimum income had failed. As one report explained:

> Pressure groups are renewing calls on the government to increase the basic pension after official figures revealed its latest attempt to encourage pensioners to claim extra benefits had flopped. . . . The government's multi-million pound advertising campaign . . . encourages pensioners to claim the minimum income guarantee. . . . However despite writing to 2 million pensioners, only 82,000 have responded. Critics say that many elderly people are unlikely to overcome the associated stigma of claiming means-tested benefits.[88]

Those who would qualify but did not claim still numbered about 750,000, many of them over eighty years old. In order to claim the full MIG, claimants had to fill in a 39-page form proving that they did not have other income or assets worth over £3,000. Possession of more than £6,000 of assets meant loss of any top-up from the MIG.

Those relying on the state pension alone in 2000 still received less than £4,000 a year – slightly less than the sum charged by stables in Britain's home counties for the livery of a horse or pony. According to the government's own surveys it was clear that about half of elderly women do not actually qualify for the full pension, mean as it is. Pension entitlement is still dependent on a contribution record, with proportionate reductions for those with less than thirty-nine years of contributions. Modest increments are available to the basic pension above certain age limits, and wives or widows can claim entitlement to the BSP on the basis of their husband's record of contributions. Obviously, a truly universal pension system would pay the same basic pension to all those over a certain age. In the UK this straightforward approach is timidly adopted for those over eighty years of age but brings a tiny increment – in some cases no more than 1p a week – and is accompanied by byzantine complications. And as a relic of the generosity of some bygone chancellor, a lucky few have been able to claim a modest supplement when they qualify for what is known as a 'Category C' pension which, as a handbook explains, is available to 'men who are at least 110 years old; and women who are at least 105 years old *or* who are married to (or in some cases divorced from) a man who is at least 110 years old *or* who are widows and whose husbands would now be at least 110 years old if they had lived.'[89] The complications involved in simply applying for the MIG were considerable, quite apart from such rarefied extras.

Disillusionment with New Labour's stinginess towards the pensioners spilled over into seemingly unrelated disputes. Thus in September 2000 Britain was brought to a halt by the pickets of truck drivers and farmers who closed the country's main fuel depots. Petrol stations ran dry, deliveries of foodstuffs to supermarkets ceased and hospitals had to use their emergency supplies with care. The bearing of the fuel protest on the plight of pensioners might not seem obvious, though naturally its spokesmen claimed that high fuel prices were especially hard on pensioners. *The Times* reported that pensioners were joining the pickets. The nation was paralysed yet, to the government's alarm, the protesters nevertheless enjoyed overwhelming approval in the opinion polls. The treatment of the pensioners had offered malcontents an issue that camouflaged more self-interested concerns. The Conservatives pulled ahead of Labour in the polls for the first time in many years. The protesters, anxious not to dissipate public support, announced after a week that their action was suspended for sixty days, giving the government time to formulate a response. The Transport union played a key role in winning the government this respite.

No sooner was the protest suspended than Tony Blair, Gordon Brown and Alistair Darling faced another challenge in the shape of a well-supported move at the Labour Party's annual conference in October 2000 to endorse a restoration of the BSP's link to the earnings index. The case for re-establishing the earnings link was strongly urged in an intransigent speech by the ninety-year-old Barbara Castle. A perspiring Tony Blair apologised for the 75p rise in the pension; he had, he assured delegates, 'got the message' and promised that generous new measures were in the pipeline to help pensioners. But Blair and his ministers pleaded for the conference to reject the 'earnings link' motion, saying that the MIG would help the poorest pensioners. Ministers ignored the aversion felt by many poor pensioners towards all means-tested benefits and took no heed of the pinched existence of even those who were not the very poorest. Barbara Castle, Jack Jones and other warhorses of Old Labour displayed a surer sense of the sentiments of middle England than New Labour, its self-appointed champions. Thus Darling declared that 20 per cent of pensioners had incomes of over £20,000 a year, without noticing that this sum was actually below average male earnings and that even this figure showed that five-sixths of pensioners were living on less than £20,000, indeed half of them on less than £10,000, even if they were not the poorest. According to information made available by his own department, 56 per cent of pensioners were among the poorest 40 per cent of the population, and 42 per cent of pensioners had less than 60 per cent of average income.[90] Darling made reference to private pensions without registering that most of these are not indexed even to prices, with the result that pensioners suffer a steady erosion of the stipends they can draw from their personal savings and so would look forward to a state pension which – like the contributions made into it – is linked to earnings levels. When the time came to vote at Labour's conference, the trade unions, under heavy pressure from their retired members, stood their ground in support of the earnings link, ensuring the passage of a motion calling for its reinstatement. This was a very public rebuff to Labour's leaders at the hands of a body which, following 'New Labour' reforms, had previously been very tame. The National Pensioners' Convention, with its 1.5 million supporters, many of them retired trade union members, was now more likely to be given air-time. And its main points were often echoed by the charitable organisations, Age Concern and Help the Aged.

Not all arguments favourable to restoring the earnings link to the BSP came from the Left. Two authors who favour entirely winding up public pension provision nevertheless pointed to the anomaly that price indexation of the BSP meant that 'under current policy the basic state pension is fixed in real terms, whereas contributions are related to earnings'.[91] The result of combining a mean BSP with an earnings-related NIC was an increasing surplus in the National Insurance accounts. In November 1999 Darling had conceded that the surplus would stand at £20 billion by year end; he faced pressure from an all-party social security committee in the Commons to use some of this money to raise the BSP by £5 instead of the projected 75p.[92] Since the public revenues were anyway enjoying large surpluses, the case for generosity towards the pensioners seemed especially strong. However, neither the Conservatives nor the Liberal Democrats moved to outflank the government by adopting the earnings link, leaving Blair with valuable room to manoeuvre.

At the time of the dramatic fuel protest the government had insisted that it could not allow itself to be compelled to drop the fuel tax by action in the streets but that it would listen to representations from the hauliers, the farmers and their supporters, and would formulate an appropriate response in its pre-budget statement in November 2000. The sixty days following the suspension of the fuel protest proved to be full of incident. In addition to the Labour Party conference, that period also included the heaviest rains for 200 years, flooding large areas of the country, and the paralysis of the entire national rail system, when an accident at Hatfield led to the discovery that throughout the network much of the track was in a dangerous condition. In these emergency conditions, and with a general election looming, the Labour Chancellor announced in his pre-budget statement an increase for the pensioners worth £2.5 billion and remitted fuel duty worth £1.7 billion through the device of a tax rebate on 'green' petrol.[93] The BSP was to be raised to £75 a week and the minimum income guarantee would be raised from £75 to £90 a week. There were to be new measures to reach those not claiming the MIG and extra money for those over seventy-five and eighty years old. The Chancellor also promised 'transitional measures' to be introduced prior to the establishment of a 'pension credit'. The increase in the BSP was well above inflation but no move was made to endorse or formalise any return to the earnings link. The plight of the pensioners had been marginal, at best, to the concerns of the fuel protesters while concern for 'climate change' had been entirely absent. By addressing these issues, the government sought to redefine the nature of the September events, the most worrying aspect of which had been overwhelming public support for the protest. It was conceded that those upset by the 75p rise for the pensioners had been right. Something had to be done for the pensioners and ways found to help the farmers and hauliers while weaning them from the most noxious fuels. This reinterpretation, adroitly presented by Transport Minister Gus MacDonald, was to have the desired effect. When the hard-core protesters sought to descend on London in a mass cavalcade of juggernaut trucks in late November, few turned out and the protest ended with a whimper.

As a by-product of the government's various travails the politics of pensions had, at long last, become central to the British political process. It has also modified the fundamental architecture of the new public pension regime. While the BSP went up by £5 the MIG went up by £14. In 2003–4 the gap between the BSP and the MIG was set to widen further with the former reaching £77 a week and the latter £100.

In their book on the first Blair government two *Guardian* writers, David Walker and Polly Toynbee, hail its pension measures as a crowning achievement. They contrive to congratulate the Chancellor both on his original plan and on its drastic revision, while condemning Old Labour attachment to the basic state pension. The initial aim, they declare, was good since it robustly targeted pensioner poverty: 'Brown was adamant that any extra for older people should go to the poorest, though it meant that the growing numbers of better off elderly would see their state support shrinking.' But there was a problem: 'However, fair, right and brave the message never flew.' The authors were impressed by Brown's generosity:

> To lift them [the poorest] above the poverty line, Labour introduced a Minimum Income Guarantee (MIG), to be uprated each year with earnings. When first paid in April 2000, it gave an immediate £5.45 a week increase to the poorest. It was linked to a campaign to find the estimated 500,000 who were not claiming all their entitlements: the downside of targeting is that it always misses some people. But all this well-targeted spending won Labour little gratitude.[94]

The authors fail to register the modesty of 'all this well-targeted [?] spending', all £0.8 billion of it, and are consequently puzzled at the ungrateful response. Because their attention is fixated on what they call 'an ever-growing tide of well-off pensioners', they do not explain that there were several million *needy* pensioners excluded by the relevant means test.

Of course the top 20 per cent of pensioners were reasonably well off, with per capita incomes averaging about £15,000 a year when Labour came to power. The next 20 per cent were living on an average of somewhat less than £10,000 a year. But the remaining six million or so pensioners were making ends meet on a pittance.[95] Those whose income came to just £5,000 including the BSP in April 1999 did not qualify for the MIG – nor would they if their assets were worth £6,000. And even those who qualified for the whole sum – £5.45 a week – would find that it did not go far.[96] Nevertheless, as Toynbee and Walker tell the story it gets mysteriously better. 'The Chancellor kept saying how much he had done – but was not believed. So then he did something that will stand as one of the great milestones of this government. At a stroke, Brown increased the MIG so sharply that it pulled all pensioners out of poverty.' No credit is given to what is dismissively referred to as the 'Old Labour pensioners lobby', an entity that had enjoyed little support from the liberal daily's senior journalists. The claim that all pensioners will be raised from poverty ignores 'the proud ones' and sets a very modest poverty threshold.

The help which New Labour had received from the philosophy of 'Old Labour', courtesy of Barbara Castle and Jack Jones, enabled it to reassert leadership over society and lay claim to the moral high ground (restore its 'hegemony', as the neo-Marxists say). It had improved the situation of current pensioners but left the new pension architecture in place. As an immediate fix this was effective, especially as Labour's main opponents were unable, or unwilling, to expose the resulting problems, but in the longer run the rise in the BSP and MIG leaves much of the rest of the new pension regime 'under water'. The publication of the consultation paper on the Pension Credit revealed that it created as many problems as it solved. The proposed credit will allow pensioners to keep 60p of every £1 of their income from savings or earnings over the basic pension, planned to be £77 in 2003.[97] Thus a pensioner who has private savings income of £23 will be able to keep £13.80, plus the MIG at £100, giving a total of £113.80. However, the savings income of pensioners not entitled to the full basic pension does not benefit from the credit until it reaches the full rate. In consequence, the Institute of Actuaries pointed out: 'Introducing Pension Credit only on income in excess of the full BSP means that pensioners with incomes lower than the BSP will still experience marginal tax rates of 100 per cent.'[98] It also pointed out that those pensioners who were in receipt of Housing Benefit (HB) or Council Tax Benefit (CTB) already had tapered credits on their income and that in combination with the Pension Credit, 'marginal tax rates of 85 per cent will apply to most tenants on low income'. About this group it was observed: 'If they have saved in a pension scheme then they will have done so without incurring much tax, but in payment their savings are taxed at 85 per cent.' Even those who keep 60 per cent of their savings will still be losing their original tax gain. The report added:

For people to be able to plan effectively for retirement, the foundation on which savings are built needs to be made more stable. Ideally this means that the BSP should be the headline benefit . . . if the Government genuinely wishes to 'reward the thrift' of those on low incomes, it cannot do so by imposing high marginal rates of tax on their savings. The consultation paper describes the Pension Credit as a 'reward' for pensioners on low and middle income. In fact, Pension Credit is a benefit taper of 40 p in the pound. . . . It will result in a smaller penalty being applied to savings than is the case presently.[99]

The memorandum registers that to make the BSP the basis of the pension regime would mean paying a higher rate to some pensioners who do not really need the extra, namely those in the richest 20 or 30 per cent of the distribution. It suggests that instead the better-off pensioners could be taxed at a higher rate by reducing their allowances.

The Pension Credit paper explains that it is hoped to find 'less intrusive' ways of establishing pensioners' incomes and to move to something much more like an income tax assessment. Presumably the levels of permitted assets will rise, as the government expects 5.5 million pensioners to qualify for a top-up. This will involve a massive extension of means-testing until over half of all pensioners are involved. It will also create some perverse incentives. Thus someone with £15,000 of assets would find it advantageous to spend it in order to qualify for the MIG. Frank Field warns that means-testing 'will create the "double dipping" problem with people taking money out of their ISAs [tax-favoured savings plans] in order to qualify for the means-tested benefit'.[100] When the stakeholder was launched in April 2001 the government's own Pension Provision Group added its voice to the chorus of criticism. Tom Ross, the group's chairman, was quoted as saying that taking out a stakeholder would be 'a very difficult choice' for 'a lot of people in the lower earnings range' because it would not offer more than the MIG. 'The aim is to get more people saving and get people saving more, but I remain to be convinced that this will happen.'[101]

In August 2001 the Institute of Public Policy Research, a Labour-leaning think tank, confirmed the sense of disarray. It observed that the government's policies on pensions and old age care, which had appeared coherent a year earlier, were now 'unravelling'. Not only did different aspects of pension policy get in one another's way but the increase in means-testing for pensions clashed with the means tests that the government had introduced for long-term care for older persons – a move made against the advice of the government's own Commission on the subject. The report pointed to research showing that the assumption of an all-round increase in care costs was anyway unwarranted, since such costs were heavily concentrated in the last months of life. The IPPR urged that new options should be considered – among them a relaxation of means tests applied to income, and an extension of compulsory saving.[102]

Following the new legislation of 1999, the implementation swerve of 2000, and the perverse features of the Pension Credit, British pension policy is in a mess. There are three public schemes – the BSP, SERPS (being phased out) and the S2P (being phased in) – and three types of regulated and subsidised private pension – the stakeholder, occupational schemes and personal plans. And because there may be many who do not receive a decent pension from the foregoing there is the MIG. Since the latter is means-tested and not a proper pension the government has still not delivered on the implicit promise of its publication, *We All Need Pensions* (1998). The fragmentation of the different schemes is likely to be reproduced in many people's lives, as they move from casual to permanent employment, or from a mainly caring role to self-employment, or from convalescence to study leave, or any one of a hundred or more permutations on the foregoing. Instead of the existing moth-eaten patchwork quilt, pension provision needs to be integrated and unified.

An earnings-linked BSP, a restored SERPS and the new S2P could all be consolidated in a US-style graduated but egalitarian Social Security system, but with the advantage of coverage for carers and the 'proud ones'. Tax could claw back much of the extra BSP paid to better-off pensioners. Christopher Daykin, the Government Actuary, has paid tribute to the effectiveness of both the state pension and SERPS because of their impressively low administrative costs.[103] And as noted above, Tony Lynes has proposed building up an investment reserve.[104] SERPS is not unpopular and will anyway be in operation for a long time yet because of a double reprieve. The Conservatives first announced the winding up of SERPS in 1985 and were then obliged to withdraw their initial proposal and simply 'reform' it because there had been too much of a furore. Likewise, Labour found it had to backtrack on widows' rights to SERPS in the autumn of 2000, its season of repentance. It was discovered in 1999 that DSS leaflets had never properly informed people of the imminent halving of widows' entitlement according to the 1986 legislation. The Treasury's initial response was to say that only those who could prove they had been misled would be compensated. There was a public outcry and the Commons public administration committee dubbed the proposal 'an invitation to fraud' with 'all the makings of an administrative disaster'. Age Concern announced that it would take legal action in the European Court. In late November, in concert with its other U-turns, the government conceded that the widow's pension would be paid in full for all those retiring prior to 2002 and that the reduction would be gradually phased in over the following ten years.[105]

The strange election of 2001 saw Labour returned to power with a large parliamentary majority but on a much lower vote, following a 12 per cent drop in turnout. Tony Blair triumphed with fewer votes than Labour had received in its 1992 defeat. This was dubbed the 'apathetic landslide' but exit polls reveal that the older voters, at least, could not be charged with apathy: 79 per cent of those aged 65 and over cast their vote compared with 62 per cent of those aged 35–64, 45 per cent of those aged 25–64 and only 36 per cent of those aged 18–24. Overall, Labour won 42 per cent of the vote, the Conservatives 33 per cent and the Liberal Democrats 19 per cent. But among older voters – those over 65 – Labour trailed the Conservatives by five points, with the Conservatives on 42 per cent and Labour on 37 per cent. The Conservative share dropped steadily in each age bracket, being under 30 per cent for all those under 44, while Labour's share rose to 47 per cent for those under 34. Among the 'middle class' the Conservatives now had only a two-point lead (38 per cent to 36 per cent), while among the 'working class' Labour led by 49 per cent to 28 per cent. The bearing of pension policy on this pattern is not simple but it seems likely that Labour would have done very much worse among the over-65s if it had not raised the basic pension and MIG. The fact that it still trailed among this group should not be set down to the traditional loyalties of the aged because there had been a marked drop in support since 1997. More likely explanations are the enduring memory of that 75p and the government's continuing attachment to the means-testing approach. Given New Labour's studied conservatism, social fear would no longer have been a factor. But for its belated turn on pensions, Labour could also have expected to do worse among those aged 55–64 (where it led by 40 per cent to 34 per cent).

The younger voters with whom Labour did best would have been much less preoccupied with pensions, we may suppose. On the other hand, fewer of this age group voted at all.[106] The election was generally interpreted as revealing an overriding desire for better public services and a spurning of the tax cuts promised by the Conservatives – the Liberal Democrats actually did better, promising to raise taxes. In one constituency a doctor who promised to campaign for the restoration of local hospital facilities was elected against both Labour and Conservative opposition.

Labour broadly hinted that it would explore private delivery of health and education; private pension delivery fits logically into this pattern. Several commentators with no ideological animus against private provision warned that the British public might prove allergic to this approach. Nicholas Timmins in the *FT*, Melanie Phillips in the *Sunday Times* and the correspondent of *The Economist* all expressed this reservation.[107] While private provision should be allowed to flourish, in this view, there should still be a publicly provided core of social provision and protection. Above all, the newly returned government should take note of widespread concern that more should be done to renovate and reward the ethos of public service, something difficult to reconcile with pursuit of the bottom line. Pension provision cannot be equated with educational or health services, yet here too New Labour could seriously misjudge the public mood if it thought that the time had come to make private provision compulsory. The record of the financial sector is anyway too chequered to inspire confidence.

Personal and occupational funds have helped to generate satisfactory retirement incomes for about 30 per cent of pensioners. The new stakeholder pension is unlikely to raise this proportion and in many cases it may even displace good public sector occupational schemes. The full or partial privatisation of public services shrinks the size of the workforce with access to established pension schemes. Employees in the newly contracted private concerns will not have such a scheme but will be offered the stakeholder instead, without an employers' contribution and, of course, with no defined benefits. The main drawback of the existing occupational schemes is that they are often less portable than is the stakeholder – but that is a question which could easily have been addressed by specific legislation. Thus the advent of the stakeholder may halt the decline of overall coverage but it will still lower, not raise, its quality. The important figure will not be the numbers enrolled in schemes of all types but the numbers who maintain membership over decades at a level sufficient to provide a good secondary pension. For voluntary schemes appealing to people who are anyway struggling to make ends meet in an insecure environment, this is a most demanding requirement.

Whatever the weaknesses of the new stakeholder pension, it possesses built-in cost-effective features which are superior to run-of-the-mill personal pensions and even some new-fangled DB schemes. One of the explanations for the weak launch of the stakeholder is the financial services industry's dislike of the 1 per cent cap on charges, a figure well below prevailing rates. This cap does not apply to dealing charges, which become a potential loophole for invisible charge gauging. From the policy holders' point of view, the reliance on 'index tracking' and passive investment formulas is particularly unsuited to turbulent markets and speculative bubbles. The rocky performance of trackers in 2000 and 2001 shows the pitfalls here: as noted in chapter 2, the tracker fund is obliged to buy bubble stocks at their peak and then sell them when they collapse. However, commercial providers will argue that if they have to supply active fund management then the 1 per cent charging cap is out of the question. Side by side with a strengthened BSP it would make sense to make available a reformed stakeholder, to be supplied by mutually owned providers. The answer to the fund management problem could be to assemble non-commercial fund managers, by drawing on the expertise available to universities, trade unions, well-established self-managing pension funds, ethical investment trusts and the like. The existing commercial managers have a long track record of underperforming the market. Regional stakeholder boards could be formed which are much cheaper, and at least no less proficient, than the commercial providers. A re-engineered stakeholder could also be made more responsive to social priorities, and become a benchmark for the performance of the entire commercial sector.

Public confidence in the existing UK personal pension regime had been further damaged by revelation of the full scale of the problems of Equitable Life, a major pension provider. When Equitable closed its doors to new business in December 2000 it was one of the largest and most respected, as well as oldest, of British insurers. Founded in 1762, it had pioneered the so-called 'with profits' fund which allowed policy holders to choose a fund which would smooth market fluctuations to achieve a more secure return. The Equitable's money managers were – and remain – responsible for handling the pensions of around a million policy holders, backed by a fund worth £25 billion. In the 1950s Equitable began to offer a guaranteed annual rate (GAR) on some annuities, set at a manageable level so long as inflation did not drop too low. Extraordinarily enough no steps were taken to ensure an offset to these commitments and the same fund was used for GAR and non-GAR policies. When inflation fell in the mid-1990s Equitable succeeded in paying the stipulated interest rate only by lowering the capital sum credited to the GAR policy holders – this reduction was achieved by denying the policy holders concerned bonuses which were received by holders of 'unguaranteed' and 'with profits' policies. A group of policy holders who believed that they had been short-changed took legal action and eventually, in July 2000, won an appeal in the House of Lords. For many years Equitable's directors, accountants, actuaries and regulators – together with the lower courts –

had been prepared to endorse its conduct. All the foregoing were aware that the size of 'with profits' funds is subject to smoothing in the long-run interests of the policy holders. But since GAR and non-GAR policy holders had different and rival claims to the same fund they did not have the same interests and one or another group was going to suffer. In making their decision the Law Lords may well not have been aware of the havoc it would lead to. *Fiat justitia ruat caelum* – 'justice must be done even if the heavens fall' – is a maxim that sounds well in the course of a speech in the Lords but not in a substantive judgement. Equitable did not warn that it might have to close its doors if the case went against it. The Law Lords, who are sometimes out of their depth in complex financial affairs, may not have realised this would be the consequence of finding against it. While the GAR policy holders were represented the non-GAR policy holders were not.

Since Equitable was a mutually owned society, there may have been a belief that the extra sum due to the aggrieved policy holders – at least £1.5 billion but possibly much more – could easily be met by sale of the society. But it turned out that no purchaser was willing to offer that price, because of the number of open-ended liabilities. The imminent introduction of the stakeholder, with its cap on charges, added to uncertainty concerning the value of Equitable's well-respected sales force. (As we will see below, anticipation of the stakeholder prompted wholesale lay-offs of pension salesmen.) The failure to find a purchaser led to the decision to accept no new business but simply manage existing policies. The effect of this procedure on the over 800,000 or so unguaranteed 'with profits' policy holders was likely to be negative. While the search continued for a new purchaser, Equitable's remaining funds were henceforth to be managed on safety-first principles, with a large proportion of government bonds, and a low rate of return. As may readily be imagined, those who took out non-GAR 'with profits' policies with Equitable could not know the risks they were taking. Even if they knew about the 'guaranteed rate' policies they would naturally assume that Equitable, a concern that virtually invented the principles of insurance, would have insured itself against adverse movements of the rate of inflation. They would also have assumed that Equitable's procedures and books had all been expertly vetted – as, indeed, they had been, including by the Treasury itself which had been responsible for the regulation of insurance houses until 1999, after which the Securities and Investment Board (SIB) had taken over. In the present context it is especially relevant since Equitable was likely to be one of the leading concerns offering stakeholder pensions. In the end Equitable's policy holders will not be left destitute but nor will they be compensated for the underperformance of their policies. In February 2002 the policy holders approved a compromise by a large majority which should avert the danger of Equitable's assets being depleted by legal disputes.

Equitable was not the only concern to offer 'guaranteed' returns, so problems could crop up elsewhere in the financial system. Indeed, many commentators have blamed the very principle of the 'with profits' policy, and declared that it would have to go. Combined with the disappointing returns of most fund managers in 2000, these events were not auspicious for the stakeholder pension. They showed the need for a new regime of fund regulation and the importance of protecting the value of the public pension, the citizen's insurance against the risks of personal provision.[108] In the wake of the government's boost for private provision, it is salutary to remember the observation of Labour's 1957 document on superannuation: 'confidence can be placed in the survival in perpetuity of a government in Britain while similar confidence cannot be placed in the survival of any individual firm.'[109]

The Labour government sought to channel new business to a financial services industry embroiled in new difficulties and contributing to the weakness of the British economy in the areas of investment and manufacturing. The private sector pension funds were being held up as a model though their workings lacked transparency; a leading firm of actuaries complained that a third of Britain's top 100 companies had failed to give adequate information concerning their pension liabilities.[110] While some funds were in surplus others could be seriously underweight. The 1995 Pension Act had laid down a 'minimum funding ratio' with a significant proportion of gilt-edged, long-term government bonds as a guarantee against sharp falls in the stock exchange. But as the 1990s closed there was a dearth of such bonds. A decline in interest rates meant low yields on the annuities used to buy pensions. The drop in shares prices in 2000–1 weakened the financial position of many funds, resulting in demands for a 'pension rescue fund', to which all would contribute, and which would step in in the case of fund failure (i.e, similar to the US PBGC discussed in chapter 3).[111] A new accounting standard, FRS17, obliged companies to report the condition of any DB pension fund they sponsored using a rigid new formula that required all assets to be marked to market at current values and all liabilities to be discounted, using the yield on bonds, to achieve a present value. Any deficit resulting from this exercise was to be registered in the company accounts. The effect of FRS 17 was to remove discretion, ban resort to 'smoothing' formulae, and reduce both assets and liabilities to current values. Because many occupational funds are as large as, or larger than, the companies that sponsor them, the impact of any deficit on the company's bottom line would, in the event of a shortfall, be very large. The new reporting standard was introduced by the Accounting Standards Board, a non-governmental body, in 2000 and was to be phased in over three years. Supposedly the aim was to enhance the transparency and credibility of occupational funds. In the aftermath of the share slide of 2000 and 2001 it exposed underfunding and persuaded more large companies to close their DB funds, and offer their employees defined contribution plans instead. The latter, however, offered less value now because of the loss of corporation tax relief and the near-halving of annuity rates. And while employers who closed their DB funds would offer a DC alternative, including the stakeholder, they contributed little or nothing to them and by definition offered no guarantees as to the final pay-out. Hence the conclusion that the government was urging people to turn to private provision just when the private sector was in greater trouble than ever before. (In chapter 7 the resulting pension panic will be considered.)

Contradictions of Grey Capitalism

Pensions policy has to be seen in the larger context of political economy if its dynamic is to be grasped. In the long run good pension provision requires a healthy economy. It can also help to supply some of the conditions that make for economic vigour and sustainability. During the first Blair government Britain's economy managed to grow, but the country's basic ills were not addressed. Investment in public services and productive facilities remained very disappointing, showing no recovery from the Conservative years. Employment in manufacturing continued to drop and productivity figures remained weak. Britain could still attract some inward investment but it was becoming increasingly difficult to identify leading sectors in international terms. British concerns in formerly strong areas like pharmaceuticals, auto components and finance were wilting. No British investment banks were left and even the retail banks and fund-managing concerns faced trouble.

Though the exchequer was running a surplus and growth continued at around 2 per cent a year the Treasury had data on investment, productivity and competitiveness that flashed a warning light. In a pre-budget statement on 3 October 1998 Gordon Brown had already noted that labour productivity in Britain was between 15 and 40 per cent below rates in the United States, Germany and France. The productivity problem was linked to undercapitalisation and to fund managers who insisted on high hurdle rates used to judge investment.[112] Even where productivity had been raised, this had been achieved by cutting back on capacity rather than through new investment. A government report in November 2000 was to show that low productivity had persisted, notwithstanding overall growth and a raft of micro-measures.[113]

In May 2000 Labour's Chancellor asked Paul Myners, a senior Gartmore executive, to explain how pension funds could be weaned away from their customary short-termism and herd behaviour. Why were they so averse to investing in venture capital funds and to taking out private equity stakes in promising unlisted companies? And why did their undoubted ingenuity not lead them to find ways of promoting stronger economic growth? Legislation had already required the pension funds to become active shareholders and, as from July 2000, to publish their investment criteria. Myners's brief was 'to look at the key decision-makers in the investment process, namely the pension fund trustees and the fund managers. It is also to look at some of the likely impediments to investment in small companies, such as trustee law and the minimum funding requirement.'[114] By commissioning this probe the Labour Chancellor acknowledged that something was wrong with the pension fund regime but failed to address the true scale of the gathering crisis.

Grey capitalism spontaneously provokes a counter-ideology articulated by those who speak for employees, pensioners and a variety of social movements. Whatever the complexion or inclination of the government of the day, these voices know that it is perfectly possible to mobilise public opinion in favour of welfare and against highly paid and irresponsible financial operators, or blind faith in the free market. The backtracking on the Multilateral Investment Agreement in 1998, and the public outcry in Britain against the introduction of GM crops in 1999, show that public opinion can upset the plans of powerful interests. New Labour had run into a lot of flak because of its shabby treatment of the pensioners. At the same time the structures of grey capital history encouraged policy holders to try to influence boards of trustees or reclaim fund surpluses. Pension funds became conduits for protest at exorbitant executive salary increases or dubious investment decisions. The Lord Mayor of the City of London used the annual banquet for the Prime Minister in 1998 to warn his own colleagues and their visitor of the new spirit abroad: 'Lord Levine flagged that the shift from the State to the private sector in providing for retirement marks a fundamental change in the way that society is organised. Because of this, society can be expected to take a much greater interest in what happens to its money, how it is managed and what power is exercised by those who control it.'[115]

In the mid-twentieth century people would say of a problem, 'the government should do something about it'. By the close of the century, and in the twenty-first, a frequent answer would instead be 'the pension funds should do something about it'. Gordon Brown exemplified this approach when he asked Paul Myners to report on ways of encouraging the pension funds to back his attempts to raise investment and productivity. Here are some other examples. A speech by Claire Short, Minister for Overseas Development, was reported under the headline, 'Pension Funds Urged to Invest in Third World'.[116] Gerald Holtham, previously director of a Labour think tank but at the time Global Strategist at Norwich Union, comes forward with a proposal aimed simultaneously at furnishing the pension annuity market with the long-term, better-yielding government bonds it craves and at funding important social programmes. His proposal was that Gordon Brown should issue, say, £30 billion worth of long-term bonds at 5 per cent. The money so raised (mainly from pension funds which need this type of bond to meet their minimum funding requirement) would then be invested to yield the government net revenue for its social fund of around $1 billion a year to be spent on pensioners or health.[117] Around the same time proposals were made that the refurbishment of the London Underground should also be met by floating a bond to be bought by the institutions; an approach advocated by the winning candidate in the London mayoral election in 2000. In the spring of the same year the government was deeply embarrassed by the decision of BMW, the German car company, to sell off the Rover complex, at the cost of 30–50,000 jobs in the west Midlands. Will Hutton wrote in his *Observer* column: 'we need to re-think corporate law and, in particular, the responsibilities of pension-fund trustees.'[118] Most of these various proposals had a somewhat ad hoc character and certainly needed scrutiny to ensure that savers' money was being well used. They addressed real problems but did not outline a coherent overall architecture. And, last but not least, all these proposals produced little tangible response, notwithstanding the fact that they emanated from people who, with the exception of the London Mayor, were in or close to the Labour administration. While pension funds can be relied on to ignite controversy – and to be called in aid as saviours – as constituted they are part of the problem, not part of the solution.

The report produced by Paul Myners in March 2001 addressed the need for a new and more responsible regime for the pension funds but in much narrower terms.[119] It called for a reform of the minimum funding requirement (MFR) to make it easier for pension funds to invest in sound or reasonable long-term assets even if these are not immediately liquid. Much of the short-termism and herd behaviour of pension fund managers stems from their need at any time to be able to show that the assets in their fund can meet future liabilities. This inhibits them from acquiring assets, such as equity stakes in venture capital funds or in private unlisted companies, which are not 'marked to market' and hence have no provable market value. Myners also called for an end to the silent levying of charges in the shape of 'soft commissions' and he recommended that pension fund trustees should receive fees and training, the better to enable them to invigilate the fund managers. With the exception of the proposed replacement for the existing MFR, Myners's recommendations took the form of advice to his colleagues in the fund management industry. New legislation would only be needed if exhortation had been shown to fail. Gordon Brown announced that he agreed with Myners's conclusions in his March 2001 budget speech.

The Labour Chancellor's cautious approach no doubt reflected a wish not to frighten the horses. The money managers are mostly embedded in the City of London which, notwithstanding the takeover of so many of its elite institutions by Wall Street and the continental finance houses, is still thought to represent the raw power of money. But the money the institutions manage comes from domestic incomes and revenues which are largely within the control of the Chancellor. So long as the government retains the power to tax – and hence to allot tax privileges – then it has great leverage over all those financial concerns that depend on domestic savings. In 2000–1 income tax supplied just over a quarter of national revenues, and corporate taxation nearly 10 per cent. This marked a three-point decline for income tax since 1979 and a three-point rise for corporation tax. In both years National Insurance contributions supplied a further 16 per cent of government revenue.[120] Tax has fallen a little as a proportion of GNP and as a proportion of the income of the wealthy. But all the major income groups pay well over a third of their income in taxes of one sort or another. This means that the power to award tax breaks gives the Chancellor enormous power. The Chancellor has also undertaken a reconstruction of regulatory institutions in the field of financial services that opens up a so-far-unused ability to prescribe new rules of operation.

Gordon Brown's legislation on financial regulation replaced a series of ill-coordinated, ad hoc bodies – the PIA (Personal Investment Authority), IMRO (Investment Management Regulatory Office) and SFA (Securities and Futures Authority) – with a revamped and unified Securities and

Investment Board. The new SIB is a public body, with an initial staff of 2,000 employees and responsibility for regulating the banks and all branches of the financial services industry. It is essentially intended to guarantee the integrity of financial institutions, to prevent banking scandals and 'mis-selling' of services. While some in the City treated it as a revolutionary novelty, the proposed role for the SIB resembles that of the US Securities and Exchange Commission. What was not at all envisioned was that the SIB or any other institution would enforce guidelines permitting and encouraging funds to pursue clear social and economic priorities. Nor was it proposed that incentives would be given to channel funds in socially desirable directions – for example, towards the regional development boards. Yet there is no reason why the new apparatus of financial regulation could not be harnessed, with appropriate modification, to such purposes.

What was really needed, of course, was a species of regulation that went beyond the minimal goal of policing crooks, sanctioning sloppy managers, or publicly upbraiding delinquent institutions, and actually served to promote socially desirable and sustainable development. The new institutions needed to effect this would also require supportive fiscal and regulatory measures backed by the Treasury, the new SIB and a new Pensions or Social Insurance Board. With some trade union support the Cooperative movement and the Social Investment Foundation had already sponsored debate on whether new incentives and tax rebates were needed to reward socially aware funds. Others had urged that the commercial management of funds should be replaced by bodies owned on a social or mutual basis, because private management of the pension funds adds a costly layer of administration and management profit. Labour's pension policy combined with the rage for web-marketing to produce a large impact on the organisation of the fund industry. Even though the take up of the stakeholder was to be disappointing it had a considerable impact on the life insurance industry, as the following report explained:

> The need to achieve sufficient scale for handling stakeholder pensions was one of the key motives behind last year's £19 bn merger between CGU and Norwich Union that created CGNU, the UK's biggest life assurer. Scottish Life, a small mutual pensions provider, also sold out to a bigger mutual, Royal London, to help deal with the challenge of the stakeholder world. In doing so it followed the example of its larger Edinburgh neighbour, Scottish Widows, which was bought for £7.3 bn by Lloyds/TSB, the bank. February this year saw Prudential, the UK's second largest life assurer, announce it would close its direct sales force with a loss of 2,000

jobs, and Sun Life Financial of Canada also decided to axe its direct sales force, with a total loss of 1,700 jobs. The following month Birmingham-based Britannic became the latest life assurer to withdraw from door-to-door selling, saying it would cut 2,000 jobs − a significant proportion of the group's total of 4,900 employees. All three groups had decided that door-to-door selling would not be viable in the new stakeholder environment. Life assurers generally agree that the stakeholder pension will not become profitable for providers until 2010, according to Cap Gemini Ernst and Young.[121]

The UK's financial services industry is still on the defensive because of widespread suspicion of its charges and low public esteem for its management practices. The introduction of the stakeholder pensions was intended to allay some of these fears. It had once again shown the enormous power of legislation, triggering a spate of mergers aimed at capturing the economies upon which it sets a premium. Now that employers were obliged to offer stakeholders to their staff, teams of door-to-door salesmen were being stood down or redeployed. The fund management and life insurance industries reckoned that by 2010 only half a dozen large concerns would be supplying stakeholders and that these will often be closely associated with provision of payroll services. If it establishes itself the new regime would reward those who adapt successfully, though resources and patience will be required.

The pension fund managers, stung by criticism of their passivity and angered by growing signs of self-aggrandisement by business leaders began to display greater concern for corporate governance issues. By 2000–1 scarcely a week went by without reports that the institutions were unhappy at exorbitant levels of executive remuneration or pointless merger projects. The criticism of Gent, and the fund manager role in the reconstruction of the Marconi board, noted in chapters 2 and 3, were emblematic of a more assertive approach. But trustees and fund managers were still generally unwilling to take a pro-active role on other issues of public concern.

Public opinion in the UK, as elsewhere, is increasingly prone to question the strategic decisions made by corporations about products, processes and the direction of desirable economic growth. Consumer resistance has been one sign of this. In 1999 all the large British supermarkets withdrew foodstuffs made using genetically modified crops in deference to widespread disquiet. An international campaign led Monsanto to withdraw its patented and sterile 'terminator' seeds. When BMW announced the disposal of its Rover operations in 2000 it strove to avoid the boycott of its products threatened by some sections of its former workforce. Fund managers now exercise caution when approaching, for example, shares in

companies implicated in research involving cruelty to animals. In February
2001 the organisers of the FTSE 100 announced the launch of a new UK
and global index FTSE4Good which would track ethical and socially
responsible funds. A Reuters report explained: '"We want it to be a step
towards encouraging companies to adopt socially responsible principles,"
FTSE Chief Executive Mark Makepeace told a news Conference, adding
that the new index licence fees will go to the United Nations Children's
Fund (UNICEF).'[122]

Will Hutton, in the course of a dialogue with Anthony Giddens published in *On the Edge* (2000), commented:

> Heineken, Unilever and Monsanto are having to adjust their corporate
> strategies to consumer power. The difficulty is that while consumers clearly
> have the power to buy or not to buy, it is pretty crude – and only arises
> when there is a well-publicised flashpoint. Consumers do not have a sys-
> tematic voice through the democratic process or in the ways companies
> make decisions. . . Consumer power is also easily manipulable.[123]

Hutton has also proposed that all enterprises should be subordinated to
social audit as a condition of being registered on the stock exchange.
Pension funds could also play a role in social monitoring as well as being
more accountable themselves. In the course of the same exchange Hutton
observed:

> Pension funds own nearly half the quoted shares in British companies. The
> question is what the law should insist should be the relationship and mutual
> responsibilities between those funds and the companies in which they invest.
> It is no longer adequate to say that they can turn up once a year if they want
> to at an annual parliament of shareholders and sell their shares whenever
> they choose, especially if there is a hostile take-over bid. At the very least the
> funds need to vote on key decisions, to play a part in setting commercial
> objectives and to ensure that executive pay is not excessive.[124]

This elicits from Anthony Giddens the response: 'I don't think you make
the best case for these possibilities. . . . It might be possible to democratise
the pension funds but for the core "stakeholders" – those whose pensions
are "at stake" – the most important thing is effective, professional management.'[125] Unfortunately no more was offered by either participant on
the important issues raised in this exchange.

A new statute for pension funds could make them more accountable
both to policy holders – who, one hopes, may often themselves be open
to persuasion on issues of public interest – and to a process of social audit
which would determine their eligibility for tax breaks. Fund managers
could be obliged to monitor the standards adhered to by the enterprises in

which they invested. These pension fund audits could be entrusted to regulatory bodies whose criteria would be set by local and national elected bodies. Those funds which, for whatever reason, did not wish to conform to such criteria would forfeit their right to tax-privileged contributions or benefits. Trade unions and social movements would be encouraged to play their part in helping to ensure the effectiveness of these arrangements.

Following a succession of disasters in 2000–1, the awesome scale of needed social expenditure in the UK was revealed after two decades of Conservative budgets. The budgets for 2001 and 2002 planned large increases in expenditure on health and education. In the context of the post-Hatfield paralysis of the rail network it was agreed that the government would have to find £60 billion of new investment as this was beyond the resources of Railtrack and the newly privatised rail companies. Social infrastructure of every type – the London Underground, air traffic control, the road network, the waterworks and sewers – was in urgent need of renovation and investment. Large sums were needed to develop renewable energy sources, an area where the UK now lags most of its European neighbours. In thrall to its Third Way ideology, New Labour had sought to plug all these gaps with public–private partnerships and new instalments of privatisation. Since the débâcle of rail privatisation the need for large public subsidies had been increasingly acknowledged, creating the predicament that unpopular and discredited private companies will receive windfalls from the public purse as the investment bears fruit. There is likely to be interest in involving pension funds in infrastructure renewal both as sources of finance and as stakeholders; David Blake of the Birkbeck Pensions Institute had already signalled as much.[126] If the government is to inject cash into these projects, then it should reacquire ownership and could vest control of it in autonomous social bodies responsible to the communities concerned. The slogan 'No public subsidies without social representation' could guide social restructuring. Pension funds – themselves subject to social audit – could thus help to recollectivise public utilities and services. In *Pension Fund Capitalism* (2000) Gordon Clark outlined some of the ways in which pension funds can contribute to urban renewal while at the same time furnishing guarantees and good returns to their policy holders.[127]

The need for massive investment in UK industry and services, in social infrastructure and R&D, has been underlined by Adair Turner. [128] But we should not expect even the most enlightened vice-chairman of Merrill Lynch (Europe) to explain that all these needed areas of investment could furnish important fields for publicly guaranteed and socially audited pension fund mobilisation. The government does not itself have to 'pick winners' – though public authorities have not in fact been so bad at this (radar, the jet engine, the modern tractor, the internet and so forth). But responsible social organisations can lay down investment principles. The government already has the power to compel employers and fund managers to adopt or shun particular practices, ranging from changes in the rules governing the type of assets in which the funds can invest to audit requirements to which approved funds are subject. As we have seen, the government has huge power over the financial services industry. Both trade unions and new social movements are pressing for fund management to be made accountable in quite new ways to policy holders and to public opinion. Beyond particular struggles over the quality of corporate governance or the destiny of a fund surplus or the ethics of investment in a dam in Turkey lies the horizon of a civic reappropriation of the power of the funds and of the regulatory regime which has created them.

These ideas will be further explored in the Conclusion. But here it is worth adding that a different and collective approach to pension funds, and a restoration of public pension provision, could help to supply badly needed cement to a social and political order weakened by globalisation and suffering from the diminished prestige of UK institutions, from the monarchy to the Houses of Parliament. When William Beveridge drew up his report in 1942 he saw social insurance as an idea that would promote social cohesion as well as social justice. In the first decade of the twenty-first century Britain's political elite, re-elected by an ever-dwindling number willing to vote, seems almost united in supposing that the UK state need discharge fewer and fewer tasks and that the social insurance principle can be discarded in favour of commercial provision for those who can pay and state charity for those who cannot. The Scottish parliament takes a less cavalier attitude. Do Westminster politicians really suppose that the UK in 2002 displays a national morale so superior to that of 1942 that they can safely push implicit privatisation to its logical conclusion? Such different figures as Richard Titmuss, Richard Crossman, Tony Benn and Frank Field were drawn to the strength of the case for funding public pensions and using those funds as part of an investment strategy, yet each was to be frustrated by economic orthodoxy, Treasury caution and special interests. In the Conclusion we will see that Keynes too campaigned for a somewhat similar package in 1940. If the winning side in the repeated clashes over social savings and pension provision had built a flourishing and successful system then there would be no more argument. But manifestly, as even the government's closest friends admit, pension policy is unravelling and its contribution to the wider political economy is dubious or negative.

Notes

1 Pat Thane, *Old Age in English History: Past Experiences andPuseut Issues,* Oxford 2000, p. 371.

2 Richard Titmuss, 'Pension Systems and Population Change', *Essays on 'the Welfare State',* London 1958, pp. 56–74; Thane, *Old Age in English History,* p. 373.

3 Draft Policy Statement on National Superannuation, Titmuss Papers, British Library of Political and Economic Science, LSE, folder 1/12.

4 Crossman's speech is given in Labour Party, *Report of the 56th Annual Conference,* Brighton 1957, pp. 119–24. Titmuss's thinking at this time is reflected in Titmuss, *Essays on 'the Welfare State',* chapters 2 and 3; Income *Distribution and Social Change,* London 1962, chapter 7, and *The Irresponsible Society,* Fabian Tract, April 1960. For his role in shaping Labour's proposal for a funded National Superannuation scheme see Hugh Heclo, *Modern Social Politics in Britain and Sweden: from Relief to Income Maintenance,* New Haven (CT) and London 1974, pp. 260–4, and Peter Baldwin, *The Politics of Social Solidarity: Class Bases of the European Welfare State 1875–1975,* Cambridge 1990, pp. 232–9.

5 *National Superannuation: Labour's Policy for Security in Old Age,* London 1957, p. 91.

6 Heclo, *Modern Social Politics in Britain and Sweden,* p. 265.

7 Ibid., pp. 99–101. The Titmuss papers held at the British Library of Political and Economic Science, LSE, make it clear that Crossman drafted much of the document, distilling material prepared by Titmuss, Abel Smith and Peter Townsend. See Titmuss Papers, folder 1/12.

8 Quoted Dorothy Wedderburn, 'Pensions, Equality and Socialism', *New Left Review,* no. 24, March–April 1964, p. 77.

9 Department of Social Security, *The Changing Welfare State: Pensioner Incomes,* March 2000.

10 Ivor Crewe, Anthony Fox and Neil Day, *The British Electorate 1963–1992, a Compendium of Data from the British Election Studies,* Cambridge 1995, pp. 6, 8, 9. In 1966 support for Labour among older voters was 51.3 per cent of those aged 65–74 and 46.7 per cent of those aged over 74 (its share of the overall vote was 52.6 per cent). This is the best Labour score among older voters for any general election for which information is available.

11 Richard Crossman, *The Diaries of a Cabinet Minister,* vol. 3, *Secretary of State for Social Services, 1968–70,* London 1977, pp. 176, 206. See also Baldwin, *The Politics of Social Solidarity,* pp. 243–4.

12 Pressure for opt-outs had already emerged in 1957 and had been expressed in the Labour conference debate; in his reply, Crossman had conceded that workers had to be allowed to continue in good schemes (*Report of the 56th Annual Conference*, p. 122).

13 Lisa Martineau, *Barbara Castle: Politics and Power*, London 2000, pp. 291–5.

14 Barbara Castle, *Fighting All the Way*, London 1993, pp. 461–8.

15 Organisation for Economic Cooperation and Development, *Ageing in OECD Countries*, Paris 1996, p. 38.

16 Reagan and Congress did trim Social Security benefits in 1983 and Balladur was to do the same with private sector pension schemes in 1993, but compared with Thatcher this was tinkering, as witness the previously cited OECD projections.

17 Richard Disney, discussant, 'Insights from Social Security Abroad', in R. Douglas Arnold, Michael J. Graetz and Alicia H. Munnell, eds, *Framing the Social Security Debate: Values, Politics, and Economics*, Washington, DC, 1998, pp. 229–37.

18 Paul Pierson, *Dismantling the Welfare State? Reagan, Thatcher and the Politics of Retrenchment*, Cambridge 1994, p. 71.

19 It was the visibility of the community charge ('poll tax'), and the possibility of refusing to pay it, that allowed it to become the focus of more general anger against the government. See Michael Lavelette and Gerry Mooney, '"No Poll Tax Here": the Tories, Social Policy and the Great Poll Tax Rebellion', in Michael Lavelette and Gerry Mooney, eds, *Class Struggle and Social Welfare*, London 2000, pp. 199–227.

20 Nigel Lawson, *The View from No 11*, London 1992, p. 368.

21 Ibid., p. 369.

22 Ibid., p. 370.

23 Ibid., p. 591.

24 Norman Fowler, *Ministers Decide: a Personal Memoir of the Thatcher Years*, London 1991, pp. 211–12.

25 Margaret Thatcher, *The Downing Street Years*, London 1993, p. 49.

26 Ibid., p. 127.

27 Ibid., pp. 314–15.

28 Margaret Thatcher, *Preparing for Power*, London 1995, p. 573.

29 Ibid., p. 121. For her time at the Ministry of Pensions see pp. 119–25.

30 Ibid., p. 546.

31 Pierson, *Dismantling the Welfare State?*, pp. 53–73, and with special reference to Britain, pp. 64–9.

32 By Anglo-Saxon politics I mean political arrangements based on first-past-the-post and winner-takes-all systems of representation, and an executive enjoying, at times, quasi-monarchical authority, even if elected on a minority of votes. For the baneful influence of such arrangements in the UK see: Perry Anderson, *English Questions*, London 1992, Tom Nairn, *The Enchanted Glass*, London 1987, and Will Hutton, *The State We're In*, London 1994. For the US see Daniel Lazare, *The Frozen Republic*, New York 1996. The political

342 BANKING ON DEATH

processes surrounding the welfare termination legislation of 1996 in the US might bear comparison with Margaret Thatcher's pension reform: see Joel Handler, 'Reforming/Deforming Welfare', *New Left Review*, second series no. 4, July–August 2000, pp. 114–36.

33 Based on figures in Crewe *et al.*, *The British Electorate 1963-1992*, pp. 6, 8, 9.

34 Thatcher, *Preparing for Power*, p. 450.

35 Ibid,. p. 382.

36 Constance Rollet and Julia Parker, 'Population and the Family' in A.H. Halsey, *Trends in British Society since 1900*, London 1972, pp. 20–63, p. 33. For class and gender mortality differences see also Julia Parker and Constance Rollett, 'Health', in ibid., pp. 321–72.

37 For the postwar gender and class gap in voting, see David Butler, 'Electors and the Elected', in Halsey, *Trends in British Society since 1900*, pp. 227–47, p. 243. But the overall gender gap closed in 1987 while the class gap closed more slowly, but was much narrower by 1997: see David Sanders, 'The New Electoral Battlefield', in Anthony King *et al.*, *New Labour Triumphs: Britain at the Polls 1997*, Chatham (NJ) 1998, p. 220.

38 Paul Johnson and Jane Falkingham, *Ageing and Economic Welfare*, London 1992, pp. 63, 65. By 1995 65 per cent of all pensioners received some money from a private pension worth an average of £78.70 per week. *We All Need Pensions – the Prospects for Pension Provision*, Report by the Pension Provision Group, London, The Stationery Office, London 1998, p. 61.

39 Crewe *et al.*, *The British Electorate*, pp. 6, 8. So Labour's support among the older voters was being rebuilt but remained below that of the Conservatives.

40 David Sanders, '"It's the Economy, Stupid": the Economy and Support for the Conservative Party 1979–94', Essex Papers in Politics and Government, Department of Government, University of Essex, April 1995; see also King *et al.*, *New Labour Triumphs,* pp. 198–9.

41 John Plender, *A Stake in the Future: the Stakeholding Solution*, London 1997.

42 Frank Field, *How to Pay for the Future: Building a Stakeholder's Welfare*, London 1996.

43 See William Hutton, 'Raising the Stakes', *Observer*, 17 January 1996; A. Grice, 'Has Stakeholding Shrunk to a Slogan', *Sunday Times*, 21 January 1996.

44 'Basic Pension Plus', *Daily Telegraph*, 6 March 1997. For an account of the scheme see also Tony Lynes, 'Supplementary Pensions in Britain: Is There Still a Role for the State?', in Gerard Hughes and Jim Stewart, eds, *The Role of the State in Pension Provision: Employer, Regulator, Provider*, Boston/Dordrecht/London 1999, pp. 75–84.

45 Bill Jones *et al.*, *Politics UK*, 4th edn, Harlow 2001, p. 174.

46 Frank Field and Matthew Owen, *National Pensions Savings Plan: Universalising Private Pension Provision*, Fabian Society, March 1994. See also Frank Field and Matthew Owen, *Private Pensions for All: Squaring the Circle*, Fabian Society Discussion Paper no. 16, July 1993, and Frank Field and Matthew Owen, *Making Sense of Pensions*, Fabian Pamphlet no. 557, March 1993.

47 Field and Owen, *Private Pensions for All*, p. 9.

48 Department of Social Security Paper no. 2, *The Changing Welfare State: Pensioner Incomes*, London 2000, p. 19.

49 *We All Need Pensions*, pp. 16, 21. This report also cites data showing that the numbers of pensioners in the poorest fifth of the population declined from 47 per cent to 25 per cent between 1979 and 1995 (p. 18), though the general increase in poverty during these years made this a very relative achievement.

50 If we look at the money paid out in state pensions, then British pensioners are worse off than their counterparts in all OECD states except Greece, Ireland and Portugal. However, the material position of British pensioners is considerably improved for about 40 per cent of the population if private pensions receipts are taken into account. Other factors which somewhat improve the relative position of British pensioners in international comparisons are their access to free healthcare, 'income support' and subsidised housing. If all these factors are taken into account, the number of old people with an income less than 50 per cent of average earnings was actually less than in West Germany in the mid-1980s. Since German wages were much higher this was still compatible with German pensioners being richer than their British counterparts. Peter Whitehead and Steven Kennedy, *Incomes and Living Standards of Older People: a Comparative Analysis*, Social Policy Research Unit, University of York, 1995.

51 Field and Owen, *Making Sense of Pensions*.

52 Barbara Castle and Peter Townsend, *We Can Afford the Welfare State*, London 1996. See also Barbara Castle, Bryn Davies, Hilary Land, Peter Townsend, Tony Lynes and Ken Macintyre, *Fair Shares for Pensioners: Our Evidence to the Pensions Review Body*, January 1998, available from Security in Retirement for Everyone, 27–29 Amwell St, London EC1R 1UN.

53 Richard Minns, *Pulp Fiction: Pensioning Off the State*, Political Economy Research Centre, University of Sheffield, Policy Paper no. 2.

54 Tony Lynes, *Our Pensions: a Policy for a Labour Government*, London August 1996, p. 9.

55 Ibid., p. 24.

56 John Denham, *Stakeholder Pensions: a Consultation Document*, Department of Social Security, London November 1997, p. 2.

57 For a detailed review and response, see 'Stakeholder Pensions; Consultation Document', Draft Response from the Independent Pensions Research Group and the Northern Pensions Resource Group. This is available from Sue Ward, 5 Goldspink Lane, Newcastle upon Tyne, NE2 1NQ.

58 'Building a Better World: the Role of Socially Responsible Pensions', a lecture delivered by John Denman, MP, Parliamentary Under-Secretary of State for Social Security, 9 July 1998, to the UK Social Investment Foundation meeting.

59 I was present at a seminar in the City of London in early 1998 organised by *Prospect* magazine where Field as minister outlined his views on pension

reform. It was noticeable, in such a context, that Field still stressed the role
of trade unions, friendly societies and other non-commercial bodies in
acting as trustees for stakeholder pensions, with no mention of the financial services industry. Despite this stance, Field did not see himself – nor
was he seen – as proposing a left-wing or anti-business policy. Such an
other-worldly approach might have been quite effective if combined with
a willingness to make clear to potential allies the issues at stake. But as it
was, the allegation that he lacked political skills was not altogether wide of
the mark.

60 David Lipsey, *The Secret Treasury*, London 2000, pp. 186–91.

61 For Field's demise as minister, see Andrew Rawnsley, *Servants of the People: the
    Inside Story of New Labour*, London 2000, pp. 109–10, 119–20.

62 *Partnership in Pensions*, Cm 4179, HMSO, London 1998, p. 34.

63 The new legislation is surveyed in David Blake, 'Two Decades of Pension
    Reform in the UK', *Employee Review*, vol. 22, no. 3, 2000, pp. 223–45,
    especially pp. 228–45.

64 *Partnership in Pensions*, pp. 41, 43.

65 The weakness of the State Second Pension was explored in a briefing paper
    prepared by the Actuarial Profession's Pension Provision Task Force, *The Size
    of the State Pension*, presented to the seminar Pension Provision: Looking to
    the Future, 28 February 2001.

66 Blake, 'Two Decades of Pension Reform in the UK', p. 233.

67 DSS, *The Changing Welfare State: Pensioner Incomes*, DSS Paper no. 2, March
    2000, p. 70.

68 *Partnership in Pensions* accompanied these stipulations, in bold type, by the fol-
    lowing declaration: 'We would welcome views from the pension fund
    industry on alternative structures which could provide comparable benefits for
    stakeholder pension scheme members.' *Partnership in Pensions*, p. 55.

69 Ibid., pp. 8, 103.

70 Some idea of the business input to *Partnership in Pensions* may be gleaned from
    such publications as *Pension Provision: Building Consensus for the Future*, Report
    of the Fabian Business Seminar, May 1998, and *We All Need Pensions*. The
    September 1998 issue of *Social Economy* ran a number of pieces devoted to the
    technical elaboration of the plan, some implicitly signalling problems with
    Field's approach.

71 Frank Field, 'A Guarantee to End Pensioner Poverty', *Financial Times*, 3
    August 2000. Field himself still supported a scheme that would be mandatory
    for employees over 25 and would deliver the stakeholder on £14,000 a year
    a guaranteed pension of £143 a week, instead of the £91 a week of the –
    government's stakeholder pension. He was the chair of the Pensions
    Reform Group which published *Universal Protected Pension: Modernising
    Pensions for the Millennium*, Institute of Community Studies, London 2001.
    This pamphlet proposed pre-funding, with the fund to be managed by an
    independent, non-commercial public body, a half of whose directors would
    be elected.

72 James Banks and Carl Emmerson, 'Public and Private Pension Spending: Principles, Practice and the Need for Reform', *Fiscal Studies*, vol. 21, no. 1, Spring 2000, pp. 1–63, p. 55.

73 These objectives are based on the work of Susan St John and Toni Ashton as reported by Littlewood, *How to Create a Competitive Market in Pensions*, London 1998, p. 117.

74 Antony Giddens, *The Third Way*, London 1999, p. 119.

75 Ibid., p. 121.

76 Ibid., p. 118–19.

77 By the close of 2001 only 570,000 stakeholder policies had been sold, and many of these were transfers from other schemes. Andrew Bolger and Nicholas Timmins, 'Stakeholder Schemes Fail to Reach Targets' *Financial Times*, 8 January 2002.

78 Following his resignation Field placed articles in newspapers ranging from the Conservative *Daily Mail* and *The Independent* to the left-wing weekly, *Tribune*. In one article he wrote: 'The proposal I have put forward is for a pension guarantee, paid from National Insurance and Investments, which links the interests of poorer and richer in a single scheme.' 'An Almost Criminal Waste of Welfare', *The Independent*, 2 August 1998.

79 Evan Davis, *Public Spending*, London 1998, pp. 260-1.

80 Ben Jupp, *Saving Sense: a New Approach to Encouraging Saving*, Demos, London 1997, p. 21.

81 Tom Clarke and Jane Taylor, 'Income Inequality: a Tale of Two Cycles', *Fiscal Studies*, vol. 20, no. 4, December 1999, pp. 387–408, p. 400.

82 'Inequality: Just Like the Old Days', *The Economist*, 21 April 2001.

83 Polly Toynbee, 'Prudent Parveen is the Chancellor's Fictitious Saver', *Guardian*, 11 April 2001. Under some circumstances Parveen might be able to draw down her stakeholder at the age of 50 rather than 65 but the lack of flexibility for someone of 28 is still evident.

84 *Partnership in Pensions*, p. iv. For the minimum income guarantee, see pp. 4, 18, 34.

85 *Sunday Times*, 16 April, 2000. Quoted in Bruce Kent, 'Why We Must Unite to Fight', *British Pensioner*, New Series 38, Summer 2000.

86 'Can We Afford to Help Today's Pensioners?', *Essex Pensioner*, Winter 1999–2000.

87 Ibid.

88 'Labour Plan to Help the Aged Flops', *Sunday Times*, 27 August 2000.

89 Richard Poynter and Clive Martin, *Rights Guide to Non-Means-tested Benefits*, London 1996, p. 112. The authors mention certain other unspecified further residency qualifications – a cemetery address perhaps?

90 Department of Social Security, *Households Below Average Income, 1994/5–1998/9*, HMSO, London 2000, pp. 114–15.

91 Alan Budd and Nigel Campbell, 'The Roles of the Public and Private Sectors in the UK Pension System', in Martin Feldstein, ed., *Privatizing Social Security*, Chicago 1998, pp. 99–134, pp. 117–18.

92 Jon Hibbs, 'Brown Sitting on £20 bn NI windfall', *Daily Telegraph*, 25 November 1999.

93 'Gordon Brown's Incoherent Cave-in: Juggling the Cash', *The Economist*, 11 November 2000.

94 Polly Toynbee and David Walker, *Did Things Get Better?*, London 2001, p. 24.

95 *We All Need Pensions*, p. 21; DSS, *Pensioner Incomes*, p. 40 (though note information here is for 'pensioner couples').

96 It is worth noting that pensioner incomes are conventionally always discussed in terms of pounds per week in homage, as it were, to the early poverty campaigners. But these campaigners, people like Maud Pember Reeves, author of *Round About a Pound A Week*, London 1914, used this reckoning because wages were then paid weekly. Today stipends are usually given in monthly or annual sums. If the colleagues of Walker and Toynbee speculated in the bar about how much they were paid, the answer might be 'I think Polly's on eighty and David's on sixty' and they would not be referring to pounds per week. In *Guardian* job ads vacancies are advertised at 40k, or 25k, or if it's a very junior post £14k. But in conversation one would avoid using 'k' as it sounds a bit crude. The fact that the pensioner organisations use the pounds per week formula regrettably perpetuates pensioner ghettoisation.

97 DSS, *The Pension Credit: a Consultation Paper*, Cm 4900, London November 2000.

98 Institute/Faculty of Actuaries, *Response to The Pension Credit: a Consultation Paper* (Cm 4900).

99 Ibid.

100 Quoted in 'Pensions: Means and Ends', *The Economist*, 18 November 2000.

101 Nicholas Timmins, 'Government Advisers Criticise New Pension', *Financial Times*, 6 April 2001.

102 *A New Contract for Retirement: an Interim Report. Incremental and Fundamental Reform Options for Pensions and Long Term Care*, Institute of Public Policy Research, London 2001.

103 Speaking on 27 January 1998; cited in Castle *et al.*, *Fair Shares for Pensioners*, p. 23.

104 *Report of the 1994–6 Advisory Council on Social Security*, Washington (DC) 1997, pp. 25–8.

105 Nicholas Timmins, 'Compensation Plan for SERPS Changes "May Be a Disaster"', *Financial Times*, 24 November 2000; Rosemary Bennett and Nicholas Timmins, 'Labour Gives Way on SERPS', *Financial Times*, 30 November 2000.

106 Alan Travis, 'Public Services the Key in "Apathetic Landslide"', *Guardian*, 9 June 2001; Peter Kellner, 'Blair Tightens Grip on Middle England', *Observer*, 10 June 2001.

107 Nicholas Timmins, 'When Public Price Becomes a Private Matter', *Financial Times*, 4 June 2001; Melanie Phillips, 'This Is a Chance to Be Truly Radical

with Public Services', *Sunday Times*, 10 June 2001; *The Economist*, 8 June 2001.

108 Will Hutton and Charlotte Thorne, 'An Inequitable Pensions Policy', *Financial Times*, 10 January 2001. The best brief assessment of the mistakes made by Equitable Life is David Blake, 'An Unfair Compromise', *Financial Times*, 29 January 2002.

109 *National Superannuation: Labour's Policy for Security in Old Age*, pp. 88–9.

110 Michael Peel, 'Third of Top Companies Give "Inadequate" Pension Details', *Financial Times*, 18 August 2000.

111 Alan Beattie and Simon Targett, 'Bid to Set up Pension Rescue Fund', *Financial Times*, 14 August 2000.

112 Gordon Brown's pre-budget speech was extensively published in the *Financial Times* for 4 November 1998 and his remarks on the fund managers were the subject of critical comment in the *FT's* Lex column on 5 November.

113 Martin Wolf wrote: 'One of the most important reasons for lower productivity in the UK is that workers have considerably less capital at their disposal . . . "Total factor productivity" – output per unit of labour and capital – is also about 20 per cent higher in the US and France (than in the UK)'. Martin Wolf, 'A Measure of Progress towards Closing the Gap', *Financial Times*, 19 February 2001. See also *Productivity in the UK: the Evidence and the Government's Approach*, HM Treasury, November 2000.

114 Simon Targett, 'The Knotty Problem of a Knighthood', *Financial Times*, 17 May 2000.

115 Anthony Hilton, 'City Must Think Hard about Shift on Savings', *Evening Standard*, 17 November 1998.

116 Simon Targett, 'Pension Funds Urged to Invest in Third World', *Financial Times*, 15 March 2000.

117 Gerald Holtham, 'Why the State Needs to Borrow More not Less', *Guardian*, 15 August 1999.

118 Will Hutton, 'Why the Wheels Fell Off at Rover', *Observer*, 19 March 2000. Hutton himself has not written systematically about what that rethinking might involve. However, this column did make the following relevant proposal: 'As a first step the publication of a social, employment, investment and environmental audit should be made a condition of a stock exchange listing.'

119 [Paul Myners], *Institutional Investment in the UK: a Review*, HM Treasury, London 2001.

120 Fabian Society, *Paying for Progress: a New Politics of Tax for Public Spending*, London 2000, pp. 62, 67, 75.

121 Andrew Bolger, 'Challenging Times Ahead as the Industry Begins to Restructure', *Financial Times*, 27 April 2001.

122 Rex Merrifield, 'FTSE Goes Green with New Ethical Indices', *Reuters*, 27 February 2001.

123 Will Hutton and Anthony Giddens, eds, *On the Edge*, London 2000, p. 47.

124 Ibid., p. 35.

125 Ibid., p. 36.

126 David Blake, 'What Kind of Pension is Best?', *Economic Journal*, February 2000.

127 Gordon Clark, *Pension Fund Capitalism*, Oxford 2000.

128 Adair Turner, *Just Capital: the Liberal Economy*, London 2001, pp. 206–27.

6

US Social Security: Tax Farmers
Besiege the Citadel

*When the politicians are ready to act, I hope that we in the
economics profession are ready to help them.*
(Martin Feldstein, 1996 Ely Lecture to the
American Economics Association)

*We refer to the tax supplement as a 'Liberty tax' since it frees work-
ers of a significant proportion of the debt that they have been passed
from earlier generations.*
(Advocates of Personal Security Accounts, *Report of the 1994-96
Advisory Council on Social Security*)

*It was one of the clearest promises of the presidential election,
solemnly sworn by both leading candidates and repeated at almost
every rally. Just four days before the election, George W. Bush told
an audience in Saginaw, Michigan, that protecting Social Security
was one of his top priorities. All Social Security taxes were 'only
going to be spent on one thing – what they're meant for – Social
Security,' he said. 'We're not going to let Congress touch them for
any other reason.'*
(R. Wolfe and P. Siegel, 'Social Security Vows Return to Haunt
Bush', *Financial Times*, 29 August 2001)

Suddenly the Social Security lockbox seems so trivial.
(Tim Russert, *ABC News*, 11 September 2001)

In January 2001 the United States acquired a President who had made two awkward promises regarding the country's Social Security programme. Like his Democratic rival, Bush promised not to use the Social Security surplus for any other spending programme. But, unlike his opponent, he also proposed a measure of privatisation.

Bush argued that individuals should be able to divert payroll taxes equivalent to 2 per cent of their income below the payroll tax ceiling – nearing $80,000 at the time of the election – to their own retirement savings account. The payroll tax overall comes in at 12.4 per cent of salary up to the ceiling, split 50–50 between employee and employer. Under the rather sketchy Bush proposal the contribution to the general programme for each employee who opted out would thus be reduced from 12.4 per cent to 10.4 per cent. Naturally this would result in a reduced entitlement, but those who opted out would – Bush claimed – be able to more than compensate for this through the returns that they would achieve from their private investments. The programme's revenues would be reduced but so would its eventual obligations – and anyway today's retirees were assured that, if necessary, the Federal surplus would be used to make up any shortfall in contributions to the programme. Such a shortfall was to be anticipated since higher earners, who contribute more in payroll taxes, would be most likely to opt out. Bush's proposals were not worked out in detail and basic awareness of the difference between this approach and that of the Democratic candidate was, according to a large-scale study, belated and uneven.[1] Gore was opposed to diverting any portion of Social Security contributions to individual accounts, but he did canvass the idea of setting up a new savings vehicle – the Universal Savings Account – which would not only be free of income tax up to $1,000 a year but would also benefit from a matching government contribution; but this arrangement would still leave all employees paying the full payroll tax and thus entitled to Social Security benefits.

Some commentators thought that the new President would not press his privatisation plan, because he had won fewer votes than his opponent and would strive for consensus, or because the slide in the stock market in 2000 and 2001 would make individual accounts unappealing, or, after the 11 September attack in 2001, because he would not wish to jeopardise the new spirit of national unity. And even if Bush went through the motions of recommending legislation to Congress he would get nowhere because no measure of privatisation would be able to command the necessary majorities. But Bush has consistently disappointed those who hoped that he would abandon what was distinctive and partisan in his programme. Evidently the Bush camp has been convinced that the best way to dispel any lingering doubts about his election was to do nothing that would even hint at a lack of legitimacy. The appointment of unabashed conservatives to key positions, the renunciation of the Kyoto accord and of the Anti-Ballistic Missiles treaty, the insistence on sweeping tax cuts and corporate give-aways, were all congruent with this approach. And Bush's success in winning support for his tax cut, including key Democrat defections, suggests that the administration's ability to push controversial measures through Congress should not be underestimated. In May 2001 the President appointed a commission to find out the best way of implementing his pledge to reform Social Security. The commission's terms of reference, composition – its members were all supporters of some species of privatisation – and schedule – it was asked to report before the end of 2001 – made it clear that the new President had every intention of honouring his pledge to work for individual accounts. Notwithstanding the Republican loss control of the Senate, there was reason to believe that, when it judged the moment right, the administration would bring forward its version of Social Security reform. When the President's Commission delivered its report in December 2001, outlining three different ways in which individual accounts could be introduced, it recommended that a year be set aside for debating the best approach, conveniently pushing the issue beyond the November 2002 elections.

The aftermath of 11 September enabled both President and Congress to invoke the national emergency to justify breaking their promise not to raid the Social Security 'lockbox' (i.e. use the surplus revenues on Social Security for other budget items). But this was a pledge that had been foisted on Bush and the Republicans in the first place, while the promise to introduce individual accounts sprang from a strong ideological commitment to the privatisation of Social Security. The subject to be addressed in this chapter is the two- or three-decades-long struggle over the future of the programme, a struggle replete with surprising twists as the advantage has switched from defenders to opponents, and vice versa. My aim will be to illuminate the forces and issues at stake in this still unresolved battle.

Bush inherited a budget surplus and a newly positive and optimistic discourse concerning Social Security. Bill Clinton's State of the Union addresses in 1998 and 1999 had proclaimed the need to use the dramatic improvement in the public finances to 'Save Social Security First'. Following the fiasco of the 1995–98 Republican offensive against 'big government', Clinton's proposal that 62 per cent of the projected overall budget surplus should be devoted to building up the Social Security trust fund was to command bi-partisan support. Conservative Republicans had complained that the payroll tax had been squandered on other programmes and should instead be placed in a 'lockbox'. Clinton adopted the term as part of his opposition to using the surplus to cut taxes. When Bush championed a tax cut he took pains to insist that it would in no way threaten the finances of Social Security. Moreover his reform proposal, by allowing individuals to build up wealth as part of the programme, would actually fortify those finances. In question-begging fashion the commission Bush established was formally entitled 'The President's Commission on Strengthening Social Security'. But, whatever the play on words, all versions of the Bush proposal would deprive the programme's trust fund of a major income stream and would mean that a significant portion of future benefits would be paid on a 'defined contribution' rather than, as at present, 'defined benefit' basis.

A structural feature of Social Security should be noted. There is no other comparable branch of government with its own dedicated source of revenue. The 12.4 per cent payroll tax is available to meet Social Security entitlements, supplemented by whatever is available in the trust fund. Even if some of the Social Security surplus is used to cover other expenditures – as traditionally happened and as was to happen again from September 2001 – then the trust fund still retains special Treasury bonds equal to the amount paid over. When Bush took office the trustees, using assumptions that some felt were too pessimistic, calculated that the proceeds of the payroll tax combined with the trust fund credit should allow benefits to be fully paid up to at least 2036 and perhaps beyond. After that the programme would still have massive revenues even if it was unable fully to meet obligations. If Congress and President concur then this source of financing can be changed, but no positive legislation is required to ensure continuation of the programme as it is. While even the military budget depends on annual appropriations this is not the case with Social Security. In this sense it has some of the qualities of a stand-alone agency like the Post Office, which also has its own sources of finance. In the case of Social Security the integrity of the programme is linked to a public perception that those who pay into this programme of 'social insurance' are acquiring rights and claims which the government is bound to uphold. Today most critics of the programme accept that this is the case, having learnt that open depreciation of pension entitlements is political dynamite. By the same token, if Bush succeeds in something like his projected reform then the programme will have been badly, even fatally, weakened.

The Reagan Revolution Stumbles

A brief review of the recent history of Social Security will show the breadth of support it can attract and the institutional obstacles to changing it, but also the emergence of new sources of vulnerability in the 1990s. In the first chapter it was explained how the programme founded by Roosevelt, and improved under Truman, was embraced by Eisenhower in the 1950s. Subsequently Republicans liked to portray themselves as champions of the senior citizen. In the hackneyed phrase Social Security had become the 'third rail' of American politics. A sizeable majority of voters could anticipate needing and receiving the retirement income Social Security provides. The programme also caters to widows and the disabled who are seen as deserving sections of the poor. Social Security is a universal benefit, something which has made it popular as well as expensive. The initiative for boosting the programme in the 1960s came from Robert Ball, the Social Security Commissioner, with strong support from organised labour. The collapse of the Studebaker pension plan in 1964 and several stock market tremors in the late 1960s helped to emphasise that other forms of saving were unreliable. Wilbur Mills, a New Deal Democrat who was Chair of the House Ways and Means Committee, helped to knit together support for the programme from a broad constituency. A similar coalition had helped to place Medicare, the programme which furnishes free healthcare to the retired, on the statute book in 1965. However, it was President Richard Nixon who signed into law the 1972 Act which extended Social Security coverage, and raised and indexed benefits. The Congressional majority would probably have been sufficient to override a presidential veto but Nixon claimed to take great satisfaction in approving it, marking the occasion with a special television broadcast. In his address to the nation the President urged his fellow Americans to abandon patronising views of the elderly and recognise their continuing potential as full members of society – Toscanini, he pointed out, was an outstanding conductor well into his eighties. By demonstrating his support for the new dispensation, Nixon hoped to cement a bond between the Republican Party and older voters, as well as to pursue his strategy of winning over Southern Democrats. The National Council of Senior Citizens, a body sponsored by the AFL-CIO, and the American Association of Retired Persons (AARP), which was thriving by offering discounted commercial services to seniors, subsequently helped to mobilise older people themselves in support of these programmes.

While broadly popular, Social Security always had its critics. Reformers on both Left and Right have periodically argued that the graduated and universal approach of Social Security was getting in the way of poverty reduction. In 1968 the Brookings Institution published a proposal by three liberal writers advocating a negative income tax as the best way to eradicate poverty. In this view all citizens lacking a means of livelihood would be paid a basic income. Those in employment would pay taxes if their income was above a certain threshold but would receive supplements, or credits, if what they earned was below the threshold. However, the Brookings authors conceded: 'In view of the controversial nature of the negative income tax and the great political appeal of Social Security in its present form, the prospects for total reform in the foreseeable future are dim.'[2]

In 1974 Martin Feldstein, a Harvard economics professor, published an article that argued that the growing Social Security programme was having the unintended effect of lowering the national savings rate.[3] Employees and employers paying into the programme believed themselves to be saving, yet the Federal government did not invest the proceeds but instead paid them out as benefits to those who qualified for Social Security. He estimated that saving was 30–50 per cent lower than it would otherwise be and that the programme represented $2 trillion of unfinanced liabilities in 1971. Feldstein did not challenge Samuelson's classic defence of pay-as-you-go financing though he did describe it as 'much misinterpreted', since there was no room anyway for a fund given Samuelson's assumptions.[4] Feldstein also conceded that the precise extent of the substitution effect was not yet clear. But Feldstein's line of thought helped to explain why the US savings rate was low, with negative consequences for future national economic competitiveness. This article contained no policy conclusion but Feldstein followed it up with another in 1975 in which he argued that the payroll tax should be increased so that its yield was significantly higher than the money expended in benefits, with the result that there would be a growing trust fund. The growth of the trust fund would increase national savings. Moreover, he urged that the trust fund should be invested in mortgages and corporate bonds as well as government securities. As a result, 'the Social Security system would accumulate its own reserves, which would offset the reduction in private capital accumulation'.[5] Feldstein's analysis and proposal were difficult to pigeon-hole in terms of

Left and Right. While his analytic points were uncomfortable for defenders of the programme, his proposed remedy – including both a tax hike and the creation of a huge publicly controlled fund – was uncongenial to its critics.

The free market Right regrouped in the 1970s with help from business people who resented the power of public agencies and trade unions. The Business Roundtable, the American Enterprise Institute, the Heritage Foundation and the Cato Institute began to question the size and workings of public services and income maintenance programmes. The Nobel Prize awarded to Friedrich von Hayek saluted an author who had always questioned the postwar Keynesian–welfare state consensus. Milton Friedman also carried the torch for unalloyed capitalism and questioned the basic principles of the Social Security programme. And so far as the broad public was concerned, raging inflation, stagnant output and increasing unemployment showed that the good times were coming to an end. This was the backdrop to the rise of Ronald Reagan and Margaret Thatcher and their efforts to cut back state provision and encourage self-reliance.

The right-wing think tanks were quite prepared to challenge the third rail and argue that individual insurance would do the job better, without an expensive and intrusive bureaucracy. As Governor of California Reagan had already expressed scepticism concerning Social Security and in 1978 California's voters endorsed Proposition 13 setting strict limits on property levies, a notable political success for those who opposed the tax-and-spend state. But while there were signs of a tax payers' revolt and distrust of conventional politicians, Social Security was still seen as a programme that was closer to the citizen and in a way above politics. Cutting welfare programmes for the poor was a different matter from axing Social Security which paid benefits – benefits earned by contributions – at almost the same rates to everyone, whatever their other assets or income. And while privatisation might later prove a godsend where state assets were concerned, since even selling them off cheaply raised money, the 'privatisation' of *liabilities* – in the shape of Social Security entitlements – was an altogether more daunting and difficult proposition.

Notwithstanding criticism of public provision, the 1970s also saw a development of the case for Social Security. In 1977 Peter Diamond, who appropriately enough held the Samuelson Chair at MIT, published a keynote paper explaining and upholding the purposes of the programme.[6] In it he argued that in the absence of Social Security there was good reason to suppose that many individuals would not make sufficient provision for old age. He pointed out that from the standpoint of the majority of individuals there were anyway thorny problems in making such provision. Unless they were very wealthy they would need to purchase an annuity to assure their retirement, yet real annuities were difficult, expensive or impossible to obtain. There was also the problem of predicting their working life in a context where they might lose their job and have difficulty finding another. In a compulsory and universal scheme all these problems were addressed. Though the finer points of the article could only really be grasped by experts, it furnished a resource for those who defended the programme. It did not directly address the Feldstein critique but it did bring forward evidence to suggest that in the absence of the programme many poorer citizens would not make sufficient savings.

When Reagan was elected to the presidency in 1980 Social Security faced an immediate and severe funding problem. The programme faced a shortfall in 1983 and the growth in entitlements under the programme was running far ahead of the trust fund's ability to meet them. In 2000 there was a surplus in the trust fund and even pessimistic projections did not claim that there would be an actual shortfall for decades. Reagan's attempt to reform Social Security set back the cause of privatisation by two decades and so its lessons are sure to be mulled over by the Bush White House before any action is taken. Moreover, this episode revealed the political resilience of the programme and the pressure to find ways to continue rather than scrap it. The much improved position of the trust fund in 2000 compared with 1980 reflects the measures to which Reagan was driven in 1983, after the failure of a radical attempt to cut back the programme in 1981–82. Income to the fund has risen both because the 1983 reforms raised the payroll tax and because a rise in employment levels has increased the number of contributors. The reform did cut some benefits, but not in the short run.

The raising of contribution rates and the protection of immediate benefit levels represented a strategic defeat for Reagan's supply-side strategy, as David Stockman, his budget director, insisted at the time. So the question arises of how and why the 'Great Communicator' was defeated at a time when the scheme's finances were tottering and free market economics was poised for a series of increasingly triumphant assaults on collectivism in all its guises.

Ronald Reagan embarked on his presidency determined to see social and welfare entitlements slashed in favour of privatised provision. While he left the details to others, Reagan was clear in 1980 that the United States faced a critical situation at home and abroad requiring a difficult combination of increased military spending, reduced taxation and deep cuts in all civil and welfare programmes. In his acceptance speech to the Republican convention he warned that the country faced 'calamity' if it did not address the 'grave threats' of 'a disintegrating economy' and 'weakened defence'.[7] This was not just the usual politician's rant since the US economy was indeed gripped by double-digit inflation while abroad defeat in Vietnam and humiliation in Iran were compounded by Cuban advances in southern Africa, Soviet intervention in Afghanistan and the victory of the Sandinistas in Nicaragua. A massive increase in military expenditure would put great strain on the Soviet Union if, with its much weaker economy, it sought to compete. And such expenditure might help to lift the US economy out of stagflation – so long as it was combined with ruthless pruning of civilian expenditures. The Federal Reserve chairman, Paul Volcker, had already begun a monetarist squeeze which would depress the private sector; the remaining task was to cut back civilian public expenditure so that there would be scope for private sector investment and growth.

Reagan's budget director was appointed in full knowledge of the fact that he was a sworn enemy of entitlement programmes of all sorts. Stockman had made his name as a Republican Congressman by his relentless opposition to big government and a grasp of free market economics acquired from a study of Friedrich von Hayek. His standing with Republicans in Congress made him seem a shrewd pick despite his youth (he was only thirty-four), and his prestige among his fellow Representatives, itself partly derived from ideological fluency and conviction. Stockman's field of postgraduate study had been theology, not economics, and he came to Hayek via an initial interest in Marxism and the Russian revolution. But even if Stockman had lacked the credentials of a free market zealot, the need to contain inflation and cut taxes while financing a military build-up would have forced any Reagan-nominated budget director to question the level of public outlays on all civilian programmes, including Social Security.

Stockman writes:

> I wanted the President and his advisers to know from the start that we would be working toward a huge spending cut total, at least by all prior standards. Raging political controversies and allegations that millions of people would be impacted or 'hurt' had to be expected. The Reagan economic policy could not be a simple matter of 'limiting the rate of increase of public spending'. . . . It amounted to a substantial retraction of welfare state benefits that people had come to feel 'entitled' to receive. I was relieved to find almost no resistance to my proposals on the part of the President and his advisers, even after I emphasised that these cuts would cause dramatic

legislative battles. Reagan paid close attention to the discussions. . . . Reagan's body of knowledge is primarily impressionistic: he registers anecdotes rather than concepts. I soon learned that it made less sense to tell him that you were eligible for a thirty-five cents a meal lunch subsidy if your income was above 130 percent of the poverty line than to tell him, 'The kids of Cabinet officers qualify'. He was not surprised by these revelations: they conformed to his a priori understanding of what outrages the federal government was capable of perpetrating . . . Reagan never flinched. Soon we reached the point where he would respond to one of my explanations with 'No question about it. It has to be done'.[8]

The inevitability of the assault on Social Security and related programmes for the elderly stemmed from their size. Stockman began his budget-making by stripping out or down programmes for the poor but he soon discovered the limitations of this exercise:

No single issue was as critical to the success of the Reagan Revolution as Social Security reform. Spending on that program alone consumed nearly $200 billion per year, just under one third of the entire domestic budget. . . . It was time to deal with the basic architecture of the Reagan Revolution, not just details, so a frontal assault on the very inner fortress of the American welfare state – the giant Social Security system, on which one seventh of the nation's populace depended for its well-being – was in order. Social Security had been born during the New Deal as a minimum, state-insured retirement pension. That idea was noble. But over the decades the system had evolved into a capricious hybrid of out-and-out welfare benefits and earned pension annuities, which were hopelessly tangled together and disguised under the fig-leaf of social insurance. . . . The problem with all this closet socialism was that it tempted politicians with something close to original sin. Unearned benefits severed the exacting actuarial linkage between what you put in and what you got out of it. Once the linkage was gone the politicians were off to the races, adding promise after promise of unearned benefits to those who retired by mortgaging the incomes of workers who were not yet born. By 1980 Social Security had become one giant Ponzi scheme.[9]

But Stockman soon discovered that even fellow Republicans did not see things this way. Thus Dick Schweiker, Secretary of Health and Human Services, proved resistant: 'Schweiker acquired a little right wing gloss by coming out against gun control and abortion; but when it came to the welfare state he hadn't really changed his spots at all. As with all quasi-conservative politicians, he accepted all the welfare state's premises, merely trying to pinch a few pennies from the resulting costs when the opportunity arose.'[10] Another formidable obstacle was the bureaucracy:

Schweiker and his people came up with forty options presented in monkish
texts that were so dense and unreadable that neither Meese nor any of the
other White House staff who were just now focusing on the nitty gritty of
Social Security had the faintest idea what the real issues were. You had to
learn a whole new language even to speak about the Social Security behe-
moth: PIAs (Primary Insurance Amount), AIMEs (Averaged Indexed
Monthly Earnings), bend points, bands, replacement rates, megacaps,
insured status – it went on and on. Which was precisely what the Social
Security priesthood wanted. . . . Frankly I was as happy as a pig in mud. I
had some really sharp people on my OMB staff who gave me crash tutori-
als in the arcana, and by dint of night after night of long homework sessions,
I'd mastered the obscure jargon and logic of the system. . . . By the end of
the week we had reviewed nearly $150 billion worth of potential reforms.
As a matter of highest priority I wanted to get at whittling down the bonus
benefits provided through wage indexing. The Social Security bureaucrats
finally came round, even offering a sneaky, back-door method to accom-
plish what it called 'freezing the bend points'. This step alone would cut
long-run pension costs by five to ten per cent.[11]

Stockman reports that the President liked the plan but that James Baker,
his Chief of Staff, had reservations. Following the announcement of the
planned cuts on 12 May 1981, 'the reaction hit with gale force'.
Congressman Claude ('Red') Pepper, an eighty-year-old 'folk hero of the
liberal and radical senior activists groups', declared the plan 'cruel and
insidious'. 'House Speaker O'Neill . . . roared that the package was "despi-
cable" and a "rotten thing to do". Organised labour had the usual
denunciations. So did Save Our Security, an umbrella organisation of
senior citizen and labour organizations dedicated to forestalling so much as
a penny of cuts in Social Security.' As opposition to the plan spread like
wild fire the White House staff sought to distance the President from it.
For Stockman the greatest blow was criticism in the Senate from his erst-
while mentor, Daniel Patrick Moynihan.[12] Eventually the Senate passed a
motion by ninety-six to zero rejecting any proposal that 'precipitously
and unfairly penalises early retirees' or that advocated reductions in benefits other than those designed to preserve the integrity of the system.[13]

In order to retrieve the situation a bi-partisan commission under Alan
Greenspan, with equal numbers of members nominated by President,
Senate and House, was charged with coming up with proposals to guar-
antee the future of Social Security. The presence on this commission of
Claude Pepper, the Florida Democrat, and of Robert Ball, head of the
Social Security Administration in 1962–73 and architect of the 1971–72
extensions, was proof that a quite new approach was to be adopted. The

commission eventually proposed a small increase in contributions (the payroll tax), the raising of the age of retirement to sixty-seven, to begin in 2003 and to be completed so as to apply to the baby-boomers, who are due to start retiring in 2007. One-half of Social Security benefit payments were to be taxable and Federal employees were to be brought within Social Security arrangements for the first time. The proposals of the commission, published in January 1983, occupied only twenty-eight pages. Legislation along these lines was speedily endorsed by Congress and President.[14] One clear result of the new legislation was a commitment to building the surplus in the Social Security Trust Fund, just as Martin Feldstein had urged in 1975; indeed, Feldstein had argued that it would be well to raise contribution rates paid by the baby-boomers, so that the programme would begin to accumulate the reserves that it would need when they retired. In 1982–84 Feldstein was brought in as the chairman of the President's Council of Economic Advisers.

A survey of the Reagan presidency observes: 'The clearest domestic winners during the Reagan era, as in earlier decades, were the elderly. In fact, the growth in pensions and medical insurance since 1965 has been so great that one cannot understand the forces shaping federal fiscal policy without first coming to terms with this basic fact.'[15] There is exaggeration in this judgement if the term 'winners' is broadly construed. Obviously, the real winners during the Reagan years were corporate executives, real estate speculators, weapons producers, junk bond kings and the like. But among those in receipt of public entitlements, the retirees were indeed more successful at defending themselves than any other group. A modification in the procedures for indexing the old age pension slightly reduced entitlements but during a period when average earnings stagnated those dependent on Social Security saw no worsening, and even some improvement, in their relative position.

David Stockman himself had been concerned at the gap between a political rhetoric which dwelt on the need to root out fraud, waste and bureaucracy and the reality that the time had come to dismantle welfare, including the welfare component of Social Security – its 'out-and-out redistributionism'. His package had cut into entitlements linked to disability and early retirement. In response, the many-million ranks of the normally non-political American Association of Retired Persons (AARP) had been roused, as had the coast-to-coast network of the National Retired Teachers Association, which denounced the plan as 'a calamity, a tragedy and a catastrophe'.[16] The fate of Social Security was of concern to every region.

Stockman's own account suggests that the so-called 'Boll Weevils', conservative formerly Democrat Southerners, were particularly allergic to his attack on the programme. Stockman notes the reaction of Republican Congressmen when he explained his package to them:

> No sooner had I finished speaking than Congressman Carrol Campbell of South Carolina lit into me like a junkyard dog. 'You absolutely blind-sided us with this Social Security plan' he seethed. 'My phones are ringing off the hook. I've got thousands of sixty year old textile workers who think it's the end of the world. What the hell am I supposed to tell them?' I was surprised to hear this coming from Campbell. He was an extremely conservative, serious minded, and smart member of the House Ways and Means Committee, who had been one of the original Reagan supporters in the House. He wanted sweeping changes in Social Security every bit as much as I did.[17]

Southern Republicans and party strategists like James Baker were anxious not to alienate the Boll Weevils since this would jeopardise the historic realignment that was bringing the South into the Republican column.[18] At least some of the redistributionism targeted by Stockman favoured recipients in poorer Southern states and was underwritten by contributions from richer states.

The ninety-six to zero Senate vote showed that Social Security's reputation as the 'third rail' of US politics was still secure. Throughout the country there was support for the programme even if there was also concern for its future. John Myles has argued that the survival of the programme during such adverse times stemmed from its breadth and inclusiveness, though he warned that the 1982–83 revision was likely to prove a 'truce', not a victory. In this view there was great merit in the fact that Social Security was a middle-class as well as a working-class programme, since all felt a stake in it. Conceptually he also saw defence of Social Security entitlements as spreading wage remuneration into the years of retirement; in this way the programme appealed to an interest common to all employees.[19]

The Social Security programme rescued in 1983 retained the essential shape imposed on it in 1971–72 and 1977, when an over-generous technical indexing mistake had been fixed.[20] The cost-of-living adjustments (COLAs) were applied to payments but the method of calculating the pension at retirement linked it to earnings. It was this 'wage indexation' that Stockman had sought to uproot. Instead, it survived together with price indexation of benefits to insure the value of Social Security pensions at a time when private pensions were badly eroded by inflation. In the years 1973–91 the public programme contributed two-thirds of the increase in the incomes of the elderly. By contrast, as Theda Skocpol notes: 'Overall, about a fifth of increased family income for the elderly between 1973 and 1991 comes from employment-based pensions.'[21]

Skocpol has also pointed to the social price of the 'politically self-sustaining' features of Social Security. Historically this programme had been anchored in the core sections of the white, male, middle and working classes who consequently feel ownership of the programme. Even with the real improvements introduced in the 1950s, 1960s and 1970s, the remaining gaps in the programme affect women and members of ethnic minorities who have weak contribution records.[22] The 1983 amendments did not rectify these shortcomings and in some ways aggravated them, since the extension of the retiring age to sixty-seven will have an adverse effect on blacks and the poor, who are less likely to reach this age than members of the white middle class. But these are statistical frequencies so that there are still many older African Americans, and older women, with full entitlement, lending substance to the idea that this is a truly national programme, in which all citizens partake.

While the conflicts of the early 1980s proved the hardiness of Social Security the assault mounted by Stockman had a hasty and improvised character. Many of his measures had an immediate and highly visible impact – notably the attempt to cut back early retirement – and it was this that stimulated the outcry against them. In this respect Margaret Thatcher had moved much more cleverly and stealthily in simply removing the earnings link, a measure which would only took effect over several years. If Stockman had largely confined himself to 'freezing the bend points' (a similar measure) he might have been more successful, though the British Prime Minister was, of course, in a stronger institutional position than Reagan, let alone Stockman, since she controlled the legislature.

Impractical Critics

The supply-siders' assault on Social Security had been encouraged by a blast against the US welfare state from the Nobel Prize-winning economist, Milton Friedman, and his wife Rose Friedman, entitled *Free to Choose* (1980). Friedman's earlier work on the economics of the life course had helped to establish his reputation.[23] The Friedmans argued that Social Security comprised a payroll tax and a system of benefits which, taken separately, would be regarded as highly illogical and undesirable. The payroll tax was regressive, and functioned as a tax on employment, while the

benefits gave a bad deal to workers and poorer citizens who tended to die
earlier than those who were better off. 'We find it hard to conceive of a
greater triumph of imaginative packaging than the combination of an
unacceptable tax and an unacceptable benefit program into a Social
Security program that is widely regarded as one of the greatest achievements of the New Deal.'[24] They also argued that a worsening dependency
ratio would impose intolerable strain on pay-as-you-go financing: 'In 1950
seventeen persons were employed for every person receiving benefits; by
1970 only three; by the early twenty first century, if present trends continue, at most two will be.'[25] (The trends did not continue and the ratio in
2001 was still three.) The authors also argue as follows:

> Workers paying taxes today can derive no assurance from trust funds that they
> will receive benefits when they retire. Any assurance derives solely from the
> willingness of future tax-payers to impose taxes on themselves to pay for bene-
> fits that present tax-payers are promising themselves. This one-sided 'compact
> between the generations', foisted on generations that cannot give their consent,
> is a very different thing from a 'trust fund'. It is more like a chain letter.[26]

As knock-about polemic this was okay but it did not address Samuelson's
point that in guaranteeing the future value of money governments are
engaged in an essentially similar enterprise. In *Free to Choose* the Friedmans
expend much space attacking inflation and urging governments to protect
the currency. Yet they insist that a currency has no intrinsic value but serves
as a means of exchange and store of value simply because society, through
the government, legislates that this is the case. As John Myles points out,
critics of programmes like Social Security are really concerned that contributors' claims are too strong, not that they are too weak. The Friedmans
urge that Social Security should be wound up and employees encouraged
to make their own pension arrangements – but they insist that all existing
claims should be honoured. They believed that winding down Social
Security would boost employment, capital formation, the growth rate and
the expansion of private pensions. But they added: 'This is a fine dream,
but unfortunately it has no chance whatever of being enacted at present.'[27]
In some ways the Friedmans were more radical than Stockman, since they
wished to see the entire programme ended rather than simply strip out
those 'welfare' elements not justified by contributions. On the other hand,
they were more aware than Stockman of the large-scale educational job still
to be done, seeing their book as a contribution to this; it was released as a
mass-market paperback and boosted by a TV series featuring the authors.

A more detailed programme for dismantling Social Security was
published in 1980 by Peter Ferrara, a young lawyer and economic researcher

attached to the Cato Institute. After a lengthy critique of the programme, it addressed the critical 'transition' problem. However attractive it might be to live in a world where pension provision was wholly privatised, it was difficult to move in that direction when encumbered with the entitlements already built up under the pay-as-you-go system. The payroll tax was needed simply to pay current benefits. Unless it was sharply increased, a measure scarcely appealing to the neo-conservative, there would be nothing left over to fund future private provision. A way had to be found for employees both to save up for their own future pensions and to finance payments to those who had retired or would do so with a significant record of contributions. Ferrara was convinced that once a privatised system was in place it would yield a much better rate of return to savers than did the Social Security programme. So, he thought, it should be possible to capture these anticipated financial advantages and use them to defray the costs of transition. Thus a cut-off age could be set – say, at forty years old – above which some continuing entitlement would be recognised. But those below the age of forty would lose all claim on the system and would instead be urged or required to take out tax-favoured private pension plans. They would supposedly be compensated and consoled for their loss of entitlement in the public programme by the prospect of better returns from the private pension scheme. A different variant of this philosophy was offered also to old employees:

> A different set of rules would apply for those between the cut-off age, estimated at forty, and age sixty. These individuals could not accumulate as much as they have been promised in Social Security benefits if they started saving and investing in the private sector at this late age. Those in this age group would therefore be given Social Security bonds that reach maturity at retirement. At maturity these bonds will equal what these individuals are currently promised in benefits under Social Security minus what they would get in the private sector if they now began saving and investing what they would otherwise pay in Social Security taxes. The individual would then be required, starting now, to save a percentage of their income each year equal to the full amount they would have paid in Social Security taxes if the current programme had continued.[28]

In this case the value of the contributor's existing Social Security entitlement is deflated (rather than simply cancelled out) by the anticipated future advantage of investing in the stock market. In both cases the line of argument requires huge numbers of people to countenance the effective liquidation of entitlements which they had already earned. It demands implicit faith in the stock market. And it grates on the old notion that a bird in the hand is worth two in the bush. The detail of the scheme is also odd for a self-described libertarian, based as it is on the state-enforced revision of entitlements followed by a requirement 'to choose alternatives from a list of low-risk, government approved [investment] options'.[29] But whether libertarian or not, these proposals faced further difficulties. They would be difficult to sell to those directly involved – the bulk of the voters – but even if this hurdle was surmounted they would not fully solve the transition problem anyway since they concentrate only on reducing the entitlement of those of working age. It would still be necessary to find a way to pay existing beneficiaries. Ferrara reminds the reader of the consoling thought that the problem will not persist since '[e]ventually all those who were sixty or over when the reform was instituted will die'. But Ferrara concedes that financing the remaining budget gap will require taking the axe to other public programmes, most of which were, in his view, unnecessary or over-funded anyway. Ferrara's attempt to solve the transition question really ends up by proving how intractable it is – in subsequent editions of the book refinements and variants have appeared in an effort to make the whole prospect of privatisation appear more convincing and feasible. But at the time the book had little impact since it appeared to fully share the provocative features that ensured Stockman's defeat. In the years 1981–83 Ferrara worked as an aide to the Reagan administration and the OMB director may have been aware of his ideas but, if so, to little avail.

The prestige of Social Security required there to be experts capable of proving that the programme was economically sound and socially desirable. The detailed arguments might not be understood by the broad public, or even by many opinion-formers, but it remained helpful that there was a body of expert opinion supportive of the principles of Social Security. The much-cited articles of Samuelson and Diamond, for example, furnished a reassuring background to the work of the actuaries and economists attached to the Social Security Administration, and to other branches of government, when they came to assess the programme's viability. The technical revision of 1977 and the amendments of 1983 were even more important because they enabled the SSA trustees and advisers to project a growing trust fund. Opinion polls had shown not declining support but declining confidence in the programme from the mid-1970s.[30] Over four-fifths of those interviewed expressed support for the principles of the programme but by the early 1980s half or more believed that they would not be realised. The fact that alarming projections could be made without authoritative contradiction will have contributed to this public mood. It had created conditions in which critics of the programme could make play with the 'chain letter' or Ponzi scheme charge. With the adoption of measures to raise revenues, public confidence in the future of the programme began to recover. In 1983 the trustees were able to project a trust fund rising to $20 trillion in 2045 and were satisfied with the programme's ability to cover its liabilities until 2062.[31]

In 1982 the National Bureau of Economic Research (NBER) sponsored a seminar on the financing of pensions and social security which suggested that a number of leading economists and pension experts still supported the need for a public programme for retirement. Robert C. Merton, using Diamond's article as a framework, found other reasons for believing Social Security to be an efficient way of tackling risk, and concluded with a sketch of a system of generational exchange in which the education of the young was supported by consumption taxes (paid disproportionately by the old) and in which retirement expenses are met from a payroll tax (paid disproportionately by younger workers). Martin Feldstein delivered a paper arguing that the wage indexation of Social Security compensated for the generally non-indexed character of private pensions. The broadly positive tone of the papers concerning Social Security may, in this case, have reflected the dramatic political events of the months preceding the seminar (it took place in March 1982, ten months after the unanimous Senate vote). It also reflected the fact that the private approach to pension provision faced a number of difficulties resulting from the weakness of stock market performance over the previous decade or more and the impact of the early 1980s recession on corporate pension funds.[32] Feldstein elsewhere reiterated his critique of Social Security's negative impact on the savings level. But, in a line of thought which developed Diamond's 1977 article, the extent of that impact was also questioned on empirical grounds by Henry Aaron of the Brookings Institution in another 1982 study.[33]

Public confidence in the future of the programme recovered in the early and mid-1980s but did not regain the very high levels of the early 1970s. That an attempt had been made drastically to reduce entitlements may have left a nagging doubt, despite its comprehensive defeat. And the Friedmans' critique reached quite a broad audience. But probably of more importance was the perception that something was still very much amiss with public finances as the Federal government ran up huge deficits and a wide trade deficit also developed. Price inflation was reined back by the Federal Reserve Bank's severe monetarist policies. This brought on a recession. Unemployment rose from 5 per cent in the late 1970s to over 7 per cent in the 1980s, leading to a jump in unemployment benefit payments. Notwithstanding the cutting of many programmes other than Social Security, public outlays on unemployment benefit, Medicare, Medicaid and housing all rose considerably between 1980 and 1983.[34] Henceforth the cost of Social Security payments would be more than covered by contributions, so that the trust fund steadily built up to $226 billion by the end of 1990. Nevertheless, Social Security could still be seen as a huge problem. It was argued by some that because the programme's finances were presented together with the Federal budget, the Social Security surplus was being used by legislators and bureaucrats to offset deficits on other programmes. And despite the growing size of the surplus, the pay-as-you-go element in its financing meant that the programme could always be found wanting if its existing surplus was measured against the future claims of those now living, or even just accrued entitlements. The surplus rose partly in response to economic recovery in the mid-1980s and partly in response to the growing contributions of the famous 'baby-boomers'. But when projections were made, less favourable demographic and economic possibilities could be conjured up.

Although the stock market recovered in the 1980s, the dynamism of the economy did not. Real GDP growth had been 4.8 per cent a year in the Kennedy–Johnson years (1961–68) and 3.5 per cent in the Carter years (1977–80) but fell back to only 2.9 per cent in the Reagan–Bush years (1981–92), or in per capita terms to only just over 1 per cent a year.[35] Social Security forecasts are very sensitive to the anticipated level of real earnings which in turn are usually based simply on assuming that the experience of the previous decade or so will be maintained for the next three-quarters of a century. In the Reagan–Bush years earnings rose very slowly, with an increasing proportion of national income going to owners of stocks, bonds and real estate. The bargaining power of employees was weakened by unemployment, government hostility to organised labour, the growth in the number available for work (the other side of the baby boom), and corporate out-sourcing, both at home and abroad. The pay-roll tax is based on employment incomes, not asset incomes. Once a pattern of slow earnings growth has established itself – as it did in the years 1975–95 – actuaries assessing the future viability of Social Security feel obliged to project it into the future. While there are certainly other factors to be considered (demographic shifts, methodological assumptions, etc.), projected income to the scheme from the payroll tax plays an absolutely crucial role, and in its turn that will reflect overall levels of employment and earnings. By 1992 the trustees' report had brought the programme's 'exhaustion year' forward to 2036, compared with 2062 as envisaged in

1983, notwithstanding the rising trust fund. Greater than expected increases in the longevity of the retired also played a part but the stagnation of employment income made the problem much worse.

The troubled outlook of the public programme could be compared with the rapid rise in 401(k) coverage in the years 1982–95, and generally buoyant stock market conditions. Conservative and neo-conservative opinion portrayed this contrast as a vindication of their past insistence on private savings as a viable alternative to the collectivism of Social Security. And to many of the newly affluent, the individual approach to retirement funding seemed to offer more choice and control. For them, anyway, Social Security offered rather meagre benefits and some could see advantages in simply making their own arrangements, paying less – or nothing – in payroll taxes. But the number of the better-off for whom this would be a major preoccupation was limited – no payroll tax was payable above a line set at roughly twice average earnings, so no one paid more than a few thousand dollars, a bagatelle to the new rich.

The Phoney Generation War

When the Friedmans launched their critique of Social Security they had argued that it was a mechanism whereby the old could exploit the young. This line of thought was developed in two complementary but distinct ways in the 1980s. On the one hand, a contrast could be drawn between comparatively well-off seniors and large numbers of children born into poor families. While Social Security had proved rather successful at preventing poverty in old age, the Federal programmes catering to poor families with children really did suffer from the assault on welfare. This contrast might have been mobilised to argue that the successful programme should be seen as a model for the unsuccessful programmes. But more often it was invoked to show that the improvement in the conditions of the elderly had occurred at the expense of other, more needy recipients.

The second way of pursuing a generational critique was to argue that Social Security failed to ensure equity between generations, in the sense that some cohorts would get a much better 'return' for their contributions than others, depending on their size, and on the economic conjuncture and the maturity of the system at the time they retired. The generations born after the baby-boomers would face steeply rising payroll taxes so that the notoriously self-indulgent boomers could continue to lead the good life – and by the time the successors were themselves old enough to retire the system would have collapsed. In 1984 Senator Durenberger, a Republican representing Minnesota, founded Americans for Generational Equity (AGE) with the declared aim of calling 'into question the prudence, sustainability and fairness of federal old age programmes'. After making quite an impact, this organisation folded in the wake of a financial scandal. The theme of affluent seniors flourishing at the expense of the young was then taken up by the Concord Coalition, a body founded by Reagan's former Commerce Secretary, Peter Peterson.[36]

Around this time the idea of generational accounting was also being introduced to mainstream economics and public administration. It involved taking economic models of income, saving and expenditure as applied to an individual's life-cycle – Franco Modigliani's celebrated 'life-cycle hypothesis' – and applying it to entire generational cohorts. Thus generational accounting would feed into the model the differential size of cohorts, changes in income, saving, birth rates and life expectancy, then match them against different patterns of taxation and expenditure. Government income and expenditure would thus be broken down into what every cohort member would pay in taxes, and receive in benefits, over the course of his or her life, to obtain a residual net tax burden. The approach was embodied in a benchmark text by Auerbach, Gokhale and Kotlikoff in 1991.[37] In 1992–94 it was adopted by the OMB and employed to illustrate points in the President's *Analysis of the Budget*. The device helped to dramatise the need to tackle the ballooning public deficit. Laurence Kotlikoff was based at Boston University and had worked on taxation with Lawrence Summers, the World Bank chief economist who had commissioned *Averting the Old Age Crisis* and who was later to join the administration. At one level generational accounting seemed simply to be a way of bringing out the impact on the individual tax payer of the astronomic numbers involved in public budget projections. Actuaries and public finance economists were bound to find the new models of interest.

The principles of generational accounting might appear straightforward but they posed major methodological problems. Thus the public money spent on education appeared in these exercises simply as an outgoing since for the most part users did not pay for their education. The implication seemed to be that the more money was spent on education the worse off the citizen became. Another conceptual problem arose when the money spent in payroll taxes was compared with cash received in Social Security benefits. The time between payment and receipt had to be adjusted for, the generational accountants believed, by deflating the benefits by a discount rate – say 6 per cent annually – to obtain the discounted present value of future retirement income. But the calculated net tax burden would differ greatly depending on the discount rate chosen. Projected into the future, generational accounting purported to show how tomorrow's workers would stagger under a rising tax burden, eventually reaching 80 or even 90 per cent of income. This bleak scenario received considerable press publicity and bolstered Republican and New Democrat advocacy of lower taxes and moves to shrink entitlement programmes ('end welfare as we know it'). However, Dean Baker and Mark Weisbrot were subsequently to show that the looming tax burden conjured up by 'generational economics' shrinks to manageable proportions if spending on education is treated as a transfer (from parents to children), if the discount rate for future benefits is lowered to 2 or 3 per cent and if runaway cost inflation in the health sector is curbed. And Peter Diamond argued that it would be appropriate to discount using the government interest rate only if this was a cost-based exercise whereas the results aimed at refer to utility not cost.[38] In fact, the results yielded by these generational models were highly sensitive to initial assumptions. But it was to take time for the mysteries of generational accounting to be probed and in the meantime it was used to weakening support for public programmes.

Those who have advocated privatisation, or even abolition, of the Social Security programme have often harped on the fact that the contributors to the scheme were receiving a poor 'rate of return'. This is a somewhat different issue to the rate of return received by the programme for its positive balances, though obviously there is some link between what retirees receive and the health of the programme. However, the return received by contributors refers to the notional rate of interest they have received when they come to draw their pension compared with the contributions they have made over the years. As we have seen, Social Security has graduated contributions according to income. Those who pay more get a somewhat higher pension but the scheme produces some redistribution from high- to low-income earners. This means that the rate of return differs for different income brackets. Nevertheless, this variation is within limits set by the gross return the scheme delivers for the contributions paid into it. In the early decades of Social Security the return was good because retirees were awarded entitlement with much less than a full lifetime of contributions, and because any PAYGO system can pay good pensions if the economy is booming and the numbers making contributions still greatly exceed those on the receiving end. The expanded and indexed entitlements introduced by the 1972 legislation temporarily boosted the 'rate of return' but placed strain on the programme's financial viability, even after amendment of the flawed method of calculating the index in 1977. If the US economy had continued growing the problem would have been manageable but it did not, and longevity continued to rise. The raising of the payroll tax in 1983 and the trimming of benefits reduced the rate of return to those who were going to retire in the twenty-first century. It meant that the long-run rate of return on contributions to the programme was around 2.6 per cent and not the 6 per cent or more that had been delivered in the early decades when retirees had been able to claim benefit without a full 37-year contribution record.

This brings us back to Baker and Weisbrot's caveat concerning the difficulty of projecting many decades ahead. Such projections are based on assumptions about future tax and benefit rates, which reflect assumptions concerning the future of the US economy which may prove wrong. Naturally it is easier to predict outgoings, based on the ageing of the population, than it is to predict revenue, which will reflect economic conditions. Even immigration will have more of an impact on the latter than the former. The large increase in employment in the course of the 1990s, combined with net immigration of about one million persons a year (most of them with many working years ahead of them), tended to belie the predictions of those who argued that Social Security would be doomed once the baby-boomers start to retire around 2010 and that the sooner it was given a decent burial the better. The privatisers tend to argue both that the projected future fiscal burden is intolerable and that future benefits represent a poor rate of return; if people had their own accounts they could both reap a higher rate of return for their contributions and reduce the burden on public finances.

It is, of course, inappropriate to use an individual 'rate of return' spread over a lifetime as a yardstick for a pay-as-you-go programme where the money coming in is immediately paid to qualifying beneficiaries. In his own way Ned Gramlich, an economist who favours partial privatisation and was to chair the 1994–96 Council of Advisers on Social Security, recognised this when he addressed what he saw as misleading evidence taken from opinion polls:

> Support for Social Security . . . is high. I think we can figure out why. The question is asked: 'Do you support Social Security?' We all start thinking about our parents and what they would do without Social Security. Of course we support Social Security. The program provides a lot of social protection. Nobody is questioning those social protections. We all believe in them deeply. So a support position is likely to elicit such an emotional response. But a better way to ask these types of questions would be 'At the margin would you do this, that or the other thing?' If pollsters ask those types of questions, they will not get emotional support. They will get people making marginal calculations.[39]

If those who contribute the payroll tax think of it as paying for their parents' needs then there is no need to calculate a rate of return on a sum of money held for twenty or thirty years. Many contribute little or nothing to their parents in old age and would find it burdensome to do so. This is not simple selfishness but can also reflect the true complexity of the life-cycle; the expense of a parent going into hospital might coincide with the expense of children going to college. To say that such arguments do not apply to those whose parents are dead or rich, or to those who have no children, does not meet the point either, since the programme can be thought of as offering a kind of cross-generational insurance. Someone who has held fire insurance for a decade without being able to claim cannot ask for the money back because the coverage has brought no benefit. Of course individuals could completely reject their ascribed social identity, in which case they can exit, but if they accept the benefits of the social arrangements into which they are born then they should admit some obligation as well. The expenses of childhood and schooling are paid for by our parents and those of their generation. Programmes like Social Security and Medicare should be there for them in their old age when they need it. This is a generational complex to which we owe our existence as individuals and not one which can be calculated away on grounds of individual marginal benefit. It takes place in a continually renewed present that reaffirms social identity and generational bonds. The precise calibration of burdens and benefits can always be negotiated but not the existence of a basic obligation. As Hugh Heclo has put it: 'The essence of the Social Security programme itself, however, is the priority of a common social bond with a common security package for all citizens. Money's worth calculations are not decisive, because they ignore the existing system's social solidarity mission – that it is not a purely cash-and-carry economic transaction but a "social" program.'[40]

There is much to be said for these sentiments. But, of course, they do not sanction any wider claim of the old over the young. Those born into a society have the right and duty to revise its arrangements. Talk of a literal or comprehensive generational compact would be wrong, since the newborn find many choices taken on their behalf. Humans are born prematurely to enable a lengthy period of learning. This 'neoteny' has a price, of which the social cost of education is only the most visible expression. But as they become adults it is up to them to play their part in reshaping these decisions, as members of the social collective, not just as individuals. The individual encounters many arrangements already in place with claims on future output: this is a character of all property claims as

BANKING ON DEATH

well as retirement systems. When addressing the justice or otherwise of burdens placed on different generations, we should bear in mind the observation of the philosopher Brian Barry, adapting John Rawls, to the effect that 'the key to justice is a willingness to claim and be claimed upon in virtue of a given principle. Justice must be "fair from both sides". . . . The point here is that we should think not of a choice made by a particular generation at a single point in time but of a collaboration over many generations in a common scheme of justice.'[41] Such collaboration, or its absence, gives rise to 'just institutions', or their absence, and there is an obligation to 'do one's bit' to sustain 'just institutions', even in the absence of mutual benefit. As I have pointed out, any actually existing generation will have some obligation to its predecessor as well as hopes for its successor. The debate on 'intergenerational justice' among philosophers was triggered by Rawls's conclusion that: 'The just savings principle can be regarded as an understanding between generations to carry their fair share of the burden of realizing and preserving a just society . . . the ethical problem is that of agreeing on a path over time which treats all generations justly during the whole course of a society's history.'[42] The stock market, on the one hand, and Social Security, on the other, represent different institutional solutions to the responsibility for future generations, one based on the inheritance of private property, the other on civic entitlements. Given the capitalist pattern of US society, the former continually generates pressures which tend to erode the latter. Such pressures can be opposed – and philosophers' debates have a contribution to make here – but the starting point will usually have to be attitudes prompted in many minds by the very texture of the dominant social relationships.[43]

The notion developed in the 1980s and 1990s that Social Security was a cruel device, whereby one generation oppressed another, reflected a consumerist and individualist sensibility nourished by the equity culture and the stock market boom. Those who imbibed the prevailing ethos could be induced to feel frustrated that Social Security was cheating them of their 'money's worth'. The individualist assumptions of generational accounting helped to inform the vivid story of the supposed betrayal of 'Generation X' by the baby-boomers elaborated by outfits like Third Millennium and then amplified in the media, with braver souls detecting some unreality in the exercise. The scene is evoked by Tom Frank:

> 'There's something just a little odd about the idea of people in their twenties obsessing over retirement,' journalist Josh Mason has pointed out. 'I have no idea what I'll be doing in 4 years let alone forty.' And yet to read any of the position papers and calls for reform generated in the mid-nineties by Third

Millennium, Generation X's very own self-proclaimed advocacy organisation, this was the issue that young people cared about more than any other. What did Generation X want? The privatisation of Social Security. Third Millennium was ostensibly bi-partisan, of course (any lobbying group intent on doing business must be), but in practice it marched in step with Wall Street PR campaigns, insisting over and over again that Congress somehow require or permit taxpayers to invest their FICA money [payroll tax] in equities.[44]

It was Third Millennium which sponsored the much-cited poll which supposedly found that more young Americans believed in UFOs than that they would ever draw Social Security. They followed up this coup with others showing that the young believed that *General Hospital* – a TV show – would outlive Social Security or that betting on the Super Bowl was safer, and other ready-made morsels for the lazy editor and columnist. As Frank observes:

> after sixty years of direct political assault from the far right it was gen-X sarcasm that blew the first hole in the walls of the New Deal citadel. Irony did what Reagan couldn't – and Wall Street sat up and took notice. Nothing punctured the airy pretensions of the welfare state, the Third Millennium episode seemed to prove, better than the dumb-shot pop-cult language of youth. The hated legacy of FDR was being driven from the field by the moronic chant of *as if*.[45]

This account deftly captures the spirit and idiom of a hip conservatism which aimed to ventriloquise the voice of youth. The staff and directors of the Third Millennium were, after all, 'a cross section of young Wall Street' and allied professions. It received contributions from a mutual fund group and had connections to the pro-privatisation think tanks.[46]

The Third Millennium polls often revealed little more than the natural disinclination of those under thirty to think about pensions, or their inclination heavily to discount pension prospects if they did. Even the famous UFO poll had not, in fact, asked a question directly comparing receiving Social Security to seeing flying saucers, and the correlation was made by Third Millennium.[47] For its survival, Social Security needs the support of a sizeable majority of voters, including those of working age. During the 1980s and the 1990s most polls showed that it held that support, but with strong undercurrents of concern, with majority opposition to a raising of the retirement age.[48] More surprisingly, those on higher incomes were more willing to see benefit cuts for upper-income retirees.[49] Skocpol further notes that, according to survey data, 'American adults between thirty-one and fifty-nine are a bit more likely to support public generosity towards the elderly than the oldsters themselves'.[50]

The Workings of the Social Security Programme

A brief description of the workings of Social Security as the century ended helps to explain why the great majority of Americans still esteemed the programme and remained sceptical of the powerful privatisation lobby. Under its provisions employees were paying 6.2 per cent of their salary up to $72,600, with a matching contribution from their employer. In return they will receive a graduated pension, based on their average annual indexed earnings over thirty-five years, plus substantial disability insurance and insurance benefits for their spouse. In 1998 the average payment received by an individual was $953 a month and a couple received $1,430 a month. Ron Gebhardtsbauer, of the American Academy of Actuaries, describes how contributions and benefits are related:

> if your average earnings are $20,000 per year, you will have almost half (actually 47 per cent) of your earnings replaced by Social Security (or almost $10,000 a year). If your average earnings are $60,000 per year, you will have only one quarter (actually about 27 per cent) of your earnings replaced (or about $16,000). . . . Generally your surviving spouse gets a benefit at least as large as your retirement benefit, even if she (or he) never paid into Social Security. If she (or he) is caring for a child or is disabled, she (or he) can get it at a much earlier age. It could be worth $300,000 for someone with a wife and kids, and would be worth much more than you paid in, if you died when young.[51]

Thus the Social Security system aims to furnish a basic income for retirees, which for the low-paid is above the poverty line and is somewhat better, but not proportionately better, for those who have contributed more. The combination of poverty alleviation, mild redistribution and social insurance has helped to promote its political survival. Every employee contributes, and all contributors and their families can claim benefit, so the programme is not seen as welfare, notwithstanding the element of redistribution. This hybrid character enrages neo-liberal (in US parlance, 'neo-conservative') critics, who would like to see a clear distinction made between (public) welfare programmes and increasingly privatised social insurance. In this view social insurance should be a commercial product and the undoubted redistribution it involves – from the short-lived to the long-lived in some cases or from the lucky to the unlucky in others – should be based on actuarial principles linked to individual calculation, not social solidarity. But public social insurance covers more risks than is possible for commercial providers and does so in ways which avoid the stigma of public charity. The public system gains from the fact that it comes to symbolise and reinforce the sense – and substance – of civic belonging. The public delivery of social insurance is cheap and efficient because it is easily combined with other administrative functions – payroll on the one hand and maintenance of a citizen register on the other. In the US case Social Security costs are around $16 per person (workers and beneficiaries) annually, against mean taxable earnings of $23,000 in 1997.[52] Those who propose commercially delivered individual accounts find it difficult to match anything like this figure. Thus Estelle James notes that recording and collection expenses alone on a mutual fund account worth $25,000 typically come in around $30 annually, out of a total cost of $463 if fees for money management, audit and brokerage fees are included.[53]

Once citizens have built up entitlements in such a system they will be inclined to come to its defence, which helps to explain public support running at over 90 per cent of those polled. It might be thought that higher-paid employees would be restive because they are being obliged to pay for protection that they are unlikely to need. Such people may be a little less committed but can still find reasons to support the programme. In an uncertain world they or their dependants might just possibly be in need of the benefits offered one day. They or their dependants will anyway receive back what they pay in, even if the 'rate of return' is low or negligible. Though some Social Security receipts are taxable they are not otherwise means-tested so those with a good private pension will still receive a useful Social Security cheque once they retire – and if a problem arises with their pension plan then that cheque will be even more welcome. The more employees earn above the payroll tax limit ($72,600 in 1998) the less they pay proportionately into the system, so that for the rich the contributions are simply small change. Last but not least, contributors may feel that this is a programme which benefits their fellow citizens.

Neo-conservative critics like to complain of the regressive features of Social Security and it is true that workers who do not go to college may contribute for longer, and yet probably die earlier, than non-manual workers. But the redistributive features of Social Security could be improved if the taxable limit was raised or even abolished. They would also be promoted if the low-paid had a credit to cover all or part of their payroll tax. As it is, redistribution is enhanced by the fact that between 50 and 85 per cent of the pension is included in taxable income. The money clawed back in this way goes to the Social Security Trust Fund. Redistribution could also be enhanced by making all receipts subject to taxation. It is estimated that Social Security raises eleven million recipients above the poverty line, and improves the standard of living of a further 33 million others; but gaps in coverage mean that about a tenth of all the elderly, many of them women, remain below the poverty line; Supplementary Security Income is paid to 6.5 million old or disabled people but its coverage is patchy and perhaps three or four million who qualify do not apply for it, perhaps because they see it as 'welfare'. Altogether 44 million persons were in receipt of OASDI (Old Age, Survivors and Disabled Insurance) benefit in December 1998, of whom 27.7 million were retired workers and 5.2 million widows or widowers, compared with 4.7 million disabled workers, 3.8 million children and 3.1 million spouses. The retired workers and their surviving spouses received 81 per cent of all benefits distributed.

The Social Security OASDI furnishes 43 per cent of the income of all those over sixty-five, with private pension and annuities supplying 19 per cent, and income from assets 18 per cent and from employment earnings 18 per cent. But these figures are skewed by the rich and those still earning. Michael Graetz and Jerry Mashaw point out that OASDI furnishes over 60 per cent of the income of those in the poorer 60 per cent of the population, and is the largest source of income for all except the top 20 per cent. Just under 40 per cent receive no pension income other than OASDI.[54] Despite its growth since the 1950s the private pension industry still plays a modest role compared to Social Security. Earlier I cited Theda Skocpol who observes that Social Security contributed two-thirds of the increase of the family incomes of older people in the period 1971 to 1991 while the increase due to private pensions was only a fifth.[55]

The comparative success of Social Security should not obscure the fact that the incomes of elderly Americans remain rather modest, exception made of the richest 30 or 40 per cent. Thus in 1996 one-half of all Social Security recipients had total incomes of less than $20,000 a year.[56] The single person whose income record at retirement comes to one-half of average earnings, either because of low pay or absence from formal employment, will receive a Social Security pension only just above the poverty level.

The overall success of Social Security in boosting retirement incomes when compared with private pensions does not, of course, mean that the latter have not significantly contributed to inequality. Nearly all those over sixty-five receive the Social Security pension which is only mildly redistributive. Improved Social Security furnishes a higher platform for all, with some able to add varying amounts of private asset income, or employment income, on top of it. A study of inequalities among the aged by the AARP shows that average income for the over-fifties rose by 17 per cent between 1980 and 1998 but it grew by 28 per cent among the top fifth of incomes and only by 11 per cent among the bottom fifth. Despite 401 (k)s, two-thirds of US households saw no growth in pension wealth between 1983 and 1998. Blacks and Hispanics, with little asset income, were particularly likely to be among the poorer two-fifths, as were women.

> Social Security . . . was never meant to be the main source of retirement income. However it provided 90 per cent or more of total income for 27 per cent of the population aged over 65 in 1998, up from 23 per cent in 1980. . . . Social Security was the sole source of retirement income for 17 per cent of those over age 65. Marcia Greenberger, founder of the National Women's Law Center, said Social Security was particularly important for women and that without it more than half of elderly women would be living in poverty.[57]

Of course, the qualifying requirements still allow poverty among elderly women and minorities but at least it is reduced by the programme.

The Advisory Council and the Clinton Proposals

The Social Security Act requires the Health and Human Resources Secretary to convene an Advisory Council on Social Security (ACSS) periodically to deliver its verdict on the health of the system. In 1994–96 a thirteen-member team met to deliberate on the future of the programme. Their deliberations were bound to be profoundly affected by the 1994 report of the SSA trustees since this charted a dramatic deterioration in the projected viability of the programme stemming from changed economic and demographic conditions. While the trustee report for 1984 had shown the recently amended programme to be in close actuarial balance over a 75-year horizon, the 1994 report showed – as its mid-range projection – a sizeable actuarial deficit equal to 14 per cent of future discounted costs. In 1984 it seemed that the trust fund would build up a surplus of about $3 trillion by the mid-1990s because the baby-boomers would then be flooding the fund with contributions as their earnings grew. But these projections underestimated the growth in longevity among those in receipt of benefit and were based on economic projections that now seemed overly optimistic. The 1994 report foresaw the trust fund peaking at a little over $1 trillion around 2008–16, and then beginning to decline as the baby-boomers retired. But the weight of economic factors, including weaker projections of income and productivity growth, had a larger impact on the eventual projected deficit than demographic changes.

There had been an expansion of employment since 1984 so that the dependency ratio in the mid-1990s was very similar to that in 1970. But the growth of earnings and productivity was at levels far below those of the 1960s and the 1970s. When these lower rates were projected forward over the 75-year period a severe funding problem appeared since the revenue coming into the system was mainly the yield of a payroll tax levied as a proportion of earnings. When the trust fund was in surplus there was also some income from interest, but at a real rate of return of only 2 per cent this made little difference.[58]

Since the Social Security Trust Fund is debarred from going into deficit the only way to fix the expected problem within the existing architecture of the scheme was to cut entitlements or to raise the payroll tax. If the level of entitlements remained the same then the payroll tax would have to rise by between 0.5 per cent and 1 per cent every ten years to keep the programme solvent. A 2 per cent increase in the payroll tax would cover projected outlays up to 2020 – eventually the payroll tax would need to rise to 18 per cent by 2070.[59] Most commentary on the trustees' report insisted on the need for prudence – especially since the figures I have quoted were the mid-range, not worst-case, estimates. And while there is strong support for Social Security there is also opposition to any increase in the payroll tax. It should be borne in mind that this is a levy paid disproportionately by the mass of employees and it is already a huge budget item. In 1997 payroll tax receipts comprised no less than $539.4 billion or 34 per cent of all Federal taxes, compared with income tax receipts supplying 47 per cent and corporate tax receipts of 11.5 per cent. Social Security outgoings were $362 billion, or 22 per cent of the total, larger than defence at $272 billion and interest on the public debt at $244 billion.[60]

These actuarial projections can be looked at in a variety of ways. Dean Baker and Mark Weisbrot point out that the projections still envisaged the scheme being in surplus up to 2030 and that by that time either happier conditions would prevail or, failing this, this government could step in and raise the payroll tax. After all, even the 18 per cent payroll tax envisaged for 2075 would be slightly below the contribution paid by Swedish employees today. They also very reasonably question whether it was sensible to project ahead for seventy-five years the disappointing 1.5 per cent annual growth of productivity achieved in 1974–94.[61] If a better rate was achieved then the forecasters' model would show rising income to the programme. (Productivity growth did in fact rise above 2 per cent in 1995–2000, only to falter in 2001.) While there was substance to these criticisms, the partisans of privatisation had gained an important advantage when the actuarial projects were published. Moreover, if escalating Medicare costs are added to Social Security costs then the financing problem will appear more serious. And for those now in their thirties and forties the health of the system beyond 2030 is likely to be a concern.

The forecasts of the actuaries were bound to be taken seriously by the Advisory Council. It is the Council's job to recommend the steps necessary to avoid the sort of problems signalled by the projections. Simply advising a wait-and-see response is impossible for them. Eventually, three different approaches emerged on the Council. Seven members, led by Robert Ball, the former Social Security Commissioner, and including two prominent trade union representatives (Gerald Shea and Gloria Johnson), outlined a 'Maintain Benefits' programme (MB). Five members, including Sylvester Shreiber of Watson Wyatt Worldwide Co. and Carolyn Weaver of the American Enterprise Institute, urged the setting up of personal security accounts (PSA) into which would be paid 5 per cent of the employee's salary, in lieu of part of their employee payroll tax contribution. The remaining two members, one of them being the Council's chairman, Ned Gramlich, advocated supplementary individual accounts (IA) to be added on to a trimmed Social Security programme financed by a continuing 12.4 per cent payroll tax. The sums placed in accounts, whether PSA or IA, were projected to earn a 7 per cent real rate of return, this being an average figure computed for US securities for over a century. Because this rate of return was much better than that hitherto earned by the trust fund, it was claimed that these approaches, plus some benefit trimming, would plug the funding gap. The PSA plan envisaged a supplement to the payroll tax and a public bond to meet the remaining transition costs. While the privatisation features of this scheme were attractive to Republicans, they were not attracted to the proposed new levy of 1.52 per cent of income over seventy-five years notwithstanding an ingenious presentation idea: 'We refer to the tax supplement as a "Liberty Tax" since it frees workers of a significant proportion of the debt they have been passed from older generations.'[62] The IA 'compromise' position seemed close to that of New Democrats and the one the Clinton administration would probably favour. It did require an increase in overall contributions, but also promised a taste of privatisation.[63]

Sheiber and Shoven have pointed out that the 1994–96 Advisory Council was the first to be so badly split and to witness such substantial support for privatising approaches. Quite apart from the context supplied by the input of the trustees and actuaries, the Council included several who were known for their advocacy of individual accounts (Weaver) or were likely to be sympathetic to them. The SSA was far less effective than on previous occasions and the staff director it appointed to help the Council departed for a post with the World Bank prior to the completion of the report. Sheiber and his co-author pay tribute to the assistant chief actuary, Steven Goss, as someone willing to explore new approaches.[64] The Council met against a background of continuing concern at the enormous size of the public deficit. No doubt the administration's 'deficit hawks' had ways of influencing appointments to the Council.

A feature of the report was that all three groups advised the Social Security Trust Fund to acquire stock market equities in order to boost returns. Whereas the MB approach would have the trust fund itself make the investments and reap the returns, the others were advocating that the investments would be made by, or on behalf of, individual contributors and the returns would eventually go to them without passing through the trust fund. By envisaging the placing of funds in the stock market the authors of the various approaches were able to capture a 7 per cent annual rate of return, instead of the 2 per cent accruing to Treasury bonds held by the trust fund. As noted above, the members of the Advisory Council could scarcely challenge the actuaries' and trustees' cautious estimates of projected income from the payroll tax, but they were not similarly constrained when it came to projecting future income from investments in the stock market. A paper delivered to the Council by Barry Bosworth, an economist at the Brookings Institution, made an impression when it argued that the trust fund could both raise the national savings rate (and hence boost growth prospects), and earn a high rate of return, if it invested reserves in the stock market. An earlier study by Alicia Munnell and Nicole Ernsberger had marshalled evidence from Japan, Sweden and Quebec to show that if pre-funding of pensions was separated from government spending the growth of a trust fund would raise saving.[65]

As we have seen, all groups on the Advisory Council counted on an average return to stock market investments of 7 per cent and any significantly lower rate would have upset their calculations. Yet this anticipated rate of return was at odds with the modest overall growth projection – less than 1.5 per cent a year – which underpinned the pessimistic projection of future payroll tax income. Baker and Weisbrot point out that the historic rate of return of 7 per cent a year, on which the projection is based, was achieved when the overall growth rate of the US economy was 3 per cent a year. They argue that if the growth rate of the US economy is less than half its previous rate over the next three-quarters of a century, then it would scarcely be possible for the stock market to maintain its 7 per cent average rate of return. Assuming that the price–earnings ratio of stocks maintained its 1998 level and assuming that the share of wages and profits in national income remained constant, then, they calculate, a 3.5 per cent rate of return on stocks would follow. If the price–earnings ratio dropped from its historically high 1998 level, and/or the share of profits in national income also declined, then the rate of return would be lower still. On the one hand, if something like the historic 3.0 per cent rate of growth was maintained, then projected income from the payroll tax would rise more than enough to assure the future of Social Security. On the other hand, if overall growth is indeed 1.5 per cent over the 75-year period the incomes of US employees will still be rising fast enough to permit them to pay a higher payroll tax and enjoy a rate of take-home pay that will increase to be comfortably above today's remuneration. These authors, who are sceptical of 75-year projections, believe that a fluctuating overall growth pattern is most likely and that the excessive stock values of the late 1990s will lead to a strong correction reducing real returns in the coming period. Their conclusion is that the 7 per cent projection is both inconsistent and improbable, and that projecting a financial balance over about three decades should give sufficient time to secure extra income, should it be necessary.[66] The stock market declines of 2000–1 reinforce Baker and Weisbrot's scepticism concerning the 7 per cent rate of return. A more cautious forecast might take into account that the United States enjoyed natural advantages in resources, territory and population over the period 1875–2000 which may gradually diminish in the twenty-first century. Moreover, there will be a need to ensure that rates of growth and productivity are sustainable and not just a statistical illusion generated by failure to take account of the destructive impact of modern technologies and blinkered consumerism. So perhaps it would be wise to plan for real long-term rates of return that are closer to 3.5 per cent than to 7 per cent. The post-bubble rate of return could sink much lower.

The MB supporters were persuaded of the need for the innovation of stock market involvement, albeit with only a limited tranche of assets, since this seemed the only alternative to major cuts in benefit or large tax increases. The MB position did identify some minor economies and favoured the phasing in of a modest increase in the payroll tax. But significant further economies would, in their view, damage the viability and popularity of the system, and immediate increases in the payroll tax were not necessary. So the MB approach concentrated on raising extra cash for the programme by placing a portion of the trust fund in the stock exchange, where it could be projected to earn the agreed 7 per cent real rate of return, helping to make good use of the surplus contributed by the boomers in their remaining working years. Given the uncertainty of the stock market, it is worth emphasising that the MB group did not propose that the returns achieved should in any way affect benefits and entitlements, which would go on being calculated in the same way as before. On this point their approach was very different to that of the PSA and IA groupings who made benefits partially or wholly dependent on stock market performance. In effect, the MB wished to preserve Social Security as a 'defined benefit' type of pension arrangement, in contrast to the so-called 'defined contribution' approach which would characterise the PSA and IA accounts. These defined benefits would remain as before. If the stock market failed to perform as well as expected, then other expedients, including, one assumes, raising the payroll tax, would have to be adopted. Another expedient might be to make benefits taxable at the full rate, with the money thus raised being returned to the Social Security account.

President Clinton chose his State of the Union message in 1998 to highlight the fate of the retirement system and to urge the need to use the improvement in public finances to 'Save Social Security First'. In his 1999 State of the Union address he was more specific, urging that 62 per cent of the budget surplus – some £2,800 billion – should be devoted to Social Security over the next fifteen years. He further proposed that $700 billion of the new trust fund should be invested in the stock market, in order to obtain a higher rate of return. Clinton's repeated attention to Social Security gave it a higher profile than at any time since the crisis of the early 1980s. He did not propose more generous terms for the old age pension and related benefits but he did insist that those benefits should be honoured. Prior to the first address in 1998 such a stance from the President had not been anticipated. The 1994 elections had given a powerful boost to the Republican Right and scepticism about all social programmes. The President repeatedly adjusted to anti-welfare initiatives emanating from this quarter, securing re-election in 1996 by first tempting his opponents to overplay their hand and then accepting much of their programme. But Clinton was eventually to decide that it would be better – perhaps even smarter – to take a different approach to Social Security. In outline, his proposals were to follow those of the Maintain Benefits group – with the commitment of the Federal budget surplus being a flourish of his own.

The proposal to invest a portion of the trust fund in the stock market aroused a storm of objections from the custodians of financial orthodoxy.

Republican Congressional leader Bill Archer responded: 'No, no, a thousand times no. If you thought a government take-over of health-care was bad just wait until government becomes an owner of America's private sector companies.' Alan Greenspan, chairman of the Federal Reserve, weighed in with his own denunciation: 'I do not believe that it is politically feasible to insulate such funds from government direction.'[67] Of course Clinton was at pains to insist that the $700 billion would be invested using the services of the financial industry and that political interference would be categorically ruled out. But if the temptation was there, would it be resisted? A *New York Times* correspondent was worried that the answer was negative: 'The danger is that Congress will meddle, for example, steering funds into environmentally-friendly companies rather than, say, tobacco companies.'[68] Finally, Milton Friedman feared that a reckless president was playing with fire:

> I have often speculated that an ingenious way for a socialist to achieve his objective would be to persuade Congress, in the name of fiscal responsibility, to (1) fully fund obligations under Social Security and (2) invest the accumulated reserves in the capital market by purchasing equity interests in domestic corporations. . . . Suppose the president's proposed policy had been followed in the most extreme form from the outset in 1937, i.e. the whole excess of the Social Security payments . . . had been invested in the stock market. . . . The trust fund at the end of 1997 would have totalled . . . approximately $7 trillion. In that case the Social Security Trust Fund would own more than half domestic corporations! To return to my fantasy, full funding would have long since brought complete socialism.'[69]

There was, of course, still reason to doubt that the proposals of a President under threat of impeachment and in his penultimate year would go anywhere at all, still less in the directions improbably conjured up by his critics. The controversy rumbled on for a few months with Greenspan using Congressional hearings to warn that public sector pension funds did not have a good track record. This allegation provoked a group of public sector funds to commission research into their performance by Keith Ambachtsheer, a pensions consultant. This review discovered that over the years 1994–97 a sample of thirty-four US public sector pension funds 'marginally outperformed' another sample of fifty-one US corporate sector pension funds on a 'cost- and risk-adjusted basis'.[70]

Clinton hoped that his concern to save the most popular social programme in America's history would play well with the public and it did. A review of the period by former White House staffers written in 2001 notes: 'By all accounts, the "Save Social Security First" policy was a brilliant political stroke, at least in the short run.'[71] Clinton's political instinct and polling research had tuned into a widespread preoccupation. A large number of voters wanted to see the future of Social Security guaranteed. The theme allowed Clinton to head off Republican clamour for tax cuts. Republicans could not flatly contradict the thesis that saving Social Security should have priority and with this conceded the surplus could be protected. Clinton urged Congress to enshrine his proposal in law but, in the circumstances, there was no prospect of the Republican majority agreeing. But while the Lewinsky affair shocked voters, the Social Security proposals had a definite impact. With his characteristic guile Clinton combined his Social Security proposals with a retirement-related savings device calculated to make them appear consumer-friendly. This was the universal savings account (inevitably, USA) to which no less than 11–12 per cent of the budget surplus was to be devoted. Under its provisions workers who saved up to $1,000 a year in a USA would have the money matched by the Federal government. This matching approach outbid the usual tax relief by offering a premium too.

Clinton's watchword 'Save Social Security First' gave shape and direction to the half-formed, unstable and possibly contradictory sentiments suggested by the evidence of opinion polls. These polls simultaneously expressed support for Social Security and hostility to tax rises. Clinton's first State of the Union message still left open the possibility of some species of partial privatisation and several commentators still believed that this was the direction towards which the President was heading. The institutes and foundations campaigning for privatisation had conducted a relentless stream of polls, framing questions in ways that foregrounded fears for the future of the programme and invited younger working contributors to consider the advantages to them of exiting the system. Polls sponsored by the Cato Institute and its co-thinkers were able to find majorities of younger working Americans who believed that Social Security would not deliver for them and who seemed willing to lose their entitlement and withdraw from the scheme. There were also majorities against any increase in the payroll tax. Other polls showed continued wide support for Social Security and opposition running at over 90 per cent to benefit cuts.[72] Clinton doubtless had polling sources of his own which further differentiated and nuanced the picture.

It is sometimes thought that opinion polls make it easy for politicians to find out what most voters want and then further their careers by offering it. But this is an oversimplified picture. On many important issues public opinion is complex, contradictory and capable of change. Sometimes politicians use polls to find out how best to sell policies to which they are anyway committed. These are policies to which powerful backers, or party activists, or the elite consensus are already committed. The task of the politician is to find the way to enlist public support for this already agreed agenda.[73] By the mid-1990s Clinton was widely regarded as the slave of his pollsters because of his willingness to sign on to stringent welfare reform. The pollsters had told him that the public wanted welfare payments to be denied to those who would not take jobs, to long-term claimants and to illegal immigrants. As a New Democrat, Clinton had sympathy for these positions anyway but could also see that they would help to steal the clothes of his Republican opponents in the run-up to the 1996 presidential election. So he struck a deal on 'welfare reform' and 'triangulated' his opponents.

The dilemma posed by Social Security was different. There was business backing for privatisation but it was not yet overwhelming. In the absence of an agreed path to privatisation the financial corporations were cautious, fearing that they could be lumbered with a large number of unprofitable small investors. Clinton had pleased this constituency by giving them something they really wanted – a large cut in capital gains tax – and for the time being most were content. Nevertheless there was still a definite ideological and cultural impetus towards privatisation. The extraordinary buoyancy of the stock market was giving added appeal to the idea that the programme's difficulties could be fixed by personal accounts. Prominent economists were coming forward with detailed blueprints. We will shortly consider the scheme drawn up by Martin Feldstein. But since Feldstein inclined to support the Republicans it was also significant that Laurence Kotlikoff of Boston University and Jeffrey Sachs of Harvard produced a partial privatisation plan for Social Security in 1997. These men were closer to Summers and other figures in the administration, and had both served, with Washington's approval, as advisers to the Russian government.[74]

At a conference held at Harvard in June 2001 former staff members of the Clinton administration presented papers explaining that plans for partial privatisation or mandatory private provision had been intensively prepared in 1997–98 but abandoned prior to the State of the Union address in 1999. A newspaper report explained:

> President Clinton and his economic advisors spent 18 months secretly discussing the elements of a plan to add individual accounts to Social Security, but abandoned it when it became clear the president would be impeached . . . Throughout 1998 a working group met once or twice a

week, with the agenda disguised on official schedules, to discuss options and
hash out details of a proposal. The president was briefed every six weeks.[75]

The so-called 'Special Issues' task force was set up by Larry Summers and
Gene Sperling, the chair of the Council of Economic Advisors. While
some of those involved favoured privatisation anyway, there was also the
political objective of devising a reform that could bring together
Republicans and New Democrats. One of the papers, written by three of
the aides involved, makes it clear that this was believed to require mandatory private accounts: 'For example, one option was for workers to
indicate their choice of a private sector fund manager on their 1040 tax
form. The working group's estimates were at the level of detail that it was
determined how many digits an ID number would have to be for each
fund and how many key strokes would therefore be required to enter all
the ID numbers each year.'[76] The team encountered great difficulty in
devising accounts that would have acceptably low operating expenses. By
far the cheapest solution was to allow the full payroll tax to be paid to
Social Security and then to subtract the amount for the individual account,
but this would involve a delay of up to eighteen months since employers
record earnings on a quarterly basis and a fully verified statement of earnings for any year is not available until August of the following year; for all
that time the contributions would not be earning an investment return.
The authors note: 'Deputy Secretary Summers was fond of saying that we
had to guard against the risk of setting up the Post Office when people
were used to dealing with Federal Express.'[77] They also worried that the
amount of government regulation involved in selecting a few officially
approved schemes might lead to political interference in business.

But it was not technical or design questions which eventually doomed
the working party's efforts. In the event Monica Lewinsky sabotaged the
privatisation cause. As the aides explain:

> Toward the end of 1998, as the possibility that the President would be
> impeached came clearly into view, the policy dynamic of the Social Security
> debate changed dramatically and it became clear to the White House that
> this was not the time to take risks on the scale that would be necessary to
> achieve a deal on an issue as contentious as Social Security reform. The
> President decided to follow a strategy of trying to unite the Democrats
> around a plan that would strengthen Social Security by transferring some of
> the budget surpluses to Social Security and investing a portion of the trans-
> ferred funds in equities.[78]

A paper by a different group of Clinton aides further explained that the political situation by no means deterred the White House from courting controversy: 'Put simply, the communications and political staff at the White House were enthusiastic about anything, including Social Security reform, that would divert attention from the scandal.'[79] Clinton evidently decided that it would be better to advocate controversial means for saving Social Security than to arouse the different sort of controversy that would have attended a privatisation bid.

Swathes of Democratic activists had been alienated by Clinton's capitulation over welfare reform but could be counted on to respond warmly to a defence of Social Security. There was still broad public support for the programme, and hostility to benefit cuts, even if significant minorities could be found to support experiments in privatisation, especially versions of privatisation which sounded as if they could be achieved without extra taxes and without any cuts in benefits. The Clinton proposal to place $700 billion over fifteen years on the stock market was adopted despite polling evidence that a majority opposed such a device. It had been supported by the MB group and thus had some legitimacy. By including the projected higher returns from that investment, and adding much of the budget surplus, Clinton was able to avoid the trimming of benefits which the MB group had also proposed. Another advantage of the investment proposal was that it would allow the trust fund to dispose of real assets held independently of the Federal budget. For as long as the trust fund was only allowed to hold government IOUs its independence would be notional. So here Clinton made a wager that his case for allowing the trust fund to invest in the stock market would eventually gain acceptance, notwithstanding doubts expressed to pollsters.

But, even granting Clinton's skill in interpreting public moods, the course on which he was embarked was a break with the tactics of appeasing Republicans with which he was by then so thoroughly identified. The extraordinary crisis which threatened to destroy his presidency made the bolder and more radical course acceptable.

Clinton evidently believed that his 1999 State of the Union message would help him to rally broad support and forestall potentially fatal Democratic defections. Some hostile commentators saw it as congruent with his opportunistic political style anyway. As David Frum put it in the *Weekly Standard* in February 1999:

> Since 1994, Clinton has offered the Democratic party a devilish bargain: Accept and defend policies you hate (welfare reform, the Defense of Marriage Act), condone and excuse crimes (perjury, campaign finance abuses) and I'll deliver you the executive half of government. Again since

1994 Clinton has survived and even thrived by deftly balancing between
Left and Right. He has assuaged the Left by continually proposing bold new
programs – the expansion of Medicare to 55 year olds, a national day-care
program, the reversal of welfare reform, the hooking up to the Internet of
every classroom, and now the socialisation of the means of production via
Social Security. And he has placated the right by dropping every one of
those programs as soon as he proposed it. Clinton makes speeches, Rubin
and Greenspan make policy, the Left gets words, the Right gets deeds; and
everyone is content.[80]

In the circumstances the President's words on Social Security would certainly not lead to legislation. All the same, they could and did help to focus
attention on the programme and puncture the pessimism and fatalism
which surrounded discussion of its future. The debate that followed
Clinton's speech put defenders of the programme on the offensive again for
the first time in many years. The new buoyancy of the public finances
made it possible to argue that general revenues should be used to fix the
programme. By this time the Congressional Budget Office was projecting
a ten-year budget surplus of no less than $5,600 billion. While Clinton had
little or no prospect of securing legislation on Social Security he could
hand the Democratic contender for 2000 an issue whose mobilising and
attractive features could offer some mitigation of the damage caused by the
Lewinsky affair, the hiring out of the Lincoln bedroom and other such
proceedings. Vice-President Gore was portrayed from the outset as a man
who had helped to fine-tune the different elements of the Social Security
package.[81] With adjustment, it was subsequently to feature as a central
plank in his presidential campaign. In this he was assisted by the decision
of Governor George W. Bush to opt for a different approach, tending
towards privatisation. Both the USA and the Bush proposal for individual
accounts invested in the stock market reflected the burgeoning 'equity culture' of a country in the throes of a record bull market, but the
Clinton/Gore package was emphatic on the need to protect the existing
level of public provision.

The Clinton plan withstood the first blast of assaults because it was carefully constructed to pre-empt the privatisers and individualists, while still
retaining the historical and popular Social Security system. The proponents
of Social Security privatisation had dwelt on the looming deficit, the
impossibility of raising taxes and the need for individuals to be able to
invest in the stock market to reap its higher rewards for themselves. The
Clinton plan met the finance gap, and tagged on USAs to give savers subsidised access to the stock market. Over previous decades the surplus on

the Social Security account had been used to offset the Federal budget deficit, making it easy to argue that it was time to prevent this from happening again by putting the surplus in a special fund, the 'lockbox', that would not be used for other programmes.

The Clinton plan, and the response by Gore and Bush, gave further prominence to the debate on Social Security which had been rumbling away since the 1970s or even late 1960s. The US political system has many regrettable features, as the forthcoming election was to show. The way that campaigns are financed stinks to high heaven. Voting levels are very low. Debased infotainment infantilises the public. The first-past-the-post, winner-takes-all system works to exclude significant minorities and to smother programmatic debate – and on occasion, as in 2000, the Electoral College fails even to award the prize to the candidate with most votes. The antique Constitution offers no protection against dumbing down and rampant commercialisation, leaving politics vulnerable to demagogy and big money. And so on. But if de Tocqueville would weep at the fate of democracy in contemporary America he would find something to respect in the debate on Social Security. In Europe the agenda is too often set, on the one hand, by the World Bank and central bankers, and, on the other, by the lobbying of the financial services industry. As we have seen, the leading parties of the Left in Sweden, Britain and Germany have rallied to some version of privatisation almost without public debate, leaving defenders of the public system stranded on the sidelines. It is quite possible that Italy, and even France, will follow suit. But in the United States the debate on the future of Social Security gives a much weightier representation to the non-commercial voice of civil society, with public funding being robustly defended by a series of special institutions and research centres. Perhaps because of its centrality in the political culture of modern America, the debate on Social Security has a depth and quality that are lacking on almost every other issue. This does not mean that there are no taboo topics or excluded hypotheses. Nevertheless, the quality of argument and the extent of civic involvement are often impressive.

Admittedly there have been some difficult passages. At one point it seemed that the personal flaws of the President, and the political flaws of this quasi-monarchical institution, would drown out discussion of the future of the country's largest social programme. On 14 December 1998 a White House conference on the future of Social Security was convened, with advocates and opponents of privatisation, experts from universities and research institutes, foreign specialists, and representatives from senior citizens' organisations, trade unions, social movements, the Quinault

Indian Nation, the Council of La Raza, and a few luminaries from the financial services industry. Because of the Monica Lewinsky scandal, just then reaching its crescendo, the conclave was barely reported. But the proceedings were posted on the web where they were copied by half a dozen sites devoted to the topic, such as National Dialogue and Social Security Network. There were also to be broadcast town meetings and printed collections.[82]

While the White House's motives in mounting its circus were diversionary, the decision to focus on the future of Social Security turned out to be shrewd. At all events, a sustained presidential focus on the programme from January 1998 to the summer of 1999, including the mid-term elections of November 1998, checked the campaign in favour of privatisation and secured bi-partisan acceptance of the view that the anticipated budget surplus should only be used for modest and selected tax cuts and that most of it should be devoted to rescuing Social Security and Medicare. This was a surprising turnaround in a decade that had been drenched in talk about the looming demographic catastrophe and the need to privatise Social Security. Even the Republican contender, Governor Bush, spoke of respecting the 'lockbox' and confined his privatisation proposal to 2 per cent of salary, as already noted (his most serious Republican opponent, John McCain, did not even go this far). Bush's variant of the IA proposal drew on the work of Martin Feldstein as well as the IA and PSA groups on the Advisory Council, and, notwithstanding the lip-service to the 'lockbox', represented a threat to the future integrity of the programme.

Feldstein, Bush and Privatisation

In the mid-1990s Martin Feldstein became a leading advocate of IA-style privatisation and in the run-up to the 2000 election he was an adviser to Bush. Feldstein claimed that the real return that individual accounts could reap on the stock market was higher than had previously been thought. He reached this conclusion by adding in as a return all taxes paid by corporations as well as their dividends and capital gains. Using this approach he argues that the total real return on capital averaged 9.3 per cent annually in the period 1960 to 1994, more than two points higher than the figure adopted by the privatising wing of the Advisory Council.[83] Governments should be willing to forgo those corporate taxes, in this view, because they would have been produced by the new IA regime and because other forms of private pension provision are tax free. In this way the problem of the transition was made a little easier.

Because of the risk and volatility of investing in shares, Feldstein usually advocates a portfolio with 60 per cent shares and 40 per cent bonds for an average return of 5.9 per cent. Jerry Seigel estimates that the real rate of return to shares has been 6.7 per cent between the 1920s and the mid-1990s, while the return to government bonds has varied between 1.7 per cent and 4.8 per cent.[84] The span of years taken for estimating real rates of return can have a big impact on the average. E. Philip Davis calculates that the real rate of return on US equities was only 4.7 per cent a year between 1967 and 1990, a 23-year period running from a strong to a weak stock market, with bad patches in between. On the other hand Davis calculates that over the same period UK equities returned 8.1 per cent, German equities 9.3 per cent, Swedish equities 8.4 per cent and Japanese equities 10.9 per cent.[85] Thus clever investors who pick the right markets might do better – or, of course, worse (Italy posted only a 4.0 per cent return in those years). Two pension fund analysts, Keith Ambachtsheer and Don Ezra, claim an average annual monetary return to US stocks of over 12 per cent between 1920 and 1996, but with an average annual volatility of some 18 per cent, compared with an average annual return of 4.5 per cent from Treasury bonds, with a volatility of only 3.5 per cent.[86] While the method of calculation used to get these precise figures is not clear, the contrasts drawn are often encountered in discussions of asset performance.

A critique of George W. Bush's proposal by several leading pension specialists underlines the meaning of volatility in equity markets:

> between 1927 and 1997, the S&P 500 stock market index declined in eight years by more than 10 per cent. The Japanese stock market fell by more than 50 per cent between 1990 and 1992, and has not recovered since. The Swedish stock market fell by 63.6 per cent (inflation adjusted) between August 1976 and August 1977. The UK stock market fell by 63.3 per cent between November 1973 and November 1974.[87]

Once again, the possibility of even a protracted bad patch is more of a problem for advocates of IAs than for those who want to diversify the holdings in the Social Security trust fund. The latter urge that it is a wise rule of investment to opt for diversification and that the addition of some stocks and shares to a programme still mainly dependent on future employment incomes would conform to this rule.

The prices for stocks in 1999–2000, as this debate raged, were reckoned to be very high, with many trading at multiples of earnings that had never been seen before, and warnings from some economists of heavy downside risks.[88] The 60 per cent drop in the NASDAQ from March 2000 and the 10 per cent drop in the S&P 500 in that year underlined these dangers. But a market crash would not invalidate the argument that over long periods – three or four decades – the rate of return on equities will be higher than the rate of return on government bonds even if the averages are considerably below those postulated by Feldstein. While individuals would be unwise to take the risk upon themselves – especially since it is associated with administrative and transaction costs which will eat away even reasonable returns – tens of millions of individuals can pool their risk through the mechanism of the trust fund. The financing problem faced by the US Social Security programme is that of balancing the books through to 2075 and beyond. This is why the MB group concluded that an investment that gave a higher return over three or four decades than Treasury bonds would be very helpful. Even in the period 1969–90 the return from equities was slightly higher than that for Treasury bonds. Indeed the Treasury bond device has really meant that Social Security contributions have been paying for other programmes.

The critics of the IA approach adopted by Bush concentrated most of their fire on the way that it threatens to ruin the finances of the programme while delivering a very indifferent prospect of a pension to those holding the accounts. Like any PAYGO scheme, Social Security absolutely requires a steady and, if possible, growing stream of contributions to pay out the benefits which it has promised. Diverting some 16 per cent of contributions from all those under fifty-five into some other programme leaves a gaping hole. Benefits for those who have already retired have to be honoured and the weight of the cut falls entirely on those who opt to have an IA. According to a thorough critique of the Bush proposals published by the New Century Fund, if all those eligible acquired an IA then they would see cuts of 25 to 54 per cent of their expected benefit. If their IA did very well they might not suffer any decline in total income, but if the market performed averagely or badly they stand to suffer a serious loss, of between 20 and 38 per cent. Apart from the uncertainties of the market, there is also the heavy cost of customising accounts for over a 100 million employees.[89] It is quite possible that only a half, or less, of those eligible would opt to divert the 2 per cent to an IA. But while this would not improve matters much for those taking the option, it could have a disproportionately negative impact on the economics of the system. Those most likely to opt out are higher earners who receive a lower rate of return from the system; allowing them to do so undermines the redistributive features of Social Security. The New Century authors remind us of these problems when they present the average anticipated retirement income in 2037 under current legislation for three categories of earner. The low earner, paid an average of $14,258 in 2000, will receive $9,618 if single and $14,427 if married; the average earner on $31,685 in 2000 will receive $15,877 if single and $23,816 if married; the high earner on $76,200 will receive $25,433 if single and $38,150 if married. The higher and lower figures represent the extremities of the system and the higher sums are taxable.[90]

The IA proposal represents a threat to the Social Security system when what it needs is an infusion of new resources. The Republicans agreed that all of the budget surplus generated on the Social Security account should be used to extend the viability of the scheme. But circumstances might arise in which it would be possible to abandon the pledge. And individual accounts, as Skocpol notes, would be 'the privatisation camel's nose under the tent'.[91] The attempt to introduce IAs, even if only on a voluntary basis, could do enough damage to Social Security to make privatisation the only option. It would allow the better-paid to exit the system as they sought the best rate of return. In its turn this would destroy the element of redistribution which makes the system work.

The supporters of individual accounts do generally support privatisation, as did five members of the Advisory Council. But privatising a PAYGO system, even one with a trust fund element like Social Security, is a formidably difficult undertaking because of the transition problem – the need simultaneously to build up a fund and to continue to pay out pensions to those who have retired, or will retire as the transition is made. The Social Security programme will be rendered a little less costly by raising the retiring age to sixty-seven as changes agreed in 1983 are phased in, but it is politically impossible as well as dishonourable to deprive retirees of benefits they have been promised.

When Milton and Rose Friedman proposed abolition of Social Security in *Free to Choose* in 1980 their aim was to return to an economy where people made their own decisions and lived out the consequences, with a negative income tax furnishing a safety net. However, as we have seen, they did not advocate repudiating or even trimming entitlements already acquired under the Social Security programme. Retirees would have to be paid what they were owed under current law and workers would have to receive a rebate equivalent to their past contributions; all this would be paid for by cuts in government expenditure, government borrowing and raised taxes. Peter Ferrara of the Cato Institute published revisions and amplifications of his privatisation proposal, all of them involving cutting back on benefits, making cuts in other programmes and, if really necessary, floating a public bond.[92] In his view, the rigours of transition were as nothing compared with the felicity of a privatised system with its multiplication of choice, scope for individual responsibility, stimulus to savings and so forth. While this vision could be contemplated with wistful longing, the perils of transition continued to daunt many otherwise sympathetic to the neo-conservative camp. It could so easily alarm seniors or furnish an excuse for new taxes. Ambitious members of Congress competed with one another to come up with more or less ingenious attempts to devise a credible path to privatisation. But what all these schemes needed was a tightly-costed plan of transition, with detailed computations of revenues and outgoings.

In the Ely lecture to the American Economics Association in 1996, Martin Feldstein returned to the subject of Social Security, this time proposing a path to privatisation based on personal accounts. His eminence within the economics profession, and his ability to mobilise technical resources for tackling the transition question, meant that his adhesion to the privatisation cause was a major boost.[93] He followed up his lecture with a stream of technical papers and newspaper articles. While committed to eventual full privatisation, he was prepared to envisage a partial approach to begin with. The IA scheme proposed by two members of the Advisory Council, and the subsequent Bush proposal, were to reflect the influence of Feldstein's thinking and his solution to the transition problem. However, to begin with, Feldstein, who was keenly aware of the funding deficit and inclined to be severe on those who sought to magic it away, still retained a preference for a modest increase in the payroll tax as the best way to get over the initial hurdle of honouring obligations to retirees and building up the new personal accounts. In a jointly authored paper he showed that if payroll tax was kept at 12.4 per cent and employees were obliged to contribute an *extra* 3 per cent into their own personal retirement account (PRA) deposits, then the combined payroll tax/ PRA contribution could steadily be reduced and the ratio between them altered: by 2050 the PRA contribution would rise to 4.25 per cent and the combined tax and contribution would fall to less than 10 per cent of earnings.[94] This would be made possible because Social Security benefits could be reduced as PRA annuities kicked in. Feldstein allowed for this tax/obligatory contribution to rise for a couple of decades or so to 15.4 per cent because he calculated that funding retiree commitments would anyway require such a rise. However, he and his co-authors also modelled a mixed system that kept the overall 12.4 per cent payroll tax level and added 2.3 per cent for PRA deposits. The approach here was to show that benefit levels ('the benchmark') could be maintained by adding the yield from the 12.4 per cent payroll tax to the yield from the PRAs, under various assumptions concerning the performance of the stock market and wider economy. Although the paper shows that the median level of benefits under this approach would reach the benchmark figure, there was a 10 per cent chance that the combined PAYGO and PRA benefit would be less than 50 per cent of the benchmark. Increasing the PRA savings rate for younger workers would make it possible to reduce but not eliminate the low benefit risk. A major feature of the paper – written during and just after the turbulence of late 1998 – is the attempt to address capital market risk. In order to remove the risk the government in, say, 2050 or 2070 would either have to raise a special tax or have to guarantee benefit payments. The possibility that the existence of a guarantee would prompt individuals to go for riskier, high-return funds, counting on the guarantee to bail them out if things went wrong, is met by the proposal that the guarantee would only cover a 'standard portfolio' of 60 per cent broad-based equities and 40 per cent bonds. The various models allowed only 0.4 per cent of contributions for administrative expenses because the system was to be mandatory and employers were to be required to send contributions to a clearing office which would then forward them to the indicated fund, comprising a choice of passively managed index funds. The assumptions about annuitisation costs also seem optimistic.

As it stood, this scheme proved not to be practical politics because it proposed tax increases and, at least in some versions, benefit reduction. But the whole exercise supposedly showed that inserting personal retirement accounts into the Social Security system could lead to a growing funded and personalised element within it, accompanied, if necessary, by a guarantee to be financed by contributions or contingency taxes. In making their calculations, the authors set considerable store by the positive impact which the new arrangements would have on savings; indeed, they enhanced the viability of their transition models by crediting government with the extra taxes that would flow from corporations as a result of the concomitant stimulus and using this extra revenue to maintain benefit levels. In the aftermath of the Clinton State of the Union message it was impossible to propose cutting the benefit and for most Republicans tax increases were excluded.

For Clinton, the booming budget surplus, and the upward revisions to which it was periodically subject, furnished the answer to the conundrum of how to fix the looming Social Security deficit. But Feldstein had very negative, if also mixed, reactions to the 1999 State of the Union message. In a piece he penned for the *Wall Street Journal* in the immediate aftermath of the speech he declared: 'Although President Clinton's Social Security proposal is terrible in itself and based on a remarkable accounting sham, it also contains and endorses the key building blocks of a very desirable reform – creating individual accounts, using projected surpluses and investing in equities.'[95] Because of the risks of politicisation Feldstein was now completely hostile to any public agency undertaking the investment programme and this feature alone of the Clinton plan would have earned the epithet 'terrible'. But he was also shocked by the accounting 'sham', 'so duplicitous it is hard to believe', of double counting the projected budget surplus. The plan only postponed bankruptcy from 2034 to 2055 by resort to a surreptitious and unhealthy injection of public bonds into the system. The double counting relies on the fact that, according to current US budgetary practice, the Social Security account is consolidated with the rest of the budget.

Under the Clinton plan two tranches of money were injected into the scheme. Feldstein comments:

> The trust fund accumulates the [first] $2.7 trillion of regular Social Security surplus. The same $2.7 trillion is then counted again in the $4.5 trillion [overall budget surplus] the President uses to finance his [second] $2.8 trillion to Social Security. Thus the President raises the Social Security trust fund by $5.5 trillion while spending nearly $2 trillion on other things, all out of a total surplus of $4.5 trillion. This amounts to the biggest and most creative budget sham I've ever seen. If the government gave $2.8 billion to private individuals, it would create $2.8 trillion budget deficits, and the national debt would rise by $2.8 trillion. But since the Social Security Trust Fund is part of government, this transfer of money (and the bonds that are bought with it) does not count as deficit or add to the national debt.

Around the same time Tony Blair, Bill Clinton's fellow pilgrim on the Third Way, was introducing *Partnership in Pensions*, which assured readers that the pensioners were to get 'a package worth £2.5 billion' when actually it referred to an increase of £ 0.75 billion over three years (and much larger claims were made by the British Prime Minister using this methodology concerning health and education). But the difference between these two smoke and mirrors operations was that while Blair exaggerated his plans, Clinton was hoping to do more than he claimed and to ensure that the surplus derived from payroll taxes actually ended up in the Social Security 'lockbox'. This effect could have been achieved by rigorously separating Social Security from the rest of the Federal budget but to have done this would have greatly diminished the size of the projected surplus and thus of Clinton's own achievement in 'balancing the budget'. Clinton was also proposing to raise extra money in the form of a bond and it was this that attracted Feldstein's ire, because it would displace saving. Indeed, from Feldstein's point of view, the rot was going to set in quite soon when the $2.7 trillion which had been genuinely saved up in the trust fund was spent on pensions. Even though this sum represented a genuine subtraction from consumption when it came in, via the payroll tax, when it went out, in retiree pensions, it would be a toll on savings.

Feldstein nevertheless saw some redeeming features:

> Bad as all this is, the Clinton proposal has put on the table with full White House endorsement the key ingredients – using the budget surplus, investing in equities and creating individual accounts – of a desirable plan. . . . The government would continue to collect the 12.4 per cent payroll tax and use those funds to finance traditional social security benefits. The government would also use the budget surplus to finance deposits of 2 per cent of each individual's earnings (up to the Social Security maximum, now $72,000) in a new Personal Retirement Account. . . . The combination of PRA annuities and Social security benefits . . . would exceed the benefits under current law . . . the funds that go into PRAs would be outside the federal budget and therefore wouldn't tempt Congress to spend more money.

So Feldstein's mixed approach could also find a use for the budget surplus and do so without encouraging profligacy. By 31 March, when the positive public reception of the President's plan was more evident, Feldstein was moved to compose an article entitled 'Common Ground on Social Security', which appeared in the *New York Times*. He spelt out his enthusiasm for the USA idea, its only demerit in his view being that it was placed outside the framework of Social Security as a stand-alone device. He hinted that Democrats and Republicans should work for a compromise, with his rearrangement of the positive features of the Clinton plan furnishing the basis.

Around this time, on 14 April, Larry Summers, the Deputy Secretary of the Treasury, and Gene Sperling, the director of the National Economic Council, gave a briefing on the USA scheme. Perhaps there was a feeling that it had been unjustly neglected in all the brouhaha about the fate of the surplus and the wisdom of state agencies investing in the market. Summers urged the importance of secondary pensions:

> There are, unquestionably, holes in our current retirement system. Seventy-three million Americans have no employer provided pension, 50 per cent have no pensions whatever. Only 18 to 20 per cent have IRAs. And our tax

system which does an excellent job for many, many Americans through the
IRAs and the 401(k)s does not provide the kind of incentive that it should
to the families who, because they have lower incomes . . . have the hardest
time saving.[96]

He went on to explain that 66 per cent of the tax spent on retirement
incentives went to the 5 per cent of Americans earning over $100,000 a
year and only 7 per cent of those tax benefits went to those earning under
$50,000 a year. These were, indeed, striking figures but a voluntary USA
programme of $1,000 a year per employee might not redress them to a
great extent unless, perhaps, they could be made mandatory. But neither
Sperling nor Summers proposed that.

Feldstein's campaign for his own mandatory approach to second pensions had continued with a signed three-page piece in *The Economist* on 13
March 1999. One of Feldstein's preoccupations was further explained by
an article entitled 'Closing the $1 Billion-a-Day gap', with its strapline
'More savings needed to cut dependence on foreign funds'.[97] Feldstein is
not an economic nationalist but he believed that the huge inrush of foreign
funds, combined with a low domestic savings rate, was storing up future
instability. In 1999 the United States ran a current account deficit on its
foreign trade of $400 billion, much of it financed by the import of capital
as Japanese and European companies and financial concerns (Daimler,
Vivendi, AXA, Sony) bought up US assets and businesses. This was the
culmination of a decade-long trend. According to Feldstein, foreign ownership of US assets exceeded US ownership of foreign assets by $1.8 trillion
by the end of 1999. Privatisation of a part of Social Security would begin
to raise the domestic savings rate and reduce dependence on this influx.

With the onset of the presidential campaign, and his own appointment
as adviser to Governor Bush, Feldstein somewhat adjusted his interventions. Bush's plan to introduce Pension Plan Accounts with 2 per cent of
the salary destined for payroll tax was similar to, but not identical with,
Feldstein's plan. As we have seen, Feldstein had envisaged the 2–3 per cent
put into individual accounts as a mandatory amount on top of the 12.4 per
cent payroll tax, not as part of it. Moreover, Bush usually implied that his
scheme would be voluntary – it was expanding 'choice'. Feldstein evidently believed that these were reasonable compromises and/or ones that
could be revised in future. But he must have been uneasily aware that if his
own transition scheme only just scraped through, Bush's reform must be
even more vulnerable. When the New Century Fund authors launched
the attack on Bush's scheme cited above, Friedman entered the lists to
defend it. Significantly, he did not question the figures assembled by the

New Century authors. He chose instead to focus on what he saw as their two crucial errors:

> The first correction is to recognise that the Personal Retirement Account raises national saving, leading to a larger capital stock and therefore greater profits. A significant portion of the extra profits would go automatically to the Treasury as higher corporate tax payments. Transferring that extra tax revenue to the Social Security Trust Fund would help to maintain both the level of future benefits and solvency of the trust fund. The second correction is allowing the trust fund to borrow when it does not have enough assets to pay benefits. Although the increase in the baby boomer retirees will cause the trust fund to run out of money under any plan, the infusion of corporate tax revenue and the growing size of the Personal Retirement Account annuities in a Bush plan eventually could buy the trust fund back to a healthy positive balance. The New Century Fund study incorrectly assumes that benefits would be cut sharply when the trust fund runs dry.[98]

The New Century authors probably failed to envisage the trust fund going into deficit since this would actually be illegal under current legislation. If the trust fund did issue bonds, then this would cut into the savings effect on which Feldstein set such great store. Feldstein here assumes that the postulated 'savings boost' of a scheme which does not raise mandatory contribution rates will be strong enough to outweigh other conjunctural factors and lead to even higher rates of growth. On the other hand, newspaper articles on such thorny issues are bound to offer abbreviated reasoning. Feldstein was more effective in attacking Clinton than in defending Bush but the Texas governor's camp gained credibility from the adhesion of the director of the NBER.

While Clinton had begun to rally public opinion to defend Social Security the defenders of the programme needed a ranking big-gun economist to counter Feldstein's stream of articles and papers. Peter Diamond drafted a report attacking privatisation for a panel of experts assembled by the National Academy of Social Insurance. But Diamond was a well-known and long-standing champion of the programme and the panel did not produce a united report.[99] At the White House conference there had been good material defending the need for public provision but also belligerent partisans of privatisation. The Cato Institute fielded a team that included Ferrara, a principal of State Street Global Investors, and José Piñera, the man who, as Pinochet's secretary for labour and social services, had introduced the AFPs. Piñera, delivering a paper entitled 'Chile's Social Security Lesson for the United States', impudently concluded: 'everyone agrees that a system like this [the Chilean system] is much more consistent with American values than a system created by a Prussian Chancellor in the nineteenth century.'[100]

'Ten Myths about Social Security'

The need to fortify the intellectual defence of public pension provision was to be supplied from an unexpected quarter in September 1999. Joseph Stiglitz, then Chief Economist at the World Bank, co-authored a paper entitled 'Rethinking Pension Reform: Ten Myths about Social Security Systems' together with Peter Orszag, a White House policy aide on secondment from the Economics Department at UC Berkeley. Stiglitz, previously based at Stanford, had established himself as a bold and innovative critic of both neo-classical and Austrian economics by showing that the information conveyed by price signals could be very misleading unless the precise context was known. He had been appointed to the World Bank at a time when it was anxious to prove that it no longer subscribed to the simplistic free market notions embodied in structural adjustment programmes. Peter Orszag had made a special study of private and public pension systems. The Orszag/Stiglitz paper was presented to a conference in Washington on 'New Ideas about Old Age Security'. As the authors made clear at the outset, their intention was to challenge myths sowed, wittingly or unwittingly, in the Bank's famous report, *Averting the Old Age Crisis*. That report had not focused to any considerable extent on Social Security in the United States and the US retirement system could not be said to be based on a 'dominant' public pillar. Yet the report had a few glancing criticisms to make of US Social Security, and its authors and sponsors were by no means unaware of the problems of the US scheme. The paper by Orszag and Stiglitz was addressed to what they saw as the errors of a privatisation model which was being indiscriminately recommended to a whole range of countries which might benefit from quite different approaches. It also objected to the tendency in *Averting the Old Age Crisis* to see all the problems of public systems as systemic and all those of private systems as remediable.

The 'ten myths' addressed by the paper are as follows:

1. 'Individual accounts raise national saving.'
2. 'Rates of return are higher under individual accounts.'
3. 'Declining rates of return on pay-as-you-go systems reflect fundamental problems.'
4. 'Investment of public trust funds in equities has no macroeconomic effects.'

5. 'Labor market incentives are better under individual accounts.'
6. 'Defined benefit plans necessarily provide more of an incentive to retire early.'
7. 'Competition ensures low administrative costs under individual accounts.'
8. 'Corrupt and inefficient governments provide a rationale for individual accounts.'
9. 'Bailout policies are worse under public defined benefit plans.'
10. 'Investment of public trust funds is always squandered and mismanaged.'

On its chosen strategic terrain the paper was devastatingly effective, a source of intellectual instruction and even aesthetic pleasure. Most of its shafts of criticism applied as much to Feldstein-type proposals and arguments as they did to *Averting the Old Age Crisis*. Only a few highlights can be signalled here.[101]

The first myth is dear to the hearts of privatisers and involves both assuming that private saving via individual accounts will not be offset by reduced saving in some other form, and neglecting the fact that national savings could be raised by putting the money in a public trust fund. Calling higher national saving 'broad pre-funding' and individual accounts 'narrow pre-funding', Orszag and Stiglitz insist: '*Privatization and broad pre-funding are distinct concepts and privatization is neither necessary nor sufficient for broad pre-funding.*' One way in which higher individual saving might be offset, and thus not lead to 'broad pre-funding', would be if the privatisation programme was financed by government borrowing, as some privatisers argue it should be. On the other hand, if the state decides to pre-fund then this can be done in such a way as to ensure that it is not offset by other expenditure. As an example they point out that 'over the last year, despite the lack of agreement on almost everything else, policy makers in the United States have largely agreed to protect Social Security surpluses from the demands of the rest of the budget – in other words, to ensure broad pre-funding.'

The second myth conflates privatisation of the pension fund with its diversification. While diversification of a fund to include equities should raise rates of return there are much stricter limits to this than is assumed by most privatisers. The costs of administration and transition reduce or cancel out the notional gain from switching from PAYGO to individual accounts. But, using both Samuelson on PAYGO and the theorems of neo-classical economics, Orszag and Stiglitz write:

> World population growth is expected to slow from 1.7 per cent per year in the 1980s and about 1.3 per cent per year currently to 0.8 per cent per year,

on average, between 2010 and 2050. As a result, global labor force growth
is expected to slow, putting downward pressure on the rate of return under
mature pay-as-you-go systems. Assuming productivity growth of 2 per cent
per year, the long run real rate of return on a hypothetical global, mature
pay-as-you-go system would be about 3 per cent a year. In a dynamically
efficient economy without risky assets, the real interest rate must exceed the
growth rate. Therefore in a dynamically efficient economy, individual
accounts – even without diversification – will always appear to offer a higher
rate of return than a pay-as-you-go system.

However, this is deceptive: 'If the economy is dynamically efficient, one
cannot improve the welfare of later generations without making intervening generations worse off . . . *higher returns in the long run can only be obtained
at the expense of reduced consumption and returns for intervening generations.*'

The third myth links to this latter point as well. It is not the PAYGO
principle but the way it was introduced which produces the problem.
Most existing PAYGO systems allowed early retirees to obtain a very good
rate of return but this necessarily reduces the rate of return from the
system for subsequent generations. In so far as privatisers fail to repudiate
already existing obligations, they have the same problem.

In addressing the fourth myth, the authors quote Alan Greenspan to the
effect that if the Social Security trust fund invested in equities it would
produce a situation where other investors would find themselves obliged to
accept lower returns because the price of equities would be raised. The
authors point out that the same objection would apply to private accounts.
They observe: 'proponents of private accounts often hail the diversification
potential of such accounts as a substantial social benefit, yet simultaneously
claim that diversification undertaken through a trust fund would yield no
benefits.' The authors themselves believe that the diversification approach
would be further enhanced by combining investments in equities with
retention of a PAYGO element since the latter is really an investment in
the productivity of future generations: 'partial funding provides access to an
asset – the human capital of the young – that is not normally tradable on
the financial markets'.

The fifth myth arises in connection with arguments advanced by Martin
Feldstein and the personal security account proposal group on the 1994–96
ACSS to the effect that the weak link between contributions and benefits
in a PAYGO system can undermine the incentive to work. The partisans
of individual accounts stress that under their approach there is a direct link
between what employees put in and what they can expect to take out
whereas the payroll tax is just a disincentive. However, Orszag and Stiglitz

argue that: 'We are ultimately interested in welfare not labor supply. It is possible to design structures that accentuate labor market incentives but reduce welfare. To do so would be to confuse means with ends.' They also point out that there is invariably a trade-off between redistribution and incentives. Helping the poorer and less advantaged will always somewhat reduce their incentive to work (or save). Most advocates of pension reform, whether by IAs or simple abolition, still favour some degree of poverty alleviation, via safety nets or negative income taxes. Orszag and Stiglitz cite a paper by Peter Diamond in which he argues:

> economists have raised the issue of the extent to which the payroll tax dis-
> torts the labor market. Suggestions that switching to a defined-contribution
> system will produce large efficiency gains are overblown. . . . Any redistri-
> bution will create some labor market distortion, whether the redistribution
> is located in the benefit formula or in another portion of the retirement
> system.[102]

The authors also refer to ongoing work by Stiglitz which shows that the Social Security entitlement linked to employment acts like a wage sub-sidy which encourages employment by strengthening the 'no shirking' constraint.

The sixth myth is related to the fifth but focuses on the way that a public 'defined benefit' plan amounts to a tax on further work by employ-ees reaching the early retirement age. Once again, Orszag and Stiglitz see a potential conflict between labour supply and welfare. An economic com-pulsion to continue working to the age of sixty-seven applied to all employees, however demanding their work and whatever their physical condition, might boost the availability of labour but would do so at the expense of unacceptable sacrifice by the individual worker. They also point out that employees need protection against productivity shocks which render their particular skills redundant, and that early retirement provisions help to supply this. And even if an existing public system was too generous in this regard, the solution would be to fine-tune the benefits it offers, not necessarily to opt for individual accounts. They point out that Sweden's new pension system provides incentives for delayed claiming of retirement benefits, with these benefits themselves indexed to earnings levels.

The seventh myth relates to claims in an *Economist* article and assumptions used by the Advisory Council on Social Security in 1994–96 to the effect that administrative costs would be kept low by commercial competition. Orszag and Stiglitz point out that such costs have been high in Britain where there is intense commercial competition in financial services. According to the ACSS, a decentralised individual plan approach would be likely to incur added costs of 1 per cent of assets annually and this would consume 20 per cent of the value of the money in the accounts. But in Britain the research of Mamta Muthi, J. Michael Orszag and Peter Orszag has identified even higher costs, which eat up 40–45 per cent of the value of the fund. This work (referred to in chapter 3 above) shows the need to take account of the loss at each stage of the process – the accumulation ratio (covering the costs of opening the account, contributing to the account, managing the account), the alteration ratio (allowance for transfers from one employer, or movement from one fund to another) and the annuitisation ratio (cost of converting the fund into an annuity). Orszag and Stiglitz believe that the costs involved here are not usually those of superprofits, which can be reduced by competition, but those which arise from 'sales and marketing costs, fund management charges, regulatory and compliance costs, record-keeping, and adverse selection effects'. Orszag and Stiglitz do concede that a centralised approach to the provision of individual accounts could help to mitigate some of these problems, citing a paper at the same conference which envisages extensive and intimate government regulation of pension providers. But if this was to be done, 'one may wonder why government interference and governance concerns are less problematic under such a centralised approach than under a public trust fund system'.

The eighth myth relates to the supposedly greater fallibility of government provision than of private provision. But, the authors observe, private providers also need to be supervised by honest and effective public authorities. 'It is difficult to know why a government that is inefficient and corrupt in administering a public benefit would be efficient and honest in regulating a private one.'

The ninth myth holds that if a public system fails then the government will be obliged to step in to save it whereas if a private system fails this will not happen. If this were true, it would also mean that public systems would tend to be more reckless since they could always count on a bail-out. Orszag and Stiglitz doubt that the government could walk away from a disaster affecting basic pension provision, especially if the private providers had received some official encouragement. However, they do concede that in former Communist states the acquisition of privatisation vouchers by pension funds may make a government bail-out necessary should the vouchers prove to be worth less than their market price: 'To be sure the pension reforms are often touted as "deepening of the stock market". Yet they may ultimately merely re-allocate losses from one set of funds [the voucher funds] to another [the pension funds] – and in a potentially regressive fashion.'

The tenth and final myth was that public trust funds would always be squandered and mismanaged. Orszag and Stiglitz reject the argument and evidence adduced by *Averting the Old Age Crisis* on this point, countering that the discussion in that report indicted the performance of some public funds in the developing world without supplying the relevant comparison with the real market rate of return in those countries. Supplying the deficiency, they give data showing that the real market rate of return in most of these countries was also negative, and that in two cases the public fund rate of return was actually better than the market rate.

Turning to the alleged deficiencies of public trust funds in the developed world, they cite work by Alicia Munnell and Annika Sundén which looked at the performance of state and local pension funds in the United States which, they point out, fails to confirm Alan Greenspan's allegation that such funds underperform the market. They cite the following:

> First, economically-targeted investments (ETIs) account for no more than 2.5 per cent of total state and local holdings . . . recent survey data reveal no adverse impact on returns as a result of the current small amount of ETI activity. Second, public plans in only three states have seriously engaged in shareholder activism. . . . The literature suggests that this has had a negligible to positive impact on returns. Third, the only significant divestiture that has occurred was related to companies doing business with South Africa before 1994. . . . Today public plans appear to be performing as well as private plans.[103]

Orszag and Stiglitz conclude by arguing that while underfunding may be a problem in several countries this does not justify the claims made for a second pillar limited to the 'private, non-redistributive, defined contribution pension plan'. While many of their points clearly related to the US debate on individual accounts they conclude by arguing that the 'conventional wisdom' on the need for private defined contribution accounts would be particularly unsuited to countries with weak financial markets and regulatory capacity.

There have been other powerful assaults on the case for privatisation and individual accounts but the paper by Orszag and Stiglitz was in a class of its own.[104] And in addition to demolishing many of the privatisers' arguments, it opened the space to argue for public trust funds as the proper custodians of the people's savings. Some of the arguments they present, not adequately represented in the above summary, make use of neo-classical growth theory. When they argue that there are zero-sum features to pension arrangements in a 'dynamically efficient economy', the defenders of privatisation, committed to view the cumulative effect of

PAYGO and similar public programmes as a drag on dynamic efficiency, might contend that this begs the question. And even those who are utterly opposed to privatisation and IAs could still believe that prevailing pension arrangements, notably the dominant forms of secondary pension, are themselves an obstacle to a dynamically efficient economy. On the other hand, the zero-sum type argument advanced in answer to myths one and two is a salutary caution against imagining that all problems can be conjured away by assumed increases in efficiency. If above-average returns are obtained by one group, then others will receive below-average returns. Above all, general pension plans – and even those of the privatisers have universalising features – have to be able to work for everyone. If all savings for retirement are eventually invested in a mixture of equities and bonds what would be the consequence for the stock market? It is estimated that Bush's 2 per cent plan would mean that only about 4 per cent of all shares were held in approved accounts in twenty years' time. But if this aspect of the programme was a success, then there would soon be pressure to raise these percentages considerably. Those who wish to raise the savings rate would presumably find ways to encourage this. If all of the former payroll tax was devoted to IAs then the time would soon come when a quarter of the stock market would be held by them. To keep costs down it is sometimes suggested that such contributions would be channelled automatically to a limited number of passive, index-style funds. Would this really promote dynamic or any other sort of efficiency?

Privatisation and the New Tax Farmers

The forced savings proposals which are often referred to as privatisation – I have gone along with the custom on occasion above – actually involve a public authority so intrusive and extensive that they would certainly have been bitterly opposed by Hayek and Mises. Indeed, something strange has happened to the rival camps of defenders and opponents of the public programme. Undoubtedly, there are real differences in their approach, but, at the tactical level, they often seem prepared to borrow from the enemy's armoury. Robert Ball, Clinton and Orszag/Stiglitz are all willing to see the Social Security trust fund invest in the stock market. On the other hand, the so-called privatisers are accepting the framework of a publicly mandated system complete with detailed supervision of asset ratios, draw-down mechanisms, charges and much else besides. Feldstein sometimes rejects the term 'privatisation' for this reason: 'Individual accounts do not mean "privatizing" Social Security. The Government would set up the accounts, regulate the investments and guarantee the benefits.'[105] From the standpoint of 'Austrian' economics Feldstein may be almost a socialist but, in truth, the sort of public regulation he proposes would ensure that the financial services industry receives a vast and continuing stream of business. The regulations would be likely to favour larger providers or those with payroll service facilities. The Clinton approach offered less to the financial services industry but some would do well out of those USAs and out of handling the 15 per cent of the trust fund which was to be invested in the stock market. At the December 1998 White House conference Ronald P. O'Hanley, president of Dreyfus International Investors, spoke in cordial tones about the need to shore up Social Security by whatever means were likely to be the most effective.

The Clinton/Gore stance on Social Security was dictated by political necessity. In one sense both were fortunate to be able to construct their position at a time of buoyant public finances since this allowed them to offer something to Wall Street, to the AFL-CIO and to the AARP and the Social Security 'defend benefits' crowd. If it ever came to legislation, the detail would be of the greatest significance and the Secretary to the Treasury would have a critical input. If Gore had won, Larry Summers, the incumbent, was expected to stay at the Treasury Secretary's post. In 2000 Summers allowed Stiglitz to be dropped by the World Bank because of his public criticism of the IMF's role in the Asian crisis. The financial services industry would not have lacked for prominent spokespersons in a Democrat administration. Daniel Gross supplies evidence for what he sees as a marriage between New Democrats and a layer of 'new moneycrat' purveyors of personal finance in the 1990s, with the latter supplying Clinton and Gore with cash contributions of such size that they often put Democrat finances ahead of those of the Republicans.[106] Jon Corzine, formerly the head of Goldman Sachs, ran a hugely expensive campaign which elected him as Democratic Senator for New Jersey. This was, perhaps, emblematic of a new willingness on the part of prominent financiers to enter the public realm, whether as politicians and top functionaries or as patrons of the arts or social commentators. Daniel Gross improbably postulates a distinction between arrogant money and humble money, with Corzine and Warren Buffett in the latter category because of their willingness to encourage others to share in their good fortune. But as he concedes, inequalities multiplied as a by-product of the 'politics of personal finance'. In truth, even the philanthropy of a genuinely enlightened financier like George Soros only highlights the chaotic and predatory character of globalised capitalism.

The AFL-CIO has also shown concern for the workings of the private and occupational pension funds. The unions have favoured making the funds more responsible both to their members and to the general social interest. Individual unions have also sponsored Housing Investment Trusts (HITs) and other Economically Targeted Investments (ETIs). The Heartland Labor–Capital Project has produced a stream of publications and reports assessing the possibilities of using pension funds – 'labor's capital' – as a gigantic lever for imposing new social priorities. But the vast public attention concentrated on the future of Social Security has not yet been drawn to the functioning of the private pension funds (though Enron's collapse may change this).[107] The political economy of these is treated only as a by-product of the Social Security debate. Yet ultimately retirement provision is a field that must be studied as a whole. Much of the employment expansion of the 1990s was concentrated on low-earning jobs, and research shows that low earners are less likely to have a second pension, and are most likely to be afflicted by poverty in old age.[108] The pattern of private accumulation will have far-reaching significance for both public and private pension funds. The trade unions have always supported the extension of funded provision and, in a long-range context, a boost to funding levels will favour labour incomes for a structural reason: because, other things being equal, such a boost will increase the supply of capital relative to labour which in turn will tend to raise labour incomes (return to labour) and to lower asset incomes (returns to capital). So long as their members are in defined benefit public or occupational schemes they will be gainers. From the early 1970s returns to capital grew strongly at the expense of labour's share, so the time has certainly come to redress the balance. This and other aspects of a new trade union strategy for pensions will be considered in the conclusion.

Gore, following Clinton, dropped that element in the plan to save Social Security which envisaged the trust fund taking stakes in US equity. From about July 1999 President and Vice-President adopted a line less likely to antagonise Alan Greenspan. The revised approach would use the budget surplus to pay down the national debt; the resulting savings in interest payments would then be credited to the Social Security account. This revision meant that the plan was no longer vulnerable to the charge of double counting. It also left Gore free to play what he believed to be his trump card – the performance of the US economy – without any embarrassing conflict with the Federal Reserve chairman.[109]

By the time that it became clear that Bush and Gore would be nominated by their parties the stock market had peaked and new technology stocks had begun a steep decline. When Gore attacked Bush's individual account approach he stressed the damage it would do to Social Security but not the rocky state of the stock market. To have drawn attention to the stock market slide would have placed a question mark over the administration's economic record. The fate of Social Security was certainly one of the central issues of the campaign but both major candidates treated it as a question apart from the prospects for stocks and shares. Norman Birnbaum has summarised the campaign in these terms:

> The presidential campaign of 2000 in its initial phases was marked by argument about the scope of public and private solutions to the problem of education, health care and retirement. The obsessive calculatedness and moral woodenness of the two major candidates rendered a conclusion obvious. Each thought it profitable to affirm the positive functions of government. True, Governor Bush suggested partial privatisation of Social Security and evoked previous support for the policy by New Democrats. Vice-President Gore responded as an old Democrat by rejecting the idea as destructive of the universal quality of Social Security, its function as national social insurance. He insisted that Social Security could be protected, best, by using government surplus to pay down the Federal debt. He did not have the imagination to suggest that Social Security funds could be invested in new national projects, for renewing infrastructure or (in education and health) reducing gross inequalities. Gore . . . joined the defense of Social Security to a profession of fiscal caution.[110]

The evidence of exit polls suggests that Gore's prominent defence of the public programme helped him to win the votes of older and – especially – poorer voters. Gore won 51 per cent support among those over sixty, to Bush's 47 per cent, with Nader on 2 per cent. If it can be assumed that the personal morality aspects of the Lewinsky scandal weighed more strongly with older voters, then Gore's gain among this group was significant. In 1996 Clinton won 48 per cent of the over-sixties vote, Dole 44 per cent and Perot 7 per cent. Of course Bush's opt-out idea was pitched at younger male voters and may have attracted some interest. According to the exit polls, Gore gained 48 per cent of the votes of those aged 18–29, Nader 5 per cent and Bush 46 per cent. In 1996 Clinton gained 53 per cent of these younger voters, Dole 34 per cent and Perot 10 per cent. So the Gore/Nader vote represented a slight drop from the Clinton score while the Bush vote represented a slight gain on the Dole/Perot score. Among those aged 30–44 and 45–59 the split was the same, 48 per cent for Gore, 49 per cent for Bush. Since the over-sixties are thought to have a better turnout, then Gore's overall lead can be attributed to his support among older voters. Rather more striking than the age cohort contrasts was Gore's 20-point lead among those earning less than $15,000 a year and his 13-point lead among those earning $15,000 to $29,999, and Bush's 11-point lead among those earning over $100,000, 9-point lead among those earning over $75,000 a year, and 7-point lead among those earning over $50,000. We should bear in mind that the 2 per cent of salary opt-out from the payroll tax becomes financially and psychologically less significant to higher earners, since this tax takes a smaller bite as their income rises above $80,000. On the other hand, Bush's tax cut would mean more to them. By contrast, the workings of Social Security would be important to poorer voters, with many heavily reliant upon it; for them, the tax cut would offer little, except a threat to Social Security and welfare. In a context where politicians seem to have less direct responsibility for the economy, this complex of issues is likely to have had a fairly strong impact on the voters' preferences. There remain the significant polarisations stemming from the rise of the Christian Right – with white Protestants plumping for Bush (by 63 per cent to 34 per cent) and African Americans, Jews and Catholics (though the last of these by only a small 2-point margin) leaning to Gore; the secular vote was split between Gore and Nader, with Gore's white Protestants being the more liberal variety. So far as Social Security is concerned, Bush's stress on self-reliance echoed a traditional radical Puritan theme while his gestures to 'compassionate conservatism' and 'faith-based welfare' may have helped him to win over Catholic votes – Dole's 37 per cent share in 1996 jumped to 47 per cent for Bush.[111]

Bush's early victory in securing a major tax cut showed his capacity to deliver on his programme. By the late summer of 2001 his success on this front looked as if it was undercutting his promise to use Social Security taxes for no other purpose. On 4 September the Senate leader, the Democrat Tom Daschle, demanded reiteration of this undertaking and claimed that he had received it on a visit to the White House. But a presidential aide offered the following gloss: "'Funding projects out of Social Security is something the President said he wanted to avoid doing," said the White House spokesman Ari Fleischer. He noted that the president had vowed to tap Social Security "only in the case of war or recession."'[112] This get-out clause – not very robust when given, because of the poor state of the economy – became even less so with the spectacular terrorist action in New York and Washington on 11 September.

The advent of recession made more problematic the Democratic approach to Social Security finances with its emphasis on 'paying down the debt' and not tampering with the 'lockbox'. The right-wing columnist William Safire complained on 10 September that too many Republicans were also hog-tied by these Clinton-era formulas:

here we are with unemployment rising smartly and consumer and investor confidence falling. . . . By these measures it's safe to say a downturn is upon us – signalling the moment for government to spend more and tax less. Why aren't we doing that? . . . The reason that good Keynesian sense is not prevailing is that Bill Clinton, eager to find a way to avoid tax reduction, spooked the nation with his phony notion of a 'lockbox' on revenues coming in from the payroll tax. It's phony because no such vault exists: no fund containing cash or gold is set aside for future retirees. . . . The only thing in the government 'lockbox' is government paper.[113]

Of course the 'lockbox' idea would have had more substance, and would not have inhibited deficit spending by the Federal government, if Social Security had had its own assets, including stocks and shares, as originally proposed by Clinton. And if the Social Security Administration had acquired a measure of operational autonomy, then it could also have acquired public bonds on better terms.

President and Congress abandoned the 'lockbox' in September 2001. If Bush manages to restore the economy he might be forgiven for dipping into the Social Security trust fund. If he does not, then it will be his entire economic programme, and its reliance on tax cuts and corporate give-aways, that will come under attack. This leaves his second pledge – to introduce individual accounts into Social Security without jeopardising the programme's finances.

The Bush Commission

When the 'President's Commission on Strengthening Social Security' reported in December 2001 it made little impact. This was partly because it was overshadowed by 11 September. But it was also because none of the three alternative methods it outlined succeeded in fully restoring the programme to fiscal balance over a 75-year period. Not only did each require a transfusion of cash from general revenues, but one cut benefits sharply, while another increased the payroll tax for those opting for an account. The Commission's first variant left contributions and benefits exactly as they were but allowed for employees to divert payroll taxes equivalent to 2 per cent of their taxable income to their own accounts. Naturally this approach did the least for 'strengthening' overall fiscal balance and required the largest 'transition investment from general revenues'. The second approach did manage to improve fiscal balance but only by radically reducing benefits. It took a leaf out of Margaret Thatcher's book and indexed benefits to future prices not wages – and even this approach did not obviate the need for cash infusions across the 75-year horizon. The third of the schemes invited workers wishing to have an individual account to pay an additional 1 per cent of their income into the account; if they were unwilling to do this then they would not be able to set one up. This scheme, in effect, contradicted the injunction not to raise the payroll tax and also required further cash injections from general revenue. In fact each approach required hundreds of billions of dollars in future subsidy at a time when the recession and agreed future tax cuts had slashed the prospect of budget surpluses. The Commission urged that the assets assembled in the individual accounts would be out of reach of the Treasury, and in that sense in a sort of 'lockbox'. As contributions went in they would count as saving. Another feature of the accounts, expressly requested by President Bush, was that the assets in the accounts would be inheritable, thus diminishing the resources available for the 'insurance' aspect of Social Security. On the other hand individuals would not be allowed to withdraw any money from their accounts until they retired, and even then they would not be able to draw it all out at once.

The commission's co-chairmen were Daniel Patrick Moynihan, the former Democratic Senator and long-term advocate of Social Security reform, and Richard Parsons, a Republican who was Co-Chief Operating Officer, later CEO-designate, of AOL Time-Warner. Its members included Estelle James, the principal author of the World Bank report *Averting the Old Age Crisis*, Robert Prozen, vice-chairman at Fidelity, and Sylvester Shrieber of the consultants Watson Wyatt. Martin Feldstein was not a member of the commission but his theoretical contributions were singled out for praise in the final report. The commission lacked a prominent economist, though it did include a Bush economic aide, John Cogan.

The commission was advised by Alicia Munnell, 'Peter F. Drucker professor' at Boston College, and a critic of individual accounts, to retain Social Security's defined benefit structure: 'Social Security's defined benefit structure, particularly with some pre-funding and investment in equities, is better than individual accounts for providing the basic retirement income. Because Social Security is a defined benefit plan, it can spread risks across the population and over generations. This means that people's basic benefits do not depend on what stocks they pick or when they buy or sell. . . . The dollar amounts are not very large: the benefit for a worker with a history of average wages who retired at age 62 in January 2001 was $892 per month or $10,704 a year. I do not think it makes sense to put this dollar amount at risk.'[114] Munnell pointed out that there was a great difference between individual accounts as an 'add on' to the existing system and individual accounts as a 'carve out'. Her insistence that the key alternative being examined was really between the defined benefit and the defined contribution approach also helpfully underscored what was really at stake. The US Social Security system already has individual accounts in the sense that each participant will have benefits calibrated according to their contributions and other circumstances – but the individual's benefits are defined and do not depend on market returns.

The commission also received testimony from Kent Smitters, a member of the Treasury task force established by the previous administration, who informed them of the conclusions reached by the 'Special Issues' group. William ('"Bill"') Frenzel, a former Republican Congressman, was struck off to head the sub-group working on administration. He reported that for cost reasons the best results would be 'achieved by the centralised rather than a more individualised or decentralised plan'. He believed that only a very few stylised choices should be offered, perhaps three or five different funds as with the Thrift Savings Plan (TSP) offered to Federal employees:

> I think members [of the Commission] also considered that there is a certain lack of sophistication on the part of a number of [potential] participants . . . even the most sophisticated of us would not know how to approach the 500, then 700 Swedish choices that we had. And looking a little further at the British one, we noted that there was a bit of rapacity, you might say, on the part of the money managers, who were anxious to get the business at whatever cost.[115]

Frenzel said that at a later point more choice might be offered in a two-tier scheme but that for the moment they should focus on making a success of the first tier. Prozen accepted the case for drastic simplification but urged a more definite commitment to a second-tier plan for those above a threshold. Estelle James observed that the cost advantages of the TSP approach were so great that it would have to be adopted but she worried: 'this kind of system also potentially poses some dangers because it is quite a centralised, concentrated system. The danger [of] political manipulation . . . could reappear there over time.'[116] She favoured moving to a second more diversified tier above a threshold but warned that the portfolios offered in tier two should not be 'too different from what is in tier one . . . There would be no point in having identical portfolios, but not too different, because the more differentiation you allow, the greater the danger that costs will escalate, that marketing will lead to this outcome.'[117]

This discussion disappointed the more eager privatisers on the commission as they saw robust consumer choice pushed over the horizon.

The report by Fidel Vargas on collection procedures was also dispiriting
since he saw no immediate alternative to allowing for an average fifteen-
month delay between contributions and the implementation of the
investor's decision: 'while I would favour real time reconciliation . . . the
mechanics of it are quite complicated. [W]e want to make sure, especially
on small businesses, that we do not place any unreasonable burden on
them.'[118] Estelle James added that there was a compliance issue since you
had to make sure that there was no collusion between employers and
employees to avoid payment. All in all 'the simplest thing was to simply
have them [employers] treat it as part of the payroll taxes they submit
now.'[119] Following further discussion of how payroll taxes and benefits were
handled by the existing system, Moynihan was moved to comment: 'I
think you will all [agree with me], that our social security system is a miracle. I mean, 45 million people all get a check on the same day of the
month all over the country. Huh?'[120]

The eventual report finessed some of the issues raised – the second tier
was to be available from the outset once an account reached $5,000. But
the failure to recommend a single scheme, and the fact that none of the
approaches solved the problem of overall fiscal balance, weakened the
impression made. A press report of the final meeting noted: 'The commission disclosed today that it would probably take $2 trillion to $3 trillion
of new revenue to shore up the system for 75 years, money that could only
come from increased borrowing, higher taxes or spending cuts in other
programs.'[121] The commission's decision drastically to limit participant
choice in tier one, and to apply stringent regulation in tier two, probably
diminished the report's appeal to free market purists. The report warned
that many would opt for the 'standard' fund offered as a default option.
Only a few commercial providers would be involved and the Treasury
would be asked to construct an inflation-indexed public bond which
would appeal to the cautious. Collection was to be centralised, for the time
being, through the existing methods for collection of the payroll tax, with
the long delay this entailed.[122] The commission's final report also suggested
some ways in which women and minorities could be given better coverage (though such issues could also be addressed without recourse to
individual accounts).

This was all a far cry from the revolution heralded by Friedman and
Ferrara, and perhaps a disappointment to some in the financial services
industry. However there were crumbs of comfort for the latter. The
report did not propose a cap on charges, as in the British stakeholder
pension, only that they be identified in an annual statement. Discussing

the problem of small accounts it observes: 'While caps on transactions fees could be used to pool administrative costs across participants, such caps could also stifle innovation.'[123] Tier 1, which will hold up to the first $5,000 of the individual accounts, will comprise three balanced funds, or a combination of the five index funds already offered to Federal employees by their Thrift Savings Plan. No doubt there are ways in which this could offer useful new business to the larger providers. The governing board, which is to vet the suppliers and their products in both tiers, is to be sworn to abstain from allowing political considerations to affect their conduct. The voting rights of the shares held in individual accounts are to be exercised by the fund managers, a proceeding which would boost the influence of those funds allowed to sell their products to the scheme.[124]

The commission report remained sufficiently positive and elastic in its conclusions to allow new legislative initiatives when the time is ripe. According to one story the President's enthusiasm for privatisation was undimmed: 'Mr. Bush seems genuinely convinced that the issue is a winner, especially among younger voters who are comfortable with investing and take a long view of Wall Street's ups and downs.'[125] Obviously the issue would go nowhere prior to the 2002 mid-term elections. And many believed the President would shelve the whole question indefinitely. Yet for Bush to abandon this distinctive issue, so dear to a powerful current of Republic opinion, would be uncharacteristic. Proposals to introduce individual accounts have in the past been supported by several prominent Democrats, among them Senator Lieberman. When Bush's controversial tax measure came before the Senate in 2001 it passed by 53 votes to 47, with four Democrats helping to supply the majority.[126] Just as Bush won over Democrats to his tax cuts so he may hope to find Democrats who will see merit in giving greater state sponsorship to the financial services industry.

If and when Bush decides to press his case he can pick and choose what aspects of the commission report to accept. He will also be influenced by his chief economic officers and advisers. Prior to the commission's report, Paul O'Neill, the Treasury Secretary, envisaged what an interviewer described as 'a sweeping revision of social security . . . and abolition of corporate income tax and capital gains tax on business'.[127] 'Mr O'Neill would include America's entitlement programmes for senior citizens in his survey. Currently, the government guarantees pensions and senior healthcare. Mr O'Neill questions this guarantee, the roots of which lie in Roosevelt's New Deal. "Able-bodied adults should save enough on a regular basis so that they can provide for their own retirement and, for that matter, health and medical needs.'"[128] Paul O'Neill is chairman of the board of trustees of Social Security.

Presumably presentation will be a bit more emollient than this if individual accounts are proposed, but their logic would indeed doom the finances of the public system. Sooner or later 'privatised' Social Security would channel all payroll tax to the financial houses favoured by the governing board. Interestingly, one of the few historical precedents for such an arrangement would be the 'tax farmers' of the French *ancien régime*. These men paid the monarch a lump sum for the right to collect his taxes, making sure in the process that they squeezed as much as possible from the contract. As with the lottery, another currently fashionable *ancien régime* device, the government will play a key role in selecting those who hold the franchises. Pressed to name today's aspirant tax farmers, one might cite Robert Prozen of Fidelity and Peter Peterson of the Blackstone group, but these individuals are to be congratulated for at least acting openly. Dozens more will appear once legislation is in place.

Of course, the privatisation cause has wealthy backers. The Cato Institute has an endowment of $300 million. Lobbyists retained under the category 'finance, insurance and real estate' spent just over $200 million in 1998 and 1999, ahead of spending on any other category including health and defence.[129] The financial services industry does not have a monolithic position on privatisation but some of the largest concerns would welcome the individual accounts, and even more would welcome a further trimming of benefits since this would make employees more reliant on their 401(k)s and the like. The industry will be very concerned at the shape of any reform. If there are to be many millions of small accounts for the low-paid and economically insecure then the providers would expect to see generous subsidies and guarantees to make catering for these new and often unpromising clients worthwhile.

When Bush came to give his State of the Union address in January 2002 the circumstances could scarcely have been less propitious for proclaiming support for privatisation. The collapse of Enron in the previous month was still attracting a blaze of publicity. The bankruptcy of the iconic Houston concern, the country's seventh largest company, had wiped out its own employees' savings and weakened a wide range of other pension funds. The media were picking over the intimate ties between the administration and the energy company – its donations to George W. Bush and the Republican party, its role as former employer to the President's economic adviser and Army Secretary, its privileged access to the Vice President's task force on energy policy, and so forth. Enron's complaisant auditors had earned fat fees as a consultant and successfully lobbied Congress for looser standards. The news that they had been busily shredding documents confirmed the worst suspicions. The company's banks, as noted in chapter 3, far from raising the alarm, had negotiated new loans and then quietly offloaded the risk on unsuspecting insurance houses and fund managers, many of them repositories of pension money. The hazards of investing – especially those facing the small saver – were highlighted by every aspect of the sordid affair. Another wide-spread business practice highlighted by Enron was the issuing of huge quantities of share options to senior management and, in individually much smaller packets, to the mass of employees. In 2000 employee stock options ran at 19.7 per cent of pre-tax profits, diluting the value of existing share-holdings in a major way.[130] According to prevailing US law such options were tax deductible but did not have to be treated as an expense on quarterly earn-ings reports. At senate hearings representatives of pension fund shareholders raised strong objections:

> Enron's demise has drawn attention to the possible abuse of options by executives who might act in their own rather than shareholders' interests if they become overdependant on share-based incentives. In testimony to the [Senate] committee yesterday Sarah Testlik, executive director of the Council of Institutional Investors, which represents large US pension funds, called executive stock option packages 'an enabler of corporate fraud' and asked congress to grant shareholders the right to vote on all stock option grants. 'Options dilute the assets of future shareholders . . . and ultimately come out of our pockets, and companies are using them like cocaine addicts,' she said.[131]

Bush could scarcely ignore the outpouring of public concern in his State of the Nation address. Nevertheless he defiantly inserted a brief con-cluding reference to individual accounts:

> A good job should lead to security in retirement. I ask Congress to enact new safeguards for 401(k) and pension plans. Employees who have worked hard and saved all their lives should not have to risk losing everything if their company fails. Through stricter accounting standards and tougher disclosure requirements, corporate America must be made accountable to employees and shareholders and held to the highest standards of conduct. Retirement security also depends on keeping the commitments of Social Security, and we will. We must make Social Security financially stable and allow personal retirement accounts for younger workers who choose them.

The account given in this chapter has explored the rival proposals for Social Security, their economic logic and potential for stimulating social resistance. Reagan began by attempting severe retrenchment but eventually sponsored the build up of a more satisfactory trust fund. The privatisation cause had real momentum in the 1990s but its most tangible opportunity, coinciding with the great stock market boom, disappeared when Clinton decided to brave out the Lewinsky scandal by ditching the schemes of the Treasury cabal and springing to the aid of the threatened programme. The events stemming from 11 September for a while concentrated the Bush administration's energies and attention elsewhere, but may eventually strengthen him. Certainly the advent of recession, the huge boost to military outlays, and the disappearance of budget surpluses weaken the finances of Social Security. Is the programme to be strengthened, or to be dismembered and handed over to the financial services industry?

If President Bush decides to move, as he has promised to do, then citizens of the United States will face something more fundamental than an economic policy option – they will have to ask themselves whether they wish to dismantle one of the few civic arrangements in which all participate, whatever their beliefs, economic condition or ethnic background. Social Security has become almost co-extensive with citizenship, helping to symbolise it and make it tangible. To allow the wealthier to exit the system, and to remove the element of redistribution and social insurance it embodies, could prove as provocative and ill-advised as any of the wild and sweeping initiatives of Reagan's wunderkind, David Stockman.

Notes

1 According to a report of a meeting of the American Association of Public Opinion Research a tracking poll involving no fewer than 80,000 voters found that the individual accounts proposal took time to register with voters: 'The poll showed that the public was unaware of the candidates' differences on that issue favoured by Bush as late as the start of October. But people became more aware through debates of Gore's opposition to investing Social Security trust funds [in individual accounts], and he was able to bring more Democrats and some independents to his side on this issue.' Will Lester, 'Poll Sheds Light on 2000 Campaign', Associated Press, Montreal, 19 May 2001.
2 Joseph A. Pechman, Henry J. Aaron and Michael K. Taussig, *Social Security: Prospects for Reform*, Washington (DC) 1968, p. 217; Rose and Milton Friedman, *Free to Choose*, New York 1980.
3 Martin Feldstein, 'Social Security, Induced Retirement and Aggregate Capital Accumulation', *Journal of Political Economy*, vol. 82, no. 5, September–October 1974, pp. 905–26.
4 Samuelson's argument was outlined in chapter 1.
5 Martin Feldstein, 'Toward a Reform of Social Security', *Public Interest*, no. 40, 1975, pp. 75–95, p. 88.

6   Peter Diamond, 'A Framework for Social Security Analysis', *Journal of Public Economics*, vol. 83, April 1977, pp. 275–98.

7   Ronald Reagan, 'Acceptance Speech', in Paul Boyer, ed., *Reagan as President*, Chicago 1990, pp. 22-7.

8   David A. Stockman, *The Triumph of Politics*, London 1986, pp. 95–6. In his own memoirs Reagan recalls an incident in the 1966 Goldwater campaign that suggests that his speeches on Social Security were capable of causing alarm. Some wealthy backers paid for a speech by Reagan backing Goldwater to be shown on national TV. The Senator's aides were sufficiently upset by a passage questioning the financing of Social Security in this speech to propose that it be dropped. The passage was eventually transmitted, with Goldwater's approval. Ronald Reagan, *An American Life*, New York 1990, pp. 140–1. Reagan also attacked Social Security while Governor of California.

9   Stockman, *The Triumph of Politics*, pp. 193–4.

10 Ibid, p. 197.

11 Ibid, pp. 198–9.

12 Ibid, p. 206.

13 Hugh Heclo and Rudolph G. Penner, 'Fiscal and Political Strategy in the Reagan Administration', in Fred I. Greenstein, ed., *The Reagan Presidency: an Early Assessment*, Baltimore (MD) 1983, pp. 56–8.

14 Report of the National Commission on Social Security Reform, Washington (DC) January 1983; Edward D. Berkowitz, 'The Historical Development of Social Security in the United States', in Eric R. Kingson and James H. Shulz, eds, *Social Security in the 21st Century*, New York 1997, pp. 22–38, p. 25.

15 Paul E. Peterson and Mark Rom, 'Lower Taxes, More Spending, and Budget Deficits', in Charles O. Jones, ed., *The Reagan Legacy: Promise and Performance*, Chatham (NJ) 1988, pp. 213–40.

16 Quoted in Heclo and Penner, 'Fiscal and Political Strategy', in Greenstein, *The Reagan Presidency*, p. 56.

17 Stockman, *The Triumph of Politics*, p. 203.

18 Paul Allen Beck, 'Incomplete Realignment: the Reagan Legacy for Parties and Elections', in Jones, ed., *The Reagan Legacy*, pp. 145–71.

19 John Myles, 'Postwar Capitalism and the Extension of Social Security into a Retirement Wage', in Margaret Weir, Anna S. Orloff and Theda Skocpol, eds, *The Politics of Social Policy in the United States*, Princeton (NJ) 1988, pp. 265–91.

20 Sylvester Shreiber and John B. Shoven, *The Real Deal: the History and Future of Social Security*, New Haven (CT) 1999, pp. 152–62.

21 Theda Skocpol, *The Missing Middle: Working Families and the Future of American Social Policy in the United States*, New York 2000, p. 72.

22 Theda Skocpol, 'The Limits of the New Deal System and the Roots of Contemporary Welfare Dilemmas', in Weir *et al.*, *The Politics of Social Policy in the United States*, pp. 293–312.

23 Milton Friedman, *A Theory of the Consumption Function*, Princeton (NJ) 1957.

24 Friedmans, *Free to Choose*, p. 134.

25 Ibid., p. 135.
26 Ibid., p. 132.
27 Ibid., p. 155.
28 Peter A. Ferrara, *Social Security: the Inherent Paradox*, San Francisco 1980, p. 329.
29 Ibid., p. 366.
30 Virginia P. Reno and Robert B. Friedland, 'Strong Support but Low Confidence: What Explains the Contradiction?', in Kingson and Shulz, *Social Security in the 21st Century*, pp. 178–94, p. 182.
31 Robert J. Myers, 'Will Social Security be There for Me?', in Kingson and Schulz, *Social Security in the 21st Century*, pp. 208–16, p. 210.
32 Robert C. Merton, 'On the Role of Social Security as a Means for Efficient Risk Sharing in an Economy Where Human Capital is Not Tradable', in Zvi Bodie and John B. Shoven, eds, *Financial Aspects of the United States Pension System,* Chicago 1993, pp. 325–58, and Martin Feldstein, 'Should Private Pensions be Indexed?', in ibid., pp. 211–30.
33 Henry Aaron, *The Economic Effects of Social Security*, Washington (DC) 1982; Martin Feldstein, 'Social Security and Private Saving: Reply', *Journal of Political Economy*, vol. 90, no. 3, pp. 630–42. Continuing controversy among economists over Feldstein's 1974 argument somewhat neutralised its impact. However, low savings were indeed a US problem. The point was: did richer citizens really save less because of a payroll tax that accounted for so little of their income? And would the low-paid save for the long term even if there were no payroll tax? Some recent information on this will be cited in the conclusion.
34 Reagan's failure to bring social expenditure under control was the theme of an article published in *Commentary* in August 1983 by Michael Novak, 'The Rich, the Poor and the Reagan Administration', reprinted in Boyer, *Reagan as President*, pp. 136–41.
35 For economic performance mapped against presidential terms see Robert Pollin, 'Anatomy of Clintonomics', *New Left Review*, second series no. 3, May–June 2000.
36 Theodore R. Marmore, Fay Lomax Cook and Stephen Scher, 'Social Security Politics and the Conflict between Generations', in Kingson and Schulz, *Social Security in the 21st Century*, pp. 195–207, especially pp. 202–5.
37 An early example of the 'individual account' approach was Michael J. Boskin, Laurence Kotlikoff and John Shoven, 'Personal Security Accounts: A Proposal for Fundamental Social Security Reform', in Susan Wachter, ed., *Social Security and Private Pensions*, Lexington (MA) 1988, pp. 179–206. For generational accounts see Laurence Kotlikoff, 'The Social Security "Surpluses"', in Carolyn L. Weaver, ed., *Social Security's Looming Surpluses*, Washington (DC) 1990, pp. 17–27, and Alan J. Auerbach, Jagadeesh Gokhale and Laurence Kotlikoff, 'Generational Accounts: a Meaningful Alternative to Deficit Accounting', in D. Bradford, ed., *Tax Policy and the Economy*, Cambridge (MA) 1991.

38 Dean Baker and Mark Weisbrot, *Social Security: the Phony Crisis*, Chicago 2000, pp. 38–53, p. 45; Peter Diamond, 'Generational Accounts and Generational Balance: an Assessment', *National Tax Journal*, vol. xlix, no. 4, pp. 597–604. Barry Bosworth and James Poterba had pointed to weaknesses of the generational accounts approach in Weaver, *Social Security's Looming Surpluses*, pp. 29–38.

39 Ned Gramlich, 'Comment', in R. Douglas Arnold, Michael J. Graetz and Alicia H. Munnell, eds, *Framing the Social Security Debate: Economics, Politics and Values*, National Academy of Social Insurance, Washington (DC) 1998, pp. 422–3.

40 Hugh Heclo, 'Comment', in Arnold *et al. Framing the Social Security Debate*.

41 Brian Barry, *A Treatise on Social Justice*, vol. 1, *Theories of Justice*, London 1989, p. 200–1.

42 John Rawls, *A Theory of Justice*, Cambridge (MA) 1971, p. 287. Problems with Rawls's approach were debated in R.I. Sekora and Brian Barry, eds, *Obligations to Future Generations*, Philadelphia 1978.

43 The terms used by the philosophers themselves are also implicated here. Barry points out that the whole problematic of 'saving' rests on certain assumptions, notably a '"process of accumulation" of capital', Barry, *Theories of Justice*, p. 193. Rawls insists that this process of accumulation comprises 'not only factories and machines, but also the knowledge and culture, as well as the techniques and skills, that make possible just institutions and the fair value of liberty.' Rawls, *A Theory of Justice*, p. 288. In the Conclusion I will return to the issue of 'just institutions' touched on here.

44 Thomas Frank, *One Market Under God*, London 2000, p. 137.

45 Ibid., p. 139.

46 Ibid., p. 138.

47 Lawrence R. Jacobs and Robert Y. Shapiro, 'Myths and Misunderstandings about Public Opinion', in Arnold *et al., Framing the Social Security Debate*, pp. 355–88, p. 364.

48 Ibid., pp. 370–3, 385.

49 Ibid., p. 387. The most likely benefit cut would be to make Social Security receipts fully taxable.

50 Skocpol, *The Missing Middle*, p. 84.

51 Ron Gebhardtsbauer, speech at seminar on Social Security in Providence, Rhode Island, 1 July 1998, National Democracy Dialogue web-site, Briefing Book on Social Security.

52 Peter Diamond, ed., *Issues in Privatizing Social Security, Report of an Expert Panel of the National Academy of Social Insurance*, Cambridge (MA) 1999, p. 15.

53 Estelle James, James Smalhout and Dimitri Vittas, 'Administrative Costs and the Organisation of Individual Account Systems', in OECD, *Private Pensions Systems: Administrative Costs and Reforms*, no. 2, Paris 2000, pp. 155–84, p. 64. Of course, strictly speaking the observation above does not compare like with like. Further information on costs of different pensions was given in chapter 2 and will be reviewed in the conclusion.

54 Michael J. Graetz and Jerry L. Mashaw, *True Security: Rethinking American Social Insurance*, New Haven 1999, pp. 102–3.

55 Theda Skocpol, *The Missing Middle*, p. 72.

56 Graetz and Mashaw, *True Security*, p. 257.

57 Sue Pleming, 'Report: Many in US Not Prepared for Retirement', Reuters, Washington, May 23 2001. A study reporting stagnation in pension fund assets for two-thirds of US households between 1983 and 1988 is summarised by Jeff Madrick, 'For Most in US No Pension Windfalls', *New York Times*, 22 February 2002.

58 Barry Bosworth, 'What Economic Role for the Trust Funds?', in Kingson and Shulz, *Social Security in the 21st Century*, pp. 156–77.

59 Bosworth, in ibid., p. 160.

60 Daniel J. Palazzolo, *Done Deal: the Politics of the 1997 Budget Agreement*, New York 1999, p. 13.

61 Baker and Weisbrot, *Social Security*, especially pp. 21–37.

62 *Report of the 1994–6 Advisory Council on Social Security. Findings and Recommendations*, Washington (DC) 1997, vol. 1, p. 111.

63 Ibid. The 'maintain benefits' proposals are outlined on pp. 25–8. The various plans are discussed in Laurence S. Seidman, *Funding Social Security: a Strategic Alternative*, Cambridge 1999, pp. 10–16, 53–5, 95–7.

64 Shreiber and Shoven, *The Real Deal*, pp. 263–89. This chapter, entitled 'Heathens in the Temple', furnishes a detailed account of the proceedings of the Council which, based as it is on quoted minutes and transcripts, is both partisan and informative.

65 Ibid., pp. 266–8. Alicia Munnell and C. Nicole Ernsberger, 'Foreign Experience with Public Pension Surpluses and National Saving', in Weaver, *Social Security's Looming Surpluses*, pp. 85–118.

66 Baker and Weisbrot, *Social Security*, pp. 88–104.

67 Congressman Bill Archer quoted by Deborah McGregor, 'Social Security Plans Opposed', *Financial Times*, 20 January 1999; Greenspan quoted by Stephen Fuller and Deborah McGregor, 'Greenspan Attacks Clinton Plan', *Financial Times*, 21 January 1999.

68 Michael Weinstein, *New York Times*, 25 January 1999.

69 Milton Friedman, ' Social Security Socialism', *Wall Street Journal*, 26 January 1999.

70 Keith Ambachtsheer, 'Public Pension Fund Power', *Journal of Portfolio Management*, vol. 27, no. 2, winter 2001, pp. 61–4.

71 Jonathan Orszag, Peter Orszag, and Laura Tyson, 'The Process of Economic Policy Making during the Clinton Administration', delivered at conference on 'American Economic Policy in the 1990s', June 2001, John F. Kennedy School of Government, Harvard University, p. 60. See the web-site at ksg.harvard.edu/cbg/econ.

72 The evidence of the polls is examined in Fay Lomax Cook, Jason Barabas and Benjamin L. Page, 'Invoking Public Opinion: Polls, Policy Debates, and the Future of Social Security', Institute of Policy Research (IPR), WP-00-5,

Northwestern University 2000; see also Benjamin I. Page, 'Is Social Security Reform Ready for the American Public?', IPR, Northwestern University, WP-99-6, 1999, Fay Lomax Cook, 'The New Politics of Social Security', IPR, Northwestern University 1998, WP-98-30 and Lawrence R. Jacobs and Robert Y. Shapiro, 'Myths and Misunderstandings about Public Opinion toward Social Security', in Arnold *et al., Framing the Social Security Debate*, pp. 355–88.

73 For a helpful discussion of the limits of polling as a guide to politicians' behaviour, see Lawrence R. Jacobs and Robert Y. Shapiro, *Politicians Don't Pander: Political Manipulation and the Loss of Democratic Responsiveness*, Chicago 2000. This study focuses on US politics in the mid-1990s for most of its examples and case studies.

74 Laurence Kotlikoff and Jeffrey Sachs, 'Privatising Social Security: It's High Time to Privatise', *Brookings Review*, vol. 15, summer 1997, pp. 16–23.

75 Glenn Kessler, 'Clinton Eyed Private Security Accounts', *Washington Post*, 29 June 2001. The paper by Douglas Elmendorf, Jeffrey Liebman and David Wilcox, 'Fiscal Policy and Social Security Policy during the 1990s', was delivered at the conference 'American Economic Policy in the 1990s' (see footnote 71).

76 Elmendorf, Liebman and Wilcox, 'Fiscal Policy and Social Security Policy during the 1990s', ibid.

77 Ibid., p. 44–5.

78 Ibid., p. 60.

79 Orszag, Orszag and Tyson, 'The Process of Economic Policy Making During the Clinton Administration', ibid., p. 61.

80 Quoted in Christopher Hitchens, *No One Left to Lie to: the Triangulations of William Jefferson Clinton*, New York and London 1999, p. 29.

81 John Harris, 'Clinton Sought Middle Ground on Social Security', *Washington Post*, 25 January 1999.

82 The White House was, of course, amplifying for its own reasons a dialogue that was anyway underway and to which many of the works I cite contributed. But for a direct and lucid engagement between two opposed authors see Henry J. Aaron and John B. Shoven, *Should the United States Privatize Social Security?*, Cambridge (MA) 1999.

83 Martin Feldstein and Andrew Samwick, 'The Economics of Prefunding Social Security', in Ben Bernanke and Julio Rotemberg, eds, *NBER Macroeconomic Annual*, 1997, Cambridge (MA) 1997, pp. 115–48, p. 120. See also the same authors' essay, 'The Transition Path in Privatizing Social Security', and the editor's introduction, in Martin Feldstein, *Privatizing Social Security*, Chicago 1998, pp. 1–29, 215–64.

84 Jerry Seigel, *Stocks for the Long Run*, Burr Ridge (IL) 1994.

85 Davis, *Pension Funds*, p. 133.

86 Keith P. Ambachtsheer and D. Don Ezra, *Pension Fund Excellence: Creating Value for Stakeholders*, New York 1998, p. 44. (I am interpreting a chart found on that page.)

87 Henry J. Aaron, Alan S. Blinder, Alicia H. Munnell, and Peter R. Orszag, 'Governor Bush's Individual Account Proposal', Issue Brief 11, The Social Security Network, The New Century Fund, New York 2000.
88 Robert Shiller, *Irrational Exuberance*, Princeton (NJ) 2000.
89 Aaron *et al.*, 'Governor Bush's Individual Account Proposal'.
90 Ibid., p. 12.
91 Skocpol, *The Missing Middle*, p. 99.
92 Peter Ferrara, *Social Security: Averting the Crisis*, Washington (DC) 1982.
93 Martin Feldstein, 'The Missing Piece in Policy Analysis', *American Economic Review Papers and Proceedings*, vol. 86, no. 2, 1996, pp. 1–14.
94 Martin Feldstein, Elena Ranguelova and Andrew Samwick, 'The Transition to Investment-based Social Security when Portfolio Returns and Capital Profitability are Uncertain', NBER Working Paper no. 7016, Cambridge (MA) March 1999.
95 Martin Feldstein, 'Clinton's Social Security Sham', *Wall Street Journal*, 1 February 1999.
96 Press Briefing by the Director of the National Economic Council, Gene Sperling, and Deputy Secretary of the Treasury, Larry Summers, The White House, 14 April 1999, from the web-site, Network Democracy Social Security Briefing Book.
97 Martin Feldstein, 'Closing the $1 Billion-a-Day Gap', *Boston Globe*, 18 July 2000.
98 Martin Feldstein, 'Bush's All Gain, No Pain, Retirement Plan', *Washington Post*, 17 July 2000.
99 Diamond, *Issues in Privatizing Social Security*. The report outlines some strong arguments but was accompanied by a disclaimer signed by three members of the panel who withdrew at the last moment after having secured several amendments to the draft, circumstances which distracted from the report's conclusions and arguments.
100 José Piñera, 'Chile's Social Security Lesson for the United States', 14 December 1998, White House Conference, Network Democracy.org/social security.
101 Peter Orszag and Joseph Stiglitz, 'Rethinking Pension Reform: Ten Myths about Social Security Systems', World Bank web-site, to be published in Robert Holzmann and Joseph Stiglitz, eds, *New Ideas About Old Age Security: Toward Sustainable Pension Systems in the 21st Century*, Washington (DC) 2001.
102 Peter Diamond, 'The Economics of Social Security Reform', in Arnold *et al.*, *Framing the Social Security Debate*. p. 62, and cited in Orszag and Stiglitz, 'Rethinking Pension Reform', p. 24.
103 Alicia H. Munnell and Annika Sundén, 'Investment Practices of State and Local Pension Funds: Implications for Social Security reform', paper presented at the Pension Research Council Conference, Wharton School, University of Pennsylvania, 26–7 April 1999, and cited in Orszag and Stiglitz, 'Rethinking Pension Reform', p. 39.
104 Deserving of special mention would be two papers which query technical aspects of the case for privatisation: John Geanakoplos, Olivia S. Mitchell and

Stephen P. Zeldes, 'Would a Privatized Social Security System Really Pay a Higher Rate of Return?' and 'Social Security's Money's Worth', Working Papers, Wharton School, University of Pennsylvania, August 1998 (though one of these authors, Olivia Mitchell, is a supporter of individual accounts and served on the Bush commission).

105 Martin Feldstein, 'Common Ground on Social Security', *New York Times*, 31 March 1999.

106 Daniel Gross, *Bull Run: Wall Street, the Democrats and the New Politics of Personal Finance*, New York 2000. I cite this because Gross is himself sympathetic to the New Democrats. The same argument has been made more trenchantly by Alexander Cockburn in *Washington Babylon* (with Ken Silverstein), New York 1997, and in *Albert Gore: a User's Manual* (with Jeffrey St Clair), New York 2000.

107 Teresa Ghilarducci is one of the few US authors to have studied the workings of the gigantic pension fund complex. Apart from her excellent study *Labor's Capital*, published nearly a decade ago, the literature on the workings of the US pension funds is dominated by European authors like E. Philip Davis (*Pension Funds*), Gordon L. Clark (*Pension Fund Capitalism*), Lucy ap Roberts (*Les retraites aux Etats-Unis*), François Charpentier (*Retraites et fonds de pension*) and Jacques Nikonoff (*La Comédie des fonds de pension*). Of course, there are US textbooks on pension funds but these tend to be assembled for and by practitioners, such as Robert Prozen of Fidelity; while such compilations are professional and informative, they do not represent independent and critical scholarship.

108 See the report of a study conducted for the Consumers Federation of America by Catherine P. Montalto, Ohio State University, 'Many Lack Enough Retirement Savings', Associated Press, 26 April 2000.

109 Henry Aaron and Robert D. Reichauer, 'Paying for an Elderly Population', in Henry Aaron and Robert Reichauer, eds., *Setting National Priorities: the 2000 election and beyond*, Washington (DC) 1999, pp. 179–82.

110 Norman Birnbaum, *After Progress: American Social Reform and European Socialism in the Twentieth Century*, Oxford 2001, pp. 364–5.

111 All above poll figures from 'Portrait of America', *Financial Times*, 16 November 2000, with Voter News Service cited as source. Similar breakdowns appeared in another exit poll cited in the *Sunday Times*, 12 November 2000, with the difference that Gore's lead among the over-sixties was 51 per cent to 46 per cent. Gore's 9-point lead among all women compares with a lead of only one point among white women but of as much as 19 points among 'working women'. Obviously many working women are not white, but for the figures to make sense non-working white women ('housewives' and older women) must have plumped for Bush.

112 Philip Shenon, 'Bush and Daschle Agree Not to Tap Social Security', *New York Times*, 5 September 2001.

113 William Safire, 'Jimmy That "Lockbox"', *New York Times*, 10 September 2001.

114 Alicia Munnell, 'Strengthening Social Security: Testimony Before the President's Commission on Strengthening Social Security', 18 October 2001. (available on the commission's web-site).

115 Transcript of the 9 November 2001 session of the President's Commission on Strengthening Social Security, pp. 59–60 (available on the commission's web-site).

116 Ibid., p. 63.

117 Ibid.

118 Ibid., p. 68.

119 Ibid., p. 77.

120 Ibid., p. 79.

121 Richard W. Stevenson, 'A Finale in Three-Part Harmony', *New York Times*, 12 December 2001.

122 *The Report of the President's Commission for Strengthening Social Security*, 21 December 2001.

123 Ibid., p. 41.

124 Ibid., p. 57.

125 Richard W. Stevenson, 'A Finale in Three-Part Harmony'.

126 Adam Clymer, 'Senate Sticks With Bush on Budget', *International Herald Tribune*, 11 May 2001.

127 Amity Shlaes, 'US Treasury Chief Mulls Tax Reform', *Financial Times*, 19/20 May 2001.

128 Amity Shlaes, 'Republicans Sample the Rhetoric of Confidence', *Financial Times*, 22 May 2001.

129 Nancy Dunne, 'Big Challenge for Lobbyists', *Financial Times*, 4 June 2001, citing as source the Center for Responsive Politics. Total spending by lobbyists came to $1.45 billion in 1999.

130 Andrew Hill and Peronet Despeignes 'Balancing Options', *Financial Times*, 19 April 2002.

131 Peronet Despeignes and Andrew Hill, 'Calls for Review of Stock Options Accounting', *Financial Times*, 19 April 2002.

The Paradoxes of Privatisation and the New Pension Panic

There is a secret agreement between past generations and the present one. Our coming was expected on earth. Like every generation that preceded us, we have been endowed with a weak messianic power, a power to which the past has a claim. That claim cannot be settled cheaply.

(Walter Benjamin, *Theses on the Philosophy of History*, 1938)

There's an iceberg dead ahead. It's called global aging and it threatens to bankrupt the great powers. As the populations of the world's leading economies age and shrink, we will face unprecedented political, economic and moral challenges. But we are woefully unprepared. Now is the time to sound the alarm.

(Peter G. Peterson, *Gray Dawn*, 1998)

Francisco Goya, *Showing Off? Remember your age*, 1815–20 (Stattliche Museen zu Berlin)

Before addressing alternatives to today's pension regimes it is appropriate to summarise the story so far, to explore the paradoxes of the argument over privatisation and to explain how the pension malaise of the 1990s became, post-bubble and post-Enron, the pension panic of the new century.

In chapter 1 pensions were seen to have been at once a gift to be bestowed and a prize to be seized, a facet of power and a capstone of social harmony, the privilege of a minority and the aspiration of the majority, deferred pay and a form of semi-socialised surplus. In their puritan, individualist guise, pension arrangements reflected and encouraged thrift and accumulation while in baroque culture they demonstrated the benevolence of power. When industrial states were pressed to furnish old age pensions to all, treasuries insisted on a contributory approach. Yet, concerned at the disturbing implications of large state-controlled funds, they shied away from full pre-funding. The pay-as-you-go financing method allowed for the construction of an immense apparatus of social and intertemporal redistribution, the product of a peculiar mid-twentieth-century moment, a time when the failure of private provision was a fresh memory and the experience of wartime collectivism an inspiration. But in countries where the stock market was well entrenched in economic life, private insurance houses, banks and brokers were eventually able to renew and, in time, vastly extend their role as pension providers, thanks to tax relief on their savings products.

In the second chapter we found that by the 1980s and 1990s the occupational and personal pension funds possessed great potential power which they used very tamely and ineffectively. Pension trustees were insulated from policy holders and constrained to adapt to the customs and outlooks of the corporate and financial establishment. The money in occupational pension funds turned out to be a cloudy species of 'grey capital' over which the policy holders, or even the trustees, had little control. Those with tax-favoured personal pension plans bore the burden of higher costs and acquired little extra control over the assets logged in their name. In fact, contemporary 'Anglo-Saxon' economies have come to exhibit a double 'accountability deficit' or agency problem, with policy-holder interests suffering at the hands of both money managers and corporate managers. The result is extravagant rewards to the managers, massive marketing expenditures, poor returns, and styles of corporate governance that flout the interests of policy holders, employees and customers. Individual 'defined contribution' plans, like 401(k)s, generally give weaker returns than corporate 'defined benefit' schemes, and benefit from lower employer contributions, but they are more flexible and portable. Public occupational schemes have given good returns with some portability. Private sector schemes often turn out to be underfunded and have poor portability. The individual plans are also vulnerable to speculative bubbles precisely because they offer no 'defined benefit'. The competitive marketing and managing of private pension funds is especially wasteful when everything is customised on an individual basis, leading to a 'cost disease' which erodes returns. Since the mid-1990s, a decline in interest rates has sharply reduced the value of the annuities that can be purchased by pension holders. However, those who have a policy, with the fiscal subsidies this involves, are certainly better placed than those with little or no provision, the situation of more than half the population reaching retirement in the United States or UK.

The third chapter explored the complicity of the pension funds in two decades of low growth, high unemployment, growing inequality and painful restructuring. The money managers became notorious for short-termism and herd behaviour. Obsessed with holding only assets that could readily be 'marked to market', they preferred to back the junk-bond kings and corporate raiders rather than to channel resources to build a productive and sustainable economy. The gain accrued to business buccaneers and highly paid brokers and money managers, the pain to millions of employees, often themselves policy holders. For many years the possibilities opened up by the knowledge-based industries were neglected – opportunities that would have been missed altogether had it not been for the universities with their programmes of basic research and their industrial parks. Once opportunities were seized by the money managers, it was often in a manner that failed to generate balanced and sustainable development or to recognise the interdependence of the 'new' and the 'old' economies or to discourage speculative bubbles. With the pricking of the bubble economy in 2000 and 2001 the institutional investors once again displayed a basic lack of coordination and commitment. Policy holders, whose returns had been below par in the boom years, now took a hit to the value of their pension funds. The collapse of Enron, the sag in the value of many 401(k)s and the parlous condition of many company pension schemes all pointed to failures in the commercial delivery of pensions.

Whatever the social price, the Anglo-American financial services industry thrived mightily in the 1980s and 1990s, but largely in a parasitic way at the expense of their host societies. The mega-salaries of the financial sector and boardroom existed side by side with mass unemployment, social cutbacks and deindustrialisation. With the lopsided recovery of the 1990s the financial services industry became more aware of the inherent limits of the pool of voluntary savers in the domestic market. Part of the answer lay in exporting the 'Anglo-Saxon' model, its 'equity culture' and flourishing private pension funds. In chapter 4 we saw that the World Bank report *Averting the Old Age Crisis* (1994) furnished the recipe for privatising pension regimes, with demolition of what it called a 'dominant public pillar' opening the way to new markets for financial products. The World Bank alternative was centrally to comprise a novel solution to the problem of sales resistance – citizens were to be forced to buy savings schemes from commercial providers. This new approach notched up a number of victories – in Sweden and Hong Kong for example – but was checked in the mid-1990s in the largest continental European states, notably France, Italy and Germany, when it ran into stiff opposition and led right-wing governments in all those countries to electoral defeat. Nevertheless, the succeeding centre-left government in Germany was itself to give ground in 2001 while in Italy the victory of the Right, which lulled electors by not talking about pensions, has produced a government which is expected to shrink pension entitlements to escape fiscal crisis. At a European level, the centre-left parties failed to come up with a concerted response to mass unemployment, technological stagnation and a drifting currency, though the French government, thanks to a *dirigiste* tradition and the 35-hour week, did better than most. Europe does have an ageing population and needs to improve – not scrap – its public retirement programmes. In chapter 4 I suggested that the pre-funding of pension liabilities and a mobilisation of those retirement funds in every region of the Union could tackle its economic underperformance and social malaise.

The fifth chapter recounted the story of pension reform in Britain, a story that has mixed, in equal parts, triumphs for 'reform' with scandal and failure in pension delivery. In her strategy of 'implicit privatisation', Margaret Thatcher successfully shrank public pension provision and offered new opportunities to the private providers. The latter's high-pressure sales tactics led to widespread pension 'mis-selling' and thus contributed to Conservative defeat in 1997. New Labour promised a 'stakeholder pension'. According to Labour's pension guru Frank Field, this meant ensuring that every citizen had a stake in a collective and portable pension fund, with the government furnishing contributions for carers and the unemployed. Trade unions, friendly societies and mutually owned financial houses were to organise these pensions and the resulting assets were to be invested in ways that promoted national prosperity. But within a little over a year this vision was abandoned because it was deemed too costly. Instead, the meagre state pension was to be supplemented by a new regulated product from the financial services industry. In 2000 New Labour discovered that it had made a major tactical blunder when it stuck to its policy of indexing the basic pension to prices, not earnings – which translated that year into a rise of only £0.75 a week. A disparate but dramatic series of protests forced the government to alter course and introduce large increases in both the basic pension and the Minimum Income Guarantee for pensioners, thus reducing the appeal of its stakeholder pension for the low-paid. Its complex 'pension credit' brought millions more within the scope of means tests. Notwithstanding the failure of the 'Third Way' to deliver on its promises, public discussion in Britain continues to witness calls for the better use of the resources presently under the lacklustre management of the pensions industry. The prestige of the latter has suffered as the pension mis-selling scandal and Maxwell affair were followed in 2000–1 by the slashing of the value of a million pension holdings at Equitable Life. The closure of many 'defined benefit' company schemes further accentuated the generalised disarray.

Indeed Britain, the premier laboratory of the new 'grey capitalism', is a poor advertisement for it. Possessed of extraordinary assets – oil wealth, a world language, innovative scientists and technologists, social cohesion, a highly cost-effective national health system – it has squandered them on reckless privatisation, deregulation, financialisation, deindustrialisation and social retrenchment. The result has been continuing sluggish growth and productivity, decaying social infrastructure, diseased livestock, demoralised research, teaching and health professionals, and a loss of strength and control in sector after sector, culminating in the self-destruction of the 'gentlemanly capitalism' of the City of London itself. The advent of a New Labour government in 1997 not only failed to reverse or arrest these developments but in several cases actually abetted them.

The citizens of the United States also paid a price for its crucial role in the 'market revolution' of the 1980s in the shape of stagnant wage rates, growing inequality, environmental deterioration, cutbacks in welfare, the criminalisation of an expanding underclass, and an intensified commercialisation of politics, culture and communication. But the scale of the country, the dimensions of its human and resource endowments, the strength and agility of its leading corporations, and the scope of its educational and military research complex set some limit on the ravages of marketisation and allowed for a broader-based economic recovery in the 1990s than was seen in Britain, though some of these negative trends persisted. While individualist and capitalist values are probably more strongly diffused in the United States than in any other country, the society would not hold together unless it had found some sources of collective identity that were not reducible to market price. The Social Security programme, together with education and some aspects of civic culture, give substance to the idea of citizenship in a country whose population is otherwise highly diverse.

The debate on the future of Social Security, central as it is to US politics, has witnessed both a clumsy, failed attempt to wreck the programme in the early years of the Reagan administration and a subsequent, more sustained and insidious, attack on it, as neo-conservatives spread alarm at unfunded liabilities, and a beguiling equity culture tempted some voters with the prospect of putting their payroll taxes into stocks rather than a public insurance programme. The late 1990s witnessed a rallying of public support for the programme by a coalition of the AARP, organised labour, Social Security experts and a beleaguered President. The plan to rescue Social Security put forward by the Maintain Benefits group on the Advisory Council (1994–96) envisaged both the pre-funding of the programme and the trust fund itself investing in the stock market, albeit with the understanding that there would be no 'political' interference in the latter. The economic case for privatisation has been subjected to a withering critique, yet those pressing for it have received a fillip from Bush's entry into the White House. They will now seek to advance their cause in and through the ongoing process of 'reform'. The report of Bush's Commission on Social Security made little impact, and disappointed naive privatisers. But the White House will not forget an issue with such powerful backing and ideological resonance.

The Inevitability of Collectivism?

In Europe and the United States, in Latin America and South-East Asia, the partisans of neo-liberalism and pension privatisation made dramatic progress in the last two decades of the twentieth century. But, somewhat surprisingly, the prize of pension privatisation generally eluded them. Margaret Thatcher made the greatest progress by carrying out a stealthy act of implicit privatisation – removing the state pension's link to earnings

levels – as one of her first acts in government. A string of political leaders
have drawn back from weakening the state pension system: Reagan in
1983, Juppé in France in 1995, Berlusconi in Italy in 1995, Kohl in
Germany in 1996–7, Clinton in 1998 and Blair in 2000. Unlike some
other welfare arrangements the state pension goes to everyone, so long as
they live long enough. The pay-as-you-go method of finance does not
seem fraudulent to many because they know that it helps to pay the pensions of their parents and those of the older generation, and that it does so
in a dignified way. Complex attempts to do 'generational accounting'
overlook the debt that each generation feels to its predecessors.

Interestingly, even the privatisers offer their own strange tribute to the
power of a new collectivism, as they devise increasingly complex ways for
the state to sponsor and regulate the pensions business. The private pension
industry has always enjoyed strong fiscal privileges. Some of the large
providers now want state enforcement of mandatory contributions – and
in return are willing to envisage additional measures of public regulation.
The mandatory principle can initially be disguised as choice by simply
allowing contributions to replace a part of the payroll tax. But since this
will be most attractive to the better-paid, it will undermine the programme's general finances. Eventually employees are likely to find that they
have to pay both a payroll tax and a levy to a private pension provider. The
more candid or clear-sighted advocates of privatisation, like Peter Peterson,
stress that:

> workers will have to keep paying for retirees in the old system even while
> they put aside extra money into the new system to pre-fund their retire-
> ment . . . In one way or another too many privatisation plans end up
> nullifying their purported objective. Sooner or later, whatever workers save
> by making smaller contributions to a pay-as-you-go plan they'll have to sac-
> rifice in higher taxes to pay off existing pay-as-you-go liabilities.[1]

Peterson, a former cabinet officer who now chaired a banking group
(Blackstone), himself embodied the neo-mercantilist outlook of today's
financial world. But at least he here confronts an issue which many, including the authors of the Bush Commission report, seek to fudge.

The new collectivism takes both strong and weak, virtuous and malig-
nant forms. Public pension provision remains large and growing, helping
to explain the fact that state expenditure has stabilised at 30 to 40 per cent
of GNP throughout the developed world, with further large sums forgone
to public treasuries as a consequence of 'tax spend'. Despite the pressures
of globalisation and social dumping modern states still need to finance a
widening range of social services if they are to maintain their competitive

position. They also face strong political pressures tending to the same end. The ageing of the population creates a need for larger expenditure on health and income maintenance for 10–20 per cent of the population. Devising entirely individual and private solutions to this challenge has not proved feasible.

Those who have rights in a private pension are themselves also locked into a type of collective structure, albeit one that can be weak or inefficient. Those in such arrangements usually do not exercise individual ownership over their pension 'pot' and, in most schemes, the fund will march on after their demise. The herd instinct of fund managers is another, often regrettable, example of perverse collectivism, as is the cost disease that afflicts the more personalised pension products. If the collective nature of pension provision is accepted and understood, then a benign and progressive potential can be developed which empowers the social individual. But that requires socialising the destructive and divisive forces of commercialism and irresponsible financial intermediation.

In the 1930s there was a classic exchange, known as the calculation debate, between ultra-liberal and socialist economists. The Austrian economist Ludvig von Mises had proved that a socialist economy would be unworkable because it would have no rational method for establishing prices, and, in consequence, would not be able to achieve that intricate coordination of different economic sectors necessary to any modern economy. The socialist economist Oskar Lange responded to the challenge by conceding that markets were good at establishing prices – even Marx had insisted that market prices reflected 'socially-necessary labour time' – but that it would be perfectly possible for a socialist economy to mimic this process while ensuring that the market was not allowed to determine the allocation of incomes and future investments. Friedrich von Hayek stepped into the argument to explain that Lange did not understand the role of entrepreneurs, that is individuals who are willing to risk their own resources and reputation backing hunches concerning new products, or services, or processes, or business methods, and prepared to accept the results, win or lose. Maurice Dobb urged the necessity of planning if large and lumpy infrastructural projects were to be successfully undertaken, while Joseph Schumpeter stressed the inevitability of 'creative destruction' in economic progress.[2]

From today's perspective there is something odd about the debate. Today, it is not socialists who advocate long-term planning but Anglo-Saxon financial officials and advocates of privatisation. The United States and UK budgets used to be drawn up one or two years at a time; it was left to France to establish a Commissariat du Plan and the Soviet government to launch its famous Five Year Plans. Now budgets in the United States and UK are routinely projected many years into the future. In 1992, for the first time, the United States Congressional Budget Office drew up a ten-year projection; then, as we have seen, President Clinton adopted a fifteen-year budget projection when he introduced his scheme to save Social Security. Clinton was himself responding to the challenge of the partisans of 'generational accounting' who claimed to show that Generation X, or even those not yet born, would, in decades to come, stagger under the burden of today's greedy seniors and baby-boomers. The Boston economist Laurence Kotlikoff, fresh from showing the Russians how to bury Gosplan, has argued that the 75-year horizon for Social Security projections is too short and the only responsible procedure is to make projections 100 and 150 years into the future. However, the advocates of privatisation remain very schematic when it comes to pro-jecting the real rate of return on capital or the share of profit in national income. In the United States many influential participants in the debate on the future of Social Security assume an average 7 per cent real rate of return on capital in projections for the next three-quarters of a century. This is said to be the long-term historical average for the United States, an average that, notwithstanding a continuing 'equity premium puzzle', will be reliably reproduced by efficient markets and does not, therefore, need to be adjusted for changes in demography, the resource base or the character of international competition.[3]

While it used to be 'market socialists' like Oskar Lange and H.D. Dickinson who urged that the state should mimic a market system, now the advocates of pension privatisation often urge that the financial cor-porations should begin to operate like public services. Citizens are to be required to purchase pensions from a financial services industry which is to conform to stringently prescribed procedures, in order to reduce costs and protect the 'consumer'. The private pension providers, creatures of gov-ernment favour, have never embodied the principles of free enterprise, even if their fund managers have wished to see the rest of the world organ-ised in a market-friendly fashion. Now the devout wish of the industry's leading lights is that the entire population be dragooned into subscribing to its schemes, so that the forward flight of the stock exchanges can be resumed. The role of governments will be to enforce this and to scurry along with safety nets in case the whole project falls out of the sky.

A striking corollary of today's curdled collectivism is the insistence on placing pension assets in index-tracking funds, as with Stakeholder pensions in the UK or many leading privatisation proposals in the United States. In their account of Social Security policy in the 1990s the former Clinton-era Treasury officials Elmendorf, Liebman and Wilcox explain:

> Early in the debate, proponents of individual accounts were arguing that there should be no restrictions on investment options. For example, Martin Feldstein initially proposed that individual accounts be administered by letting people invest in the same broad set of investments options that are available to the holders of IRAs, and that funding for these accounts should be handled by a tax credit. But in response to concerns about administrative costs and naïve investors, most Republican plans (including the main legislative proposals) ended up restricting investment choices to a few broad indexed funds similar to the choices offered under the Federal Thrift Savings Plan.[4]

The report of the Bush Commission on Social Security in December 2001 was entirely to confirm this observation. Sylvester Scheiber, a member of the commission, had signalled one reason for a collective approach. In a work he co-authored with John Shoven we read that the solution to the cost problem is to emulate the scale economies of large 401(k) schemes where the employer furnishes a subsidy: 'If we can find a relatively efficient way to group workers into large systems, the cost of the remaining administrative functions should be even lower.'[5] If employees of the same or an affiliated workplace are to be brought together in this way and given a stake in the same plan then, notwithstanding individual accounts, they will have some interests in common and an incentive for joint action.

Advocates of privatisation now generally favour *mandatory* private schemes partly because only this universal approach enables them to capture scale economies and thus tackle the cost disease which afflicts voluntary private pensions. Another feature of this hybrid approach is the offering of only a few standardised options. As Estelle James and her co-authors explain, the lowest fees are to be obtained when 'worker choice is constrained':

> Mandatory IA [Individual Account] systems can be structured to obtain scale economies in asset management without high marketing costs, by operating through the institutional market. In other words, they can offer workers an opportunity to invest at much lower costs than would be possible on a voluntary basis. To accomplish this requires aggregating numerous small accounts of a mandatory system into a huge block of money and negotiating fees for the investment function on a group or centralised basis.[6]

James cites the example of the way the Swedish second pension board, PPM, channels contributions to fund managers:

The PPM records these contributions, aggregates the contributions of many individuals and moves them in omnibus accounts to the mutual funds chosen by the workers. Indeed, the funds will not even know the names of their individual members – a procedure known as 'blind allocations'. All fund switches will be processed by the PPM. These features reinforce the bulk buying power of the public agency and further discourage sales commissions.[7]

The same authors voice a fear that such government regulation might in time generate unappealing features – becoming subject to 'value judgements and/or political pressure'. But they are not worried by the prospect that really huge sums of capital will be invested according to the heedless principles of the index-tracker funds. From the individual's point of view, trackers have the disadvantage that they buy stocks when they are doing well and sell them when they decline, and thus, in turbulent markets, they lock the investor into a costly pattern of transactions. There are now both many indices to track and many tracking methods, so there could be a wide variation in their performance. Some advocates of privatisation, Feldstein being one, advocate a government guarantee in case of bad performance, but only if the investor conforms to a prescribed asset allocation. This qualification is designed to prevent the moral hazard that some will choose high-risk, high-return stocks, secure in the knowledge that they will be all right even if the gamble does not pay off.

From the social point of view, tracker funds also have serious drawbacks. The existence of large resources operated according to tracking principles will exacerbate market swings. This type of investing contributes to herd behaviour, privileging a very narrow species of information – what others are doing. However, paradoxically, 'passive investment' could eventually encourage shareholder activism. This is because the institution committed to a broad index cannot simply sell the shares of companies whose policies and practices it finds misguided or disreputable. If its concerns, or trustee concerns, are intense, then it will have to seek change by taking the path of shareholder activism. There is evidence that the growth of institutional activism in the UK in 2001 reflected, in part, the restiveness of 'passive' money managers who found their funds dragged down by the bear market.

The growing 'financialisation' of the Anglo-Saxon economies has been accompanied by gestures which seek to indicate that the forces of creative destruction can, after all, be tamed and directed. In July 2001 the FTSE, seeking to improve on the Dow's sustainability index, launched FTSE4Good, an index that would select stocks in the UK, US, continental European and global stock markets, screening out those which do not work towards environmental sustainability, respect stakeholders or uphold human rights. Companies involved in tobacco, armaments or nuclear power were all to be excluded. The UK list included 290 out of the UK's All Share Index of 757 companies. It was claimed that the stocks which met the standards of the FTSE4Good index had outperformed the FTSE 100 and the FTSE All Shares indices over the previous five years. On the other hand, in 2000 the performance of the selected stocks had been worse because of their disproportionate concentration in the technology sector.[8] Whether or not socially responsible investment is in any way effective will be discussed in the conclusion. At least the appearance of a bench mark index for 'socially responsible' funds represents a dawning awareness in the business community that narrow fixation on the bottom line arouses public unease.

A promising logic has also been spotted by some in the workings of the public sector pension funds. Thus Keith Ambachtsheer, an independent pensions consultant, has praised these funds, many of them distinguished by their record of active management, as the harbinger of a new, more acceptable investment style. As noted in the last chapter, Ambachtsheer carried out a survey which found that the performance of a sample of thirty-four public funds compared well with a sample of fifty-two corporate sector pension funds. He observed:

> If we are right, the world's public sector mega-funds are well positioned to promote the financial interests of their principals in coming decades. This is only part of the good news. By doing so, they will be furthering the financial interests of citizens at large as well. They will do so both as knowledgeable transactors when trading government and corporate securities, and as informed holders of these securities. As knowledgeable transactors they will be a stabilising influence in frothy markets driven by short-term investors (whether retail or institutional) whose main focus is price momentum. Against these kind of transactors, superior fundamental information and disciplined buy-and-sell strategies will win the day over the long term. The globe's financial markets benefit through lower volatility and securities prices that eventually reflect fundamental value.[9]

The optimism is no doubt misplaced, since it takes no account of instabilities inherent in today's anarchic global financial structure. And the account of the funds themselves is too flattering. But public sector funds are removed from the crasser pressures of commercialism and do feel some need to justify their conduct to policy holders and a wider public. The members of such schemes should indeed expect them to be run as knowledgeable, committed and socially responsible transactors.

A similar line of argument to Ambachtsheer's has insisted that, if they are really to live up to the best interests of policy holders, today's mega-funds must aspire to be 'universal owners': 'The fundamental characteristic of the universal owner is that it cares not only about the governance and perform-ance of the individual companies that compose its portfolio, but that it also cares about the performance of the economy as a whole.'[10] This is held to be true partly because of the huge size and diversified nature of the typi-cal institutional holding. While the holdings of large private investors are usually concentrated in a few sectors the institutions should, in principle (according to this view), be concerned about the health of society as a whole. For them there can be no 'externalities': 'pension funds can be con-cerned with vocational education, pollution, and retraining, whereas the owner with a perspective limited to a particular company or industry would consider these to be unacceptable expenses because of competi-tiveness problems.'[11] If offered as a description of today's institutional investing this would be risible. But as a critique of the workings of the 'prudent expert' doctrine, and an argument in the mouth of those campaigning for pension funds to become socially responsible investors, it has merit.

In the age of globalisation the discourse of economics has become hegemonic but it does not, as some suppose, invariably endorse pension privatisation. Some economists now believe that they can demonstrate why existing commercial pension arrangements lack the long-term per-spective that alone can yield the best outcome for all generations. In this view it can be shown that optimum results can be obtained by income smoothing using a combination of safe and risky assets over three genera-tions. Thus Franklin Allen and Douglas Gale compare the possibilities of insurance open to an individual with those which could be made by a 'long-lived agent or planner who maximised the long-run average of expected utility'. Individuals maximising their own expected utility across a two-generation horizon might, these authors contend, behave very differently from the planner, who 'would have an incentive to accumulate large stocks of the safe asset in order to provide insurance against rate of return risk.'[12] They go on to argue:

> a market equilibrium will not be ex ante efficient in general, because agents are not allowed to trade before they are born. Hence, all trades are under-taken by an agent after the state into which he is born has been revealed. In other words, the birth state . . . is a 'pre-existing condition', against which an individual cannot insure. However, a planner could provide such insur-ance by making appropriate transfers between the old and the young at each

date. Thus . . . the planner could achieve a Pareto improvement from the ex ante point of view. However, the expected utility will be even higher if intergenerational smoothing is carried out, accumulating reserves of the safe asset and using them to smooth fluctuations in consumption. Intergenerational risk-sharing by means of transfers between old and young at each date does not remove the aggregate uncertainty caused by the randomness of the aggregate endowment. Intertemporal smoothing eliminates this uncertainty, at no cost in terms of long-run average consumption.[13]

Allen and Gale do point out that the long-term advantages here might be spotted by a financial intermediary. 'Given the opportunity to make individuals better off, some institutions will try to exploit that opportunity and capture part of the surplus. One possibility is that a long-lived intermediary is set up to provide insurance against uncertain returns by averaging high and low returns over time. Such an intermediary could hold all the assets and offer a deposit contract to each generation.'[14]

The 'with profits' funds offered by UK insurance houses – many of them in the past owned on a mutual basis – perhaps corresponded to this formula. But as Allen and Gale observe, the workings of such procedures will only be stable if protected and enforced by the public power. In particular, intertemporal risk sharing will present some individuals with arbitrage opportunities: 'Taking advantage of arbitrage opportunities is rational for the individual but it undermines the insurance offered by the intermediary. For these reasons an open financial system may not be able to provide intertemporal risk smoothing, although it provides a tremendous variety of financial instruments.'[15] The case for a long-lived planner harbouring reserves would be even stronger if account were taken of the inevitability of unpredictable external shocks.

The line of thought explored by Allen and Gale echoes the stress in Samuelson's classic 1958 article concerning the superior insurance which can be made from a three-generation perspective. It presents a case for a degree of collective protection of pension arrangements with the aim of securing an advantageous result for all of the generations. It also uses asset accumulation and different types of asset to furnish better forms of intertemporal risk sharing. It demonstrates how misconceived is the World Bank's antagonism to the 'dominant public pillar' in pension provision, while itself recognising the necessity of funding if differently situated generations are to be catered for equitably.

The US National Bureau of Economic Research has published a series of studies probing alternative methods of pension delivery which have allowed Martin Feldstein, John Shoven and others to refine their case for privatisation. Some of these studies have turned up arguments supportive of forms of public or non-commercial provision. Thus Henning Bohn has urged that PAYGO systems may not be as vulnerable to changes in the size of age cohorts as has often been thought because of alterations in factor-prices that will flow from the demographic shift itself. A reduction in the size of the available labour force will trigger a rise in wages, in this view, which in turn will boost payroll tax receipts. Bohn's conclusion is that 'members of a small cohort generally benefit from being in a small cohort even if the government operates a DB social security system. . . . Large cohorts are, however, worse off than small ones if there is no DB social security: their high labor supply drives down the wage rate when the cohort is young; their desire to save reduces the return on capital as they age.'[16] The precise impact of labour supply on factor price changes is a topic where varied estimates are to be expected; Bohn's model assumes something like a 'closed economy' (e.g. without immigration or international capital flows) so a more open context could weaken some of the factor price changes he postulates. Varying cohort sizes remain a factor that PAYGO systems must reckon with. But it is remarkable that the countervailing tendencies Bohn cites have been so generally neglected in previous discussion of the topic.

In the same NBER volume Antonio Rangel and Richard Zeckhauser argue that while the market is bad at intertemporal risk sharing, so are governments responding to self-interested electors. In both cases the risk-sharing mechanism is exposed to the danger that a cohort will seize a temporary advantage.[17] But governments can and do set up protected types of collective property which thereby become administratively, legally and politically difficult to divert to other ends. This is the positive aspect of trustee law. Public funds set aside with their own administration, constitution and social purpose, are difficult to tamper with. Even the privatisation zealots of the Bush commission found themselves taking the Thrift Savings Fund, the US civil servants' pension fund, as their model for the first phase of their individual account proposals. Relatively autonomous social funds can be protected in this way while their constitutions still enshrine appropriate forms of accountability. Of course a really determined government could always undo even an institution of this sort. Electoral behaviour may often be fickle or foolish yet it doesn't generally bear out the single-minded and consistent pursuit of individual advantage postulated by Rangel and Zeckhauser's model.[18] Their approach cannot explain why the French governments of the 1990s, or the US administration of 1999, abandoned plans to weaken public provision, or why the UK government in 2000 felt it had to introduce a big and previously uncontemplated rise in the state pension. It is true that another NBER author is able to document benefit trimming of public pensions in such varied polities as the United States, Japan, Italy, France, Germany and the UK but most of the rule changes which produced this trimming were carried out with little fanfare and several had the aim of 'saving' the public scheme.[19]

As the discussion in chapter 6 has shown, the work of Joseph Stiglitz has tended to justify a greater role for public authorities, seeing governments as differently situated from private organisations because of their greater powers, privileged access to information and longer time horizons. States, or the public bodies they mandate, can supply the coordination needed by large-scale enterprises and are placed to internalise, and thus confront, what will appear to commercial organisations as external costs and opportunities. Moreover the state can allow for decentralisation if it wishes and so capture potential gains from market organisation:

> Whatever can be achieved within a decentralised mechanism can be achieved within a centralised framework. The argument underlying this is simple. A centralised system could, in principle, organise itself in a decentralised way so that, if there were advantages to decentralisation they could be attained. But the centralised authority can do more (and our earlier discussions suggest that it might well be desirable to do more, to intervene to counter externalities or to coordinate).[20]

However, Stiglitz did not regard this as a knock-down argument since it still had to surmount the problem of commitment – of ultimate responsibility for the allocation of investment. If the public authority, the centre, had this power what would prevent it from continually second-guessing investment decisions, or from doubling its stakes to recoup if its investment wagers failed to prosper? One aspect of the discussion which follows will be an attempt to see whether part of the solution to these problems would be to endow semi-autonomous social savings funds with some of this power of commitment, making them answerable not to the government of the day but to their own members and to rules of social audit.

Saving, Funding and Investing

We have seen that the partisans of privatisation have waged an incessant propaganda war against public pensions on the grounds that they inhibit national savings and that, in an ageing society, they become ruinous. Such advocates frequently exaggerate or misrepresent – and never investigate the co-responsibility of Anglo-Saxon pension funds and consumerism for low savings and poor economic performance in 1973–96, and for the subsequent economics of bubble and bust. The low, or even negative, rates of savings in the United States and UK economies are a problem which cannot indefinitely be avoided by the import of capital. Research in the UK shows that while payroll taxes may indeed substitute for some types of saving, matters are not improved by pension privatisation. A study of savings patterns in the UK, where opt-outs became more generous in the 1980s, concludes that 'contracting out to a personal pension has a positive wealth effect, which tends to reduce saving.'[21] The alternative, to be explored below, is to make sure that funds built up from payroll taxes and National Insurance contributions are made available to democratic institutions charged with responsibility for socially-prioritised investments.

The economist's notion of saving simply refers to factor income that is not spent on current consumption. It is important because too much consumption will crowd out investment and/or generate inflation. Because of credit arrangements and the import of capital, those making investments do not need to be directly connected to those making the savings. The former simply need to have a good business proposition. Nevertheless, those who extend credit will need some collateral, and funds which gather up savings also help, by boosting liquidity and bolstering confidence. The government generates potential saving through its taxes, but cancels this out with its expenditures. One might have thought that those who lament low levels of savings and investment would target the spendthrift habits of the wealthy, and the weak investment record of the state. But a surprising amount of attention is in fact devoted to the inadequate savings record of the poor, who are deemed to be putting aside much too little and whose improvidence, supposedly cushioned by programmes like Social Security, menaces national prosperity. Researchers have discovered that many on low or middling incomes heavily discount the future: 'we believe that there is a significant group of households with savings rates too low to be explained by conventional life cycle models'.[22] In the merciless prose of the modern economist they explain:

> For hyperbolic agents, short-run discount rates are higher than long-term rates, so decision-making is time inconsistent. When combined with costs of planning, this gives rise to much inaction: people procrastinate on making decisions that require immediate effort. In these types of models, people suffer from self-control problems and thus fail to follow through on plans to save. If individual savers have trouble doing so because they lack information, or because of these dynamic inconsistencies . . . then the justification for government policies to encourage saving becomes stronger.[23]

Moreover these authors point out that means tests supply a positive deterrent to savings and that '[w]elfare recipients can be legally prosecuted for saving above the legal limits.' Their solutions include 'removing all asset-based means tests', 'improving financial education' and 'an expansion of Social Security saving, either through subsidized saving accounts or personal equity accounts.'[24] (This presumably means either as an add-on or as a carve-out to Social Security, but it could equally cover the trust fund investing in equities). Research like this is congruent with the view that Social Security reform can lead to increased savings, boosting the rate of contribution by some combination of carrot and stick. In its turn this will lead to a larger funded element, whether public or private, which will create economic room for investment.

But the making of investments does not just arise from propitious general conditions, such as low interest rates or the absence of crowding out. It requires highly specific decisions and commitments. Some of this has a fairly routine character – replenishing wear and tear on existing facilities – and some of it will be more innovative. At the limit, all investment involves a wager that whatever is being built will, one day, prove to be socially useful and productive. In chapter 3 I pointed out that high finance is much better at spotting an existing misallocation of resources and rectifying it through arbitrage than it is at sponsoring the wager on investment in something new. The institutions and money managers are simply too big and far removed to be able to perform this task satisfactorily. Stiglitz sees banks as having been better at monitoring investment, though he always stresses the failure of both market theory and central planning theory to grasp the particular nature of investment opportunities in any real economy.[25] However, if there was broader and more egalitarian participation in funded pension provision, then community- or workplace-based pension funds might help to supply the missing links and to reconnect individuals with decisions about savings and investment.

Pay-as-you-go (PAYGO) principles played a progressive part in extending pension coverage in the middle of the last century and will continue to make a vital contribution to pension finance. But PAYGO will not be able fully to cover the cost of both basic and secondary pensions for a population with varying cohort sizes and a rising proportion of dependants. In a healthier pattern of economy, and with sanctions against ageist hiring practices, larger proportions of those over fifty and over sixty would be able to find work. But a drop in dependency rates remains unlikely and, in some ways, undesirable. Today's employees need lengthier initial education and training, with refresher courses or new starts at intervals throughout

their working lives. At the age of fifty-five or sixty-five there are many who
would welcome 'active retirement', especially the possibility of work
undertaken for its intrinsic satisfactions rather than simply as a source of
income. Finally an ageing society does mean many more of the older old
who will aspire to live independently and with dignity. All this will need
resources. The perspective of the 'long-lived planner', and a preparedness
to invest in the future, point beyond the foreshortened horizon of early
PAYGO or of the two-generation model of life-cycle economics. The
advocates of compulsory private pensions and of elaborate attempts to
overcome the vices of commercial competition do not always exaggerate.
Indeed, in their own backhanded way, they sometimes recognise that the
scale and type of needed provision demands something more than privatised calculation and individual planning. In societies rightly concerned by
the ebbing of community spirit, here is an issue that requires, and would
reinforce, generational solidarity, independent civic institutions and an
enlightened public power.

Individualism, consumerism and commodification remain powerful,
even hegemonic forces, in the first decade of the twenty-first century. But
they have helped to create such a dangerous and divided world that their
influence will be increasingly contested. In Britain and the United States
politicians seek to respond to a widespread desire for better public services.
More public money for education, for the National Health Service in the
UK, for Medicaid and Medicare (e.g. to cover prescription charges) in the
United States, for railways in the UK and for airline security in the US, all
testify to politicians' desire to be seen responding to the new mood. Such
diverse and unsettling events in 2000 and 2001 as Britain's rail breakdown,
California's power crisis, the attack on September 11th, the collapse of
Enron, the Argentinian default, the steep decline of the stock markets, and
the onset of recession, helped to dramatise the vulnerability of an economic system weakened by pervasive de-regulation, privatisation and
commodification.

The shrinking of 401(k) holdings in 2000 and 2001, and the underfunding of many DB schemes in the private sector, swiftly dissipated the
euphoria of the late 1990s bubble. Groups of employees were less likely to
trust their managers and more likely to insist on collective representation
as these schemes entered troubled waters. When the Argentine government seized pension assets and froze current accounts in December 2001
it soon discovered that it had made a fatal mistake. As the citizenry poured
into the streets in protest, President De la Rúa was forced to resign. Since
Argentina and its finance minister, Domingo Cavallo, had pioneered

dollarisation and privatisation this was a major blow to the laissez-faire creed. In Italy the new premier, Silvio Berlusconi, announced that his government would not be privatising ENI, the state oil company, as some members of the previous Centre-Left government had proposed, and that pension reform would, in the first place, target the workings of the company retirement reserve scheme.[26]

At the level of ideas the advocacy of public programmes has found a more attentive hearing and gained in sophistication. The intellectual balance was tilting back towards defenders of Social Security, with economists like Peter Diamond and Alicia Munnell, Dean Baker and Mark Weisbrot, Peter Oszag and Joseph Stiglitz, helping to marshal a strong case. In the *New York Times* Paul Krugman attacked the proposals of the Bush Commission, as did a technical paper from the Century Foundation and a spirited polemic by Thomas Frank in *Harper's*.[27] As we saw in the last chapter philosophers have also explored the meaning of justice between generations, although they sometimes return the problem to the economists by insisting that justice is served by the economic institutions which do most for the poorest. When free market economics prevails, this apparently egalitarian prescription can lead to toleration of much inequality, as it did in the 1980s and 1990s. But when the results of laissez-faire turn out to be very different from those promised, then other economic models can gain a hearing and economics itself be called to justify itself in terms of such concepts as justice, citizenship, human solidarity and cultural self-realisation.

In Europe the sociologists Pierre Bourdieu and Peter Townsend helped to rally public opinion in defence of pension provision by appealing beyond individualism to a notion of social citizenship. In 1995 in France and in 2000 in the UK social movements extracted major pension concessions from government. The idea that economic arrangements should be tailored to serve social ends and that 'atomistic calculation' can generate absurdities was advanced by Michael Prowse, a *Financial Times* columnist, in the following terms:

> How extraordinary to think that millions of adults, nominally citizens of a single state, must nevertheless make individual provision for retirement. . . . They must pay the transaction costs of personal investment over a 40-year period. . . . They must try to provide security for themselves without knowing how stock markets will perform. . . . In choosing a private pension provider, they must make one of their most significant financial decisions. And yet there will be no rational basis for it. Past performance is no guide to future performance as the Equitable Life saga illustrates . . . Over a forty

year period many private providers will not only perform badly, they will go bust. Now consider the advantages of a generous state pension. Although nothing is certain in life, it is more logical to rely on the state than on any particular private institution. It can certainly commit itself to pay pensions indexed to overall economic growth. . . . There is no compelling economic evidence that such a scheme would undermine work incentives. . . . Perhaps even more important, generous collective provision for retirement would be a symbol of social maturity. The fact that we could agree on an income-linked scheme for all would show that we are not beasts of the jungle, but rational – perhaps even civilised – beings. Now why cannot a Labour government understand such logic?[28]

The award of the Nobel Prize for Economics to Joseph Stiglitz in 2001 (and Amartya Sen in 1998) could be seen as recognition that alternatives to neo-liberalism were needed. But the real and enduring consequence of all this remains to be seen. Western governments and international organisations remain wedded to a basically neo-liberal model (the famous 'Washington consensus'), even if that model has failed New Zealand and Argentina, and has had to be tinkered with in the UK and United States. In a climate of recession and budget constraints the siren song of privatisation and commodification will continue to tempt political leaders.

Events themselves can prompt diverse responses. In the aftermath of 11 September defenders of public services were able to argue with some success that airline security should be a public responsibility or that the overall level of medical services should be raised to reduce vulnerability to bio-terrorism. But the Social Security privatisation lobby had its own egregious response to the disaster. Meredith Bagby solemnly informed the Bush Commission: 'The Gen X firefighters and policemen who lost their lives on September 11th made the ultimate sacrifice for democracy. A request to their contemporaries to forgo a small amount of Social Security money decades from now would be a well-timed yet minuscule sacrifice by comparison, and would not be rebuffed.'[29] While few are likely to be persuaded by this strange logic the real message was that the privatisation lobby remained as perversely dedicated as ever.

Pension Panic and New Prospects of Reform

Some writers have argued that more than a decade of widespread infatuation with stock markets has created a 'mass investment culture' that instinctively supports individual and private solutions to all questions. Thus

Adam Harmes warns that it is not so much the diffusion of share ownership as the 'naturalisation of the stock market in everyday life' that changes the values and perceived interests of voters, fostering a readiness to go along with privatisation and deregulation. He points out that publications like *Business Week* and *Fortune* have won a wider readership, and the TV business channels have blossomed. In this way the 'norms and practices of finance capital' have become deeply embedded among 'broad layers', so he believes, 'in a way that a downturn in the stock market cannot destroy'.[30]

There can be little doubt that there has indeed been a diffusion of such a 'mass investment culture', but I believe that in the conditions of what I have called 'grey capitalism' the implications are less stable and unidirectional than Harmes claims. In the months following the collapse of Enron in December 2001 there was an outcry directed at bankers and auditors who had let the directors of the company raise huge loans and imperil the retirement funds of their own – and many other – employees. Opinion polls showed that many believed that the malpractices of Enron's management were to be found in many other companies and had only been possible because of the complicity of its auditors, lawyers and bankers. The Enron collapse drew attention to a series of other cases where the financial services industry had been found wanting. Lax auditing had contributed to failures at Cendant, Sunbeam, Waste Management and Global Crossing. The New York office of Credit Suisse First Boston had been fined $100 million for awarding hot new issues to favoured clients during the share bubble, Goldmann Sachs had been fined by the Tokyo stock exchange for 8,000 illegal trades, while in London Merrill Lynch Mercury Asset Management had paid £80 million to the Unilever pension fund to compensate for chronic mismanagement and underperformance. Over the four years prior to Enron's collapse over 700 US companies had been forced to restate their accounts.[31]

While the evidence of wrongdoing and indulgence was quite sufficient to prompt public anger, Enron's collapse also crystallised more widespread anxieties and fears concerning the prospects for pension funds and 401(k)s, given the prevailing laxity and worrisome outlook. When such large companies as Global Crossing, K-Mart and LTV filed for bankruptcy around the same time as Enron their employees' retirement plans were also hit. Even employees who felt secure in their employment could still be left with a much smaller pension fund. The business press sought to console fund holders with the thought that a recovery was on the way but, aware that this might be a long time coming, they also lambasted the people and institutions that had allowed the disaster to happen. Some writers even dwelt on structural novelties: 'For a long time we thought that the fundamental conflict in capitalism was between owners and workers. Enron proves that the real conflict is between insiders and outsiders. The losers in the Enron case are both stockholders and workers.'[32] In this case the *insiders* would include the banks, like J.P. Morgan Chase and Citibank, that had off-loaded their risky Enron loans on insurance houses and fund managers (ultimately, therefore, on retirement funds, whose beneficiaries would be the *outsiders*). Workers who are also indirect or small-scale shareholders are now very numerous but their 'outsider' status is preserved by their lack of real control over the assets lodged in their name, even if the latter are in a 401(k).

In February 2002 *Business Week* ran a cover story on 'The Betrayed Investor' in which it reported that 81 per cent of investors lacked confidence in those running 'Big Business' and were 'angry and disillusioned'.[33] The report tended to elide the difference between avid day-traders, punished for their speculations, and the great mass of those holding 401(k)s and similar plans who were saving for their retirement and had no intention of 'playing the market'. The great majority of the 45 million holders of 401(k)s never change their provider and rarely alter the balance of their portfolio. (One of the reasons the funds spend so exorbitantly on advertising is that they know that if they can win a new customer they should be able to retain him or her for life.) It is these people who now felt betrayed by those entrusted with their savings. *Business Week* nervously observed that these people are mostly 'baby boomers who grew up in the era of protests and social activism'. The journal reported a poll of 'professional investors' which revealed that those working for the fund industry wished to pass on some of the blame – 43 per cent were 'extremely concerned' at the potential for 'widespread reporting fraud'. The truth would probably be that they were themselves mostly only 'half-insiders', aware that something was amiss, hoping to gain anyway and comforted by the thought that everyone else was also heavily committed.

Even activist retirement funds that were in a good position to know what was happening at Enron chose not to become whistle blowers. The California Public Employees Retirement System (Calpers) had invested in Jedi, one of Enron's off-balance sheet partnerships, in 1993 and had had difficulty, as noted in chapter 3, in withdrawing its capital in 1996. It knew that Enron's Chief Financial Officer, Andrew Fastow, was also an officer of the LJM3 partnership and decided in December 2000 not to take a stake in it. But Calpers did nothing to publicise its concerns.[34] As the Enron scandal unfolded much was made of the fiendish complexity of the company's 'aggressive' accounting strategies. Yet many of the main deceptions practised by its executives, and condoned by its auditors and bankers, were among the hoariest ruses known to the financial fraudster. One would expect any halfway competent and independent analyst to spot the large gap between reported revenue and actual cash-flow, to suspect that 'hollow swaps' were artificially boosting turnover, to worry about the purpose of the off-balance sheet partnerships, to wonder whether it was right to book loans as hedges or trades. Half of Wall Street was involved in selling stakes in Raptor, Chewco, Jedi, LJM and the rest, or in off-loading Osprey bonds.[35] It was greed and safety in numbers, not devilish cunning, that explained Enron's success in duping so many.

As might be expected, the *Wall Street Journal* did not feel unduly chastened by the débâcle, retaining an undimmed enthusiasm for the working of 401(k)s – 'one of the great inventions of modern capitalism' – and hostility to any further regulation. The editorial's refrain was that risk was unavoidable and that alternatives to 401(k)s were also risky:

> there are risks to any investment that seeks to benefit from America's capitalist prosperity. The old fixed pension arrangement so favored by the anti-401(k) brigades carry the risk that the entire company, or industry, can get into trouble. Those pensions obligations then become 'unfunded', which is worse for workers who have no diversification choices at all. Just ask America's steelworkers.[36]

Here, at least, the *Wall Street Journal*, had a valid point, though it was cold comfort for many of the 40 million or so employees who were members of defined benefit schemes, notably those in the private sector. The plight of the steel workers will be addressed in the conclusion; here it is only necessary to observe that the bill for Enron was picked up by all types of pension fund, whether DB or DC.

The demise of Enron, coming just a few weeks before the report of President Bush's commission on Social Security, was a major setback for the cause of privatisation. It was said of the Enron employees that now they had 'nothing other than Social Security' to fall back on. The proposal that even this basic pension should also be exposed to Wall Street was difficult to make. The Enron affair prompted a raft of proposals aimed at calling boards of directors to account, establishing a new regulatory structure, reducing workers' exposure to the fate of their employer, tightening reporting standards, guaranteeing the independence of auditors, and so forth. While the legislative consequences are likely to be modest in the extreme the issues ventilated had far-reaching implications. By calling into question the working of nearly every key institution and practice of

corporate governance and finance, the end-result of Enron was not to
'naturalise' the workings of the corporate and financial system. Rather it
was to present a stark portrait of the cynicism and greed of members of the
corporate elite as they sacrificed and misappropriated the savings of millions
of workers. Many respectable institutions, and a swathe of politicians, had
been caught up in the venality and obfuscation. If some 85 million other
employees did not feel exposed because of their own pension holdings –
whether DC or DB – the bankruptcy would have made less impact.
President Bush himself was, as we have seen, sufficiently abashed to declare
that 'corporate America must be made accountable to employees and
shareholders and held to the highest standards of conduct.'

British pension funds suffered some losses from Enron but this was not
their major headache at the time. The downfall of the energy company
coincided with growing awareness of a pensions crisis, signalled by front
page headlines in the popular newspapers as well as in the financial press.
Thus the *Daily Mail*, the self-appointed 'voice of middle England', under
the headline 'Pensions: the Crisis Deepens', ran a story which explained:
'The growing scale of the crisis in pensions is exposed today as figures
show one in three company schemes has been scrapped in the last decade.
The revelation adds to fears that an entire generation is facing cash-
strapped retirement. . . . Astonishingly 58,000 company schemes have
been wound up.'[37] The *Mail* followed up the story with a four-page supplement entitled 'Shameful Betrayal of All Our Futures', containing a
manifesto and promises of a campaign to come. Among a score of proposals, the manifesto called for 'final salary' (i.e. 'defined benefit') schemes
to be protected and declared: 'Millions of pension savers are trapped in old-
style schemes laden with charges and penalties. First all transfer penalties
should be removed. . . . Second all disguised charges and penalties should
be removed to bring these contracts in line with stakeholder.'

The *Financial Times* reported in February 2002 that Alistair Darling,
the pensions minister, had responded to mounting confusion and anxiety
by commissioning two new reviews of every aspect of pension policy.
There were to be, it was said, no 'no-go' areas.[38] The state pension
might be reprieved and the newly-minted pension credits and guarantees
abandoned. The paper's pensions correspondent contributed an article in
which he warned that the closure of 'defined benefit' pension schemes
in such established companies as BT, Sainsbury, Whitbread, ICI and
Lloyds/TSB was an ominous sign of the impending destruction of schemes
catering to 8 million employees. The effect of these closures could be
compared to the 'healthy terminations' which swept the US corporate

sector in the 1980s (see chapter 2). As the correspondent explained: 'To many members – those in their forties and fifties – this will feel like theft. A contract in which the job would deliver a dependable pension has been broken. Legally, it is likely that the companies are on firm ground – although the issue has yet to be tested in the courts.'[39]

In the first instance the closing of schemes was hitting the private sector, but public sector schemes were increasingly vulnerable as the public-private boundary was broken down by the out-sourcing and privatising of public services. The decision to fold traditional schemes had been prompted by several developments – the withdrawal of relief from advance corporation tax (ACT) and a succession of two bad years for the fund managers played a part. But perhaps the critical factor had been the introduction of a new account standard, FRS or Financial Reporting Standard 17. The promulgation of FRS 17 in November 2000, to come into force over a three-year period, was designed to show the cost of a company's commitment to fund employees' pensions, valuing fund assets at current price and with liabilities discounted by the yield on corporate bonds. Any shortfall was to be registered on the balance sheet. Since, as noted in chapter 2, pension funds are often larger than the company sponsoring them, FRS 17 can make a large impact on the bottom line. ICI, one of the companies to close its scheme in early 2002, had registered a pension fund shortfall of £453 million under FRS rules. A survey of 500 of Britain's largest companies by William Mercer, the pension consultancy, found that 52 per cent of them suffered a reduction in assets in their pension funds because falling stock market prices had wiped out the effect of any new contribution made.[40]

While FRS 17 created a new problem by specifying a rigid formula, its effects really reflected British employers' success in claiming legal custody of the pension schemes they sponsored. And the shortfalls often reflected an option to take a contribution holiday in the years of booming stock markets. The *Financial Times* correspondent pointed out that the great disadvantage of the switch to 'defined contribution' was likely to be a sharply reduced employer's contribution: 'The brutal fact is that when employers do make the switch they tend to contribute less.'[41] Moreover those taking out a defined contribution scheme might well face a continuing slump in annuities rates when they came to retire.

UK pension worries were compounded by the confusions and disappointments of the government's attempt at reform. The take-up of its Stakeholder pension had been modest. Few of the 570,000 policies taken out in 2001 were from those on lower incomes, the group that had been targeted, and many had been conversions from other schemes. Neither employers nor providers were keen on the Stakeholder terms they had been obliged to accept and the government had studiously avoided compulsion. The other ingredients of Britain's new pension regime – especially the pension credit – combined great complexity with widespread means testing.

In an editorial the *Financial Times* composed its own advice to the minister under the misleading heading 'Back to Beveridge'. It recommended the scrapping of the complex legislation which Darling himself had so recently placed on the statute book. Instead, it argued, the government should perform 'radical surgery', eliminating the state second pension and slowly raising the qualifying age for the basic pension to 70 years of age, meanwhile restoring its value 'back to a level where it provides just enough to live on'.[42] This would give everyone who could do so a powerful incentive both to save and to continue working.

In both the United States and the UK an alternative to full or partial privatisation could be a scaling back of state provision – by raising the age of entitlement to 70 or (in the US case) weakening the link to earnings, so that workers are obliged to save more in private plans and, if they can, to go on working throughout their sixties. This approach, congruent with the tradition of the 'residual liberal' welfare state, might even deliver as much worthwhile business to the financial services industry as the World Bank-style mandatory approach. While voters may not be entranced, it is the sort of reform which could be encompassed in a succession of seemingly modest amendments. In the context of a gathering pension panic, politicians might be unwise to reduce public entitlements, but this might seem to them preferable to extending compulsion. So while 'Individual Accounts' remain in contention, 'implicit privatisation' could prove to be the fall-back option.

The case for privatisation has placed great, indeed quite exaggerated, emphasis on the prospective burdens of an ageing society. The critics of privatisation have consequently been drawn to protect the principle of public provision by defending the existing workings, and sometimes finance, of public retirement programmes. In this way it can sometimes appear that the Left is the conservative force, justifying existing arrangements, while it is the Right which has raised the banner of reform, or even revolution. In my view critics of privatisation do sometimes sound a little too reassuring. They do not fully bring out the inadequacy of prevailing levels of public provision and do not fully confront the funding problems which would beset better provision. In the conclusion I will argue that it would be good to fund public provision more generously and that existing levels are quite inadequate in the UK, and only a bare minimum in the United States (and in the case of many older women and the lower-paid not even that).

However, the biggest failings of pension provision are to be found in the costly and unequal access to secondary pensions, something highlighted by the dismal performance of many 401(k)s and company schemes. Advocates of Social Security 'reform' have often claimed that private pension delivery is itself the model and in no need of fundamental transformation. This is becoming increasingly untenable. Ideally primary and secondary pension provision should instead be thought through as a unified and necessarily interconnected field. Whatever the failings of public delivery, they pale beside those of the private sector.

While the case for privatisation often harps on impending deficits, some of its proponents have been, consciously or otherwise, motivated by a quite different fear. In 1990 Carolyn Weaver edited for the American Enterprise Institute a volume on the future of Social Security significantly entitled *Looming Social Security Surpluses*.[43] These surpluses 'loomed', perhaps, because they gave substantial leverage and leeway to the Social Security Administration and to those who directed the trust fund. While pre-funding might simply push extra business the way of favoured financial houses it might also be carried out in different ways which would strengthen the public programme.

Pre-funded pensions can take a variety of forms. In the debates traced in this book such varied advocates as Richard Titmuss and Rudolf Meidner, Frank Field and Tony Lynes, Michel Aglietta and Joseph Stiglitz, Peter Diamond and Alicia Munnell, have contemplated the advantages of collective versions of what is now known as 'asset-based welfare'.[44] Of course the aim of these different advocates was to harness pre-funding to public programmes rather than to commercial delivery. The public and planned approach recommended by these advocates fits in well with the economic case for the 'long-lived planner'. And matters often work out better for the individual if the asset-holder is, in fact, a collective entity, enabling risks and skills to be pooled to everyone's advantage.

It would, no doubt, be possible to persuade a commercial organisation to play the part of the long-term planner sketched out by Allen and Gale, so long as guaranteed fees were available stretching far into the future. Perhaps it is visions of this sort which today's aspirant new tax farmers harbour. Their late eighteenth-century forebears also proposed extremely ingenious schemes for salvaging the public finances and paying for programmes of civic improvement and welfare.[45] Indeed it was only the contingent costs of military adventures and the unexpected popular appropriation of the idea of civic rights – not anything intrinsic to the schemes of the tax farmers – that eventually derailed the *ancien régime*. Agreeable as it may be to imagine Alan Greenspan muttering 'Après moi le déluge', we live in different – but not more stable – times.

When Clinton's Treasury experts met in secret to address what they publicly flagged under the enigmatic rubric 'Special Issues', they were preoccupied, so they tell us, to prevent their exercise in partial privatisation from pushing the programme onto a 'slippery slope' which would end by destroying its integrity and viability.[46] Unfortunately, they discovered that what some of them deemed a 'slippery slope risk', others found a promising avenue of reform, and vice versa. It is possible that there is another, and to some even less welcome, 'slippery slope', namely that leading from today's hybrid and artificial 'privatisation' towards new forms of collective involvement in the management of economic resources and processes. If there are to be government-mandated, government-devised and government-guaranteed pension funds owning decisive chunks of the economy, why should not the generality of citizens exercise democratic oversight and ensure that these arrangements benefit them and their families rather the financial services industry?

It would be cowardly to conclude this book without furnishing my own view of the progressive way to resolve today's pension problems. But I must warn the reader before I do so that, because of the subject's complexity and my own limitations, I will only be able to furnish a sketch. In the conclusion I register some of the key links but will only skate over a number of questions that should ideally receive more exhaustive and specialist treatment. My aim is to show that our current economic potential, and our obligations to the future, could be brought into a far happier and more fruitful relationship.

Notes

1 Peter Peterson, *Gray Dawn: How the Coming Age Wave Will Transform America – and the World*, New York 2000, pp. 104–5.
2 Ludvig von Mises, 'Economic Calculation in the Socialist Commonwealth', and Oskar Lange, 'On the Economy Theory of Socialism', in Alec Nove and D.M. Nuti, eds, *Socialist Economics: Selected Readings*, Harmondsworth (UK) 1972; Friedrich von Hayek, 'Economics and Knowledge', *American Economic*

Review, 1945. I review this debate in 'Fin de Siècle: Socialism after the Crash', in Robin Blackburn, ed., *After the Fall*, London 1992. See also Andrew Gamble, *Friedrich von Hayek*, London 1996, and J. O'Neill, *The Market: Ethics, Knowledge and Politics*, London 1998.

3 See the correspondence between Dean Baker and Martin Feldstein available on the web-site of the Center for Economic Policy, Washington DC. This web-site also contains Baker's correspondence with Stephen Gross, the Deputy Actuary of the SSA.

4 Douglas W. Elmendorf, Jeffrey B. Liebman and David W. Wilcox, 'Fiscal Policy and Social Security Policy in the 1990s', paper presented to the June 2001 Conference on 'American Economic Policy in the 1990s' at the Kennedy School of Government, Harvard University, pp. 55–6.

5 Sylvester J. Scheiber and John B. Shoven, *The Real Deal: the History and Future of Social Security*, New Haven 1999, p. 360.

6 Estelle James, James Smallhout and Dmitri Vittras, 'Administrative Costs and the Organization of Individual Accounts Systems', in OECD Private Pension Series, *Private Pension Systems, Administrative Costs and Reforms*, no. 2, Geneva 2000, pp. 18–84, p. 35. Estelle James was, of course, also a member of President Bush's Commission on Social Security as well as having been the coordinating editor of *Averting the Old Age Crisis*.

7 James et al., 'Administrative Costs', p. 42.

8 Pauline Skypala, 'Tough Standards for Inclusion Leave No Room for Complacency', *Financial Times*, 14 July 2001.

9 Keith Ambachtsheer, 'Public Pension Fund Power', *The Journal of Portfolio Management*, vol. 27, no. 2, winter 2001, pp. 61–4.

10 James Hawley and Andrew Williams, 'The Emergence of Universal Owners: Some Implications of Institutional Equity Ownership', *Challenge*, vol. 43, no. 4, July–August 2000, pp. 43–61, p. 44.

11 Robert Monks and Nell Minow, *Corporate Governance in the 21st Century*, Cambridge (MA), 1996, p. 121.

12 Franklin Allen and Douglas Gale, 'Financial Markets, Intermediaries, and Intertemporal Smoothing', *Journal of Political Economy*, no. 3, June 1997, pp. 523–46, p. 533.

13 Ibid., p. 534. 'Pareto optimality' exists when economic welfare cannot be improved for one individual without reducing that of another.

14 Ibid., p. 539.

15 Ibid.

16 Henning Bohn, 'Social Security and Demographic Uncertainty: the Risk Sharing Properties of Alternative Policies', in John Y. Campbell and Martin Feldstein, eds, *Risk Aspects of Investment-Based Social Security Reform*, Chicago and London 2001, pp. 203–41, p. 205.

17 Antonio Rangel and Richard Zeckhauser, 'Can Market and Voting Institutions Generate Optimal Intergenerational Risk Sharing?', in Campbell and Feldstein, *Risk Aspects of Investment-Based Social Security Reform*, pp. 113–52.

18 The model developed by Rangel and Zeckhauser involves only two overlapping generations which, as they point out, renders it less likely to be able to identify the rationale for cooperation between generations. The evidence of voter behaviour cited in chapters 5 and 6 found little evidence that generations constitute electoral blocs. And in 1979, when older voters in the UK plumped for Margaret Thatcher, they were to discover that they had voted for removal of the 'earnings link' that protected the value of the state pension. On the other hand the survival (so far) of US Social Security has demonstrated politicians' inclination to respect the generational alliance that supports the programme. Nevertheless, the vagaries of electoral politics, the lumping together of many different issues in campaigns, and the failure to confer adequate institutional independence to pension arrangements, often do render public pension programmes more vulnerable.

19 John McHale, 'The Risk of Social Security Benefit-Rule Changes', in Campbell and Feldstein, *Risk Aspects of Investment-Based Social Security Reform*, pp. 247–82.

20 Joseph Stiglitz, *Whither Socialism?*, Cambridge (MA) 1994, p. 64. This book was a critique of both free market and market socialist approaches. For an interesting assessment see John Roemer, 'An Anti-Hayekian Manifesto', *New Left Review*, no. 211, May–June 1995, pp. 105–30.

21 Richard Disney, Carl Emmerson and Matthew Wakefield, 'Pension Reform and Saving in Britain', *Oxford Review of Economic Policy*, vol. 17, no. 1, spring 2001, pp. 70–94, p. 91.

22 Annamaria Lusardi, Jonathan Skinner and Steven Venti, 'Saving Puzzles and Saving Policies in the United States', *Oxford Review of Economic Policy*, vol. 17, no. 1, pp. 95–115, p. 111.

23 Ibid., pp. 111–12.

24 Ibid., p. 113.

25 E.g. Stiglitz, *Whither Socialism?*, pp. 15–20, 27–44, 226–7.

26 In its initial formulation Berlusconi's proposal aims to create a new commercial system of secondary pensions not by reducing state benefits but by winding up the arrangements whereby Italian employees pay 8 per cent of their salary into company reserves at a low rate of interest and receive, in return, a lump sum as severance pay (TFR) when they leave the company. The proposal will run into opposition from several quarters, including employers. If eventually introduced its final shape may in practice weaken state benefits. James Blitz, 'Berlusconi Proposes Private Pensions Revolution', *Financial Times*, 22 December 2001.

27 Paul Krugman, 'Laissez Not Faire', *New York Times*, 11 December 2001; Thomas Frank, 'The Trillion Dollar Hustle', *Harper's*, January 2002.

28 Michael Prowse, 'The Only Way Out of the Pensions Jungle', *Financial Times*, 11–12 August 2001.

29 Quoted in Thomas Frank, 'The Trillion Dollar Hustle'.

30 Adam Harmes, 'Mass Investment Culture', *New Left Review*, new series no. 9, May–June 2001, pp. 103–24, pp. 123–4.

31 'The Lessons from Enron', *The Economist*, 9 February 2002; 'A Bleak Winter for Credit Suisse', *International Herald Tribune*, 12 February 2002.

32 E.J. Dionne, 'Shareholders and Workers in the Same Camp', *Washington Post*, 20 February 2002.

33 'The Betrayed Investor', *Business Week*, 25 February 2002.

34 Diana B. Henriques, 'Big U.S. Pension Fund Kept Silent on Enron Conflict', *International Herald Tribune*, 6 February 2002.

35 Andrew Hill and Stephen Filder, 'Enron Ties Itself Up in Knots', *Financial Times*, 30 January 2002; David Kay Johnson, 'How Offshore Havens Helped Enron Escape Taxes', *New York Times*, 18 January 2002; Daniel Altman, 'How Enron "Hid" Debts in the Open', *International Herald Tribune*, 18 February 2002; James K. Glassman, 'Even Amateurs Can Detect Problems by Counting the Cash', *International Herald Tribune*, 18 February 2002.

36 'Raiding Your 401(k)', *Wall Street Journal*, 20 December 2001.

37 Darren Behar and Matt Kovac, 'Pensions: the Crisis Deepens', *Daily Mail*, 20 February 2002.

38 Nicholas Timmins, 'Pensions Industry Braced for Radical Shake Up', *Financial Times*, 15 February 2002.

39 Nicholas Timmins, 'Pension Decisions That Ministers May Pay For', *Financial Times* 11 February 2002.

40 Philip Coggan, 'Accounting Rule Will Unbalance Company Assets', *Financial Times*, 22 February 2002.

41 Ibid.

42 'Back to Beveridge', *Financial Times*, 18 February 2002.

43 Carolyn Weaver, ed., *Looming Social Security Surpluses,* Washington (DC) 1990. In fairness it should be said that this volume included some good work supportive of Social Security, notably the contribution by Alicia Munnell and Carole Ernsberger, 'Foreign Experience with Public Pension Surpluses and National Saving' (pp. 85–118). This text showed how trust funds run for public pension programmes had boosted savings in Japan, Sweden and Quebec.

44 See Sue Regan and Will Paxton, *Asset-Based Welfare: International Experiences*, London 2001. Most arguments for asset-based welfare argue that since most poverty and social exclusion derives from lack of assets the best antidote is to find ways to endow all with assets (say baby bonds or a lump sum on reaching the age of 18). The advocates I cite above have favoured universal and collective asset endowments – though eventually these translate into individual incomes.

45 Perhaps because they were uneasy at their status as financial parasites the tax farmers sought to justify themselves by publicly identifying with good causes. Many tax farmers sponsored the Amis des Noirs, France's anti-slavery society. More generally the holistic views of the Physiocrats owed something to the perspective of the state financiers. One should not expect today's financier-politicians or philosophers to have a monolithic position in favour of privatisation and the free market. In the grey capitalist *ancien régime* George Soros,

Jon Corzine and Maria Cantwell may aspire to play the role of Clavière, Brissot de Warville or Turgot.

46 Douglas W. Elmendorf, Jeffrey B. Liebman and David W. Wilcox, 'Fiscal Policy and Social Security Policy During the 1990s', paper presented at the conference 'American Economic Policy in the 1990s', Harvard University, p. 58.

Conclusion:
Good Pensions and Responsible Accumulation

Being in too much of a hurry to repay a debt is a form of ingratitude.
(La Rochefoucauld, 1703)

We must teach the petrified forms to dance by singing them their own song.
(T.W. Adorno 1948)

Empire cannot be resisted by a project aimed at a limited, local autonomy. We cannot move back to any previous social form, nor move forward in isolation. Rather, we must push through Empire to come out the other side. Deleuze and Guattari argued that rather than resist capital's globalisation, we have to accelerate the process. . . . Empire can be contested only on its own level of generality and by pushing the processes that it offers past their present limitations.
(Michael Hardt and Antonio Negri, *Empire*, 2000)

'*Let us not destroy the wonderful machines that produce efficiently and cheaply. Let us control them. Let us profit from their efficiency and cheapness. Let us run them for ourselves. Let us oust the present owners of the wonderful machines, and let us own the wonderful machines ourselves.*'
(Ernest Everard in Jack London, *The Iron Heel*, 1906)

Francisco Goya, *Content with her lot*, 1815–20 (Rotterdam, Museum Boijmans von Beuningen)

B oth the UK and the United States face a crisis in pension provision, notwithstanding attempts to present them as a model for the rest of the world to follow. The basic state pension in both countries is modest, a little over or under the poverty threshold. Citizens have been urged to rely on the financial services industry for commercially-delivered second pensions. Nearly a half of those reaching retirement have no such provision. Even those who do, often have much less to show for it than they thought. Their fund, depleted by charges or 'under-funding', yields only a scaled-down income. A sharp drop in interest rates and yield ratios means that annuities and investment portfolios produce much less income. In interviews people are prone to express the view that they will experience hardship if their income drops by significantly more than a half consequent upon retirement.[1] Yet, while failing to furnish decent coverage, the Anglo-Saxon pension regimes also fail to generate adequate levels of national saving and in this way store up further problems for the future.

Let us explore some of the basic principles that should guide pension finance and provision. Inescapably I will be schematic here, but with the aim of establishing appropriate correlations and orders of magnitude. This book has ranged over a wide variety of pension regimes, so it would be wrong to conclude with a 'one size fits all' formula for pension reform. In a rapidly changing world, where access to information is uneven, it is important to proceed in a way that maximises popular understanding. This will usually mean starting off from existing arrangements for pension provision and changing them in clear and intelligible ways, for example by widening coverage, removing excess charges, empowering savers and pensioners, or securing more adequate pre-funding. Many existing forms of pension provision represent a historic social conquest, which should be strengthened and safeguarded. But at the same time I will be arguing that increased pre-funding can often reinforce the viability of a pension regime and that assets linked to the dynamic advance of an economy are preferable to government paper.

My main reference point will be existing arrangements in the United States and Britain. However, this does not mean that countries that do not at present possess an 'Anglo-Saxon' style economy should first introduce a market free-for-all in order later to impose genuine social and stakeholder controls upon it. Starting off from the given balance of economic and social forces in a country, it should be possible to find ways in which the social need for retirement income and associated costs of ageing can be linked, through a new regime of savings, to the social control of the accumulation process. It could well be that other social programmes could also be buttressed in this way, but here we are concerned with an area of social provision that is large and which, of its nature, needs to be planned for decades ahead. There are few countries where some older people are not among the poorer and more disadvantaged, and in many countries they comprise a significant proportion of the poorest. But the case for alleviating child poverty will also be pressing. More generally, the pattern of class and geography plays a huge role in maintaining social exclusion. Nevertheless, as I will try to show, pension provision can be tackled in ways that both help the pensioner and contribute to the wider search for a more responsible and equal world.

I assume that those who reach their mid-sixties, and want to retire, should be able to do so with an income that is sufficient to enable them to go on participating in society. And since the retired have more free time their ability to contribute, whether on a paid or unpaid basis, will often be enhanced rather than diminished. Contemporary social anthropologists tell us that, in modern conditions, the retired are able to play a more positive role in their families and communities if they have economic independence and are not a burden upon their children.[2] Moreover, if the aged find that they have surplus resources they are highly likely to pass them on to the generations beneath them – indeed they do this even when they have no surplus and it means accepting a real sacrifice. With increased longevity, the traditional two- or three-generation extended family is likely to become a three- or four-generation structure – what Peter Laslett terms the 'bean pole' pattern – further complicated by the infrequency of lifelong monogamy. The reciprocal structure of the traditional peasant or artisanal family seems often to have been undergirded by the elders possessing property in land or tools, expertise or symbolic value. The downside of this was that the elder person could impose marriage partners on, or otherwise constrain, the next generation – and there were always those marginalised because they were younger sons or maiden aunts. In the modern world only a more democratic family structure is acceptable. The proper funding of pension provision could play its part by enabling older people to contribute in a dignified way and on their own terms.

It has been estimated that for those in employment about 20–30 per cent of their income is taken up by employment-related expenses like travelling, buying lunch or purchasing appropriate clothes and equipment.

Furthermore those who have reached the age of sixty-five have often acquired a residence, or household furnishings, and no longer have primary responsibility for young children. If those who retire receive a total replacement salary of 70 per cent of their former earnings (up to a ceiling of three times average earnings) or 70 per cent of average earnings, whichever is the higher, they should be able to retain their former level of life and economic independence. This total could come from a basic pension and a secondary pension linked to contributions. To encourage later retirement, those who continue working after sixty-five years of age can be offered better rates, and those who voluntarily retire earlier could receive lower rates. But there should be a principle that pensions to which people have contributed should be paid even if the pensioner decides not to retire but to pursue a new occupation. This is not only elementary justice but also allows pensioners to accept a less well-paying job without loss of income.

Existing basic state pensions should be raised until they are at least 40 per cent of average earnings, made available to all citizens, regardless of their contribution record or their possession of such non-income-generating assets as a place of residence. The basic pension should be supplemented by pre-funded secondary schemes, with the state making contributions for those unable to do so themselves. These should aim to replace about 30 per cent of pre-retirement income. In the context of an ageing population all this will require raising considerable sums of extra money by a mixture of capital levies, taxes, contributions and investment income, all of which will enable pre-funding to be achieved at the same time as honouring, indeed improving, current pension provision.

The Rationale for Pre-Funding

There is scope for some increase in taxes and in contributions to social insurance. The public provision of welfare rights based on progressive taxation enjoys more support than New Democrats or New Labour allowed in the 1990s. Insecurity now afflicts the better-paid as well as the low-paid. Given the scope for raising tax rates on the rich and the existence of a still fairly broad band of middle incomes there is a tax basis sufficient to improve existing social provision.[3]

Nevertheless, pension provision is a special case. It is not just another public programme but is the main or only source of sustenance for a large and growing sector of the population. According to the 1998 UN estimates, those over sixty-five already comprise 15 per cent of the population of the developed world and according to the 'medium scenario' this proportion will rise to 20 per cent in 2020 and nearly a quarter by 2030. Let us assume that those in retirement are broadly the same in number as those over sixty-five – with early retirees balancing out those who continue working after sixty-five – and let us also assume that the retired should receive on average 70 per cent of average earnings. Then some 17.5 per cent of national income should be devoted to pension provision, and other income maintenance schemes for the retired, over the next generation. This sum is more than half of US public revenue and a little under half of UK public revenue. As an order of magnitude it is an uncomfortable sum to extract solely from tax sources. This is where special pre-funding, ear-marked levies and investment come in.

We should also bear in mind that the public finances will simultaneously be meeting other costs related to the pressures of an ageing population. Advances in medicine and public health extend life expectancy – and allow us to remain fit in old age[4] – but entail rising medical costs. And since health care tends to be labour-intensive this supplies a further reason to expect costs to grow. The annual medical expenses of those over sixty-five years of age tend to be about four times as large as those under sixty-five. The trustees of Medicare, the US medical programme for seniors, forecast that its budget will be equivalent to 6.5 per cent of GNP by mid-century. While US medical costs are poorly controlled by its privatised system, Medicare is a partial and inadequate programme, leading its recipients to spend over a fifth of their income on extra medical services. If all medical costs are added to retirement income then the proportion of national income absorbed by the over-65s in the advanced countries could rise to between 22.5 and 25 per cent of GNP.[5]

There will also need to be much more public expenditure on sub-sidised child-care if the burden this places on women is to be alleviated and what Esping-Anderson calls the 'low fertility equilibrium' of advanced societies – with its accentuation of the ageing effect – to be avoided.[6] The heavy cost of bringing up children is believed to be a major factor in lowering fertility. Additionally, child poverty must be removed and educational expenditures will increase as more and more people prepare themselves to enter the knowledge society.

There are presumably good reasons why, in nearly all countries, public pensions are largely financed through contributions clearly linked to this purpose. Existing 'National Insurance Contributions' or 'Federal Insurance Contributions' (the payroll taxes destined for Social Security) were separated from general tax revenue and identified in this way in deference to the widespread acceptability of these programmes. Any device which renders the public finances more intelligible should be welcomed. Indeed, there is a strong case for enhancing the separate identity of provision for old age and disability. In the UK Demos and the Fabian Society have recently canvassed the advantages of 'hypothecated' or ear-marked taxes. While governments everywhere acknowledged the appeal of this approach when they established social insurance, they often could not resist raiding the piggy bank, albeit in the disguised form of paying only a low rate of interest into the fund.

Since pensions are such a large and predictable item, and since there are many urgent calls on general tax revenue, it seems wise to find ways of funding them that are not part of annual budgets. While a basic state pension can largely be financed by existing payroll taxes, neither Social Security in the United States nor the BSP in the UK are adequate by themselves and anyway need improving. Pay-as-you-go will continue to make a vital contribution, but if retirement incomes at a much higher replacement rate are desirable, then other sources of finance will have to be found. There is scope for raising the contribution rate from higher earners, but also for reducing rates for low-income earners, so these changes are likely to cancel one another out.

Today the great burden of taxation falls on individuals and there are few who do not contribute substantially via consumption taxes, payroll taxes (in the United States) or national insurance contributions (in the UK), and income tax. The pre-funding of pensions would require extra revenue streams. The fact that most of the baby-boomers are still in employment, with many at the peak of their earning power, means that there should be an excess of revenue over outgoings on the US Social Security current account down to around 2010 or later. Subsequently interest accruing to the trust fund will mean that income should exceed outgo for several more years and the trust fund will not be run down until around 2036. But these sources will, at best, only be able to cover the basic pension and may not even be sufficient to finance needed improvements to it. In the case of the UK the situation is worse than in the United States because no trust fund has been built up.

The contribution made by corporations to retirement schemes has plummeted in the last two decades and should be raised. Much of the needed pre-funding of pensions could most appropriately be met by requiring corporations, as in the Meidner scheme mentioned in the introduction, to issue new shares – say at the rate of 10–20 per cent of their profits annually – both to the existing trust fund and to a range of regional pension boards.

Essentially this levy would serve as a special type of employers' contribution but with the advantage that, like the options now offered to employees, it would not subtract from cash-flow. One of the problems with employee stock options is that they concentrate rather than diversify risk. If companies contributed shares to pooled funds instead, the employee benefit would be greater. The shares contributed to the pension fund would have to be held for at least five years before they could be sold. Private companies would issue profit-linked bonds and concerns below a certain size would be exempt.[7] In traditional, but now increasingly rare, DB pension schemes the employers' contribution was as large as that made by the employee; the proposed share levy would ensure that employers once again were making a significant contribution. There would also be employee contributions but at 10 per cent of profits the share levy alone would raise £10 billion a year in the UK and $73 billion a year in the US. Over 15 years, assuming returns of 5 per cent annually, this would build to a fund of £237 billion in the UK over $1,727 billion in the US, rising to £357 billion and $2,607 billion respectively over 20 years.

One of the aims of pre-funding of pensions through employee and employer contributions would be to reduce or remove the claim of pensions on public revenues to the benefit of other programmes, such as education, health and child care. While a share levy, accompanied by the inability to sell the shares for a period, could boost the funds available to a pension fund it would be difficult or impossible to apply this type of finance to other public expenditures. If a further source of capital was needed then another appropriate financial device might be to pledge the anticipated yield of a tax on that portion of rising commercial site values which reflect public investment in transport, cultural facilities, urban renewal or the rescue of ecologically degraded areas (on this more below).

There is, famously, no such thing as a free lunch. If income-bearing assets are to be accumulated by pension funds, then they must be found from somewhere. In some cases current contributors will need to defer compensation. But since the burden of financing pensions lies in the future then arrangements capable of generating future income streams are perfectly acceptable components of the pre-funding strategy. The share levy would spread a sliver of capital value from existing owners to the pension funds. Rich individuals who hold shares would lose a tiny amount each year while share-owning pension funds would gain more than they lost – up to the point where all shares are owned by pension funds. Individuals with only a few shares would probably gain more than they lost, so long as they were benefiting from a pension fund. In the long run such a process would help to spread economic power to the whole population as Social Funds acquired a significant proportion of corporate assets and helped to defray the new costs of providing for an extended life-course, incorporating further education, active retirement and sophisticated medical care, for larger numbers of long-lived persons. Increased social provision would thus be achieved by scaling back the claims of the wealthy and restoring the employers' contribution.

The perspective of the long term needs to be strengthened within prevailing forms of public provision. The market alone does not act like a long-lived planner nor, often, will modern states, increasingly permeated by market principles and steered by governments facing elections every few years.[8] There are signs that once people have the opportunity to register the failures of privatisation, deregulation and out-sourcing, resistance develops. In some areas a direct state role can simply be restored, but often it will be possible to improve on historical formulas of public delivery and responsibility. In the provision of public services less bureaucracy and paternalism will often be in order. But, where pension provision is concerned, an element of bureaucracy and paternalism could be desirable, preventing policy holders and contributors from selling the assets being held for their retirement. The challenge here can be seen as that of finding the shape of 'just institutions' which might encourage us towards solutions that will benefit all. In many ways the institutions of democratic capitalism, Anglo-Saxon style, expose long-term welfare arrangements to special risk – market arbitrage and political raids motivated by vested interests and wealthy minorities. Ultimately sovereign states can do as they like, of course. But autonomous pension bodies, accountable to their members but permitted to dispose of assets only on an actuarially fair basis, could offer an element of protection, functioning as an institutional defence for retire-ment funds.

Successful and popular pension and social security systems in France and the United States have incorporated, as we have seen, an element of autonomous administration as well as self-financing. This helps to differ-entiate them from state-administered benefits which sometimes encourage a passive and clientelistic relationship. As for commercial undertakings, they have some of the latter defects together with the added disadvantage of being run in the interests of their owners. I will later have something to say about the scope for variety and participation in the constitution of pension funds. Here it is simply a question of differentiating them from the state, on the one hand, and from business, on the other. It is also worth adding that in the US case the integrity of the Social Security Administration is still compromised by the practice of consolidating its funds with the rest of the public budget. A rigorous separation would be far preferable to the purely notional 'lockbox' of a candidate's promise.

Any proposal for favouring a funded element in pension provision has to meet the objection that there is something illusory about the setting aside of pension funds since, eventually, the cost of furnishing pensions will have to be met out of current production. In other words, the income stream to be received by tomorrow's pensioners will represent a claim on the production of the future, and the existence of a pension fund will not necessarily make it easier to meet that claim.[9] However, this is not a well-framed objection since some types of pre-funding could reduce the claims on future resources of wealthy capitalists and rentiers, and encourage a more productive economy. If employers, employees and the state help to build up a fund to assist the paying of pensioners this will reinforce the latter's future claims, and help address the problem of cohorts of unequal size.

More generally and strategically the building up of such pension funds could help to meet the costs of future pensions for three reasons: (1) because the funds raise the rate and quality of economic growth, as a well-managed fund should – an issue to which I will return; (2) because the funds reduce, as they are very likely to, governments' recourse to borrowing. The existence of the pension fund will offset the pre-existing public debt and, as Asimkopulos puts it, 'future generations of workers will be better off if the public debt they inherit is lower.'[10] If the public debt is lower, or if it is entirely extinguished and replaced by public assets, future generations will find it easier to meet their obligations to pensioners and to plan for their own future. Meeting the needs of larger proportions of pensioners will still require an effort but at least the beneficiaries will be more deserving than today's rentiers and financial industry. And finally, (3) because the consumption of the wealthy is restrained, as a consequence of the capital levies, without subtracting from investment.

Some might conclude that if a crucial advantage of pre-funding is the reduction of national debt, why not simply pay down that debt and forget about pre-funding? The difficulty here is that even if political leaders solemnly swear that they will reserve the social security or national insurance surplus for the payment of pensions, they may forget all about their promises at the first emergency, just as President Bush and Congress did in 2001, and 'jimmy the lockbox' rather than find some other solution to their fiscal problem (and reneging on the 'lockbox' promise was clearly about to happen even before 11 September). Pre-funding creates a pool of resources which can be used to enhance the long-run performance of the economy, by favouring well-judged investment in physical plant, or social infrastructure, or research and development, or urban renewal, or education and training. Depending on the economic conjuncture, or the resource endowment of a particular region, a different combination of the foregoing may be appropriate. Part of the advantage of pre-funding is that it allows such choices to be debated and made. Sometimes the pre-funding will take the form of a subscription to public bonds raised to address a particular social issue, and in other cases it will be for investment in company stock, or venture capital. Over time the funds will hold a diversity of assets whose exact mix can be altered as circumstances change.

A supplementary pension system could be set up in such a way as to encourage higher contributions from those in a position to make them while still embodying an element of redistribution. Research now makes it clear that people's ability and propensity to save is not simply related to income. An extra contribution of, say, 2 per cent of salary could be phased in for those earning over 70 per cent of average earnings. If there is some broad link between what a person contributes and what they or their family eventually receive, a universal pension scheme can both encourage additional voluntary payments and encompass mild redistribution. Even commercial insurance schemes redistribute (e.g. from the healthy to the sick, or from those who die young to those who live longer). The gearing of interest rates, administrative charges and rebates can be adjusted to favour those with below-average incomes or suffering misfortune. To have some of the features of a solidarity fund is part of the nature of a pension arrangement. In many cultures to be a recipient of charity has been dishonouring – today the stigma of being on welfare lingers. A pension system that encompasses redistribution over the lifetime of the individual, over the cycle of generations, and between rich and poor, can ensure that the potential injury in the gift relationship is neutralised. The anthropologist Keith Hart has described how West African village work teams achieve this by tending the provision grounds of the infirm and elderly under the guise of mutual cooperation and collective house keeping.[11] The addition of assets deriving from the share levy would help to ensure that the pension system both gave good value to contributors and helped to redistribute.

Secondary Pensions for All

The new pensions funds would need to be set up and regulated in such a way that they were answerable both to their own members and to the community as a whole. Accountability to their own members will be enhanced if they are based on occupation, locality or affinity group. Accountability to the wider community can be promoted by pensions boards which would oversee a registry of pension funds, rules of investment and mechanisms of social audit. Only duly registered and audited funds would have access to fiscal privileges. Today's regime of grey capitalism is defined by indiscriminate tax breaks, many of them swallowed by the charges of the commercial providers. The tax-free nature of contributions, and sometimes of aspects of accumulation and pay-out as well, creates an ecological niche which is filled by the pensions fund industry itself, leaving little or nothing of the benefit to the policy holders. In principle the tax concessions could be confined to funds which meet specified and audited criteria of social responsibility and good husbandry. The need to control the cost disease of private provision has already persuaded some pension reformers to propose conditional tax concessions; it is an approach that could be developed on a broader front and not limited just to charges, important as these are. The new approach could allow pre-existing schemes to qualify for new concessions – such as relief from dividend tax – conditional on meeting audit standards. These standards could include mildly egalitarian rules governing contribution and benefit rates, adherence to an anti-speculation code, an investment policy discouraging anti-social objectives and rewarding social commitment, and a democratic structure of internal governance in which commercial practices are minimised. Each of these components will be separately discussed, though it would be vital that they work together and fit coherently within the overall structure of fiscal policy and monetary regulation.

In arguing for conditional tax concessions – favouring pension funds which meet audit standards – I am assuming, for the moment, that income tax and corporation tax will remain important sources of revenue. Some wrongly claim that globalisation has spelt the death of direct taxation. Although indirect taxes have grown in importance, income tax still supplies about a quarter of central government revenue in Britain and the United States. Campaigns for a flat rate of income tax or for a consumption-only tax have got nowhere. Notwithstanding the rise of globalisation the taxation systems of the OECD countries have retained their bite. In the UK, a fairly exposed or open economy by the late 1990s, direct taxes still supplied a half of government revenue: income tax 25 per cent, National Insurance 10 per cent, and corporation tax 15 per cent. Because the US Federal government does not levy a sales tax it is even more reliant on direct taxes. Large corporations and wealthy individuals certainly make extensive use of tax havens and all available tax loopholes. But such corporations and the members of the corporate elite need the security, facilities, markets and sources of finance which only proper states belonging to the OECD can supply. Indeed even the most important tax havens – places such as Monaco, Liechtenstein, the Isle of Man, the Channel Islands, Bermuda, the Cayman Islands, Gibraltar, and so forth – are invariably themselves dependencies of an OECD state (very often the UK). Tax havens are a problem and should be closed down. But they do not prevent states from exercising great leverage, if they wish to do so, over corporations and the wealthy.[12] The attempt to track the funds of criminals, terrorists and drug smugglers has led to a tightening of reporting standards. Those possessing, or responsible for, large sums of money are by nature timid and fearful. The security they crave often exposes them to a measure of taxation. So does their desire to make use of their wealth. And where accumulation takes the form of windfall gains from rising property or share values then these, too, can be taxed. As for the mass of citizens, they have little opportunity to avoid taxation of their incomes and expenditures. Recourse to the tax havens only makes sense to those with large asset-based incomes and the resources to pay expensive legal and accounting fees. The continuing vitality of the tax system helps to maintain the attractions of the tax-breaks on which pre-funded provision has been built.

Governments do still have the power to tax but that does not mean that its effects are straightforward. Thus, Paul O'Neill, Bush's Treasury Secretary, has argued that corporation taxes are simply passed on to consumers in higher prices. There is some truth in this. That is why it is better to oblige corporations to pay in shares, not cash, on the Meidner model, as I have proposed. Such asset levies would anyway require investment boards to manage them and beneficiary bodies that represent all citizens. The proposed pension board and Social Funds would fit the bill perfectly. And since ownership of the means of production exercises a claim on future income streams, its transferral from the hands of the wealthy to Social Funds benefiting the future pension needs of the generality of citizens would be entirely appropriate.

Income tax remains highly 'progressive' in that there are higher rates for those who earn more. Thus in the United States in the mid-1990s the top 1 per cent of income earners paid 30 per cent of all income tax while the top 10 per cent of income earners paid 60 per cent of all income tax.[13] As Bush's tax cuts are phased in this will diminish a bit but income tax will still take more from the better-paid. In the UK the richest 10 per cent paid 50 per cent of all income tax in 1999–2000.[14] (By contrast, National

Insurance and Social Security contributions, paid by the mass of employees, are not inherently 'progressive', and only become mildly redistributive because of their benefit conditions). The availability of tax breaks on pension fund contributions or 401(k)s inescapably subtracts from the progressiveness of the tax system, giving larger absolute and relative gains to the higher-paid. But the existence of ceilings, above which further tax breaks are not available, limits their regressive impact. Indeed, one reason why the rich do better out of the 'tax spend' than the poor is simply that they are more likely to take part.

US Social Security, as we have seen, is mildly redistributive, and could be made more so by raising the income level below which contributions are payable. The redistributive features of the scheme come from the fact that everyone is covered, including survivors, even if not as generously as would be desirable. But much of the $100 billion a year or more of US tax money spent on subsidising pension plans and 401(k)s goes to people who are already better off. Likewise, the £12–17 billion of tax concessions lavished on British pension schemes. It would clearly be fairer to confine tax breaks to pension schemes which embrace all earners, or to reorganise second pensions so that everyone benefits from them. And if tax breaks were available only to non-commercial organisations this would prevent commercial providers becoming the main beneficiaries of the concessions rather than the policy holders. It is doubly appropriate to insist on a professional rather than commercial approach to fund management if the design of the secondary funded scheme is to be universal and mandatory. If citizens are obliged to take part in a scheme, then they should have a real stake in its management and success.[15]

Ensuring a reasonable approximation to egalitarian outcomes in pension provision would require some vigilance and ingenuity if the social funds employed are diverse, since some will perform better than others. Even pension associations elaborated with good objectives could find it difficult to counteract unequal endowments. Some regions or employee groups would be well placed to run their own schemes, but others would need publicly subsidised professional help.[16] There is bound to be some unevenness in performance and a well-designed structure could prevent major fluctuations and inequalities. However it should leave room for variations that are quite deliberate, so that funds can negotiate their own trade-off between returns and social investments with non-pecuniary advantages. Requiring individuals to have a variety of funds would diversify their risk.

The pension board would maintain panels of financial advisers to help citizens to register with three funds, linked, perhaps, to their former college, their employer and their place of residence. Alternatively Citizens' Advice Bureaux, post offices or Social Security offices could be upgraded to take on this role. Entitlement to the public pension and other benefits would be maintained but it would now be supplemented by the yield of the three extra funds. The proceeds of the Meidner-style share levy, and the taxation of windfall gains in commercial property values, would furnish a supplementary contribution and would finance credits covering the full amount of the minimum contribution for those outside employment or on low incomes. Thus everyone earning less than, say, twice average wages would receive a portion of credits, on a tapering scale, stemming from the Meidner levy and commercial property appreciation tax. The trust fund for the public pension would also benefit from the capital levies. Individual contributions to the public pension would be paid on a gently rising scale. There would be a minimum rate of contributions to the supplementary funds for all those over twenty-five years old but individuals could choose to contribute more if they wished up to some limit. Benefits would be available on both a defined benefit and defined contribution basis, with each individual having at least one of the former. Holders of defined contribution plans would be obliged to hold a high proportion of government bonds as their plan approached maturity (in order to minimise the danger that their pot would be hit by an adverse market) and to purchase an annuity when maturity was reached (to ensure that future livelihood needs really would be met).

The provision of employment-related, residence-related and alumni funds would permit low administration fees and encourage the involvement of those concerned, though some funds of a more nomadic character would also be available. Everyone would have such a set of funds but they would only need to keep in touch with one office maintaining their Social Fund accounts if they so wished. Contributions and credits would be paid to this office, for onward transmission, and benefits claimed from it. In order to keep costs down, and to promote participation, switching between funds could only be made at specified intervals, or, where appropriate, after a change of occupation or residence. Funds would be required to maintain interactive web-sites, to keep their members informed, to give them an opportunity for face-to-face contact, and to give them a voice and a vote in deciding investment principles. Reconnecting the mass of citizens and employees with the processes whereby strategic economic decisions are made will not be easy and will require trial and error. But it also promises the avoidance of the wasteful mistakes and missed opportunities which today plague economic strategy and performance.

Which organisations should be allowed to sponsor and to manage the pension funds which would benefit from Social Fund contributions and tax favours? Municipal and regional authorities already sponsor their own pension organisations for employees, and those which are self-managed have a generally excellent record of pension delivery. The residence-related funds might be sponsored by these authorities or by local educational or research institutions. Some funds may be too small to manage their own investments but there is plenty of scope for joint, professionally run, not-for-profit agencies to offer their services to smaller funds. In Italy locally owned public bodies in Emilia-Romagna made a dynamic contribution to the development of their region. In Quebec activist pension funds helped to supply finance to local enterprises and to the Hydro-Québec project, developments which in turn underpinned the 'Quiet Revolution' of the 1960s and 1970s.[17]

Trade unions have a special responsibility for the active representation of policy-holder interests and the monitoring of fund compliance with social objectives. They would have much to contribute to an improved pension regime. But it is vital that the interests of those outside unions are recognised and met.

Other organisations with relevant experience include US thrifts and mutual companies, UK building societies and mutually owned insurance companies. The considerable success of TIAA-CREF in the US, and of USS in the UK, shows how effective non-commercial fund management can be (although the former does channel contributions to commercial firms). Existing US 'mutual funds' would have to be reorganised in order to qualify for tax relief. The reorganisation would require limited management fees, opportunities for their members to have a real say in running them, and compliance with other features of the new pension regime. As existing commercial providers have hijacked the mutual concept, it would be quite appropriate to take them at their word and require them drastically to prune their management rake-off.

When developing and assessing their investment programmes funds would be able to draw on the knowledge and experience of those professionally engaged in social, scientific and cultural research and education. The endowment funds of colleges and research foundations are generally well-run and this expertise could be shared. While economists, accountants and actuaries would obviously have a special contribution to make they should generally be required to explain and submit their advice to a wider forum. Individuals would be free to choose to join any qualifying fund but would have to remain for a minimum period. Affinity groups would be able to sponsor funds so long as they met criteria of technical competence and did not operate discrimination on grounds of race, religion or sex.[18] The members of funds would receive regular information and free advice. They would be encouraged to participate in the running of the fund subject to limits established by a pension board concerning overall accumulation ratios elaborated to ensure the ability of the fund to meet its long-term obligations. While informed participation would be facilitated it would not be mandatory.

A basic state pension indexed to earnings, combined with the prospective income from three funds, might obviate the need for a guaranteed minimum income for pensioners, or the latter could become the safety net feature of the secondary system. A premium should be placed on simplicity, visibility and an absence of any disbarments except other tax-declared income. The retired person could receive the basic, state-guaranteed pension from his or her Social Fund account(s). The guarantee could be specified as a proportion of average earnings, say at least 50 per cent, thus setting it above the level of US Social Security or the 'minimum guaranteed income' in the UK.[19] The best arrangement might be for a state supplement to be paid to a person's principal pension fund to cover any shortfall. Retired persons would receive the full proceeds of their fund group but in the event of this falling below the guarantee they would be entitled to a top-up payment. When the economy is growing then the proceeds of the pension funds should generally be larger than the guaranteed minimum and the pensioner would share in the general prosperity; but if the funds are depressed for any reason then the state pension supplement would act as a safety-net for the individual and a stimulus for the economy.[20] In 'grey capitalism' politicians claim that the state must bail out banks and funds which are in trouble because otherwise pensioners will suffer. In a genuine stakeholder regime the state might also bail out beleaguered funds; it would not subsidise speculators and would be entitled to seek explanations for poor performance. In fact only the state can offer pensioners a guaranteed minimum and the fact that it offers such insurance would justify redistribution through a levy on the best performers.

The share levy would enable all those over a certain age – say twenty-five – to be brought within the scope of the secondary scheme with the pension boards making payments for carers, students, invalids and the unemployed. Employers who already maintained a good pension scheme might be exempted from up to 50 per cent of the share levy. Their employees would retain their rights in the employer's scheme but gain rights in the new scheme which they could take up in the event of losing or leaving their job. It should be left up to the members of existing schemes whether they wish to merge them with the new arrangements. However such schemes could be required to conform to all or part of the investment code if they wished to continue enjoying full tax benefits. They could also be legally compelled to give representation to their members on the boards of trustees. There should be new rules concerning holding shares in the sponsoring company. In chapter 2 I noted that too many US workers today either have 401(k) accounts stuffed with their employer's shares and options, or belong to an underfunded company scheme. Companies where more than half of 401(k) holdings were in the employer's shares in 2001 included Coca-Cola, Proctor and Gamble, Pfizer, General Electric, Texas Instruments, McDonald's, Enron, Ford, Qwest and AOL Time Warner.[21] The collapse of Enron demonstrated the doubling of risk this entails for employees. Henceforth the amount of retirement savings that can be held in the form of an employer's shares should be limited to 10 or 15 per cent (more on this below).

The number of good defined benefit schemes in the private sector is now in decline in both the UK and the United States. Companies find it increasingly awkward to run a pension fund side-by-side with a business, with the over- or under-performance of the fund flowing directly to their bottom line. It is true that in the US they can still derive some benefit from this by entering optimistic projections of fund returns, and other cosmetic measures.[22] But regulators and tax inspectors are tightening reporting standards in this area. And there is anyway a problem both for companies and for employees, since the cash-flow of DB schemes fits awkwardly with the business cycle. Thus in chapter 2 we saw that the existence of pension fund surpluses in good years allowed many companies to claim contribution holidays. But these holidays are less needed in periods of general economic buoyancy. When recession looms the fund needs injections of cash and yet this is when companies find this more difficult. So long as it exists the DB scheme will constitute a claim on the company's assets. From the employee's point of view, this claim often turns out to be illusory. If the company is healthy then the claim will not be exercised; if it is not then employees will find themselves pressured to permit contribution holidays in order to prevent forcing their employer out of business. While there is no reason to wind up good and well-funded DB pension schemes, the share levy method of supplying the employers' contribution will at least allow them to do so in a way that does not strain their cash-flow in bad times and does not put their employees in the unfortunate position of having to waive contributions in order to save their jobs.

These points were underlined in late 2001 by the plight of many US steel workers who were members of underfunded DB pension schemes. They found that the DB members' claim on company assets was impossible to exercise in the one situation where they really need it, namely when their employer goes bankrupt. In chapter 2 it was pointed out that the Pension Benefit Guaranty Corporation sometimes allowed companies in serious difficulties to delay or skip contributions to the pension fund. In a sense, it was pointed out, this amounted to an inferior species of 'industrial policy', enabling companies to survive a bad patch. In the 1980s the PBGC's tolerant attitude probably did help companies to survive, and thus save jobs, at least for a while. But, in effect, such a policy also doubles employee risk and indulges failing management. By November 2001 twenty-five US steel concerns were operating under Chapter 11, prior to formal bankruptcy. In nearly all cases their pension funds were seriously depleted. LTV threatened, and then carried out, a bankruptcy that threw 7,500 workers out of their jobs and caused a loss of benefit to 52,000 retirees, as the PBGC insurance did not cover all aspects of the company scheme.[23] In its own way the plight of thousands of steel workers was just as bad as that of those who lost their jobs at Enron, though it received much less attention.

A socially responsible industrial policy should not commit workers' savings to keeping afloat businesses in a declining sector. But such a policy could very well use those savings to diversify the regional economy or enhance its facilities. When a large business fails there is no reason why local homes and social infrastructure should all also be abandoned; yet, with sovereign disregard for anything but the bottom line, that is the judgement the market often makes. Boosting a region's educational system, communications, research facilities and cultural endowment can often powerfully enhance the prospects of economic growth, as the experience of Bavaria, Quebec, Catalonia and Emilia-Romagna have shown. The very tentative moves towards industrial policy made by the Swedish wage-earner funds did not prevent an exodus of capital from the country in the late 1980s and early 1990s and did not have a major impact on the restructuring of Swedish industry. But the research institutes set up with money from these funds did eventually contribute in significant ways to the growth of Swedish knowledge-based industries.[24]

Some Approaches to Social Audit and Regulation

The issue of exorbitant executive pay and outrageous rewards for money managers highlights the need for new and tougher standards throughout the world of institutional investment. Pension funds could, if their trustees wished, or if their members' views were consulted, act against the unsavoury spectacle of executive greed. In both the UK and the United States teachers and academics are well-placed to lead the charge.

G.A. Cohen has put his fellow political and social philosophers on the spot by asking *If You're an Egalitarian, How Come You're So Rich?*[25] The query is pointed because so many such philosophers accept one or another version of John Rawls's argument that the only justifiable inequalities are those which improve the position of the poorest, but they then smuggle back in significant inequality on the supposed grounds that talented people have to be heavily bribed to give of their best. Chief executives and senior money managers are very much better paid than philosophers, even those at the top of their profession. Recently, as we saw in chapter 3, money managers have been objecting to the pay-offs which boards award to CEOs and financial officers, especially (though not exclusively) where these reward poor performance (as they often do). But the money managers themselves are just as flagrantly overpaid and the discrepancy with performance is often just as glaring (once again, chapter 3 cited many examples).

Two remedial steps could be introduced quite easily by money managers and pension trustees. The managers could be mandated not to vote for any board which offered remuneration and options above, say (for starters), $1 million a year. And trustees could stipulate that they would not award mandates to managers who did not adopt some more stringent limit for themselves. There is anyway little or no consistency in the performance of managers, which is why index tracking has caught on. Passive investment on any scale is socially undesirable but the pains required of an active manager are not so arduous as to justify the compensation they receive. Their overpayment is a by-product of an unhealthy and malfunctioning regime of institutional property and should be rectified by the measures proposed – measures which will benefit and empower all shareholders. Stringent controls on the issuing of share options to executives would also check a source of great abuse. So G.A. Cohen's egalitarian impulses are highly relevant. As it happens, political and social philosophers, who invariably hold policies with TIAA-CREF or the USS, have the power to move against the extraordinary excesses of the corporate and financial elite. There are already groups of concerned TIAA-CREF members who are working to improve the social criteria which guide its investment policy.[26]

A feature of the economics of the bubble and post-bubble was an explosion of new financial products and new techniques of intermediation.

Investors responded to the hedge funds' claims that they can extract continuing high returns from a falling market. Convertible bonds (i.e. bonds that turn into shares at a strike price) have appeared to offer insurance against downside risks while remaining open to gains on the upside. Exotic new forms of spread betting have gained great respectability in the financial centres.[27] Hans Eichel, the German Finance Minister, has pointed out that hedge funds are exempt from the disclosure requirements and investment restrictions which bind other financial institutions. He suggested that appropriate regulations should be drawn up and agencies established. He also urged that financial authorities should have the power to regulate 'short-selling' (i.e. selling borrowed shares with the aim of driving down their price).[28] Robert Hunter Wade further proposed that undisclosed and unregistered contracts – such as derivatives – should have no force in a court of law.[29]

As noted in chapter 3 the collapse of Enron in December 2001 underlined the difficulty of tracking the activities of enterprises at the forefront of futures trading. While criminal deception, and grossly deficient audit and regulation, created much of the problem, the complexity and novelty of many of the company's trades also helped to bemuse some of those who, directly or indirectly, lent Enron money. Enron's large political contributions had brazenly promoted de-regulation. So even hard-headed analysts with experience of deceptive accounting were baffled by informational black holes.[30] In effect Enron operated like a financial concern but could exploit the fact that it did not have to obey the reporting and regulatory rules that bind banks and finance houses. Those 'insiders' who should have smelt a rat – Enron's own auditors, lawyers and bankers – either failed to do so or brazenly abetted the Enron board.

After the Enron scandal the need for a thorough overhaul in accounting standards was widely recognised. It was proposed that accountancy firms should no longer be able to carry out consultancy work for the companies they audit, with the conflict of interest this sets up. Companies could also be prevented from hiring former employees of their auditors, and there should be tighter rules to combat regulatory 'capture'. Members of regulatory bodies should not subsequently be allowed to take up lucrative board positions in the industries they were regulating. In the Enron case, as we saw, all these elementary principles were flouted. Andersen earned more money from Enron as a consultant than as an auditor. A stream of senior Andersen employees joined Enron. And Wendy Gramm moved from a post as Federal futures trading commissioner to a position on the Enron board, after having exempted energy trading from regulation.

The United States now lacks regulation adequate to the era of electronic communications, financialisation and derivatives. The Gramm-Leach-Bliley Act (1999) gave its blessing to the rise of financial services while failing to create the new, unified regulatory regime they minimally require.[31] Potential conflicts of interest were created when the Glass-Steagall distinction between commercial banks and investment banks was removed, opening the way for hybrids like Morgan-Chase and Citigroup. Moves to ban auditors from working as consultants for their clients were frustrated after strenuous lobbying by the big five auditing concerns. A Congress beholden to special interests denied the Securities and Exchange Commission the powers it needs and placed its faith in allowing the financial and insurance concerns to regulate themselves. The SEC itself was established in 1933, notwithstanding Wall Street's reservations, and soon proved its worth. Its powers now need to be dramatically enhanced and its director changed. Harry Pitt, appointed by Bush to head the SEC, was one of the lobbyists who successfully headed off the attempt to restrict auditor's consultancy work. If the SEC was in more credible hands then it could be entrusted with allocating auditors to companies, with a subsidiary rule that the auditor change every four years.

Improved financial audit would help to monitor compliance, award tax concessions and establish overall parameters. Finding ways to improve reporting, audit and regulation standards will be demanding but far from impossible. If auditors really were appointed by shareholders, if non-executive directors reported regularly to shareholders and if audit contracts were for only a limited term then audit procedures would be more effective and independent. But all this is unlikely to happen unless pension fund trustees, and any fund managers they appoint, are rendered answerable to policy holders or plan members rather than to company boards. The best antidote to audit malpractice would be a reformed and independent body of institutional investors. This is the crux of the problem of the 'accountability deficit', not the technical considerations sometimes urged. The compliance apparatus that already exists in the financial sector could be far more effective. Contrary to what is sometimes claimed, the movement of money or the purchase of futures in today's electronic markets can easily be monitored: e-mails remain in the system and phone calls are recorded. While paper documentation is vulnerable to the shredder, and electronic communications to erasure, both processes leave an awkward trail.

The UK experience with the regulators of former public utilities may be mixed but it shows that they are quite capable of curbing monopoly pricing, allowing for future investment needs and monitoring the service supplied.[32] The pension board and social audit bodies I am proposing for the pension funds would have a different but comparable set of duties. They would obviously work together with existing financial services regulators but their focus would be different. They would have to be properly financed themselves, partly out of general taxation and partly from some appropriate hypothecated source (the yield of a tax on share-dealing?). The pension board and its ancillary social audit arm would pursue priorities laid down by elected authorities, and would be able to accumulate the practical experience and theory needed to steer investment in desired directions. But the audit body would not itself have the power to commit investment resources, which would remain with enterprises and the funds whose support they might attract. In this way enterprises and funds would still remain the crucial source of innovation and initiative.

The 'ethical' and 'social' funds have already established some guidelines for conducting social audits of companies. They usually ask an independent specialist panel to undertake the necessary research and rankings. But at present there are no widely accepted practices and procedures governing this work. Progressive lawyers have begun to explore ways in which policyholder interests could be defined so as to reflect the 'whole person', principles of environmental accounting have been elaborated and there is debate on the fundamentals of audit.[33] But much remains to be done. At present there are no clear criteria for establishing whether ethical or social funds really live up to their claims and the public relations profession is getting ever more skilled at the cosmetic presentation of crude and unchanging corporate reality.

Most 'ethical' and 'social' funds apply extremely modest criteria, and invest in concerns that are simply willing to negotiate. But these approaches can sometimes be justified. Since the pension funds together own such a large proportion of all shares, and since share-switching is expensive, they may use 'voice' rather than 'exit' in their attempts to influence company policy. Portfolio composition does play a role. 'Ethical' funds shun companies engaged in particular practices – say, arms production, the use of child labour and environmental degradation – while 'social funds' make positive decisions to reward companies they believe to be behaving well or moving in a socially-desirable direction.[34] *Business Ethics* reported that the UK-based Stewardship Fund, operated by Friends Provident, had assets of around £1 billion, with companies screened out for poor quality or service, lack of equitable relations with staff or the community, or a poor environmental record. Nike had been dropped because of bad labour conditions in its East Asian suppliers' factories. The Stewardship Fund also shuns

investment in arms or gambling casinos. However, those who on principle
oppose investment in any capitalist enterprise would have to look elsewhere; Stewardship's top holdings were in the stock of Coca-Cola,
Microsoft, Merck and IBM.[35] 'Ethical' funds, like trade unions, are seeking
to change the policies of corporations via pressure and negotiation.
Sometimes they will hold shares in a company about whose practices they
have doubts and use their voting strength to raise issues with the board or
at AGMs. They would clearly become far more effective if backed by
favourable legislation and if they were themselves subject to audit.

The adoption of modest criteria, and a negotiating approach, is not necessarily wrong so long as a coherent and cumulative direction emerges over
time. The best way of ensuring this, and awarding tax concessions to particular funds, would be to introduce a publicly-vetted 'kite marking'
system, ranking those funds deemed to be of 'social investment grade'.[36]
The new institutions that would regulate and monitor the pension funds
would themselves need to be democratically accountable and there would
be a range of differing emphases. The element of public subsidy entailed
by tax-exempt status would help to ensure that funds shouldering the
burden of social investment were not penalised by lower returns.

Under the arrangements I am proposing registered funds would purchase securities with net contributions but would also be in receipt of
shares from the pension board which would range across the economy.
While some funds might be allowed discretion – where their members had
strong ethical objections to involvement in companies of a particular type –
the majority would receive their entitlements by a system of more or less
random allocation. However fund members who would like to see their
savings used to improve corporate behaviour should bear in mind that their
fund could well have more of an impact on the conduct of a given corporation as an 'activist' shareholder than it would by refusing to purchase
its shares (though, of course, the fund could, if it was unhappy with the
company, both be an activist shareholder with the shares it was allocated,
and refuse to build on its stake by purchasing more shares). Allocated
shares could help to remedy the problem registered by Michael Calabrese,
namely that 'screened funds have no ownership rights at the companies
they most want to change.'[37]

The modus operandi of pension funds as financial institutions would
also be a proper subject of regulation and differential taxation. Just as the
Tobin tax proposes to discourage purely speculative cross-border financial
transactions, so pension funds could be encouraged to shun speculation and
demonstrate commitment. While speculative practices and 'churn' could

be penalised by a small tax to be paid by all who trade shares, the pension funds might be bound by rules relating to turnover. For example, the qualifying funds might also be required to commit to holding a proportion of their assets for, say, five years and to make net sales of, say, no more than a tenth of their holdings in any year. Alternatively transactions in excess of such norms could attract a tax. The thresholds could be set at rates which take account of the overall economic climate. Because funds have a stream of income from contributions, and may need to sell assets to meet obligations, they have considerable scope for adjusting the balance of their portfolio. They would thus still be able to threaten divestment and to contribute to the rational reallocation of capital. Adherence to the responsible investor code would be an example of using social property as a lightning rod to earth the otherwise menacing storm clouds of speculative capital. The large pension fund consultants, such as William Mercer, Frank Russell and Watson Wyatt, have built up expertise in the monitoring of pension fund managers which could be drawn upon. Their data banks and analytical models would furnish a helpful starting point for the work of the pension board and audit panels.

The foregoing is just a tentative sketch and the precise institutional complex could vary considerably from one country to another, enlisting the cooperation of whatever social organisations have a good local network. While I have suggested that pension funds should gain access to appropriate financial and technical expertise, the debate on the principles informing investment strategies should not be monopolised by professionals. The wishes of informed citizens should ultimately be decisive when it comes to taking account of social and ecological questions. Funds would also need to be insured and a safety net established for those in danger of losing out, without giving encouragement to the reckless use of assets.[38] In such ways it would be possible to foster a prudent use of resources without weakening the egalitarian logic of the scheme.

Mutuality and Accountability

It has been suggested that the most appropriate bodies to act as trustees and managers of tax-exempt pensions, and those eligible for credits, would be non-commercial and socially-owned or 'decommodified'. Mutual societies or friendly societies, in which each participant is an equal member, would qualify. US 'mutual funds' would not be eligible if they continued to pay exorbitant fees to the sponsoring financial corporations. UK mutuals are, in principle, membership bodies – though the United States does also have genuine not-for-profit mutuals, credit unions and 'thrifts' run independently of a commercial sponsor. Legislation should confine all tax concessions to socially-owned bodies so that public subsidy does not underwrite the profits of the large banks or stoke wasteful competition among them.

The mutual idea has been under assault in Britain in recent years but in July 1997 the attempted privatisation of the country's largest building society, Nationwide, was defeated by a large majority of its members despite the fact that a positive vote would have meant a windfall of £1,500 or more for each of the 1.5 million voters. In the following year a similar attack was beaten off by a smaller majority.[39]

Awareness of individual and immediate pecuniary interest is strongly encouraged by the society in which we live. But it remains the case that perceptions of interest are socially-constructed and open to more generous, enlightened and far-sighted definitions. In the case just cited the Nationwide's management came to the defence of the mutual concept and trounced the carpetbaggers and corporate raiders. Political debate and government legislation also play a vital role in promoting – or inhibiting – collectivist perceptions. To its shame Britain's 'New Labour' government, with its vaunted commitment to the 'Third Way', failed to legislate to protect mutual organisations from unscrupulous bounty-hunters, often backed by respectable and wealthy institutions. Thus in March 2000 the Monaco-based carpetbagger Fred Wollard launched an attempt to demutualise Standard Life, an Edinburgh-based insurance company founded in 1880 and with 2.3 million policy holders; it transpired that Barclay Global Investors was behind the bid and stood to gain £20 billion if it was successful. The financial press pointed out that even if the board of the mutual concern won the vote it would still remain vulnerable to takeover because it had sanctioned a modest valuation of its worth in order to reduce the size of potential windfall payments, and thus reduce the temptation facing its policy holders in the privatisation vote.[40] It did win the vote by a convincing margin – a majority, not just the blocking 25 per cent. Once again this was a remarkable tribute to the support for the mutual concept to be found among policy holders. But, for the reasons stated, Standard Life could face other challenges. In a number of cases boards have themselves initiated privatisation, claiming that they were simply bowing to the inevitable. While it would be good to protect genuine mutuals from carpetbagger raids it is important that members retain the ability to call boards to account. At the limit they should be able to dismiss an entire board, and introduce far-reaching changes to its constitution. But this should not extend to allowing members to vote themselves windfall payments arising from privatisation, a proceeding which could be made illegal.

There are still several hundred building societies and life insurance houses organised on a mutual basis in the UK, many with a strong regional character; they could organise their own pension funds or offer facilities to other bodies to help them do so. In the United States there are genuine mutuals in the insurance sector, some of which offer pensions, while occupational schemes run for public employees have demonstrated the viability of non-commercial custodianship and delivery. The Vanguard group, a major pension provider, is mutually owned and has often been able to contain costs better than its rivals.

The principle of mutual ownership, though valuable, will not obviate the need for rigorous and independent auditing of the organisations concerned. Just because a pension fund is sponsored by a friendly society, trade union or building society does not mean, unfortunately, that its management will be immune to incompetence, neglect of policy-holder interest, favouritism or corruption. As fund managers handle large sums of money, and devote a portion of them to undertakings that involve risk, the danger arises that they may pursue a personal agenda rather than the good of all their members. Over a century or more British building societies have developed traditions of service, and devised methods of audit, which kept this problem under reasonable control. Even so, such bodies need to demonstrate that they really do serve the community, and give fair and equal treatment to members and potential members. In the case of building societies this has meant banning discriminatory practices – such as 'redlining' to exclude people from what are deemed unfavourable districts. Likewise, mutual insurance houses also have to take care that they do not practise implicit discrimination against high-risk groups. In principle, a universal system should make it easier to negotiate and resolve such issues. Of course, genuinely difficult questions are at stake here which have to be addressed by any type of social insurance and provision.

A different problem is posed by managers who are encouraged to enrich themselves quite legally by betraying the raison d'être of their institutions – demutualising the organisations of which they were custodians. Sadly the leaders of some large trade unions in South Africa behaved in a similar way. In this case some key trade union leaders, white as well as black, pursued a strategy which led them to well-remunerated private sector financial posts without conferring any substantial or lasting benefit on the mass of trade unionists. Trade union pension funds were in several

cases used by their officers to advance their own financial careers. Cyril
Ramaphosa's National Empowerment Consortium negotiated the acquisition of shares with borrowed money in the mid-1990s; in the course
of 1997–98 these shares lost value and they may have to be handed back to
those who financed their acquisition in the first place. The trade union
pension funds may not actually have lost money but they have failed to
gain as much as they should have from their dramatic new leverage in the
post-apartheid order.[41]

If there are to be a variety of fund-sponsoring and managing organisations, then any body which has popular roots and structures of
accountability could be registered, so long as it is willing to submit to
appropriate auditing procedures. Trade unions should be in the front rank
of those seeking to promote a longer-term and more socially responsible
view, even if it sometimes means asking their members to put group solidarity ahead of immediate personal gain. In the United Parcel Service
dispute of summer 1997 one of the key union objectives was that UPS
employees should be members of the Teamster inter-company pension
fund and not of the UPS fund. The UPS management was able to claim,
not entirely implausibly, that its fund would be financially stronger than a
union fund based on a mixed bag of mainly smaller outfits. Nevertheless,
the UPS workforce distrusted the management and opted to strengthen
the union fund by adhering to it. It is worth noting, incidentally, that UPS
itself is a corporation owned by (a part of) its large workforce, namely a
core of permanent employees. Schemes that promote employee ownership
entail risks for those concerned, since their savings and employment eggs
are thus placed in the same basket, and for others, since such employees are
encouraged to identify with corporate selfishness and exclusion. In the
UPS case it took a dramatic strike to remind core worker-owners that the
plight of the majority of temporary and part-time workers had a claim
upon their concern. Legislation to favour pension fund groups should
seek to ensure that the best breaks are available to those run on egalitarian
and inclusive grounds.

Efficiency and Social Objectives

The approach outlined here is not intended to slight the need for any
economy to make efficient uses of resources. References to two or three
'bottom lines' only help if it is grasped that a numerical calculus works for
economics but not for many cultural, humane or environmental values.

Over time an economy has to produce the surplus required for further investment and to cover the costs of social reproduction in its widest sense (education, health, culture and so forth). And it should achieve this surplus without jeopardising future sustainability (but note that many types of resource efficiency, e.g. fuel efficiency, can be reconciled to sustainability).

Many enterprises will have to produce a surplus even if some do not. The fact that an enterprise does not employ child labour, or emit poisons into the air, or pay exorbitant executive salaries, or discriminate against women or minorities, may be very positive, but does not absolve it of the need to use its resources as effectively as possible. If management can only make a profit by flouting these norms, then it is bad management and others should take its place. Enterprises which make innovative as well as profitable use of resources, while respecting such norms, should be encouraged since they will be able to give back more to the community. There will necessarily be many cultural and social institutions which it would be inappropriate to subordinate to profit criteria but they should also be expected to make good use of any social subsidy they receive, to furnish decent conditions for their employees and to be responsible stewards of the assets and facilities entrusted to them.

The philosophy of 'stakeholding' introduces and validates the notion of a wider sense of corporate responsibility but can pose a problem of indiscriminate pluralism. A report for the UK's Royal Society of Arts and Manufacturing states: 'There is nothing in company law to prevent directors having regard to other interests if they judge reasonably and in good faith that to do so is conducive to the good health of the company. Indeed, for directors not to give appropriate weight to all the company's key relationships may well be a breach of their fiduciary duty.'[42] This is a heartening thought, but we know that in practice boards of directors are more attentive to some than to others. As noted in chapter 2, the structure of capitalist social relations embodies a process whereby alternatives can be arbitrated and decisions imposed. In its own way this is a strength not a weakness. The arrangement I am advocating certainly envisages registering the views and interests of those whom Sheldon Leader has called 'secondary stakeholders'. But the main thrust of my argument is the need to change the composition and modus operandi of those Leader calls the 'sovereign stakeholders', namely the shareholders who possess the ultimate power of decision.[43] If policy holders were closer to being owners, they would find it easier to favour decisions that were not determined simply by the bottom line, just as individuals or families who own an enterprise may decide to plough back all profits into it or to establish a foundation.

Infrastructure Bonds and Taxes on Economic Rent

The balanced pursuit of economic viability and social priority will require entrepreneurial skills and the taking of risks. This means there will be failures as well as successes. But as it happens there are large and important areas of investment in social infrastructure which commercial investors and money managers have found difficult to tackle because of their short time horizons. Gordon Clark points out that pension funds have a scope and scale well adapted to urban regeneration but the competitive tender model of awarding contracts has made it difficult for them to play their part.[44] This is an area where governments have a lively interest in seeing projects funded and should be prepared to offer their own investment guarantees.

While there remains a strong case for pension funds investing in equities – notwithstanding market turbulence and on occasion with the aim of curbing it – pension funds are in many ways appropriate holders of public bonds, with their guaranteed rates of return and redemption values, so long as the money raised by the bonds is used to make a tangible contribution to a better future. The practice of issuing low-grade government IOUs to public pension trust funds, which are then used to cover current account deficits, should be abandoned for a more classical conception of the rationale of the public bond. Pension trust funds should be able to acquire bonds on good terms and the money raised by these bonds should be devoted to specified improvements in social infrastructure. In 1999, as noted in chapter 5, Gerald Holtham, then economic adviser to the Norwich Union, lamented the scarcity of long-term public bonds in the UK and proposed that the government float a series of bonds maturing in twenty-five or thirty years to underwrite the cost of modernisation programmes for health and education. [45] In this case the government would be pledging its own future tax revenues, since both education and health care would remain free at the point of delivery. But in some cases public investment will or could boost future revenues or taxes generated by the project undertaken.

Thus if pension funds help to fund urban renewal, the recovery of blighted land or improvements to communications then their investment could be rewarded in full or in part by revenue from taxation of the resulting increase in site values and commercial property. Samuel Brittan has argued that such a desirable type of tax is applied to what economists call 'economic rent' and explains: 'This is not the rent that you or I might pay for our home or office, which includes a charge for the use of buildings or other structures. It is the price for the use of pure space. This will be far higher in a thriving urban area than in a Highland bog. And within urban areas the scarcity value can be much increased by the provision of new public transport facilities or an arts centre.'[46] Brittan points out that California's Supreme Court in 1979 provided a basis for taxes based on 'special benefits assessments'. The financing of loans for improvements to public transport in this way could also be geared so as to allow for reasonable fare levels.

The British government announced plans in 2000 to channel some £20 billion or more of public money into the country's now privately-owned but manifestly failing and underfunded railway system. The government refused calls to renationalise the rail companies, notwithstanding the large majorities for this course of action revealed by opinion polls. It also hoped to raise £40 billion from the private sector. The public injection of funds was to be either simple subsidy or soft loan – yet the rail companies, most of which have made windfall profits and delivered poor service, were to reap the benefit of the resulting investment. It would be far better to use this massive injection of funds to bring all the rail concerns once again under one common management, and to use the public subsidies to attract the needed funds for upgrading the rail system from the pension funds. Such funds, raised by special issue rail bonds, could bring the UK rail network to the level of efficiency and safety already achieved by the main continental European rail systems. Such modernisation, so long as it took account of environmental concerns, would help to alleviate traffic congestion and reduce the emission of greenhouse gases. The rail bonds could be made available only to the pension funds and could carry a government redemption guarantee. In October 2001, the government responded to mounting public concern by putting Railtrack, responsible for line maintenance, into receivership and announcing that henceforth it would be a not-for-profit entity. However the companies that operate the trains remain in private hands and will benefit from a programme of public investment which could rise to £34 billion.[47]

The Blair government has had recourse to Private Finance Initiatives (PFIs), and Public-Private Partnerships (PPPs), rather than public bonds, in financing investment in public services, whether transport, health care, crime control or education. Private construction companies are invited to build and manage new hospitals, schools, or transport facilities in return for handsome guaranteed future revenues. The private finance obtained in this way is more expensive than is money raised by the floating of public bonds but does not immediately show up in the public accounts, which pleases

the Treasury. The extra cost is held to be justified on the grounds that
private contractors are more likely to deliver on time and cannot claim cost
over-runs. The government also finds it convenient that promises of future
revenues, unlike public bonds, do not show up on current budgets, thus
helping to keep the public sector budget requirement at low levels. The
experience of using commercial contractors to build and run hospitals
and prisons has belied many of the claims made to justify the expedient.
The contractors have all too often cut corners to reduce costs, offered poor
working conditions, undermined the morale of the workforce and strained
relations with the surrounding community.[48] Where supplementary
finance is needed for capital projects in the public sector then the sale of
infrastructure bonds to pension funds, with interest and redemption guaranteed by the government, remains the best way of proceeding. Of course,
the modus operandi of public works departments may need improvement,
but this problem can be tackled by making better use of independent
professional surveyors.

Public enterprises and not-for-profit organisations will not function
well simply because they lack direct commercial motives. All will depend
on whether their employees and managers are given the right type of
incentives, whether they offer decent working conditions and whether
they are accountable to the communities they serve.[49] Pension funds
managed by mutual concerns will be able to use their financial leverage to
promote good working practices. In recent decades a proliferating audit
culture has sought to mimic commercial criteria in the provision of public
services with often counter-productive results.[50] Social audits are best
conducted not by teams of highly paid experts dispatched from central
government but by local communities. Pension funds could play a useful
part in furnishing finance and expertise in public construction projects and
for public services. Where there are private commercial organisations
with vital knowledge, experience and resources then it would be possible
for community-based pension funds to buy them up and use their
power as owners to introduce new working practices and relationships
with customers.

Economically Targeted Investment

While pension reform should aim to raise rates of growth there will sometimes be a trade-off between the immediate rate of return and the quality
of growth. One strand of the argument I have been developing is that

funds operating according to clear social criteria, and oriented towards sustainable technologies, would have intrinsic merits, even if the immediate 'rate of return' was low. A disappointing financial return to an investment in social housing or regional diversification is likely to yield social gains nonetheless, compared with the pure loss of an ill-judged currency speculation. Thus London has faced a crisis of personnel in public services in recent years because those qualified to fill such posts cannot afford the astronomic price of houses or rented accommodation in the capital. The pension funds could help to build low-cost housing, and would merit government support and guarantees if they did so.

Economically Targeted Investments (ETIs) have the objective of strengthening or diversifying a local or regional economy. Pensions funds which have made such investments have usually allotted only a small fraction of their holdings to them (on average about 2.5 per cent) and have submitted the projects concerned to independent panels for vetting. ETIs may still have about them an aura of naïve good works – or self-interested log-rolling – but their record is an increasingly positive one. The regional control of investment funds makes it possible for the funds concerned to gain from access to local knowledge and local trust networks. These have proved themselves to be considerable assets, making possible significant contributions to local employment and facilities.[51] In chapter 6 I cited a recent study of ETIs by Alicia Munnell and Anika Sindén which reported 'no adverse impact on returns'.[52] A major constraint on the investment policies of the large commercial pension funds has been that they concentrate on a fairly narrow band of asset types, mainly those well-documented and easy to monitor. One of the reasons why public sector pension funds have done well is that they do become knowledgeable transactors. Outfits like Calpers or the Retirement Systems of Alabama (RSA) do not confine their investments to their own region but a range of their investments have benefited from local knowledge. In New York the Bureau of Asset Management (BAM), which acts as an adviser to five of the largest New York City pension plans, has proved itself skilled in assembling urban development projects as investment vehicles. Gordon Clark notes:

> With respect to the New York BAM, there are a number of advantages to such an arrangement. Because of their scale and independence from private investment management firms, their knowledge base is more extensive about the margins of, and intersection between, markets . . . The fact that they have close, intimate and long term relationships with their trustees adds to the confidence that outside organisations place in their developments.

The fact that they [Bureau employees] are paid by salary, rather than a pro-portion of the brokered deal, also adds to the perception of independence when compared to private investment companies.[53]

Ambachtsheer and Ezra, advocates of 'pension fund excellence', tell us that funds which found a way to engage in 'economically targeted invest-ment' in their own regional economy only 'underperformed' the bull market by an extent similar to that of most prudently diversified funds. They add: '[w]hat has not materialised are massive raids on pension assets by pension system outsiders such as politicians or other power sources with possible ulterior motives'.[54] Funds investing in their own region are more likely to display long-term commitment and take an active interest in the fruits of that investment. Studies comparing the performance of socially screened investment portfolios as against unscreened portfolios have found there to be little or no difference in overall performance.[55] Some analysts even claim to detect an overall positive correlation between companies' responsibility to the environment and good treatment of their employees, and their long-run rate of return.[56] Matters are probably more complicated than this but recklessness and abuse could well be poor strategy in the long run. Even if this is not the case in today's world then at least the public authorities should be seeking to make it so by penalising polluters or those who batten on inhumane labour standards.

In chapter 2 we saw that the pension funds operated by the financial ser-vices industry have regularly underperformed the market by 50 to a 100 basis points or more. And we saw that sponsoring corporations have underfunded or even purloined their employees' pension funds. The par-tisans of pension privatisation, as we have seen, often now recommend the holding of pension assets in passive index funds, to be tossed about like driftwood in the stormy seas of globalised capitalism. The reforms I advo-cate aim to strengthen the hand of workers, policy holders and electorates, and progressively to remove funds from the power of an irresponsible financial system. That such an approach might sometimes mean under-performing the benchmark indices is a possibility that does not call it in question, so long as the chosen strategy is endorsed by those concerned, is executed in good faith and tends towards its declared goals. And as pointed out already, the overall aim would be to put available resources to good use and to generate sustainable growth. Existing national accounting conven-tions and statistics furnish only a very approximate guide and the purpose of the regime of social and economic audit would be to introduce needed corrections and revisions.

Pension funds are already hugely important, so it would be essential for the goal of social responsibility to be pursued in a well-informed and conceptually rigorous fashion. Market prices are not just a delusion but approximate to social cost. They should be revised to take account of costs they are not good at measuring, such as the using up of non-renewable resources, but they cannot be entirely disregarded without unfortunate results. Likewise profit and loss. The existence of a social audit would not mean exemption from standard accounting procedures. Funds would still have an incentive to pursue good returns, but not at the expense of other social goods. In the construction of portfolios the funds would be encouraged to find a balance of different types of assets, some held for yield and others because of their promise or social utility. Across the economy as a whole the objective would be sustainable growth.

Those who defend the commercial delivery of pensions like to insist in a supposedly hard-headed way that if the aim is to ensure good pensions then there must be a single and solitary goal, the best rate of return. Introducing other 'social' objectives, they say, simply generates confusion and sub-optimal performance. It is certainly the case that all proposals for reorganising pension provision should meet a stringent test of adequacy and reliability. Those who risk people's savings in pursuit of pet projects or private utopias would not be easily forgiven. Investments should be rigorously and independently screened to make sure that their social risk and reward profiles are reasonable. But the world we live in is one of uncertainty and it would not be reasonable to insist on uniformly good results. And even the most specific of investments will have implications and corollaries beyond the rate of return. To some small extent it will be helping to create one type of world rather than another. Often the social consequences of investment are easier to establish than its prospective rate of return. Over the economy as a whole, and over the long term, sustainability requires positive rates of return, but these rates would not be genuinely positive if they were achieved by ignoring ecological degradation or the liquidation of social assets.

Corporate executives and public relations departments are often already quite keen to present themselves as socially responsive, hence the new art form of the socially sensitive 'mission statement'. The more hard-nosed type of business analyst or neo-conservative find the resulting pious waffle irritating and ridiculous – and it is sometimes easy to see their point. Digby Anderson, a writer for a free market British think tank, goes further and argues that mission statements are often positively misleading and get in the way of thinking about what the true purpose of a commercial undertaking must be. Large amounts of well-paid person-hours are expended to produce claims such as that of BP-Amoco to be 'a force for good in all we do'. Corporations, he insists, are there to look out for their shareholders and not to play God. He suggests that a truthful mission statement should read: 'Our company is there to make money for share-holders. It will only make money if it pleases customers more than its rivals and keeps its workforce happy enough to attract a good and loyal one. However, when actions that benefit the customer or employee diverge from those that benefit the shareholder, our duties are unequivocally to the shareholder.'[57] While one appreciates the candour of this statement, it is unlikely to catch on. When pondered it has a chilling effect. It also assumes a homogenous and well-defined shareholder interest which in practice rarely exists. The approach I advocate here seeks to appeal to an enlightened and long-term shareholder interest, defined by a well-informed and vigilant shareholder body. And public policy, by restricting good tax breaks to funds which emerge well from a social audit, could also play a key part in shaping the shareholder perception of even narrowly economic advantage.

The 'social priorities' model will not find it easy to overcome the complexity and opacity of links in a market society between savings decisions, on the one hand, and actual investment on the other. Buying shares in a company puts money in the hands of the seller not the com-pany. But, as was argued in chapter 2, buying a company's shares helps to maintain or raise the share price, which in turn will improve the company's credit position, putting it in a better position to make investments. But since much investment is financed out of retained profits it is not directly amenable to manipulation by fund managers. There is bound to be trial and error in the effective application of social criteria and an awakened public opinion would be an indispensable ingredient of a progressive learning curve. But then the implementation of such reforms is likely to stimulate awareness and controversy surrounding key business decisions. Notwithstanding the many real complexities of any market economy, especially in today's more globalised world, a genuine 'stakeholder' scheme that embraced the bulk of pension fund assets could have a large impact, especially if bolstered by government action and new audit proce-dures. In effect such institutions could themselves help to structure the market in new ways, even more radically than used to be the case in Germany and Singapore.

A responsible or socialised pension fund regime could be defined as one which defied the grey capitalist context by offering both communities and the mass of employees the opportunity to shape the pattern of investment and business practice in their region and in the wider economy of which it is a part. Fiscal redistribution could be reinforced by a growing employee and citizen stake in the economy. There is currently huge dissatisfaction with the norms of corporate governance and the practices of shareholder democracy. Today shareholding is far more widely diffused than ever before but the powers of shareholders are diverted or muzzled by money-managing institutions with their own corporate agenda. The approach I am advocating would require resources to be made available so that policy holders could develop a collective view of their interests and wishes. Policy-holder AGMs, making use of electronic communication, could furnish an occasion for the membership as a whole to decide its priorities. In giving a say to policy holders the principle of one person one vote should be adopted, since each person's savings are important to them.

In the introduction I cited figures for the distribution of global wealth which showed that rich individuals control as much property as do pension funds and charitable institutions. Indeed, if we take account of the fact that wealthy individuals also make considerable use of the tax breaks available for retirement savings vehicles then it is clear that individual wealth is still considerably larger than pension fund wealth. Furthermore the rich can, for a price, gain access to some scale economies in financial management. But all of these circumstances do not nullify the huge leverage that still accrues to pension funds, which already constitute between a quarter and a third of the major share markets and which form part of a tax-exempt institutional sector which often has majority status. This money enjoys fiscal privileges because it is subordinate to special regulations which could be brought closer to the general social interest they are anyway meant to serve. The scale of the pension and insurance funds is such that they do have strategic initiative and this would be steadily increased by the proposed share levy.

Pensions and the Global Economy

In principle the pension funds that I have been advocating would be based within a given tax jurisdiction. Rudolf Meidner proposed that national share levies should be based on the proportion of profits or turnover attributable to the Swedish operations of a company. A similar restriction – together with Meidner's provisions to prevent manipulation of profit data – would be appropriate for the capital levies which would help to finance the new pension fund regime proposed here.[58] The shares contributed to the pension board would be either stock in the country-specific subsidiary or in the parent coporation. The world's top 100 companies, holding 5 per cent of the world's capital stock, and responsible for somewhat more than 5 per cent of world output, employ 12 million workers in the countries where they are based and just under 6 million elsewhere. And there are 44,500 companies which have at least one foreign subsidiary in which they hold at least 10 per cent of the stock. These companies are responsible for 22 per cent of world output; they have 17 million foreign employees producing 7.5 per cent of world output.[59] Most employees in the more advanced states have an interest in raising standards of social protection throughout the multinational enterprise which employs them, since this will counteract downwards pressure on their own pay and conditions. They are also likely to discover that a management that exploits vulnerable workers in one area is unlikely to be a solicitous and responsible employer in another. The willingness of international companies to recognise unions in their subsidiaries has already been, and will continue to be, a crucial issue for employee-influenced funds.

Pension funds established for the workers of transnational corporations and their subsidiaries might also naturally develop an international membership and investment policy, even if they were bound by the tax regime of the countries where they operated. At the present time, as has already been pointed out, multinational concerns tend in practice to have special links to one or another of the major states, even if their formal registration is in a tax haven. Pension funds need security and for this reason will also be obliged to base themselves in one or more properly constituted jurisdiction. But, subject to this restriction, pension funds might also play a positive role in developing cross-border patterns of investment, with 'twinning' arrangements similar to those set up by municipal authorities.

To the extent that individuals are seen to 'earn' their pension entitlements through their own contributions this could help to abate hostility to immigration. Europe's welfare states benefit from the presence of immigrants but the design of their civic arrangements often does not make this visible, and it falsely appears that the newcomers are simply subtracting from available resources. The element of ethnic or racial animosity should, of course, be confronted, but, at the same time, welfare and pension arrangements can help to make it clear that the immigrant community is usually making a significant net contribution, that it helps the host society to address the issue of a rising dependency ratio and that immigration significantly boosts the resources available to finance retirement.[60] Migration to rich countries will most probably continue to rise anyway since, with the gap between rich and poor so great, it is difficult to control – and will become more difficult as uneven development gives more of the excluded the motive and resources to migrate. The great majority of migrants still have many years of work ahead of them and many are quite, or highly, skilled. Since rich societies are thus acquiring 'human capital' nourished by the society of origin it would be important to ensure both that retirement savings could be remitted to the latter, that elderly parents be allowed to join their sons and daughters, and that a portion of the taxes paid by the migrant workers return to their countries of origin.

To the extent that collectively owned and managed pension funds are established the anti-social power of finance capital in a globalised context can be diminished.[61] Tax incentives for funds which invest in their own regional or national economy could help to dampen speculative movements. When necessary, regulatory measures could limit the inflow or outflow of capital. Willingness to regulate capital flows should not mean hostility to cross-border investment. If a developing country prevents the outflow of hot money it is keeping cross-border investment higher than it would otherwise be. In principle overseas investment, by allowing capital to flow to where it can obtain a better return, can benefit both recipient and donor, supplying the former with scarce capital (and sometimes expertise), while affording the investor the advantages of diversification as well as the return. For pension funds in the advanced countries to invest in the developing countries will often be mutually beneficial and the pension board could be charged with exploring and promoting such opportunities. However these general considerations assume the health and efficiency of the investment regime in both donor and recipient areas, something which cannot now be assumed. In the 1980s and 1990s UK institutions placed about a third of their investments overseas, notwithstanding evidence that the returns were often below par because, as noted in chapter 2, the British fund managers were less knowledgeable than the local investors and poor at market timing. The large occupational pension funds deemed an investment in real estate in Chicago or Brussels, or in Japanese technology stocks, a better proposition than attempting to regenerate the economy of Britain's own rustbelt regions. If public policy had instead helped to foster a responsible pension regime the latter option could have been more appealing. Over time domestic returns would have risen and, before long, the absolute value of capital export could have been greater and better judged. While there can be an economic rationale for overseas investment of pension funds, achieving the right balance will require planning, forethought and an analysis of the domestic alternatives that accords due weight to social costs. Pension funds in developed countries should be encouraged to allocate a portion of their investments to developing countries but not to condemn their own communities to neglect and decay.

Capital controls, 'Tobin taxes' and other such measures have their place in any attempt to discourage speculation.[62] But an essential element in any strategy to regulate capital must be an element of de-commodification or socialisation, since only this can 'neutralise' the floating electric charge of capital by tying it to the 'earth' of mutual or public property, which can no longer be bought and sold. In this way the cumulative effect of the proposals advanced here would be to achieve 'complex socialisation'. Socially owned and publicly regulated pension funds reduce an economy's vulnerability to the forces of globalisation by removing assets owned by the pension funds from the free play of the financial markets. At the same time these pension funds would be required to achieve a socially desirable mix of domestic and overseas investments. Enterprises would still decide whether or not to invest in plant or equipment or training, but advantageous capital costs could greatly influence such decisions. Indeed the pension boards could have such wide-ranging influence that they would supplement some of the steering functions once monopolised by treasuries and central banks.

Since the breakdown of the Bretton Woods agreement in the early 1970s, and subsequent waves of deregulation, global financial turbulence has much increased and growth slowed. The breakdown no doubt itself reflected fundamental imbalances, and by the beginning of the twenty-first century these take the form of global over-capacity in a world where there are still billions of poor people. A development pact between the developed and developing countries would help to lever the former out of recession and underperformance as well as to equip the latter to tackle poverty. These desirable goals will require subordinating global financial flows to regulatory monitoring and restraint. John Eatwell and Lance Taylor have urged the need for capital and exchange controls, for currency bands, for the establishment of a global 'lender of last resort', and for a World Financial Authority, developed from the basis already provided by the Bank of International Settlements, which would promote 'efficient risk management techniques for *all* major institutions, banks, mutual funds, highly-leveraged institutions (e.g. hedge funds), insurance and pension funds, and covering all onshore and offshore and on-balance-sheet and off-balance-sheet operations'.[63] The authors recognise the difficulty of monitoring on such a scale. National institutions of the sort proposed here would help underpin such an effort.

Jane D'Arista has proposed that there should be a public international investment fund for emerging economies which would establish rules that tended to stabilise foreign portfolio investment flows while also furnishing some insurance coverage to investors. The proposed closed-end fund would protect emerging economies from abrupt fluctuations in capital flows and would be capitalised by holding government securities of the major industrial countries, furnishing 'a floor against losses for the beneficiaries of pension and other pooled funds'.[64] The aim of such an international investment fund would be to encourage the capacity of emerging economies to manage inward investment, offering investors some guarantees but not allowing instant withdrawal. Such arrangements would need to be negotiated in ways acceptable to all concerned.[65]

Though I have couched my argument in terms mainly appropriate to the developed countries the need to assert democratic social control over accumulation is just as urgent in developing societies. In the first chapter I argued that the mobilisation of savings was an important component of the South-East Asian development model, and here I would add that similar institutions might well play a positive role in any development strategy. The challenge of an ageing society is by no means confined to the developed world but in time will have to be addressed everywhere. At the present time the World Bank urges poorer countries to privatise their pension arrangements and to avail themselves of the expertise of the large financial concerns. But does it really make sense for the citizens of a country in, say, West Africa to look to Fidelity or Merrill Lynch to handle their pension arrangements rather than to their own government and public institutions? In the short run they may well be persuaded that it is safer to place their savings in New York or Boston, London or Geneva, supposing them to be significant enough to interest the concerns in those financial centres. Entrusting their savings to local bankers or politicians may well appear, in given conditions, quite foolhardy. But then their real problem is to change those given conditions. Stashing their money away abroad will simply help to perpetuate the unreliability and incompetence of local institutions.[66]

In many parts of the Third World the extent of indebtedness to the developed world is a major factor enfeebling and compromising the local state, whose most important social role has become that of collecting taxes to service the debt. Simply abolishing the debt, however, may bring relief only to the elite that controls the state and not to the mass of citizens. Kevin Danaher has proposed that instead of simply cancelling the debt it might be preferable to transfer it to the hands of the citizens of the indebted country, thus furnishing them with a potential lever of influence over their own elite.[67] One way in which this could be done would be to transform discounted debt into pension or social funds held in trust for the generality of citizens. Such a transfer would then give an incentive to the development of popular social organisations, sponsored by local credit unions, trade unions, and peasants' associations, with, perhaps, the ILO supplying technical assistance. There is no doubt that the absence of public pension provision in many parts of the Third World is a major and grow- ing problem, both for the elderly themselves and for their relatives and communities. And it contributes to the lopsided development of the inter- nal market, depriving it of purchasers of local goods and services. The relentless pressure of the 'structural reform' sponsored by the IMF and World Bank has, of course, taken a toll on all forms of social expenditure. By the mid- or late 1990s some officials of these organisations felt obliged to acknowledge this. But with the departure of Stiglitz from the World Bank in 2000 the emphasis once again swung away from public pension provision and back to providing new opportunities for the financial services industry.

Pension delivery inescapably contributes in a major way to the extent and composition of demand, while pension financing has major impli- cations for savings and investment. Improving the outlook for the aged in developing and intermediary states could help to establish a more effective, because domestically-embedded, model of economic advance. The absence of pension provision may sometimes be a cause as well as an effect of a weak economy. Thus in Russia during most of the 1990s the value of the state pension fell to derisory levels, seemingly (and really) because of the terrible condition of the country and the callous- ness of IMF-sponsored 'shock therapy'. In 1998 the value of the rouble collapsed and the Russian government reneged on its loan obligations. A very modest economic improvement took place as imports became expensive and exports more competitive. Under the administration of Prime Minister Primakov, and following a recovery in the oil price, it was decided to pay Russia's elderly a slightly better pension. By the end of 2000 there were signs of a still limited but slightly stronger recovery, in part fuelled by 'babushka economics'. The financial crisis and the new tilt of government policy had produced a marginal redistribution away from the comprador bourgeoisie and towards pensioners. In the process the composition of demand was changed. The pensioners did not spend their money on Mercedes Benz or Armani but on local food- stuffs and manufactures. The resulting multiplier effects furnished a lift to other sectors.[68] It is likely that many transitional and developing – not to say developed – economies could achieve a healthier composition of domestic demand by curbing the compradors and supplying the aged with a decent pension.

Macro-economic Imbalances: Keynes's Neglected Remedy

But if pensions help to shape demand, their financing helps to shape savings and investment. While the South-East Asian experience shows that public pension funds can free resources to build infrastructure, in the developed economies there is another, related aspect of macro-balances to be considered. The introduction and governance of a universal stakeholder pension fund regime would both facilitate and require management of the trade cycle. Interestingly enough, Keynes himself proposed such a mechanism as a necessary complement to the demand management more familiarly associated with Keynesian economics. In chapter 4 I noted that the expansionary policy associated with the short-lived German Finance Minister Oskar Lafontaine was being described as a new Keynesianism because it concentrated on expansion and opposed the cautious monetarism of the European Central Bank with its recurrent anxiety about inflation.[69] In a number of his later writings Keynes saw the expansion of demand via extensive public works programmes and better welfare provision as only the first steps towards a more equitable and well-regulated economic system. In 1940 he advocated the introduction of employee-controlled institutions which would assist with the task of containing inflationary pressures and ensuring future welfare. The outbreak of hostilities in 1939 immediately created the necessity for wide-ranging government expenditure but also, in his view, the need for coherent economic planning to avoid the danger of inflation. The idea that Keynes was tolerant of inflation dangers is quite incorrect. He pointed out that if wages rose faster than output, as was likely to happen with the expansion of wartime expenditure, then this would impose sacrifices and uncertainty on the bulk of the population.

In his pamphlet entitled 'How to Pay for the War', Keynes proposed that the remedy for inflationary pressure was to pay wage rises partly in the form of deferred entitlements. The latter were to be paid into funds controlled by the trade unions, friendly societies or other social bodies. The funds would be redeemed in the future, after the war, from a 5 per cent levy on capital. He explained:

Considerable choice could be allowed to the individual in what institution his deferred pay should be deposited. He might choose his friendly society, his trade union, or any other body approved for the purposes of health insurance; or, failing such a preference, the Post Office Savings Bank. This then would be encouragement to the working man's own institutions to take charge of his resources for him and, if desired, a considerable degree of discretion could be allowed to such bodies as to the conditions in which these resources could be released to the individual to meet his personal emergencies . . .[70]

To propose mutually owned pension funds as a further receptacle for such deferred pay is a logical extension of Keynes's line of argument. Like the 'deferred pay' proposal, it would add a further instrument of macro-economic management. It would also serve a very similar social purpose. After all, he recommended his war fund on the grounds that this arrangement would make it clear that the economy was being run in the interests of working people and would powerfully assist the construction of a more just and equal social order: 'the accumulation of working class wealth under working class control [could induce] an advance towards economic equality greater than any we have made in recent times.'[71] Thus Keynes hoped not only to abate the inflationary danger but also to introduce a new tool of macro-economic management and to promote the basis of a more equitable political economy.

Unfortunately, the social democratic and Keynesian policies of the post-war era failed to enlist the mass of working people in the consolidation of a new pattern of political economy. Demand management, nationalisation of particular sectors (often those facing losses), ambitious welfare programmes, still left untouched the central dynamic of the private accumulation process. The social weight of organised labour did help to buttress the new priorities for a while but in one country after another the welfare state and full employment were to be eroded by financial counter-measures such as hyper-inflation and capital flight (Britain in the 1970s, France and Sweden in the 1980s and 1990s). It was not rising wages which destroyed the 'golden age' but rather the ability of corporations and capital to outflank well-organised labour movements. Governments that failed to find a route to the socialisation of the accumulation process, or to engage the mass of working people in the new social dispensation, became over-reliant on taxation, leading to overtaxation of middle-income earners in order to pay for welfare programmes burdened by the cost of rising unemployment.

Some analysts warn that the aggregate operations of pension funds have huge implications for the functioning of stock markets and economies whether this is recognised as an opportunity or not. In the West the combination of a demographic shift and a commercialisation of pension provision could aggravate economic shocks, in ways that are quite ignored by the proponents of pension privatisation. The rise of pension funds sends huge tidal waves of cash into and out of the funds, with potentially large and distorting effects on equity valuations. In one demographic phase the surplus of contributions over payments could stimulate a runaway equity boom. But once the baby-boomers begin reaching retirement age the fund managers will need to become net sellers to finance their pension commitments. In other words, unless vigorous and enlightened steps are made to counteract this automatism demographic shocks will be fed into the financial system, adding a new layer of instability. Jan Toporovski argues that the 1990s bubble was fed in part by institutional demand and that pension funds themselves sometimes contributed to a 'Ponzi finance' logic in the capital markets, with effects similar to that of a pyramid selling scheme.[72]

In its present unplanned form the contribution of pension funds to macro-balances could exacerbate problems rather than help resolve them. There is now some evidence of a link between demographics and stock market prices, mediated by the pension funds and the like. Thus Michael Mosebach and Mohammed Najand estimate that in February 1997 65 per cent of all US full-time employees participated in a 401 (k) plan or its equivalent, implying a total investment of some $266 billion annually with penalties for any early withdrawal. At this level, they calculate, there was a significant inflationary impact on share prices.[73] In the UK the danger of demographic shocks being fed into the markets has been stressed by a veteran fund manager, Malcolm Crawford, who points out that when the baby-boomers begin to draw down their savings in a few years' time a heavy downwards pressure will be exerted on stock prices.[74] Such effects could be offset by share buybacks but the possibility is certainly one which further underlines the need to bring pension funding within the scope of financial management.

At a time of huge uncertainty concerning international stock markets it would be quite wrong to propose that citizens place their faith in funds quoted on the exchanges. However, it would be equally wrong to treat stock exchanges, and their roller-coaster behaviour, as facts of nature which should never be challenged by public policy. For the many millions of policy holders methods of invigilating and protecting their retirement funds now seem even more urgent than before. Of course uncertain

markets can still deliver rewards, which is why the crash of 1987 did not
slow the advance of the pension funds. Pension funds accumulate investments over relatively long cycles enabling the individual to reap the average
of decades of growth. But this is precisely why the short-term regime of
grey capitalism is particularly ill-adapted and vicious. The measures advocated here seek to counteract the speculative structures which make for
crisis and chaos. Above all, they seek to lend more stability and coherence
to what is now an anarchic accumulation process. Pensions coexisting
with capitalist anarchy tend to be vulnerable, whether supplied by the state
or by private funds. A transitional regime would aim methodically to
address all sources of instability and inequity until a properly socialised
accumulation process had been reached.

Some US critics of proposals to invest part of the Social Security trust
fund in the stock market have shown that this would have yielded a bumpy
ride over the years 1954–97. Thomas MacUrdy and John Shoven argue
that such a strategy amounts to obliging the trust fund to swap a safe asset,
government bonds, for a risky asset, private securities, and that over periods as long as a decade this could have produced worse results.[75] (These
two authors do not contest the long-run prospect of better returns from
investment in equities but believe that it would be best to allow holders of
individual accounts to make the choice of risks for themselves.) The
argument against asset swaps does not apply to the approach I have been
advocating here, since the main source of the equity holdings in the
pension funds will be new securities issued by corporations, not taxation. The proposed capital levy is raising assets which could not have
been obtained in other ways and could not have been converted into
public bonds.

Resisting Grey Capitalism – From Within

At this point it is necessary to confront the philosophical objection that
even the best and most inclusive and accountable system of 'socialised
pension funds' would remain deeply beholden to capitalist concepts and
methods of organisation. Rather than a real alternative, what we have
here, it could be objected, is, at best, popular capitalism, invigilated more
or less effectively by government and such social movements as are able to
make themselves heard; and, quite possibly, the result will simply be a further commitment to the most negative aspects of contemporary capitalism,
with the savings of many millions entrusted to the lottery of the stock

markets. Such a line of criticism points to real dangers – dangers which will be all the worse if nothing is done to discipline and replace the spontaneous workings of the capital markets. A reinvigoration of public bodies and state enterprises will certainly be indispensable but by themselves such desirable developments will be vulnerable and ineffective unless there is a reckoning with financial power, a reckoning which will be promoted by accountable pension funds. The simple fact is that we are already immersed in the world of grey capitalism. It is this morass which is our starting point and extracting ourselves from it will be a demanding task.

Many unions already hold shares as a way of acquiring information and the right to attend AGMs. Since they have long bargained to gain funded pension packages for their members, this is a logical next step. Thus the International Federation of Chemical, Energy, Mine and General Workers Unions (ICEM), with twenty million affiliated members, fought in the late 1990s to break the deadlock between the mining company Rio Tinto and the Australian mining union. As one part of that campaign ICEM, with backing from the TUC in the UK and the AFL-CIO in the United States, helped to bring together a coalition of shareholders, which urged the company's AGM to pass a resolution committing it to observe ILO labour standards. The large Australian institutional investors handling employee 'super' funds were approached by campaign staff and a number agreed to support the resolution. When first put at the 2000 AGM, the resolution obtained 17 per cent of the votes, a score reckoned to be good at the start of a campaign of this sort. Another resolution, also supported by the campaign, asking for the appointment of independent directors to the board and addressing other governance issues won 20 per cent of the votes. A further 8 per cent of the shareholders formally abstained as a way of signalling their desire for a new management approach. The campaign continued, reaching other parts of the Rio Tinto empire. After rallies in Sydney and Los Angeles timed to coincide with the Rio Tinto AGM, the company agreed to commence negotiations with the union representing the US Borax workers in California.[76]

Using the shareholder avenue is not a substitute for other forms of pressure available to employees or campaigners but can be a powerful addition to them. However, presenting arguments to shareholders, even when they are fellow trade unionists, will tend to influence the language and concepts used. For example the point might be made that adopting better practice will not hurt profits, or that if it does hurt profits there will be some offsetting gain. While this could lead to a softening or fudging of issues it could also be a spur to reach out beyond the local and sectional

horizon of a particular work group to the larger context and consequences
of the proposed course of action. So while there are dangers in the activism
of worker-shareholders they are outweighed by opportunities and advantages. This approach would, of course, require that the power pension
funds should be democratised so that contributors and beneficiaries had
more scope to influence the actions of trustees and money managers. At
the present time many employee pension funds are managed, as we have
seen, by large financial institutions. But the failure of these money managers to check the rapacity of the corporate elite, or to contain their own
costs, makes them vulnerable to demands for reform. It might be thought
that the corruption of trustees was part of the problem but, interestingly,
this is not the case. Corporate sponsors nominate their own employees to
the post of trustee, and in adjusting the pension scheme to the needs of the
corporation they are just doing their job. So what are needed are new
structures of accountability that render trustees accountable to the full
membership of the scheme, both retirees and those still in employment and
contributing to it. Actuarial rules enforced by auditors would set some
limits on broad categories of investment to ensure that the scheme was not
skewed inappropriately to the short or long term. But within such limits
the fund trustees would be encouraged to make choices reflecting the discussions among their members and the various communities of which they
were a part.

   Thus the investment of fund resources could help to promote the ability of communities to respond to the challenges of flexibility in a global
division of labour in constant flux. Some procedures I have advocated, such
as those designed to discourage financial speculation, would seek to make
market mechanisms less jumpy and erratic, and easier to monitor and
anticipate. Free market mechanisms frequently overshoot first in one direction and then another – economists can formalise in 'cobweb' diagrams the
systemic features of such market failure. But it is ultimately neither desirable nor possible to avoid change, since our techniques, tastes and the
environment are all subject to expected and unexpected flux. Risk-pooling
is a necessary response and requires a collectivity willing to undertake
and guarantee it. But those capable of risk-pooling might go one better and
employ at least some of their collective resources to prevent avoidable
accidents and to promote desirable alternatives. Richard Sennett has
described the evolving discussions of a group of IBM main-frame programmers in upstate New York who had been made redundant in the early
1990s. First they blamed the loss of their jobs on the premeditated mach-
ination of their managers, but many of the latter were also soon dismissed

and anyway managers were themselves responding to processes over which they had no control. Then the redundant programmers moved to blame outsiders and aliens – the new Jewish CEO who had no commitment to them and the programmers in India who would do their work for a fraction of the pay. But eventually they became dissatisfied with narratives that portrayed themselves simply as passive victims and began to argue that, if only they had had the initiative and resources, they could have devised a new role for themselves and their colleagues. But in Sennett's account these programmers were willing to confront their own failure without shame or embarrassment. After all flexible capitalism generates losers as surely as it promotes winners, with the former often outnumbering the latter. While Sennett's companions recover in talk a sense of connectedness, ultimately they have no possibility of acting together even though they are active as parents and citizens. So they retreat into a resigned and private salvation.[77] The institutions which I have been sketching in this conclusion would encourage those bound together by a sense of place, or profession, or a common past or future, to help them devise their own solution. While only a tenth of the contributions paid by, or on behalf of, a fund member could be held in the enterprise for which they worked, funds organised on the basis of residence, occupation, education or affinity would allow for investment in parallel networks. In helping their neighbours contributors would also be helping strengthen and diversify themselves and their communities. While such networks would sometimes be deeply embedded in a region or industry they might also have strong links to people in other parts of the world or in other fields of work. The funds' rules should facilitate a species of 'neighbourly' cross-investment that would pool resources and opportunities as well as risks.

Some may come across the wider political and social implications of tax-exempt funds in their capacity as trade unionists and employees of a large corporation. Others may do so as members of educational or charitable institutions. In the 1980s and early 1990s the campaign to urge companies and investment funds to break any connections they had to the apartheid regime in South Africa involved many different organisations and eventually proved highly effective. The number of funds claiming to operate a social or ethical screen of some sort has not declined since the heyday of the South African divestment campaign. But their focus and effectiveness is more in question. Sometimes their claims are overblown, and supposedly ethical funds are launched by the large commercial providers as little more than a new marketing ploy. Clearly, funds which wish to claim ethical or social status should submit to independent evaluation.

The Canadian economist Jim Stanford has written a sharp critique of
the functioning of actually existing ethical and labour-sponsored funds. But
though he identifies many real problems he does not, it seems to me, sustain a case for entirely rejecting these approaches. Since there are more
consumers than investors, he says, it makes more sense to count on consumer groups than on ethical investors. Choosing to engage business elites
on the terrain of AGMs and financial power is wrong-headed and will
never make much impact on wealthy individual investors. As an argument
about today's large corporations this has much cogency. One might add
that, despite the rise in the number of shareholders, there are also more
employees than shareholders, and that the holdings of many small shareholders are quite insignificant vis-à-vis corporate wealth. Outside the ranks
of top management there are few employees whose salary or wage is not
very much larger than their share income. But these points do not alter the
fact that pension funds already have great financial power and could be
induced to use that power in more responsible ways. The best way of
advancing such a goal is to combine and coordinate different dimensions
of social activism, whether linked to trade unions, pension funds, community organisations, issue groups or consumer groups.

Stanford charges that many self-described ethical trusts in Canada, once
they have made their share selection, have then adopted a completely passive stance. He cites the officer of one such fund declaring: 'It is not
within our mandate to take an activist stand on particular issues.'[78] As a
blanket position this must be wrong. On the other hand social funds probably do have to be selective. The presumption should be that the issues
they select are the ones which are most calculated in any given situation to
join up with wider progressive campaigns. So one year the emphasis might
be mainly on attacking the exploitation of children and the use of toxic
production processes, the next on refusal of labour rights, extravagant
executive compensation or discrimination against older workers.
Presumably a ratchet effect should be aimed for, such that each period's
gains are maintained and built upon. The fact that social funds must prioritise issues if they are to be effective does not make them any different
from trade unions or single-issue campaigns. And, like the latter, they
may sometimes be right to settle for real gains in one sector while postponing engagement in others.

Because of their modest size, and because they operate according to no
independently-vetted standards, it is not difficult to criticise today's social
funds for their limited impact and ambitions. Jim Stanford is often able to
show the difficulty ethical funds have making a difference – and the failure

of some of them even to try. He does not challenge the remarkable contribution of the Quebec Pension Plan to regional development but he does criticise the investment record of Canada's labour-sponsored funds and public sector occupational funds. In these cases the activities of the funds cannot be described as insignificant but nevertheless they arouse his distrust – either because they have condoned or encouraged anti-social business practices, or because they set up potential conflicts of interest. A difficulty arises because many of Canada's supposedly 'labour-sponsored' funds are, in fact, sham 'rent-a-union' outfits in which commercial pension providers pay nominally trade union bodies (small provincial branches, professional athletes' associations and so forth) for the right to use their name in marketing their products. They do not provide for member representation and have no social objectives. The legislation permitting labour-sponsored funds failed to establish a body that would vet their bona fides. In an effort to retrieve the situation the genuine labour funds formed the 'Labour-Sponsored Investment Alliance', with a 'defining statement' that committed them to control by the sponsoring trade union and to a variety of social goals. The investment record of the five main funds which form the Alliance was financially positive in the 1990s, with the Quebec Solidarity Fund obtaining an 8.70 per cent annual rate of return in 1995–98. Over the same period Working Opportunity obtained 5.82 per cent annually, the Crocus Investment Fund 9.40 per cent, and the First Ontario fund 3.44 per cent, compared with a return of only 0.16 per cent annually for the rent-a-union funds. Stanford has estimated that the labour-sponsored investment funds have created 15,000 to 25,000 new jobs, though two of the funds argued that the impact was greater. The Working Opportunity Fund of British Colombia has turned down over 1,000 firms as investment prospects since it was formed in 1992 and has selected 41 concerns based in its own province.[79]

Even the genuine labour-sponsored funds are seen by critics such as Stanford as enticing workers into the delusions of share-ownership. The fact that large numbers of today's workers have an interest in a pension fund certainly complicates matters for those who are critical of capitalism and the big corporations. Workers with a stake in a pension fund will be less likely to yearn for the day of capitalist collapse than the class warriors of the early twentieth century. If consulted on investments, they may side with the bosses rather than fellow workers. Trade unions and progressive campaigns will find that they have a demanding educational task ahead of them when they seek to enlist the support of the broad membership. But at least pension funds are long-range and quasi-collective in character, furnishing the occasion for an argument framed in wider terms than immediate material interest. Thomas Frank, like Stanford, believes that wider participation in pension funds, in the shape of mandatory accounts, is a device whereby Wall Street aims to get its hooks into the American proletariat: 'With our Social Security money invested in Wall Street, its priorities will become the nation's priorities; its demands for de-regulation, de-unionisation, low wages, and generous "stimulus" packages whenever the Dow looks a little weak will be recast as the demands of little old ladies in Beardstown and blue-collar workers in Providence. Who would dare to legislate for high or minimum wages, say, or arctic wild life, when such a move could be construed as an attack on the nation's beloved retirees.'[80]

Frank is, of course, right to attack the privatisers' designs on Social Security, which should continue to benefit from the full measure of FICA contributions. And he is also right to warn about the insidious manipulation of supposed pension fund interests. But Wall Street had ways of imposing its agenda long before the rise of the pension fund. Workers are not likely to be stampeded quite as quickly as Frank fears. Workers who are employed by a company whose products pose health dangers may still continue to work for it, and to support it publicly, because their very livelihood is at stake. But the extra income that will accrue to a pensioner, either now or in the future, as a result of oil drilling in the arctic, or a reduction in the minimum wage, or a union-ban at a given corporation, would be very notional. At most it would be imperceptible and quite possibly it would be negative. The corporation which drilled in the arctic might, after all, become the target of shareholder activists and see its share price sag. We do not have to endorse Robert Monks's theory of the 'universal investor' (referred to in chapter 7) to see that workers may well perceive an individual and social interest in a pattern of economy that does not wipe out wild life and that does not rely for its profits on low wages or poor conditions. About half of all US workers already participate in a pension scheme and it would be wrong to suppose that they are thereby irredeemably committed to Wall Street. Arguments framed in terms of a general social interest, and of the need to protect the planet's resources, have quite broad appeal and can be mobilised against corporate recklessness and rapacity. Frank was not addressing the particular structure I have been outlining; the mechanisms of social audit and conditional tax relief would give further support to the more enlightened approach. Ultimately the mass of citizens will have to be convinced of progressive goals whether there is widespread participation in pension funds or not. Even supposing that the pension funds were all wound up, and American workers able to consider the prospects for arctic wild life without the distraction of pension fund involvement, crass calculation might lead them as *consumers* to conclude that gas would be cheaper if the arctic deposits were tapped; this sentiment is more of a problem than pension-fund holdings, though still not one that is invincible.

Progressive advocates should be encouraged to spell out a positive vision for their community and region, and for their relationship with the world. This is more difficult than framing a wage demand but could involve reaching out to valuable new allies and partners. Anyway the traditional capitalist structure has disappeared, or is fast disappearing, partly thanks to the struggles of yesterday's class warriors. Neither Stanford nor Frank is proposing that today's workers should be asked simply to give up their pension funds. Obviously to do so would be to invite rebuff. In fact better would be to appeal to these workers to opt for social investing. So, as Jim Stanford himself finally concedes, the wisest course is to explore ways in which employee funds can be integrated with credit unions and his proposed 'new model of social investment and community entrepreneurship'.[81]

It is probably more appropriate to aim for *socially responsible* than for ethical fund management. The ethical acquires its true meaning and intelligibility, Alain Badiou has argued, in quite specific situations and it applies to courses of action as a whole. The brandishing in the abstract of supposed ethical imperatives too often displays a lack of awareness of context, and a one-sided fixation on the negative.[82] It can imply that a set of rules of avoidance is a prescription for the good life. The activity of investment management is too general to be able to offer real ethical guarantees but it could be animated by a positive world-view. Stanford points out that some ethical funds have had a religious inspiration. Sometimes the resulting proscriptions could well be justified in terms of social responsibility – for example, the bans on investments in armaments or child labour. But there is evidence that policy holders generally feel it more appropriate for their funds to take account of social consequences than personal dimensions of ethical choice – for example, to support investment policies aimed at regional regeneration rather than to boycott investment in alcohol-related industries. Thus Anne-Marie Darke, CEO of the Australian fund HESTA-Ecopool, explained to an interviewer the results of an attempt to find out members' view of the principles they would like to see in operation:

> It was interesting to see the response we got. People overwhelmingly supported having such an investment option within our suite of options: but when we tested the screens, obviously our fund covers [workers in] health

and community services, and I guess most people would have put money on
that tobacco would have been one of the top items of exclusion. And in fact
it was near the bottom of this research, and the environment, closely followed by human rights, were clearly those screens that people favoured. And
the rationale was that they are issues that affect all people, so it's a societal
issue, whereas tobacco, gambling, alcohol are individual issues . . .[83]

Nevertheless, businesses which condone or profit from cruelty to humans
or other sentient beings also frequently arouse revulsion. Badiou does not
regard Marx and Engels as committed to abstract moralising yet the authors
of the *Communist Manifesto* included the following as one of a list of ten key
demands: 'Free education for all children in public schools. Abolition of
children's factory labour in its present form.'[84] Marx and Engels believed
that children would benefit by learning about the activity of production –
hence their qualification – but deemed the exploitation of children to be
worth singling out for abolition in their programme of transition. It is also
interesting that while they advocated state ownership of the transport
system and central bank they did not propose the suppression of all market
relations. Those who seek to establish socially responsible funds may be
excused for not seeking to tackle everything at once. On the other hand,
they will find that child labour conducted in atrocious conditions (i.e. not
simply occasional help in the harvest or shop) is far more widespread
today than it was in 1848, giving socially responsible investors reason to be
vigilant.[85] The purely ethical course of action might be simply to boycott
any concern implicated in child labour. The more socially responsible
funds might discover that such an approach would deprive poor families in
poor countries of their only income. They would, instead, promote the
employment of older workers and insist on specific age limits, hours and
conditions of work, and access to school for younger workers.

    In the wake of the Enron scandals, in which as we have seen it figured,
the California Public Employees Retirement System (Calpers) announced
that it was going to pull out of all its investments in Thailand, Malaysia,
Indonesia and the Philippines mainly because of concerns about social
conditions in these countries. A report explained: 'Calpers latest move follows a review of its "permissible countries" criteria which, for the first
time, gives equal weight to issues such as labour standards as well as market
regulation, investor protection and accounting transparency.'[86] Another
report concerning the new approach added that Calpers would now use
ethical screens for US companies and pointed out that Calpers's announcement sent stocks falling in the Philippines, Thailand and Malaysia.[87]
Whatever Calpers's motives may have been, the fact remains that it is one

of the largest funds in the world, managing $151 billion assets itself as well as using other fund managers. Its decision is not unambiguously positive. Nevertheless it is a striking victory for the movement for social responsibility in investment and one which, if followed up, could well be refined and improved. The countries targeted in the move maintain special export zones where social protection of the workforce is particularly weak. Altogether there are believed to be some 27 million workers in 800–1,000 special export zones worldwide.[88] The ban on labour organisation in these zones has been an intense concern of the anti-sweat-shop movement, and Calpers's decision is certainly a success for this campaign.

The developing philosophy of ethical investment could be seen as a new version of the puritan impulse in pension provision, and the social investment approach, together with the new stress on the role of the 'long-lived planner' cited in the previous chapter, could be seen as a new variant of the 'baroque' impulse, echoing, in modified form, the use of these terms in chapter 1. Historically the puritan and baroque impulses helped, unintentionally, to foster the capitalism of the eighteenth-century Atlantic world but they also helped to inspire critiques of it. The anti-slavery movement, and the welfare proposals of Paine and Condorcet, could be seen as examples of this and as part of an attempt to challenge the destructive, oppressive and inhumane consequences of rampant commodification and laissez-faire capitalism. These were, of course, Western cultural movements and in the age of globalisation there will be many other sources of resistance to the false antithesis of individual and society encouraged by neo-liberalism.

In the context of classic capitalism workers were obliged to sell their labour power in order to provide food and shelter for themselves and their families, and capitalists, who controlled access to employment, were able to extract a surplus from a seemingly equal and fair arrangement. In today's world welfare reform, competition between differently-situated groups of workers and the deprivations of unemployment mean that these constraints continue to structure social outcomes without the employer or capitalist appearing to dictate them. There are those whose labour helps to reproduce capital and there are those condemned to idleness because they cannot do so. The result is a pattern of inequality and exclusion, both within the advanced and industrialising countries, and between them and the rest of the world. These are outcomes which are not the result of evil intentions on the part of those who benefit from them. The employer who gives work may feel like a benefactor even if his employees are denied a say in the disposition of the surplus. And all those enmeshed in market relations feel responsibility slipping from them in a process of serial alienation.

The manager who lays off workers or shuts down a plant will often feel he or she has no choice. The aim of the new institutions I have been proposing would be to go beyond sporadic and ad hoc attempts to discourage or suppress particular abuses and to give communities and working collectives the resources to begin to structure social relations in a new way. Those who direct enterprises would increasingly have to respond to market opportunities in ways that withstood social scrutiny and attracted the support of financial bodies responsive to the generality of employees and citizens.

Employee Share-ownership?

The idea that there can be a progressive potential in worker ownership of assets naturally raises the question of the desirability of enterprises wholly or partly owned by their own workers. Surely it is better for workers to control their own bosses than to invest in other concerns? Perhaps if worker ownership took only this form then awkward conflicts of interest would be avoided? Once again, we find that Marx strove for a balanced approach. He regarded worker cooperatives as occasionally useful, if limited, experiments within capitalism because of the experience that employees would gain from them. But he was not a proponent of workers' self-management or share-ownership. In his terms surplus value might arise at the point of production but it was only realised in a wider circuit of accumulation that involved the economy as a whole. To seek to trap and control surplus value at the point of immediate production of commodities was a mistake and an illusion. Surplus was only realised in the working out of the wider accumulation process. The labour expended in producing a commodity was only validated as being 'socially-necessary' at the point of sale or use. When Marx wrote of management by the 'associated producers', he was referring to a standpoint that was itself not that just of a particular workers' collective but rather of a social interest embracing that of all producers, and their families, as a whole. We could conclude that in so far as this wider social interest would require preliminary institutions to embody it, then mutually owned pension funds could add something critical to the required mixture, along with other forms of civic economy and productive self-government.

While employee-ownership schemes do not offer a plausible route to the construction of a general social interest they should not be wholly spurned. For employees to have a stake in the company for which they work can have significant advantages. It should furnish them with more information and influence over management plans. It allows them to share in the success of their company and should reinforce their motivation. And while responsive management can be fostered by other means, the possession of shares by workers can give the latter extra leverage.[89] In a previous section it was noted that employee share-ownership schemes (ESOPS) have serious defects. Firstly, workers' savings are tied up in the company for which they work, increasing their exposure to risk, and secondly, self-investment will foster enterprise egoism. But this does not mean that workers should not have *some* of their savings invested in the company for which they work. Any strategy which hopes to bring about a better world does well to enlist on its side the employees of the major multinationals and financial institutions. Many of them could be attracted to mixed or parallel funds that include stock in the company for which they work but also stakes in a much larger basket of enterprises and assets.

I have urged that the entitlements embodied in employees' pension schemes should be recognised as a specific social form of private property. As things stand at present policy holders do not normally exercise anything like full property rights over the assets held by the fund to which they belong. They have no influence whatsoever over the disposition of the assets in their account. In fact, this notion of an individual account is often itself a fiction, as particular assets are not ear-marked to particular individuals in most pension schemes. Policy holders cannot sell the assets in their pot and they generally suffer a loss if they merely wish to switch from one scheme or plan to another. The investments held by a fund are subject to conventional valuations and, in the case of defined benefit schemes, to actuarial manipulation of the claims placed upon them. The assets held to service policy-holder claims usually return to the general pool at the holder's death in both 'defined benefit' schemes and in the annuities bought by those cashing in 'defined contribution' schemes. Pension entitlements in public schemes are usually not fully backed by assets but they are individualised. The old 'flat-rate' pensions once paid in the UK or New Zealand have now been replaced everywhere in the advanced countries by graduated and individualised schemes. The pension entitlements I propose will vary according to the individual's contribution record and the performance of the funds they have chosen. But at the same time these individual variations allow weight to egalitarian and social considerations, and rest on a guaranteed basic entitlement.

I have recommended that the claims of policy holders should be stronger than they are and, in certain respects, that their rights should be closer to individual property rights. But ultimately the social character of 'ownership', or policy-holding rights, in a pension fund should be maintained and clarified. This specific form of property should receive certain privileges and guarantees partly because it serves the purpose of ensuring against the needs of retirement and partly because it is invested in accordance with social priorities. Today certain types of tax-favoured saving – 401(k) schemes in the United States and Stakeholder or personal pension plans in the UK – are closer to the model of the commercial unit trust or 'mutual fund' account. This more individualised form of saving is likely to earn somewhat lower returns than those achieved by the large collective funds, and its greater flexibility may be offset by the erosion of principal. But workers may well wish to be able to identify their holdings and to transfer them from one fund to another from time to time. In the interests of cost containment I earlier suggested that such switches should be limited to once every five years. In this way a degree of individualisation of fund accounts could be reconciled to scale economies and some standardisation. If the members of a pension scheme were unhappy about the policies it pursued they would be encouraged to play an active part in it. On the other hand, there would be no obligation to be a financial expert. All schemes would be obliged to obtain professional advice and to conform to basic principles of diversification. Audit procedures would ensure that these principles were adhered to. The auditors would also help to ensure that current members did not pressure trustees to pursue investment policies that were tantamount to winding down the scheme in favour of current consumption.

In the introduction I pointed out that capital – whether held as shares, bonds or real estate – can be seen as a claim on future streams of output and income. Returns to capital often comprise between a fifth and a third of national income in any capitalist economy. The world's peoples now face the prospect of meeting the cost of an ageing society in which the elderly will need a larger share of total income. Devoting a major portion of the returns to capital to meeting these costs, as the reforms advocated here seek to do, seems a logical and equitable proceeding. In the process it would be highly desirable to mitigate – and so far as possible abolish – all those practices of today's capitalism which generate insecurity and inequality while fostering a reckless plundering of natural and human resources. The complex task of devising effective and egalitarian forms of social ownership and economic governance will have a vital role to play.

But today's starting point is still that of 'grey capitalism'. When employee funds invest in private corporations then they will, as things stand, suffer from market fluctuations, which in a capitalist trade cycle can be severe. Depressions can last a decade or two, though eventually counteracting tendencies will assert themselves, as capital is devalued and restructured. There are, of course, already several standard devices used by pension and insurance funds to mitigate the uncertainty of trade cycles. Funds can be required to hold a proportion of government bonds as a hedge; policy holders can be obliged to invest in more than one fund in order to spread risk. The government can erect a safety net for badly hit funds – though it should then take them into social ownership. But if the whole economy sinks then the employees and policy holders still suffer. This is one reason why it is necessary for there to be a satisfactory minimum guaranteed and indexed pension, as indicated above. But recessions do not have to be regarded as a force of nature. While some unevenness of development is inevitable the grotesque disparities and wild swings typical of today's globalised capitalism should be combated by public policy and institutional innovation.

The main threat to sustainable and steady growth in the world economy at the start of the new century came from unused capacity, yawning inequalities, widespread poverty and the bubble economics of disorganised capitalism. More egalitarian social arrangements at a national and global level would help to restore demand while the construction of funded and socially responsible retirement programmes could help to contain inflationary pressure and prioritise social need. Public programmes to develop alternatives to fossil fuels, to recycle waste, to develop the potential of bio-technology in ethical ways could all furnish an economic stimulus. Pension funds could subscribe to public bonds that paid for these programmes. To the extent that public authorities encourage such expenditure and more committed forms of investment there will be a tendency for fluctuations to moderate but it would still be necessary to insure against turbulence, especially in any transitional phase. If such reforms are not adopted, or are not effective, then major stock markets will continue to experience shocks and disturbances like those of 1929, 1973, 1987 and 1997–98 and 2000–1. Eventually fund values may recover but in the meantime many lose out – workers lose their jobs, Third World producers lose markets and policy holders lose the value of their savings.

The distempers of globalisation certainly require global solutions and new institutions of global economic governance, some examples of which were given in a previous section. But pending their elaboration there is much else to do. Global solutions will be either facilitated or impeded by the success or failure of local, regional and national

institutions in fostering a more responsible and sustainable path of accumulation. Despite the growing importance of pension provision it is still
only a part of the story. The initial difficulty is to identify immediate
improvements that will lead to structural advance. The mixed pension
regime I have been advocating – combining a mainly PAYGO basic
pension with a funded secondary pension – should provide immediate
improvements, even within a still-capitalist context, while paving the way
for a more responsible economic pattern. Financing citizens' future
retirement partly by future public revenues and partly by asset income
involves an advantageous type of diversification, since, short of economic
collapse, a fall in one source of finance need not be directly linked
to a contraction in the other. According to some analysts, the macro-
economic effect of a long-term build-up of pension funds would be to
lower the price of capital and improve the return to labour. Certainly the
years after 1973 witnessed a massive increase in the available labour
force – thanks to the baby boom and the entry of women into employment – which contributed to reducing the return to labour and boosting
that to capital. Other things being equal, the funded approach to pension
provision should help, over the long run, to raise returns to labour, as the
cost of capital is reduced by growing supply. (In a lopsided way, even the
US fund growth of 1997–2000 was accompanied by an increase in
labour's share of national income.[90])

A major source of inequality in the recent past has been the fact that
the pensions paid to some – the better-off 40 per cent of pensioners –
derive from the forward momentum of the accumulation process while
those of others have trailed behind because they have no stake in
that process. Even if the twenty-first century opens with a decade of
recession, as some now predict, it remains likely that shares will once
again perform better than government bonds over a period of twenty or
thirty years. Sharp market fluctuations herald capitalist restructuring
not collapse. Occupational and personal pensions have been popular
precisely because they promised employees a share in economic prosperity and some insurance against short-term fluctuations. Some
pension consultants claim that good returns on equities and bonds,
multiplied by compound interest, meant that many of those who retired
in the 1980s and 1990s received in benefits three or four times as much
as they originally contributed.[91] Such good returns are unlikely to be
seen again in the near future. But pension funds and regulatory boards
could be encouraged to foster investment-led growth, and a recovery of
profitability. This in turn would assist share price recovery.[92]

From Responsible Accumulation to the Socialisation of Capital

The shape of the future of our societies is set by the accumulation process and the priorities which it dictates. The method adumbrated here is that of giving priority to an incremental but deliberate 'socialisation' of the accumulation process, asserted in the first instance through the elaboration of new rules and practices, new powers and institutions, relating to planning for the future. This is not a concern only of older employees, since socialisation of the investment process would furnish the instruments to tackle many urgent social problems in the present. Funds which were responsible to the wider community could combat unemployment, help clean up the environment and combat anti-social management practices. Regulations which are only promulgated and enforced from the heights of government power are often ineffective or counterproductive. If civic monitoring is lodged within civil society itself it will have a much greater chance of being effective – though of course argument will still be needed to win popular majorities for progressive policies. In this model the plans and programmes of governments and international agencies would be dove-tailed with the planning of individuals and families.

It is sometimes thought that Ludwig von Mises and the Austrian School economists were implacably opposed to planning of all types. In fact Mises recognised that workers did wish to plan for their future and he believed that they should be encouraged to do so.[93] Providing for income in retirement is an example of such planning and, as we have seen, there is a powerful case – now pressed on the Right as much as on the Left – that the fate of future generations should be taken fully into account. While Mises would scarcely have embraced anything like the complex socialisation I have outlined, it nevertheless offers real opportunities for individual and generational planning while simultaneously combating the irresponsibility of the fund managers speculating with other people's money and futures. Empowering the ultimate holders of institutional funds would aim to reintroduce the notion of responsible and committed ownership.

Michel Aglietta has urged that subordinating the pension funds to social control could furnish a vital ingredient in a new regime of accumulation.

> If the labour unions recover influence over the division of income it will be because they have become aware that the control of company shares is the vital battle to wage and win . . . In effect the conversion of contractual savings into property rights over enterprises implies a decisive change

in the government of enterprises. The latter are decreasingly ruled by their own organisation, as was the case with the managerial capitalism of the Fordist epoch, and increasingly subject to the pension funds.[94]

Aglietta believes that a new regime of accumulation based on responsible retirement funds could be established essentially within capitalism. Indeed, such a move would save capitalism from its own destructive tendencies. Responsible pension funds could indeed help to address problems in today's capitalism but there may be outcomes other than those Aglietta envisages. The mounting of a concerted reform across a broad front, under the pressure of awakened social movements, might overflow capitalist constraints. Indeed self-managed social funds might complement other progressive anti-capitalist strategies in essential ways. Thus by employing large assets in a responsible way they could complement and complete that 'socialisation of the market' argued for by Diane Elson.[95] Likewise such funds could supply forms of financial commitment to the tools of macro-economic regulation proposed in John Roemer's model of 'market socialism'.[96] Finally accountable social holdings could add a new dimension to the 'rotating capital funds' which Roberto Mangabeira Unger has proposed.[97] Ownership and entrepreneurship by public bodies will surely have a place. Together such measures could become stepping stones to a progressive 'socialisation of capital'.

Some anti-capitalist activists may find the overall approach I have been advocating objectionable, since it seeks to appropriate institutions and practices which they regard as inimical to their project. Yet there have always been strong currents within the historic anti-capitalist traditions – Marxism, anarcho-syndicalism and social democracy – which have identified a progressive side to the complex organisation of capitalist society. Indeed, Marx's idea that socialism could only be built on the basis supplied by developed capitalism has yet to be faulted. In his view the challenge was not to annul the complex coordination of capitalist society but rather to harness the higher social productivity capitalism had made possible to a truly human – we might today say a sustainable human – future. The very term 'socialism' was first put into circulation by the followers of Fourier, Saint-Simon and Proudhon who instead of spurning high finance sought, too naively and indulgently, to adapt the techniques of the financier to the proletarian cause. Fourier championed the idea of what he called the 'joint stock communal counting house', a financial facility which would furnish credit, act as a depository, organise trades and manage agriculture.[98]

The historic socialist and Communist movements, however, found it easier to make headway in regions – or areas of social life – where capitalism was little developed. The challenge of old age provision today is, by contrast, that of framing appropriate and responsible institutions in a sector where advanced financial techniques are already well established.

Marx himself saluted the advent of the joint stock company as a step towards the socialisation of capital, writing: 'This is the abolition of capital as private property within the confines of the capitalist mode of production itself'.[99] Both parts of this judgement have to be held in balance. Marx was not endorsing the joint stock company but he was highlighting the tension between capital and private property which it embodied. We can be confident that Marx would similarly have regarded the rise of grey capitalism as a development of huge importance, with a progressive as well as a reactionary aspect.

It could be that the approach I have advocated would achieve only a middling score on the measures of 'de-commodification' that Esping-Anderson used to evaluate welfare arrangements. So long as there is some relationship between contributions and entitlements then we do not have full de-commodification. But the focus here would be upon the pension itself, whereas the arrangements I have been outlining aim at a more fundamental dimension of de-commodification, namely the de-commodification of ownership of the means of production. Pension fund property would be tethered to accountability and social use. It would no longer be bought and sold with the sole goal of maximising accumulation. On the other hand, market mechanisms and prices would remain until superior methods could be found for furnishing a standard measure of cost and value. It is not possible to plan economic activity without prices. If technical improvement is to be allowed for – for example, improved ability to tap renewable energy sources – economic planning cannot be specified simply in terms of given relationships between physical quantities. So while there is good reason to strip pension funds of some commodity features, wholesale de-commodification is not yet feasible or desirable, and 'complex socialisation' is the best path.

A responsible financial system might well find a useful purpose for many of the instruments and devices of finance capital. The international credit card agencies and investment funds now possess a global network capable of processing formidable quantities of information, a resource that cannot simply be ignored or suppressed. While it would be absurd to espy a progressive content in every last exotic 'product' of the financial 'industry', the fact remains that derivatives could only be harnessed to the genuine reduction of uncertainty if they were accompanied by guarantees and embedded in a context that was not itself completely commodified and financially leveraged. In the absence of any equivalent to the guarantee of bank deposits, or the lender of last resort, those purchasing derivatives to reduce risk find that they are taking a bet on the ability of the seller to deliver. Furthermore, in today's global market place financial arbitrage reaps what are often hugely disproportionate gains from spotting asset price anomalies. The challenge is to develop a global framework of exchange that is more stable without being rigid, whose anomalies can be rectified with less expense and disruption, and which is protected by insurance and embedded in de-commodified structures. By themselves socialised pension funds will not be enough and new institutions of global governance are badly needed. But they could supply one component of a more responsible structure.

Seen statically, the ideas I have expounded above amount to arguing that the workers and citizens should, collectively, take over capitalist institutions and not only run them but subordinate them to new rules of management and investment. I myself believe that such a profound, if also curious, alteration in property relations almost certainly could not be sustained without provoking a fundamental rupture with capitalist social relations. To the extent that socialised pension funds, or a regime of accumulation based on employees' funds, failed to go beyond 'ethical capitalism' to the suppression of the fundamental mechanisms of capitalist competition, it would be exposing itself to subsequent social recidivism. The capital levies I have proposed would progressively diminish the importance of the capital disposed of by very wealthy individuals, or powerful corporations controlled by a family or founder.

Such institutional proposals are made not as an alternative to social movements, class mobilisations and political campaigns but as a complement to them, and a way of building on resistance to those forms of capitalist accumulation which are trampling on historic social conquests and which menace the fragile envelope of a humanly habitable planet. Among the debates which would help to instruct such a groundswell of resistance would be whether or not to proceed to the construction of a post-capitalist socio-economonic order. At each stage it is only necessary to reach agreement on the next practical step, allowing a generous coalition to build around it. Agitation for the progressive use of the shareholder power of employees is not a magic bullet. It represents only one further addition to a broad programme of proposals and needs to be integrated with other reforms, such as taxes on speculation, reductions in the length of the working week and the introduction of a basic citizen's income (part of which could, perhaps, be linked to stakeholder social insurance).[100]

Willingness to seize the progressive potential of funded pension provision requires us to recognise that the overall significance of a social measure cannot simply be read off from the politics of those who first introduce it. As we saw in chapter 1, state pensions were first introduced in continental Europe by Bismarck, in Britain by a Liberal government. The German Social Democrats did not oppose such pensions simply because they were inaugurated by the Imperial Chancellor, nor did British socialists oppose the operation of a pensions systems based on the capitalist state; in both cases criticism from the Left argued that the initial level of benefit was far too modest. In both cases, as Wolfgang Abendroth pointed out, the pension system did act to cement popular loyalties to a social and political order that was headed towards the terrible slaughter of the First World War.[101] On the other hand, if the pension and social insurance arrangements had been much more generous, as the Social Democrats urged, then there would have been less public money for armaments, and if the Social Democrats had been in government then perhaps the drive to war might have abated. The nationalisation of industry is another programmatic measure that has been carried out by right-wing as well as left-wing governments, and in both cases the results were not always empowering for the workers involved. It is in the nature of both class struggle and political competition that there is a tussle over the specific direction and use of any new social measure. It is the contribution made by the measure to the overall relationship of social forces and relations that will determine whether it has a broadly progressive character.

With pension provision, I have suggested, there is often wisdom in starting from the institutions which have already won a degree of popular recognition and understanding in each state or region. Institutional innovation is indispensable but should usually build on and develop existing forms of social solidarity and popular understanding so long as these have a broadly egalitarian character. Existing state pension schemes should not be neglected but, rather, strengthened by the progressive addition of a funded element, with every care taken to protect or enhance the position of those presently excluded from employment. Existing private pension schemes should be required to respect social priorities and to give proper representation to policy holders if they are to continue to enjoy fiscal subsidies. Where enterprises hold reserves in trust for employees' pensions they should likewise be obliged to make provision for employee representation and social audit. Where there are more and less egalitarian ways of gearing the working of a funded pension scheme the former can be encouraged. But the overall impact of any scheme will also depend on the balance of social forces. The approach urged here seeks to empower communities and working collectives and to encourage them to find allies at home and abroad rather than to embark on an illusory attempt at collective autarchy.

The classic devices of social insurance and commercial insurance were able to furnish a pension because large numbers of those who contributed died before they reached pensionable age, and many others only drew it for a year or two. But the economics of 'banking on death', and the 'mortality bonus', can no longer be counted on. The great majority are going to need their pension and hope to live on it for many years. Of course eventually they will die and mortality rates will still help to regulate pension provision. But as the revolution in longevity takes place people will want to make the best of it and invest in life. They may hope to explore some new occupation or pursuit, or to work on a part-time or voluntary basis, or to see the world. Many will help with the care of grandchildren. All will hope to stay fit. They will also hope to see their children and communities prosper. These are modest and reasonable aspirations which should be met. But, as things now are, they are beyond the scope of existing public provision and will be met, if at all, only for the minority. Public support for retirement, and for services caring for the elderly, faces retrenchment and austerity nearly everywhere, and private provision will not be able take its place.

The institutions of grey capitalism set the scene either for continuing free market mayhem, affecting those of all ages – or for debates, conflicts and campaigns that could lead to the progressive socialisation of the accumulation process. The measures I have advocated address the need to make more provision for the new life-course in a society where people will live longer and need more time for study. They necessarily begin to socialise the accumulation process, furnishing communities, working collectives and concerned citizens with the opportunity to resist the divisive and dangerous dynamic of capitalism. By smoothing income over the life-course, furnishing opportunities to defend the social fabric and empowering the citizenry, they seek to ensure that the free development of each is the basis for the free development of all.

Notes

1 Evidence bearing out these observations will be found in Nicholas Timmins, 'Closure of Final Pay Pensions a "Disaster"', *Financial Times*, 10 February 2002.

2 Martine Segalen, 'Introduction' to Marianne Gullestad and Martine Segalen, eds., *Family and Kinship in Europe*, London and Washington 1997, pp. 1–13.

3 A strong case for moving to a higher tax regime was made in Bob Rowthorn, 'Saving the Welfare State: Why Taxes Have to Go Up', *Social Economy*, autumn 1993. He urged that welfare expenditure should be sufficiently well-financed to furnish benefits attractive to those on middle incomes and to bring the disadvantaged up to their level. In the mid- and late 1990s New Labour shrank from advocating such a change of course but it will eventually have to decide on entry to the eurozone, with its more generous welfare regime. For the logic of the latter see Matts Persson, 'Why are Taxes so High in Egalitarian Societies?', *Scandinavian Journal of Economics*, vol. 97, 1995, pp. 569–80.

4 Research confirms that fitness in old age is increasing as well as longevity. Between 1982 and 1999 the prevalence of chronic disability among all US citizens over 65 declined by 25 per cent, or 0.6 per cent a year. (This trend was only observed among blacks over 65 in the years 1989–94.) By 1999 80.3 per cent of the over-65 population were not disabled in any way; the proportion receiving institiutional care dropped from 6.8 per cent in 1982 to 4.2 per cent in 1999. See Kenneth G. Manton and XiLiang Gu, 'Changes in the Prevalence of Chronic Disability in the United States Black and Nonblack Population Above Age 65 from 1982 to 1999', *Proceedings of the National Academy of Sciences*, vol. 98, no. 11, 22 May 2001, pp. 6354–9.

5 See Robert William Fogel, *The Fourth Great Awakening and the Future of Egalitarianism*, Chicago 2000, pp. 196–202. Fogel also makes the point that the growth of GNP in future decades will make rising pension and health care expenses much easier to cover, but in his view new institutions, similar to the Asian Provident Funds, will be required to make sure this happens. The orders of magnitude I indicate are also broadly consistent with the evidence advanced by Dean Baker and Mark Weisbrot, *Social Security: The Phony Crisis*, Chicago 1999, pp. 55–68. The study cited in the previous footnote pointed out that projected Medicare costs do not take proper account of declining disability among the elderly (Manton and Wu, 'Changes', p. 6357). However they also noted that the declining number of the elderly receiving institutional care was partly caused by an increased number in 'assisted-care facilities' or 'residential care', which do entail some expense (p. 6358).

6 Esping-Anderson argues that, with rising female employment, women are strongly discouraged from having children if there is an absence of affordable child-care. He cites this as the explanation for the steep fertility decline in Catholic Italy and Spain, concluding:.'[T]he long-term welfare state

consequences of population ageing give a new urgency to nations' fertility performance. Basically, if contemporary welfare states discourage fertility, be it directly or indirectly, they will undercut their future financial viability.' Gosta Esping-Anderson, *Social Foundations of Postindustrial Economies*, Oxford 1999, pp. 67–8.

7 A variety of technical difficulties are addressed in Rudolf Meidner, *Employee Investment Funds: An Approach to Collective Capital Formation*, London 1978. The actual operation of the Meidner scheme at least showed that a levy of this sort could work. Note that I am proposing that all the proceeds of the share levy would go into general social funds; in Meidner's original proposal an initial tranche went into enterprise level funds.

8 There is now a growing literature on all these phenomena. I would single out the following as particularly cogent: Colin Leys, *Market-Driven Politics*, London 2001; Peter Self, *Roll Back the Market*, London 1999; and Allen Shutt, *The Trouble with Capitalism*, London 1999. Also worth consulting is a textbook which explores the pros and cons of market models in a somewhat too balanced fashion: Alan Shipman, *The Market Revolution: a Price for Everything*, London 1999, pp. 389–474.

9 Opponents of privatising Social Security frequently make use of this argument. Simply looking at production and distribution, abstracted from the social relations which help to constitute them, has its uses but also its limitations. It renders invisible capitalist institutions, and capitalist claims on future streams of income. Central to the approach I am advocating here is a willingness gradually to transform capitalist claims in ways that transfer assets to the pension funds.

10 A. Asimkopulos, 'Financing Social Security: Who Pays?', *Journal of Post-Keynesian Economics*, vol. 11, no. 4, Summer 1989, pp. 655–60, p. 656.

11 Keith Hart, personal communication, but see the discussion of the gift relationship, exchange and reciprocity in Keith Hart, *The Memory Bank, Money in an Unequal World*, London 1999, pp. 192–9.

12 For a useful identification of the problem by an IMF official who estimates the value of offshore holdings at $7-8 trillion, see Vito Tanzi, *Policies, Institutions and the Dark Side of Economics*, Cheltenham 2000, pp. 215–26. Tanzi has some proposals for mitigating what he calls 'tax degradation' and 'tax competition'. The wider issue here is, of course, that of the continuing powers of the state in the epoch of globalisation. See Daniele Archibugi, 'Cosmopolitics', *New Left Review*, no. 4, July-August 2000, and Grahame Thompson and Paul Hirst, *Globalisation in Question*, London 1998.

13 Daniel Gross, *Bull Run: Wall St, The Democrats and the New Politics of Personal Finance*, New York 2000, p. 20.

14 David Smith, 'Richest 10 per cent Pay Half of All Income Tax', *Sunday Times*, 7 May, 2000.

15 The question still remains whether a better device than the income tax can be found. It is possible to formulate 'progressive' versions of a consumption tax, with taxes assessed on the basis of annual or quarterly spending, and with a

rising rate of taxation. I believe that the essentials of the approach advocated here could be combined with a consumption tax but it would imply a discriminating approach to the border between savings and expenditure, a critical area for consumption tax advocates. See Laurence S. Seidman, *The USA Tax: a Progressive Consumption Tax*, Cambridge (MA) 1997.

16 In Britain some unions already give modest support to such a body; Union Pensions Services provide comparative details on occupational pension schemes, assessing their quality and performance from the members' point of view. They are based at 50 Trinity Gardens, London SW9 8DR.

17 Kevin Pask, 'Late Nationalism: the Case of Quebec', *New Left Review*, no. 11, September–October 2001, pp. 35–54, pp. 43–4. See also Alicia H. Munnell and C. Nicole Ernsberger, 'Foreign Experience with Public Pension Surpluses and National Saving', in Carolyn Weaver, ed., *Social Security's Looming Surpluses*, Washington (DC) 1990. pp. 85–118, especially pp. 107–14.

18 The qualifying funds would enjoy considerable privileges giving them exemption from general taxation, so they should, in principle, be open to all comers. There would no doubt be a tendency for people to plump for well-regarded funds but their openness would dilute any tendency to generate long-term inequalities.

19 The approach I am outlining here links up with the case for indexation of the basic pension to earnings, since it gives pensioners, and the funds representing them, an interest in the advance of employee earnings. Since these funds would be influential economic actors it would help to strengthen ties of solidarity between the two groups.

20 One example of how a top-up might operate is given by Fakenham and Johnson, 'A Unified Funded Pension Scheme', pp. 23–5. Note that this solution could, at least for a time, render unnecessary the payment of contributions on behalf of those not in employment. For another approach to achieving a guaranteed minimum within an integrated pension policy see A.B. Atkinson, *State Pensions for Today and Tomorrow*, London School of Economics, Working Paper, Welfare State Group, June 1994, especially pp. 21–9.

21 'When Labour and Capital Don't Mix', *The Economist*, 15 December 2001.

22 See, for example, Floyd Norris, 'Guaranteed Profits: The Fiction of Pension Accounting', *New York Times*, 7 December 2001.

23 Robert Guy Matthews, 'LTV Seeks to Shut Down Its Operations, Asks Court Approval for Sale of Assets', *Wall Street Journal*, 21 November 2001.

24 The reasons for the ultimate frustration of the labour-movement-sponsored industrial policy and of the wage earner funds in Sweden are explored by Jonas Pontusson, *The Limits of Social Democracy: Investment Politics in Sweden*, Ithaca 1992, especially pp. 127–61, 186–219. It is, perhaps, useful here to quote his summary: '1. The reform offensive failed because business mobilised against it. 2. The reform offensive failed because the SAP leaders and the government did not share labor's ambitions. 3.The reform offensive failed because the systematic power of capital thwarted the effects of the legislation

that labor achieved. 4. The reform offensive failed because labor lacked an alternative industrial strategy and hence failed to take advantage of the new opportunities created by new legislation.' (p. 225). While some business resistance was inevitable, the sources of failures could have been anticipated or avoided.

25 G.A. Cohen, *If You're an Egalitarian, How Come You're So Rich?*, Cambridge (MA) 2000.

26 Prior to the 13 November 2001 annual shareholder meeting of TIAA-CREF in New York, leaflets and e-mails called on members to vote to divest from Unocal and Nike. They claimed that according to the fund's own survey 81 per cent of those who opt for the Social Choice Account would like to see their savings channelled to companies with an outstanding record on social issues; but this Account only achieves a 'one-heart' rating on a scale of 1–5 'hearts' from an independent rating agency. The leaflets advised those in search of further information to contact NeilWoolman@Manchester.edu.

27 Even a managing director at Morgan Stanley was alarmed: 'The hedge fund mania that grips the US and Europe is rapidly assuming all the characteristics of a classic bubble. . . . The bubble is all about the fallacy of composition, which states that individuals' actions are rational, or would be if others were not behaving in the same way. . . . The belief that hedge funds can make money come rain or shine has not been tested in a bear market – but with an ugly market environment, the collapse of technology and private equity returns plummeting, hedge funds have become the new asset class of choice for the world's aggressive money. Originally the domain of wealthy individuals, hedge funds are attracting money from foundations, endowments and pension funds. There is now more than $400 billion (£290bn) of equity in about 6,000 hedge funds, completely unregulated and highly leveraged.' Barton Biggs, 'The Hedge Fund Bubble', *Financial Times*, 9 July 2001.

28 Hans Eichel, 'The Dangers of Hedge Funds', *Financial Times*, 7 February 2002.

29 Robert Hunter Wade, Letters, *Financial Times*, 9 February 2002.

30 'The Amazing Disintegrating Firm', *The Economist*, 8 December 2001.

31 Gary Silverman, 'Banks Break the Old Boundaries', *Financial Times*, 18 January 2002.

32 Below I will consider the case for 'de-privatising' some public utilities (e.g the British rail companies) but the regulators should stay. For an account of the workings of utilities' regulators in the UK see Paul Cook, 'Privatisation in the UK: Policy and Performance', in David Parker, ed., *Privatisation in the European Union: Theory and Policy Perspectives*, London and New York 1998, pp. 218–41.

33 See, for example, Alex Arthur, 'Evidence and Argument: Another Look at Audit Fundamentals', *Critical Perspectives on Accounting*, vol. 12, 2000, pp. 247–67; Carlos Larrinaga-Gonzalez and Jan Bebbingdon, 'Accounting Change or Institutional Appropriation? A Case Study in the Implementation of Environmental Accounting', *Critical Perspectives on Accounting*, vol. 13, 2001, pp. 269–92.

34 Eric Becker and Patrick McVeigh, 'Social Funds in the United States: Their History, Financial Performance, and Social Impacts', in Archong Fong, Tessa Hebb and Joel Rogers, eds, *Working Capital: the Power of Labor's Pensions*, Ithaca and London 2001, pp. 44–66; see also Amy Domini, *Socially Responsible Investment*, Chicago 2001, and the magazine *Business Ethics: Insider's Report on Responsible Business*, published from Minneapolis (MN).

35 *Business Ethics*, July–August 1998.

36 For 'quality assurance' benchmarking see Guy Palmer, ed., *Quality Assurance or Benchmarking? Presenting Information About Pensions*, London 1998.

37 Michael Calabrese, 'Building on Success: Labor-Friendly Investment Vehicles and the Power of Private Equity', in Archong Fong *et al., Working Capital*, pp. 93–127, p. 120.

38 For a unified and funded pension plan which helpfully tackles some technical questions not addressed here, see Jane Fakenham and Paul Johnson, 'A Unified Funded Pension Scheme for Britain', Welfare State Programme Discussion Paper, WSP/90, London School of Economics, 1993; the same authors summarise their approach in an article in *Soundings*, Issue 4, Autumn 1996. However, these authors take for granted current financial institutions and do not mention the possible role of pension funds in fostering a wider social political economy. Even within a 'harmonised' European approach to social policy there could be considerable variation so long as its fiscal impact was broadly similar.

39 For an account and defence of the mutual ownership concept, where each member has an equal vote, see Christopher Hird, 'Building Societies: Stakeholding in Practice', *New Left Review*, no. 218, July–August 1996, pp. 40–52. Following the Nationwide vote, British mutuals began taking market share from their demutualised competitors and featured well in 'best buy' surveys. See Christopher Brown-Humes, 'Future of Mutuality', *Financial Times* survey, 10 March 1998.

40 James McLean, 'Takeover Threat if Standard Beats off the Carpetbaggers', *Evening Standard*, 12 May 2000.

41 Victor Mallet, 'Stock Declines Threaten Black Ownership Deals', *Financial Times*, 14 October 1998. This article claims that no one has actually lost money in the 'black empowerment' schemes, though evidently a handful of former trade union leaders have enriched themselves. The complex pyramid of holding companies and investment vehicles, tying together some union-owned enterprises with the financial structures of 'black empowerment', was described and criticised by a special correspondent in 'Union Investment: New Opportunities, New Threats', *SA Labour Bulletin*, vol. 20, no. 5, October 1996. See also Ravi Naidoo, 'Union Investment: Can it Drive Transformation?', *SA Labour Bulletin*, vol. 20, no. 3, June 1997. These articles stressed the absence of union membership control over investment companies and trust funds set up in their name and the predominance of inappropriate commercial investment criteria. To the extent that it was openly and legally pursued, the project of strengthening a black business leadership would not be any more objectionable than any other capitalist activity. Indeed given that

South Africa was probably not in a position to break with capitalism some promotion of black capitalists would simply redress racial inequality. But for trade union leaders, whether white or black (several have been white), to enrich themselves at the expense of their own organisations would be a quite different matter, especially since much use was made of an anti-capitalist rhetoric. And even if breaking with capitalism was unrealistic at least such leaders could be expected to resist a wave of privatisation and deregulation which weakened overall economic performance. The trade union-influenced pension funds might have contributed to a far more progressive strategy of development than that actually pursued.

42 Royal Society of Arts and Manufacturing, *Tomorrow's Company*, London 1995, p. 12.

43 Sheldon Leader, 'Participation and Property Rights', *Journal of Business Ethics*, 21, 1999, pp. 97–109.

44 Gordon Clark, *Pension Fund Capitalism*, Oxford 2000, pp. 21–34.

45 Gerald Holtham, 'Why the Government Needs to Borrow More, Not Less', *Guardian*, 16 August 1999.

46 Samuel Brittan, 'How Land Taxes Could Pay for Urban Renewal', *Financial Times*, 30 August 2001. Brittan was responding to, and drawing on, a pamphlet by Don Riley, *Taken for a Ride*, published by the Centre for Land Policy Studies, 7 Kings Road, Teddington, TW11 0QB.

47 Since privatisation in 1994–6 public subsidy for the railways has grown steeply and the quality of services deteriorated: see Christian Wolmar, *Broken Rails*, 2nd ed., London 2001.

48 Allyson Pollock, Jean Shaoul, David Rowland and Stewart Player, *Public Services and the Private Sector*, November 2001, published by Catalyst, PO Box 27477, London SW9 8WT.

49 For an analysis of good and bad practice in this area see Steven Rathgeb Smith and Michael Lipsky, *Nonprofits for Hire: the Welfare State in the Age of Contracting*, Cambridge (MA) 1993.

50 Michael Power, *The Audit Society, Rituals of Verification*, Oxford 1997.

51 See Randy Barber and Teresa Ghilarducci, ' Pension Funds, Capital Markets, and the Economic Future', in Gery A. Dymski, Gerald Epstein, Robert Pollin, eds, *Transforming the US Financial System: Equity and Efficiency for the 21st Century*, New York 1993, pp. 287–319, especially pp. 298–305.

52 Alicia Munnell and Anika Sundén, 'Investment Practices of Local Pension Funds', cited in Peter Orszag and Joseph Stiglitz, 'Rethinking Social Security Reform', R. Holzmann and J. Stiglitz, eds, *New Ideas About Old Age Security*, Washington 2001.

53 Clark, *Pension Fund Capitalism*, pp. 197–8. The activities of the RSA and Calpers are enthusiastically recounted in Gross, *Bull Run*, pp. 27–54; for a more critical account see Teresa Ghilarducci, *Labor's Capital: the Economics and Politics of Pension Funds*, Cambridge (MA) 1992, and the various contributions to Archon Fong, Tessa Hebb and Joel Rogers, eds, *Working Capital: the Power of Labor's Pensions*, Ithaca (NY) and London 2001.

54   Ambachtsheer and Ezra, *Pension Fund Excellence*, p. 221. On p. 15 these authors contend that today's US commercial funds have missed the maximum growth pattern by about 66 basis points or 0.66 per cent annually. In footnote 7 on p. 230 they cite a study of a portfolio of Economically Targeted Investments (ETIs) engaged in by public employees' pension funds in the Great Lakes region which earned a return that was 'four percentage points below stock market returns over a five year period'. Thus by their own calculations the putative underperformance of targeted investment is the same as that for the average commercial fund, with the boost to employment and amenity in the Great Lakes area being pure bonus! However, there are quite legitimate objections that can be made to expecting employee savings to carry the burden of social investment while allowing capitalists to ignore them. The special tax breaks to social funds would be complemented by a broader regulatory structure that would apply to all funds and corporations, as argued by Robert Pollin in, 'Finance and Equality', *New Left Review*, no.114, November–December 1995, pp. 26–61.

55   L. Kottsman and J. Kessler, 'Smart Screened Investments: Environmentally Screened Equity Funds that Perform like Conventional Funds', *The Journal of Investing,* Fall 1998; John B. Guerard, 'Is There a Cost to Being Socially Responsible in Investing?', *The Journal of Investing*, Summer 1997.

56   See, e.g., Edward Alden, 'Go Green, Invest and Prosper', *Financial Times*, 23 January 1999. Some evidence for this is also supplied by Domini in *Socially Responsible Investing*, pp. 159–62.

57   Quoted in Lucy Kellaway, 'Statements that Sum up Mission Impossible', *Financial Times*, 20 March 2000.

58   Meidner, *Employee Investment Funds*, pp. 61–8.

59   Bob Sutcliffe and Andrew Glyn, 'Still Underwhelmed: Indicators of Globalization and their Misinterpretation', *Review of Radical Political Economics*, vol. 31, no. 1, 1999, pp. 111–32, p. 125.

60   In the aftermath of a Danish election which saw an anti-immigrant party garner 14 per cent of the vote, and several of the major parties adjust to anti-immigrant sentiment, Martin Wolf, who regards much higher levels of immigration as desirable, observed: 'It is no accident that mass democracy, the welfare state and immigration controls came to the advanced countries at roughly the same time.' Martin Wolf, 'Fighting for Economic Equality', *Financial Times*, 28 November 2001.

61   An analogous point is made by Erik Olin Wright in his discussion of John Roemer's 'Coupon Socialism', in *New Left Review*, no. 210, March–April 1995, pp. 153–60.

62   The Tobin tax, named for the US economist James Tobin who proposed it in the 1970s, would place a small tax on the financial transactions between currencies. For a discussion see Keikki Patomaki, *The Tobin Tax: How To Make it Real*, Project Report by the Network Institute for Global Democratisation, The Finnish Institute for International Affairs, Helsinki 1999.

63 John Eatwell and Lance Taylor, *Global Finance at Risk: the Case for International Regulation*, New York 2000, p. 226.

64 Jane D'Arista, 'Financial Regulation in a Liberalised Global Environment', Working Paper Series III, May 1998, Center for Policy Analysis, New School University, New York.

65 The recent experience of CDC Capital Partners, the British government's investment fund for the developing world, shows pitfalls to be avoided here. This organisation began life as a wholly state-owned body, the Colonial Development Corporation, and had built up assets of over £1 billion by the late 1990s. The government explored the idea of opening the CDC to external investors, including pension funds, but a Commons committee objected that this would not be compatible with CDC's aid objectives. The real problem seems to have been CDC's turn to inappropriate business criteria and detailed control, arousing criticism both from Greenpeace and from local communities in Papua New Guinea where it operates palm oil plantations. Michael Peel, 'Greenpeace Groups Attack Ethical Fund' and 'When Contracts Fall Foul of Local Culture', *Financial Times*, 30 July 2001. However while particular commercial practices have been criticised the provision of capital and expertise has not.

66 A valuable report on the African experience was supplied by Eric Adjei's paper, 'The Politics of Pensions in Africa: in the Eye of the Storm', delivered at the 17th Congress of the International Association of Gerontology in Vancouver, July 2001. Adjei directs the Social Security and National Insurance Trust in Accra, Ghana. In a World Bank collection Iglesias and Palacios observe that most poor countries favour investing pension funds locally and comment: 'This is poor policy in the light of the limited options available in most countries especially when funds are large relative to local capital markets.' Augusto Iglesias and Robert J. Palacios, 'Managing Public Pension Reserves', in Robert Holzmann and Joseph Stiglitz, eds, *New Ideas About Old Age Security*, Washington (DC) 2001, pp. 213–53, p. 230.

67 Kevin Danaher, 'An Alternative to the Debt Crisis', in K. Danaher, ed., *Democratising the Global Economy*, Monroe (ME) and Philadelphia (PA) 2000, pp. 190–3.

68 Robert Cottrell, 'Russia's Cold Warrior', *Financial Times,* 4 January 2001; the case for a more 'Keynesian' approach to Russia's economic reform was made by, among others, Stanislav Menchikov, *Catastrophe or Catharsis?*, Moscow and London 1992.

69 Wolfgang Munchau, 'Return of Keynes', *Financial Times*, 26 October 1998, p. 22.

70 John Maynard Keynes, 'How to Pay for the War', in *The Collected Writings of John Maynard Keynes*, vol. IX, *Essays in Persuasion*, London 1972, pp. 397–439, p. 403.

71 Keynes, 'How to Pay for the War'. Keynes put forward these ideas in a very public campaign of articles in the press and meetings with ministers, TUC officials and the like, but failed to win the support of organised labour or the

Treasury, who opted for rationing and mild inflation as the way to deal with the problem of excess demand. Nevertheless his campaign helped to establish the need for budgeting to grapple with social issues. See Robert Skidelsky, *John Maynard Keynes: Fighting for Britain, 1937–1946*, London 2001, pp. 46–72, 87–90.

72 Jan Toporovski, *The End of Finance: Capital Market Inflation, Financial Derivatives and Pension Fund Capitalism*, London 2000.

73 See Michael Mosebach and Mohammed Najand, 'Are Structural Changes in Mutual Funds' Investing Driving the US Stock Market to its Current Level?', *The Journal of Financial Research*, vol. XXII, no. 3, Fall 1999, pp. 317–29, p. 318.

74 Malcolm Crawford, 'The Big Pensions Lie', *New Economy*, vol. 4, no. 1, Spring 1997, pp. 39–44.

75 Thomas E. MacUrdy and John Shoven, 'Asset Allocation and Risk Allocation: Can Social Security Improve Its Future Solvency Problem by Investing in Private Securities?', in John Y. Campbell and Martin Feldstein, eds, *Risk Aspects of Investment-Based Social Security Reform*, Chicago and London 2001, pp. 11–32 and, for technical criticism of their argument, pp. 29–41.

76 'Stunning Shareholder Protest Vote at Rio Tinto AGMs', Coalition of Rio Tinto Shareholders, www.icem.org. This web-site also gives the strategic perspective on globalisation of this organisation and news of campaigns similar to that at Rio Tinto. For other examples of trade union use of shareholder power, and of various snags and pitfalls, see Marleen O'Connor, 'Labor's Role in the Shareholder Revolution', in Archon Fong, *Working Capital*, pp. 67–92.

77 Richard Sennett, *The Corrosion of Character: the Personal Consequences of Work in the New Capitalism*, New York 1998, pp. 118–35.

78 Jim Stanford, *Paper Boom*, Ottawa 1999, p. 349.

79 Tessa Hebb and David Mackenzie, 'Canadian Labour-Sponsored Investment Funds: A Model for US Economically-Targeted Investments', in Archon Fong, *Working Capital*, pp. 128–57, p. 143.

80 Thomas Frank, 'The Trillion Dollar Hustle', *Harper's*, January 2002, p. 38.

81 Stanford, *Paper Boom*, pp. 382–3, 385–412. Though this author could have given more space to ways in which pension funds could 'do it differently' his criticisms and alternatives are a valuable contribution, reflecting Canada's considerable experience with the issues I am addressing. It should be noted that according to Stanford pension funds are much less important in Canada than they are in the United States or UK, owning only 12.3 per cent of corporate equities (p. 262).

82 Alain Badiou, *Ethics*, London 2000.

83 Anne-Marie Darke, interviewed by ABC National Radio's Background Briefing, 25 November 2000.

84 Karl Marx and Frederick Engels, *The Communist Manifesto*, with an introduction by Eric Hobsbawm, New York and London 1998, p. 61.

85   Kevin Bales, *Disposable People: New Slavery in the World Economy*, Berkeley
     1999; International Labour Organisation, *Child Labour: Targeting the Intolerable*,
     Geneva 1996.
86   'Calpers Asian Retreat a Victory for Ethics', *Financial Times*, 22 February 2002.
87   'US Pension Funds Slash Holdings in Southeast Asia', *International Herald
     Tribune*, 22 February 2002. Note that Calpers was just setting a new course at
     this time following a bitter public row over whether its Chief Investment
     Officer should be allowed to earn more than any other state official (his
     salary was $260,000, a pittance by Wall Street standards). The fight was
     resolved by the resignation of the manager concerned after a trustee decision
     to lower his compensation. 'Investment Chief at Calpers Quits After Ruling
     on Pay', *New York Times*, 14 November 2001.
88   Naomi Klein, *No Logo*, London 2000, p. 205.
89   Advantages explored in Robert Oakeshott, *Jobs and Fairness: the Logic and
     Experience of Employee Ownership*, Norwich 2000. See also Corey Rosen and
     Karen M. Young, eds, *Understanding Employee Ownership*, Ithaca (NY) 1991.
90   See Philip Coggan, 'Workers Grab a Bigger Slice of the Pie', *Financial Times*,
     9 August 2001. I say lopsided because better-paid employees did much better
     than the low-paid, as Coggan points out.
91   Ambachtsheer and Ezra, *Pension Fund Excellence*, p. 40, basing themselves on
     the experience of the last few decades, claim that 60 to 80 per cent of benefits
     paid derive from fund earnings, not the original contributions, though they
     do not seem to have properly allowed for inflation. That capitalism generates
     profits and capital growth over the long term for capitalists should not be sur-
     prising, since if this did not happen for any extended period the whole
     economy would grind to a halt. Following the 1929 crash the stock market
     needed twenty-four years to reach its former level. Nevertheless, over thirty
     or forty years the odds would have to be on a substantial recovery. In the
     1990s over-optimistic judgements of the stock market were encouraged by
     Jeremy Siegel's *Stocks for the Long Run*, New York 1994. This book showed
     the buoyancy of US stocks between the 1920s and 1990s notwithstanding the
     slump, and this seemed impressive. But over longer periods, and taking
     account of over twenty other stock markets, the ability of shares to outper-
     form government bonds is less clear-cut. See Elroy Dimson, Paul Marsh and
     Mike Staunton, *Triumph of the Optimists*, Princeton (NJ) 2002. These authors
     find the average return to shares does exceed that to bonds by an average of
     4.6 per cent. But this is only half the 'equity premium' usually claimed and
     there can be periods of a few decades during which no such premium is
     observed.
92   Some authors point to sharp share-price fluctuations as a decisive argument
     against employee pension funds ever holding equities; see, for example, Dan
     Atkinson and Larry Elliott, *The Age of Insecurity*, London 1998, pp. 284–5,
     and Doug Henwood, *Wall Street*, New York 1997, p. 303. The arguments
     made by these authors against privately-run schemes are generally cogent.
     More generally these two books furnish vivid and compelling accounts of the

reckless speculative frenzies to which the markets are prone, and which it would be the purpose of the approach proposed here to bring under effective control. But to the extent that they oppose all pension fund investment in equities on grounds of risk they go too far. From the standpoint of the argument of this book it should also be noted that many of the shares in the proposed funds would have been acquired by allocation not purchase. Furthermore the institutions proposed seek to use the shares in the funds in ways which recognise the employees' interest in reducing stock market volatility and restoring general economic buoyancy.

93 Ludwig von Mises, *Social Action*, Chicago 1947, pp. 61–70.
94 Michel Aglietta, 'Towards a New Regime of Growth', *New Left Review*, no. 232, November–December 1998. See also Aglietta, *Le Capitalisme de demain*, pp. 34–41, and the Postscript to *The Theory of Capitalist Regulation*, second edition, London 2000.
95 Diane Elson, 'Socialisation of the Market', *New Left Review*, no.172, November–December 1988, pp. 3–44.
96 John Roemer, *The Future of Socialism*, London 1994.
97 Roberto Mangabeira Unger, *Politics: the Central Texts*, London 1997, pp. 350–61, and *Democracy Realized*, London 1998.
98 *Selections from the Works of Fourier*, with an introduction by Charles Gide, translated by Julia Franklin, London 1901, p. 131–4. See also Charles Fourier, *The Movement of the Four Seasons*, introduced by Gareth Stedman Jones and translated by Ian Patterson, Cambridge 1997, and for the early French socialists see G.D.H. Cole, *A History of Socialist Thought,* I, *The Forerunners*, London 1953, and II, *Socialist Thought: Marxism and Anarchism*, London 1954.
99 Karl Marx, *Capital*, vol. III, London 1991, p. 567.
100 The call for the 35-hour working week has been widely taken up in France, Italy and Germany. For 'participatory budgets' with special reference to the Brazilian experience see G. Baiocchi, 'Brazillian Cities in the Nineties and Beyond', *Socialism and Democracy*, no. 31, November 2001, and for 'associated democracy' see Paul Hirst, *From Statism to Pluralism*, London 1997.
101 Wolfgang Abendroth, *A Short History of the European Working Class*, London 1975.

Index